Granny Tyler peered suspiciously up at him. 'How come you do know so much?'

'I read a lot!'

Doctor Who and the Image of the Fendahl
by Terrance Dicks

1

Foreword

Matthew Waterhouse

There's a little company in America which releases old indie horror films on VHS. Their belief is that these cheap, grainy movies are creepier on tape, with its shaky, lo-fi, white-flash texture, than the glossy, antiseptic cleanliness of DVD. Enough people agree to keep the company afloat. I can't say I have bought any of these films but I find the concept endearing. I guess I am quite a lo-fi person.

In much the same way, I think it's charming that the new, digital version of *Doctor Who* has caused a surge of interest, modest but real, in the speedily written and cheaply printed paperback novelisations of the seventies and eighties. I do hope that there are new, young fans among the readers of the recent reprints and the listeners to the long line of audio readings. Perhaps some will get to know the book versions of old stories alongside the TV versions or even before, just as I knew *The Crusaders*, *The Zarbi*, *The Web of Fear* and so on from their novelisations.

Doctor Who makes total sense as a book character. The old BBC drama department was a pretty literary place and this influence seeps into *Doctor Who*, a lot more bookish than American series which many people regard as its equivalents like, say, *Star Trek*. *Star Trek* is essentially a journey through the tropes of Hollywood movies. Each new planet in *Star Trek* is its own film set. But *Doctor Who* is a journey through history and literature. Its sources are books. There's a lot of Victorian science fiction – Wells, Verne – and Victorian gothic in it: *Doctor Who* was steampunk before the idea existed. A bit of Rider Haggard, more than a bit of Arthur Conan Doyle, the characters of both Holmes and Professor Challenger. Even the influence of Conan Doyle's rip-roaring historical novels can be traced, novels like *The White Company*, a gripping example of 'ye olde historical romance'. Quite a lot of Robert Louis Stevenson who, if he had been born eighty years later, would have been a masterful *Doctor Who* writer (he was terrific at scary!)

There are the pulps of the thirties, forties, fifties and sixties too. When Philip Hinchcliffe was asked to become producer, he was already familiar with the nineteenth century writers so the first thing he did was read a big pile of science fiction books of the twentieth: it was these that convinced him he could work in the genre. Terrance Dicks once said to me that his hope as script editor had been to recapture the thrill of the stories he'd read as a boy. It seems appropriate that Terrance would later script edit, and for a while produce, BBC's Classic Serials strand: Dickens and Wells and others.

Because it drew so much on pulp fiction, it's appropriate that *Doctor Who* should be transformed into pulp fiction itself. If its first home is the TV studio, a comfortable home from home is that of the penny dreadful, of cheap paper and glue.

For some unfathomable reason, I hated W H Smith, the obvious place to find *Doctor Who* books in Southern England when I was a child. This prejudice remains. It is a joke with my friends that if a town has a branch of Smith's it is my idea of suburban hell. This mysterious dislike did not apply to the railway bookstalls, only the high street shops. I spotted the first 'new' Target books (following the three sixties reprints), *Doctor Who and the Auton Invasion* and *Doctor Who and the Cave Monsters* at the Smith's bookstall on Brighton station. Most of the other early ones I bought not from a bookshop at all but a little stationers called Clark's, which smelt of pencils and envelopes. It had a half dozen spinners displaying randomly arranged paperbacks: TV books and Agatha Christies and Ian Flemings and biographies of film actors and Peanuts comic strip collections and hospital romances all mixed up together. Then a little bookshop near my house opened up, one of a number of small, narrow shops in a conversion from what had been the waiting room and ticket office of a bus terminus. It was called Bestseller, and its stock was hardly more adventurous than Clark's, but Bestseller was run by a nice middle-aged woman who was happy to check her microfiche list of forthcoming books and tell me the very date the next Target instalment was due. I would turn up on publication day, sometimes browsing for around an hour or more waiting for the afternoon delivery. During my long wait, I was often the only customer, so it was no surprise when Bestseller closed to become a hairdresser, which it remained until just a couple of years ago, when the whole building was bulldozed to make way for a Waitrose. But meanwhile a bigger, more ambitious independent bookshop opened a few minutes' walk further up the road. It was called Halcyon Books. It clung on, every so often changing hands, until Waterstone's put paid to it a decade ago, despite a local campaign and an attempt to turn upstairs, formerly the children's section where the *Doctor Who* books were shelved, into a coffee shop. I went into this a couple of times when visiting the town as an adult: two round tables in the upstairs bay window, covered in red and white checked table cloths; a little cup of coffee accompanied by one of those malty biscuits with a 3-D picture of a cow stamped on the front.

By this time, I had lost track of *Doctor Who* books, which had long since moved from Target to another publisher and from the children's section to the science fiction section. They had ceased to be

3

novelisations of TV programmes, which had pretty much been used up, and instead were New Adventures...

*

I bought the Target books as soon as they came out but I didn't always read them immediately. Do you remember how, in *Charlie and the Chocolate Factory*, Charlie Bucket spins out the pleasure of a Wonka bar by eating only a tiny morsel each day, anticipating day after day after day of choccy pleasure? I liked putting the Target books aside until, after a few months, a pile had grown, so in the summer holidays, the programme off the air, there would be maybe half a dozen waiting to be read.

But Charlie sometimes goes to the other extreme, ripping the wrapper off and gobbling the whole bar in a few mad, intoxicating indulgent chunks. Some of those books – *The Auton Invasion, The Space War, The Talons of Weng-Chiang, The Abominable Snowmen, The Doomsday Weapon* – I began to read within moments of getting back from the shop and had turned the last page by sundown. (Incidentally, I always liked it when the novel had a different title from the serial, though I never understood the point of the change. What is wrong with *Doctor Who and the Web Planet*? *Doctor Who and the Frontier in Space*?)

There was excitement to be had even before the new book was opened: the gorgeous painted covers. These paintings were a vital part of the magic and energy of the novels, each new artist, like a new producer or script editor or, for that matter, a new Doctor, putting his own stamp on the series. Marvellous artists like Chris Achilleos (those speckly black and white faces with coloured surroundings), Andrew Skilleter, Alister Pearson and Jeff Cummins brought the stories to life. It is not a good thing to judge a book by its cover, but it's okay to appreciate a good one.

There was a bleak period when these lovely cover paintings were scrapped in favour of photographs. Peter Davison's agent, I'm told, objected to a proposed painting and this message got mangled on its way back to Target to mean he objected to *all* cover paintings. When you are used to covers which evoke atmosphere, evoke the essence of the piece, then a photo of an actor, even one as photogenic as Peter Davison, seems a bit flat. A photo is only a photo; a painting is a story. Still, all was put right in reprints, when the Fifth Doctor got some of the very best cover paintings ever, including an *Earthshock* cover by Alister Pearson which is a classic.

Cover paintings are an integral part of the spirit of pulps, as anyone who has seen back issues of *The Shadow* knows, or old 1950s American paperbacks. I like very much that the VHS releases of the TV episodes

4

continued the pulp spirit with painted covers of their own. It's sad that the DVDs and modern novels use photographs. The extraordinarily expressive face of Peter Capaldi cries out for Jeff Cummins's painterly brush.

The contributors to the splendid book you hold in your hands have set out to express their affection for a particular entry in the series. Me, I can't pick out any particular title as having greater or more unusual significance. In any case, my first *Doctor Who* novel, *The Crusaders*, was still in its pre-Target Book incarnation, no footnote about 'The Changing Face of Doctor Who' required. Much of their 'meaning' may be in the sheer quantity, the piles and piles of them. The meaning may be in the mass. After I had been cast in the series, I re-read a lot of them, in an eccentric, possibly misguided, spirit of preparation and research. This continued into the early days of rehearsal, the books disguised by orange faux-leather covers so I could read them at lunchtimes in the pub round the corner from the rehearsal rooms at Acton. Perhaps I imagined that this research would impress my fellow artists! I wonder if Peter Capaldi has read a few in recent years. I bet he read them in the seventies.

Target books are eminently practical technological devices, easy to carry and suitable for reading anywhere. In bed; on the train; in the back of the car; in the supermarket while your mother does the shopping; in the bath; at granny's house while *Emmerdale Farm* is on; at school concealed behind your book of maths problems; at choir practice while faking interest in a psalm; lying on your tummy on the grass, ladybirds walking across the pages. Reading outdoors is appealing, but a lot of tiny living entities can think of nothing better to do than come and sit on cheap paper, turning 'Doctor' into 'Do¶tor', 'Dalek' into 'Daleω', 'K9' into 'θθ'. Almost certainly a creature will take up lodgings on an open page, and refuse to move when you're ready to turn to the next one. Of course, you don't want to squash it because that will leave a mark. You develop a strategy to make it fly away. You shake the book, gently at first, then more and more forcefully, then enough to cool down a bar in the tropics. The insect will just sit there, rubbing its feelers together. You blow on it, soft then hard. It stays put. You suppose it's used to attaching itself to a leaf and remaining through wind and rain and storm. Even a big puff of human breath is just a spring breeze. So then you have to flick it with your fingernail, at the correct angle to lift it from the page. A miscalculation and the stain is just as bad as if you had slammed the book closed right at the beginning. And, being a science fiction enthusiast, you suddenly wonder what it would have been like if you had been shrunk down to the size of the insect (by the Master's shrinking ray, maybe) and flicked off the book yourself, by a giant person or even, irony of ironies, a giant insect.

Also, if you are a true collector, you have to buy another copy.

Much as I loved the Target books, they disappeared from my life, becoming only a childhood memory. I never got rid of them but I never opened them either. (They stayed at my parents' house.) It did not cross my mind that I would have a reason to think about them again.

Until I got a message from BBC Audio asking if I would like to read one for a CD release.

Too bloody right I would!

They asked me to make a list of favourites of the episodes I was in, which I did, adding that all of them were sufficiently favourites that I would be happy to read them. (Unfortunately, the audio producers will not let a regular TV cast member read a story in which his or her character does not appear.) I must admit I was pleased not to be asked to read *Earthshock*, just because it seemed too predictable a choice. I was utterly delighted when Eric Saward's novelisation of his original script for *The Visitation* was chosen. They sent me a reproduction of what was plainly a second-hand copy, the price top written in pencil in the corner at the top of the first inner page.

If you are fond of *Doctor Who*, recording an audio novel is almost criminally pleasurable. It is very nice to be paid to do something that is so much fun. I lived with the novel for a week or two, thinking about pace and rhythm and assorted character voices. Then I went to a cosy little studio. A producer sat the other side of the glass and I simply started reading the story. We worked fast: the three hours plus of *The Visitation* were recorded in less than four hours' studio time. (We started at ten and finished at three thirty, and there was a coffee break after each chapter and a lunch break.)

All actors like showing off and the reader of an audio book gets to use a lot of his range. He plays everyone: the Doctor, the companions, the villains. In this case, the cast of characters includes a wicked, genocidal alien and also an actor-cum-highwayman, a comic character one could imagine in a Perry and Croft sitcom set in the fifteenth century. (The novel's highwayman is discernably different from the one in the TV serial.) There's the doomed family and servant of the big house in that wonderfully shadowy, candle-lit opening chapter. The book is abundantly atmospheric. I like the emphasis on the utterly alien beauty of the Terileptil - 'beauty' is a word used several times to describe him.

A while later, I was asked to read another classic Target novel. This was *Full Circle* by Andrew Smith. Another example of a novelisation by the original script writer, this widely-loved book expands on and adjusts the TV serial even more than *The Visitation* does, hewing closer to Andrew's original vision. It is quite sophisticated in science fiction terms, belonging, I suppose, to that sub-section of the genre known as 'biological science fiction'. Usually, this deals with sexuality. The first story of its kind I know of is *My Sister's Brother* by Philip Jose Farmer from the mid-fifties, about an affair between a male human astronaut and a Martian woman which results in a child. Farmer invents a whole alien reproductive biology. (This was all regarded as rather shocking at the time.) The most famous example must be the *Star Trek* episode by Theodore Sturgeon about Mr Spock's mating ritual. There's not a great deal of sex to be found in *Full Circle* (or any!) but the revelation that the Marshmen and the Starliner humanoids share the same DNA is very cool.

The same studio, the same lovely producer, the same good vibe. Another vast cast to play: the bureaucrats of the Starliner, the teenage rebels, the Marshmen – who, towards the end of the novel, are allowed to voice their own point of view, which is moving and adds a whole extra dimension to the piece.

Yup, recording these Target audios was spectacularly enjoyable.

The *Full Circle* audio was packaged with Andrew Skilleter's marvellous painting from the book cover, of three Marshmen, the middle one looking at the observer, at once monstrous and vulnerable, hands in air in what may be threat or may be terror, but the eyes showing more fear than malice. The first edition of *The Visitation* had had a photo cover and I was thrilled to see, when I received my comp of the audio, that this was blessed with a glorious, brand new cover painting by Nicholas Spender of a burning London, flames billowing into the air making the sky a looming orange, houses crumbling, in the distance a blazing church with fire in its windows, a cloaked, sharp-toothed Terileptil to the front left, a wooden cart filled with rats and, behind it, the TARDIS, rats scurrying over the roof; a painting so perfectly in-keeping with the Target spirit that, holding it, I felt exactly as I had at thirteen, looking for the first time at the gorgeous image on the front of the newest novelisation!

Editor's Note

There is little I could say about the Target *Doctor Who* range that isn't said more eloquently in one of nearly 200 essays contributed to this book by over a hundred writers.

The publisher and chief editor of the *You and Who* books was, at first, sceptical that we would attract this level of interest and felt that *You on Target* would be a slim tome covering only the most significant of the books. The size and diversity of the finished product is testament to the power these books still have on the nostalgia centres of the brains of *Doctor Who* fans of a certain vintage.

As usual, all proceeds from this latest entry to the *You and Who* bibliography will be donated to charity. The charity I chose for *You on Target* is Tree of Hope, who offer hope to the families of seriously ill and disabled children in the United Kingdom and Ireland who need specialist medical treatment, therapy and equipment. By enabling families to raise money towards these important ends, under the banner of a registered charity, they have been a lifeline for hundreds of children and their families for over 25 years.

Thank you to everyone who contributed; to Matthew Waterhouse, David J Howe and Nigel Robinson for their very special essays; to J.R. Southall at Watching Books; and of course to my wife Nina for tolerating me spending time editing a book about a long-finished series of books spun off from a TV series...

I believe this book is fairly comprehensive, but inevitably there are books missed: the novelisations of *The Sarah Jane Adventures*, for example; *Shakedown* and *Downtime*; audio-only novelisations... and probably some books I don't even know exist. Furthermore, I originally finished editing this book in 2017, but they keep announcing more and more books! Even now, we know there are novelisations coming out later this year, but we've decided not to delay publication any longer.

Let's agree that the book is long enough as it is!

Christopher Bryant
2020

Dedication

Almost all of the essays written in this book were written before 29th August 2019, when Terrance Dicks passed away at the age of 84.

Unsurprisingly, his writing and his inspiration are already the focus of so many of the essays that we didn't think we needed to add anything else in tribute to the great man.

The whole book is in tribute to the writers who brought us the Target novelisations, and none more so than Terrance Dicks.

You on Target is dedicated to the memory of Terrance Dicks.

Introduction

David J Howe

It was a Thursday ... good things always happened on a Thursday ... and I was on holiday down in Newquay in Cornwall. My parents always holidayed there as my grandmother had a house there, so it was cheap and easy and, being by the sea, was also good for kids. We would all get out every day and walk down to the town, past Narrowcliff and sea vistas, past the imposing hotels and down into a wonderland of shops and amusement arcades and beaches.

One of the shops was W H Smith – it was the only bookstore in the town – and even at the age of about 14 I was a bit of a book connoisseur. I was also a lover of the TV Show *Doctor Who*, and a couple of years earlier had delighted in finding a copy of *The Making of Doctor Who* – my first glimpse behind the veil of the show, and also my first inkling that there were more *Doctor Who* adventures than those I was happily watching on television at the time. In fact I remembered some of them: *Evil of the Daleks*, *The Tomb of the Cybermen*, *The Invasion* ... images and memories from these haunted my mind.

So on this particular Thursday in 1974, I was wandering in W H Smith, looking to see if there was anything interesting to buy, when my eyes fell on the *Doctor Who* logo. Black. On a book cover. Now back then, this was unheard of. There were no *Doctor Who* books ... only that amazing *Making of* book ... so what was this? I picked it up and studied the cover. It was *The Curse of Peladon* and the cover artwork showed me the fantastic creatures from this story.

It was a tale I remembered well as it was the first that I had ever audio recorded off the television! My dad wanted to watch *UFO* as I recall, which was on ITV at the same time as *Doctor Who* and so he rigged up a little microphone thing in the back room, and recorded the sound of *Doctor Who* for me as I was distraught at the thought of missing the show completely while *UFO* was on. So the sounds of that adventure stayed with me: the hissing background throb of Acturus, the sonorous drumbeat tones and hissing voices of the Ice Warriors, and the squeaking panic of Alpha Centauri. It remains a favourite story to this day.

And now there was a book of it! I had to have it. I can't remember if I had to go back home to plead for funds, or whether I had the required 35p in my pockets (we would go out and haunt the amusement arcades, obtaining forgotten pennies from the deposit slots of penny falls machines, or larger coins which had been abandoned in one armed bandits, and then use that money to buy sweets and toys – we also used to retrieve abandoned Corona lemonade bottles from the bins as they had 5p return value on them) but I bought the book, and was enthralled.

I guess it must have been a few days later that I headed back to W H Smith to see if there were any more – some titles were mentioned in the book I had – and lo and behold there were! So I managed to get them as well ... and over the next few months slowly grew my initial Target collection. The only one I couldn't find was the very first, *Doctor Who and the Daleks*, but I eventually got this a couple of years later from a small shop while on holiday in North Wales.

Thus started my love affair with the Target books. Everything about them was perfect, from the brilliantly rendered cover artwork by the exotically named Christos Achilleos, to the prose and the design (though to my young self, such things were at the time unknown – I just knew they looked *great*).

I remember the following year, again checking in the shop on holiday and finding a copy of *The Giant Robot* and being horrified. They had changed the artist! But by then I wanted to know more and so wrote off to the publishers, joined the Target Book Club, got some newsletters and some covers, and found out what was coming up and - more importantly - which titles I had missed. I loved it and was a regular correspondent with Sandy Lessiter (who ran the club), asking more and more questions and trying to get covers and information in advance.

So the wheel turns, and my love affair with the books continues, and I write articles for *Doctor Who* magazine about them, and then I realise that I have enough material to compile all this together into a single book ... and there was really only one title that this book could have: *The Target Book*. One thing I wanted to do was to try and emulate certain nostalgic aspects of the range and so we arranged all the covers side by side in the back, much like the lovely cover spread on the back of *The Doctor Who Monster Book*, and also created some covers which never were from unused artwork. I think that the book hit the right nerve with readers as there have been many lovely comments about it. We produced two printings of the paperback and two runs of different limited edition hardbacks before it sadly went out of print. Happily, the book gained a new lease of life in 2016 with another run of hardback editions.

Now I find that I am not the only one with stories and memories about these books: this publishing phenomenon which got so many kids reading, which was a small juggernaut of inspiration and design and artwork and stories, which inspired so many children to try writing their own *Doctor Who* fiction, and which led to many of them now writing for the television show itself, and penning the books and

11

comics and audio stories.

Contained in this book that you hold in your hands are more stories and memories and inspirations which that book range has generated. Every book has its fans, and here they are, talking about the stories which mean most to them ... it's an amazing legacy of work, and one which I'm sure the publishers of the books over the years never even considered might exist. They were just publishing a range of books ... to us it was something magical and spellbinding.

I don't know why so many people found the books on holiday. Maybe they were only distributed to seaside towns! I for one am glad that they were.

Chapter 1

The Journey Begins

1973

The first three *Doctor Who* books, previously published by Frederick Muller in the 1960s, are reprinted. The Target imprint acquires the rights to novelise television stories from *Doctor Who* thanks to the range's first editor, Richard Henwood.

Also in 1973

Strikes lead to a three day week in Britain... the World Trade Centre opens in New York... the UK joins the European Economic Community... *The Exorcist* is released in cinemas... Picasso dies... Peter Kay is born... Pink Floyd release *The Dark Side of the Moon*... Katy Manning leaves *Doctor Who*...

An Exciting Adventure in WH Smith

Doctor Who in an Exciting Adventure with the Daleks
by Ken Shinn
Favourite *Doctor Who* book: *Timewyrm: Revelation* by Paul Cornell

I am sitting in a crowded civic hall in Southwark. I can only guess what kind of crowd normally fills it: perhaps councillors, or some of those other politicians that I glance at occasionally on the evening news. Today, though, is Saturday, 1st July, 1972. The crowd around me is composed of other primary school children like myself – in fact, some of them are friends of mine from Dog Kennel Hill – and their parents and other family members. The stage in front of us is occupied by some other grown-ups who do look like councillors, although I reckon that most of them are teachers. Some are even dressed in those dark gowns that Nigel Molesworth has already taught me that teachers always wear, even though I've only seen my headmaster wear one, and only rarely then. All of my teachers wear tweedy suits or twin-sets, with the occasional younger, more rebellious one favouring polo-necks.

My own parents are with me, reassuring me that I just need to walk up on to the stage when my name is called. I know that my brother has definitely been to an event of this kind before and managed okay, so I can't let the side down. I am nervous, but it's an excited sort of nervous. Because, for the first time in my life, I am here to receive a prize.

Why have I won a prize? Let me explain. At school, my favourite subjects are reading and writing. My class is currently working through Sheila McCullagh's books about *The Three Pirates*. Everybody, boys or girls, loves pirates – but these pirates are even better than the usual. They don't just get involved in sword fights and treasure hunting – their world has the supernatural in it as an easily-accepted feature. There are real mermaids. There's a real griffin. It's a heady mixture of 'real' and 'fairy tale', and I love it. I tear through these books in classes, to the point where I'm at least a couple of volumes ahead of everyone else, and my teacher – with an equal mix of delight and concern – suggests quietly that I slow down a little to let my classmates keep up. And, as a natural accompaniment, we're encouraged to write. To keep a diary. And to create stories. One of the exercises that has stayed with me is that great old standard, What Will Happen To Me When I Grow Up. My piece flits from job to job to encompass whatever takes my fancy, and a lot of it comes from the television that I also enjoy. I recall that I'm destined to end up as a

14

SHADO interceptor pilot on Moonbase, and that when the hostilities presumably cease I end up, in my impossibly old fifties, as a bespectacled glass-blower, due to an item on *Blue Peter* that fascinated me.

I find imagination and inspiration in both books and television, as well as a hell of a lot of interesting things to 'borrow'. Much like a certain Doctor 'borrowed' a certain magic box. But let's not get ahead of ourselves here.

You see, we've had a writing competition in our school recently. One of the suggested subjects was 'Meteors'. Well, of course, I battened onto that one like a remora to a shark. I love all things Space and Science Fiction. The resulting masterpiece is – shall we say? - derivative. The gogglebox has allowed me to absorb so many great works of fantastic wonder, often in the company of my Mum's dad, who is the kind of grandfather that every small child of my stripe dreams of having: kindly, intelligent, possessed of an impish sense of humour and just that little bit odd. Not barmy, or creepy, you understand – but with that slight air of the dreamer. The imaginer. Grandy Wal, as we fondly know him, has a love of fantastic fiction as well. The bookshelves in his Deptford flat are crammed with all sorts of the stuff, from trashy horror potboilers – *Witchfinder* by Brian Ball – to classics by Wells, Wyndham and many others. We visit that flat on alternate weekends, usually after a trip to the swimming baths: on others, such as this one, he comes to visit us in Peckham.

My tale tells of how a race of evil aliens – much like the ones in *UFO* – stage an invasion of Earth. They use spaceships disguised as meteors in order to land on our world, much like the Martians in George Pal's *The War Of The Worlds*. They promptly begin all-out attacks on the planet's major cities, and standard military ordnance quickly proves useless against them and their lethal laser weaponry. Science is called in. A desperate but determined team of boffins, led by Professor Quatermass, battles to find a solution before all is lost. The Prof discovers a serendipitous answer and the world is saved because the otherwise invulnerable aliens can be killed by being sprayed with brine (as in the widely-derided film of *The Day Of The Triffids*).

The more astute reader has probably already noticed that a certain key figure is absent from my work. A fellow named Doctor Who. Want to know why? Because *Doctor Who* frightens me, in a way that other science fiction doesn't. I can't explain why. I can just about bluff my way through excited playground conversations about it, as long as I let others do the bulk of the talking. It's an almost primal fear. Close to a phobia. Phobias are irrational, though. Quatermass would know that, and would overcome any that he had, as he had ultimately overcome Martian mind control, by facing them calmly and scientifically. This evening, the newspaper informs me, BBC1 is showing a film entitled *Dr. Who and the Daleks*. Maybe, I reason, the time has come to watch that with Grandy Wal and the rest of my family. To take the first significant step towards quelling the fear.

But first, I have a prize to receive. The clouds gather for a perfect storm.

Eventually, my name is called. I manage to make it up the stairs on to the stage, accept my prize from the nice man who hands it to me, not be embarrassed by the applause, thank the nice man, and make it back to my seat without crying, wetting myself or throwing up. That really wasn't so bad. But what is this prize? Only now do I allow myself to relax. To look around. To take stock.

As this was a writing competition, the winners were quite understandably given books as prizes. *Charlotte's Web* is very popular among the winners, probably because a much-publicised cartoon feature film of it has just been released. A large number of them also plump for something called *The Hobbit*. As so often, I'm an awkward kid. Yes, I love reading: but there's no one book that I really wanted enough to ask for as a trophy. What have I been presented as my award?

It turns out to be an envelope. Inside is what looks like an expensive birthday card. The picture is a 3D image of the first lunar landing. Inside are several stamps of different colours, with monetary values printed on them. £2. £1. £1. 50p. 50p. I have just received my first Book Token. My parents explain that I can exchange these stamps for books in the shops. My Dad slyly observes that my indecision has actually benefitted me – rather than just the one book, this will let me get a lot of them – and I don't even need to spend them all at once, if I can't find enough books that immediately excite my attention. And you know what? He's right!

I am therefore a young child, who likes to read, handed the means to get myself many books. Sod sweet shop rampages, this is the real deal. Hyped beyond measure at the thought of such power, it's a good thing for me that my family needs to do some shopping on the way home, meaning that they'll stop at the shopping centre at the Elephant and Castle. Because that shopping centre, as I already know, has a branch of W H Smith. And that W H Smith has many, many books to choose from. An ideal safety valve – without it, I'd probably have exploded from the excitement...

The book stacks form a wonderful labyrinth. My seven-year-old self can't see over any of them, even on tip-toe, but they've thoughtfully laid out a large display of children's books on low shelves and a table. I can't remember all of the books that I exchanged tokens for that day – I don't even think that I managed to spend the whole fiver's-worth at once – but three I'm pretty sure about. One was a very early prototype for those 'choose-your-own-adventure' books that really came into vogue about a decade later, *Mission to Planet L*. The second caught me with its dramatic painted cover of a screaming man in a Mini hurtling over a cliff edge, and its breathless, exclamation mark-adorned title, *Narrow Squeaks!* – a compendium of fictionalised accounts of true-life miraculous escapes from various misfortunes. And the third...

As an adult, I can see the flaws in the cover art. Why is the TARDIS purple? What's up with those carnival-coloured Daleks? Why does the Doctor have galaxies in his coat? But as a child, it gripped me with its simple, direct power. The TARDIS, pulsing into existence to save the day: the Daleks, looming and blasting away at unseen targets; and, wise, calm, and heroic-looking (for all that he's an old man, not like Pertwee at all, oh no), the Doctor taking centre-stage. Above it, the stark title in bold, black capitals: *DOCTOR WHO AND THE DALEKS*. The exact same title as the film that I'm bracing myself to watch tonight. Maybe even the same story. A perfect case of serendipity. I add it to my other booty with trembling fingers. After I've seen the film, I promise myself, I'm going to read this.

I can barely wait till dinner is done. My family crowds the front room for the grand old ritual of Saturday night television, and the reassurance of my family around me helps my resolve, as does the fact that the film doesn't have the frankly terrifying title music of the television version. The mix of slapstick comedy among the tense travails and explosive, fire extinguisher-punctuated action eases my worries further, and Cushing's genuinely charming portrayal reminds me somewhat of my own Granddad. It is a film that is very difficult for a seven-year-old not to love. I come away from it almost bouncing with glee. Internally, I resolve to start watching *Doctor Who* properly on telly when it comes back on. In the meantime, to cement the foundations of my new-found fandom, I have a book to read.

Interesting thing about this book. While it does make a fan out of me, it chooses to test my loyalties in a very unusual way: trial by ordeal.

Firstly, the title page tells me that the cover is wrong: this book should properly be referred to as *Doctor Who In An Exciting Adventure With The Daleks,* but that's nothing compared to what's to come. The mysterious Mr Whitaker introduces me to Ian, Barbara and Susan not in a comedy sequence involving a squashed box of chocolates in a warm, cosy living room, but on a foggy common late at night, where Ian finds Barbara wandering semi-conscious by a wrecked lorry with a dead squaddie inside. It's less Aaru and more Euston Films. At least when the Doctor finally shows up, he'll be the nice, friendly old cove

17

from the film, right?

> *'The point is, can I let you go now? I don't think I can. I'll just have to take you both with me.'*

In the parlance of times future, this book is gleefully wrenching me out of my comfort zone. This Doctor is a frighteningly unknown quantity – quick to anger, deliberately inscrutable, apparently far more physically powerful than such a frail old man should be. He's as super-intelligent as the film's portrayal, but that just concerns me all the more. This Doctor is someone whose bad side is not something that I'd like to experience, but I have the horrible feeling that I could readily do so. The inspired use of Ian's first-person narration makes it very easy to put myself in that place. I'm made privy to his thoughts, his feelings and even his night terrors. The whole thing feels less jolly, less safe, than on celluloid. And it takes its time. Incidents that took seconds on screen take whole chapters here. Initially, this puzzles me, even irritates me a little. Why is it taking so long to unfold? It isn't until I find myself becoming much more intrigued with this version that I finally glimpse the answer.

This is a book about things that I'll only be able to put proper words to as I grow older. Characterisation. Atmosphere. A growing sense of dramatic tension. One thing that it does is something for which I'm very grateful – it expands my vocabulary. Indeed, overall, it never talks down to me. It assumes a certain amount of intelligence, knowledge, and inquisitiveness on my part. That's a gift that can't be appreciated enough.

The first voyage in the TARDIS becomes a piece of genuine wonder: the antique furniture that clutters the vast control room, rubbing shoulders with unknowably advanced technology, the amazing oil and hot water shower/massage cubicle, the moment when the Doctor, finally becoming a little more affable, produces what look like white Mars bars that taste perfectly of bacon and eggs that are as filling and nutritious as the real thing. It almost comes as an irritant when the Ship lands and we make the trek through the petrified forest to that shining metal city.

What of the Daleks themselves? The film makes them, as they should be, marvellous villains of the most colourful sort, easy to boo and hiss, to cheer as they're finally foiled. Creatures of pantomime. Fascinating as they are, they can't frighten me now. Can they?

> *'The answer came through the front entrance slowly. A nightmare answer that had the blood draining away from my face and the skin stretching around my eyes.'*

Assisted by Arnold Schwartzman's scratchy, moody, black and white illustrations, now I begin to fear. This story doesn't just make the Daleks properly frightening – intelligent, scheming, ruthlessly

18

deadly - it takes the bold, splashy cartoon of the film and transmutes it alchemically into something so much darker, so much more intense. The Thals, when we meet them, are given names and characters. Temmosus doesn't just wander into the Dalek control room looking about in slightly gormless silence before being promptly shot down. He attempts, in a breath-taking moment, to talk peace with the Daleks in a speech of courageous eloquence. And the Daleks' response, as he stares them down and awaits their answer, is as shocking and brutal as it could be.

'The planet Skaro is ours. And ours alone.'

All bets are off. There can be no happy, easy answers. From here on in, the story becomes not some simple action-adventure, but a genuine, taut struggle for survival. Whitaker isn't so much teaching me some harsh truths as rubbing my nose in them as if I were an errant puppy. His tone is uncompromising and refreshingly free of condescension or didacticism. He is treating me as an intelligent adult. Many years later, Virgin's New Adventures novels announced themselves proudly as 'stories too deep and too broad for the small screen' and sometimes they were. But they weren't the first to do that for *Doctor Who*.

This is an intelligent tale, but also a powerfully emotional one. Love, pride, hate, fear – they're all here, along with every other feeling that you could think of. The blows are never softened. Antodus doesn't get his own *Narrow Squeaks!* style escape in this version – his end, when it comes, is an unforgettable moment of drawn-out horror that even the original TV rendition (when I finally saw that) can't hope to match. Poor Elyon is hauled off to his agonising demise and Whitaker adds a subsequent battle between the torch-wielding Ian and Kristas and an enormous, savage monster that Ray Harryhausen would surely have given his eye teeth to bring to life. The scaling of the mountain becomes a genuinely gruelling struggle against the merciless elements. As we reach the climax, we are given something that the television version hadn't - a Dalek leader, who is also – such a simple, unexplained, brilliant conceit! – a glass Dalek! It's an image almost more suited to the bluntly-moralistic world of the fairy tale than to science fiction. This Dalek feels more like Rumpelstiltskin or some evil wizard, a being of pure, uncompromising hatred and fury. Finally, even in chains, the Doctor speaks with the voice of genuine heroism against it.

'Stop this senseless slaughter,' he bellowed.

The Doctor speaks heroism and Ian enacts it. With the help of Barbara and their Thal allies, a full-scale battle ensues which eclipses both the other versions, packed with individual incidents – Ganatus bronco-riding a Dalek which throws him off and wounds him, Kristas

19

like some unstoppable alien Obelix smashing in the domes of other Daleks with his handy metal canister – before the Daleks' power is finally broken. And – unlike either other version – Whitaker doesn't want to just run away and leave us with a rushed ending. He gives us a proper epilogue, with genuine emotional punch. Friends say their goodbyes; there is even doubt on the part of Barbara and Ian as to whether they should stay here.

It was a marvellous tale back in 1972 when I first read it. Eager to share it, I badger my class teacher into reading it as our end to the school day, in the same place as such wonderful stories have been read aloud to us as *Rikki-Tikki-Tavi* and *Charlie and the Chocolate Factory*. She gives it a try, but the reading is met with polite bemusement from my classmates and the very next day she returns the book to me with a polite apology and a new story is begun at the end of the afternoon. 'But when do the Daleks show up?' is my friends' constant, frustrated refrain. Maybe, like me, they've been slightly spoilt in terms of pacing by the film version. The Daleks don't actually show up in the book until page 56. It all feels a little unfair, but I swallow my disappointment and carry the book home carefully with me. I want to read it again soon. I hope maybe some of my friends will find a copy of it, read it in their own good time, and become as enraptured by it as I was.

Whatever the case, it definitely made me a convert to the cause. This imaginative, intelligent, moral story, aided and abetted by the film, has ensured that *Doctor Who* has a new fan. Years later, in 1985, my then-girlfriend at college, taking a PGCE, reveals to me that *Doctor Who in an Exciting Adventure with the Daleks* is the current book that she is reading to her primary school charges. I find myself hoping that mid-1980s Liverpudlian kids enjoy it more than early-1970s London ones did. Either way, it is a delight to find that it still endures.

Just last year - my original, prize copy of the book long gone after many house-moves - I'm browsing the marvellous Barter Books in Alnwick with my current girlfriend. Clutching my pile of acquisitions, I crouch down to the lowest shelves, and there – before my seven-year-old's height's eyes – is a copy of the BBC Books reprint. A smile crosses my face and becomes a grin. This one isn't going to be lost. I add it to my stack before heading to the till.

The adventure continues.

> 'Barbara said, 'Can we stay with the Doctor, Ian?'
> I saw Susan and her grandfather smile at each other. I got up and walked over to Barbara and took her hand lightly. I felt her fingers pressing into mine. Asking for comfort? Affection? I still didn't dare hope it might be love. Only time could tell. I turned and faced the Doctor with a smile.
> 'We stay with you,' I said.'

Ugly Bug Ball

Doctor Who and the Zarbi by Tim Pieraccini

Favourite *Doctor Who* book: *The Making of Doctor Who*
by Terrance Dicks and Malcolm Hulke (1972 edition)

No one expected the 1970s boom in *Doctor Who* merchandise. Its most exciting manifestation was the wonderful Tenth Anniversary Special...and *The Making of Doctor Who* — its two most exciting manifestations were the Tenth Anniversary Special, *The Making of Doctor Who* and the Weetabix — its three most exciting manifestations were...

I'll come in again.

It's taken for granted that Dalek and TARDIS are words that everyone knows, but it occurred to me recently that the word Zarbi has similarly been with me my whole life. It turns out, as with so many things (anyone remember when Draconian seemed like a whole new word, and not a description of government policy?), that the word already existed, in French, and means 'strange' or 'bizarre'. Apt enough for the atmosphere of Vortis, whether or not that's where Bill Strutton actually got it from.

I can't be sure I saw *The Web Planet* on broadcast; my earliest TV memory is the Cybermen falling to their own weapons in *The Tenth Planet*, so I certainly saw some Hartnell, even if I don't remember the Doctor himself. Of the earlier stories I have no memory at all, though the fact that we were watching the show in 1966 suggests that perhaps we did a year earlier (I suspect only because there was no alternative that appealed to my parents, neither being science fiction fans. My father's only comment on *Doctor Who* was to say he might start watching when he first saw Leela, and the only thing I remember my mother saying was that *The Five Doctors* 'didn't seem to be about anything').

As with many fans of a similar vintage, I suspect, my early impressions of both Hartnell and the Zarbi come from the magnificent, if eccentric, 1965 *Doctor Who* Annual. In this I suppose I fell victim to the BBC's master plan (was there one, or did I dream it?) to push the Zarbi as the next great monster - not one, but two Zarbi stories, even if the later one was, oddly, clearly written/set before the earlier - since at the time I viewed them as the principal antagonists of the Hartnell Doctor. This was a view not necessarily undermined by the first three books in the Target range.

Personal snapshots of my Target experience:

The Curse of Peladon was the first book I ever ordered by post, being unable to find it anywhere in the shops. After getting the book, I received a further communication from Target asking for an extra 10p: my dad said, 'Oh, I don't think they'd be asking you to send just 10p...oh, they are...'

For many years I carried within my copy of *The Abominable Snowmen* an autograph of Kevin Keegan, obtained at Hamley's – I was not a football fan (let's face it, the football results on TV Saturday teatime were a kind of sophisticated torture—you know what I'm talking about. Would they never end?) but my brother was, and perhaps it seemed odd for only one of us to go up.

I recall reading *The Daemons* on a boat across the Thames; a very grim, grey day, but fortunately not heavy enough rain to interfere with my reading. I don't remember my family's reactions to my lack of interest in the London scenery.

I was gently reprimanded by the Deputy Head for reading *The Cave Monsters* at school when I was 13. How would he have felt to know I read through most of the range again in my early twenties – and possibly damaged my eyesight doing so (reading for an hour first thing every morning to not recommended, children)

The early 1970s were the golden age of my personal fandom. Aside from the books I mentioned earlier, we had the Holiday Special with the then-rare Delgado picture I copied for one of my *The Key to Time* contributions a decade later. *The Sea Devils* was repeated at the drop of rain on a cricket pitch. Armies of aliens were made, following the templates of the Weetabix figures (folding sheets of paper over several times so I could cut out five or six figure shapes at once and then fill in the details) and vast newspaper bases constructed for them to wander (has the Daily Telegraph ever been put to better use?). My best friend, who lived handily just across the road, even devised a way to make sliding doors for the bases. Or was that me? It's so hard to recall exactly where the ideas came from... We also disagreed about what the Yeti looked like, without realising that their appearance had changed between stories – but that was nothing compared to the confusion about story titles caused by the Tenth Anniversary Special and the lack of titles in *The Making of Doctor Who* (at the age of 9 or 10, I was far from certain what an 'insane warmonger' was).

But of course, the biggest thing was Target – exciting enough to be reminded of the Autons crashing put of the shop windows or to be told futuristic guerrillas could scarcely imagine pyjamas, but actually to be able to revisit Det-Sen monastery and the moonbase ... and to go even farther back, to the earliest years...

I wish I could say I read the original 1960s editions of those three novels, but I think the truth is I only picked them up on the Target re-issue, and possibly only after *The Auton Invasion* came out. I do have a Green Dragon edition of *The Crusaders* which seems to stir memories, so perhaps I had that one earlier. This would account for the sense I always had that Hartnell, Ian and Barbara were 'my' TARDIS team, in a way even Pertwee/Jo didn't quite manage. Certainly David Whitaker's sketches of how Ian and Barbara had developed during their travels made a deep impression on me, and I'm sure he was responsible for my lifelong devotion to Barbara Wright. More importantly, perhaps (at least in terms of this article), Whitaker's brief exploration of the characters at the beginning of one novel informed my reading of them elsewhere, most significantly in the Zarbi book.

It's an odd beast, Bill Strutton's novelisation. It alternates between being really well-written and, apparently, the work of someone not used to expressing themselves in narrative prose. It followed the structure of the TV serial (6 chapters), even if much of the detail of events and dialogue was different. It's not my favourite novelisation – top two places would go to the Whitaker books, with some competition from early Dicks and Hulke – but it does, for me, have a special relationship to the TV story. I believe it was Paul Cornell who said the Pertwee TV stories are disappointing partly because the books are so good – and in a similar but actually completely different way, I think anyone who watches *The Web Planet* without having read the novelisation is losing out.

It may, in fact, be essential to read the novelisation first. This may simply be a product of the way my mind works, but seeing the unfamiliar names on paper (Vrestin, Hrostar, Nemini, Hetra, Hlynia, Hilio, Prapillus) fixed them in my mind much more strongly than just hearing them in passing could ever have done. It was easier to remember who was who amid a plethora of similar-looking Menoptera: Prapillus is fixed as old the moment he appears, not something that necessarily comes over immediately on TV. Similarly, Hrostar is described as proud, and scornful, and much is made of the beauty of his wings (and of Vrestin's, later). Speaking of Vrestin, it came to me, when considering the obvious main difference between the character on TV and in the novelisation, that despite its lack of diversity by modern standards, *Doctor Who* didn't do too badly in terms of gender-bending – not just Vrestin, but Alpha Centauri, Eldrad, Kronos...they all play with gender identity. These tiny touches in the book bring about an intimacy and sense of involvement with the characters that is probably lacking for most people when they watch the TV serial. *The Web Planet* may be my favourite Hartnell serial, and I think it owe much of that to the novelisation.

And if nothing else, it gave me some life advice I still use – swallowing whenever my ears sing...

23

The Magic Dragon

Doctor Who and the Crusaders
by Stephen Hatcher
Favourite *Doctor Who* book: *Short Trips: The Centenarian*
ed. Ian Farrington

I'm going to start with something of a heretical admission. The Target novelisations have never really meant that much to me.

I suppose by the time the Target range started in 1973, I was approaching 15 and had moved on to more 'adult' books from Ian Fleming and Edgar Rice Burroughs to Arthur C. Clarke and Robert Heinlein, often scouring charity shops for second-hand SF short story anthologies. Although I had finally become a regular viewer of *Doctor Who*, there really wasn't room in my life for it to invade my reading time, the exception being Hulke and Dicks' wonderful *The Making of Doctor Who*, with Pertwee and a Sea Devil on the cover, which played a major part in turning me into a fan.

The only two *Doctor Who* novels that I ever owned during my childhood were those two paperbacks that came out when I was younger, back in the sixties – *Doctor Who in an Exciting Adventure with the Daleks* and *Doctor Who and The Crusaders*. (For some reason, the third sixties book, *Doctor Who and The Zarbi*, never made it into paperback stage and so never crossed my path.)

I was an avid reader from an early age, oddly enough becoming a fan as much of particular publishers as of the work of individual writers. The first book I ever read on my own was, in common with so many British children, by Enid Blyton: *Mr Galliano's Circus*, published by Armada Paperbacks, who quickly became my favourite publishers before being supplanted later on by the wonderful Puffin Books, the children's imprint of Penguin. Armada, with their fabulous, bright covers introduced me to the Anthony Buckeridge *Jennings* stories, *Biggles* by Captain W. E. Johns, the famous Armada Ghost Books and a number of wonderful *Thunderbirds* and *Stingray* novels by John Theydon. Then of course, there was David Whitaker's novelisation of the first *Doctor Who* Dalek story, with its striking cover, devoid of Daleks, but with Hartnell's Doctor complete with flowing white locks and the immense swirl of a red-lined purple cloak.

All these books were among the most treasured possessions of my reading-obsessed childhood, which is why I still cannot understand to this day how I came to allow myself to be persuaded, in the interest of creating storage space in my admittedly tiny bedroom, to donate a large box of them to the children's ward of Warwick Hospital. How I regret even now that minor act of philanthropy – as well as my later decision to donate my entire collection of Gerry Anderson *Century 21* Mini-LPs to a jumble sale in aid of the Labour Party. (Mind you, at that same jumble sale I bought my first Wisden Cricketer's Almanack, thus beginning another life-long obsession.)

However, *Doctor Who and the Crusaders*, also by David Whitaker, was not one of those lovely Armada paperbacks. A little research reveals that Dragon Books was in fact founded by one Gordon Landsborough in 1966 after he had sold Armada Publishing, which he had also founded a few years earlier. Given this fact, it becomes less surprising that *The Crusaders* was one of the new company's earliest releases, along with lots of Enid Blyton, various classic authors, Edgar Rice-Burroughs' *Tarzan* novels and Anthony Buckeridge's less successful *Rex Milligan* books. That's quite a roster, but although I certainly spent a fair bit of pocket money on Green Dragons, I never found these books as appealing as Armadas. A lot of this must be put down to the covers. In place of the sumptuous full-colour illustrations of the Armada books, Dragon books were predominantly white, with a colour illustration that took up just over half of the front cover. *The Crusaders* sports a bizarre depiction of a long-legged, rather athletic-looking Hartnell, sprinting away from a group of crusader knights across a field of oddly blue grass. It just isn't impressive - in fact, the whole range looked cheap and shoddy in comparison. Although it was never going to be among my favourite editions, *Doctor Who and the Crusaders* took its place alongside Whitaker's earlier novelisation on my heaving bookshelf, only to be lost in due course to the young patients of Warwick Hospital.

It wasn't until many years later that this book was to enter my life again. The 1993 30th Anniversary of *Doctor Who* having rekindled my love for the show, I came to the realisation that there were an awful lot of books out there that I would quite like to own. Initially, I settled for factual books – Howe, Stammers & Walker, Peter Haining et al. Then I dipped my toes into the Virgin New and Missing Adventures. The collecting bug bit. The annuals..? No, I wasn't really interested in buying them, yet within a couple of years I had a full set, even the rare ones. Now how about those Target books? In those days it wasn't uncommon to find them cheaply in charity shops and second-hand bookshops, but even so, there were just too many for me to contemplate acquiring the lot. It didn't take me to long to do just that – even all the alternative editions and covers, among them the Green Dragon edition of *The Crusaders* (in nice condition). Childhood memories were unearthed just in time for the relevant chapters to fill in more than adequately for the missing TV episode, as part of a marathon *Doctor Who* watch.

There it sits to this day, on my still heaving bookshelf, together with the 1973 and 1982 Target Books editions (the latter signed by Jean Marsh) and the 2011 BBC Books reprint, not to mention the BBC talking book read by William Russell. In preparation for this article, I re-read the book in its entirety for the first time since the 1960s, but this time in electronic form on my Kindle – who would have imagined that in 1966? Come to think of it, the rather imaginative David Whitaker might well have done. As a novel it really holds up rather well – fast paced, action packed and all that. As a novelisation of a television story, it is even better, being faithful to the original plot and characters (Whitaker's own TV scripts), without feeling perfunctory as some novelisations can. Any additions are limited in scope and just feel right – primarily emphasising the romantic relationship between Ian and Barbara that had been established in the previous book, but never on TV, and allowing Ian and Saladin to share a scene – an odd omission from the televised version. I don't think there have been many editions in the Target range that come close to this book in terms of quality. If *The Daleks* is a successful novelisation in a different mode – making many changes from the TV version in order to make a better book – *The Crusaders* sets the pattern of faithful re-tellings that the majority of the Target output would follow. It is a very important book for the range.

Finally, a note of thanks to John Allard. John is not someone I know; I have never met him, nor have I ever corresponded with him. I know nothing about him other than that at some time in the last 50 years he used what looks like a John Bull toy printing set to mark with his name (not very neatly) what later became my copy of *The Crusaders* as his own. Whether he was the original owner or a later custodian, my gratitude goes to him for helping to keep it in the good condition that it is. Many thanks. I hope that in your time, you got as much pleasure out of the book as I continue to do.

Chapter 2

The Invasion

1974 – 1981

Beginning with a run of novelisations of recently-aired stories from Jon Pertwee's time as the Doctor, Target publish between 7 and 11 *Doctor Who* novels every year. Following the departure of Richard Henwood, the range has four different editors during this time. 40 of the 64 books published during these years are written by Terrance Dicks. Six other writers account for most of the others. Cover artwork is initially handled by Chris Achilleos, but other artists such as Jeff Cummins and Andrew Skilleter join the range too.

Also in these years

The Labour governments of Harold Wilson and James Callaghan give way to a Conservative administration which will outlive the Target imprint... Apple Computers formed in Silicon Valley... Cinema changes forever thanks to films like *Jaws* and *Star Wars*... John Lennon is shot... Prince Charles marries Lady Diana Spencer... *Bohemian Rhapsody* enjoys its first stint at number one... Liverpool become the first club to top the First Division ten times... Tom Baker spends seven years in *Doctor Who*...

In the Beginning is My End

Doctor Who and the Auton Invasion by Steven B

Favourite *Doctor Who* book: *Castrovalva*
by Christopher H Bidmead

Somewhen in the lost dimension of youth, I fell into the vortex of *Doctor Who*. I came in to it via half-formed remembrances of after-school television repeats, and – more influentially – a veritable treasure trove of by-then already long-neglected Target novelisations that were housed in a cosy primary school library; a strangely comforting place, which allowed access to its inner sanctum only through a set of battered blue double doors...

In truth, I never quite managed to escape.

My introduction to what has been the longest mainstay and one of my greatest passions in life happened early on an unseasonably cold February morning, in a seaside town on what – to many of you – will be the other side of this good planet. Simply seeking refuge from the weather, I instead collided with something that I impossibly, immediately, and actually recognised upon first sight. It wasn't just this book that exercised such an influence upon me, of course, as I soon came to formulate through that library's collection an understanding of and love for the conventions that the Target range established for itself: the now-naïve yet bold designs with that iconic logo; the dots-as-starfields covers and those oddly charming blurbs on the back; their infrequent and ultimately non-existent illustrations; and, of course, The Changing Face of Doctor Who.

Like the days of the Doctor himself, I experienced his stories like crazy paving, taken all out of order and context. Each Target title listed on the inside cover of those first editions held promises of tall tales and close scrapes: but these were adventures that hadn't happened – not yet, not to my mind, at least. I used to go hungry on occasions, so that I could save up that little bit more pocket money so as to join him on his next adventure. It's tragic to admit now, but I even lost blood standing up for my hero in the playground when it was pointed out one too many times that reading was 'uncool' and reading *Doctor Who* books was even 'uncooler'. How could I not? I believed in and wanted so desperately to believe in a hero like the one that I found in those books, and the truth is that I still do.

Some of the titles of these unknown adventures seemed alluringly bizarre and terrifying, others impossible and contradictory. What, I would wonder, was a *Ribos Operation*? How could there possibly be a story with *Three Doctors*? I soon became enthralled by the idea of stories about brains in jars and monsters stitched together from other creatures, of the great war between ants and bumblebee people that was driven by a sinister influence, of abominable robot yeti in the Himalayas and a greater, ancient horror... But first and always, this: *Doctor Who and the Auton Invasion*. It was the only place that the whole story of *Doctor Who* could have begun (for me).

In the same way that, at the same age, modern music began (for me) with David Bowie, so *Doctor Who* began (for me) with Jon Pertwee and the UNIT era. What came before – including the Beatles/the black-and-white years – was undoubtedly important, and something that I learned to greatly appreciate and enjoy in time, but – back then – the story began where I found it, at the point in time at which I recognised that this message that was utterly and intriguingly alien was also familiar enough to act as the perfect entry point for someone who, it turned out, was desperate to learn all about a strange and quaint little British cultural phenomenon.

I don't believe I have been alone in pinpointing *The Auton Invasion* as providing that moment to *Doctor Who* at large. It's little surprise that so much of this story is so often borrowed from every time that *Doctor Who* reboots itself. Whether it is the Eighth Doctor dressing himself in the hospital having forgotten who he is or the use of the Nestene Consciousness and the crash of dummies through shop windows in *Rose*, this story provides a narrative template for introducing the idea of the Doctor and the very peculiar nature of those alien threats. How do we tip our hat to the idea of starting all over again when the time comes to do so? We go back to the first time we did it and we say 'thank you', and 'we remember'.

Terrance Dicks' first novelisation – like the many that came after it would undoubtedly have been for many others – was the pretext for me not only becoming a reader, but later an English undergraduate, then a teacher of Literature, and now even a writer. I didn't like books before I picked up *The Auton Invasion*. There was cricket and football to be played and a bike to learn to ride instead, a beach upon which I would run with my pals in the sun. So this was my beginning, one that would later lead me to an understanding and appreciation of the realms of myth and literature, history, philosophy, and television – especially British television. Through it, I would come to travel to the ends of the earth. Our world view is enlarged by that which we are fortunate enough to have catch in our imagination. This was the start of it. Terrance Dicks - thank you for what you have gifted me. We all should thank you. And why you are still waiting for your knighthood for what you have contributed to children's literacy everywhere is one of those irritating mysteries that, if this were one of your books, you would have already wrapped up by now.

Steven Moffat has suggested that *Doctor Who* is the one television show that will never die. To grow up, as many of us did, in love with this show is to have been attuned, however unconsciously at first, to the truth that, in this form, our culture has discovered and perfectly distilled the modern, televisual incarnation of the one story that humanity has told itself over and again for millennia: of Campbell's monomyth of the wise man from distant parts who arrives unannounced, does the most wonderful and inexplicable things, and then – before anyone can thank him, or even ask him why – disappears into the ether from whence he came.

Doctor Who is so lasting because it is both resonant and powerful, compelling enough to attract the attention of a child and simultaneously complex enough in its multiple layers of meaning to arrest that attention well into adulthood. Moreover, it employs the most tried and truest narrative structure that we as a species have developed and refined since the time of the cavemen, allowing us to dress it up in whatever conventions, norms, costumes, tropes, trappings and standards each era thinks is most relevant and appropriate in order to bring that story to life once more. I would never have understood that if it wasn't for that chance encounter with *The Auton Invasion* in a public school library all those years ago. Though the friends and loved ones I have met along the way may have come and gone, through all the places I have lived, seen, and ultimately left, and of all the people I have been, *Doctor Who*, in its eternally shifting and reshaping nature, has remained the one constant in all my lives. How lucky I have been to have once picked up that battered brown book whose pages led me to a world bigger on the inside than I could ever have imagined.

Below the Surface

Doctor Who and the Cave Monsters
by Ian Millsted
Favourite *Doctor Who* book: *The Target Book*
by David J Howe

There are some books that you always remember; always associate with the place you were when you read them. I was working on a fruit farm when I read Kerouc's *On the Road*. H.G. Wells' *The Island of Doctor Moreau* was read while on holiday in the south of France. And *Doctor Who and The Cave Monsters* by Malcolm Hulke? Where was I when I read that? Underwater. Well, technically: below sea level on a ferry, crossing the North Sea from Harwich to Sweden. You were probably expecting greater synchronicity than that. Either I should have been reading *The Sea Devils* on the ferry or I should have been reading *The Cave Monsters* somewhere dark and subterranean. But life never fits that well.

The copy of *The Cave Monsters* I read back then is the copy I still have. I think I got it from a jumble sale. There were always decent bargains at the jumble sales in Danbury, where I lived then. It is certainly a second-hand copy and still has the name of the previous owner marked on the title page. So, J. Moore, whoever you are, thank you for dispensing with the book. If you ever read this, please at least be aware it ended up with someone who read and enjoyed it and has looked after it pretty well. I finished it before we reached Sweden and brought it back and it has survived numerous house moves since. There were, by the way, no cave monsters on view in Sweden. Far from.

The book itself is great, but you probably already know that. If not, don't take it on trust from me; stop reading this and go and get a copy. Yes, you don't get Fulton Mackay's performance as you would in the TV version, but you do get plenty of Malcolm Hulke fleshing out Liz Shaw and the Brig and the Silurians. Especially the Silurians. Last words should go to Mr. Hulke.

'The Doctor started up the car again and continued along the main road in silence.'

Colony Collapse

Doctor Who and the Doomsday Weapon
by Chris Kocher
Favourite *Doctor Who* book: *Timewyrm: Exodus*
by Terrance Dicks

Growing up as a *Doctor Who* fan in rural Pennsylvania in the mid-1980s, things were never easy.

It can be hard to remember now, with the relaunched show not only embraced again in the UK but also part of the pop culture in the US and around the world. Back in the eighties, though, not a lot of other teenagers seemed to know what *Doctor Who* was. I had only one friend as fanatical as me - perhaps even more so - and that might be one of the reasons we're still friends today. (In fact, we travelled together to London for all the 50th anniversary hoopla in 2013.)

One good thing we did have: *Doctor Who* on the local public television, one episode every weeknight at 7:30pm. After having heard my friend talk about the show for years, I finally tuned in just in time for *Warriors' Gate*. Man, was I confused. I somehow missed *The Keeper of Traken*, so my next story was *Logopolis*. Then I was really confused! I was intrigued enough to keep watching, though - and thus a love affair was born.

The public TV station continued to show *Doctor Who* one episode at a time through Sylvester McCoy's first season then cycled back to *Spearhead from Space*. Then, something happened that would shake my world to the core: the station began showing Jon Pertwee's stories in omnibus format on Saturday afternoons, like some kind of B-movie meant to fill time until the more intellectual stuff came on. Still, it was better than nothing, right? Except whoever was programming the station's schedule could not cope with the varying story lengths. Four episodes, or even five, seemed to be fine, but any more than that and the stories would have to be split over two consecutive weeks, generally in the most awkward way possible. The action would reach what I later came to realize was an episode cliffhanger, then just go black: no end credits, nothing - just the station's 'Saturday Matinee' bumper and the next programme.

There were also scheduling mistakes, the biggest of which affected the Doctor's first trip off of Earth since his exile. The station broadcast the first four episodes of *Colony in Space* one week, then the following Saturday aired episodes 3 and 4 again. I must have tried to call the station a dozen times to tell them about the error, but I got no response and the following Saturday we saw *The Daemons*. A classic, to be sure, but still frustrating when a third of the previous story hadn't even been shown. The Master had the Doctor and Jo at gunpoint! How would they ever escape?

At the time, I figured that was the end of it. Sure, there were commercial releases of a few *Doctor Who* stories, but I didn't know a good way to get a hold of them. (Besides, *Colony in Space* would not come out on VHS for another 15 years!) My friend and I would get sketchy bootleg videos from a guy in Ohio, paying top dollar for episodes he'd taped off of TV, as well as grainy and almost unwatchable versions of orphaned episodes from the 1960s (like *The Web of Fear* part one) that were probably ten generations from the original master tapes. *Colony in Space* never seemed important enough to buy that way, compared to Hartnell and Troughton gems we'd have no other way of seeing.

The solution presented itself almost by accident a few months later. My mother would occasionally take me to the library in a nearby city about a half-hour's drive away. It had many more books and seemed more cosmopolitan than the smaller one closer to our home. The library was housed inside of an old Gothic church, and I loved just browsing through the stacks or finding an obscure title that hadn't been signed out for fifty years or more.

In a bunch of spinner racks stuffed with random paperbacks, I found a scattered assortment of Target novelisations, among them *Doctor Who and the Doomsday Weapon* by Malcolm Hulke. Considering the different names for the book and the TV story, I can't recall how I figured out it was really *Colony in Space*. I guess I recognized the Master and the Primitive shown on the cover, then saw the title page where it mentioned the original serial's name. I checked it out from the library immediately - at last, I would know how the story ended!

We should acknowledge at this point that *Colony in Space* is hardly a beloved story in the *Doctor Who* canon. *The Discontinuity Guide* offered a measure of praise for its ambitions but dismissed it as 'rather like watching socially-aware paint dry.' In 2015, an interview in the *Radio Times* with current honcho Steven Moffat asked what *Doctor Who* episodes he'd watched lately: 'Heroically, I got all the way through *Colony in Space* recently. That's a test.' (He added, though, that 'I loved it at the time' - which I suppose proves 1980s producer John Nathan-Turner's well-worn axiom that 'the memory cheats.')

For all of the faults in the television version, though, the novelisation allows Hulke to alter, expand upon and enrich his original script. Some scenes that played out on TV - and seemed pretty important - are summarised offhandedly, while other scenes (such as the Doctor having to arrange the funeral for two slain colonists) are added. Throughout the course of the novel, we learn a lot more about the Earth that Ashe and his intrepid colonists left behind (short

33

answer: crowded, noisy and awful).

The biggest changes happen at the beginning, though, before settling down to the plot we're familiar with. Chapter one gives an extended look at the Time Lords' reaction to the secrets of the Doomsday Weapon being stolen, including a primer from an ancient 'Keeper of the Time Lords' Files' (perhaps a forerunner to the Keeper of the Matrix) and his young protégé on how TARDISes work, why the Doctor was exiled and the Doctor's long-running feud with the Master. There's also a 'Who?' joke thrown in for good measure. (Apparently the kid - 'a mere 573 years of age' - slept through most of his studies at the Academy.) Hulke also rewrites the canon so that *Colony in Space* is Jo's first story, with the Doctor and the Brigadier both offering condescending exposition to this silly young thing about what's going on with UNIT and the Master. That change must have been puzzling to my young mind.

Near the end, the story's climactic meeting with the Guardian is described quite differently from what we saw on TV: he's an impressive being of light rather than a short little frog-man who trundles out of the wall at the opportune time. Perhaps most surprising, however, is when Ashe is confined to quarters and reads one of the two books he brought with him from Earth: the Bible, which was 'largely about someone called God.' Apparently the entire human race has gone atheist? Still, reading the Gospels inspires the thinking that leads Ashe to his fate: 'Why, he asked himself, should anyone willing give his own life for other people?' This short passage, just a paragraph, must be one of the few references to Christianity in the *Doctor Who* canon.

Reading *The Doomsday Weapon* opened a door to the wider world of *Doctor Who* that extended beyond the hundreds of episodes that were broadcast on TV. I started collecting and voraciously reading all the novelisations I could get my hands on. I found and joined a couple of national fan clubs - Canada's *Doctor Who* Information Network and the Friends of *Doctor Who* in the US. I started mailing off for 'zines that featured original *Doctor Who* fan fiction and I even tried my hand at a few early stories, all of which were rejected because, let's be honest, they were terrible. (I later wrote things I'm more proud of and edited a fiction 'zine called *Ninth Aspect*, imagining a ninth Doctor for a TV series that had never been cancelled - yes, very nerdy!)

In the end, then, I learned a lot from the Target books, and it all started with *The Doomsday Weapon*. Thanks, Mac - you'll always hold a special place in my personal *Doctor Who* canon. Oh, and as fate would have it, I waited nearly 25 years to see those last two episodes of *Colony in Space*. The ending definitely looked better in my imagination. Of course it did.

Dalek Days

Doctor Who and the Day of the Daleks
by Chris Omega
Favourite *Doctor Who* book: *Fury From The Deep*
by Victor Pemberton

In 2008, I returned home from a difficult job I had had for a number of years. I had saved enough that I had some time to decompress and to do a project or two. I decided I wanted to use Openoffice and Lulu and make my own pocket Target *Doctor Who* Novelisation guide. I had never written a reference book (or any other book) so it was kind of a learning experiment as well.

One of its purposes was to carry it in your pocket while searching out the books to complete your collection. Unfortunately, I used a copy of it as recommended. I was hitting every bookstore I could find in an attempt to complete my Target collection. I also started buying book lots on eBay and before too long I had them all. After nearly three decades of searching whenever I came across a used bookstore, my quest was over, a quest I'd had since I was a young child. I found another person who was as much of an addict as I was and we even made mock-ups of the New Zealand novelisations that looked like a 'blue spine' version, so I truly had every televised story. I topped off my collection with the Peter Davison Target Book Poster I saw as a kid, but it was basically all over. I never thought about how I would miss the quest.

There are certain Target *Doctor Who* stories that really stand out from my childhood. *Fury from the Deep* was one: the foam and beach scenes I imagined are still vivid. *Day of The Daleks* is another. I spent years (decades to be honest) afterwards searching for 'Terrance Dicks' at every library and book store I went to. It seemed to me that Terrance and *Doctor Who* books were synonymous. In my searches I came across the American Pinnacle version of *Day of The Daleks* - I didn't realise at first just how inaccurate the cover art was on the Pinnacle books and wondered why there was a Neanderthal on the cover.

I think *Day of The Daleks* was the first Target book I really became engrossed in. I had read *The Ice Warriors* but I don't think it painted the picture for me that *Day of The Daleks* did. The time rebels are the biggest thing that stands out in my memory from just over 30 years ago when I was still in grade school. I also remember that when I was still fairly young and saw the televised *Doctor Who* episode, I thought I must have been thinking of another 'of The Daleks' episode or something. At the time I didn't realise just how much more could be in

35

the books than was in the televised version. I also didn't understand why there were only two or three Daleks and Ogrons in the televised version. The Special Edition did a good job beefing it up a little: the futuristic city seemed out of place, but the rest was a good idea and they did a much better job adding segments in than George Lucas did in his movies.

If ever I got rid of my *Doctor Who* collection, the one thing I would have to keep is my Target collection, or at least one copy of each as I still have a few hundred doubles/triples/etc - at one time I bought out a large number of a mail order retailer's back stock of them so I even have a number of brand new spares. Selling these is more pain than what people are willing to pay for them is worth to me at this point. The VHS videos my brother and I made from PBS broadcasts as kids are now pointless and largely effectively blank, but I can't even get myself to throw them out.

The Target novelisations however will never lose their intrinsic value. The missing episodes still live in the books and the books contain so many scenes that the show never had. When it comes to which Target novelisations you should read, listen to what Terrance Dicks said about *Day of The Daleks* in his DVD commentary about the televised version: 'Read the book.'

Sugar, Old Spice and Cigarettes

Doctor Who and the Daemons by Matt Barber

Favourite *Doctor Who* book: The *About Time* books
by Lawrence Miles and Tat Wood

In the mid-1990s, a year before his death, Jon Pertwee toured a one-man show around the country. This was a mixture of tried-and-tested songs, anecdotes, skits and stand-up, honed through a career as an entertainer and a retirement as the elder statesman of *Doctor Who*. He performed a show at my sixth form college in Andover, Hampshire and my dad took me to see him. This was my second experience of seeing an actor from my favourite television series, the first being four years earlier in Swindon where I met Nicholas Courtney, Pertwee's successor as elder statesman. Despite being born in 1977, three years after he changed into Tom Baker, my 'live' experiences of the series were all Pertwee: home counties, UNIT, Bessie speeding along west country lanes and, when I passed my driving test, a pilgrimage to Aldbourne where 'The Daemons' was filmed.

The Daemons resonates with me more than it has any reason to. It's rightly regarded as an atypical *Doctor Who* story, and comes during a period that's rightly regarded as atypical in the series as a whole. A ruffled and authoritarian conservative who defeats villains using a mixture of patronisation and social rank-pulling, was as unlike the mercurial Troughton or the Victorian alien Hartnell as you could get and was a sharp right-turn for the series. But I love it because of how I *experienced* it; I love it because of how I came into direct contact with it.

I remember the one-man show as being bittersweet. Even before I became aware of Pertwee's penchant for performing as himself at conventions, I could sense his stage persona masking his true self. He wasn't just an actor, he was an entertainer, an old-school performer and, as such, I got the impression that he rarely switched off. He was Jon Pertwee only during his private times, but in public he was *Jon Pertwee* - star of *The Navy Lark*, the Third Doctor, Worzel Gummidge. This is what I saw on stage, even as he sat and spoke directly to us of his childhood and his war experiences. I look on the internet to try and pinpoint when I saw him and it states that 'in 1995, Pertwee starred in a one-man show called *Who Is Jon Pertwee?*' This is a good summary: Pertwee didn't just appear, he 'starred' in the show. And that title *Who is Jon Pertwee?* asked a question that was never really answered on stage – but then I met him in the interval, briefly. I saw him during his down-time and experienced five minutes of what felt at the time like the real Pertwee...and he signed my copy of *The*

Daemons by Barry Letts.

I didn't go in alone. Even though I was old enough to shave, I still retained a pre-teen shyness and I was (and am) prone to being star-struck to an extreme degree, so I took my dad with me. I had my book in a pocket. The Target books were perfect for this – flexible and compact and very pocket-friendly. We went to the lobby and asked whether Pertwee would mind meeting us. A thirty second wait then the response: Pertwee would but, we were warned, he was very 'down-to-earth'. I'm still not entirely sure what this meant but I can still remember the roughness of his hands: hands of an adventurer rather than a soft-living entertainer. He was smoking and drinking a coke: two vices, sugar and nicotine, that spiced his dressing room and gave an edge to his voice. I brought out my copy of *The Daemons* and he signed it 'To Matthew, all good wishes, Jon Pertwee (Dr Who no. 3)'. The book inspired a conversation between him and my father about the filming Pertwee had done in Hampshire, Wiltshire and Somerset: I occasionally corrected their inaccuracies, at the time I thought helpfully, in retrospect I suspect irritating. Then we left, our audience at an end and the book safely stowed.

If all this sounds rather like a religious encounter then it's because it was, albeit in a condensed, secular sense. Meeting Pertwee, the physical act of encountering him one-on-one, was like reaching into the television, like stepping into the stories of my past and finding them to be 'down-to-earth' and smelling of sugar, old spice and cigarette. It must be a little like when a Catholic meets the Pope and discovers that he isn't a cold marble statue but has warmth, texture, skin and an odour.

When I got home, I didn't put my copy of the book in its usual place. Instead I upgraded it to a place on the shelves with my 'important' books: my first editions and rare leather-bound copies of inherited literature.

Here's my confession: I've never fetishized the Target novels. I read the comments on the Facebook threads about how much the novels meant to people when they were learning to read, about how much nostalgia they have for them and how much of the books they can quote verbatim, and I just don't share that. For me they were disposable, although I had, and still have, an almost pathological drive to keep books in an immaculate condition. For me they were quick and cheap reads but nothing more, maybe because the videos came at just the age I had money to buy them or maybe because I became just as interested in what happed behind the cameras. But my copy of *The Daemons* was different. It wasn't a Target novel anymore, disposable but desirable, cheap but priceless. It had, alchemically, transformed – *transubstantiated* - from a Target novel into a relic, an object that had shifted beyond its physical form into something transcendent. This one Target novel is my connection with Jon Pertwee and with the brief memory of meeting him.

When he died in 1996, I wrote my first and only letter to *Doctor Who Magazine* relating my conversation with him. I wrote it with the book in front of me as a touchstone and closed my obituary by saying that the overall impression I'd got from the encounter was that he had been a thoroughly nice person, but this wasn't entirely true. Sitting here staring at the pen-marks he made just for me, so close to his death, my impression is of the 'down-to-earthness' revealed in that moment, a glimpse behind his stage, his Time Lord persona. Sitting here, I can still remember the layers of texture that made him real to me: the roughness of his hands, the gravelled sound of his voice and the smell of cigarette smoke.

Growing Up with the Doctor

Doctor Who and the Sea-Devils
by Angela Pritchett
Favourite *Doctor Who* book: *The Dinosaur Invasion*
by Malcolm Hulke

Growing up thirty miles outside of a major city in Virginia in the early 1990s meant that I grew up without the internet and cable. I was also an only child, so to stay entertained, I read a lot (and watched local television, which was not much to write home about). I grew up in a family of avid readers: my great-grandmother, grandmother and father are all bibliophiles and they passed that love on to me at a very young age. We still pass around books once we finish reading them to this day.

I was very lucky my father was a huge science fiction and mystery fan, which meant I had a lot of fantastic books to read. Science fiction books and television shows have always been something the two of us could share in, and some of my fondest memories involve my father and I watching the television on the weekends, or going to a local science fiction convention for the day so we could hear the actors and writers speak.

I actually read the novels before I discovered *Doctor Who* on the local PBS channel. My father travelled a lot for work and always brought books home from his trips: I had a wonderful collection of *Tin Tin* and *Doctor Who* books, *The Sea-Devils* among them. I was so happy the Target books were written on a level that young fans could engage with (since I was maybe seven or eight when I read my first) while still being interesting enough so my father could also enjoy them. I can still remember my fascination of seeing some of the characters for the first time on the television, since I only had the covers, a few drawings in the books and my imagination to go by (and what an imagination that was!) - the Sea Devils always seemed a lot more terrifying in my mind.

One thing these books showed me was that women could be useful and deep characters in these stories. They weren't just there for show, they weren't the princess in the castle that needed saving (even if, occasionally, the Doctor had to step in and help them get out of trouble) and most of the time they were in the trouble with the Doctor and working together to get out of it. These ladies were often educated and had careers outside of helping the Doctor on his adventures. They were headstrong and thought for themselves, they did not always do as they were told; to a young girl growing up that meant a lot. They gave me characters to look up to, which at that time were few and far between in the sci-fi I knew.

The Sea Devils showed me that average girls could go on to do fantastic things and be able to stand up for themselves. Jo was not always the strongest lady in the *Doctor Who* world, but she would at times stand up to the Doctor, and being a young girl and seeing another, who is just a normal person, going on amazing adventures and helping the Doctor fight monsters that are threatening the earth, like the Master and the Sea Devils, was really inspiring. Reading about Jo escaping through a vent when being captured showed me that ladies could be the heroes just as much as their male counterparts, and while the Doctor was the hero of the story, the female companions were just as important.

Growing up female and a huge fan of science fiction, I learned from a young age that it wasn't cool to be interested in that type of stuff, but I was never one to let people tell me what to like and what not to like. I went on to work at a comic shop (where I would play the owners' *Doctor Who* videos while I was at work) and also went on to cosplay as some of my favourite characters, all because I grew up reading (and later watching) *Doctor Who* and other genre shows. I did not always fit in, but I knew what made me happy, and I ended up making some of my friends into fans as well, since they embraced my weirdness instead of pushing it away. It makes me incredibly happy to see those friends getting their children into it.

I am very happy that today we live in a world where people are more open to all types of interests and you can be a male or female who likes *Doctor Who*, whether you are reading classic Target novels or watching the show on the television. Boys and girls, young and old can all love it equally without being judged for it. It makes me happy to see young children come into the school I now work at excited about *Doctor Who*, wearing shirts with Daleks on them; I even had a young girl dress as the tenth Doctor for 'Blast from the Past Day'. To see both boys and girls actively excited about the show (and the books I recommend to them) is really awesome, since twenty plus years ago that would not have always been the case.

The Target novels helped me learn about the wonderful world of *Doctor Who* and opened me up to some amazing stories. I am very happy to have been able to discover these books as a child, and go along on adventures with the Doctor and his companions while sitting in the comfort of my room.

I Don't Think You're Ready for This Yeti

Doctor Who and the Abominable Snowmen
by Nick Mellish

Favourite *Doctor Who* book: Will Brooks's *500 Year Diary*

I was roughly nine years old when I struck gold, or so it felt at the time. It was a horrible, wet, windy and frankly miserable grey day in Lancing, the village where I grew up, and there was a car boot sale on the seafront. I walked to the beach green with my mum, to be greeted with a dozen cars and people wearing waterproofs as the rain started to lash down heavier still and the wind picked off a handful of stray paperbacks along the way.

(It was probably *How to be a Wally* by Paul Manning, wasn't it? That always seemed to be on sale at an endless stream of table sales as a child of the late 1980s. Nowadays though, you never see it anywhere. I wonder what the book of this new generation will be—the one that is always on sale at such events. Will it be *The Da Vinci Code* by Dan Brown? Perhaps, but I think its equivalent is liable to be *Eats, Shoots and Leaves*, and in years to come anyone even scanning Lynne Truss's name will find that their mind instantly conjures up wafts of orange squash watered down within an inch of its pulp, fairy cakes, dusty village halls, and that inevitable raffle that you always seemed to be one number away from winning.)

Despite the rain, I felt warm enough in my blue coat and plodded along with Mum, avoiding mud, looking at table tops carefully laid out and knowing that the fifty pence piece clutched tight in my hand would be spent elsewhere, unable to meet the car owners' gaze at my betrayal. I bent my head down low and walked on, glimpsing dolls and workout videos, Soda Stream makers and a box full of Target books, ugly green vases and LPs, knitted bears and – wait up, what was that box?

I ran back and looked: there, sat before me, was a box absolutely full of *Doctor Who* novelisations. I recognized the names, of course: Terrance Dicks, Malcolm Hulke, Terrance Dicks, someone else, Terrance Dicks and just beneath that, a couple of works by Terrance Dicks.

I knew, right there and then, that I had to have this box. It was important to me; more so than saving up my pennies to get the *Mr. Men* books with the matching spines (I still covet them, all these years on); more even than that VHS of *The Twin Dilemma* which had been in my sights for an age now: a regeneration story, a Doctor I hadn't seen,

42

a new title sequence *and* it was exclusive to Woolworths! What could possibly go wrong?

I pleaded with my mum, but she was already handing over money for the box. I realised that I'd prayed on my knees for nothing and, absently swiping off clumps of mud from my tracksuit bottoms, I held her hand as we traipsed back along the seaside, where home and the fire and the promise of a chicken sandwich awaited.

Once I was back and changed and bathed, I greedily pored over the books: oh, there were so many! Cybermen and an exploding tenth planet! Giant spiders and robots alike! The triple-whammy of the Death, Day *and* Earth Invasion of the Daleks! A War Machine that looked like it could 'brrrrm' right through anything, but more specifically the looming, giant head of William Hartnell!

It wasn't these that caught my eye though. No, it was the sight of a Yeti that grabbed me. I'd seen clips of them in the underground in Kevin Davies's superb *Thirty Years in the TARDIS* and had watched Jamie and some monks catch one in a net thanks to *The Troughton Years*, rented time and again from my local branch of Blockbuster before securing it on my tenth birthday. I'd glimpsed a paw in *The Five Doctors* and even been promised that they made a cameo appearance in *The War Games* thanks to *The Doctor Who Yearbook*, but even back then the sight of an over-exposed one dancing on screen for a heartbeat or two was a bit of a disappointment.

Still, Yeti! Yeti were good, and Yeti were right in front of me and written about in a book. Not only that, but a book by Terrance Dicks, the man who had written *The Five Doctors*, which at the time was pretty much my most favourite-ist thing in the whole wide world ever. It was, frankly, a no-brainer which book to read first: *The Abominable Snowmen* it was. I remember being a bit daunted that it was word-heavy and looked rather big, but I was a good reader and this was the Yeti and I was determined; and but a few pages in, a man had been savagely karate chopped to death by one of the abominable snowmen. Frankly, this was all I had wanted and more.

I read it, slowly, over a few weeks. I remember now Travers finding a real Yeti at the end; Victoria being possessed; the death of a monk mid-way through. Of course, years on I remember these things due to having heard the soundtrack and watched the recon(s) - and re-read the book, too - but my mind can still specifically recall the first time I stumbled upon these scenes: in bed, at school, whilst sat upon the toilet (though not in Tooting Bec, I'm afraid). It was so engrained in my mind that when, a few years later, I happened upon Telesnaps from the story in the pages of *Doctor Who Magazine*, it already looked and felt familiar.

If it wasn't for *The Abominable Snowmen*, I'd not have been brave

43

enough to read more novelisations: and what wonders they were! If it wasn't for *The Abominable Snowmen*, my *Doctor Who* fandom would be a far lonelier and poorer experience, because that book opened up a whole world of excitement and further books to me. Just seeing its cover sends shivers of remembrance through my body. (The sense of nostalgic recollection, not the Sylvester McCoy story. If nothing else, unlimited rice pudding is a bugger to wash out of this new top of mine.)

Even better, once my dad knew that I'd contributed my pocket money to the cost of the box, he kindly went to Woolworths when he was away for work that following week, and purchased *The Twin Dilemma* as a treat. I eagerly ran to the video machine and put it on.

Sorry Dad, but I think Mum won this round.

Among the Barbarians

Doctor Who and the Curse of Peladon
by Robert Mammone
Favourite *Doctor Who* book: *Alien Bodies*
by Lawrence Miles

Let's get some context. We're in Australia and it is the Year of our Lord 1983. Alan Bond's *Australia II*, that fabled yacht with a mysterious winged keel, performs a miracle and claims the America's Cup. Back home, Australia is in the throes of a devastating drought. In February, partly fuelled by that drought, a disastrous series of bushfires on Ash Wednesday in Victoria and South Australia claim the lives of 75 people. Mid-way through the year, the Federal election result sees Malcolm Fraser forfeit the prime ministership as his Coalition government loses its majority in the lower house. And in a small primary school in a central Victoria town called Ararat, little old me is in the final stages of a campaign of bullying that stretches back to late 1981.

Let's get some more context. Prior to 1945, convicts and chancers from the British Isles settled Australia. After 1945, with the realisation that Australia stood almost alone in a tough neighbourhood and needed greater economic development and expansion, the government of the day threw open the floodgates to wider European immigration. My parents, both born in 1946 to peasant farmers in southern Italy, came out with their families in the late 1940s. Along with them came hundreds of thousands of their compatriots, along with Greeks and Yugoslavs and Maltese, utterly transforming the ethnic mix of Australia for the better. They assimilated, more or less, adopted the language, more or less, put their heads down and worked like dogs to make better lives than their shattered homelands could offer, and in the process wove a gleaming thread into the broader tapestry of Australian history.

Nothing changes without resistance. Well, not really resistance, but a sort of sullen acceptance. From this distance it's hard to say what the real thoughts of the Anglos were as they observed these new arrivals move into the poorer parts of their cities (which, ironically, are now some of the pricier areas to buy into). There was certainly name-calling and there were likely more than a few punch-ups. I've uncles on my mother's side who would happily belt up any idiot who stood around abusing them for not being locally born and I know for a fact in the mid-1980s my father grabbed a racist Australian-born farmer by the throat and pushed him into a wall. But as the years rolled by, those locals exercised by the arrival of foreign-speaking types moved on from the southern Mediterraneans and after 1975 they

45

lit into the Vietnamese refugees fleeing the Communist victors.

The town I was born in had an influx of refugees and migrants after the war. My best friend at school, Tommy, was the son of Yugoslav-born parents. I had Italian friends and Greek friends and, memorably, a Turkish friend. We had pasta at home, I had pies at school; I stubbornly refused to learn Italian and I had a great old time being a kid living in the country. Then my parents decided to change professions. They sold their vineyard and bought a motel. We moved four hours south to a place called Ararat, in the Victorian goldfields. A runt of a town, really; a very distant suburb of the far larger, far more cosmopolitan city of Ballarat with some astonishing Victorian architecture. Ararat was a pale shadow of Ballarat, fringed by houses containing what we indelicately today call white trash.

I should point out here that while I was deeply upset about moving, I have never blamed my parents for what happened when I changed schools. In taking on the risk of leaving behind their family and friends in search of a better life, I can only salute them. They were working to ensure their children had all the advantages of life their poorer upbringing never allowed them.

So Ararat. Not quite a one-horse town, but it did die after lunch on Saturdays as the shops closed until they re-opened on Monday. It was home to Aradale, a mental hospital for the criminally insane. In my more uncharitable moments, I would think that perhaps the inmates and the locals had swapped places. Viewed from the highest point outside the town limits, Ararat sits in a dry, nondescript valley. It was a place to live, a place to pass through on the way to Ballarat and thence Melbourne, the sort of place where the Victorian government saw fit to build a new prison on the outskirts. Yes, that's right; the locals were just good enough to provide a crop of prison guards to patrol their peers.

In addition, it was monocultural. At least, that's my memory. It's surely possible that aside from one Greek family - who owned (ironically) the local fish and chip shop, and whose daughter, Tania, was in the same class as me - we couldn't have been the only immigrant family. But it bloody well felt like it. We moved to Ararat over the school holidays in August 1981. Aside from Tania and myself, every single person in that class, perhaps twenty other students, had Scots, Irish or English blood seething through their veins. Now while you could certainly hate them for the attitudes they expressed, you couldn't blame the kids per se for having those attitudes. No one is born racist or ignorant. It comes from what kids hear at home around the kitchen table. So when young Rodney Cameron or Michael Gimmell called me a wog or a dago or (for the love of God) a spaghetti muncher, it's not because they crawled dripping from their mothers' wombs

46

with a hatred for non-Anglos. You can only blame their parents, just as you blame parents today for inculcating a hatred of, say, Muslims into their kids.

To a shy, bookish, introspective ten-year-old, that sort of hair splitting didn't matter a jot. From a school where everyone was different to one where everyone was the same, and where some of those people found entertainment in baiting me, tormenting me and hating me simply for being different, for having a different sounding surname, for having a slightly darker tone to my skin: it was simply devastating.

Now you might say, why didn't you tell someone? Why didn't you tell your parents, or your teachers? Perfectly reasonable questions, if you've never been a child. Why I never spoke up at the time haunts me today. I don't have a good explanation other than to say I was ten, then eleven, and I simply didn't know better. Perhaps it was shock; a slow, rolling paralysis that stilled my tongue, that allowed me to sit in class, day in day out, hoping, praying at times, that they wouldn't start up again. Sometimes they didn't, sometimes they did. Waiting for the sword to fall was like a slow corrosive, eating away, hollowing me out and leaving behind panic and pain. Which isn't to say that I spent my school days curled in a ball hiding from reality. While the Michael Curries of this world stuck the knife in, I got on with school. I made some friends, particularly Jason Marshall, who became a nurse in later life. While it was Jason I have to thank for the idea of buying *Doctor Who* novelisations, it was thanks to my school librarian that I originally began my obsession with them.

I can't remember her name. Her son was a para-Olympian swimmer, representing Australia. She's probably dead now, but the memory of her kindness towards me still lingers. I loved our one-room library, with the children's books occupying one wall. Outside, in the corridor, was another wall of books. I can't remember if they were part of the library. I can only imagine they were. She fostered in me an interest in writing. In fact, as memory serves, she submitted a story I wrote to the teacher's union magazine. Once she realised that I liked *Doctor Who*, she allowed me to look at the novelisations as they came in from the wholesalers before they were covered in plastic and placed on the shelves. I remember particular excitement picking up a copy of *Tomb of the Cybermen* – the image of the cover, with its blue background and Cyberhead encased in ice is still strong.

Those novelisations came to dominate my reading life, or so it seems. I remember picking up *An Unearthly Child* as part of a four-book haul one day, wondering what mysteries the nondescript cover contained. I remember how the week my brother was born I purchased and read *The Invisible Enemy*. The novelisations, like for so many other

47

fans, instilled in me an interest in reading, in the possibility of writing, and in the pre-VHS era, a chance to experience stories I had never seen.

So, you might be screaming, where does *The Curse of Peladon* come in?

By the time of my last year at primary school, my principle tormentors, a pair of twin boys a year ahead of me, had moved on to the local high school. With them gone, the responsibility devolved to Rodney Cameron. He was essentially top dog of my class, the leader of a pack of boys who would follow him around, laughing as he tossed off what seemed like scintillating witticisms, but no doubt were the boring platitudes of a country hick with the worldview of a dormouse. Look, he was just a kid with a big mouth and a sort of crude charisma. Kids our age were looking for a structure in their schooling lives, and the kids around me were attracted to Rodney. Doesn't mean they were as bad as he was, but they were what we quaintly today call enablers. I don't have any particular memories of him saying anything to me: it was just the constant pressure that he might say something that was enough.

That pressure built and built and built until one day, I just stood up and walked out of the classroom. I went for the set of shelves outside the library. I grabbed a book, a copy of *The Curse of Peladon* and flicked through the pages. It was a completely random choice, but perhaps a fated one. Simply holding the book, looking at the illustrations, helped calm me. The television story isn't great, and it shows on the page - a re-written script, with average internal illustrations. However, for this one brief moment in my life, it was a lifejacket in a dark and stormy sea. Then my teacher, Mr Dunn, who also doubled as the town mayor, walked down the corridor and ordered me back inside.

Things didn't really improve until after the end of the mid-year holidays. I refused to go to school on the Monday. In tears, I sat at the top of the stairs until my parents managed to coax from me what was wrong. I have no recollection of their immediate response, but my next memory is of myself and Dad sitting in the principal's office, me on Dad's left, watching on as he told the principal in no uncertain terms he needed to sort the issue out, or my father would do it himself. While Dad would never have belted Rodney and his cronies, it was enough of a threat for the principal to haul the offenders in. The upshot of that was that for the remainder of my time in Ararat, my former tormenters treated me as they always should have - a peer, a friend, and not someone to laugh and mock.

Now you could say that blindly clutching for *The Curse of Peladon* had symmetry with what I wanted – the notion the story embodies is a group of disparate races coming together to accept the Peladonians

48

into their ranks as one of their own. You could do that, if you wanted. Really, it was just blind luck. But, when I think back to those two years, one of the memories that always comes is of that moment, in that corridor, clutching a *Doctor Who* book and finding a little peace of mind.

A Corner of the Universe

Doctor Who and the Cybermen
by David Tudor

Favourite *Doctor Who* book: *A Celebration* by Peter Haining

Garston Library in south Liverpool was a wondrous place. I visited many times in my youth: evening walks on dark, misty weeknights past endless terraces lit by orange streetlights, accompanied by my dad and older brother, armed only with a sense of expectation of the delights I would find inside. Surrounded by iron railings and a small, rather weary-looking garden, the curious Victorian mix of sandstone and mock-Tudor contained a world of discovery within its musty, oak-lined shelves.

While dad enhanced his already considerable knowledge in the pages of reference books, and my brother satiated his thirst for music trivia in pop encyclopaedias, I was drawn to one particular dark, shadowy alcove. Skimming past 'Dahl', I would usually select a title by 'Dicks', for here it was that I would find row upon row of *Doctor Who* novelisations, most of which were penned by that ubiquitous wordsmith. But one evening, my eye was drawn to the red spine of a novel written by another: *Doctor Who and the Cybermen* by Gerry Davis. Carefully, I drew the book from the shelf and turned it round to look at the cover: I gasped.

It was often the covers which attracted my attention and sometimes I would take them home merely to gaze at those exciting images on the front: I never got past the first page of *Pyramids of Mars*, for instance, because I could not tear my eyes from that iconic jacket illustration. But *The Cybermen* depicted something more startling: I had been enthralled and terrified by the silver giants since their recent, triumphant return in *Earthshock*, and here, looking very different, were two fascinating, seemingly golden (the irony was lost on me) creatures, standing in space. And one was pointing directly at *me*. Obediently, rather like a boy possessed, I produced my tattered library card and took the book home.

It is at this point that I must make a guilty confession: *Doctor Who and the Cybermen* is perhaps my favourite children's book. Why should I feel guilty? Perhaps it's because I feel that my favourite ought to be one of those aforementioned Roald Dahl stories. Maybe it's the nagging remorse that my favourite *Doctor Who* novelisation wasn't written by the prolific Mr Dicks – it's rather like admitting that your favourite Queen song wasn't composed by Freddie Mercury (this is also true). But no, to my shame, the most influential book I discovered during my formative years (aside from perhaps *Mr. Impossible*) was

50

this cheap 1970s adaptation of a black-and-white science fiction serial.

Gerry Davis opens his book with a brief but fascinating account of the Cybermen's creation, before throwing the reader – quite literally – into the TARDIS 'cabin' and introducing a motley crew of central characters: the Doctor, of course, curiously given virtually no introduction or description; Jamie, the young refugee from the Highlands (his speech even written in 'authentic' Scots), apparently new to the team; Ben, a 'young cockney sailor from East Ham' who proves an engaging, resourceful protagonist; and, most delightful of all, the long-legged, mini-skirted Polly, a character for whom Gerry Davis particularly seems to enjoy writing. Polly is the only female character in the story, but she plays a vital role, most critically devising the chemical cocktail which proves so effective against the Cybermen. She's a confident, adorable character, and in Davis's hands, it is difficult not to fall in love with Polly.

Davis's prose style may not be the most adventurous, but he ably masters the template, exemplified in a hundred other books by Terrance Dicks, which made the Target books so successful: simple, straightforward retellings of the original TV serials, rattling along at a thrilling pace. Description is this author's forté and the moonbase in which the time travellers find themselves is a tantalising, if occasionally unreliable, technological utopia, typically scientifically accurate in its realisation. It is a place filled with darkness and shadows, brilliantly captured in those evocative Alan Willow illustrations which lend set pieces an eerie visual reference point: Ralph's encounter with a Cyberman in the food store is particularly chillingly effective. Despite the scale of Davis's moonbase and its enormous 'doughnut-shaped' Gravitron, it is still a dark, dingy place, with nightmarish alien giants seemingly waiting in every nook and cranny.

Doctor Who and the Cybermen kept me engrossed through cold nights, the bedside lamp casting its own menacing shadows on the bedroom walls; the book even gave me solace during a short illness (measles, rather than space plague). Eventually I acquired my own shiny new paperback copy of the book, purchased with a whole three weeks' pocket money from the school book club, a pleasing Friday lunchtime retreat which allowed to me to start building my own collection of Target novels. However, my mum and dad put a stop to my *Doctor Who* reading for a while following a period of sleeplessness and nightmares (my folks wouldn't have it that this was actually caused by watching *Arthur C. Clarke's World of Strange Powers*) and a vicious, unprovoked attack on my mum's vase of decidedly deadly daffodils (which was rather more difficult to blame on the spooky science-fiction visionary). They eventually relented, though, and my

51

literary travels through time and space and to the library resumed. However, my trips to that particular corner of the universe were about to come to a halt.

As I write this, it is exactly thirty years since I last set foot in Garston Library. We moved away at the start of 1986, settling in Oswestry, a small market town on the Shropshire/Wales border and a world away from urban Liverpool. Of course there was a library (a very good one) and yes, a section in which I discovered even more new and exciting *Doctor Who* books. However, as adolescence began, my journey to seek out these titles became ever more difficult, for they were situated upstairs, in the most frightening place: a small area devoted to children's books. My desire to indulge in these stories was greater than ever, especially with the arrival of new adaptations of long-forgotten 1960s serials. But to retrieve them, as a shy teenager, was a dangerous quest fraught with the perils of negotiating screaming toddlers and pre-schoolers before sneaking my treasure down to the issue desk, at all times risking the ultimate trap: being spotted by one of my schoolmates. No wonder then that I turned more and more to rediscovering those old adventures through the slightly less hazardous means of home video.

Those years of gorging on the Doctor's fight against the universe's most terrible things were brilliant. I mean, truly enriching. Black-and-white worlds of monsters and moonbases and much, much more were brought vividly to life by authors to whom I will always be grateful, authors such as Gerry Davis. Those adventures started right there on those dusty shelves in that old library in a corner of south Liverpool. The shelves are possibly now lined with tales of Harry Potter, or hunger games, or even Haynes car manuals for all I know. But it would be nice to think that somewhere, in a dark, musty alcove, those terrifying dehumanised monsters of plastic and steel, the Cybermen, are still there, in the shadows, waiting...

The Only Copy Signed by Peter Davison

Doctor Who and the Giant Robot
by Robert Smith?

Favourite *Doctor Who* book: *Remembrance of the Daleks*
by Ben Aaronovitch

May 6th, 1983: my father came home with the most amazing news: Peter Davison was in Australia, he was signing in the shopping mall just one suburb over — and did I want to go? I was overwhelmed with joy at this. The concept of actually meeting Doctor Who in person was astonishing.

At the mall, I saw Peter Davison sitting up on a small stage, signing books for people. There were *Doctor Who* books for sale, so Dad said I could buy one to get signed if I wanted. This was even better news, so I went over to the rack and looked through them. There was a blindingly obvious choice for such a momentous occasion: *Doctor Who and the Giant Robot*.

I stood in line for a while until it was my turn. I handed Peter Davison the book with the front page open for him to sign, and he asked me my name. I told him and then he flipped to the front cover briefly and said 'That's not one of mine, is it?' I said no, wondering if maybe I'd committed a faux pas of some kind. But weren't all the Doctors the same person? Besides, I just really, really wanted *The Giant Robot*. He grunted and then signed it anyway.

There were more people behind me, so I turned to leave, but it suddenly occurred to me that there was something I needed to do. I needed to touch Doctor Who. So while he was signing the next girl's book, I reached out and slid my index finger quickly but gently along the middle part of his little finger. I then ran like I'd never run before.

Afterwards, Dad said that what I should have done was to offer my hand for him to shake, saying 'It was very nice to meet you.' That seemed like precisely the sort of manly thing that Dad would do that never occurred to me. It did make sense, but I wasn't sure I would have had the courage to do it. However, he did say that Peter Davison might have talked about me touching his finger to other people afterwards, which was an idea I really loved. The concept that I might have done something memorable enough for Peter Davison to mention to other people was an amazing one. I was ecstatic at having not only met Peter Davison, but gotten *The Giant Robot*, had it signed and even touched him. Wow.

A great many years later, I actually told Peter Davison this story, to which he reacted only very mildly, as though small boys touching his finger was the kind of thing that happened to him all the time (and, for all I knew, it was). Janet Fielding was there and asked how old I was. When I said 11, she'd laughed and said she was hoping I'd been 23 or something. Whatever. I still own the only copy of *The Giant Robot* signed by Peter Davison.

Monsters Never Looked More Menacing

Doctor Who and the Terror of the Autons
by Matt Badham
Favourite *Doctor Who* book: *The Three Doctors*
by Terrance Dicks

The memory cheats, lies, blusters, erases and distorts. My own memory of the Target books is of my sister reading them to my brother and me at bedtime when we were both children. They were a storytelling experience for me rather than a reading experience. In my memory, I see her sat by our bunk bed, hunched over a book as I, a frightened child, huddle under the covers and quake as the Zarbi, Daleks and, for some reason, a lone Cyberman creep through my mind. This memory is, most certainly, a construction; a memory of several memories with a side-order of invention to boot.

I have another memory of the Target books, however, one in which I have more confidence. This involves sneaking into said sister's bedroom and poring over their covers: miniature works of art that deserved to be hung, in my opinion, in the most prestigious art galleries in the world. The *Mona Lisa*? Pish and tosh! Give me the cover of *Death to the Daleks* any day of the week instead.

Sneaking into my sister's room while she was out was a favourite habit of mine. She's ten years older than me, an avid science fiction and fantasy fan, and that room was an Aladdin's Cave of comics and books, all pristinely arranged and maintained. I had to be very careful when I read them to make sure that I didn't damage the spine or cover because then the game would have been up and the consequences would have been dire. I was forbidden to go into my sister's room without permission or to touch her stuff and as my mum's main source of childcare, she wielded a lot of power. The consequences of crossing her could be pretty catastrophic. I suppose I was a fairly sneaky child, because I spent years doing so without ever being caught... or perhaps she knew and let me get away with it (although somehow I doubt it).

The Target books were, by far, my favourite bit of her collection, mainly because of their fantastic covers and the fact that they gave me a glimpse into stories that I was sure, at that time, I would never see. *Terror of the Autons* is a case in point. It's one of the covers that lingers in my memory after all these years, depicting as it does a cyclopean and cephalopodan alien staring out while below, in comic strip-style, a single panel shows the Pertwee Doctor rushing into a room in a vain effort to stop the saturnine Master from pulling a lever and... well, I'm not sure what he was supposed to be doing but it's a dynamic, dramatic cover nonetheless. In my memory, the Nestene Consciousness never looked slimier and more menacing, its massive tentacles probing the edge of the book's cover as it considered its impending conquest of the Earth. The Master, meanwhile, is as suave, as deadly and as in control as he's ever been. Inside, we got the closest my generation of fandom ever thought they would get to seeing this story on screen: tiny black and white illustrations picked out and realised scenes from Terrance Dicks's wonderfully efficient and atmospheric prose – examples include Jo's shocked countenance as the Doctor peels the face from an Auton disguised as a policeman (although going by the illustration it's actually more of a yank than a peel) and the moment the troll doll attacks and kills Farrel Senior.

I was almost afraid to Google the Target novelisation of *Terror of the Autons* to find out if my memory had once again cheated and that the cover was actually a damp squib. I shouldn't have worried. Although perhaps not quite as dynamic as I remember it being, it's a fantastically creditable piece of art, especially when you consider that it was no doubt done to a ferociously tight deadline. But then, isn't that the story of *Doctor Who* in a nutshell? Of creators working to strict deadlines to conjure up bizarre new worlds for the Doctor and his companions to visit, armed with nothing more than whatever resources the BBC had thrown at them – which were often more suited to soap operas and sitcoms than fantasy television – as well as their own imaginations. In this way, I suppose, the Target illustrators had one up on their counterparts at Television House, their only budgetary restrictions being the limits of their imaginations and prodigious abilities.

The Target covers are a massively important part of the visual tapestry of *Doctor Who*, which is, and always has been, a fantastically visual show. That visual tapestry continues to inspire and delight a new generation, at least in my house. It was Joe, my eldest, who reminded me of the power of the imagery of *Doctor Who*. My reaction when I see a Dalek nowadays is, 'Oh, it's a Dalek.' His reaction when he first saw a Dalek, even before he had seen a single episode of *Doctor Who* was the age-appropriate equivalent of 'What the ---- is that?' It reminded me that with familiarity comes, not contempt necessarily, but a kind of indifference. The Dalek, like the Mini or postboxes or the map of the London Underground, is a design classic and the thing about design classics is once we become familiar with them, we tend to forget what made them so beautiful and striking in the first place. What must it have been like to first glimpse a Dalek in the sixties before they had become such a recognizable part of our culture?

For me, being a *Doctor Who* fan is about being open to the show's potential despite the limitations it has imposed upon it by things like scheduling and budget. It's about knowing that even though the Nestene Consciousness is represented on television by some less than effective CGI or a gurning Jon Pertwee wrestling with rubber tentacles, the true Consciousness is a monstrous part-crab, part-octopus creature whose single eye blazing with menace stares out while the Doctor and the Master engage in an action-packed battle of wits below...

The Mystery of Grandma's Gift

Doctor Who and the Green Death
by David M Barsky
Favourite *Doctor Who* book: *Day of the Daleks*
by Terrance Dicks

Truth be told, I have never actually read Malcolm Hulke's novelisation of *The Green Death*.

Growing up a *Doctor Who* fan in the early 1980s was certainly a confusing endeavour, especially if you lived in the United States. Granted, I still feel greatly fortunate having been able to watch *Robot* through *The Invasion of Time* on a seemingly unending Monday-to-Friday loop, but I knew absolutely nothing of the Whoniverse beyond this syndicated television package. Of course, the regeneration scene at the top of *Robot* befuddled me. I recall it was mostly annoying, mystifying at best. What was going on? Why did the Doctor have grey hair? Certainly I was missing something as the dialog indicated these characters have had a past. However my nine-year-old brain could never have possibly imagined that there had been another actor to play the character, much less three. Nonetheless, I watched and re-watched this cycle of stories for a blissful couple of years, always trying to decipher the riddle of (what I'd later learn was) Tom Baker's first scene.

I know many British fans of the same age would have killed to see the Fourth Doctor's stories so often back then, but at least they had a sense of the programme's history, with older brothers and sisters, mommies and daddies, aunties and uncles to fill them in. Most importantly, the UK had Terrance Dicks and the other Target-writing regulars.

North America did have a sampling of these nifty little books. Some time before the Target novels were known this side of the Atlantic, we had ten novelisations to call our very own. Published in 1979 (the same year I began watching the show), Pinnacle Books offered seven of Target's novelised adventures from the Tom Baker stories I knew and loved. However, the titles numbered One, Two, and Three - *Day of the Daleks*, *The Doomsday Weapon*, and *The Dinosaur Invasion* - were new to me. Although these strange titles were sequentially numbered before the stories I was familiar with, they did nothing to explain why Tom Baker's hair was grey at the start of *Robot*. To me, they were just straight-to-print untelevised, original adventures – a phenomenon I was familiar with as a *Star Trek* fan. Printings of *The Dinosaur Invasion* certainly could not be of help as the pre-title page blurb declared: 'This episode features the fourth Doctor Who, who has survived three incarnations.' Even if I had known that this was actually a third Doctor title, I hadn't an inkling of what the word 'incarnation' meant, nor had I bothered to look it up.

Those books were all I had for a long, long while. That all changed during one Sunday visit from my grandmother. Unsure that I had ever even mentioned *Doctor Who* to her, it was a great surprise when she presented me with two *Doctor Who* Target books that deepened the mystery of my favourite TV show - *The Sea Devils* and *The Green Death* - along with two other potboiler sci-fi books which I never read: Peter Heath's *The Mind Brothers* and *Assassins from Tomorrow*. I'll never forget my first thought upon seen this confounding treasure: 'What are these weird *Doctor Who* books?'

'Wow, thanks, Grandma! Where did you find these?'

'In a bookstore on Broadway.'

All I knew about Broadway Street in South Boston then was that it was the place my grandmother shopped for hours and would buy me the most god-awfully ugly and uncomfortable clothing. I never had been there, nor did I ever want to go.

'They had all kinds of *Doctor Whos*. Dozens of them!' I can still remember her waving her arm through the air, as if to enhance the very length of space the volumes took up on the bookstore's shelf.

My mind went wild, conjuring images of a floor-to-ceiling monolithic wall full of *Doctor Who* titles. I briefly pictured myself there, gazing at the spines of epics I could not possibly name yet couldn't wait to discover. The reverie soured quickly as I thought: 'If there were so many of them then why the hell did you buy this other crap? Why not two more *Doctor Who* Books?' Even at that young age, I knew a potboiler when I saw it. Peter Heath could never be Philip Hinchcliffe.

I thanked her again, adding: 'I would love to have them all.'

She made no response. She just wouldn't bite on that not-so-subtle hint.

I just had to see more of these books. Everything about them was different, yet familiar. There was no Pinnacle logo on the spine, but another circular emblem: a target. The *Doctor Who* logo on the front of the Target books was different from the Pinnacle books, but the same as the one on the TV. These had to be official in some way.

I could not get over the number of books my grandmother had guessed at. Dozens. The books she brought helped to confirm this as *The Green Death*'s back page had more tantalizing titles of tales unfamiliar. A space war? Bloody stones? A *tenth* planet! An entire library out of reach to me but so seemingly easily (and unfairly!) obtained by the rest of the world if the back cover were to be believed. The UK, Australia, New Zealand, Malta!

Malta? I was not only a sci-fi nerd by that time, but a geography geek to boot, yet nowhere in the map of my mind could I place this land I must get to. This land of very affordable books.

'Look, Grandma! They're only ninety-five cents in Malta!'

'Ooh. Let's go there and buy them all!' she humoured. I was so ready.

My mother, having overheard all of this, decided to inject some deflating sanity to our musings.

'You're not going to Malta, you'd have to fly,' she said.

Ok, so?

'And these books are probably imported from England so they'll be hard to find here. That's why there is not a price for the United States on the back.'

Way to kick me while I'm down, Mom.

Further examination of the pages within revealed another wonder: pictures! None of the Pinnacle books had those. But even the illustrations of Jon Pertwee did nothing to clue me in to the show's grand past. In fact, none of the captions even mentioned that it was, in fact, Doctor in the pictures! All I thought was: 'If that's the Doctor then someone is really, really bad at drawing Tom Baker.' Had Grandma bought me two more *Doctor Who* novels that day or at any time within the next year, chances are that at least one would have had the third Doctor on the cover, further confusing the issue. Heaven only knows what would have become of my sanity had one of the titles been *The Three Doctors*!

So why didn't I read *The Green Death* despite it being so new and interesting? The best reason lies within the pages of Chapter 4. The illustration 'Boss started to talk to him through the earphones' on page 36 just plain freaked me out. By this point, *Doctor Who* had shown me a woman fried by the hand of a grumpy lighthouse keeper and servants screaming in pain at the very sight of Sutekh. Why had this bothered me so much? There was just something about this guy's googly-eyed gurn that totally got me. Perhaps it was the dribbling drops of sweat forever frozen upon his face. And what could that weird jagged line emanating from his head possibly represent? Whatever the case, the haunting image discouraged me from ever opening the book again. Sadly, its less intriguing sibling, *The Sea Devils,* suffered the same fate solely due to guilt-by-association.

These two odd volumes sat apart from my prized Pinnacle releases until *Doctor Who*'s 20th anniversary, when everything *Doctor Who* exploded, and for many of us in North America the show's past became clear. Peter Haining's tome, *Doctor Who - A Celebration* listed all of these amazing past televised adventures as well as detailing which stories we would most likely never see at all! True and proper Target novelisations soon followed the Haining volume, right in my own suburb's local bookstore. Dozens of them - just like Grandma had said!

I bought six of the novelisations on the day I discovered them in my local bookstore and happily placed them beside the two my grandmother had brought me about a year earlier. But there was a problem. My old copies of *The Green Death* and *The Sea Devils* were both taller and wider than this newly-purchased batch. I remember my mother telling me that they were imported, which led me to conclude the obvious: England made their books bigger. This really angered me, as I would have to buy new, smaller copies of those titles from my local bookstore so they would look nice and pretty all in a row.

Once I had bought them locally, and confirmed the new volumes fit properly on my shelf with the others, I threw away the two misfit books my grandmother had so thoughtfully purchased for me.

Since I then believed they were the hope to have a complete run of stories, I subsequently went on to collect all of the *Doctor Who* Target novelisations, even though a handful of the televised adventures never made it to book form. The program and its Target line had spawned a completionist bibliophile and this has spilled over to other genre properties that I love.

However, *The Green Death* does not stand alone as the only Target book I haven't read. In fact, I have never read a single one of the novels outside of the ten released under the Pinnacle imprint. My reading tastes had simply moved beyond them shortly after I acquired that first batch of Targets at my local bookstore. My opinions of books adapted from films and television programmes as literature had soured as I began to discover the likes of Clarke and Asimov.

Malcolm Hulke could never be Robert Heinlein.

Adventures on This Planet of the Spiders

Doctor Who and the Planet of the Spiders
by N. Siân Southern
Favourite *Doctor Who* book: *The Horror of Fang Rock*
by Terrance Dicks

I once worked at a children's holiday camp in the Normandy countryside. It was a business running on a shoestring – the English owner openly told us eight educational presenters that she hired British teens because French teens wouldn't deign to do the nerve-shredding forty-hour weeks for less than minimum wage. Rats scurried in the walls where we slept in the crumbling French chateau, and at the bottom of those four steep flights of stairs and across a field lay some all-purpose, functional-style utility buildings where we presenters would herd the children after a day's sightseeing, while the teachers would collapse into cracked leather armchairs in the company of our Francophile employer to drink Kir Royales.

I was supervising thirty over-excited twelve-year olds in some sort of activity. I think we might have had the souvenir shop running: mugs and notepads and things emblazoned with the camp name. It may well have been the backup plan after an organised game of Lotto failed, and the kids were milling round as I was sat behind the table, a faux -wood patterned chipboard thing.

Then I looked down. A slender, black spider about the size of a fifty-pence piece was picking her away delicately across the edge of the table.

'Look!' I said. 'She's carrying her eggs on her back. She must be looking for somewhere safe to go!'

'Wow!'

'Cool!'

'Ohh!'

About half the kids – boys and girls – surged forward to spy on the little lady, following my finger as I pointed out the transparent sack of eggs on her back, marvelling at a small, everyday wonder of nature. The other half of the kids shrank back against the back wall, shrieking, their hands crossed protectively.

On reflection, I think that moment was a fair representation of people in general. Half are fascinated by spiders, overcoming the caveman instinct to shriek like a banshee when, say, they feel a small thing scuttling over their scalp while they're drowsily naked and waiting for the shower water to warm – a hypothetical example, you understand – overcoming the instinctual fear in order to marvel at the intricacy and beautiful otherness of a specialised, clever organism...and the other half who don't.

The loss is theirs, I reckon.

Doctor Who and the Planet of the Spiders pits the wily, ruthless, marvellous spiders of Metebelis III against the Doctor, and it's a fantastic tale. Of course it is: look at the complexity and ability of a common-or-garden spider, and then add a human-level intelligence: what other creature could be such a worthy adversary?

The truth is, I didn't need to read the blurb or to have seen the drama. I (shock, horror) haven't actually watched that many episodes of classic *Doctor Who*. I was the generation born to view the best bits, the onscreen regenerations, the rare companion deaths on Top 50 compilation shows, and wish I'd been there to experience these moments first time round. My *Doctor Who* was on the printed page, and I didn't think of the books as novelisations, just stories with promising titles and spine-tingling cover art.

Where to begin? Not in numerical order, not when you had to hunt the blessed things out (Church Hall sales) or were faced with a wall of choice and too little money (the second-hand bookshop on Turl Street in Oxford). More like eenie, meenie, miney, mo.

Then came the day I saw *Doctor Who and the Planet of the Spiders*. Eenie meenie be damned; some titles promise so much, and this one delivered. Not just the spiders: throw in mesmerism, psychokineticism, mysticism, old and new friends, greed, sacrifice, subterfuge, madness, bravery, a sparkling blue crystal, another planet, the deepest, darkest jungle of this planet – new for the novelisation – and this story's a cracker.

(I'll add that I was especially glad to see Welshman Professor Clifford Jones make a brief appearance in the novelisation. When you come from a country with a population of just three million, you make the most of every fictional ambassador, despite the inevitable author's comment on the language and/or accent.)

Spiders were my way in, but the story made me stay. At the risk of getting poetic and seeing things that aren't really there, *Doctor Who and the Planet of the Spiders* is itself a spider's web. It's intricate: so many characters are woven together and given fresh facets of personality. These include the blue crystal from *The Green Death*; Jo Grant; Mike Yates, last seen leaving UNIT in disgrace; even Metebelis III itself, now totally transformed. These disparate characters are drawn together, slowly, slowly, towards the true spider-in-the-web, the Third Doctor's regeneration. This is a rich story and I gain a new insight or perspective every time I read it.

This means I've read it many times.

I'm nearing the end of a manuscript. It's a speculative fiction novel about betrayal, multiple dimensions and giant predatory spiders. I can't say that *Doctor Who and the Planet of the Spiders* inspired it – I had the meat and bones of my story long before I picked up that Target book – but when I read Terrance Dicks's book it's tempting to think as the Doctor does, of influence stretching both forwards and backwards through time, travelling every which way like the TARDIS. The spiders of Metebelis III make a future appearance in the guise of the time beetle in *Turn Left*, because why use a fantastic idea like a back-hopping invertebrate puppet-master once only?

Planet of the Spiders reminds me that the universe of *Doctor Who* is rich and complex, just as the real world is. You needn't look up at the planets and stars for wonder. Just look down.

Name, Address, Telephone Number required

Doctor Who and the Three Doctors
by Todd Beilby

Favourite *Doctor Who* book: *The Sixties*
by David J Howe, Mark Stammers and Stephen James Walker

'Which came first, the chicken or the egg?' This age-old question has been asked since the dawn of time and I think I can adapt and apply a similar question to my love of *Doctor Who* – 'Which came first, the novelisation or the TV show?' The truth is, I really don't know. For me they have always gone hand in hand; there was never a time in my childhood that I can't remember watching the TV series or reading a Target novel.

I know that many fans can remember their first TV story. I can't. As a child growing up in the late 1970s, in Australia, *Doctor Who* was always there for me, stripped 5 nights a week at 6pm or 6.30pm. Unlike others, I simply can't pinpoint that exact moment I first encountered the Doctor, so what was televisual and imagined in my mind tend to overlap.

Some things do stick vividly in my memory more than others. I knew that that there were more than two doctors - Tom Baker, Jon Per-twee (or was it Pert-wee) and a silver haired guy before him. I remember giant spiders, the giant robot, the huge Wirrn queen and the Daleks. Funnily enough, I clearly recall that I knew the Daleks before I knew Davros – but it wasn't from *Death to the Daleks*.

Unsurprisingly, I don't know what my earliest Target novel was, however as a young child of around 5 or 6 years old, I would write my name, address and telephone number into the front cover. Later, I would add in the class I was in at school (6A) and my teacher's name. If, Heaven forbid, I lost one or someone broke into the house to steal them, I could be contacted by various means to ensure they were returned!

My copy of the novel *Doctor Who and Daleks* has got my first home address and phone number in it so it has to be one of the first I bought. I remember knowing the story and being really excited when Channel 7 (one of only four channels we had at the time) was showing the movie as their Saturday or Sunday matinee. I actually thought that *Doctor Who* started as a blockbuster film and then was adapted into a television show.

My thirst to experience more *Doctor Who* led me to buy the novels whenever I saw them, but there was one novelisation that I was truly excited to own – *The Three Doctors*! I had no idea that there was another Doctor Who between the old white haired guy and Jon Pertwee.

My original version of the novel is the one with the purple cover and Hartnell wearing that funny hat with a scarf. I always thought that this was rather strange, after seeing the show some time later and not seeing him wear it. The novel has my required name, address and telephone number in it but no class details, so it was bought early when I was quite young.

For me, like so many, the *Doctor Who* novels encouraged me to read and learn new vocabulary. (I wasn't an avid reader; I had a few *Secret Seven* novels and the *Wishing Tree* adventures but those were bought for me, rather than me earning pocket money to buy them.) I was always so eager to dive into the adventure that at times it didn't bother me if I didn't totally understand the terms been used to describe people, places or things. I was totally excited to be absorbed in a new adventure, where my mind could take me to create a land of make believe and imagine the most fantastic places as they were described. Sometimes in my excitement I would also skim read paragraphs, eager to get to the end of the chapter, especially if I didn't understand the words used. No, I didn't go and look up the terms in a dictionary or ask my parents, it never crossed my mind. This was my own little world, secret and special to me.

I don't why and I don't know how but one of my most vivid memories as a child was discovering two amazing facts reading this novel. Firstly, not only were there two other Doctors, but the third one had two companions – Jo and Bessie! I couldn't understand why Bessie didn't say much. I completely failed to comprehend that an 'Edwardian roadster', as she was described, was a car! For months, I dreamt of seeing this story with the Doctor's two companions. Needless to say, I was bemused when first I saw the television version. It makes me laugh now when re-reading the novel that Bessie is referred to as 'car' on numerous occasions - in fact, on every occasion she is mentioned. How could I have overlooked this? Why had my mind simply blanked these passages out as a 5 year old child?

Thinking about this novelisation always makes me smile and remember fondly a happy time when a naïve, innocent young mind was trying to reconcile new words, exciting adventures and big dreams to sort out all of the information required to become what he didn't know at the time he would be, a *Doctor Who* fan.

Thank you Target, and thank you Bessie, for letting me remember my childhood and the dreams of a young boy. You were brilliant in all your forms and definitely no ordinary car.

Nessie, the Doctor and Me

Doctor Who and the Loch Ness Monster
by Earl Ecklund III

Favourite *Doctor Who* book: *A Celebration* by Peter Haining

For as long as I can remember, I have loved books. For an only child growing up alone in a single parent household, books were my entry to other places and other worlds. It began mainly with comic books (*Amazing Spiderman* #158 bought for me by my cousin was my first) and then slowly grew into other realms. While many of the books from my youth are gone now, one I still have almost forty years later is the American edition of *Doctor Who and the Loch Ness Monster* by Terrance Dicks, published by Pinnacle Nooks as one of ten books put out in the late 1970s. I no longer recall where it was I first came across my copy. All I do recall is that as an obsessed ten year old I had to have any book ever published about Nessie, even if the book was strictly a work of fiction. The cover boasted a quote from Harlan Ellison, a name that meant nothing to me at the time, and featured art depicting Nessie and a strange looking alien creature. I read it with glee and quickly became enthralled.

It featured a strange man named the Doctor who travelled with a pair named Harry & Sarah. They arrived in Scotland because some chap called the Brigadier had requested their presence. Something was destroying oil rigs and the Doctor's help was needed. As it turned out, a strange alien race called the Zygons was behind it all. They could change appearance and Nessie was their 'pet'. In the end, the Doctor saved the day.

After reading this, all I knew was that I wanted more. My Grandmother was kind enough to buy me a few more and listen to me as I read them out loud and struggled over unfamiliar words like 'Dalek'. Unbeknownst to her and everyone else, I was hooked for life on this *Doctor Who* thing and yet I didn't know what it was really. It was only once a schoolmate showed me something called *Doctor Who Weekly* his parents had bought him in Canada that I began to be aware there was much more to this than just the ten books I read often.

I was fascinated by this revelation that a magazine existed and it had pictures of things called Sontarans and Ice Warriors. For the first time I discovered *Doctor Who* was actually a TV show and there were more books to be had. When I was twelve, my mother took me up to Vancouver, BC for a week during the summer. Among the places I insisted we had to go was the simply-named Comic Shop on W. 4th; here I found copies of *Doctor Who Weekly* which I bought up. Another place I insisted on going to was White Dwarf Books on W 10th. There I found a couple of *Doctor Who* books with which I was unfamiliar (*The Monster of Peladon* stands out in my mind) and I quickly bought them as well. Around this time, a local TV station out of Bellingham, WA (located about 3 hours north of Seattle and near the border with Canada) began airing Tom Baker stories late on Saturday nights. I struggled to stay up that late and watch the fuzzy signal in the basement but my appetite for more *Doctor Who* had been whetted.

Around about 1982, I made my weekly trip to my favorite Comic Book Store, Golden Age Collectables in the Pike Place Market and saw a new display which to my surprise was packed with *Doctor Who* books, as a US company had finally got the rights to distribute Target Books. Every week I would buy one or two more and read them by the end of the day. Around this time, I picked up a copy of the Programme Guide, which back then was in two volumes, and for the first time I was made aware of the exact names and order of all the stories. As a result, I began to create my own system of cataloguing the books by Doctor and Story. Thus *Doctor Who and the Loch Ness Monster* in my system was '4, 6' for it was the sixth story of the fourth Doctor. I would pass the time memorizing the exact order of the stories and checking them off as each one was issued in book form.

As the years went along, my collection grew until the sad day came when the Target imprint ended. I never parted with my *Doctor Who* books and they followed me everywhere I went over the years. For many years they sat in a series of boxes in basements until finally about a year ago I got them out and put them in my spare room where they sit still to this day. Now I can take the time to give them back the love and joy they gave me as a child growing up. Most of all, I can relive those days of the Doctor fighting the Zygons, thrilling in the prose of Terrance Dicks as he took me to so many faraway places and made me dream of greater things. If not for the mystery surrounding Loch Ness I would have never discovered one of the great joys of my life, so thank you Nessie.

A History of the World in 10½ Chapters

Doctor Who and the Dinosaur Invasion
by Nathan Bottomley
Favourite *Doctor Who* book: *Human Nature* by Paul Cornell

66 million years ago

Somehow, the pterodactyl was glad to be back. It had been a very difficult day.

Just this morning, it had been sunning itself in this sandy clearing. It must have fallen asleep, for the next thing it knew was that it was somewhere else, in a giant underground cavern. There was some kind of mammal there, a mammal with a head covered with a shock of white fur. The mammal was holding a searing bright light, which had sent the pterodactyl off screeching to the roof of the cavern. But then mammal had gone away, and the pterodactyl had settled down to wait for sunrise.

Still, that's all over now, it thought. But this very thought was interrupted by a loud, high-pitched buzz. The pterodactyl looked up to see two more of the brown-coloured mammals, appearing out of nowhere in a swirling eddy of light. It couldn't understand the ugly noises coming from the mammals' mouths, of course, and it couldn't admire the highly polished fingernails of one or the expensively cut lounge suit of the other. But it knew that they would attract the attention of the Monster, who would soon be along to enjoy them as a between-meals snack. So it flew off, the tip of one leathery wing grazing the cheek of one of the mammals as it went. The Monster was coming.

Silence. A sound of thunder.

12 January 1974

At teatime today, Part 1 of *Invasion (of the Dinosaurs)* is broadcast for the first time.

(I will turn five in three months, but I don't appear in this chapter of the story.)

This six-part story will not become an instant classic. Last year's finale, *The Green Death*, featured simple rod-and-string puppet maggots and psychologically scarred an entire generation of children. No one will be scarred by the puppet dinosaurs in this story, because they are plangently, lamentably bad. They float in mid-air, amateurishly CSO'd onto poorly-directed location footage. They burst suddenly through cardboard walls. Instead of roaring, they actually seem to be saying the English word *ROAR*. One dinosaur retreats out

69

of shot, pulled by the tail by an off-screen hand. Another two dinosaurs fight, menacing each other with bendy rubber teeth. (Or are they snogging? It's honestly hard to tell.)

19 February 1976

Malcolm Hulke's fifth *Doctor Who* novelisation is published: a version of *Invasion of the Dinosaurs* called *Doctor Who and the Dinosaur Invasion*. Unlike the televised story, it's a triumph – and not just because it doesn't include a single puppet dinosaur.

Consider how it reveals the backstory — the evacuation of London and the mysterious appearance of the dinosaurs. Rather than hearing about these events in some fairly unremarkable expository dialogue, as in the TV version, chapter 1 of the novelisation (London Alert!) shows us these events through the eyes of Shughie McPherson, a young unemployed man from Glasgow, who has come to London with some mates to see the Cup Final. He wakes up in a London that has been completely abandoned: terrified by the sight of the broken body of a young milkman, he falls to his knees and recites the Lord's Prayer before being attacked and killed by an unseen dinosaur.

In the televised version of the story, there is no one as interesting or skilfully characterised as Shughie McPherson. Nor has anyone like him appeared in *Doctor Who* before.

Malcolm Hulke is brilliant at backstory and characterisation. There's an entire chapter in *Doctor Who and the Cave Monsters* devoted to the odd, one-sided relationship between Dr Quinn and Miss Dawson. In *Doctor Who and the Doomsday Weapon*, we learn all about Jane Leeson — a character who gets a couple of minutes of screen time on television — what her life was like on a miserable, overcrowded earth, how she met her husband, and why she left to colonise the planet in whose soil she will finally be buried. And in *Doctor Who and the Sea-Devils*, we learn how Colonel Trenchard aspires to be a hero and how he is tragically killed by his own buffoonish incompetence.

21 June 1978

Here I am, appearing in the story at last. I'm ten years old, and tonight I will watch my first episode of *Doctor Who*.

A couple of weeks ago, my best friend at school showed me my first ever Target book. It was called *The Doctor Who Monster Book*. Somehow, Luke and I managed to spend hours of class time looking through it, when, presumably, we were meant to be doing mental arithmetic, or reading English books, or doing whatever the hell you do in Fourth Grade in primary school. It had a picture of Tom Baker on the front cover, apparently drawn by someone who had never actually seen him.

Because it was a Target book, many of the pages reproduced Chris Achilleos's cover art for the novelisations. On pages 52 and 53, you could see the classic cover of *Doctor Who and the Dinosaur Invasion*, depicting Pertwee's Doctor, his hand protecting his face, as a Tyrannosaurus Rex advances on him from behind and a pterodactyl snaps at him with an almighty Roy-Lichtenstein-inspired KKLAK!

However, the stars of the books were the Daleks. Five pages were devoted to them, chronicling their exploits in every *Doctor Who* story of the sixties and seventies, culminating in the Doctor's attempt to avert their creation in *Genesis of the Daleks*. Tonight's episode, Luke tells me, is called *Death to the Daleks*.

I go home after school, and announce to my family that at half past six, on Channel 2, we will be watching Part 1 of my first ever *Doctor Who* story.

It will change my life.

Later in 1978

At ten years old, I am already a voracious reader. Summer is hot in Sydney, and we are lucky enough to have a swimming pool in the backyard. Sometimes I come home from school and sit on the top step of the pool and read. I'm often reading a Target novelisation.

By now, I've got quite a collection going. I get a couple of dollars a week in pocket money, in exchange for simple chores like wiping up the plates after dinner and not coming downstairs to annoy my parents after bedtime. I use that money to buy novelisations. David Jones at Warringah Mall has a bookshop, just near the butcher. We go there every week to buy meat, and after that I choose five or six novelisations and put them on lay-by until I can save up enough money to take them home with me. I write my name and phone number on the first page of each book. Soon, I have dozens of them.

April 1979

I'm in an airport in the United States somewhere. My family are here on holiday: perhaps we're travelling across the country, from LA to New York, I think. In my bag, there is an exercise book in which I use a biro to write an account of the trip; there are also a few Target novelisations from my collection.

My edition of *Doctor Who and the Dinosaur Invasion* doesn't have the cover with the pterodactyl saying KKLAK! It's a later edition with a T. rex on the cover, based on a painting by Charles R. Knight, standing in front of a building I will later learn to identify as St Paul's Cathedral. This is my first vivid memory of reading a Target novelisation: Sir Charles Grover, with his expensively cut lounge suit and delusions of grandeur, tells the Doctor that he is 'in time to be present at the most important moment in the world's history.' The Doctor, unimpressed as ever by the most important moments in the world's history, replies, 'On the contrary. I am in time to prevent a crime.'

71

I think I might be in love.

Interlude: Nathan meets Tom Baker

It's March 1980, the last year of primary school. I'm still friends with Luke. He has told me that Tom Baker is visiting Australia, that he's coming to Warringah Mall and he's making an appearance in the Grace Brothers car park. My father has agreed to let me go.

The night before, in preparation, I watch a new *Doctor Who* episode, Part Something of *The Creature From The Pit*. I also go through my collection to find a novelisation for Tom to sign. I settle on *Doctor Who and the Talons of Weng Chiang*: it has the best likeness of Tom on the cover. He is dressed like Sherlock Holmes, staring grimly out of the picture with his piercing brown eyes.

My mother is in hospital for the first time. Over the next ten years, she will often be in hospital. Now, in the distant future, I still remember going to see her years later, reading *Doctor Who Magazine* on the bus, clutching it in my hand as I go to visit her in the room where she will eventually succumb to the cancer that kills her.

That's still ten years in the future. Right now, I'm in a long queue at the rooftop car park. Luke and his sister Rachel are with me. Immediately behind me in the queue is a boy who I will actually meet and befriend many years later: Richard Stone, now one of my co-hosts from the podcast Flight Through Entirety. He has just about forgiven me for what happens next.

Many more people have turned up than the organisers expected, but we're not very far from the front. Behind us, the queue snakes off into the distance. Ahead, I can see Tom in the distance, wearing his costume from last night's episode. While we wait, I talk to Luke about my mother's trip to hospital. I am overheard by a kindly old lady who is walking up and down the queue to keep everything running smoothly.

It takes an hour, I guess, but now we're just about standing in front of Tom himself. An announcement is made. Tom needs to leave now, and so the people in front of us will be the last people to get to speak to him. At this point, the kindly lady intervenes. 'This boy's mother is in hospital,' she says, so I'm allowed to go up and speak to Tom. No one behind me in the queue will get that opportunity.

I can't remember what I said. But I do remember Tom signing my Target novelisation and saying, 'Your mother's in hospital? Well, you know, if you ever need help, let me know. I'm a Doctor.'

His eyes are piercing and blue.

5 November 1984

In Sydney, in the late seventies, Channel 2 shows repeat after repeat of *Doctor Who*, four or five nights a week, at 6:30 PM, just before the news. They start at *Spearhead from Space*, go up to the most

72

recent episode with Tom Baker, and then back to *Spearhead from Space* again. Weirdly, they leave out anything scary, anything only available in black and white and anything with the Master.

Tonight, they're showing *Invasion of the Dinosaurs* for the first time. Part 1 is still only available in black and white — the colour version was deliberately incinerated — and so they're renumbering the episodes to make it a five-part story. Watching Part 2, now re-branded as Part 1, is the first time I ever see the televised story, which opens with the Doctor and Sarah inexplicably menaced by an unconvincing puppet Tyrannosaurus.

26 June 2010

I'm all grown up now. Crazily, I got rid of my whole collection of Target novelisations years ago. Now the books are available in a completely new format — audiobooks. And so I start my collection up again, buying a copy of *Doctor Who and the Dinosaur Invasion*. Unlike my previous copy, this has the orange cover with the pterodactyl going KKLAK! It's read by Martin Jarvis, who played Butler in the episode.

Martin Jarvis is, of course, superb. He does great accents for poor old Shughie McPherson and his mates, and great voices for the Doctor, Sarah and the Brigadier. More impressive, of course, is his note-perfect Martin Jarvis impersonation. Butler is much kinder and more working class here than the posh and distant character he was in the televised version. Hulke has given him a livid facial scar, to help us to recognise him when other characters don't know who he is. When Sarah taunts him about that scar, she is embarrassed to learn that he got it saving a terrified child trapped on the ledge of a high building.

Hulke has a genius for backstory and characterisation.

January 2016

Now, in the distant future, my iPhone contains dozens of audio versions of Target novelisations, even ones that I have never owned before, like *Doctor Who and the Cave Monsters*, tantalisingly referred to in a footnote in Chapter 3 of *The Dinosaur Invasion*. My favourites are always the novelisations by Malcolm Hulke. I have all of them now, except for *The War Games*. (Why don't I have that? Wait here a second while I go and put it on my Audible wishlist.) But my favourite audiobook is still the first one I ever bought.

5 billion years from now

The sun expands, and the Earth is destroyed, but nobody watches it happen. The Doctor is there, with his new best friend Rose. Later, or earlier, they will go out to get chips.

Discoveries in the Snow

Doctor Who and the Tenth Planet
by Cory John Eadson
Favourite *Doctor Who* book: *From A To Z* by Gary Gillatt

If you discover *Doctor Who* at an early enough age, you tend to go through three main stages of fandom. The first stage is simple. It's pure enjoyment. You know next to nothing about the history of the show, nothing about the subtle references and connections to past stories. You just watch it and relish the adventure and the excitement.

The second stage is the self-discovery phase, where you start to dig deeper into the history of the show. You unearth interesting facts that you never knew before, perhaps even misinterpret some of them and let your imagination fill in the gaps.

The final stage is, of course, the 'true-fan' stage. That moment when you are so well-versed in *Doctor Who* lore that you can rattle off the names of all the actors who have played the Doctor, and you can do it backwards.

For me, it was the middle stage that I found to be the most exciting. I was thirteen years old, the year was 2004, and *Doctor Who* was still full of mystery and surprise to me. I had only been a fan for a year or so, I had yet to encounter all of the previous eight Doctors, and I certainly didn't know the 'rules' of the show. Perhaps the biggest discovery I made occurred during the earlier part of the year, a discovery that both excited me and fuelled my imagination. I didn't unearth this knowledge through the internet, or even through watching the show itself. It was through a Target novel.

It was a beautiful summery day, like all the summers of our childhoods. The sky was a clear blue, and there was probably a chorus of birdsong as well.

I was sitting in the garden, about to devour *Doctor Who and the Tenth Planet*, a wonderful novel by Gerry Davis, which boasted the tag-line 'THE FIRST CYBERMEN ADVENTURE' on the cover. I loved the Cybermen, and was extremely interested in finding out more about their origins. My interest was also piqued by the blurb, which announced that this was 'the last thrilling adventure of the first DOCTOR WHO'. I had never seen a William Hartnell story before, so this was to be my introduction to his wizard-like Doctor.

The biggest surprise though, came from turning to the title page, and seeing this gobsmacking sentence: 'THE CHANGING FACE OF DOCTOR WHO: The cover illustration of this book portrays the first

DOCTOR WHO whose physical appearance was later transformed when he discarded his worn-out body in favour of a new one.'

Now, I was fully aware that many different actors had portrayed the Doctor over the years. I never thought for a second, though, that the changeover from one actor to another would actually be incorporated into the show! My imagination was suddenly on fire. I had images of the First Doctor actually peeling away his skin, shedding his old body, and a new chap emerging from within!

In an instant, the whole Universe of *Doctor Who* was suddenly even more weird, even more incredible and magical than I expected. I suddenly realised that the book I was holding was a very special one indeed, almost reverential to a young, fairly inexperienced fan as myself.

There was more surprise, of course. That wonderful page discussing the creation of the Cybermen (which I didn't already know, my only prior encounter with them being the fun *Revenge of the Cybermen* television story) frightened and exhilarated me. How horrific, to replace your body parts and organs with metal and plastic! They were more than just robots, they were *us*.

All of this only added to my excitement of reading the actual novel, which now had an almost funereal quality to it since I knew how it was going to end. And what a romp it was! *The Tenth Planet* will never be the absolute pinnacle of *Doctor Who*, either on television or in novel format, but Gerry Davis certainly knew how to craft a good, solid adventure. The characters leapt from the page, the action sequences sizzled, and he even made better use of the fact that Hartnell was physically ill during the televised version, by incorporating little First Doctorish slips of the tongue into the dialogue of the novel – referring to Ben and Polly as Ian and Barbara, for example.

This of course all built up to the grand climax and, indeed, my first experience of what would later be known as regeneration. Interestingly, we don't actually 'see' the regeneration in the novel. The Doctor merely wanders off for a lie down, and when his companions go to find him, he has a new face! I found this to be wonderfully intriguing, and I had a little shiver of excitement when the Second Doctor introduced himself as 'the new Doctor'.

It was later that year that I finally got to see *The Tenth Planet* on television, via VHS. Having already read the novel, it was a joy to see these characters come to life on screen. William Hartnell captivated me from the very beginning, and the Cybermen were utterly terrifying. Then of course there was the regeneration, one of the few sequences that has survived from the mostly-missing episode 4, which was weirder and more vivid than I could ever have imagined!

Today, people can Google just about anything – you can have the entire history of *Doctor Who* uploaded on a single page in seconds – but nothing quite beats making those discoveries yourself. Opening a book and unearthing a revelation so huge, it completely changes the way you look at something. As a thirteen year-old boy in 2004, I suppose I was spiritually connected, in that sense, to all of the fans who grew up in the 1970s. Those people who didn't have the luxury of the internet at all. Those people who actually had to do their own research, make their own discoveries. That sort of Whovian archeology is both priceless and magical, and is a key factor in why I am so deeply connected to *Doctor Who* now. I joined this wonderful Universe at the very end of the 'wilderness years', or, as Paul Cornell more accurately described them, 'the theme park years'. I grew up with the Target Novels, with dusty old videos and magazines and reference books. And I am all the richer for it.

Doctor Who and the Tenth Planet remains a very important, very special book to me. Despite all the death and chaos it contains, as people struggle to survive in an enclosed Arctic base, I am transported back in time to a warm summer's day, where, deep within me, the seeds of a lifelong fandom were being sown.

It is Very Cold at Sea

Doctor Who and the Ice Warriors
by Anthony Brown
Favourite *Doctor Who* book: *The Myth Makers*
by Donald Cotton

July 1976, the peak of the ladybird summer, and a yellow Fiat Mirafiori is heading up the A12 towards Harwich, en route for the overnight ferry to Denmark. On board are two parents, a nine-year-old boy and a five-year-old girl, plus assorted bears. Not on board, owing to quarantine regulations, is neither the four-year-old West Highland Terrier who joined the family a year earlier, nor, as is suddenly realised, any books. Cue a sudden diversion from Parkeston Quay to the Harwich branch of Woolworths, where books can hopefully be obtained. My sister quickly settled on *Mr Daydream*. For me, the choice was more of a dilemma.

Going for a *Doctor Who* book seems to have been a given. I'd got my first one the previous Christmas, when a book token had 35 pence left over after I'd got my last outstanding *Secret Seven* book and the print version of *David Attenborough's Fantastic Animals*. Which one to go for? Well, *The Three Doctors* obviously, as it featured three Doctors. I must have liked it, but clearly not enough to get another one over the next six months. So even though a mere 27 titles had been released by that date, there was a bit of a choice on the shelf. Eventually, I went for *The Ice Warriors* for two reasons.

First of all, while the back cover didn't even mention which Doctor it featured, it did stress the involvement of Martians, and as a space-mad kid I was well aware that NASA's Viking probes were days away from making the first real landing on Mars – a key stage towards my own inevitable trip to the Red Planet sometime in the 1990s, courtesy of the new world of regular space-flight that the shuttle would definitely have inaugurated by then. Secondly, my parents were buying, and *The Ice Warriors* was five pence more than *The Doomsday Weapon*, which remained frustratingly elusive in later years, leading me to feel that I was being punished for my mercenary decision as *The Ice Warriors* appeared regularly in the book stores.

With books safely bought, we headed down the few miles of road remaining to the port, where the ship waited at the quayside. Towering over ramps and cars, it wasn't the ferry we'd expected from past trips to the Isle of Wight and across the channel, large enough for a couple of unpleasant cafés and a poky duty-free shop. Instead the Winston Churchill, launched in 1967 and run by the Danish-owned DFDS seaways but named in honour of the then newly-deceased

British Prime Minister, seemed more like a cruise ship, a comparison intended by her designer. Even better, thanks to one of those tricks you could still pull off in those days, we weren't in one of the lower deck cabins below the car storage. Instead, by going into the head office around the corner from his own workplace, Dad had got us into one of the handful of hull-side cabins on A-Deck, not far below the bridge and with a staircase at the end of the corridor leading straight up to the Saga Lounge and Bar at the ship's prow.

It was all a bit of a dream come true, really. Best of all, the bunks all had individual lights, which meant it was possible to stay awake reading into the small hours, when I hoped to be able to spot the Dana Regina coming the other way as we passed en route (not possible of course, as the shipping lanes safely ran a half mile or more apart). Which finally brings us back to *The Ice Warriors* and those time-zone-shifting small hours.

Brian Hayles's adaptation of his original script is one of the best in the range, faithful but fine-tuned in a way that meant that when the episodes themselves finally turned up twelve years later, they almost felt as if they'd mistakenly used a draft script for the recording. It's not that there's anything wrong but lines lacked that final finesse, dramatic confrontations lacked that little trick of timing, the characters didn't quite have that last inch of depth, and of course the CO_2-related global cooling science is totally wrong, whereas the book gets it right.

Circumstances helped as well: the constant throb of the Churchill's engines echoed the low vibration of the Ioniser, and the cabin lights would dip and ebb in sympathy with the uncertain supplies from the base's reactor. Outside the porthole were the cold, occasionally stormy, waters of the North Sea (and if you went out on deck, the biting wind), as hostile as the frozen wastes of the new Ice Age outside the dome of Britannicus Base. In midsummer there weren't any icebergs out there, but that didn't stop you thinking that there might be... and of course, on arrival in Denmark itself, the Viking museums and the salvaged ships they contained were a perfect echo of the Viking-like Ice Warriors themselves.

It had been six months between *The Three Doctors* and *The Ice Warriors*. With Professor Branestawm and Hugh Walters's UNEXA books as rival attractions in the school library, it would be the next Christmas before I added to my *Doctor Who* library but after that the floodgates opened and by the start of 1978 there were only twelve books I didn't have. *The Dalek Invasion of Earth* turned up in a pokey little newsagent next to Sainsbury's and Granddad got me *Planet of the Daleks* from, all places, a book stall in the local barber's shop. That was a completist purchase, as I already had it inside the Marks and

Spencer *Dalek Omnibus*, and the same went for the Target version of *The Daleks*, which looked better on the shelf than the disintegrating 1964 edition I already had. Pretty soon my father grew sick of my whines about those last ten books and went through the Yellow Pages. With a list and a map itinerary in hand, he turned the next weekend into a forced march around Colchester's dozen bookshops. All came up dry until the only one left was an outlier beyond the ancient city walls. As it was the Christian bookshop, I didn't see much point in inflicting more work on my ten-year-old aching legs, but Dad insisted on finishing the job.

The Sign of the Fish held the expected racks of worthy religious tracts, analyses and Christian-inspired stories, such as *The Chronicles of Narnia*. But a little unit behind the door also held a few shelves of secular tracts which the owner nevertheless felt espoused the right principles for life... including a shelf full of *Doctor Who*, including three of those precious missing titles. In addition, the proprietor was enough of a fan to know which stories hadn't been novelised and which were coming up.

There was just one problem. I hadn't been expecting success from our quest, so I only had the funds to get two of the books. I can't be the only fan who ever had that dream where you find a stock of as-yet-unreleased titles, only to find that you can't afford them all, and – worse – that some of them disappear every time you look away to add up your funds. Again, Dad's pockets came to the rescue. He couldn't understand why I was getting *Planet of Evil* and *The Web of Fear* when *The Zarbi* was both the cheapest and the largest of the three (answer: I hadn't taken to the first Doctor so far) so he got it for me as well.

Seven to go, and thanks to my new friend at The Sign of the Fish I knew that most of them were going to be available within months. *The Green Death* and *Day of the Daleks* turned up rapidly. Then *Revenge of the Cybermen*, *The Dinosaur Invasion*, *The Tenth Planet*, and *Planet of the Spiders*. Two of them had new covers, which was irritating, but they were there. That just left *The Doomsday Weapon*. Once again, this was more a matter of completism than need, as I'd moved to secondary school in the autumn, and had read the copy in their library. Then a classmate decided to give up on this *Doctor Who* thing and sold his books, so I got a second-hand copy then, after two years and four months of regrets. The irony was that the non-canonical opening chapters meant I didn't like it at all, so I'm not sure I've even read my copy.

The Ice Warriors was another matter – read and re-read until the spine split and a later edition was bought to serve as its stunt double. It's a story that centres on a battle to save the last vestiges of civilisation against the forces of nature and the last echoes of a dead

world – a battle against the notion that everything ends, threatened
by the last survivors of a world that lost that battle, and complicated
by the clashes of human personality.

Well, the Clarks bookshop where I bought *The Three Doctors* fell
victim to the Waterstone's revolution and closed on the day space
shuttle Columbia disintegrated in January 2003. The logos engraved
into the upper floor windows survived afterwards though, until the
demolition balls moved in last month so the building could be replaced
by a fancy new food plaza. If the Harwich branch of Woolworths
survived, it will have finally gone with the rest of the chain during the
credit crunch. The Winston Churchill herself was transferred to
another route in 1978, when DFDS's new flagship came into service –
the Dana Anglia, later to star in the ill-fated BBC soap opera *Triangle*.
In 1979, she became the third item on the BBC news on the day that
Lord Mountbatten was assassinated, after running aground just
outside Gothenburg. The end eventually came in an Indian scrapyard
in 2004.

The Christian bookshop survives though, albeit moved to new
premises without that little doorway shelf decades ago. So all that's
really left, aside from the die-cast model of the Churchill on the shelf
to my left, is that battered copy of *The Ice Warriors*, slotted into its
chronological place among all the 150-plus books that followed it – and
the Proustian memories of that beautiful ship in the dead of night its
pages still evoke.

'Script-to-Book-and-never-mind-the-detail style'

Doctor Who and the Revenge of the Cybermen
by John Rivers

Favourite *Doctor Who* book: *Revenge of the Cybermen*
by Terrance Dicks

The title of this essay is a quotation from Keith Miller, author of the fanzine *Doctor Who Digest* and, during the mid-1970s, secretary of the Official *Doctor Who* Fan Club. The style that Miller is referring to was that which he attributed to Terrance Dicks, specifically about writing *Revenge of the Cybermen*. Miller preferred the 1976 novelisation to the TV version; understandable when Miller's original review of the four-part story, broadcast the previous year, was just one word: 'Yeauch'.

I'm not going to trouble you with tales of summer holidays spent reading Target novels at my Nan and Granddad's in New Milton; you'll be spared exciting discussions with librarians over microfiche about where they could order a copy of *Doctor Who and the Cave Monsters*. *Revenge of the Cybermen* itself is so dripping in lore that it overshadows my inconsequential memories. A Robert Holmes script redeveloped from a Gerry Davis idea that tantalisingly featured a space casino, this story took the base-under-siege plot, kicked it up the arse so it starts with episode 4 and instead plunged the Doctor, Sarah and Harry into the end-game of two opposing sides ready to commit genocide. Fantastically shot on location in Wookey Hole, but fraught with all the technical challenges one might expect with filming in a cave system, the director Michael E Briant declared that the shoot was cursed. (He blamed an arrowhead he'd found and then taken home with him.) Lis Sladen nearly drowned and Briant claims to have had an encounter with a ghostly frog-man. Then consider the cast - David Collings, Kevin Stoney, Michael Wisher - and 'HARRY SULLIVAN IS AN IMBECILE!' Is there a more *Doctor Who* story than *Revenge of the Cybermen*?

The novelisation then has a lot to live up to. My copy is the paperback (1983 reprint, cover art by Chris Achilleos, 128 pages, UK: £1.25, Australia: $3.95, Malta: £M1.25c). It is compact, solid and dependable. It was the first Target novelisation I ever bought and therefore one of the few I kept. In fact, it's my favourite one of the lot.

Its chapter list is a rollercoaster: 'Return to Peril', 'The Cybermat Strikes', 'The Living Bombs', 'Rebellion!', 'Explosion!', 'Skystriker!' Dicks even creates the title 'Attack of the Cybermen' before Saward and Levine tried it. The final chapter, promisingly, is titled 'The biggest bang in history' conjuring images of universe-shattering thrills, rather than the sordid allusion that Steven Moffat made as he closed the eleventh Doctor's first series.

Then there's a page of myth making. 'The Creation of the Cybermen' details the making of the 'dehumanised monsters' concerning the men of Telos (it charmingly forgets Mondas) who were determined to become immortal. These days we're used to aligning the development of the Cybermen with our own fears around surgery, artificial intelligence and the melding of machine and man. There's something more mythical though in using it as a quest to live forever, a conceit Dicks uses again in *The Five Doctors*. Here Dicks tells us that the quest for immortality eventually gives way to something else: 'And like all human monsters, down through all the ages of Earth, they became aware of the lack of love and feeling in their lives and substituted another goal – power!' What I love about this description is that Dicks defines the Cybermen in terms of the materials used: 'plastic and steel' and 'silver', which has arguably had an impact on the show in later years: *Silver Nemesis*, *The Age of Steel*, *Nightmare in Silver*. No one ever wants to do a story with 'plastic' in the title though, not even for the Autons.

The stage has been set in epic fashion then for the story itself. As Miller points out, Dicks adapts the shooting scripts. We're lucky that back in 2001, BBC Books published this script along with the others in season twelve, so you can see what did and didn't make it to the screen. This makes comparisons with the novelisation quite straightforward. Some differences are obvious. For example, Dicks supposes the Cybermen use guns rather than the head-cannons they have onscreen (which I always imagine whenever anyone says 'head-canon' - one of fandom's more nauseating neologisms). We understand more about the intentions of the Vogans in the book than onscreen, as chunks of their dialogue are reinstated concerning Vorus's ambition and willingness to kill Kellman if it means taking out the Cybermen in the process. Another amusing moment when the Doctor tells Lester that if he puts a component back into the sabotaged transmat the wrong way around he'll destroy the Beacon also makes it back into the story.

Other moments, Dicks chooses to excise. Some of these are useful: for example in the script, after transmatting down to Voga and curing Sarah of the Cybermat venom, Harry is suddenly overcome with gold fever, like a grizzled nineteenth century prospector.

> 'I'm going to faint...Look, gold, Sarah! Gold! Gold! Gold! Lots of lovely...Lovely beautiful gold. Tons and tons of glorious gorgeous gold...'

The broadcast version cuts this out and Dicks chooses not to have it occur in the novelisation either. Harry's unimpeachable character is restored.

Other excisions perhaps don't work as well. The shooting script clearly specifies the *Macbeth* quote after the Doctor kills one of the Cybermen and in the episode it's brilliantly acted by Tom Baker and Lis Sladen. Here Dicks ignores the Shakespeare and simply has the Doctor say, 'Well there's one down, come on!' Perhaps here Dicks favoured pacing over the Doctor's own eccentricity. Another surprising moment is that the imbecile line, again in the shooting script, has been replaced with 'Harry Sullivan is an idiot!' in the book. Maybe Dicks thought this would be more easily understood by the younger reader or he simply had a different shooting script to work from. Either way, the version that happens on screen is certainly the more impactful.

Re-reading the novel as an adult, I'm sometimes struck by the shortcomings and idiosyncrasies of Dicks's writing. Repetitive description is one example: on page 18 he writes, 'The asteroid hung in space, its scarred and pitted surface dark and mysterious' - then on page 21, 'Forgotten on the screen, the asteroid Voga hung mysteriously in space'.

(Dicks also isn't afraid to communicate when something is happening just out of view of the main action by placing a whole paragraph in parentheses. Again this could be a time-saving method to favour the pacing of the book.)

When the Doctor, Sarah and Harry first explore Nerva Beacon they come across a truly grim scene:

> 'The corridor was full of dead bodies. Corpse after corpse, a long line of them stretching ahead, twisted and contorted in the ungainly attitudes of sudden death. Sarah buried her head in the Doctor's shoulder. "They're all dead. Everyone on this space station must be dead..."'

For a book nominally aimed at children, that is a powerfully horrific moment. The next paragraph though begins with the line:

> 'But Sarah was wrong.'

Depending on your perspective, perhaps depending on your age, that is either a line that is completely surprising to you and urges you to read on and discover just who is alive or it undercuts the horror of the previous paragraph by having the narrator rubbish the mystery of what the characters are seeing and in fact their authority. This is the problem of having to adapt from a screenplay that is cutting between scenes. Our protagonists don't discover the remaining Nerva crew for themselves; instead we cut to an exposition scene explaining what the crew are doing on board.

From that last example, one could conclude that *Revenge of the*

Cybermen is a book that is very much in the style that Miller suggests. That's not completely fair, though. Dicks takes time to establish mythos, reinstates key moments of dialogue and delivers it all at a blistering pace. While reading the book, you forget the dodgy Cyber-accents and the ponderous, sparse Carey Blyton music. You are swept-up in the plans of both sides to annihilate the other with Dicks being perceptive enough to include the phrase 'mutual destruction' and allude to the Cold War.

Revenge of the Cybermen isn't a book written by someone who is ignoring the 'detail'; it's been written by someone who is including just enough 'detail'. It's a book that focuses on quickly delivering a set-up that is executed at breakneck pace. Yes, it misses some key lines from the broadcast version, but those are quite small and don't prevent the narrative from flowing or stop the action in any way. Neither the broadcast version nor the Target novelisation is better - instead they complement each other and are both extremely enjoyable.

Now, if you'll excuse me, I need to see why the Brigadier's calling me from somewhere near Loch Ness.

Everybody Needs a 303

Doctor Who and the Genesis of the Daleks
by Gary Russell
Favourite *Doctor Who* book: *The Target Book*
by David J Howe & Tim Neal

Information is a very important thing. Without it, we know nothing, we can plan nothing and we can explain nothing. Today, if we want to know what the next *Doctor Who* novel or gift book is going to be, we click the internet and everything we need is at our fingertips. Similarly, pretty much everything you need to know about the history of *Doctor Who* books is available at the touch of a button. It's just taken me 13 seconds to find out that *Genesis of the Daleks* was published on 22nd July 1976.

The significance of that to twelve-year-old me is that back then, we didn't have such information. The only way young Target enthusiasts could get information was two-fold. Firstly, some, not all, of the books used to contain the ALSO AVAILABLE IN THE TARGET RANGE page, which would list other books: *Doctor Who* titles, *Agaton Sax*, *The Story of the Loch Ness Monster* and so forth. They would also sometimes say IN PREPARATION, and these would often be the next couple of books due. A Target novel that didn't offer up such tantalising glimpses was, frankly, a disappointment. The other way of finding out information was to regularly check with your local book shop and ask to see the latest Wyndham List (aka Target List) – a three-monthly pamphlet sent out by the publishers listing all their forthcoming titles, usually with pictures of the cover, a majorly exciting part of the information-gathering process.

However, somehow silly old Gary and his school friends (big Target *Doctor Who* fans all) managed to miss the announcements about *Genesis of the Daleks* coming out as a book until one Thursday afternoon, a group of us got together and went for a cycle ride (yes, it's the 1970s, kids did that - it's what passed for fun back then, just go with it) and found ourselves in Cookham Rise, a strange area in Berkshire notable for being attached to Cookham (posh) and Cookham Dean (ultraposh and full of olde worlde cottages). Cookham Rise (not posh, all modern and new, the only place with shops) was what the Cookham/Cookham Dean inhabitants referred to as being full of the 'common, council estate types'. Cookham Rise had no council estates to speak of but was looked down upon for being developed post-war and having a large Cash-and-Carry, which brought an inordinate amount of traffic to Cookham's windy, not-built-for-anything-wider-than-a-bicycle roads. Totally frown-worthy, as a result. Cookham Rise also had a little Post Office-cum-Corner Shop that sold Letraset 'rub down Super Action Transfers' which is what we were searching for on this jolly summer holiday afternoon.

Instead, tucked away in the corner next to a Betty Maxey illustrated *Famous Five* book and a Roald Dahl box set was *Doctor Who and the Genesis of the Daleks* by Terrance Dicks, with its mustard gas-toned painting by Chris Achilleos showing Davros, a Dalek and Tom Baker (who looked like he may have drunk <u>all</u> the coffee) trapped in a goldfish bowl.

So here was the quandary. Three boys: one copy of *Genesis of the Daleks* (45p) versus a number of Super Action Transfers (35p). Who was going to buy what?

It's funny what people will do in a situation like this. Fight for it? Toss a coin? In a gentlemanly way say 'No, Martin, you have it, for I wish to rub down colourful transfers of *El Cid* rather than re-discover how Davros created the Daleks and put Doctor Who inside a goldfish bowl'?

To be honest, I don't recall the outcome, other than I went home with just 5 pence change from the shiny 50p in my pocket and a new *Doctor Who* book whilst *El Cid* lived to fight another day still inside Cookham Rise Post Office.

So, why am I telling you this? What significance does this one book have out of so many that punctuated my childhood collecting spree? (I tell you this, I can recall exactly where and when I got each and every Target novel up to around *The Masque of Mandragora* - that's how important these novelisations were to me and thousands of other kids up and down Britain who could probably all do the same.) Well, let's fast forward a month or so, to late August that year. Gary, you see, apart from rabidly loving *Doctor Who* book hunting and Letraset Super Action Transfer sets, wanted to be an actor. Foolish boy. But he had been indulged and as he was shooting towards his 13th birthday, had done some West End theatre work and had now been cast in the BBC's new children's TV version of E Nesbit's *The Phoenix and the Carpet*. Which is of no real relevance to this story except that before filming commenced (and yes I mean filming, not studio work), a week was to be spent reading the scripts with the other actors and plotting out the pre-filmed sequences rather than just going on location, plonking down four kids and a wooden bird and saying 'off you go'. Thus we traipsed up to the BBC's rehearsal room in Acton, my ever-patient mother and I, for the first day, 25th August 1976. Cue the morning's read through of a couple of episodes, cups of orange squash, meeting cast and crew and generally larking about. Then it was lunch time.

The Acton rehearsal rooms were a weird building, each floor consisting of three large rehearsal areas with heavy soundproofed double doors with tiny glass windows in them, next to which was a small blackboard that told you what show was being rehearsed, who the director and production manager was. There were seven floors of that, then at the top was the restaurant which, by the nature of covering the same floor space as three rehearsal rooms was pretty large, had a rooftop bit with tables outside and a pretty sheer drop to instant death if you were daft enough to climb over the low red railing. So there we were, queuing up for our first ever BBC lunch. And the door to the restaurant opened and a tall man in a grey checked jacket, jeans and lots of dark curly hair walked in. 'Oh look,' I said to my mother as casually and quietly as I could (which probably wasn't very) 'that's Tom Baker.' Like all good mothers, mine told me not to bother him and let him eat his lunch, so we went and sat at a table. But fate wasn't having any of it, and TV's Doctor Who sat at the table behind us, so his back and mine were pretty close. I stared at my food, really really stared because I couldn't look anywhere else without giving away I was actually pretty much hyper-ventilating. He. Was. Behind. Me.

After a few minutes (or was it a lifetime?) my mum fished into her purse and brought out a pen and a receipt. Seriously, a receipt, probably from W H Smith or something. Crumpled, small and just awful. But it was all she had and frankly, I wasn't proud. So I waited till Doctor Who finished his food and then I pounced. Pen. Smith's receipt. Enthusiasm. Big smile. Please sir would you sign this appallingly grubby piece of paper because you are Doctor Who and I like your show and I don't really do autographs but you're Doctor Who and I am more in love with your television programme than life itself and I think I may be about to have a stroke at twelve and three quarters but you are Doctor Who and...and...

Now I'm pretty sure I actually just asked for his autograph, but all that was absolutely going through my head.

'No.'

Now, that's a pretty devastating response to anything when you are twelve and three quarters. When TV's Doctor Who says it to you, you kind of want to die. Preferably quickly, before your heart breaks into a billion sharp pointy pieces.

'No, no I won't sign a receipt.' And he passed this evil, accursed, awful, hateful piece of paper and clearly the world worst, most unattractive biro back to me. Then he looked me up and down. 'You must be an actor.' I managed a nod. 'You must know your way around this big building.' I nodded (a lie, but you're not really going to say 'No TV's Doctor Who, I've been here three hours and I barely know how to find the lavatory' – you just nod). 'Well, if you can come down tomorrow to room 303 at eleven o'clock, I'll sign something for you then.'

And he went back to eating.

I went back home that afternoon (I don't remember *anything* more about work that day) and grabbed my latest piece of Doctor Who wonderment - Genesis of the Daleks, 45p, by Terrance Dicks with TV's Doctor Who trapped in a goldfish bowl, and the next day, at 11am (thank you Phoenix and the Carpet producers for letting me go a-wandering) I was outside room 303, tippy toeing up to stare through the window, looking for TV's Doctor Who who had made me a promise. The door opened and someone walked out, so I slipped in (security not being something TV types were big on back then) and I got to watch a few minutes of what I now know to have been Bernard Horsfall and Angus Mackay and Tom Baker doing a scene from The Deadly Assassin.

Clearly someone eventually wondered why a child was standing sheepishly by the door and brought it to people's attention, at which point Tom Baker waved me forward. 'You came,' he said. 'I wasn't sure if you would. Well done finding us.' I just smiled, said thank you and offered up Genesis of the Daleks, 45p, by Terrance Dicks with TV's Doctor Who trapped in a goldfish bowl. Which he signed to me. I was ecstatic. He then picked up a brown case, like an old medical doctor's bag, and brought out of it a pristine copy of a yellow Doctor Who Poster Magazine (only 25p, no goldfish bowls but a decidedly odd carrot-nosed Axon on the front) and opened it to the huge poster of himself and signed that to me too. He then folded it back up, shook my hand and with my two autographed treasures, I left him to his work.

I think I was still smiling the following morning.

It's now 2016 - that was forty years ago. Forty years! That yellow poster magazine is safely in a box in my spare bedroom in my home. That copy of Genesis of the Daleks (45p etc etc) sits on the shelf with all my other Doctor Who books.

And that memory of an actor's generosity, kindness and bloody brilliance to a twelve-year-old nobody will never, ever fade.

DOCTOR WHO AND THE
GENESIS OF THE DALEKS

To Gary from
who on earth is
Tom Baker?
august 26th 1666.

THE CHANGING FACE OF DOCTOR WHO
The cover illustration of this book portrays
the fourth DOCTOR WHO

An Adventure for 2-6 Players

Doctor Who and the Web of Fear
by Drew Meyer
Favourite *Doctor Who* book: *All-Consuming Fire*
by Andy Lane

The Doctor, in any of their incarnations, is a universe-spanning super-intellect, impossible to predict, infuriatingly clever, infinitely resourceful, and painstakingly dramatic. They're the smartest being in most rooms and capable of changing personality each time you meet them. The Doctor's a magnificent character to observe as an audience, but a little harrowing when it comes to role playing games (unless you're Riley Silverman).

While reading *The Web of Fear* I realized the story is a beautiful mess of ideas and practically screams to be made into an RPG. It reads like a true dungeon crawl, exploring the London Underground with bizarre monsters lurking around every corner. It embraces science fiction by making the monsters both mythical and robots, and the monsters have futuristic weapons which fire webs... WEBS! There are a number of main characters who are not the Doctor, one of which is a traitor.

There are some fun *Doctor Who* RPGs out there, but none that fit on a single page... until now. This version borrows heavily from the games of John Harper and Grant Howitt. All you need are 4 six-sided dice (D6).

The Adventure

The robotic Yeti have infested the London Underground with a poisonous web which restricts movement. You have been tasked with retaking the tunnels.

Rather than have the players take over the roles of existing characters from the story, they'll be playing one of the many unnamed proto-UNIT military-approved individuals tasked with defending the Goodge Street Fortress and retaking the London Underground.

PLAYERS: Character creation

1. Choose a STYLE for your character: **Brash, Brave, Curious, Independent, No-Nonsense, Rookie**, or **Veteran**
2. Choose a ROLE for your character: **Engineer, Reporter, Scientist,** or **Soldier**
3. Choose your number, from 2 to 5. A high number means you're better at MILITARY (intuition; endurance, will power; action). A low number means you're better at

INTELLIGENCE (technology; science; calm, precise action) (intuition; diplomacy; seduction; wild, passionate action)

4. Equip your character with whatever you and the Great Intelligence deem fit for whatever ROLE you selected. Give them a name!

5. Create two TRACKS of 3 points-one MILITARY and one INTELLIGENCE. Your CHARACTER starts at '0' for each, but if they reach 3 on either, your CHARACTER suffers a fate.

HOW TO PLAY

Whenever the **PLAYERS** encounter a challenge, they roll dice to see what happens. If the **CHARACTER** is **PREPARED** for the situation add +1D6 (for a total of 2D6) and if the **CHARACTER** is an **EXPERT** in the situation, add another +1D6 (for a total of 3D6). Any one **PLAYER** can **HELP** by describing how their **CHARACTER** can help the other **CHARACTER,** thereby adding +1D6 (for a total of 2D6-4D6). The GI can **REMOVE** dice if the **CHARACTERS** find themselves in less than ideal conditions. **PLAYERS NEVER ROLL LESS THAN ONE DIE.** Roll the dice and compare EACH roll to your number (2-5)

If you're using **MILITARY** you want to roll **UNDER** your number
If you're using **INTELLIGENCE** you want to roll **OVER** your number

If NONE of your rolls succeed the GI tells you how the situation has gotten worse. Gain a point on the appropriate TRACK.
If at least ONE roll succeeds, you have managed in your task, but there's a complication.
If at least TWO rolls succeed, you did what you were trying to do.
If at least THREE rolls succeed, the GI rewards you with additional results.
If you roll your number exactly, you've achieved **MILITARY INTELLIGENCE**! The GI rewards you with additional positive results.

If your **CHARACTER** ever reaches 3 points on their **MILITARY TRACK**, they die.
If your **CHARACTER** ever reaches 3 points on their **INTELLIGENCE TRACK**, they have become the **TRAITOR** and must spend the rest of the session betraying the party.

GREAT INTELLIGENCE: HOW TO RUN THE GAME

It is recommended that whoever is running this adventure (the GI or Great Intelligence) be familiar with *Doctor Who and the Web of Fear*, however you don't have to follow the novelisation's narrative. Play to see where the story goes.

Possible Encounters
Crates of Explosives: Strategically placed to detonate remotely to bring down walls to halt the spread of the web.

Electrified Third Rail: A hazardous trap for the unsuspecting.

Glass Pyramid: The web will follow any Yeti carrying a glass pyramid, effectively blocking off that tunnel for the purposes of travel. Pyramid can be destroyed by gunfire.

Traitor: Any **CHARACTER** that fails 3 times on **INTELLIGENCE** rolls becomes the **TRAITOR** and can sabotage efforts (reducing the number of dice **PLAYERS** can roll)

Web: Deadly space fungus controlled by the Great Intelligence, the web moves slowly through the tunnels, blocking travel. Anyone entering it 'is never seen again'. The Yeti can move freely through the web. It absorbs radio waves and prevents long range communication.

Yeti Patrol: Strong and well armoured – cannot be harmed by machine gun fire. Hand grenades repulse but do no lasting damage. Occasionally found carrying a glass pyramid. Yeti are directed via control sphere implanted in their chests.

IF the Great Intelligence WANTS to follow the original story, then:
Act One:
The base of operations is the Goodge Street Fortress, commanded by Captain Knight. Within the Fortress are several notable rooms: Operations, the Commons and the Laboratory. Also within the Fortress is an ammunition supply.

You don't need an elaborate map for the game: there are plenty of images with the appropriate map online if you search 'London Underground map 1967.'
Events/Missions
Detonate Explosives to Halt Web: Bring down walls to keep web from spreading.

Holborn Fight: Meet with an ammo delivery truck near Holborn and return to the Fortress.

Lay Telephone Line: In aid of communication.

Act Two:
Witnessing the dangers the Yeti pose, the players have enough information to formulate a plan of action. It's possible that the Doctor, busy within the laboratory, developing a way of jamming Yeti

92

transmissions and a control unit to switch them off, will take no part in the plan of action. Military characters can attempt to get ammunition, set traps, retrieve the TARDIS, and/or defend the Fortress.

Events/Missions

Laboratory: Medical or Science minded players can attempt to help the Doctor and Anne Travers with their inventions.

Retrieve the TARDIS: Colonel Lethbridge-Stewart is looking for men to help retrieve equipment from the TARDIS the Doctor could use to re-programme a control sphere. The TARDIS, which resides near Covent Garden, is heavily guarded by Yeti.

Travers is kidnapped: (The kidnapping should occur when the players aren't in the lab, so they don't feel as though the narrative is bossing them around.) Act Two can end with a possessed Travers returning to the Fortress to deliver an ultimatum to the Doctor.

Yeti Destroy the Ammunition Supply: The traitor granted them access to the Fortress.

Yeti Models discovered: There are four little Yeti models with which to summon the Yeti. The traitor will strategically place them to cause the most damage. Discovery of the models leads to the realisation that there's a traitor among the players.

Act Three:

Both the reprogrammed control sphere and the control box are finished. The web finally reaches the Fortress, destroying it and moving the characters to the finale with the Great Intelligence. The players can retrieve Professor Travers and/or Victoria, escort the Doctor to Piccadilly Circus, or plan an alternate mission.

Events/Missions

Test the Control Box: Get close enough to a Yeti to insert the reprogrammed control sphere.

Throne Room of the Great Intelligence (Piccadilly Circus): Up to three Yeti, the traitor, and the Giant Glass Pyramid/ Knowledge Draining Machine.

Web reaches the Fortress: With the Fortress destroyed, it moves the characters to the finale with the Great Intelligence.

Player Characters who survive have impressed Colonel Lethbridge-Stewart. They gain experience and are invited to join the newly promoted Brigadier Lethbridge-Stewart as the first members of UNIT in the follow up adventure: *The Invasion.*

'The Space War'?

Doctor Who and the Space War
by Iain McLaughlin
Favourite Doctor Who book: *Doctor Who in an Exciting Adventure with the Daleks*
by David Whitaker

Every Saturday, pocket money clutched in my sweaty little hand (or stashed in my sweaty little pocket), I would go to the end of a display stand in Dundee's John Menzies where the *Doctor Who* books were kept, in the hope that there would be one I didn't have. This was before the internet told us everything that was going to happen so a new release always came with an element of surprise. *The Space War* was a particular surprise. You see, I had *The Making of Doctor Who*, so I knew there wasn't a story called *The Space War*. However, I also knew there wasn't a story called *The Auton Invasion* but that was a great novel, so The Space War came home with me. Obviously I paid for it first.

Reading *The Space War*, I started to realise the difference in quality between the books. By then some of the Target books had started to feel slimmer, but this one felt different. The page count was on a par with some of the others and the size of type wasn't smaller. No, the reason this book stayed in my hands longer was that I kept going back and looking at bits of it again. I kept re-reading passages. It had detail.

That was probably when I started to look at authors' names. For me, the selling point had always been *Doctor Who* in the title. Now, I started to see patterns. With Malcolm Hulke's books you got more of this kind of depth and detail. I found myself rereading the books that gave more detail and background. By the latter half of the 1980s, as the Target range rebounded from its skinny phase with heftier, more involved releases like *Remembrance of the Daleks* and *Fury from the Deep*, I still read the books as they came out, but my literary appetite had broadened.

I was also writing for a living. I started as a staff writer at the age of eighteen and I've written for a living ever since. Whether I'm writing a short comic strip, a long comic, a novel, a TV episode, a radio play or a short story, I am always influenced by something I learned from those Target novelisations which, like *The Space War*, had detail, the little extras that bring a character or a situation to life. As my tastes in reading broadened, I started to see that I was captured more by books with this depth than by books that didn't have it.

I started reading Ian Fleming's books when I was about eleven or twelve. I wouldn't class them as great literature but I do put them, for the most part, far above average thrillers. Fleming would spend time on little details about food and etiquette and tailoring. He built and embellished the world James Bond lived in, and gave us more insight into 007 as he did so: his snobbery, his often bizarre views, in particular his attitudes to women... I was lucky enough to have the chance to write a short story for a James Bond anthology in 2015. It was a book with many different takes on Bond and I wanted mine to read like Fleming. Understanding the way in which Fleming detailed those things made it far easier to write in a way which echoed Fleming without in any way parodying him.

Matthew Reilly is an Australian thriller writer. His books read like movie scripts. That's not meant as an insult in any way. He writes fast-paced stories that sprint from one set piece to the next. *Ice Station*, the first of his novels I read, is silly but hugely enjoyable. However, over the space of a few years, I found myself enjoying his books less and less. The reason was that he was paring back his writing to dialogue and what was needed to move from one bit of action to the next. All of the characterisation and character background was dropped in favour of pace and set pieces. The action hadn't changed but I found that I didn't care what was happening because I didn't care about the characters he was writing. In one of his later books, one of the characters is beheaded and it's supposed to devastate the hero. It barely affected me as the reader because so little had been given to the characters in the text.

Compare this with the background we get to the Draconians in *The Space War*. Malcolm Hulke fleshes them out and makes them into a real civilisation we can believe in and care about. Or compare it with the background given to Dr Quinn in *The Cave Monsters* or Butler in *The Dinosaur Invasion*. Reilly stripping away all of the characterisation acted as a reminder of why Malcolm Hulke's novelisations so grabbed me when I was a kid. And Mac Hulke wasn't the only one. When he had time to write and space to play with, Terrance Dicks delivered delightful additions to the characters, as did Ian Marter. David Whitaker's two early novels were full of beautiful characterisation. Most of the later novelisations gave their authors a longer page count and the freedom to embellish characters and plots and they were all the better for it.

The snobbery in literature towards novelisations is clear and unjustified. Yes, books like *Battlefield* are based on extant works but many in the range are infinitely superior to a lot of novels. It doesn't matter what the source material is. These are excellent books and they paved the way for the New Adventures, the Missing Adventures, the Telos novellas... when I came to write *Blood and Hope*, I was influenced by the likes of Hulke, Marter and, of course, Dicks. Terms like 'spin-off' didn't come into my mind - I was just writing a book - but when I was writing it, I remembered *The Space War* and I had a flick through it a few times during the writing of the book.

I recently wrote *The Forty Nine Steps*, a sequel to John Buchan's *The Thirty Nine Steps*, and I wrote the opening chapter from the point of view of a night watchman. He's not a major character or an important one: he was there to see the big action set-piece and in a lot of books he might have been glossed over, possibly not even given a name. Instead, I took time with this character. I gave him a name and a wife. I explained why he had chosen his job and even why he had the newspaper-reading habits that he did. I took that from another Malcolm Hulke novelisation, *The Green Death*, in which one of the characters was noted as having a fondness for reading comics. He liked the pictures and didn't have to worry about reading the words. It was a small bit of characterisation that added so much to a character who wasn't really that important. It just made for a better, more interesting book.

A friend of mine always reminds me that the devil is in the detail. He's right, but as a writer the good is in the detail as well. All those little additions that give background and depth, they are what lift a work and give it a heartbeat. Those are the things that make it breathe. Those are the things that I always try to add to my work, whether it's a novel or a short story or a radio play, and it is a lesson I started to learn all those years ago when I bought a *Doctor Who* book with an unfamiliar title.

I've taken a lot from my favourite TV show. *Doctor Who* and its novelisations constantly grabbed my curiosity and made me find out about Aztecs, the crusades, the Reign of Terror, Mars, any number of things. It was responsible for my love of reading and it opened up a lot of doors for me professionally: I've written novels, short stories and audios based in the *Doctor Who* universe so I owe a big chunk of my career to Malcolm Hulke and *The Space War*.

If you don't like my work, now you know where to place the blame.

Planet of the T. Dicks

Doctor Who and the Planet of the Daleks
by Will Ingram

Favourite *Doctor Who* book: *The Discontinuity Guide*
by Paul Cornell, Martin Day and Keith Topping

My wife, with whom I live, would doubtless say I own far too many *Doctor Who* books. Almost an entire six-foot bookcase in our bedroom is double stacked with the buggers, including a full run of the Targets.

I think the first Target novel I ever read was *The Five Doctors*. I wasn't one of the very first to read the novel, in advance of its TV premiere, but it must have been only a few months after: we had recently moved house and Colin Baker had just taken over on TV. To my delight, the local library had a fair few of the Target books on its shelves. The policy of the day allowed each person to take three books out, but somehow our parents had persuaded the staff to allow my sister and I to take out their share as well, so we both used to come out with six books at a time. Though I did like to dip into the non-fiction section, on a few occasions I emerged with a stack of six Targets. I was pleased to discover among them *The Five Doctors* with its super-shiny cover. That was one of two books I must have taken out the most; several times to read, and – to be bluntly honest – several more times just to gaze upon in awe. We had no VCR in those days, so you had to get such thrills however you could.

The other book I got out the most was a thing of beauty, WH Allen's *Dalek Omnibus*. The cover showed a re-imagined Dalek invasion of Earth with the gunmetal-grey variants blasting away amid burning buildings. As well as the Terrance Dicks novelisation of this story, the tome included two of Dicks' other Dalek adaptations, namely *Day of the Daleks* and *Planet of the Daleks*. The pedant in me even then was irked by the transposition of the blurbs of the latter two stories on the book's rear cover.

An irritating habit I picked up in my teens and am still occasionally prone to today is getting part way through a novel and then getting side-tracked, leaving it so long that the narrative has been forgotten, and it's too late to resume, instead having to start it again. The worst example of this was stalling at around eleven hundred pages into the paperback edition of the 'complete and uncut' edition of Stephen King's *The Stand*. I blame life for having too many good distractions. An early version of this was manifested by the *Dalek Omnibus*. I polished off *The Dalek Invasion of Earth* keenly, and then, uninspired by 'Moni sat up and looked around cautiously', felt rather deflated. I told myself that this story couldn't possibly be as good as the previous

97

one, so I'd give it a miss. The final tale never even got a look in and the thing was returned to the library. I really cannot explain why, but when the book came home again, *exactly the same thing would happen.*

Then one day, as Moni sat up for the umpteenth time, my stubborn gene finally kicked in and I somehow mustered the curiosity to see what he would do next. To my surprise, the story turned out to be even better than the opening salvo, a real time-travelling paradoxical mindbender, and I kicked myself for not reading it sooner. So, a valuable lesson learned there then? You'd think so, wouldn't you?

Three or four years must have passed, and I'll estimate that in that time I probably read *Day of the Daleks* about five times and *The Dalek Invasion of Earth* at least a dozen. I kid you not, at that point I probably could have recited great chunks. The *Dalek Omnibus* continued to go back to the library two-thirds read and it would be a few more cycles before I finally got round to reading *Planet of the Daleks*. A faithful adaptation and a damn good read, *Planet of the Daleks* might just be the most typical of all the Targets – pushing boundaries or trying something different it certainly is not, but it is as warm and friendly, and assuring as the range would ever be.

The novel structure is textbook Terrance Dicks. Six TV episodes are perfectly split into twelve chapters. He is a master of using the spare chapter ends to provide additional cliffhangers. Many of those here read like they come out of a Fighting Fantasy book, only missing the words 'Your adventure ends here'. Typically, Terrance's descriptive prose evokes an atmosphere far beyond the confines of the presumed TV budget (though it wasn't until the 1993 repeat that many of us got to see it confirmed).

It's basically Terry Nation's Greatest Hits reworked into Terrance Dicks' Greatest Hits. I was pleased to have finally experienced the tale and it didn't get skipped any more.

In January 1989, I had an interview during which my intellectual worth would be established, for entrance into a private school. I remember having to come up with as many uses for a coat-hanger as I could as quickly as possible. I'm not sure whether or not the idea of strangling chickens with it endeared me to them. The other thing that sticks in my memory was that I was to discuss some of the books I had read. The preparatory notes advised 'candidates should be reading a wide range of literature, not just *Doctor Who* books'.

They clearly had not read enough of them.

In defiance at this snobby attitude, I decided I would try to read the lot. During my seven years at the school, probably a good two-thirds of the fiction I read were Targets (stitch that, Headmaster!) A cynic could argue I restricted my development in some way, that I should have read more Dickens and Dumas (I did try some), but it's far more likely they helped me to find myself instead. What we choose to do in our spare time says vastly more about who we are than what other people, be they parents, teachers or anyone else, tell us to do.

As I started to buy my own copies at jumble sales, and their numbers steadily grew, the trips to the library declined and became less Target-centric. For a while I would display my collection proudly, propped up against the wall so that you could see the covers – this habit would continue until I had too many to do it with, even over multiple shelves. They ended up overlapping each other in a kind of Target book domino rally tribute. On at least one occasion a line of them actually toppled over, so perhaps this was not such a good idea. I was never that fussed back then about keeping my books pristine and I shudder slightly now about the casualness with which I crammed such hard-to-find titles as *The Wheel in Space* and *Fury from the Deep* into my holiday stash and was unfazed by sand, dirt or misplaced buttocks taking their toll. I was however aghast when *The Curse of Fenric* somehow got soaked in orange juice on the floor of the coach on the way back from a ski trip. I did manage to replace that one.

Many titles (including, at last, a standalone *Planet of the Daleks*) came from a second-hand bookshop in Molesey which was something of a Mecca to the 14-year-old me. I would cycle there every few weeks and get a small pile of Targets at almost every visit. It was only when I discovered the internet that I realised how lucky I was in scoring cheap copies of many rare titles there. The other source to which I am forever indebted is a chap called Ari Ercole. Ari had amassed a large selection of Target books and looked after them very well indeed, save for stamping his name and address inside them. I am terribly grateful that Ari had taken the decision to donate his collection to the local Cancer Research shop where I would find them being regularly drip-fed onto the shelves. It was there that I perfected the art of the Target-seeking skim-glancing of large quantities of book spines in a relatively short time. I probably should have asked them to bring the lot out for me in one go, but it never occurred to me (and I wouldn't have had the money anyway). If, however, Ari's parents had made the donation without his knowledge, then he has my sympathies. And Ari, if that's what happened and you're reading this, then I'm terribly sorry but you can't have them back now.

After I left school, I had one last summer of significant freedom. It was an important time in my life, the tide turning in many ways. That summer, I discovered the music of Genesis, particularly their 1970s albums, which was an absolute revelation (no pun intended). I had found my second great fandom, and the best news would turn out to be that there was room enough for both. However, when the spark of inspiration ignites a brand new obsession, it is inevitably going to push other things aside, as happens when first embarking on a new relationship. And it did feel that the Target books were going to be put to one side, at least temporarily. By that point, I was shy of less than twenty to complete the collection (it did happen eventually, via eBay) and the New Adventures and the ranges that followed had long since taken over my *Doctor Who* reading. The book collection didn't follow me to my university lodgings, but my music collection did.

Still, I never lost the love. I'd frequently pop into charity shops when passing, even in that wonderful summer, full of so many other distractions. On one particular day and decided to pop into the library on the way home. It'd been some time since I'd been a regular visitor, recent loans tending to be music albums rather than books. I thought I'd have a look through the sale of withdrawn items and my eyes were quickly drawn to a familiar volume. It was battered, it was tired, it had many loose pages, but it was the *Dalek Omnibus*. The same old copy I'd taken home so many times in the previous decade. My old friend! It cost me just 15p to reunite with this piece of my childhood, a piece which once taught me a very important lesson about perseverance.

It's Doctor Who I live with, not with whom I live.

A (post-processualistic) Tale of Two Libraries

Doctor Who and the Pyramids of Mars by Al No

Favourite *Doctor Who* book: *Who on Earth is Tom Baker?*
by Tom Baker

0000

It doesn`t matter how many hedgehogs there were. I`ll say there were three, because that`s how many I remember. Two small snuffly bundles traipsing behind a larger one, clambering awkwardly onto the gentle cement slope of the wheelchair ramp. Like me, they were getting out of the rain for a moment.

Moving slowly, I used my thumb to turn the volume of my Walkman right down in case the high tickity sounds scared them off. Under the corpse-light of the porch, I was probably shadowed like an abandoned pile of blankets.

The four of us sat there in the cold, early morning stillness, listening to the rain hiss against the stones and splash off the leaves of the incongruous palm tree.

Then the police turned up.

The hedgehogs scuttered away guiltily. I jumped up, the bottles of wine like bricks in the pockets of my long woollen coat, my legs burned with a sudden and blunt orange gasp. I pulled my hat down, vaulted over the railings and the library wall and ran off through someone else's car park toward an estuary.

False time travel's easy. We call it memory.

0001

Twos complement each other nicely. It's easier to bounce things between two surfaces, whether those surfaces are ideas, minds or a library wall and wheelchair ramp.

I grew up in two different worlds; two different countries; two different cultures. The person typing this is a different person to the one they used to be a century or so ago. Bits rot and names change. Not just names, but memories too. Everything I'm typing is true, whether it happened or not.

From jumping between worlds and identities like a superhero, or a thief, I learned how to develop a repertoire of language and reactions. I learned which subjects were safe and which were taboo; how to live out of separate boxes depending on the caprices of an emotionless and arbitrary calendar.

As a, largely, only child, I quickly got good at amusing myself. Trees, cliffs, comics, the underside of piers, rudimentary paths, drawing and books were all unexplored places you could tame and claim and lose yourself in. If you didn't get caught by a bear or a dinosaur or a mummy or something, you were fine. Being young, you knew you'd be fine, because bears, dinosaurs, mummies and somethings only carried away supporting characters in your story.

That confidence took a thorough denting when, not yet out of my teens, I found myself homeless.

0010

Libraries are an obvious extension of language, which, seeing as fire's plagiarised, remains humanity's greatest achievement. Language – and there are various forms – is truly magical. We can change perception, reality, the world and the future through language. It's an elegant, intricate, exquisite thing and we're lucky to have it.

Libraries are where we keep our ancestors alive.

Thousands of years ago, which may as well be right because you can't go back, I lived in a house on top of a hill and next to a park. This was only true in one of the worlds I grew up in. One road-crossing away there was a chemist that isn't there anymore. Today it's a tapas bar, the upper levels converted into luxury guest rooms with commanding estuary views. I once borrowed a copy of Peter Benchley's *Jaws* from the elderly lady who'd haunt the tourists, if only ghosts were real. If you travel back even further, about a century, you'd find it was once a Royal Library and Reading Room.

Now, retrace your steps, head down the hill and, at the gap in the wall, turn right and head into the trees. Run down the path until you run out of park, then turn left and head up the hill that's there (don't forget to Splink when you hit the crossroads), keep heading up until you spot the incongruous palm tree on your right and then stop.

The square stone building sleeping behind the tree used to be this world's library. Now it's flats.

Last century, that journey was an adventure. The bag filled with books to be returned banged against my back as I ran down one of the many, many routes that only children know about. Wade through the garlic and stinging nettles and pull yourself up onto the wall, run along and leap out to the tree branch. Fighting the bark that came away like frayed rope, I'd pull my legs up before the dragon's curled fangs closed around them and dragged me down into the lava. I bounced from one tree to another, then onto the stegosaurus's back, making my way around the bony plates that jutted up like random stones from a wall.

Moments later, still unnoticed by anyone, I'd run up the gentle cement slope of the wheelchair ramp, turning slightly so my shoulder pushed the stiff, stiff door open and then plunged into the library's porch/reception area. I ignored the posters and donor card displays and, panting and sweating, breathed in the warm mingled smell of paper and ink and dust. I rummaged through my bag as I walked round the glass-free window on my right and turned into the children's library at the rear of the building. I'd take out the books I took out yesterday and proudly return them to the beautiful lady with long, long, long hair. She'd smile, glide through the card trays and return my worn and dog-eared green library cards. Grinning, I'd choose some places to hide tonight. Sometimes I'd been to them before. Usually not.

The other world was across water and I only visited it twice a month. There was a library there too. It was like a bungalow, but had a huge children's area filled with books that simply didn't exist in any other reality. Titles and covers so dramatic and exciting and rich with colour they almost brought on some sort of attack. Because I was only occasionally real here I could borrow books, but wasn't allowed my own tickets, and I couldn't take these books back to the other world to read. Everything kept in different boxes, you see.

0011

Archaeology's a nightmarish discipline: piecing together stories from discarded objects, places and people; sifting through layers of physical time; digging backwards through the past. It's strictly analogue. Bring sensible shoes, wet weather gear and make sure to pack a lunch.

History's changing all the time. Yesterday's Modern Studies are tomorrow's tedious exam questions. Tragedy and cataclysm lose colour and horror with distance: even if there's a definite line that can be traced to show how a bullet fired on a Sunday morning in 1914 directly killed millions and named a Glasgow band, it's hard to make that real to people who don't remember a time before DVDs. To a child thundering through 1980, 1911's as distant as an Egyptian god is to one born after the Millennium Bug chewed our species to pieces.

History's modernised and moved into the digital age. It's possible to remotely view recent memories of a world you think you grew up in. It looks wrong though. Buildings are gone, foliage is huge, hills are shorter than you remember. We click our way through streets that don't feel real and wonder whether we know any of the blur-faced people captured in the windows of this glacial zoetrope.

We're an arrogant lot. We forget how fragile and brief our lives are. Time-lapse a street over a century and watch as the skyline shrinks and undulates. There's no sense of scale. We're all renting these buildings, this land, this space. We're temporary. It's a terrible and humbling thought.

After one particular adventure, I plopped my books on the library counter and didn't get a smile in return. The beautiful librarian with the long, long, long hair wasn't there. Instead I was faced with a cold stare and a beard. Rather than return my library cards, the man picked up the top book, flicked through it and asked me a question. I answered him. He swapped books, skimming though right to the end of this one. Settling on page 117 he asked me to, 'Name the character who rises stiffly from his throne.'

I told him. This went on for a while until the man stopped, sighed, flicked through the racks and returned my cards. Within a week I was issued eight new bright pink library cards and allowed to access the adult area. I only found out why this weird stuff had happened over a century later.

0100

I'd thrown myself out of one world, riding a second-hand bike down the hill next to the park as though it was a time tunnel. After a month, I wound up living in a new reality. I got two jobs and collected education certificates that would unlock yet another alternate future, one that would eventually lead to a strange reality where I'm typing the words that you've just read. Whether or not you're reading this/them on a screen or a page doesn't matter. The keyboard's translating my thoughts into ones and zeroes and then those're decoded so you can read them. It's magical. Really, truly magical.

Our memories seem mostly to be manufactured. We reinforce things and events and turn them into little fictions, anecdotes that highlight the humour, romance, science-fiction and horror. You can't trust memory: it lies like an eyewitness.

Somewhere, I'm still running toward the estuary. It wasn't a world that was happy with homeless people, especially ones with long coats, longer hair and hats that stood in for personality. I dodged the police and hid in the bandstand overlooking the estuary that Anthony Hopkins and Emma Thompson would film a scene in a few years later. I hunkered down, huddled against the ancient wind that'd bent once-hopeful saplings into genuflecting trees, and finished the wine. In that long, dark night of the soul – most of which can wait for another day – the place that'd offered safety, shelter and security... Well, it was so obvious that I only noticed it while typing this.

You see, it doesn't matter how many hedgehogs there were. It just matters that they were there. Being there's all that ever matters, all that ever has. After all, you can't trust memory.

Time travel's easy. We teach it in schools and hide it in libraries.

Reach Out and Touch Me

Doctor Who and the Carnival of Monsters
by Christopher Bryant
Favourite *Doctor Who* book: *The Writer's Tale: The Final Chapter*
by Russell T Davies and Benjamin Cook

He was standing right in front of me, within arm's length. I could have reached out and touched him.

I didn't, obviously. That would have been weird.

It was only my third convention. Many fans are used to hobnobbing with the *Doctor Who* great and good and think nothing of cuddling up to Sophie Aldred for a photo op, or quizzing Andrew Cartmel about his masterplan. I'm not one of those. Standing in a hotel near Gatwick airport, I found myself in the perfect position to talk to one of my literary heroes and time, for a moment, stood still.

This was May 2017. I was forty years old.

What would I have said to him? Would I have explained that *Carnival of Monsters* was the first proper book I remember reading? That it led me on to become a voracious reader as a child? That I spent most of the 1980s devouring his books (and those of his Target stablemates) over and over again? That I associated trips to the library on Pen y Dre with the legend DIC DOC on the spines of hardback books? That he inspired a love of reading which led to English A Level, an English degree, a job teaching English? That I now encourage primary age children to read? That I am writing books and short stories and editing anthologies of essays by *Doctor Who* fans? That all of this is down to his writing, reaching out to my young mind and touching my imagination?

I didn't say any of this, of course. It would have been nothing he hadn't heard before. Terrance Dicks is used to having ageing *Doctor Who* fans gushing at him. He adapted sixty-four television serials into book form for money and, far more than the excellent work he did on the TV show itself, it made him into a living legend.

I let him walk down the corridor and didn't say a word. So I'll say it now.

Thank you, Terrance.

What I Want To Be When I Grow Up

Doctor Who and the Seeds of Doom by Sami Kelsh

Favourite *Doctor Who* book: *City of Death* by James Goss

It's hard to believe now that I came as late as I did to the *Doctor Who* party. I could tell you that I tucked into my first Target novelisation as a Who-obsessed primary schooler on a camping holiday in northern Québec, but I won't, because I didn't. I saw it from time to time when I was very wee, and then not again for many years. I bought my first Target novelisation second hand for $3 in a comic shop in Toronto in my mid-twenties, read it on a hot day in Starbucks and then drew a quick sketch of Roger Delgado on the back of a serviette. I hope some clever barista held onto that serviette. It may well be worth tens of Canadian dollars by now. Indeed, I came to *Doctor Who* properly as an adult, when things like DVDs had become readily available, and with an erratic academic and working schedule, I had hours to myself to pore through endless series. This is how I watched *Doctor Who*, and I loved every moment. It was exciting and familiar. It was as though I had, it turned out, been a *Doctor Who* fan all along, waiting to come home.

The most interesting thing to me on most DVD releases quickly became the commentaries. Those little, magical behind-the-scenes glimpses we'd had before suddenly became so much more comprehensive, and I was enthralled. The anecdotes from the actors were at times both enlightening and hilarious, but the people I really wanted to hear from were the people at work behind the scenes: the writers, directors, and producers. I wanted to absorb every kernel of knowledge that I could from these people so I could be a better writer, so I could think like someone who wrote for television. I wanted to write for a medium where there was music and pictures, and actual people speaking my words, and I had a lot of ideas for what I'd do if it were up to me to shape a series of *Doctor Who*. Never mind the fact that was I well into adulthood with a university degree under my belt, I basically wanted to be Philip Hinchcliffe when I grew up.

The next logical step in my diabolical plan was to get credentials under my belt: undergraduate English degrees like mine were a dime a dozen, but if I could persuade a good university that it was worth taking a punt on a Canadian photographer with a minor in psychology, then a Master's in film production would put me in good stead as a prospective *Who*-maker, surely – or at the very least, set me on the path. I sent applications to two well-respected schools in New York

106

City, and hoped for the best.

It was at a convention in America that I happened upon the novelisation for *The Seeds Of Doom*. While my favourite *Doctor Who* tended to be of the Troughton and Pertwee vintages at the time, *The Seeds Of Doom* ranked up there as a shining example of just how good Crazy Eyes Bob Dylan and his Magic Scarf could be, and the novelisation boasted such a handsome cover: it certainly leaves the prospective reader with no doubt that the story is going to take turns being thrilling, scary, and sometimes gross.

(And that there's going to be an aeroplane and a big house in it at some point. I only wish that nasty old Scorby and his Beard Of Evil had made it onto the cover.)

It so happened that its author, Philip Hinchcliffe, was a guest at the convention. I had had no plans to say hello: for someone who gets nervous when a barista asks for my order, I had nightmare visions of blurting out 'PHILIP HINCHCLIFFE, I WANT TO BE YOU WHEN I GROW UP OK THANKS' or something equally embarrassing. But then there was the pressing issue of this rather nice copy of *The Seeds Of Doom* that had insinuated itself into my hands and whispered, 'I'm worth more to you than the latte you were going to buy with the last of your small banknotes,' as if to suggest that the Hinchcliffe connection was nothing less than serendipitous. I had to introduce myself.

So I steeled myself, took a deep breath, and said hello. Never mind the fact that I was, at the time, wearing a reasonably accurate recreation of an old-school UNIT uniform. This fact did not escape Mr Hinchcliffe's notice, and to my mild embarrassment, he asked about it.

'I'm meant to be Sergeant Benton,' I said.

'You're much prettier than Sergeant Benton,' he smiled.

'Thank you,' I smiled back, 'but don't tell Sergeant Benton. It'll hurt his feelings.'

'I wouldn't dare,' he said.

He signed the inside cover of my book. He even spelled my name correctly. I thanked him, and scampered off, beaming.

Back home, I awaited a response to my graduate applications. The good news was that the film schools wanted me; they thought my vision was worth nurturing. The bad news was that, as a good for nothing foreigner, I would have paid through the nose to pursue an education in filmmaking, with no recourse to student loans or grants, and without being able to work legally: looking at the possibility of six-figure tuition fees and New York rent, I abandoned the dream and chose to come at it another way. If I was going to run *Doctor Who*, I'd have to start by being in the right country, so I quit my job and moved

107

to England. I started writing, I became a journalist, and I found myself volunteering to visit the set of *Doctor Who* in Cardiff, and sometimes to interview its cast and crew. I embarked on a project to photograph as many people who were connected with *Doctor Who* as I could. I kept writing *Doctor Who*, and sometimes, things I wrote about *Doctor Who* made it into books. I was going to be the next Philip Hinchcliffe after all, albeit the long way round.

I'm still working on it.

It All Begins with the First Line

Doctor Who and the Dalek Invasion of Earth
by George Ivanoff
Favourite *Doctor Who* book: *The Dalek Invasion of Earth*
by Terrance Dicks

'Through the ruin of a city stalked the ruin of a man.'
What an utterly brilliant opening line. So evocative. So intriguing. So unexpected. The greatest opening line from the Target range and, in my humble opinion, one that stands its ground among the great opening lines of literature. It grabbed me when I first read it, and it still resonates with me now, haunting me all these years later.

I am haunted by a ruined man in a ruined city.

A ruined city may be a staple *Doctor Who* image, but a ruined man... that's rather more frightening. It's a perfect synergy of images. With this one sentence, Terrance Dicks sets up an atmosphere for the story. That first line epitomises his approach to this novelisation. He follows the plot as televised, but tweaks little things and adds to it in small, subtle ways.

The televised episode begins on the banks of the Thames, a roboman approaching the water and ripping off part of his helmet before plunging in. Dicks begins the novel just a little earlier. He spends two short paragraphs describing the roboman's walk through a devastated London to the Thames. It makes all the difference. Four sentences is what it takes to give readers a sense of scale that the television series could not afford. It immediately makes the whole thing grander and more epic.

Budgetary limitations stifled the impact of numerous scenes in the televised serial. With prose, Dicks is able to expand the scale, increase the spectacle and drama, and replace poor visual effects. The failed attack on the Dalek saucer is so much more epic and exciting in prose than in the rather confined space of the studio in which it was shot. Dortmun's death is more dramatic and therefore more emotive. Thanks to this book, and other Target titles, the *Doctor Who* that existed in my teenaged mind was so much more spectacular than the *Doctor Who* that existed on screen.

Dicks also takes the time to fix a problem with the original series. Since Hartnell took a holiday, the Doctor is absent from episode four ('The End of Tomorrow'). This is covered up by having him faint at the end of the previous episode and then being left behind for a little while. Dicks reinserts him into the narrative, having him defuse the Dalek bomb, rather than David. Given that the Doctor is the hero of the story, this makes far more dramatic sense.

Prose is also able to delve into a character's thoughts more readily than a televised drama. Yes, film and television can resort to a voice-over to convey an inner monologue, but this is difficult to pull off and often comes across as clunky and intrusive. In the pages of a book, however, you can be privy to any character's innermost thoughts. Dicks takes advantage of this — not in a big way; but with little insights that add depth and believability. Perhaps the most obvious of these is the relationship between Susan and David, which he subtly builds from the word go.

Reaching the end of the televised serial, you could be forgiven for thinking Susan's departure rather abrupt. Had she really fallen in love with this guy? Yeah, sure, they had a little snog and a bit of a laugh — but is that depth of emotion necessary for a lifetime commitment really there? The book gives you that little bit extra, making Susan's departure more believable for me. Early in the story, when David returns to the resistance headquarters after his reconnoitre, he holds Susan's hand as he emphatically tells her how Ian and the Doctor might be rescued. That didn't happen in the serial. It's a small thing — just one sentence — but it lets the seed of a connection between the two. (Although as an aside, with the televised version one could possibly read things into the way Susan holds David's gun while he polishes it.)

After the failed attack on the Dalek saucer, when the Doctor, Susan and David are travelling together, we get some insight into her feelings for David:

> 'Somehow she had grown to rely on David, to trust his judgment in every crisis. She felt safe when they were together. That was why she didn't want to leave him. Perhaps there were other reasons too...'

A little while later, when the Doctor sees Susan and David kiss, we are privy to his thoughts:

> 'He looked closely at Susan. How deeply was she involved with this young man? For some time now the Doctor had been aware that Susan was fast growing up, and that their wandering way of life posed problems that would one day have to be faced...'

Dicks is subtle and never overplays the additions. It is a fine line with these novelisations. Add or change too much and you risk slowing the story down (remembering that these books were primarily aimed at kids); don't add anything and things just aren't convincing.

Perhaps one of the most startling things Dick does in this novelisation is to briefly give readers a monster's point of view. The Slyther is an alien creature kept as a pet by the Black Dalek, which hunts stray humans at the Dalek mine:

> 'It lay curled and asleep on one of the throbbing machines. The

machine was warm, and it didn't care for the cold on this planet. Suddenly it quivered and woke. Its keen hearing had picked up voices ... human voices. And humans meant food.'

I had forgotten about this when I came to re-read the book in my forties. It surprised me! What a daring thing to do. I can only compare it to Malcolm Hulke's *Doctor Who and the Cave Monsters*, where he gives the Silurians individual names and allows us to see things from their perspective. In the actual episode, the Slyther is a bit rubbish, really. Poorly realised and ineffectively shot, it is not in the slightest bit threatening. Dicks brings it to life, makes it a creature to be feared and even gives it some motivation. It is his Slyther that lives in my memories, as I do my best to forget the crappy on-screen version.

Dicks also updates elements to the current (1970s) mythology of the series. In the book, the Daleks say 'Exterminate' more frequently than in the serial. Why? Because by the time Dicks wrote the book, this had become the Daleks' catchphrase, used far more frequently than in their earlier appearances. So Dicks brings things up to date, giving readers the Daleks they are more familiar with. The only place where I think Dicks's approach doesn't work is with Susan's actual departure. The words that the Doctor speaks on screen are so iconic and so ingrained into my fanboy mind that I feel changing them in the novel was a mistake. But that is a small quibble.

Doctor Who and the Dalek Invasion of Earth, after all these years, still stands out in my mind as a favourite of the Target range. It was first published in 1977; I'm not certain exactly when I first read it, but given that my copy is the 1979 second impression, and that it was one of the first Target books that I read, I'm estimating some time in 1979/80. One could argue that there are better books in the range, but this one remains my favourite and I will undoubtedly read it again in the future. I must note that I have a great deal of respect for Mr Dicks as a writer. In fact, I can honestly say he is one of my writing heroes. Since becoming an author myself, I have marvelled at his ability to work on so many and varied a project, with never a drop in quality — a goal for which I aim in my own career.

Most of my memories of *The Dalek Invasion of Earth*, with the exception of the Doctor's departing speech, are of the book rather than the serial. Since getting the DVD, I have watched it as many times as I have read the book, if not more...yet it is the book's images that endure. And it all begins with that evocative, intriguing and unexpected first line — a line which I quote as an example when running creative writing workshops; the sort of opening line that I strive for in my own work; a line that, after all these years, still haunts my memories.

Cover me, I'm going in

Doctor Who and the Claws of Axos
by Christopher Payne
Favourite *Doctor Who* book: *Turn Left* by Andy X Cable

'Daddy, which story is this?'

'*The Claws of Axos*.'

'Is that the Master?'

'No, that's Bill Filer, he's chasing the Master.'

'Is that a Krynoid?'

'No Freddie, that's an Axon when it's a monster.'

'Isn't the Axon the gold man?'

'Yes, and a red monster.'

'The Krynoid?'

'No. There's no Krynoids in this one. It's...'

'Is that Benton?'

'No, its Mike Yates, from UNIT, the Brigadier's friend.'

'Daddy, which story is this?'

And so on.

It's easy to get confused, especially when you're young like my three year old son and especially with *Doctor Who*. The covers of those oh-so-wonderful Target books could sometimes be a cause of great confusion, but most fans today remember those covers fondly and they provide as much excitement now as they did when seeing them many years ago. But were they wonderful? Or did they just make things confusing? As if we were in part four of *The Stones of Blood*, let's examine the evidence.

The Weirdly Drawn Prosecution. *The Auton Invasion* and *Terror of the Autons* had four covers between them, all showing four different types of squid and not a single Auton. On one cover, the Doctor is shown in a very small picture, apparently singing opera to the Master. *The Dinosaur Invasion*'s three covers show realistic, scary dinosaurs attacking famous London landmarks, which is completely not what happens on screen. *The Claws of Axos* (2nd edition) features two Krynoids and no Doctor, which did cause confusion but allowed the reader to put any Doctor into any particular story (imagine Hartnell trying to execute a Venusian aikido chop on Sea Devils).

The Rose Tinted Defence. The first twelve covers by Chris Achilleos showed just how thrilling and exciting these stories were going to be long before the days of top loading, big buttoned, £450 VHS players. *The Ambassadors of Death*'s funky cover shows just how thrilling and exciting Jon Pertwee's bouffant is going to be; the monstrous cover to *Timelash* shows just how thrilling and exciting this story could have been and the final thirty four covers by Alister Pearson all showed just how thrilling and exciting these stories were now that we had all seen them hundreds of times.

<u>The Verdict</u>. The covers of the Target range were amazing and exhilarating and as a young child or a mature fan (is there a difference?) they make us desperately want to lose ourselves in these books, even *The Twin Dilemma*.

Boxed Memories

Doctor Who and the Ark in Space
by Alex Rohan
Favourite *Doctor Who* book: *The Witch Hunters*
by Steve Lyons

I don't actually recall a time when I wasn't a fan of *Doctor Who*.

I made my world debut in 1970, just hours before Jon Pertwee's Doctor made his. Growing up in Australia, the middle child of three, my growing fascination with the series was nurtured by two important institutions in my life. The first of these was the Australian Broadcasting Commission, which, after attempting to drop the show in the mid-1970s, suddenly realised the error of its ways and programmed the series four or five nights per week for months on end. Having caught up on three series of Tom Baker serials, the ABC started showing Pertwee repeats and then started on Tom's again.

The other institution was Target Books. In 1978, my parents returned to Melbourne from a brief scouting trip to Brisbane in search of a place to live when our big move happened later in the year. A gift was taken from a suitcase and placed in my hands: a book with an exploding Dalek on the cover. I recognised the title: '*Death to the Daleks*'. That was the one where the Daleks had bullet guns, wasn't it? And the weird maze city? Oh yes, and that huge snake thing that screamed and destroyed Daleks! Wow, now I had a book of it that could bring the story back to me any time I liked! The very idea was as thrilling as the photorealistic cover.

It was read and re-read in the days that followed. Can I get another one? Please? I really wanted one with the new, younger Doctor, so not long afterwards I was delighted to get bang up to date with *The Talons of Weng-Chiang*, which I'd seen for the first time earlier that year. The acquisition of this book made me realise there was a long list of other books in the front, near the title page. Hmmm. Maybe you could collect them. Is that list complete? There were a lot of titles I recognised but a lot that I didn't, some of which just sounded weird. *Doctor Who and the Abominable Snowmen*? Didn't Tintin meet one of those once? And what's a Zarbi?

Christmas 1979 was our first in our new home city: sunny, humid, leafy, suburban Brisbane, rather than grey, miserable, cold Melbourne. Our new home was twice the size of our old one and I had a whole room to myself, rather than sharing with my little brother. I sat in the lounge room downstairs, surrounded by shredded gift wrapping and shiny new presents. 'Merry Christmas,' smiled my sister, dropping a present in my hands. I could see straight away it

114

was going to be a book. I ripped it open excitedly to find to my delight that I held a garish yellow copy of *Doctor Who and the Ark in Space*. I remembered this one well! But... hang on. I sniffed. I brought it to my face and inhaled more deeply, with some suspicion. Why does it smell funny? 'Sorry,' my sister apologised, seeing the puzzled look on my face. 'I spilled perfume on it.' I sniffed it again. Actually, I thought, that's not too bad.

The story was even better than I remembered, despite it being written by not-Terrance-Dicks. The characters and dialogue sparkle on the page and the book revels in some of the gorier aspects of the production that would've seen the show banned from television forever had it been made that way. The stomach-turning description of Noah's transformation from human to alien insect will live with me forever.

It's 2006. I'm a grown man with a room full of *Doctor Who* videos, an expanding collection of DVDs and magazines, every Target novelisation, every Virgin novel, every BBC novel. I'm also a grown man in my mid-thirties with a loving, beautiful wife, a boisterous three-year-old son, a decent-sized mortgage and a new baby on the way. It's time for hard decisions. The collection has to go to make space, and quickly. It's obvious that the amazing new series will overwhelm the market and pretty soon hardly anyone will want original series stuff. Despite good offers, I don't want to break up the Target novel collection. It sells as a single lot for what seems like quite a lot of money, given that many books have dog-ears, broken spines and the occasional pencil mark where I'd noted where the episode breaks were. The books are carefully loaded into some old wine boxes to be loaded into a car and taken away forever. I linger on a few.

The Hand of Fear. Mum bought this for me to read on the long, long drive from Melbourne to Brisbane when we moved to Queensland. I was commanded not to read it straight away, so I left it next to my bed and moved briefly on to other things. When I returned, it was gone - the removalists had packed it away! This time, I thought, it was me who was packing it away, but for good this time. *Into the box.*

The War Games. My Dad read it to me while I was miserable in hospital, having broken my arm badly whilst on holiday. It had been one of dozens of Target novels my parents bought me to help keep my mind off the injury. *Into the box.*

The Dinosaur Invasion. I remember reading this one in the waiting room during the next twelve months while the arm was subjected to excruciating physiotherapy. I didn't remember this one. Had Target just made up? No, it couldn't have been, it said 'based on the BBC serial *Invasion of the Dinosaurs*' on the title page. Why had the ABC denied me this one? Maybe it cost too much. It must have been amazing! 'Hi,' greeted the physiotherapist, 'how are you? Oooh, that book looks scary. *Doctor Who* fan, are you? Come on through.' Shudder. *Into the box.*

Death To The Daleks. The one that started it all. That cover still looks amazing. I loved to stare at it, trying to work out if it was all art or whether an explosion had been painted on a snapshot of a Dalek. Either way, it was utterly spectacular. *Into the box.*

The Five Doctors hardback. The silver cover, the lovely Skilleter artwork, the excitement of reading a *Doctor Who* novelisation of a story that hadn't been on TV yet! And it had all of the Doctors! Sort of. *Into the box.*

One left. *The Ark In Space*. I furtively look around to check if anyone's looking, open the book, pull it to my face and breathe deeply. It still smells faintly of thrills, horror, delight, sweet childhood joy, and of course a teenage girl's cheap perfume.

Into the box.

Kindling the Sacred Flame

Doctor Who and the Brain of Morbius
by Neil Chester
Favourite *Doctor Who* book: *The Web of Fear*
by Terrance Dicks

The Brain of Morbius changed my life. I know it sounds like hyperbole, but the more I think about it, the more sure I am of it.

Doctor Who and The Brain of Morbius was published when I was 6 years old. By this point I was already a confirmed *Doctor Who* fan – my first ever clear fan memory was the excellent cliff-hanger where Sarah's face fell off, although I'd definitely been watching since before then as I remember pretending to hide from sinister, lumbering Mummies. My little brother was 'published' in March 1977, some three months before the novelisation of *The Brain of Morbius* and I'd be lying if I said that I wasn't a little disappointed that he wasn't a girl, preferably one that we could call Sarah...

This novelisation was, to my mind, the first proper book I was given. My parents were keen to encourage reading and would always read to me before bed. I had the usual slew of picture books that I enjoyed reading and there was a whole hundred-acre wood full of *Winnie-the-Pooh* books, including the various poetry collections featuring James James Morrison Morrison Weatherby George DuPree and beds of delphiniums (blue) and geraniums (red). There were also lashings of adventures for *The Famous Five* and, the crowning glory, Eric Thompson's superlative *The Magic Roundabout* books. To this day I don't think that I have ever seen my mother laugh as much as when trying to read the section from *Dougal Round the World* in which the whole team attempt to assist Ermintrude the cow (wearing a yashmak, of course) onto the back of a camel. Needless to say, every time they pushed her up one side, she came sliding down the other side – hilarious stuff for both a six-year-old and his mother.

These were all great books, but, to me, *The Brain of Morbius* was something different. These others were all children's books – they were either about children or they were explicitly for children, filled with amusing animals and charming illustrations. *The Brain of Morbius* was an adult book based on a scary, adult television show. You see, for me, as a child, *Doctor Who* was never a children's show. Nowadays it's generally regarded as 'the children's show that adults love' or, at best, a family show, but to my six-year-old self, it just seemed so very grown up. There were no children in it (the usual sign of a children's show is that the heroes are kids and the adults are all a bit stupid. Or sinister. Or sinister and stupid.) It was all about a brave,

117

clever, funny, slightly scary adult and his lovely, brave, reassuring friend. The show was properly scary and exciting and full of very grown-up sounding dialogue with long words. I was lucky that my parents were allowing me to watch this sophisticated, frightening, thrilling, grown-up show. And then they bought me a book about it!

I can't remember the exact circumstances leading up to me getting the book but I can still, nearly forty years on (eek!) clearly remember being handed it for the first time. My parents had been out somewhere, almost certainly to get my baby brother checked for something, or vaccinated against something, and I was left in the care of one of my grandmothers. My parents came back to collect me and told me that because I'd been good they'd got me a present. I remember holding my hands out and the slim, bright yellow book being put in my outstretched hands. A book. A book about *Doctor Who*! I remember the Doctor's face grinning out at me from the front, surrounded by crackling yellow energy, and looming over a monster that I vaguely remembered seeing on television. I was so excited. I had no idea that there were books about *Doctor Who*. Mum and Dad explained to me that it was a *Doctor Who* story from the television that had been made into a book so that it was possible to experience the story again and again. What a fantastic idea!

I was eager to start reading it straight away: however, it was a little beyond my six-year-old reading skills and so it was agreed that Mum would start reading it to me at bedtime. I think that, for the first time ever, I was actually looking forward to going to bed. And so a routine was established, and that night Mum began - 'Kriz was dying...'

I think that Mum must've read *The Brain of Morbius* to me about five or six times before I was able to read it for myself. I no longer had time for bed-time tales of Pooh Bear or cows being pushed on to camels – there was *Doctor Who* to listen to instead! Mum was never really a fan of the book though – I seem to remember that she though it was a bit too scary and gruesome, starting, as it did, with the decapitation of a dying insect man, and continuing with hideous stitched-together monsters, hook handed henchmen, disembodied brains and considerably more gothic trappings and gory death than even Enid Blyton could muster. Needless to say, I loved it. Even the chapter titles were exciting and stimulated the imagination – 'The Horror Behind the Curtain', 'Monster on the Rampage', 'Deathlock!'

It was my enthusiasm for the book, coupled with Mum's slight distaste (or at least, fatigue with it after the third or fourth reading) that galvanised me into wanting to read better. I was eager to read it for myself and so I practised and practised, reading it out loud to myself at first. *The Brain of Morbius* kindled in me a real love of reading that *Winnie the Pooh* simply hadn't managed. The writing style

118

and sentence structure seemed so grown up when compared to the children's books that I was used to reading and that added challenge just spurred me on (as did the often obscure words – not many of the other six year olds at school knew the word 'capacious' and I even sort of knew what I meant, even if I did think that it was pronounced 'capshus'). Terrance Dicks, effectively, taught me to read and expanded my vocabulary in the process.

As a family, we were keen library users, partly because my aunt worked there and partly because it was cheaper, for young parents with a six year old and a new baby, than buying new books. Once I discovered that the library had a stock of other *Doctor Who* stories, I became an avid reader, regularly coming away with two or three of the slim hardback books. Thrilling adventures involving Daleks, Cybermen, Autons and Yeti, with different Doctors, with unfamiliar companions, faces and mannerisms, but still, unquestionably, the same man, travelling in his trusty TARDIS. One book that particularly caught my imagination was *The Web of Fear* and on every foggy day I imagined Yeti lurking just out of sight in the mists. Some, like *The Cave Monsters* and *The Crusaders*, were a bit wordier and, to my young self, drier; some had pictures in them; all of them opened out the universe of *Doctor Who* and the world of reading to me.

Soon, I was using my pocket money to buy my own Target books and was reading and re-reading them voraciously. I doubt, without *The Brain of Morbius* catching my interest at just the right time, that I'd be as avid a reader as I am today - and I probably wouldn't have quite such a good vocabulary either. Thinking about it, I probably wouldn't be a librarian either. So, on reflection, I think it's fair to say that that simple, slim volume, novelised by Terrance Dicks from a story by Robin Bland, probably did change my life.

In preparation for writing this essay, I got my Dad to dig the book out of the attic for me. I even got Mum to re-read it before they posted it on to me. Despite the fact that she and Dad are both much bigger fans of *Doctor Who* now that then were in the 1970s, I don't think that Mum's opinion of the book has changed much – it's still a bit too gory for her. The extremely battered state of it – fragile, creased cover, back hanging half off – shows me just how much I read it as a child and how much I loved it. In fact, it's cold and grey outside...I might just stay in and give it a quick re-read...

Sacred Fire! Sacred Flame! Sacred Fire! Sacred Flame!

Scribbles and Shibboleths

Doctor Who and the Planet of Evil
by Johnny Spandrell

Favourite *Doctor Who* book: Oh, you'll work it out.

Oakleigh Primary. A pretty little school, part of a leafy outer Melbourne suburb. Diverse community, mix of modern and historic classrooms. A warm, welcoming place.

At least, that's how it looks from the website. I've never actually been there. I would never have come across it all, except that it's the place where my copy of *Doctor Who and the Planet of Evil* came from. Published 1977, hardback, first edition. A thing of beauty, with a big ugly wolfman on the cover.

Since I was a kid, I've read *Doctor Who* books. (The first: *Doctor Who and the Zarbi,* paperback, umpteenth reprint. Spoilt by my sister writing a bogus dedication from Bill Strutton on the title page. I was livid.) Just as important as reading them, was collecting them. I wanted the full set of tiny little paperbacks with spines all the colours of the rainbow (and white).

The quest had begun. For years I scoured bookshops and department stores and garage sales and my world in general for those vivid little tomes. The ones I couldn't find, I'd borrow in small piles from my local library, whose collection consisted of exotic hardback editions. It was extensive too - although it lacked a *Planet of Evil,* it did have a rare Frederick Mueller edition of *The Zarbi,* which, to my life long regret, I didn't steal. Amazing, mysterious things, those hardbacks. Where did the library get them? They were never in the newsagents or quaint little book exchanges I got chased out of. I sullenly settled for buying paperbacks, but in truth, I was addicted to the hard (cover) stuff.

By the time I reached adulthood, I was concentrating on girls and beer but also celebrating my complete collection of *Doctor Who* paperbacks (I know, right? What a catch). The quest was completed, but I faced a new problem. I had nothing more to collect. I had to make do with new adventures and missing adventures and what have you. But it wasn't the same.

I couldn't kick the habit. I kept combing second hand bookstores searching for spines with little Target logos atop. I bought copies of books I already had, but with different covers. Hell, I bought copies of books I already had with the *same* covers just because I couldn't leave them behind. At one stage, I had three identical copies of *The Zarbi.* Plus my original copy, by that stage in tatters, Fake Bill Strutton's message angrily ripped out.

Every so often, I'd find a lonely hardback on those shelves and I'd snatch it up, greedily. They were rare treats, often 'ex-library', a term sneered at by serious collectors. These were well-worn books, often a bit battered, often covered in clear plastic, lending slips still glued to the back, stamps and stains throughout. I didn't care, I loved them all. As my collection grew, I wondered how hard it would be to collect all the hardback editions... and lo, the quest began again!

This time though, the task was much harder. My paperbacks search, back in the day, had been for cheap, mass market products. The hardbacks had much smaller print runs and were often distributed only to libraries. I was now searching for collector's pieces via eBay and Abebooks and other obscure corners of the web. The copies I found were old, imperfect and often pricey. Whether to drop $100 on a roughed up old copy of, say, *The Power of Kroll,* became a familiar dilemma.

It took me years. It cost me stupid money. But over time, I got them all. (Well, all except those Frederick Mueller editions of *The Daleks, The Crusaders* and my old friend *The Zarbi.* Even I couldn't stretch to those eye-watering prices.) And although I found plenty of handsome, well-kept copies of later books (harvested from collections of fans whose love had grown cold), the ex-library ones are my favourites because, shabby and dog-eared though they are, these books have histories. People have read them, loved them, taken them home, carried them in school bags, spilt tea on them, lost them down the back of the couch. They've been held in the hands of fans, pored over again and again. These stories have stories.

Who, for instance, at Oakleigh Primary School read, loved and coveted this copy of *Planet of Evil?* Who crossed off the other books they'd read on that list at the front? Was it even you, reading this article right now? Or did you once clutch some other book in my collection? Perhaps you are Kevin C Wood from Lincolnshire, who wrote his name so carefully in my copy of *An Unearthly Child.* Hello Kevin! Lovely handwriting. Did you get in trouble for defacing a library book? Or perhaps you're Kathleen Robinson, formerly of East York public library. Kathleen, I need to know: did you really borrow *Planet of the Daleks* 8 times? Or were you just practicing your signature on that library slip, in preparation for opening your first bank account, or in case you married that dreamy Robinson boy from down the road?

Or maybe you're the mysterious frequenter of Leeds library who studiously wrote the numeric ranking of each Doctor on the frontispiece of each book, a shibboleth to other fans. 'First,' you printed seriously in biro on *The Keys of Marinus.* 'Fourth,' in *Meglos.*

If you went to Mapleridge Senior Public School, Ontario, I have your copy of *Pyramids of Mars.* No, you can't have it back. If you frequented

Transvaal Public Library, you might have thumbed my copy of *The Ultimate Foe*. My copy of *The Romans* comes from Hong Kong, *The Five Doctors* from Manitoba, *The Rescue* from sunny Toowoomba. From all around the world, they've flown to me in Sydney, Australia.

I love that so many people have held these books. I love the marks and scribbles they left behind. Every now and then, there's something special. 'To Margaret,' a dedication reads on the front page of *The Deadly Assassin*. 'Happy times. Tom Baker.' Oh, Margaret. How could you ever give something so glorious away?

The quest is over now. I buy the occasional new series book, but they don't have the same appeal. I read, but don't collect. Except for last year, when three smart new additions hit my shelves. Replicas of those first three books, the ultra-rare Frederick Mueller ones, completing my collection at last. Wonderful - even if they don't have library stamps, tears, coffee cup rings, enigmatic written messages and all the rest. I'll just imagine they come from Yorkshire public library.

Of course, one of those books is another copy of *Doctor Who and the Zarbi*. Well, you can never have too many.

How I Learned to Judge a Book by its Cover

Doctor Who and the Mutants by Tim Gambrell

Favourite *Doctor Who* book: *Evolution* by John Peel

This is the story of how a seven-year-old boy made a discovery, judged several (as it turned out) books by their covers, annoyed a teacher and became a *Doctor Who* fan.

At my primary school, we had something called The Wise Owl Book Club. It was run by Miss Jolliffe, who taught the third year juniors. You had a green membership booklet, like a birthday card, with printed squares; every Monday, you'd bring in some money and go to her classroom at lunchtime, where she'd put stickers on your card equivalent to that money. Each sticker was worth either five or ten pence. Woe betide anyone who offered anything other than a multiple of ten as she peered at you over the top of her half-moon spectacles. The idea was that over time you filled each square with a ten pence sticker (or two five pence stickers) until you had enough to buy one of the selection of books that she'd display each week. Old 'JJ' (as she foolishly told us she was known to her friends one day) would relish crossing off the stickers on your card when you made a purchase. She'd also relish commenting to those, such as myself, who only brought in five or ten pence that week that 'it isn't going to get you a book very quickly, is it?' Perhaps the judgemental old cow should have asked my parents instead, who could have informed her that buying books was a treat for us, something to be relished and looked forward to over time, and that we didn't have a lot of extra money to throw about. But I suspect this wasn't a legitimate concern on her behalf, it was an opportunity to make a small boy feel bad about himself. How very nurturing of her.

It all kicked off around the start of the school year in 1981, as I moved up into the first year juniors. There was a big launch event in the school hall, where parents were invited along in the hope that they'd buy in to the scheme. There was also the opportunity to buy books then and there - like The Book People do these days at large offices. I was walking around with my mum, who had an eye on Christmas. She said I could have two books now as a treat and two for Christmas. Awesome. I distinctly remember two adjacent tables which enraptured me completely. One had a *Multicoloured Swap Shop* annual on it. The other had *Doctor Who* books. Hang on - wow! Stories about or from my favourite television programme? This was something I'd never even dreamt existed.

123

I can see it now, there were three volumes on the table: *Doctor Who and The Mutants*, *Doctor Who and The Time Warrior* (both by Terrance Dicks) and *Doctor Who The Programme Guide Vol. 2: What's What and Who's Who*, by Jean-Marc Lofficier (my mum's name was Jean, so I assumed this author was a lady). What were these curious things? They all had awesome covers!

The Programme Guide fascinated me. It had the newer logo above a gorgeous blue-tinted illustration of all the Doctors so far on it, including the guy from *All Creatures Great and Small* that my hero Tom Baker had changed into earlier in the year. But this book wasn't a story: it had lists and information in it that I could refer to so I could find out all about older adventures, previous Doctors and places and monsters I'd never seen - plus the ones I *had* seen when the programme had been better and scarier (i.e. when I'd been a bit younger). There was a whole universe waiting to open up to me.

The Mutants and *The Time Warrior* both had exciting-looking monsters on the cover. I didn't recognise the story titles and had no idea which of the Doctors on the cover of *The Programme Guide* would be in them. *The Mutants* (for years mispronounced by me as 'Muttants') won out because the monster on the front looked really scary – much better than anything from the recent season 18. So those were my 'buy now' choices. My mother wasn't convinced by *The Programme Guide*: 'It's not a story book,' she said. 'I know,' I replied. 'Are you sure it's what you want though? How about this one instead?' she asked, offering me *The Time Warrior* with Linx's three-fingered mitt reaching out towards my neck. I was sure.

Now, what about Christmas presents? The *Multi-Coloured Swap Shop* annual was a dead cert. I loved that show on Saturday mornings. I was going to add *The Time Warrior* to it - simple. But then I noticed a little white pocket-sized book called *Rocks and Minerals*. I was suddenly gripped with an outrageous notion: this book might help me identify rock formations on other planets, if I was an intergalactic explorer like the Doctor. My mother, obviously thinking that I was developing an interest in geology and not wanting to encourage me to narrow my outlook, didn't try to persuade me in favour of *The Time Warrior* again, but just asked out of courtesy, 'Are you sure that's what you want?' I umm-ed and ahh-ed. *The Time Warrior* did have a great cover. And it was *Doctor Who*. But no, I'd made my decision and the information about alien planets held within my little rocks and minerals book would allow me to talk knowledgeably to my friends if playing *Doctor Who* in the playground - or to just generally impress people. And it fitted in my pocket. Just.

I was now in possession of my very first Target novelisation and my very first reference book. Further, I was armed with the knowledge that the programme had an existence beyond the television screen. I held my copy of *The Mutants* a lot, studying the cover, reading and re-reading the blurb. It mentioned a 'Jo'. I had no idea who this was, but my assumption that she was the companion of the time was confirmed when *Carnival of Monsters* and *The Three Doctors* were shown in November that year as part of 'The Five Faces of *Doctor Who*' repeat season. I'd often toy with reading *The Mutants*, but it was a longer book than those I was used to reading at school; the concepts were probably a bit advanced for me at the time and what I did read was just a lot of people talking to each other. I wanted a story about the mutant monster on the front rampaging and doing nasty things with its pincers to threaten the Doctor and his friends. To be honest, I don't think I ever read it fully as a child. Owning *The Mutants*, though, wasn't about reading it. It was there should I choose to, and I was sure I'd get around to it eventually.

But I'd pour over *The Programme Guide Vol. 2* endlessly, absorbing all the older story titles, seeing how much *Doctor Who* there used to be on the telly, imagining what all those other stories might have been about from their exciting titles (*The Dominators, The Space Pirates* – cor!), picking out the stories I could remember and looking up names and places. This, surely, is the point at which I stopped being an engaged viewer and became a fan, when I actively started to absorb information and be interested in the history of the show.

The Time Warrior remained on the display table, taunting me week after week at the Wise Owl Book Club. I looked at it often, reading and re-reading the blurb, trying to decide if I'd like it or not. 'Why don't you buy it?' asked Miss Jolliffe. I bought other books instead, such as the glorious *The Ark in Space* and *The Three Doctors*. When we were asked for feedback, I recall requesting a wider selection of *Doctor Who* books. Miss Jolliffe starchily informed me that I hadn't bought all the ones currently on the table yet, and more wouldn't be forthcoming until I had! So, gauntlet down, I had to buy *The Time Warrior* when I'd next saved up enough. Typically though, when I arrived to do so I found that it had gone. Argh! There was someone else interested in *Doctor Who* books at my school? I never did find out who this person was, so I couldn't reach out to them in solidarity. Even at such a tender age, I was already accustomed to being a loner as a fan. Since Tom Baker had left the show, the kids at my school had stopped playing *Doctor Who* in the playground, or even talking about watching it. Even the kid who'd set up a petition to bring back K9 had since left. (By the way, I eventually picked up *The Time Warrior* about twenty years later from a second-hand stall.)

I still have that same copy of *The Mutants*, number 44 in the Target Library, price £1.25. I took it off the shelf again recently, reading it all for possibly the very first time in one hit. And I'd still argue that the cover, with its wonderful Jeff Cummins artwork, is not fully representative of the story: the mutant creatures are the subject of much of the book's dialogue but they hardly appear at all. To a seven-year-old expecting a marauding monster yarn, it's a bit too allegorical, nay philosophical, in its subject matter. But that's not the book's fault. Essentially, the cover did exactly what it was meant to do – attracted attention and prompted a sale!

To a forty-something looking for a quick afternoon's escapism, I found the novelisation to be a pretty dull and perfunctory read, I'll freely admit. It's a shame because the Third Doctor stories, in my experience, tended to fare better than most in print as Terrance Dicks and Malcolm Hulke nipped, tucked and embellished here and there with their hindsight hats on. But it doesn't matter what I think of *The Mutants* now; it isn't a question of content or quality, it's about what the book signifies. It opened the doors of perception and led me to uncover a wider world of imagining and reading for pleasure – that's why it is such a key book for me. It presents a curious dichotomy that I can follow a line of reading and appreciation back to a book that I struggled with as a text. It's as if I became an avid reader in spite of *The Mutants*, not because of it.

Following that line of reasoning, I could sit the book alongside the Gutenberg Bibles or William Caxton's early print editions – that is probably the most ridiculous claim to literary importance that you'll read this year, but my personal logic is sound. Just as the Gutenberg scholars and Caxton's printing press opened up the commodification of books and facilitated the spread of literacy, so *Doctor Who and The Mutants*, for me, opened up a wider world of literature and escapism – through *Doctor Who* and beyond into classic science fiction and classic literature. I became the capable, avid reader I still am to this day, with Bachelor's and Master's Degrees in English under my belt, and a healthy love of diverse literary styles and genres. I can thank *Doctor Who* and Terrance Dicks for that far more than any of the teachers from my school years.

Oh, and thanks also to my mum for buying them for me.

The Redundant Tautology

Doctor Who and the Deadly Assassin
by Scott Varnham
Favourite *Doctor Who* book: *Adventures with the Wife in Space*
by Neil Perryman

My first run-in with Target novels was only a few years ago. I was never part of the generation that had them as their only means of repeating *Doctor Who* stories. There's no grainy picture of me reading *Doctor Who and the Daleks* on a beach somewhere. For the first few years of the Doctor's new life, I was aware that the books existed but wondered why I'd want to read novelisations of existing *Doctor Who* stories, books which are aimed directly at children.

On Twitter's recommendation, I got a batch of the reprints. They hooked me from the minute I read the first page. I quickly realised that reading the books gives the reader a much better idea of what the writer intended, rather than watching the screen version where the effects can sometimes let them down. Once I'd read the novels, I felt no need to go out and watch the televised version. To this day I've not seen *The Deadly Assassin*, or several of the other Target novels I own, on screen. This seems a bit of a weird attitude to other *Doctor Who* fans, but then we're all a bit of a weird bunch.

Until July 2013, I'd only read the BBC's shiny new reprints. At that year's London Film and Comic Con, I was walking past *Star Wars* actors, such as the stunt double for Uncle Owen's charred corpse and the guy who played the third Stormtrooper from the left in a famous scene, when I saw it peeking out at me from a dealer's table. Maybe it was the title, with its infamous tautology (debate still rages whether you are a deadly assassin by definition), that caught my eye. We may never know. One thing that definitely caught my eye was that the book was as battered as fish and chips. The vendor relieved me of £4 and I left with a copy of the book that has helped to define the mythology of the show I watch today.

Now I pick up a Target novel whenever I see one out in the wild. Indeed, one of the highlights of going to the *Doctor Who* Experience was finding some as-new novelisations dirt cheap. I picked up a few good 'uns, like *The Sun Makers* and *The Armageddon Factor*, bolstering my collection considerably; I now have around 15 vintage novelisations. (I'd list them all but I'm not being paid by the word.)

It was only later that I realised just how influential this story was. Here for the first time was talk of the Eye of Harmony and the regeneration limit for Time Lords - I was aware of these concepts before, but there's a world of difference between reading a dry, academic entry on some Wiki page and seeing these concepts in context, reading how they are conveyed for yourself. Considering most of these elements were made up wholesale because Robert Holmes needed plot devices to get characters from A to B, it's a pretty solid foundation for the show as we know it today.

I should also make some space to celebrate Terrance Dicks here. For a range that he was pretty much paid to churn out, he brought innate talent and hard work to it. Terrance Dicks did a wonderful job here -- as he always did -- of adapting Robert Holmes's script and tailoring it to his target audience, resulting in a book that can be read by those of all ages. Whether it's a well-crafted sentence, a compelling action scene or more character development, the reader can find it in here. One has to wonder how well he'd do at adapting some of the current stories: *Mummy on the Orient Express* would be right up his street.

Even though the actual serial was written by Robert Holmes, *The Deadly Assassin* will stand as a small part of Terrance's huge legacy to literature. This does sound like I'm eulogising him while he's still around, but warning if I gave him his due would writing just by dealing with a master of the genre. In the minds of his fans, his books will live a long life only equalled by that of the Doctor.

Jeff Cummins and the Velvet Underground

Doctor Who and the Talons of Weng-Chiang
by Sean Alexander

Favourite *Doctor Who* book: *Doctor Who and the Daleks Omnibus*
by Terrance Dicks ed. Terry Nation

My story begins in the Copthorne in Newcastle, late October 2013.

It's Sunday night and the hotel bar is bare but for a few straggling convention attendees, whiling away their final hours of shared love and friendship before wending their way home to humdrum reality. I'm sat alone, writing notes for my impending dissertation deadline ('Dada and the Post-Punk return to Ideals of Revolt and Rebellion', if you're interested) and I'm only occasionally distracted by the occasional snorting cacophony of group laughter or the sight of Anneke Wills (looking a bit squiffy) being cuddled by yet another adoring fan. Basically, just a typical Dimensions warm-down evening.

My phone chimes. Well, I say chimes. It actually makes that 'breaking news' noise that BBC News likes to catch your attention with when it has some news of the, er, breaking variety. Feeling a trifle bored by yet another account of Dada poetics (and wondering how I'm going to get Johnny Rotten *and* Sid Vicious into the same sentence as these proto-surrealist artists) I swipe my phone to see what monumental cultural event has distracted me.

THE SINGER AND SONGWRITER LOU REED, BEST KNOWN AS LEAD SINGER OF THE VELVET UNDERGROUND AND FOR HIS COLLABORATIONS WITH DAVID BOWIE, HAS DIED AFTER A SHORT ILLNESS AGED 71

I feel a twinge of sadness. While being far too young to remember Reed in his decadent pomp, I was at last initiated when Reed's work – and in particular *Perfect Day* – experienced a renaissance in the mid-90s thanks to its use in the seminal *Trainspotting*. This and the counter-cultural icon *Walk on the Wild Side* were Reed's anthems to the romantic and the disaffected; songs for those who didn't fit in because they were different. In short, Lou Reed (along with his BBC obituary stablemate David Bowie) was a voice for gender-crossing 70s youth; his songs about addiction and loneliness tapped a rich vein of despair in New York and far beyond. This was a man who, musically and culturally, made a difference. One who was more than deserving of his latter-life renaissance in the hearts of poets and dreamers.

As I often do in these circumstances, I felt a compulsion to share the news of a celebrity's passing with the nearest person next to me. I don't know why, perhaps it's to mark the death of someone who (whether big or small) changed the world in some way, who made a contribution. A moment to share in reflection the impact their art made, before we turn back to our humdrum lives and chalk another famous person's passing down as one more road sign along the inevitable road to old age.

Sat behind me at the bar were two gents to whom I'd paid scant attention when I walked in earlier. They'd been talking and drinking quietly, with none of the explosions of convulsive guffawing that had otherwise broken my communion with the Dada poets of post-World War I Europe. Approaching, I waited patiently for a natural break in their chatting until they realised they had become the centre of my attention and looked up slightly bemused, as though I was going to impart the dreadful news that the bar was about to close.

'Hi, sorry to interrupt, but I just thought you'd like to know that Lou Reed has died.'

The face of the ̶̶̶̶̶̶̶ ̶̶̶̶̶̶̶̶̶̶̶ ̶̶̶̶̶̶̶ ̶̶̶̶ ̶̶̶ ̶̶̶̶̶̶̶ ̶̶ ̶̶̶̶ ̶̶̶̶ who I now recognised from sitting at a stall in the hotel lobby over the previous two days – crumpled his face with a look of genuine sadness and regret, as though he'd lost a personal friend. All three of us spoke for a few minutes about our Lou Reed recollections – mine being somewhat more recent and therefore lacking in profundity – before I excused myself back to the world of anarchic art I'd left behind me. I didn't read on for much longer, and retired to my room unaware that I has just met the man who first made me fall in love with Target books.

Our memories by their very nature become hazy and prone to after-the-event embellishment over time. But I'm as sure as I'm sitting here that the first *Doctor Who* paperback I ever received was *Doctor Who and the Talons of Weng-Chiang*, whose slightly creased and well-thumbed pages I'm looking at now. I would have been five years old and already well on the way to being a lifelong devotee, but for me the Target novels were first and foremost the thrill of seeing that new cover in the local bookshop, of begging my mum or my auntie for 60p (a fortune in 1977; quite possibly two whole months of pocket money) so that I could rush home with my paper bag of delight and gaze upon its lines and curves.

And the first of those for me was Jeff Cummins's cover for *The Talons of Weng-Chiang*.

Now, this may seem disingenuous, but at the age of five I wasn't really a reading person. Sure, I would skip through every new Target to find occurrences of the word TARDIS and the familiar descriptions of the Doctor and his current companion. But despite the huge contribution that Terrance Dicks made not just to a publishing phenomenon, but to the literacy education of thousands of youngsters, I can't pretend to say that reading the books was ever my priority. I just liked looking at the covers.

My emotional investment in these books can be put solely down to one person: my mum. Being an only child to a single parent in the late 1970s didn't exactly hold the status of a badge of pride, but the importance of being and feeling loved certainly did. My mum worked hard so she could look after us both and even if she was out a lot at night pulling pints and giving amateurish psychiatric advice – leaving me to be tucked in by my nan – I still knew that she was working to a higher purpose, which was to make me as happy and as content a child as she possibly could. Often, this involved treats.

Some of my clearest memories are of her coming home from a lunchtime shift down the Dublin Packet with a small paper bag sticking out of her handbag which I (of course) tried desperately to pretend not to have noticed. The waiting was tortuous, but eventually she'd ruffle my hair and tell me to close my eyes while she put a surprise in my hands. Most days, it was a brand-new Target paperback, and among so many, those I remember the most are *The Hand of Fear* (the shadow of that giant stone hand dwarfing the Doctor and Sarah) and *Death to the Daleks* (which had a Dalek's head exploding: how incredible was that?) - but the very first one was the Jeff Cummins-wrapped paperback for *The Talons of Weng-Chiang*.

As my collection grew, every summer holiday and day-trip to Chester became a hunt for the latest releases. Even relatives would set off with suitcases packed and handwritten lists of the latest releases, to return with a new find or three. Like most fans, the need to catalogue my treasures became a daily task. Transmission order or Target release order? And if the latter, do you subscribe to the latter-day numbering system or start with David Whitaker's *The Daleks* (as opposed to the official No.1 in the catalogue, the alphabetically superior *The Abominable Snowmen*)? On such decisions were many a winter evening frittered away.

I think many fans have that one item about which we can say with certainty: 'This is where it all began' and for me as for so many others, this was a Target book. Sure, as we grow older more demanding and cerebral tomes surpass the humble Target range in our daily attentions (Phil Sandifer's *TARDIS Eruditorum* volumes being my current favourites). But we never lose that sense of warmth and love that we first experienced with our formative object. The smell of fresh paper, the exhaustive list of other titles in the range - marked with felt tip as we ticked each one off - and that occasional need by the

131

publisher to explain about 'The Changing Face of Doctor Who'. That was why we got hooked, as much as any idiosyncratic descriptions of the TARDIS's take-off noise or Peter Davison's face.

It was only at breakfast the next day that I discovered the identity of the man to whom the news of Lou Reed's death had seemed more than just the passing of a cultural icon. Jeff Cummins was charming, modest and just a little taken aback by all the adulation he'd received that weekend for something that was just a series of jobs to him. He even laughed when I said I had his cover for *The Talons of Weng-Chiang* on a T-shirt (whilst looking understandably curious as to what percentage cut he should be getting for those), and that given the right company people talked about his art in the same way gallery curators would about a Matisse or a Rembrandt. I consumed his every word with at least as much passion as I was devoting to my bacon and eggs, all the while thinking to myself I was having breakfast with the man who painted the first piece of art I recognised as such.

That early morning feast ended far too soon and we went our different ways with Jeff's warm handshake and appreciative words of thanks still palpable in both hand and heart. I had little time to think how serendipitous sharing my sad news had been the previous evening. Jeff never had the honour of illustrating a Lou Reed album cover but he certainly did a fair few for the likes of Paul McCartney, David Essex and Kiss. The sad news I had imparted had not only been of particular relevance to Jeff and the work he'd done, but also allowed me to meet someone who had a formative influence on my young life. My only regret was that I hadn't packed that T-shirt so he could have signed it.

So, thanks Jeff. But more importantly, thank you Mum. And Adam, my uncle who spent his holidays scouring WH Smiths and Menzies for those elusive new releases instead of enjoying much deserved rest and relaxation. Although I stopped buying the Target paperbacks aged 17 (foolishly cowed by the fear that girls wouldn't fancy an already spotty adolescent obsessed more by *Delta and the Bannermen* than Madonna), I fortunately saw sense, so now my shelves remain crammed with Target books, including early 1990s reprints and their later BBC equivalents. And I still wear that T-shirt, as a reminder of when happiness was as simple as a freshly printed book and a loving look from a parent. Happy Times and Places indeed...

(In memory of Lou and all those perfect Target days.)

To 44 Hill Street and Back

Doctor Who and the Masque of Mandragora
by Russell Cook
Favourite *Doctor Who* book: *The Loch Ness Monster*
by Terrance Dicks

Someone once said that the memory cheats, fragments of happy experiences creating rose-tinted visions leading to well-rehearsed anecdotes, stories that are told and embellished when you are always in the kitchen at parties. However, I know that my memory isn't trying to pull a long woollen multi-coloured scarf over my eyes when I remember the irritating and pushy ten-year-old circa 1977 trawling the various bookshops and department stores in search of the latest Target *Doctor Who* book release.

At that time, they were being published thick and fast and no sooner had I digested Castellan Spandrell's comments about the Universe not being big enough for both the Doctor and the Master on page 121 of *The Deadly Assassin*, than I was off on the bus to Poole Town centre yet again. On the occasions when the journeys yielded no books, I stomped through the shops leaving harassed shop assistants in my wake, but one fateful Saturday, just as the Doctor of our TV screens was defeating the evil Fendahl with rock salt, the Beales department store bookshop came up trumps. Brand new shiny copies of *The Talons of Weng Chiang* took pride of place in the children's fiction department and I had already acquainted myself with chapter one ('Terror in the Fog') as I went to pay.

'You're the first to buy one of those!' said the lady who ran the small book department, bringing me back from Victorian London with a jolt. My smile gave it all away. 'Another one for your collection?' she continued; I nodded. 'Those books are very popular; in fact I'm just putting an order through for next month's book.'

What did she say?

'Do you want to know what the title is?' she continued.

I managed to squeak 'Yes' and as I did so, she reached behind the till and produced a four page, red coloured A4 catalogue headlined 'December 1977 Wyndham New Title Listing'. Smiling, she passed it over to me. There it was: 8th December, *Doctor Who and the Masque of Mandragora* with the by-line 'The Tardis Lands in 15th Century Italy' and the Doctor's perplexed face surrounded by four Mandragora masks staring out of the red logoed cover.

'Can I have this?' I uttered bravely, referring to the catalogue as I handed over 60p for the book that I still clutched in my hand.

'Sorry, I haven't phoned the orders through yet, but you can have

133

this one.' And she passed over another catalogue from July/August 1977. Wyndham, then with a different logo, were publicising *Doctor Who and the Planet of Evil*. 'Can the Doctor leave Zeta Minor Alive? Find out on 18thAugust', but I knew anyway that because that was three months ago.

I read and enjoyed *The Talons of Weng Chiang* but my thoughts as I contemplated, along with the Doctor and Leela, 'The Monster in the Tunnel' were back a few hundred years in Renaissance Italy. I felt I had an advantage, knowing when the book would be published, the actual day Philip Hinchcliffe's second offering was to take pride of place amongst all the other Target paperbacks in bookshops and department stores up and down the country.

There was another reason why I was looking forward to this book more than any other: I had never seen part one of the story when it was shown on television. We had been on a family holiday in Austria and were travelling back the day the first episode was due to go out, but there were flight delays so we never made it home in time. A few days later and back at school for the Autumn Term, I was eager to find out what had happened (I'd seen the premiere in the window times 'Mandragora energy! Get Down Quick!'). Stories drifted around the playground – a new brown wood panelled control room? The fourth Doctor in the third Doctor's clothes and the first Doctor's sonic screwdriver in a drawer in the console? Then again, was any of this true? My friend Bruce, who told me all this, had convinced me a year before that the Zygons would be returning and that the Target book (the originally titled *Return of the Zygons*) would be in book shops any day now. Bruce was confident in his predictions, though and I never saw any reason to disbelieve him.

I got *The Masque of Mandragora* on the Saturday after publication - by this time, the 'new' console room was old news and also a thing of the past - and it wasn't until I eventually saw the episode in the early 1980s thanks to those fondly remembered days of pirated videotapes. ('You are lucky, it is only a third generation copy and not on Video 2000!')

The arrival of *The Masque of Mandragora* on the shelves in that cold, wet winter of 1977 marked the beginning of another obsession: in the years that followed, I was still collecting the novelisations but now I was armed with what I termed publishers' catalogues. Consequently, I was even more annoying because, thanks to the help of a pile of stamped addressed envelopes, monthly handwritten letters from the one-hundred-and-twenty-six-page-obsessed boy would fly off to Wyndham Publications Ltd, 44 Hill Street, London W1X 8LB asking for the latest advance information. Usually within a few days, I would get the latest catalogue in the post, often accompanied by a friendly letter thanking me for my interest, always with a note on how I could order any of the myriad of titles on offer from Wyndham, WH Allen, Tandem and later Star, Comet and of course, Target. I had advance information and could pester shop staff as to where copies of *The Hand of Fear* were (18th January 1979, 'The power of the evil hand controls Sarah's mind') or why hadn't the reprint/reissue of *The Deadly Assassin* (15th February 1979, 'Will the Master's Doomsday Plan destroy Gallifrey?') with the new cover arrived on the shelves?

Eventually, in the late 1980s, the catalogues slowly came to an end: from the heyday of the glossy colour A4 booklet to a glossy colour A4 double sided page. The last one I got was promoting the publication of *The Space Museum* ('The Doctor saves his companions from being exhibits in the museum') and for the next book, *The Sensorites*, I have the book but no catalogue. At the time I wasn't too concerned: I had grown up, was at college, there were more pressing matters, often found at the bottom of a pint glass. However, I can pause for a moment and look up to the shelf above me: the Target books are there and, somewhere in the middle, sits the original 1977 edition of *The Masque of Mandragora* and every time I look at it, wonderful, happy memories flood back of a childhood enriched by the word 'novelisation'.

The Facing of the Future

Doctor Who and the Face of Evil by Ken Shinn

Favourite *Doctor Who* book: *Timewyrm: Revelation*
by Paul Cornell

Books, among other things, can be great friends. Especially if you're a thirteen-year-old being bullied at school.

This bullying varied, but some of it was the good old silent treatment, a symbolic banishment, a shunning of the unlike. Along came Terrance Dicks' excellent novelisation of *The Face of Evil*: as clever and gripping as Boucher's original, it delights in throwing in neat bits of retro-continuity - the original adventure wherein a post-regenerative fourth Doctor makes a terrible mistake occurs off-stage during his first tale. In that light, the story is also about his acceptance of responsibility and the importance of putting things right, a valid message to any adolescent heading towards the unknown future of adulthood.

Ultimately, though, Dicks takes the wise route of making the story very much about Leela: her decisions and her choices. Thirteen-year-old me in 1978 put aside little inconveniences such as her gender, age, raw strength, savagery, and disconcerting sexual appeal, and saw her simply as me. An awkward outsider squaring off against the big, bad world. I may not have had her sheer physical competence and courage, but I could fully empathise with her feelings of isolation, as well as her healthy mixture of scepticism and curiosity. Dicks, with one of his masterstrokes, wrote a good few key scenes to place her point of view as the most important. Her initial trial is a fine example, but not the only one. Even with a single tiny paragraph, he placed us firmly in her animal-skin boots:

> Leela turned away contemptuously. 'Cowering down there won't save you.'

In the end, offered a position of power and prestige as the one to reunite Sevateem and Tesh, she decides to do what she wants: to head off to bigger, and more rewarding, adventures.

> Leela saw an important-looking switch. Darting forward, she grabbed it.
>
> 'No,' yelled the Doctor. 'Don't touch that...'
>
> But it was too late.

Where did she go? Out.

What did she do? Everything.

Thanks, Uncle Terrance

Doctor Who and the Horror of Fang Rock
by Dean Hempstead
Favourite *Doctor Who* book: *The English Way of Death*
by Gareth Roberts

I love second-hand book shops. The moment that you step through the door, your senses are invigorated by the smell of ageing pages, print and binding glue. The anticipation of finding a long-forgotten treasure or even a new author or set of books to collect – it's magic and unlike any other feeling I have experienced.

Over the years, books have become a passion of mine that has never waned. The excitement of holding a book in your hand and wondering what treasures lie within is an obsession that was started by Terrance Dicks all those years ago. When I was about six, my Granddad had introduced me to *Doctor Who*, and along with my Uncle Peter, had already taken me to see *The Empire Strikes Back*. I realised quickly that I was addicted to stories. The weekly *Doctor Who* episode, the odd film here and there and a handful of other TV shows were never quite enough for me. What do I do in between? My imagination was hungry for more.

One day in class, our teacher handed us a pamphlet for a book club that we were asked to take home to our parents. I took it with little enthusiasm (there was always some dull piece of paper that I seemed to need to take home for my mum to sign – I struggled to remember and many times she found them too late, crumpled and neglected in the bottom of my school bag). However, on this occasion, something caught my eye on the page as I was about to stuff it into my bag. I saw the Doctor. Well, not just the Doctor, but MY Doctor. A mysterious and moody picture of the fourth Doctor held my gaze, with some rope slung over his shoulder and an ominous looking lighthouse in the background. I could not take my eyes off of it. The realisation dawned on me that there were *Doctor Who* books. This was too exciting to contemplate. I could actually own a piece of my favourite TV show and keep it in my bedroom. I was always happy in my own company. This would become ever more apparent when I discovered books. I carefully folded the piece of paper, placed it in my bag and resolved to show mum as soon as I returned home from school.

When I got home, I enthusiastically showed my mum the pamphlet. My eyes must have been wide with so much hope as I handed it to her, hoping that she would encourage and feed my thirst for books. Mum agreed that we could order both *The Horror of Fang Rock* and *The Masque of Mandragora*. The next day I returned to school with a cheque and order form which I gave to the teacher. She could tell that I was incredibly excited and she revealed that the school actually had some of these books in the library that I could borrow. So at the first available opportunity I began scanning the shelves and very quickly became adept at spotting that famous Target logo on the spine. I remember that I found quite a few and I was told that I could only take three at a time. So I would return home and read them feverishly each evening, so that I could return them and borrow the next exciting instalment. I hated returning the ones I had read, though. I wanted to keep them on my shelf, so that I could read them again as they were so exciting. Some of them had drawings in!

Soon enough, my books arrived. They came wrapped in brown paper. There was something about this neatly-wrapped parcel, the aroma of the brown paper and Sellotape that had been used to carefully conceal the magic within. Looking back now, it seems like such a simple thing – that neatly wrapped parcel. However, I think it was a precursor to the obsession that was about to begin.

After school I dashed home, completed my homework, ate my dinner with relish and returned to my room around bedtime to begin reading *The Horror of Fang Rock.* I read the book cover to cover twice before the week was out. The Target books had become an obsession. The best bit was that I could put these on my shelf when I had finished them. I would lay there sometimes, looking longingly at the shelf, imagining it full of *Doctor Who* books. I resolved that from this point I was going to save up as much pocket money as I could to order some more.

Soon after, Mum realised that I was not buying as many sweets as I used to. She must have thought that something was wrong. Once I explained what I was doing, Mum had an idea. The next time we went to town, she said that we could have a look in the second-hand bookshop to see if we could get any more, as they would be a lot cheaper in there. So the next time we went to town, in Maldon where we lived, we visited the bookshop and found the relevant section (they were in the sci fi section, which made me feel grown up). Very soon, I was scanning the shelves with the same skill that I had learned in the school library. Mum was very encouraging and thought that it couldn't be a bad thing to be so enthused by reading.

Over the next few weeks, my imagination was taken on many exciting adventures and my bookshelf became fuller week by week. The bookshop must have had quite a stock of them, as I always found a few new ones on every visit to add to my collection. Eventually, I needed a second shelf. Every place we visited as a family – we used to holiday a lot in the Lake District, Cornwall and the Isle of Wight - we would find bookshops to go in and I would spend ages scanning the shelves for that wonderful logo on the spine.

As I reached my teens and completed my collection, I read them less and less. I became obsessed with girls and then got caught up in the adult world of trying to hold down a job. I remember taking life far too seriously in those days, especially when I got laid off. There I was, very young and unemployed and it seemed like every job I tried for required experience. I had no money and quickly became fed up. I was young, insecure and uncomfortable in my own skin. I reached rock bottom and during this time made the decision to sell my Target novels. I rarely looked at them these days. I sold them back to the second-hand bookshop that I had originally bought most of them from. I regretted it once they were gone, but I had some money in my pocket.

Years later, visiting Milton Keynes with an ex-girlfriend, we were walking through a shopping mall and at its centre was a large bookstall. There were hundreds of books piled high. I still enjoyed reading (I was just less obsessive about it) so I headed over to the stall and something very familiar jumped out at me: the Target logo on a spine of a book. All of a sudden, I noticed they had about twenty books with this once-loved logo on the spine. I began examining them and was drawn in immediately by their pure magic. I was compelled to smell them because I had this nostalgic memory of the bookshop where I first bought these books many years ago. People must have thought me very peculiar as I stood there sniffing these books. I thought they were wonderful. It was like I had travelled through time. I remembered everything that I loved about these books. I bought every one that they had and resolved to start a new shelf as soon as I got home.

Soon after, when we were visiting my parents in Maldon, I decided to re-visit the second-hand bookshop where I used to buy my books all those years ago when I was a child. I began searching the shelves and very quickly noticed that there were loads of them. I was intrigued as to how they had so many. Each time I found one, I would look through it just to check that there were no pages missing. I was unprepared for what happened next. I looked through one of the books and there was my name in pencil on the inside of the cover. It was one that I had sold to the bookshop years ago. I couldn't believe that it was still there.

Once I had found all of the books that were there – there were still a few missing that I needed (*The Wheel in Space* being one of them – grrrr) - they were very quickly put on my new shelf with the ones that I had found in Milton Keynes. I still needed to complete my collection however. At this time, eBay was still new and somehow felt like cheating. I would miss out on the thrill of the chase!

I did, after a considerable amount of time, find all of the books that I needed in bookshops, with the exception of one. That pesky *The*

Wheel in Space. I ordered that one online and paid quite a price for it, but it was worth it to complete my collection.

Of course, since then, there have been many other *Doctor Who* book ranges and I enjoyed collecting those just as much – but it was not the same as finding that logo. That logo, and the name Terrance Dicks on the cover, symbolised everything that was wonderful about *Doctor Who*. So thank you, Uncle Terrance, for writing all those books. For encouraging me to read. I am still having the most wonderful time, reading adventures of the Doctor and beyond.

Target and Me: *Doctor Who* Books Down Under

Doctor Who and the Tomb of the Cybermen
by Antony Howe

Favourite *Doctor Who* book: *The Sixties*
by David J Howe, Mark Stammers and Stephen James Walker

Target books began being released in Australia around June 1975, the month I came to the end of a very long exhausting backpacking trip in neighbouring New Zealand. On the rebound from a dead end bout of love insanity, I reverted to fan-boy insanity, and was finding items of *Doctor Who* merchandise in the most out of the way corners of what is now the template of Middle Earth. It was there I first saw some Target books in a rickety rotating stand at the rundown ferry terminal linking the main islands. I may have had enough money left to buy one, but I am not sure. I wish I could remember the first Target book I ever got ... but my memory, normally excellent, fails me there. Back home, after a serious illness, I wrote to the publisher of Target in London, and in early 1976 the Children's Books Editor ('Sue', I think), was very encouraging of my youthful enthusiasm and sent me some advance info, probably on *The Doctor Who Monster Book*, with, I think, a poster of the cover artwork.

It was not a good time to be a *Doctor Who* fan in Australia. For years the ABC had been increasingly erratic with scheduling the series, not even running complete seasons and leaving stories out due to the government censors objecting to such dire issues as black magic in *The Daemons*! Yes, we had the benefit of repeats, but these were often muddled up, or not even advertised properly so you missed them. By the mid-1970s they screened it so infrequently that we were several years behind Britain's current material. In 1976 only half the first Tom Baker series was screened in Australia, and I discovered the ABC had decided not to buy any of the subsequent stories. (This situation was only sorted out in 1978 by a change in ABC management.)

Fan life in Australia was (and still is) very different from being in a small, densely-populated island like Britain. We are a continent where the distance from one side to the other is like flying from London to Moscow. Couple this 'tyranny of distance', as we say, with a far smaller population base than the UK and USA, and it was hard to build a fan club here, so most were basically little more than a one-city organisation. Most Aussie fans didn't know the series was in fact at death's door here. The club I formed did become national, is still around today and will be forty years old soon.

141

Down Under became like Alice's looking glass, as things were curiously reversed. Here the books often revealed the stories to us well before they were on TV. All the books of Tom's later seasons were greatly desired, being stories we feared we would never see. In 1976, at university, I founded the Australasian *Doctor Who* Fan Club with some student friends from the larger Sydney University Science Fiction Association (SUSFA), and in that pre-video era, where the past Doctors were lost in the mists of time, we were always especially keen when Target brought out a 'classic' 1960s story. I clearly remember the thrill when a fan gave me the new *The Dalek Invasion Earth* at a club meeting (thanks Tim). For several years, there was only one classic a year as the Tom Baker stories presumably had better sales, and by about 1980 older eras seemed to be totally avoided. *The Tomb of the Cybermen* was the sole classic to come out in 1978. It was great to read these stories which were at best distant memories.

I started my fanzine, *Zerinza*, which had a regular section of book reviews. The local distributor for Target here was a firm called Rical, who were very helpful, supplying review copies for our fanzines which was vital as we were mostly impoverished students in those days. We often especially appreciated the novels by the original writers of their own scripts, such as Gerry Davis with *The Tomb of the Cybermen*, which I reviewed very favourably. I especially praised the increased page count, which had jumped up to 140 pages, an all-too-rare occurrence.

> 'Reviewing these books, one sees that no matter how good the writer, he is bound entirely by having to accurately transcribe the script, making originality impossible [except with] visual descriptions, often lacking in a script. Here Davis succeeds [and there is] a feeling of foreboding all through the novel. [Despite the] guest appearance [of the Cybermen, the] real conflicts are in the human interactions [including] the usual crop of megalomaniacs [who] plague the Doctor's efforts to save humanity from itself. Why no shades of grey? Toberman is a rare exception and his loyalty and strength of character at the end save the day. [However,] the Doctor is poorly described. He could have been any one of the four Doctors.'

This sort of complaint about the characterisation of the Doctor is in a number of the reviews I flipped through when writing this memoir. Most Target writers ignored the personality quirks that made each Doctor distinct, sadly leaving him as a more standardised character. Only the cover art showed you who was Who.

Although I did not write many myself, I did a lot of 'polishing' over the next eight years of reviews by fans such as Dallas Jones, Patricia

Fenech, my mother and a couple of others. In the earlier reviews, in the late 1970s, there was often praise at a job well done, with just occasional quibbling. A lot of the books were actually very good mementoes of the series. But in the 1980s, many of the reviewers were less satisfied; praise was often out of gratitude that anything was better than nothing.

Terrance Dicks was the main author of a slew of books, and often stood in the firing line of reviewers. Undoubtedly badly paid, he had the task of rushing out books every month or so, year after year. Having read a variety of Doctor Who scripts I can say for a fact they are fairly bland, just a thin barebones outline, and turning this skeleton into a proper work of rounded writing is time-consuming, as my mother found when she wrote a fan novelisation of *The Daleks' Master Plan* from Ian Levine's notes. She had a huge amount of work to do as so much needed to be added, and it had never been screened in Australia so none of us had the faintest idea how most of it looked.

I am sure Rical were somehow involved with the PR tour of Australia by Tom Baker in February 1979. The TV network seemed to handle it, but it was a helpful PR woman at Rical who told me about it in advance, and she was a key ally in my gaining access to conduct a long interview with Tom Baker during the busy tour. This is when the *Doctor Who* club I had been running in Sydney on a small scale for years was suddenly launched into being a really national club with key fans interstate linking us all together; when they came to Sydney for work, to see relatives, or go to big shows and concerts, they also came to visit me and I stayed with several in their cities, sometimes taking Target books to sell at local meetings. Many friendships were made that have survived to today, nearly forty years later. The club soon had hundreds of members all over the continent, and even in many neighbouring island countries, from Singapore to Fiji and down to New Zealand.

From this, my involvement with Rical grew and they helped me out with hundreds of copies of Target books to sell at a club meeting in a city hall for the show's anniversary in November 1979, which started my move into merchandising for club members. We did this again when Jon Pertwee visited Sydney and kindly attended a fan event I organised. With the help of a dedicated band of volunteers, his visit was a great boost to the club and I thus met new friends who helped run the club over the next five years.

I don't recall the exact date, but months later, in the early 1980s, Rical went bankrupt, which meant there would be no distributor of Target books Down Under for the foreseeable future. When companies go bankrupt, their assets are sold to pay off debts as fast as possible, so absolutely everything sells - stock, furniture, the works - often at absurdly cheap prices. I was unemployed and I needed to make a bit of income, so I decided to take advantage of this opportunity to buy a bulk lot using savings. I cannot believe I was so reckless now, but in the end I bought about nine to ten thousand copies of Rical's *Doctor Who* books! This vast pile was freighted to my address and stored in the garage for the next few years (the car had to sit outside). There was a near disaster as my severely autistic sister when watering the garden went into the garage to spray the hose around! After a near heart attack, I was relieved that hardly any books were damaged, protected by thick wrapping. I also ended up with about a dozen cardboard stand up PR images of Daleks, which loomed up in the garage out of the shadows for years, as if it was a scene from a never-made classic, *Tomb of the Daleks*! They were to grace club functions for many a year until they fell apart.

Target had taken over my family garage, the house and all spare time. Standing behind tables covered with Target books is burned in my memory. Selling all these was a very slow process and became a really frustrating time. But it was a great way to meet up with fans. I was now unofficially Target's main distributor in Australia for about eighteen months until a new agent was appointed. In a stroke of luck for me, the new agent was Carnation, a tinned milk company! To sell books around a continent you need to have an experienced network of travelling reps who would drive thousands of kilometres a year to visit shops in rural towns, delivering advance copies, making deals and actively seeking coverage from the media. None of this ever seemed to happen. They seemed to think they could just sell, lazily, to a few department stores in the bigger cities.

Carnation also never got any of the back items needed by shops to replenish their main stocks. By 1981 there were about sixty titles, yet I was the only person in the country with a large range of older stock. Because fans usually buy the new titles as soon as they come out, I only had a small market for these older titles and had to research in dozens of Outback phone books in libraries and post offices, ending up with a potential mailing list of a few hundred regional book shops all over the continent. I did mass mail-outs of catalogues offering special deals, especially before Christmas, which worked, thank heavens.

Carnation gave up, and a far older firm, Gordon and Gotch, took on the Target franchise. I was lucky as before they really got going, I had sold most of my huge mountain. The last catalogue is dated December 1985.

I will always associate the first half of the 1980s with Target books as a near daily part of my life. Little did I realise my involvement with these books would be so unusual and take up so much space and time out of my life and house.

144

Passing It On

Doctor Who and the Time Warrior
by J.R. Southall
Favourite *Doctor Who* book: *Doctor Who in an Exciting Adventure*
with the Daleks
by David Whitaker

I loved the Target books, but they went through a phase around the turn of the 1980s – in tandem with the TV series, so it seemed to me – where they weren't very good. There were three that irritated me in particular. *The Robots of Death* was a story that I had especially fond memories of, but the novelisation was bland and thin. *Image of the Fendahl*, which I remembered less clearly and was thus more eager to read, was beyond slender. And *Destiny of the Daleks* was a story I'd just watched and only partially enjoyed, and the adaptation added barely any more depth than a simple script book might have. Where were the back-stories that had so vividly brought earlier characters to life in books like *The Cave-Monsters* and *The Dæmons*?

The Time Warrior was one of the last of the run of good Target books, and had appeared in 1978, less than a year before *The Robots of Death*. Similarly to the Cybermen books, it included a prologue which sketched in the background to the Sontarans and their never-ending war with the Rutans – although what was different in this case, was that this history was related during an exciting action sequence explaining how Linx had come to find himself in the Middle Ages in the first place. To a ten-year-old reader, the context of the Sontaran-Rutan war was almost as thrilling as the story itself, although *The Time Warrior* was a serial I barely remembered and for many years, I assumed that should I ever get the opportunity to watch the story, it would begin with Linx in the cockpit of his spaceship, a microsecond from obliteration.

Needless to say, it didn't.

The Target books that followed *The Time Warrior* had the feel of stories that had been written by more interesting writers, before being passed on to Dicks to novelise, without allowing him room to devise interesting back-stories for the characters and situations.

How ironic to discover, years later, that this was in fact almost literally the situation with *The Time Warrior*.

Death of a Dalek

Doctor Who – Death to the Daleks
by Sean Alexander

Favourite *Doctor Who* book: *Doctor Who and the Daleks Omnibus*
by Terrance Dicks ed. Terry Nation

Sometimes you buy a book simply because of the cover. That was certainly true when I first saw the cover of *Death to the Daleks* in the now-long-since-gone bookshop in Stanley Street. Perusing the shelves for any gaps in my collection had become an obsession bordering on the compulsive, my day made if I came home with even one fresh Target purchase. So when the startling sight of a Dalek's exploding dome seared into my retina, I grabbed it and begged for the money from my mum (a then-purse-worrying 75p ... a pint of beer was probably about the same price).

I was usually a bit disappointed when my haul only included a Pertwee, Troughton or Hartnell, as these were the days for me when the only Doctor was Tom Baker. But looking at this most Munch-esque of covers – the exothermic bonce showering the background with *The Scream*-like expressionism – I notice now that the poor Dalek is reflexively blasting its gun, as though in its death-throes it performs the most instinctive of actions before shuffling off its poly-bonded-carbide coil.

For the attentive, this was the 1980 third impression of Terrance Dicks' 1978 novelisation. 23 years later, Alister Pearson's jacket for the blue-spine reprint elects instead to transcribe two stock publicity photos of Bellal giving us his Tommy Cooper impression and a burning, dome-less Dalek, quite probably the same one as in 1978. This time the flames are less expressionistic and more 'refillable lighter', as the Dalek shell resembles one of those burning metal bins that protesting strikers stand around whilst warming their hands and eliciting encouraging beeps from passing motorists.

The novel? This is full-on, late-1970s production line narrative, with chapters (roughly) matching episode breaks and the resident Doctor described as having a 'young-old' face. There's no 'Escape to Danger' – Chapter 7's 'Escape to the Unknown' proving far more reassuring - but the 'Probe City - one, Dalek United - nil' joke still makes me smile. As do memories of first seeing that cover in 1980.

A Village Without a Future?

Doctor Who and the Android Invasion by Josh Zimon

Favourite *Doctor Who* book: *The Discontinuity Guide*
by Paul Cornell, Martin Day and Keith Topping

I clicked off the seat belt and grabbed the handle to the back seat of my mother's old station wagon. It was windy outside on a late autumn day in 1982. We walked into the New England Mobile Bookfair, which was neither mobile nor a bookfair: just a messy old bookstore with books strewn everywhere. I walked in and looked for the searching books, which were huge and the writing extremely small. I went to the 'D' section and went down the list to *Doctor Who*. Pinnacle books. 10 different *Doctor Who* books. Aisle 8. I walked down to aisle 8 as quickly as I could, passing several piles of other books as I entered the thin aisle.

I moved my finger along the shelf that was just about eye-level for me. There it was: *Doctor Who – The Android Invasion*. I pulled it out to look at it and sat down in the aisle to read the first page. Yes, it was the story I had seen on TV. I closed the book and ran over to my mother and put the book in the basket.

I wasn't a voracious reader when I was a kid and I know that she appreciated the fact that I suddenly had interest. While I already knew the conclusion, I didn't know what to think about reading the story off the page. I was excited to sit and read it and see how different it was going to be from what I saw on TV. So I arrived home, laid on my bed and begin turning the pages.

The Tom Baker Doctor with Sarah Jane Smith is my all-time favourite Doctor/Companion combination. Season 13 is where they built the most realistic chemistry of any two characters ever in the series. Season 13 was choked with classics such as *Pyramids of Mars*, *Brain of Morbius* and *The Seeds of Doom*. These three stories represent an era of the show, and while this time in the show is well appreciated, no one ever mentions *The Android Invasion* in the same breath.

The Android Invasion is a story by Terry Nation, the creator of the Daleks. He loved to create a world and a group of aliens who use science for evil. In this scenario, a group of aliens from a planet that is ravaged by nuclear war is looking for a new home. They hijack an Earth astronaut (Crayford) and brainwash him into believing that they saved his life and want to leave their war torn planet to share Earth with humanity. A great idea! But then...how do they do it? They create android copies of all of the humans in the small town where Crayford is to arrive. As the Doctor and Sarah make their way through the fake town, they see some very strange behaviour from the residents and

147

fresh minted money, a page-a-day calendar with only one day and an unused dartboard in a pub.

Terry Nation builds on this mystery in the first part, but then makes the situation patently obvious in the second. The android copy of Sarah is so laughingly obvious that you have to figure the average ten-year-old would have known it right away even from reading the book. In addition, the Kraals' plan does not meet the over-thinking test. To disseminate a virus using human copies from one small town is a bonkers idea that no-one over the age of 10 would ever accept.

The best dialogue in the TV version comes when the Doctor is captured by Styggron and tied to a granite pillar in the centre of town with a bomb placed at his feet. In the book, the Doctor simply says calmly, 'A matter dispersal bomb?' What I missed in the book was Tom Baker saying, 'Ah...an MD bomb.' The one thing about the books is they are built from the scripts and sometimes the interpretation of the author. Terrance Dicks kept mostly to the script here, restricting the amazing Tom Baker's input to a minimum.

That said, there is a charm about this wonderful book. Somehow, Dicks recaptured the bonkers Terry Nation ideas and naturally puts them together into a reasonably-paced story. He crafts a very dramatic (although unsatisfying) ending with a few sentences to explain what happened after Styggron's head went into the virus phial. That said, the book ends with the reader wanting more, as if it not only skipped the end of the TV version, but was also so abrupt, it almost felt like there should have been another chapter!

After reading *The Android Invasion*, I noticed the subtle differences in Terrance Dicks' dialogue to what I had seen on TV. I decided that the very next time *The Android Invasion* was on, I would follow the TV show with my book. (In the Boston area, on WGBH TV back in the late 1970s and early 1980s, *Doctor Who* was on episodically every weekday at 7pm. They repeated Seasons 12-15 over and over until 1982, when they began to show Seasons 16-18.) Once I had done this with *The Android Invasion*, I started to do it with other books too. It made for a different viewing experience. I had started my collection and, within a couple of years, more Target books were available. As my shelf of books grew, I put them in order of broadcast. Whereas in the past all I had was a listing of the stories and their number of episodes, now I had a shelf filled with the stories in their right order. It was only later in life, when the DVDs were available, that I could repeat this process.

The books were only the beginning of my personal *Doctor Who* collection. Without them, I most certainly would not have appreciated digging back into the classic series later in my life. I won't forget the excitement of going to that bookfair with my mother, reading it on the bed, and then following along with the TV episode.

Scary Sontarans under Spooky Lights

Doctor Who and the Sontaran Experiment
by Suky Khakh
Favourite *Doctor Who* book: *A Celebration* by Peter Haining

We lived in a two up, two down terraced house in the seventies. No central heating, a coal fire and draughty windows and doors. If my whole family were not in the living room then the coal fire would not be lit. The main reason was to save on fuel and money. The coal fire would be lit on the evenings, using the free newspapers that were pushed through our letterboxes, when both my mum and dad would be back from work and my siblings and I would have returned from school. The rest of the day, the coal fire would remain unlit and we would walk round with thick jumpers or sit under huge blankets to keep warm. I can remember there used to be constant electricity blackouts where the whole of Bilston town would go dark. We would light up the house with a couple of candles in the front room and a couple in the kitchen, but the living room would be lit by coal fire. This would give an eerie glow to the room which would be ideal for reading scary books.

For a seven or eight-year-old, the scariest books I would read were the Target *Doctor Who* books. As I sat, I could imagine the story on the back wall where the shadows from the coal fire would flicker. Maybe I saw a Dalek shooting its gun stick but instead of the electrical discharge as described in the books, maybe it shot out a hot burning stream of fire! Or there was a planet burning away as it had been destroyed by Sutekh. My imagination could run wild with all the scary scenarios that I could dream of as my family sat next to me eating their tea or playing card games. If not read at home during the day, they would be read at the Gurdwara (Sikh temple) or in class at school. I was determined that the first book that I would ever own would be a *Doctor Who* book.

The reason that I had a fast turnover of library books was that I was a secret night-time reader. I shared a massive, king sized, bouncy mattress bed with my two brothers and my father. I would insist on being next to the wall by the window where all my borrowed library books were on the window sill. As soon as I heard my father snoring, I would slowly push back the thick curtain and the net curtain to let in a bright light from the electric street lamp right outside the bedroom window. I would sit up, carefully trying to make sure that the springy mattress didn't make too much noise as to wake one of the others sleeping in the bed. A book would be taken down from the sill and I would start reading. I would not read a *Doctor Who* book by street lamplight in the middle of the night for many years as I would get scared because all my family were asleep and the shadows on the bedroom wall were from a monster getting ready to kill me. This was the main reason that for many years the only secret books I ever read in bed were by Enid Blyton. You can't get terrified from an Enid Blyton book. I would borrow them from the library (usually five at a time) and return within a couple of days. It helped that the library was situated almost at the back of my home in an old mansion house, where it still is to this day (although our family left the terraced house nearly forty years ago).

I don't know what time I used to read to but I'm pretty sure it was well after midnight. Once I had finished a book, I would start on another until I felt myself going to sleep and that's when I would call it a night. Most mornings I would wake up bleary eyed and still tired from my late night library sessions. Occasionally, one of my brothers would wake up and spot me reading but wouldn't say anything in case he woke up our father. But if Dad ever saw me reading there would be a few choice words said which would wake up everyone in the house.

Our Saturday morning rituals were always the same for the first few years of my life – a lot of yelling to get out of bed followed by pushing and shoving (and a lot of shouting) to be the first into the downstairs bathroom. The next stage would be crying when you had to watch Noel Edmonds on *Swap Shop* instead of Chris Tarrant on *TISWAS*. Finally, we would eat our breakfast in silence once my mother had got to the end of her tether and decided to clout the loudest or nearest child as a warning to stop all the others from giving her earache. As we sat in front of the television munching on our Shredded Wheat soaked in hot, sweet stewed tea, I would look forward to walking up to the shops in Bilston where there was a newsagent in the indoor market area that sold books.

The whole family would get ready to walk to town: every child old enough would have to carry a shopping bag, so the more hands that were available, the more shopping could be brought back. One of the other main reasons that all the kids were expected to go to the market with my parents was that my parents could hardly speak English. Like most first generation immigrants from India, they had picked up a smattering of English to get by ('Hello', 'Goodbye', 'How Much?') but for more in-depth conversations, as the eldest I would be volunteered to do the translating. With hindsight I should have used my translating skills at Parents' Evening at school!

As my parents went from one market stall to another, I would already be thinking about the most important shop, the biggest newsagent in the town centre. It contained sweets, chocolates, toys, comics and books. I knew I could just walk around the corner to Woolworths for most of these things but they didn't have *Doctor Who* books. We hardly ever went in, but on one of the few times my dad had taken me in there, at the bottom of one of the shelves I spotted the Target sign on one of the spines. Whoever came up with that distinctive Target logo at the publishers was a genius. For years at the library and other book shops you would be able to spot a *Doctor Who book* simply by looking for the logo on the spine of the book. It just glowed, beckoning me to it.

The book that had this particular Target logo was *Doctor Who and the Tomb of the Cybermen*. I had never borrowed this from the library and asked my father if I could have some money to buy it, but as money was tight I was told I couldn't have it. This became a regular request and each week I was refused. Then, on one of these weekly trips, I discovered that somebody had bought the book that I most coveted. I sulked for the rest of that day and then for every subsequent trip to town. I had lost out on owning my own *Doctor Who* book and I was going to make sure my parents knew about it. Of course my parents had more important things to worry about and so ignored me.

After a few months, after another mammoth shopping session, the whole family were passing the town centre newsagent when I spotted a glowing Target logo on the book stand. I stopped and looked at my mother and asked if we could go in. She reluctantly nodded and I ran in, leaving shopping bags on the floor outside. It was *Doctor Who and the Cybermen* by Gerry Davis – another book that I had not yet read. I picked the book up, read the blurb on the back and then, knowing I would be refused if I asked for any cash off my parents, I put it slap bang in the middle of the Mills and Boon romances. If I left it with the kids' books, a child with slightly richer parents would buy it and I would lose out on another book.

For the next few weeks, I went without my weekly packet of Polos and comic until I had enough money to buy the book. I hadn't told my parents I was saving for it and they didn't ask. Once I had enough, I told my Dad the truth. I'm sure he looked at with me with pride for saving my money but it might have been more like 'Hurry up, so I can get home and rest!' I rushed into the newsagent and started looking for the glowing Target logo. I couldn't see it. It was gone. I scoured the Mills and Boon shelves. It was not there. It was a disaster. I had saved for so long and I had missed my only chance to own a *Doctor Who* book. I was going to cry. I could feel myself welling up as I turned away from the romances. And then, from a corner of my eye, I glimpsed a glowing logo on the children's shelf. It was a shiny Target logo. I wiped away the solitary tear on my cheek and picked up the book: *Doctor Who and the Sontaran Experiment* by Ian Marter. Not the book I had hidden but just as good.

I wanted a blackout that night so I could read by coal fire light. I sat in the living room waiting for the electricity to be switched off, but nothing. I asked my Mum if I could switch off the light and read by the fire light but all I got from her was a stern look. As soon as she left, I switched off the lights but immediately had to switch them back on again as my brothers started shouting at me. As I got into bed that night, I looked at my windowsill and realised that I had read all the books on there. I had been so excited to get my first *Doctor Who* book that I had forgotten to go to the library to change my books. I had nothing to read except my scary *Doctor Who* book.

I lay in bed waiting for my dad to start snoring so I could reach across and start reading a scary book at night. The low rumbling from the other side of the bed meant that my reading session could begin. I opened the curtains, letting the light in and I opened my book. After a couple of hours, I looked up at the shadows on the bedroom wall. I couldn't see any evil Sontarans crushing poor, defenceless humans whilst Sarah Jane Smith looked on terrified. There wasn't a gigantic, massive floating robot terrorising the Doctor. In fact, there weren't any frightening shadows on the wall.

I drifted off to sleep whilst still reading and woke up in the morning. My book had been placed back on the windowsill. When I went downstairs, my dad asked if I had enjoyed my new book and I looked at him wondering how he knew that I had been reading last night. Dad had woken up when one of my brothers had kicked him in his sleep. He looked across and saw me fast asleep whilst gripping my *Doctor Who* book. He took it out of my hand and placed it back on the windowsill and tucked me back in. I got a telling off but I could tell he was happy that I had enjoyed my book. From that day forward, I could read any book under that street light. No book held any fears. I devoured *Doctor Who* books before moving onto thrillers, crime stories and the occasional horror novel.

I don't read by street light any more, but I do still see shadows on my bedroom wall which I imagine to be anything from deadly Daleks, scheming Cybermen, 'orrible Ogrons and scary Sontarans. I still have that very first *Doctor Who* book I bought. It has a handwritten note inside the front page which says, 'This book is owned by Suky Khakh'.

How I Learned to Stop Worrying and Started to Swim

Doctor Who and the Hand of Fear by David Geldard
Favourite *Doctor Who* book: *The Five Doctors* by Terrance Dicks

I was never any good at sport. I come from a very sporty family but no matter how hard I tried, it never seemed to work for me. I've always been too tall, too awkward and too clumsy, and I have flat feet. It didn't really bother me at primary school because I loved to read. I would often stare out of the window, hoping that it would rain heavily just so we would have to stay inside and read. Either that, or I would be staring outside and daydreaming about what it would be like if the TARDIS suddenly materialised in the playground.

The only sporting activity I did want to take part in, however, was swimming. I can still picture my brother and me in the shallow end of Stockport Swimming Baths, having private swimming lessons whilst a group of rowdy older lads were being constantly told off in the deep end. I had been getting very good at the breaststroke and it was now time to swim sans armbands.

But I couldn't. Despite much encouragement, every time I tried it I panicked, stopped, started sinking and got a nose full of chlorine. So I ended up going home feeling frustrated.

My Mum then made a bargain with me. 'I'll tell you what,' she said, 'If you manage to do it next week, I'll buy you a *Doctor Who* Target book.' Now at this stage in my life, that was possibly the most exciting sentence I could have heard. It's hard to believe, in the world we live in now, that a child could get so excited about a piece of literature...

I'd always loved *Doctor Who* from the moment I first saw it, when the Fourth Doctor and Leela met the Rutan in the lighthouse at Fang Rock. Being four years old at the time, I wasn't entirely sure of what was happening, but I had worked out the Rutan was killing people and it frightened the life out of me. The music and the opening titles seemed so eerie and otherworldly! I was hiding behind my Mum and Dad's 1970s white leather sofa with absolutely no idea that other kids across the country were doing the same. Fang Rock wouldn't be the last story to terrify me. There was also the bit in *City of Death* where Julian Glover removes his mask. Then there's the scene in *The Leisure Hive* where Tom Baker seems to have his limbs removed – and not forgetting the unlikely scare that was Erato from *The Creature from the Pit*.

Nowadays, that last one seems particularly laughable, but it was the 1970s and I was only a nipper. The Daleks never scared me, unless

153

I was face to plunger with them at the *Doctor Who* exhibition in Blackpool. After mithering my Mum and Dad for hours to go, once in there I was so nervous I'd go through it at breakneck speed. It was a relief to get to the merchandise shop at the end.

I was slightly confused by how much I loved something that scared me so much. Tom Baker was MY Doctor but after his regeneration, BBC2 decided to show 'The Five Faces of *Doctor Who*' – a repeat season featuring all of the Doctor's previous incarnations. This turned me from a kid who loved *Doctor Who* into a kid that was *obsessed* with *Doctor Who*. I was completely mesmerised by the first episode, which seemed so atmospheric and magical. I was amazed by the different Doctors, companions, monsters and TARDIS interiors. My teacher even passed on concerns to my parents about the level of my obsession.

Whenever I went to visit my Grandparents, I would ask them if I could read my Uncle Alan's *Doctor Who* books. He had the 1976 Annual (with its freaky, surreal and frankly disturbing artwork that seemed to be a world away from the TV series), *Doctor Who and The Ice Warriors* by Brian Hayles, *Doctor Who and the Doomsday Weapon* by Malcolm Hulke and, best of all, *Doctor Who and the Day of The Daleks* by Terrance Dicks (I was convinced that Jon Pertwee had a moustache on the cover of that one). I remember being totally engrossed in them and my Grandma turned to me and said, 'Oh, you can have those if you want them, Alan doesn't bother with those anymore.'

They were just simpler times. One Christmas, I got a Target box set featuring *The Giant Robot*, *State of Decay*, *Logopolis* and *Time-Flight*. Boxing Day is my birthday and so the next day I also got *The Mutants* and *The Leisure Hive*. To a nine-year-old *Doctor Who* fan at the time, this was the equivalent of a substantial lottery win now. Many hours were spent in my bedroom reading these books or listening to the *Genesis of the Daleks* tape. Sometimes I'd listen to my own audio recordings I'd made from the TV. These often had an unwanted cameo appearance in the background from our neighbour Sue who had come to use our phone. Some of the tension of the *Logopolis* regeneration had been somewhat lessened by Sue in the background telling her Mum about what she had made her husband, Derek, for his dinner. Upon the release of *Logopolis* on DVD, I half expected that conversation to be included as an Easter Egg.

I soon decided, from many trips to the library, that Terrance Dicks was my favourite author. All the other kids at school wanted to be Bryan Robson or Lee Majors, but I really wanted to be Terrance Dicks. I would spend hours writing my own stories in exercise books. They were nearly all set in various areas of Stockport and were all multi-Doctor adventures, including my all-time classic, *The Dalek Invasion of Celtic Street*. (PLOT: the Daleks invade Celtic Street. The TARDIS materialises outside the local off-licence. The Time Lords decide the Doctor needs help from his previous selves. The Doctor beats the Daleks. The Fourth Doctor buys some Jelly Babies from the off licence before he leaves.) No fear, Mr. Dicks, your job was safe.

So all I had to do was swim a width of the pool and I got a Target book. I closed my eyes, took a deep breath and told myself I could do it. As if there had been a moment of divine intervention, I soon found out I was swimming like Duncan Goodhew. My mother couldn't believe her eyes; she still talks about it now. I really wanted that book I'd been promised and nothing was going to stop me.

The next day at Banks Lane School, all I could think of was: 'I wonder which book my Mum will buy me?' The day dragged as I clock-watched. As soon as the bell went, I ran across the field to my Mum. 'Did you get it? Which one did you get, Mum?' My Mum smiled and handed me *Doctor Who and the Hand of Fear* by Terrance Dicks. I was so happy I gave her a big hug and couldn't wait to get home and read it.

The cover featured the Fourth Doctor and Sarah Jane cowering under the shadow of a giant hand, which in hindsight was slightly misleading, but the story was no disappointment. It featured a villain called Eldrad (for whom I had a soft spot because it is one letter away from being an anagram of my surname), her/his creepy detached-but-moving hand, mind control and a quarry! Best of all, it had the very moving scene at the end when the Doctor has to go home to Gallifrey and leave Sarah Jane behind. It was no surprise when Elisabeth Sladen passed away that BBC4 chose to repeat this story. For me, it has to be the most emotional companion exit. I always felt like Sarah Jane was the Doctor's favourite and I was always disappointed that she never got to see Gallifrey. I re-read that book several times.

When I was eleven, I started losing interest in *Doctor Who*. I saw *The Twin Dilemma* and just decided it wasn't for me anymore. The repeats of *The Avengers* on Channel 4 had taken over as my number one Cult TV fix. I was getting more and more interested in pop music, computer games and *Monty Python*. In a fit of premature maturity, I chucked out most of my *Doctor Who* books and magazines. My interest wouldn't be rekindled until ten years later when I discovered the UK Gold repeats. Fortunately – and with thanks to my very understanding wife Carol and the modern wonder that is eBay – I have them all again.

They say you should never meet your heroes. Well, I did. I met Terrance Dicks and he is a really nice bloke. I told him how his books inspired me to read and write, and how my job now is to help children with their literacy skills. However, I didn't tell him how he helped me swim.

A Lifeline, Stamped and Sold

Doctor Who and the Invisible Enemy
by Paul Holmes
Favourite *Doctor Who* book: *Ace!*
by Sophie Aldred and Mike Tucker

Like an awfully large number of people, I haven't used a library in years. I will champion their existence, but I've been absent from my local library since the turn of the century. There was that one dash into a small library in West London to tweak a job application on one of their PCs, but my overriding memory of that visit was being impressed that I could have a library card featuring a koala bear on the front. The internet came along and filled the requirements for fast information, and working life as an adult introduced me to the concept of buying my own books with the wage I earned, though these days I am frequently too busy to read them.

However, back in the early 1990s, my local library was the most special place to be, especially on a Monday night, when it rocked the status quo by staying open until 7:30pm. Heywood, a small industrial town in the borough of Rochdale, Lancashire, has never really had much going for it, now less than ever, but in those days the local library was a wondrous environment jam-packed with the kind of books every nerdy child would ever want.

I'd become a *Doctor Who* fan in 1988, just before my fourth birthday. This was almost entirely down to the fact that our family had recently got our first VCR and they decided to use the machine to record the new series as it clashed with Corrie on 'the other side'. This was probably the best entertainment-based decision anyone in my family could or will ever make. As an introduction to the series, *Remembrance of the Daleks* is hard to beat. It's got Daleks for a start. Having watched every episode of the serial intently, and with room on the tape for three more, *The Happiness Patrol* was also dutifully recorded, and my parents made the surprising decision to let me keep the tape, and get a new one to record the rest of the series. Around this time, they also picked up a couple of the recent releases in the blossoming VHS range: *Day of the Daleks*, *The Ark in Space* and the brand new title, *The Talons of Weng-Chiang*. I loved them, too, and quite frequently cite them as evidence whenever I tell people the seventh Doctor's era isn't just great to me because he was my Doctor, because I found their usually more precious third and fourth Doctors almost in tandem.

Then, the following year, *Doctor Who* was taken away from us all. Without this new-fangled thing called BSkyB, I'd survive on the odd

VHS release we could afford, but there was another source for my regular fix until I was old enough to buy the televised episodes myself. Heywood Library had a rather healthy selection of *Doctor Who* books from a company called Target. At first, I was unaware that these were novelisations of TV episodes. Best of all, because they were in the children's library, and hardly any children knew or cared what *Doctor Who* was by the early 1990s, I seemingly had them all to myself.

Every two weeks, I would agonise over the titles, wondering which one to take home next. I'd go running into the library, deliberately avoiding the children's section, and try to pick out a 'proper' book to read, quite often some young adult novel that the library assistant would refuse to believe an eight or nine-year-old was reading already. As I'd become obsessed with Hammer Horror, I'd almost always renew Christopher Lee's 1970s autobiography *Tall, Dark and Gruesome*. Really, someone should have just given me that book, as few other people ever got to read it. I'd also probably grab the *Halliwell's Film Guide* or something else from the reference section, already eager to sponge up knowledge and make my own lists of films I wanted to see.

Finally, I'd casually meander into the children's section and spend a good twenty minutes looking at every single *Doctor Who* book on the shelf. They were always along the bottom near the entrance to the section, for some reason, which meant I'd be sat cross-legged in front of them, my head tilted to one side, working out which ones I hadn't read yet and which ones I wanted to read again. When I had made my selection, I'd pick it up, check it once more to be sure, then get it stamped out and rush home to start it straight away.

By the mid-1990s, this simple pleasure was under threat. New books were coming in and the *Doctor Who* ones, tied to an obsolete TV show, were probably not being loaned as much as the rest. The need for space forced the library to start to sell off old titles. They had a perfect right to dispose of them, and a lot of books went on to new homes very quickly.

One day, I walked in to see the library's copy of *The Invisible Enemy* on their 'For Sale' table. I looked straight at my mum. She knew before I could open my mouth. The answer was yes and this was going to be the best 50p I'd ever spent.

At the time, *The Invisible Enemy* was one of the few that the library had left that I hadn't read. I'm an adult now and I know that the story is far from popular in print or in its original format. Back then, I had no idea and I was hooked. The Doctor got possessed! By a yucky insect-thing! He met K-9! Leela threw a knife into someone's back! I read that book cover to cover, over and over again, for over a month. I couldn't put it down. As the only visual element besides the pictures in my mind, the front cover image burned itself into my retinas.

Then, one day, *Doctor Who and the Dinosaur Invasion* turned up on the 'For Sale' table. That came home too, and briefly replaced *The Invisible Enemy* in my affection. Let's be fair, here: it had dinosaurs, and I was completely unaware of just how rubbery the ones on television had been. *Kinda* soon followed suit, but didn't click in the same way (nor has the televised story in the years since). There were more, too: *Warriors' Gate* and *The Sun Makers* were both a little drab, making me go back to *The Invisible Enemy*; *The Keeper of Traken*, *Four to Doomsday*, *Earthshock*, *The Seeds of Doom* and *The Visitation* were much more interesting. There had been more in the library, but others were buying them too, and it was pot luck if they'd be there when I went in. At one point, I tried going in every night on the way home from school, but they always seemed to be sold when I wasn't looking. So I'd return to *The Invisible Enemy* and its cohorts, keeping me company in a time when *Doctor Who* felt dead in the water.

In most cases, the words on the page and the vision I had of them far surpassed the eventual actuality. When I finally saw *The Invisible Enemy*, it seemed a bit of cheap filler at a time when the series was struggling to find a new identity. Subsequent attempts to watch the story again have always floundered. It's just not that interesting, despite a good cast and some great ideas. But the hazy memory in my mind of that Target novelisation... now that's still something to be cherished. The nightmare world inside the Doctor's brain, and the vile-looking creature I imagined the Nucleus to be, somehow more horrid than the faint one on the cover. How those infected with it looked with their overgrown eyebrows.

I considered returning to the novelisation many times over the years to see how it holds up with wiser eyes. Maybe it'd hold up better than the TV version? I could learn its deepest, darkest secrets, revel in its finest metaphors, embrace the elongated passages and beloved Terrance-isms. In the end, I couldn't do it. I read the opening chapter and decided to leave it there. But the book will exist forever in the back of my mind as an exciting adventure that became exclusively mine for 50p thanks to my local library. And perhaps that's the way it should always stay.

Every inch of *Doctor Who* gets analysed over and over again. I'm often part of that analysis, myself, though I have set myself a rule to watch every new episode with my critical brain off, to try and hold on to my inner child who just enjoyed the ride. To some extent, my relationship with this Target novelisation is an extension of this. Long ago, contact was indeed made, a lifeline was established, and the memory of it shall forever linger. It's slightly fuzzy and out of focus, but every now and then, that's exactly what I need to remember most.

Valley of the Lost

Doctor Who and the Robots of Death
by Kevin Jordan
Favourite *Doctor Who* book: *The Brain of Morbius*
by Terrance Dicks

My history with *Doctor Who* is a long one, going back at least as far as the transmission of *The Monster of Peladon*, when I first became a regular viewer of the show. I clearly remember...

But this is not that story.

I was a voracious reader as a child, hoovering up every SF and fantasy novel I could find (good and bad). My local librarian knew me by name, I was there so much. So when I discovered the Target novelisations it was like manna from heaven: novels I could read about my favourite TV show – what could be better? I collected as many as I could find and...

Hang on, this is not that story either.

No. This is a tale of past mistakes and second chances. The tale of when I effectively let go of *Doctor Who*.

It's June 1995. I'm 28 years old and, well, things are changing. I've moved house three times in the last three years and I'm about to do it again. This time it's primarily because I got married in January and we want a place we can call 'ours'. In the last eighteen months alone I've been through some personal problems, helped (or hindered) my fiancée through being very ill in hospital and to be honest this feels like it could be the fresh start we both need. Little do we both know that in a mere three months' time my wife will fall pregnant with our first child – and that will turn out to be a very challenging period indeed. But for now, it's time for clear skies, fresh horizons and a positive step into the future.

The thing is, this younger me has always had a complicated relationship with change - especially clearing out the old to replace it with the new. I liked the familiar around me. I held onto stuff like a comfort blanket. I think it came from my dad, who never threw anything away. 'It'll come in useful one day,' he always said. That's probably why in 1995 I have a myriad of shelves with hundreds of paperback books and video tapes and boxes full of even more comics. I'll want to read them again one day. Just because there weren't enough hours in the day didn't mean that they had to go on the scrap heap, did it? These were my memories. Large parts of my life were bound up in those pieces of paper and cassettes of tape.

But sometimes I just had no choice. Here I was beginning a new phase in my supposedly adult life. The problem was, we just didn't have room for everything in the new house. Most of the videotapes can stay (the wife enjoys a good movie and has become a bit of a *Star Trek: The Next Generation* fan). The comics are not up for discussion. But the novels? Hmmmm. I spend what feels like hours looking through the shelves, deciding what I can bear to part with. I suppose all the *Conan* books could go back to my brother – they had been his in the first place after all. Did I really need all those *Perry Rhodan* novels?

'What about these *Doctor Who* books?' the someday ex-Mrs Jordan may have asked (I could be putting words in her mouth here; my memory is a bit patchy). I look at the few slim paperbacks on the shelf.

Wait a minute. A few slim paperbacks? What kind of *Doctor Who* fan ARE you?

Ah, okay...um...right. The thing is, there is an earlier part to this story. Another very similar and important moment of change. One echoes the other across time. Come on, if *Doctor Who* is a series all about time travel, grant me a bit of artistic licence. Cue the wheezing, groaning sound...

It's late 1991. I'm 24 and I've moved into a jointly purchased house with two friends. Things are going well (that'll soon change). Despite my share of the mortgage and bills, I've got enough disposable income to treat myself. Books and comics and videos and – well, you get the idea. But this isn't my house to scatter belongings where I like. Basically, I've got one bedroom to put all my junk in and despite a convenient set of built-in shelves there isn't enough space (have you detected the theme yet?). The comic books are taking over and those are the things I want to keep right now. Something has to go.

I looked at all the Target *Doctor Who* books I'd brought over from my parents' house, stacked in a corner of the room. Those multi-coloured spines, the lettering and logos never quite matching up. There were a lot of memories tied up in those volumes, a tale behind the purchase of almost every one. Family holidays where I spent so much time looking in bookshops that my parents almost wished they had booked me into WH Smith for two weeks instead. I'd collected almost the whole set (I never did get the last handful) but, let's be honest, I'd lost interest in *Doctor Who* a while back. The series had ended in 1989 and, like a plant without water, my fandom had withered away. Oh I still 'liked' the show, in that I preferred SF and fantasy television over any other genre, and it was always there, a bit like background chatter in the dark recesses of my subconscious – but something had just...gone. It wasn't special anymore. Besides, who needed novelisations of old TV episodes anyway, especially a kids' show?

Remember I said earlier that I don't like change? Well, there is a flip side to that. Sometimes I make spontaneous emotional decisions. On a sudden impulse, I gathered up the Target books, shoved them in a spare box and jumped in the car. I drove to the second-hand bookshop in Southend-on-Sea where I have spent many lazy afternoons browsing the shelves. The owner takes a cursory look at the full box as I hand it over. 'Hmmm', he says, making some comment about *Doctor Who* books being difficult to sell (he'd make a fortune now). 'This is a sizable collection. Are you sure?' I waffle about how I really need the space and, finally convinced, he takes the box into the store room and I walk out and don't look back. That was it. They were gone. No regrets.

Except, when I got home and climbed the stairs I found that I'd missed one. One solitary novelisation looking up at me from the floor - *Doctor Who and the Robots of Death*. I picked it up and shoved it on a shelf and went down the pub with my friends.

More wheezing, groaning noises...

Back in 1995, I looked at the singular book shelf amongst many. There were a couple of early Virgin New Adventures (where did they come from?) and the Jean-Marc Lofficier episode guides plus *The Robots of Death*. I stared at the cover by the vastly underrated John Geary. It still buzzed with barely contained electricity, the micro dots on the Doctor's face combining to make an almost photo-realistic image. It really is excellent – despite the huge memorable crease down the cover where I once sat on the book by mistake.

I cracked it open and flicked through the scant 102 pages, the edges slightly yellowed, the paper slightly rough under my fingers. By now, Mrs Jordan had got bored with my indecision and gone back downstairs. I settled onto the carpeted floor and begin to read. Fourteen concise chapters, each no more than eight pages long - it might be one of Terrance Dicks' shortest novels, but it certainly evoked the episodes from television. This was good stuff! Memories of Tom Baker and Louise Jameson and emotionless robots with fizzing red eyes come flooding back and along with them a kind of faint ache deep inside.

'Are you still up there?' came the voice of She Who Must Be Obeyed, shaking me from my reverie. I took one final look at the cover and placed the book with the others on the pile in the hallway. Inside me an elastic band anchored to a part of my youth has been at full stretch for four years. It finally snaps and vanishes. The next day, my wife takes the stack to the charity shop and a few weeks later we move house. I never see that book again.

The years pass. Children arrive and good stuff and bad stuff happens, as it often does in life. The relationship ends and I change house again - and not once do I think of that £1.35 Target book and its bright green background, or any of its companions. I move on to other things - other series and other passions.

But that's not the end of the story. The Doctor always finds a way.

More time jumps. Flashes forward:

2003 – I pick up a couple of Classic Series DVDs on a whim. A single flame begins to flicker in the dark.

2004 - *Doctor Who* is returning and thanks to the amazing Neil Perryman and his series of blogs, I'm actually thinking properly about the series for the first time in almost a decade. That flame is burning slightly brighter now.

2009 – I've started buying the odd old edition of the New Adventures and Eighth Doctor books. Novels I've never read before. The flame spreads.

2013 – The fiftieth anniversary and I'm definitely back in full fandom mode as I zoom around the country attending as many events as possible. It's not a flame now, it's a roaring fire.

2014 – On January 1st I start watching every single *Doctor Who* episode in order for the next 800 days.

2015 – I start my own blog and – stop!

There's something missing from all this fannish exuberance. A gap at the heart of things like an old wound that just never quite healed up and gives a slight twinge every now and again. An image of three concentric circles in blue, yellow and red reverberates around my skull, bouncing through the empty space within, and with it a word: 'Target'.

It was time to admit my biggest failing and rebuild a childhood collection.

I start looking and reach out to the people I know. Within a few weeks, an online friend sends me around a dozen of his duplicates and I'm up and running. It's a good beginning but there is one book I need to get to make this right – to make it 'official' that I was going to attempt this, no matter the cost in time or finances. You know the one I mean...

The slim package drops through my letterbox and I scoop it up. Gingerly I open the padded envelope and slide the contents out. I catch a glimpse of red eyes in a golden face before I turn it over to read the blurb on the back. Both it and I are twenty years older now but I think the book has aged better than me. I stare at that marvellous cover. It's wonderful certainly, but there's something slightly 'off'. Something not quite right. Then I realise - there's no crease down the middle.

I open the book to page 7 and begin to read:

'Like a city on the move, the Sandminer glided across the desert sands.'

The Island of Fan-Doom

Doctor Who and the Image of the Fendahl
by Jonathan Morris
Favourite *Doctor Who* book: *The Dalek Invasion of Earth*
by Terrance Dicks

About a dozen years ago, I was at a party somewhere in London, celebrating something to do with *Doctor Who*. I can't remember precisely what it was but I celebrated it heartily, drinking until I was very much in that state where the interval between 'thinking of things to say' and 'saying them' is no interval at all. I remember that Paul Cornell was there with the legendary Terrance Dicks, and he was asking people to talk to Terrance because he was feeling a bit left out. The problem was, everyone was far too intimidated to approach him because although Terrance is a very approachable person he is also, to a generation of *Doctor Who* fans, something of a God. When somebody is responsible for making you fall in love with literature, of turning you into a voracious bookworm, it's quite hard to think of what to say to them. When you're a small child, the names of authors on book covers are burned into the core of your being; you don't imagine them ever being real people you might get to meet in a pub. Terrance Dicks is one such name, up there with Roald Dahl, Enid Blyton and CS Lewis. His name just transports me back to childhood when I would sit absorbed in his books for hours, re-reading them again and again, my imagination running wild, filling my mind with the stories. Taking them into my heart.

But there Terrance Dicks was, an embodiment of the contradiction in terms that is a 'living legend', and he was feeling a bit left out. And so, emboldened by alcohol, I approached him with some other fans – we may have formed a 'throng' – and struggled to think of anything to say. For all of us it was a very awkward social situation to be in (and these are people for whom any social situation is very awkward) – because all the normal conversational gambits such as 'Hello', 'So what do you do?' or 'How do you know Tom?' all seem absurd, because this is Terrance Dicks you're talking to, the name from your childhood, not a stranger.

So instead – this is why I mentioned the alcohol earlier – we just asked him questions about *Doctor Who*. He took it in good spirits: he knew we were all fans, we all knew he was Terrance bloody Dicks, there was no point in dancing around it and trying to be grown-up and professional. I think, actually, he found it rather flattering. When it came to my turn, I asked him the question I have always wanted to ask him, which was: 'You know the bit with the chessboard in *The Five*

Doctors, where the secret to how to cross it has something to do with pi? Well – how does that work, exactly?'

His reply was typically concise, consisting of five words: 'I', 'have', 'no', a word that I'm sure you will be able to fill in yourself, and 'idea'. He went on to explain that he'd just made it up as a puzzle that the Doctor and the Master would be able to work out, which was probably too complicated for mere mortals to understand.

Anyway, having broken the conversational ice, I suddenly found myself Talking To Terrance Dicks...or at least, he was staring at me as though to say 'Is that it or do you have any more?' So I had to rack my brains for another thing to ask him and my brains came back empty, which is how I ended up asking him: 'You know, Terrance, when you were writing the *Doctor Who* books in the late 1970s, do you ever wish that you had been given more time to do them?'

'No, not really, I felt I always had enough time...'

'No, I mean, that you were limited, in the number of pages that you had to tell the story, that you couldn't do a better job...'

Terrance was now looking at me with great amusement. 'A better job?'

'I mean, no, the books were still great, but with say, *The Image of the Fendahl*, don't you wish that if you'd had more pages you could've done more with it?'

'You know,' said Terrance. 'Nobody ever mentions *The Image of the Fendahl*. I remember thinking I did a really good job with that, that it was one of my best ones.'

'No, I mean, I enjoyed it too, but...' And then I ground to a halt. The other fans in the throng – which may have included Paul Cornell and Steven Moffat, amongst others – were shaking with laughter as they had watched me break the conversational ice and plunge into the frozen lake below.

'I think maybe you should stop digging,' said Paul, throwing me a lifebelt.

And that is the story of the first time I met Terrance Dicks.

I think he may have been taking the p slightly by saying it was one of his best books. But who knows? Because, reading it again for the first time in thirty years, it's a very efficient piece of work. My only memory of reading the novel as a child was being intrigued by the hardback's cover illustration, which looked crude and unfinished compared to the covers by Chris Achilleos and Jeff Cummins. I love John Geary's mysterious, gothic cover for *Doctor Who and the Ribos Operation* but his artwork for *Doctor Who and the Image of the Fendahl* just looks like he had been given no reference photos. The novelisation itself, though, is by no means crude or unfinished.

What leaps out, reading the book now that I am familiar with the

164

television version, is how Terrance sorts out the story. He tidies up the plotting, fills in the holes and clarifies the characters' motivations. He goes through the script with a script editor's eye for detail and logic, and – as he did when he was script editor of *Doctor Who* – whenever the story doesn't quite work as well as it might, he comes up with clear, simple solutions. But he's not only looking at it with a script editor's eye. He's looking at the story with a *Doctor Who* fan's eye. He's got a very clear idea of who his readers are, what they want from the book and how to give it to them. They want the story told as straightforwardly and concisely as possible; they're not interested in long, flowery descriptions or characters' childhoods, they just want to know what happens. And they want it all to make sense, for the villain's plan to be clear, for the Doctor's plan to be clear, for everything to fit together.

The television version of *The Image of the Fendahl* doesn't quite do that. The structure is a bit off – the Doctor is a bit peripheral as the focus is on the scientists, and given that Stael and Fendleman are both obsessive, power-mad scientists there's a little bit of redundancy; a skills overlap. There's also a muddle over what causes the Fendahl to return – is it the skull, the Time Scanner, the Time Fissure, Fendleman, Thea, the Coven, or a combination of the above? Which is a shame, as otherwise it's an extremely good story, packed with terrifying ideas about ancient evils, all very Hammer Horror.

Terrance sorts it all out in the novelisation. Whilst Stael and Fendleman are both madmen, they are madmen with distinct agendas. The scene where the Doctor appears to be let out of a locked room by nobody in particular is cleared up (he gives the door a hearty kick and it swings open); Terrance explains where all the guards disappear to (in preparation for the Black Mass, Stael has sent them all back to London); there's a whole page explaining how Stael ended up in charge of a Black Mass. Terrance explains that the 'Priestess' and Fendahleen fail to notice the Doctor and Leela entering the cellar because they are 'absorbed in the ghastly ritual of transformation' and adds that Granny Tyler senses a 'darkness' like a 'cloud of evil' in the cellar. Most importantly, by dividing the story up into chapters, he creates extra cliff-hangers, moments of tension; most noticeably, at the end of chapter ten he turns a fairly anticlimactic moment in the television story – the Doctor deactivating the Time Scanner – into a moment of high drama as the Doctor declares that he has been too late to stop the Fendahl. 'I'm very much afraid that this planet of yours is doomed!'

Admittedly, it leaves a lot of the atmosphere to the reader – but it's a very dialogue-led story, where the horror is more in the creeping dread and the ideas than in the spectacle. That said, Terrance is a master at solving the problem of writing scenes where there isn't an

165

observer – these scenes are a real pain to write, believe me. And he adds one or two moody touches – the novelisation opens with a deliberate misquotation of *The Rime of the Ancient Mariner* by Samuel Taylor Coleridge (the lines are also quoted as some atmosphere-generating shorthand in Mary Shelley's *Frankenstein*). But my favourite bit, on re-reading it, is a moment on page 57, where Terrance explains why Leela knocks out a guard rather than using her knife. He writes, 'She felt rather proud of herself – she was really getting quite civilised!'

I'm not convinced it's one of Terrance's best books – he's set an extremely high standard elsewhere. As a child I always thought he wrote the best *Doctor Who* books, and as an adult, I realise I was not mistaken to hold that view. So I'm sorry if I was rude to you, Terrance. But on other hand, you gave me something that you've given countless readers over the past forty years. You gave me a good story.

Hungry for the Games

Doctor Who and the War Games
by Ian Wheeler
Favourite *Doctor Who* book: *The Key to Time*
by Peter Haining

There was always a kid at school who had more *Doctor Who* stuff than you did. In my case, it was a guy called Edward. When I went round to his house, he would lay out his collection of Target novels on his bed for me to admire and drool over. *Planet of the Spiders, The Giant Robot*...stories which were too long ago for me to remember and featured Doctors I had never seen. How I envied his collection with their brilliantly painted covers and funky 70s logo. If only I could have a collection of *Doctor Who* books of my own.

They were available at the school library as well, of course, normally hardbacks with their beautiful dust jackets. I'll wager many a copy found their way into a young fan's blazer pocket, never to return to the shelf from which they came. Most of them were written by Terrance Dicks and, though it may be a cliché, they really did help me to learn to read. I read *The Stones of Blood* in a single afternoon once, sitting on an old mattress in our attic and delightfully detached from the outside world. Dicks was the Master of Fiction as far as I was concerned - only Enid Blyton and Willard Price came close.

So it was perhaps inevitable that I would one day begin my own collection of Target *Doctor Who* books. I remember going into WH Smith (early 1980s, I think) with my Dad and what a big deal it was for me to select my very first title. I plumbed for *The War Games*, perhaps because it featured an older Doctor and seemed to represent a time long ago of which I couldn't possibly have had any first-hand experience.

The cover intrigued me. Soldiers from different periods of history, including a dashing military figure from the First World War. (When I would finally get to see the story many years later, I was bemused to see that Carstairs looked nothing like the image on the cover but was in fact played by the same bloke who played Colonel Crichton in *The Five Doctors*!). The reason the mix of historical figures intrigued me was that I had always had, and continue to have, an strong interest in history and I was keen to see how one story could incorporate characters from Roman times, the American Civil War and World War One - only *Doctor Who* can do this!

There were two ways of experiencing a Target novel - you'd either seen the TV story or you hadn't. Each book would be a very different experience depending on which category you were in. Reading a

167

Target novel when you had already seen the story on TV was fine. You were reading an adaptation and often it would expand on the episodes in question. Particularly later in the show's history, great stories such as *Remembrance of the Daleks* and *Ghost Light* (and not so great stories such as *Battlefield*) would be considerably fleshed out and expanded.

If you hadn't seen the TV version, reading the book was an altogether different and arguably more rewarding experience. Basically, you had to create a movie in your head. Oh, you'd have a bit of help. The cover picture and perhaps a few internal illustrations if you were very lucky, maybe the odd publicity shot you'd seen in *Doctor Who Monthly*. Perhaps a few passed-on memories from an older brother or sister. Other than that, you were on your own.

The versions I created in my head were far, far superior to the reality I would later see on video or DVD. My *Revenge of the Cybermen* (circa 1984), for example, was a gem. No sparse, cheap looking sets, no dodgy seventies-looking clothes for Sarah and Harry. As for my *The War Games* - well, that was something to behold, like *Doctor Who* directed by George Lucas or Peter Jackson. I often 'cast' real life actors as the characters I imagined in my head, so Carstairs was more David Niven than David Savile. It certainly never occurred to me that it would one day be possible to own a personal copy of all ten episodes of the story on a couple of wafer-thin shiny metal discs. I assumed those ten episodes would stay in the BBC archive forever, gathering dust. When I did finally watch it, it was good, but not as good as the version I'd created in my mind from the book. That was often the case.

So began my journey. I collected more and more Target books and arranged them on my bookshelf in the correct order when they started numbering them. For those that weren't numbered, I would tape a number to the spine myself. Mainly bought by myself, sometimes bought by my brother or an auntie for Christmas, the collection grew and grew. Yes, the Target novels in general and *The War Games* in particular were a pretty important part of my formative years. And it was only 85p! Imagine getting a book for that amount of money now. It's great to see that they've kept the old cover for the audio book – I hope it continues to entertain *Doctor Who* fans for many years to come.

An End and a Beginning

Doctor Who and the Destiny of the Daleks
by Simon Hart
Favourite *Doctor Who* book: *Cybermen* by David Banks

July 1990. It's my birthday and, as usual, there's a Target book-shaped present waiting to be unwrapped from my brother and sister. This time, I knew exactly which one it was going to be. There's only one it can be: *The Mysterious Planet.* The last one. I knew that there were going to be a few more released but from this point on, but from here on, I'd have a complete set. I unwrapped the little package and I grinned. I was right, they'd found the last book I needed! My set was complete!

My Target book collection began on my sixth birthday in 1981. I had money to spend, and Dad took me into town to see what I might like, though I think I was pretty sure what I wanted: *Doctor Who* books! We went to Bracknell's two books shops – JW Smiths and WH Smiths – and I looked through the books on the shelves and picked the ones I hadn't already read and the ones that had the most exciting looking covers: *The Three Doctors, The Brain of Morbius, The Giant Robot* and *Horror of Fang-Rock* among others. A little collection with matching Target logos that sat on a shelf in the living room for a long while then moved up to my own bedroom as the collection grew.

And it really did grow. I was given Target books for certain milestones: *The Stones of Blood* for passing my first swimming test, *The Invasion of Time* for the second. Friends and family would look out for them for me. I had duplicates that I'd swap with friends at school; we'd pick up second-hand copies of the books at jumble sales, school fairs, Bracknell market's second-hand book stall and charity shops. I quickly became very adept at spotting a Target logo in a sea of other books, often upset to find out it was one of Terrance Dicks's *Mounties* series or *The Story of the Loch Ness Monster* (that one was always around!)

Target books filled hours of long journeys, came to school for quiet reading time, filled rainy Sunday afternoons and pages of exercise books where I'd note down the ones I'd got and the ones I needed. I'm sure my parents were thrilled with how they kept me quiet for vast swathes of my childhood!

Christmas was the best time though. Every year we'd get to October and my Aunty Linda would phone us up and ask me to write her a list of *Doctor Who* books I hadn't got. She'd then diligently go to WH Smiths in Yeovil and check what they'd got on the shelf and if they didn't have them, she'd have four ordered in for me for my present. It was always exciting opening that present and finding out which ones she'd found for me that year. Almost invariably it would turn up in my stocking, almost as if my parents knew that that would be the one that would keep me in bed for a few hours longer, reading whichever one grabbed me most that particular Christmas morning.

The move from primary school to secondary school didn't change my passion for the show or the Target books, but did mean it was slightly more hidden than it had been before. So much so that it took until the end of my first year for me to discover that my friend Richard was also a fan. This spurred on the next phase of my obsession with the Target books. Pretty soon things became competitive and a race started between the two of us to see who would complete the collection first.

I lost by about a year.

That didn't really matter, though. It was fun turning up at school (a Target book always fitted neatly into the inside pocket of my school blazer) with a book that he'd not got and showing off that I'd got hold of it or finding a variation we didn't know about with a different cover or of course that I walk to WH Smiths after school together on a Friday afternoon to see if we could find the latest release and which of us got hold of it first. *Silver Nemesis* was found on a geography field trip in Reading town centre, *Terror of the Vervoids* turned up unexpectedly in JW Smiths (who'd stopped stocking the books for a while), an unexpected glut of older titles appeared in our new Hammicks bookshop, *Kinda* in the new Safeways superstore. Happy days!

Richard was an artist and so the cover artwork was something we'd always discuss. We both had favourite artists and covers and we'd spend hours debating which book had the all-time best cover. Jeff Cummins (who'd painted the covers that had attracted me when I started my collection off) was a huge favourite, as latterly was the wonderful work of Alister Pearson whose photo-realistic style greatly appealed to us both. We'd really look forward to seeing the forthcoming covers in *DWM* and *DWB* and wonder if we'd recognise the photo references that had been used.

It was with the covers that my Target book story began back in the summer of 1980.

We'd gone to visit my Uncle Graham and Aunty Chris. My cousin Adrian was (and indeed still is) a huge *Doctor Who* fan and he was ready to give his little cousin a big push into becoming another big fan of the show...not that I needed much of a push, as I'd already fallen in love with it pretty quickly after my Mum had introduced me to it at the start of season 17 the previous autumn. Adrian very kindly offered to lend me one of his Target books that Mum could read to me. He gathered a selection from his shelf and laid them all out on the floor

170

of his bedroom and said I could choose one to borrow.

I wish I could remember which ones I turned down, but all I can remember now is the one I *did* choose, *Doctor Who and the Destiny of the Daleks* by Terrance Dicks. Rather neatly, it became both my first TV story and my first Target book. I can remember making the connection between the cover and the story I'd seen the previous year and Daleks were always exciting anyway. It might not be Andrew Skilleter's most accomplished *Doctor Who* painting, but there's something magical about it for me. I still like the rather pensive looking Tom Baker and the Daleks in the smoke, sucker arms extended. Maybe it's a last vestige of childhood excitement still hanging in there? I like to think so.

The pattern for the next couple of years was quickly set. Mum read me a chapter an evening, so each book would last about a fortnight. I'd sit next to her, enthralled by all these wonderful stories. Fortunately, Mum had the good idea of asking in the library if they had any more *Doctor Who* books we could read. The Librarian found many hardbacks on the shelf and popped them all on a table for me to choose from. I remember clearly the wonderful Chris Achilleos covers for *The Web of Fear*, *The Claws of Axos* and *The Dalek Invasion of Earth* being amongst them, Jeff Cummins' *The Talons of Weng-Chiang* and Mike Little's lurid *The Deadly Assassin* cover too. I think I chose *The Web of Fear* that time, but we worked our way through them and many, many more over the next few years. Mum even recorded herself reading *The Invasion of Time* to me, which I listened to many times, much to her embarrassment!

It's by no means an original thought to share that I desperately wanted to learn to read well enough so that I could read the books on my own. I wanted to read them quicker than the one chapter a night regime we had with my Mum. And from *Doctor Who* I moved to Terrance Dicks' *Ask Oliver* series because they were shelved next to his *Doctor Who* books, then to Roald Dahl and *The Famous Five* and *The Secret Seven* and *Dragonfall 5* and I became a voracious reader.

Recently, we moved house. One of the most pleasurable things about this was putting my Target books back on the shelves. They might be battered and have seen better days, but there are memories related to every single one of them and I wouldn't ever part with them.

171

How Dare You, Ian Marter

Doctor Who and the Ribos Operation
by Erika Ensign
Favourite *Doctor Who* book: *Companion Piece*
by L.M. Myles and Liz Barr

Don't get me wrong, you were great as Harry Sullivan, but your grasp on *The Ribos Operation*, arguably the greatest story in the history of *Doctor Who*, is weak at best.

Because it's my favourite story, I was looking forward to the novelisation. I knew you were the kind of writer who adds context and extra flavour to your books. What better than to have more of what I love? Perhaps a sharp stick in the eye.

A few of the changes were fine. Give K9 an extra-long adventure trundling through the city and zapping guards? Sure! Add a scene where Unstoffe returns the shrieve's stolen clothes? No problem. But when you mischaracterise the Doctor and Romana's relationship, turning their banter to bicker and Romana into a nag, not reflecting the wry humour that makes Mary Tamm's performance so great! With all due respect Mr. Marter, one does not rewrite Robert Holmes's dialogue! You might as well rewrite Shakespeare, you clueless bounder. And how did you make the scene with Unstoffe and Binro so flat and perfunctory? I simply, as they say, 'cannot even' with this.

The moment I truly gave up on this book was when I realised you clearly did not understand the story itself. When Garron takes the Graff and Sholakh to see the crown jewels (and, of course, the jethryk), Book!Garron is positively shocked and angered to see Unstoffe in a shrieve's uniform.

Um, what?

TV!Garron was annoyed with Unstoffe, yes. But that was because Unstoffe's 'initiative' led him to try selling a map to a non-existent mine, not because Unstoffe was there in the first place. Of course Unstoffe was there and dressed as a shrieve - this was part of the plan from the beginning! Had they asked a real shrieve about the jethryk, the jig would have been up, and our charming rouges would be facing the wrong end of a laser spear.

While that scene should have been the last straw, I kept reading while my will to live slowly deserted me. In the end, I made it just over half way through the book before I gave it up as a waste of time. Life is too short for hate-reading a bastardisation of one of my favourite things.

Our Secret Handshake

Doctor Who and the Underworld by Tony Green

Favourite *Doctor Who* book: *The Cybermen* by Gerry Davis

By anyone's standards, in 2013 Doctor Who was a rock star. He had literally thousands of fans worldwide, millions of people followed his adventures and most normal people on the street knew who he was. By his 50th birthday, he was packing venues both in the UK and overseas and the news media were buzzing with excitement at the idea of commemorating this impressive milestone. It was the best time ever to love him...it was the best time ever to be a fan.

By anyone's standards, in 2013 I was not a rock star. To me - an (almost) middle-aged civil servant with aspirations to be a playwright - the world of *Doctor Who* was never further away. Strangely, for all the breakthroughs in communications and information technology that fans were enjoying, the programme seemed as distant and out of reach as it had done when I first became a 'fan' in the early 1980s. Okay, we could meet other fans far more easily (because there were more of them). We could discuss the show on any number of forums (because there were loads of them) and we had virtually instant access to any number of old stories, recordings and merchandise (because it was everywhere). However (and possibly because of this), my voice suddenly seemed very small indeed. Upon reflection, this is because being a *Doctor Who* fan had become 'easy' – in fact it had become almost fashionable. As a result there seemed to be nothing special in being one anymore – you were just another face in a very big crowd.

We members of the 'old guard' can always take a personal pride in not letting the Doctor down or giving up during the so-called wilderness years. Like war veterans who still wear their medals with pride even as the society they fought to defend largely ignores them, we can talk of still buying *Doctor Who Magazine* in 1995 or not letting our DWAS membership slip in 1998 when hope seemed forlorn and the flame was not burning remotely brightly. In many cases, there was the feeling that this loyalty should be rewarded but, ultimately, nobody would care. And we few, we unhappy few, didn't even have medals.

This is nothing new in the world of fandom – and by this I mean *any* kind of fandom. Consider the fans of Chelsea football club who supported it in the 1980s and 1990s – the barren, trophy-less years when a Russian oligarch's billions were the deranged dream of a madman. These same people now tread a bitter path to join the queue behind thousands of 'glory hunter' fans and pay through the nose for tickets to see a team they had been faithful to all through its dark days of mediocrity. They tut and curse that, in the arrival of success at the club, something had been taken from them, their fealty had been ignored; they were literally and figuratively now just faces in the crowd.

Many *Doctor Who* fans are no different. You see them still, searching the faces at a convention for a single person they recognise, muttering 'It's not like Panopticon 5 – that was for the *real* fans!' Or having a conversation with a fan at a party and wearily rolling their eyes as it transpires that this 'fan' knows nothing of the events at Fang Rock or Traken and only wants to talk about Weeping Angels. And In some extreme cases, success is just as feared and resented as failure – in the same way that, for other veterans, winning a war can be just as costly as losing one.

But there are a few precious things that still set us apart - us heroes. The Target books are one of them; a boon that only the old guard really enjoy or understand. As I sit on my train (which runs from London to Cardiff) during my morning commute, I can fantasise about sharing a carriage with Stephen Moffat, or Mark Gatiss or Nick Briggs – the superstars of the new era. I can imagine introducing myself as a fan and laughing their secret, thinking that I was one of the 'new breed' – just another face in the crowd with no scars of battle and no understanding of Peladon, Galaxy Four or wheezing, groaning noises; as separate from them as the old school Chelsea fan is to the multi-millionaire owner of their favourite club.

There is little I can do to prove them otherwise – knowledge of the show matters not. No – in order to prove yourself as a worthy member of the old guard you needed something uniquely 'us' – and that thing is Target books. These pennies from heaven; impossible to replicate, of no interest to the internet generation; a bond that crosses years; a medal after all. Target novels are the knowing nod that the old guard can give to one another, saying a silent 'I was there'. Target novels are a veterans' club that is unique and satisfyingly exclusive.

Because of this, even the unloved stories, those rarely talked about even by the old guard, can become magical. A case in point is *Underworld*. Any fan or even casual viewer can watch *Underworld* now on DVD. Seeing and having an opinion on a classic story no longer separates the new fans and the old - but the Target novels do. Because of this, the story of *Underworld* is as unique and evocative as any other. So I would talk about the beautiful covers, or the way the novelisations made some stories even better and created a link to the show long before home video or organised fandom. And they would nod, content that I was a man worthy of their time and tolerance.

And we would talk about *Underworld* - not just the tale of a borderline clanger in the drab vault of Season 15, or an unloved DVD dumped into a boxed set of other unloved DVDs, but a story of how all

174

these wonderful books are special – and that makes the stories they depict more special for it. Me, Stephen, Mark and Briggsy (as he lets me call him in my mind) would talk together, we would laugh, and we would be part of a family that is not exclusive to television producers or series superstars. For a brief instant, we would all just be members of the old guard.

When I got off at Reading, they would bid me farewell with the pleasant memory of meeting a real fan just like they were. I was no face in the crowd.

And when I got home, I would pick up my copy of *Doctor Who and the Underworld* and thank it for helping me connect with these people. With a smile of nostalgia, I would pull it from my shelf, noting that I didn't need to think too hard about how I came by this book or the story attached to it. As I opened the cover, I would confirm my suspicions with a sad shake of the head. There was the sticker on the front clearly labelling 'my' copy as PROPERTY OF PINKERTON PRIMARY SCHOOL LIBRARY. This is because, as it turns out, aged eight, I was not only a creative and imaginative child who sought any and every opportunity to be lost in the world of the Doctor Who novels. I was also a thieving little Shobogan.

As the Third Doctor says in *The Five Doctors*: 'I'll return it at the first opportunity.'

Don't It Make Your Brown Eyes Brown

Doctor Who and the Invasion of Time
by Alan Stevens
Favourite *Doctor Who* book: *The Myth Makers*
by Donald Cotton

One day in 1980, I went into WH Smith and purchased *The Invasion of Time*. To be honest, I only got it because I'd read all the other Target *Doctor Who* books of stories I hadn't seen on television. Also, some misguided Auntie had recently bought me *Doctor Who and the Sontaran Experiment*, so I'd at least have the complete Sontaran oeuvre.

That night, I turned to chapter one, 'Treaty for Treason', read down to 'The human was a girl called Leela. She was tall and strong, with brown eyes...' and stopped.

Leela had blue eyes, and had done since the closing minutes of *The Horror of Fang Rock* when they had changed from brown following the pigmentation dispersal caused by the flash of the exploding Rutan mothership. I checked the front cover ... and yes, this had indeed been written by Terrance Dicks, the very writer who had also scripted the original TV version of *The Horror of Fang Rock* and the subsequent Target novelisation.

What was going on? Had Leela's eyes drifted back to brown again? As the one and only BBC transmission of *The Invasion of Time* had concluded approximately two years earlier on 11th March 1978, there was no way I could check. All I could do was believe in Terrance; after all, he must surely know what he was doing, and his following description of Leela pacing 'up and down the control room like a great cat' appeared to encapsulate the character perfectly.

So I moved on, but reaching page 31, stopped again at this exchange between the two elderly Time Lords, Gomer and Savar:

> 'I'm making a study of what I call wavelength broadcast power transduction.'
> Savar covered a yawn. 'Really?'
> 'I've noticed lately, say over the last decade or so, an enormous fluctuation in relative wavelength transduction over a particularly narrow band...'

Is Gomer referring to power being transducted (the action or process of converting that power into another form) over a

176

wavelength as a broadcast...or is he referring to the broadcast of power over a wavelength via transduction, but then, if you broadcast over any wavelength it's going to involve transduction of some form, so to call it 'wavelength broadcast power transduction' is to create a tautology. Was Gomer meant to be stupid, or an enormous pseud?

I read on to page 60 and found this exchange between the Doctor and Cardinal Borusa:

> Borusa said thoughtfully, 'So, the Vardans can travel along wave-lengths (sic) of any sort. And since an electrotemporal field is needed for communications, they can read thoughts.'
> 'At almost any distance—if their attention is concentrated.'

Then on page 90, K9 tells the Doctor:

> 'Master, I have located the wavechannel being used by the invaders. It is an outer spatial exploration and investigation channel, number 87656432 positive.'

Adding, on page 91:

> 'The circuit is used by the Academy for instruction in exploration.'

So this must have been the 'narrow band' Gomer was referring to, across which power was being transducted...but then this seemed to contradict what Rodan of space traffic control had stated earlier, on page 49:

> 'Nothing—nothing—can get past the transduction barrier.'

So if this was the case, why did the Doctor have to hide his thoughts from the Vardans once he had landed on Gallifrey and was shielded behind the transduction barrier? Also, how can a wavechannel be used to explore and investigate outer space? We're not talking about a radio telescope, but a wavechannel that can somehow pick up information and broadcast it back to the Academy. None of this was making any sense at all. What was I missing?

Then one evening I happened to tune into an episode of Carl Sagan's *Cosmos* that dealt specifically with Red Shift, Blue Shift and the Doppler effect.

I began to sweat as I once again took *The Invasion of Time* down from the book shelf, flicked to page 47 and read the conversation between the Doctor and K9:

'Suppose I can throw a mirror cast? A shadow shift to create a false image for space traffic control?'

'The plan is feasible. I suggest you proceed as follows—' The Doctor held up his hand. 'Can I finish, please? I shall reflect the transmission beam off the security shield, feed it back through a linked crystal bank and boost it through the transducer...if you destroy Security Control after I feed in the doppler effect and eliminate the Red Shift then surely the Invasion must succeed?'

I then applied my newfound knowledge. In this circumstance, I reasoned, when mentioning the Doppler effect, the Doctor must be referring to the shift in electromagnetic radiation emitted by the Vardan fleet as it moves relative to Gallifreyan space traffic control. As the fleet approaches at near lightspeed, there would be a move to higher electromagnetic frequencies, which would be seen as a shift to the red spectrum on approach and to the blue spectrum, or lower frequency, when receding. So why would the Doctor need to feed in the Doppler (sic) effect, if the Doppler effect is already there? Also, if he eliminates the Red Shift, does this mean he's going to introduce a Blue Shift instead, to make it look as if the Vardan fleet is moving away from Gallifrey?

Then another problem struck me. I turned to page 49:

There was a buzzing from the instrument console. 'Oh, not again,' said Rodan wearily. 'Excuse me.' She touched controls and one of the monitors lit up. It showed a series of brightly coloured dots moving across a dark background. Rodan spoke into a communications unit in the same bored voice. 'Traffic control here. Yes, I have them on tracking. Clearance authorised.' She switched off the communicator. 'Primitive space fleet, neo-crystalline structure, atomic power and weaponry. On its way to blast some planet into dust, I suppose.'

Is this meant to be the Vardan fleet? If not, then where did the Doctor's 'false image' go? However, if this is the Vardan fleet, then it doesn't fit with the description of their flagship given on page 53:

The space ship was enormous, terrifying, a long, sleek killer-whale of space. Its hull-lines were sharp and predatory and it bristled with the weapon-ports of a variety of death dealing devices. Everything about it suggested devastating, murderous power.

Also, how many Vardan ships were there? On page 8 it states:

> On the screen, against a backdrop of stars, was a visual display of the Vardan battle fleet, squadron upon squadron in the typical Vardan V-formation, heading remorselessly towards Gallifrey.

And then on page 53 we have this:

> Lights began flashing madly on Rodan's console, and she stared incredulously at the instrument readings. 'It can't be...no one would dare.' She flicked the communicator switch.
> 'Space traffic control here. An alien space craft, two spans distance course zeroed in to Gallifrey. Raise transduction barrier to factor five. Repeat factor five. Immediate and urgent. Red Alert, repeat Red Alert!'

So the Vardan space fleet now appears to consist of only one ship.

Although I had encountered discrepancies in previous Target books—for example, if both *Doctor Who and the Terror of the Autons* and *Doctor Who and the Doomsday Weapon* are to be believed, Jo Grant joined UNIT twice—what I was finding in *The Invasion of Time* appeared to be massive internal continuity errors. Here's another example. On page 97 it states:

> the Doctor grabbed K9 round the middle and with a grunt of effort set him upon the Presidential desk.

However, on page 110, it reads:

> In the Chancellor's office, the Doctor lifted K9 down from the desk.

This suggests that Cardinal Borusa took K9 off the Presidential desk, went to his own quarters and put him on his own desk!

We also have the case of the disappearing Jablif. On page 105 we are told:

> The Doctor pounded along the corridor with Leela, Rodan, Andred, two of Andred's men and an Outsider called Jablif close behind him.

179

But on page 108, this happens:

> Leela, Andred, Rodan and the two guards hurried through the door and the Doctor counted them in. 'Five, four, three, two, one... One, two, three, four, five, no more.'
> He slammed the door behind him and bolted it.

Where did Jablif go? He turns up again on page 114, just in time to get shot:

> Andred and Rodan managed to follow K9 to safety, but the loyal guards were shot down in the fighting, and Jablif, the Outsider, fell, badly wounded.

Also there is the matter of the Great Key. The Doctor tells us on page 113:

> No president can have total power without the Great Key, isn't that so? To protect the Time Lords from dictatorship, he gave the Great Key into—other hands.'

However, all the Great Key does is power the De-mat gun, a weapon that can de-materialise its victim, but so what? How is that the ultimate weapon?

Then, after the Doctor's final confrontation with the Sontaran Commander Stor, we get this on page 139:

> In the vast, shadowy Panopticon, everything was quiet. Stor was gone. The fusion-grenade was gone. Even the De-mat gun had disappeared. All that remained of it was the triggering device, the Great Key of Rassilon. It lay on the floor, close to the outstretched hand of the Doctor, who lay still as death.

Following which, on page 140, the reader is informed that the Doctor has lost his memory of recent events and that, according to Borusa, this was caused through 'the wisdom of Rassilon.' So does that mean that Rassilon built properties into the Great Key to ensure that whenever the De-mat gun was fired into an exploding 'atomic grenade' the bearer would lose his memory and the rest of the gun would vanish? If so, why?

I decided to return to the beginning and read the book all over, but this time checking every fact with my science teacher, Mr Lewis.

'Sir, can your eye colour be made to change from brown to blue by staring into a very bright light?'

'No.'

'Are you sure?'

'Yes and for God's sake don't try it yourself, you'll damage your retinas.'

'Okay, if a man had the ability to transmit himself across a wavelength, would he also be able to read your mind?'

'Where are you getting this from?'

'*Doctor Who.* If you change Red Shift into Blue Shift would it make a fleet of space ships look like one space ship to a female traffic controller?'

'Are you serious?'

'Yes, of course I'm serious. If I counted down from five to one and then back up from one to five very fast while standing in a lead lined room, could that make someone disappear?'

'Eh?'

'What does wavelength broadcast power transduction mean?'

'Nothing at all. It's gobbledegook. What do you expect me to say?'

'I expect you to say it makes sense!'

Mr Lewis gave me a pitying look and walked off. It was at this point that my poor child brain was faced with three options:

a) Continue to believe that the book was error-free, and I had simply failed to comprehend it.

b) That I should start hating *Doctor Who* for having betrayed my trust.

c) That I should learn from the experience, and realise that something being written down in a book didn't make it automatically true or free from mistakes.

I chose the first option, because after all, the blurb on the back of the book does state that 'Terrance Dicks is a skilful professional story-teller' and that's a quote from 'British Book News', whoever they were.

Bloody Marvellous

Doctor Who and the Stones of Blood
by Nick Mellish

Favourite *Doctor Who* book: Will Brooks' *500 Year Diary*

My name is Nick and I am in a very lucky position. Back in my early twenties, I was able to successfully pitch an article called Target Trawl for the Canadian *Doctor Who* fanzine *Whotopia*. The premise was simple: once an issue, I would read and review one or two Target novelisations, working my way through them in publication order.

That was lucky thing number one. Lucky thing number two was that people seemed to like it, so much so that now, in my early thirties, I am in the process of finishing up a book containing all the previous articles spruced up and tweaked, with reviews for every novelisation not already covered along with some extras, including the two audiobook-exclusive novelisations by David Fisher of *The Stones of Blood* and *The Androids of Tara*.

The *Stones of Blood* as it originally stood came at a time in the run of novelisations where they were being written and thrown out with few flourishes. Most were novelised by Terrance Dicks at a rate of seemingly three a day, and whilst Dicks is a great writer, the workload most definitely showed. It's not that Dicks' novelisation of *The Stones of Blood* is bad at all: it isn't. It accurately tells the story originally televised: that, and nothing else. It is what it is, and what it is, is merely ordinary, which is a shame as *The Stones of Blood* definitely isn't an ordinary story: it's a very good one, a cut above many others in Season 16.

It's lucky, then, that Fisher got to tackle it again years later. Much is the same: it's nippy still, it tells the story we've seen on screen, and it gets the job done rather well. It's the tiny moments that make it stand out: the parts where Fisher dips into the history of the stones and the mysterious Vivien Fay. The insights into the characters' minds and experiences; the depth in sentences that let it shine. It fits neatly with the start and end of the Target range, when authors really let rip and expanded, contradicted, experimented and had fun with the adaptations. It feels full of heart in a way many didn't.

When I started writing *Target Trawl*, I was warned by everyone that the middle period for the novelisations would be a hard one to do anything interesting with, and that's not unfair. I know that articles on stories such as *Time and the Rani* have alone commanded up to two or three sides of virtual A4 paper, whereas *The Keeper of Traken* had but 25 words. Frankly, there is just more to say on one than there is on the other because there is more in the telling, for better or worse.

182

I'm lucky to be in a position where I've been able to read them all, luckier still to be in one where I've been able to talk about doing so, and as fans we're terribly lucky that David Fisher came back to say, 'No, it's okay, I can do this properly, let me show you how...'

It's stories such as *The Stones of Blood* that stand tall amid the many. How lucky we are to have it told twice over.

The Quest is the Quest

Doctor Who and the Androids of Tara
by Mark Smith
Favourite *Doctor Who* book: *A Celebration* by Peter Haining

The first single I ever bought was *The Funky Gibbon* by The Goodies and the first LP I ever bought was *Zenyatta Mondatta* by The Police, but for the life of me I cannot remember the first Target *Doctor Who* novelisation I ever purchased. I have plenty of memories of buying them. I bought *Doctor Who and The Revenge of the Cybermen* in a discount book store in Bourke Street, Melbourne and the 1982 reprint of *Doctor Who and the Crusaders* in Myer Northland. But my most memorable purchase is the one that caused me the most trouble!

In 1984 I had started high school and was introduced to Geoff, who was two year levels ahead of me and in my eyes was the superfan of the school. It was Geoff who introduced me to Minotaur Books in Melbourne, who were (and still are) purveyors of all things sci-fi. The shop had a shelf that we used to go for miles, fully stocked with *Doctor Who* books. In Australia at that time, there was a dreaded three-month wait for the latest novelisation to appear after its UK release. Canny Minotaur air-freighted the latest novelisations from the UK, happily passing on to their customers a hefty $1 surcharge on top of the $4.95 (Australian) recommended retail price. Never ever get between a retailer and a fan!

The first book I purchased from Minotaur was Peter Grimwade's *Mawdryn Undead* and from then on, every Saturday afternoon I would make a trip into town and spend my (meagre) earnings from my delivery job buying a book a week in order to complete my collection as quickly as possible. By mid-1985, I looked at my then-ninety-strong stockpile of books on my bookcase with a sense of pride. However, there was a gap: not a Douglas Adams/Eric Saward type of gap, but a gap in the shape of the novelisation of *The Androids of Tara* which, unlike that particular segment of the Key to Time, was proving to be very elusive indeed.

Amongst my (albeit) small number of fellow *Doctor Who* fans in high school, this book took on near-mythical status and the only person I knew who had obtained a copy was of course Geoff, whose sister lived in country Victoria and had stumbled across a copy in a newsagent. Thus he was able to claim proudly that his collection was now complete.

One Saturday afternoon in mid-1985, I asked my good friend Andrew to accompany me on my usual Minotaur run. Andrew, along with my other friends Mick and Glenn, had come from different

184

primary schools but found each other through a mutually shared love of those ABC televisual staples regularly repeated between 6:00 7:00PM weekdays: *The Goodies*, Kenny Everett and *Doctor Who*. But their love was not as obsessive as mine (in fact, one kid told me that he used to like the series until he met me and as I was always talking about it, he had gone off it!). Andrew was a recent convert (he even audio taped *The Twin Dilemma*, which goes to show that the difference between madness and dedication is wafer-thin) and he had amassed his Target collection at a faster pace than me, but just like me, he had an *Androids of Tara*-shaped hole on his bookshelf.

Upon disembarking from the tram in Ye Olde Melbourne Towne, we made our way up Swanston Street towards Minotaur. I was (and still am, thankfully) rather lanky and my legs strode purposefully towards my destination. I entered the store slightly ahead of Andrew and made my way to the novelisations shelf. I rapidly scanned the titles (which were lined up in alphabetical order and not story order as it should, by divine right, be) and there under 'A' was a single solitary copy of *The Androids of Tara*.

My heart stopped. I did a double take, then a triple take to make sure I wasn't imagining its presence. But there it was, bathed in a shimmering glow, calling out to me. With ninja-like reflexes, my hand lashed out and snatched it off the shelf. At last, after all this time, I held a copy of *The Androids of Tara* in my hands, staring at the admittedly strange cover depicting a Fourth Doctor with slightly Auton-esque features.

By this time, Andrew had arrived in the store and asked, 'What do you have there?'

I tried to say, 'Nothing to see here, move along,' but didn't. I showed him the cover and the look on his face spoke volumes as to his disappointment and betrayal.

'You ran here on purpose so you could buy the book,' he blurted out.

'No I didn't,' I replied (I wasn't going to make matters worse by mentioning that my legs were much longer than his) and then I walked calmly to the counter to make my purchase.

Once we left the shop, an uncomfortable atmosphere pervaded our forty-minute tram ride home. My attempts to engage him in conversation were batted off with abrupt one-word answers. This stone cold silent treatment also extended to the walk back to his house. I knew that Andrew could be a bit moody but here I was copping the full brunt of it and I didn't want the seemingly innocent task of buying a book to complete a collection to get in the way of our friendship.

I said to him, 'Give me $5 and you can buy it from me.'

He stopped in his tracks, thought for a moment, then pulled out his wallet and handed over the five dollar note. I handed over the green and white Minotaur bag and straight away his demeanour changed. He had gotten his way and now held my prize in his hands. When we got back to his house, we went into his bedroom and just like the Key to Time itself he slotted the book between *The Stones of Blood* and *The Power of Kroll*, completing his collection. More importantly, at least to me, our friendship remained intact. In the months afterwards, I maintained my vigil for another copy of *The Androids of Tara*, but to no avail.

Teenagers are fickle creatures and move onto the next thing rather quickly. Four months after acquiring the book, Andrew had gone off *Doctor Who* completely and the next big thing in his eyes was the WWF (World Wrestling Federation). His excuse was that he was more enamoured of Nicola Bryant than the Sixth Doctor and he then made the decision to start offloading the merchandise he had obtained now that his fleeting interest in *Doctor Who* had died. One day, I decided to help him out with his after school job (posting marketing material into letterboxes) and when we got back to his house, he walked into his bedroom and handed over *The Androids of Tara* in lieu of payment.

I was ecstatic that the book had been returned to its rightful owner and when I got home I slotted it in between my copies of *The Stones of Blood* and *The Power of Kroll*. I stood back and admired my complete collection. (The book itself could be described as 'workmanlike' - the embellishments to the script are subtle but not expansive - but nevertheless it is an entertaining read.)

During the remainder of the 1980s I kept watching the show (much to the dismay and protest of my McCoy era-bashing school mates) and I kept buying the books, where the 'hardest to obtain' mantle passed to Philip Martin's *Mindwarp* and then Terrance Dicks' *The Wheel in Space*. Luckily, I obtained these with less drama. My mates Mick and Glenn would take great delight in re-arranging my Target novels out of transmission order: 'No, *The Curse of Peladon* does not follow *Earthshock*. Get it right!'

As for Andrew, he left school at the end of year 10 and although I did catch up with him a number of times afterwards, unfortunately over time we lost touch. In the early 1990s I was told that Andrew had died in very tragic circumstances. Re-reading *The Androids of Tara* for this essay did bring back a lot of fond memories of our times together.

I have sold, bought and in some cases re-bought many items of *Doctor Who* merchandise over the years but the one thing that I have never let go are my Target Books. Some of the spines are sun-worn, but I can never part with them as they played a major part in my teenage years. Along with memories of great friendships, reading these small slivers of *Doctor Who* history developed my larger love of reading, and for that, I love them to bits.

It's This, or it's Ray Bradbury

Doctor Who and the Power of Kroll
by Stephen Dowell
Favourite *Doctor Who* book: *The TARDIS Eruditorum*
by Philip Sandifer

The first *Doctor Who* book I owned was a used copy *The Doctor Who Monster Book*, bought at a school jumble sale in the autumn of 1977. That was the year I got into *Doctor Who*, after previously cowering behind cushions when the programme had come on. What led to this volte face I have never been able to determine, though I have a sneaking feeling it may have been due to the programme being heavily trailed on Swap Shop. I can dimly recall clips from *The Masque of Mandragora* being played on there, sandwiched between phone-ins with Brian Jacks and Keith Chegwin legging it about a playing field in Dumfries, which I am guessing would have piqued my curiosity. *The Monster Book* then was a reference text while I waited each week for another episode. It would also fuel anticipation that some of the monsters reproduced in papery black and white images would return. Of course, this was an anticipation that was almost completely starved for two years while we got Seasons 15 and 16. The anticipation would manifest itself in odd ways, the most memorable being a brief moment at the end of episode 2 of *City of Death* where I was certain that Linx was going to reappear.

This is where the novelisations helped. The next *Doctor Who* books I owned, bought for me by my mother out of the blue one Saturday afternoon, came from the newsagents where she worked. They seemed to sell every kind of magazine possible (I would later buy copies of *Fangoria* and *Starlog* there) and it also did a trade in selling paperbacks cheaply, piling them up in baskets out the front so customers would have to rummage through to find what they wanted. There was no system or order - once the books were gone, they were gone. So I came to own slightly weather-beaten copies of *The Claws of Axos, The Brain of Morbius, The Crusaders, The Mutants* and *The Cybermen*. These were shelved next to a tatty copy of *The Daemons* which a friend's brother had donated to me. I tried to ignore the crayon scribbled on the back cover.

Emboldened by my tiny library, I attempted to position myself as the premiere *Doctor Who* follower of the school playground. I held this post for probably one day before being usurped by John Coal arriving at school with copies of all the books featured on the back page of *The Doctor Who Monster Book* in perfect mint condition. I stared at his pristine copy of *The Tenth Planet* with envious eyes. Newer titles were needed.

This is where the annual family holiday helped. We had settled into an annual routine when it came to our summer holiday: Pontins, Prestatyn Sands. Apart from being the filming location for *Holiday on the Buses*, which the camp was still trading on years later, this was also the place where I was first able to choose a novelisation. Each day I would visit the camp's supermarket to peer at the spinning rack of paperbacks with its small but vital selection Chris Achilleos-covered Target books. I was promised I could have one as a holiday treat and all that was left was for me to make my choice: this choice took days while we went swimming or donkey derbying. Eventually the selection was made: *The Auton Invasion*. I had achieved a microscopic victory in my quiet (and undeclared) war against John Coal but there was still a nagging feeling: yes, the book was new, but it dealt with an old story. It wasn't current.

This is where the public library helped. The estate that I grew up on may have looked like the centrepiece of a concrete salesman's brochure, unrelenting in its greyness, but it was blessed with a superb library. Its healthy supply of Doctor Who novelisations were all shelved neatly away in the first bookcase of the children's fiction section and the titles rotated in and out on a regular basis with some books more heavily desirable than others. Everyone had to adhere to the three loan limit – and don't even think about trying to take out three *Doctor Who* novelisations at a time. That would just lead to a disapproving parental frown and a suggestion that perhaps some variety was needed, so I would have to select something else, inevitably one of Willard Price's interminable adventure series, last borrowed, and no doubt hastily returned, in 1972.

The library eventually became wise to the popularity of the novelisations, first by introducing an 'If you like this, then try this' scheme. This usually meant you would find a copy of *The Android Invasion* propped up next to some junior science-fiction collections or an Asimov, its glorious Chris Foss painted cover giving no hint to the dry-as-sawdust content. (Invariably the *Doctor Who* book would be snaffled away by an eager reader, leaving the whole display looking off-kilter.) The library's second plan was to introduce a *Doctor Who* readers club: a title would be read, a chapter a week, to a group of easily-pleased fans on Saturday afternoons in the summer months. The readings would be prefaced by craft sessions 'where robots could be built' (reality: cardboard rolls and egg boxes taped together with varying degrees of success). Needing to find something to do on a Saturday afternoon that did not involve watching *World of Sport*, I naturally attended these clubs.

To the library's surprise (I expect), this club was a success, to the

188

extent that the local newspaper took a photograph. I still have a copy of the photo: I'm there, trapped in a black and white image, one of twenty children all spending a couple of hours on a Saturday listening to a librarian read through *Doctor Who and the Loch Ness Monster*. But it was listening to this read though that I discovered that for all my self-proclaimed status as an authority on *Doctor Who*, there were still areas of the programme about which I knew nothing. Who the hell was this 'Harry' fella the librarian was telling me about? To my mind Tom Baker was current, so therefore his time on the show should hold no surprises for me. In my head his period was all mapped out via the companions: Sarah Jane, Leela, K9, then the two Romanas. I found that I was getting less excitement from reading stories from the past – I wanted to relive something I had recently witnessed.

This is where the 1980 family holiday to Prestatyn helped. Obviously there was only so much that Pontins could do to keep everybody confined to their camp – there are only so many tea dances and bingo a family can endure. Usually by the Wednesday or Thursday we would venture beyond the camp gates (gates that were crowned with barbed wire 'for our own safety') to see, as my Dad put it, 'what the town has to offer'. This usually translated into wandering up and down the high street looking for somewhere to have lunch. Dad would stop at the first place he found and make very agreeable noises about the menu taped in the window. We would agree that a plate of sausage, egg and chips would indeed be splendid. But rather than go straight in we would always just walk up to the end of the street to see if there was anything else. This happened every time we visited a holiday resort and every time, thirty to forty minutes later, we ended up back at the first place we had looked at.

This time, we stopped in at a bookstore before returning back to the first place we had looked at. While my brother immediately charged towards the railway books (he was and still is a rail enthusiast) I felt the gravitational pull of a whole stack of *Doctor Who* novelisations. This was an impressive selection – better than the library could offer. Multiple copies of some titles, many very recent, stories I had seen only in the previous year. The crunch moment arrived: Mum informed us that we needed to get a move on as these were the dark ages when restaurants and cafes often did unspeakable things like closing after lunch-time! It was time to make up my mind. The spines were all lined up before me and I reached for the story that made a massive impact on me over Christmas 1979: *The Power of Kroll*. (Later re-watching on DVD will reveal plenty to make one blush with embarrassment, but this is 1980 where the most futuristic thing is a Gary Numan album.)

Kroll's tentacles are entwining themselves around my hand, the memories of that story rushing back through my fingers. The book is mine. Then, faintly, I hear my Dad, who has another book for my consideration: Ray Bradbury's *The Martian Chronicles*, which we watched on TV that summer, reprinted in a new tie-in edition. I had been just as taken with that show as I had been with *The Power of Kroll*.

There is an alternative pathway where I put back *The Power of Kroll* and go with the Bradbury. How that works out is hard to say – perhaps it takes me further away from *Doctor Who* and closer to science-fiction literature in general? Or am I so confounded by Bradbury's flowery prose that I retire from science-fiction entirely? (Unlikely in all honesty, but you never know.) Perhaps this is one of those 'fixed points in time' that we hear so much about these days – that buying *The Power of Kroll* is what must happen and no amount of Ray Bradbury TV tie-ins are going to change that. So, with time moving against me, the decision is made: *The Power of Kroll* became the first book I ever purchased with my own money.

What follows from that decision? A steady and continued love for the *Doctor Who* novelisations naturally. Christmas 1980 will be the first time I ask for novelisations as gifts and like the dormant Kroll, my tiny library grew and grew. However, everything comes to an end and by 1984 I am buying and reading my last novelisation, *Inferno*. Blame it on a change in the family holiday routine maybe: in 1983, we travelled instead to Malaga on the Costa del Sol. In need of a book to read, I panic grab *The Shining* at the airport. It may have been an entirely different reading experience to a 130-page *Doctor Who* book, and I may have harboured illusions that I was now reading something more grown-up. Still, it was those novelisations that laid the strong foundations upon which all future reading would be built.

Armageddon? Out of Here!

Doctor Who and the Armageddon Factor
by Dylan Rees

Favourite *Doctor Who* book: *Script Doctor*
by Andrew Cartmel

Poor old *The Armageddon Factor*, a story liked by few and loved by fewer. With its overacting, shoddy sets, over-stretched story and unsatisfactory resolution, it probably ranks along *Underworld* and *Meglos* as one of the three big clangers of Baker's tenure: the three who fail to rule. When fans discuss Season 16 it is often said that the Key to Time season was 'a wasted opportunity' or 'a failure', but what I think they actually mean is 'The Key to Time season is a lot of fun before the Bristol Boys come along and bugger it up at the end!' This should have been the crowning jewel of the season, an epic finale, the ultimate battle of good versus evil, but instead it's corridors and control rooms.

As a child growing up in the late 1980s and early 1990s, it was pretty well known that Tom Baker's tenure was the golden era of *Doctor Who*. Most of the people who knew this cared nothing for the distinction between Hinchcliffe, Williams and Turner, couldn't tell their Morbius from their Mandrels. They just knew that Tom Baker's seven-year run was the best *Doctor Who* there was. And who was I to disagree? All the fourth Doctor stories available on VHS were from the Hinchcliffe/Holmes era until 1991 so it was a long time before it became obvious to my young eyes that not all was great in the Baker era.

However, my local library had a number of hardback Target novelisations, mainly stories from the Graham Williams era. I can still vividly recall the terrifying red-eyed Nimon peering at me off the shelf; Tom Baker's smug face as an enormous squid scaled an oil rig behind him; my mother struggling to pronounce Romanadvoratrelundar. I loved them all with their glorious covers and promise of adventure, the allure of the hardback somehow more appealing that the paperbacks I picked up in the shops. All except one: for some reason, the library only held a paperback copy of *The Armageddon Factor*. With its puny page count and its pastel-coloured cover, there was no promise of monsters, just a bored-looking Tom Baker standing in a generic sci-fi room. I never finished it, I never liked it

When the Key to Time season finally arrived on VHS in 1995, *The Armageddon Factor* and I still just didn't get on; it remains to this day the damp squib at the end of a fun season which not even a Terrance

191

Dicks novelisation could save.

My final childhood memory of this story is from 1997, when *Doctor Who* stories were repeated in their entirety on UK Gold on a Sunday morning and my mother would use this as a good excuse to get me out of bed: I'd happily watch any *Doctor Who* even if I already owned it. On this particular Sunday, *The Armageddon Factor* was scheduled to run, but owing to the tragic death of Diana, Princess of Wales, this omnibus re-run (which features the death of a princess) was replaced by *Planet of the Spiders* (which opens with a car crash). So unloved is *The Armageddon Factor* that it wasn't even rescheduled, just quietly dropped as they moved onto the next season.

Poor old *The Armageddon Factor*, unloved in book form, on screen and on VHS. Certain stories go through a revaluation in the eyes of fans, but I fear this one will always be the clunker that couldn't.

Based on the BBC Television Serial by Terry Nation

Doctor Who and the Keys of Marinus
by Andrew Curnow
Favourite *Doctor Who* book: *The Gallifrey Chronicles*
by Lance Parkin

I always press PLAY on the DVD of *The Keys of Marinus* with great enthusiasm. It never lasts.

The mix of wobbly sets and over-earnest am-dram acting are too much to overlook, and although I don't begrudge letting Billy Hartnell take a fortnight off, I don't approve of the attempt to fill the gap with the gung-ho Altos, a would-be hero with an aversion to wearing trousers. It's a story whose reputation would have been greatly improved if some over-zealous BBC employee had consigned it to the furnace instead of *Marco Polo* or *The Savages*.

Whatever. I still come to it each time with an optimism which I know is misplaced - and it's all because of how much I loved it that very first time I experienced it, not as a creaky set of telerecordings, but through the Target book version that I got for Christmas 1980.

Philip Hinchcliffe's adaptation doesn't, to be honest, expand very much on the original scripts. There's no Hulke-style prologue on the creation of the Conscience Machine, nor any attempt to flesh out just who and what the Voord actually are (although we do learn that they favour the BXV sub-oceanic assault craft and that their attack on Arbitan's island takes place at 701 zeniths precisely, which is nice). Instead, what the book does is to give the story a breathless 'RKO serial' type of pace, along with a sense of scale which 405-line weekly television could never hope to achieve. If I'd been older, I might have questioned why the Morphotons give Sabetha a genuine key rather than just an illusory one; or why the block of ice entombing the third key and its guardians comes with a handy melting device, or...

There are lots of perfectly reasonable questions which might fairly be asked, but which didn't matter when I was nine and rattling through a brand new story at a rate of knots. Experienced over a few days between Christmas and New Year, rather than over six long weeks in 1964, the story never lets up. There's no time for quiet reflection because with a quick twist of the travel dial, pop! we're straight into yet another adventure.

It also opened my eyes as to what *Doctor Who* can do, which is of course pretty much everything! On TV I'd seen such extremes as multiple Mona Lisas and a scheming, shape-changing cactus... Now I

193

discovered that *Doctor Who* could also be a quest story. It could explore ecological disaster and snowy wildernesses. It could be a courtroom drama or a horror story or a love story, it could debate good versus evil, free will versus control - and somehow, almost impossibly, it could do all that (and lots more!) in just 128 pages.

P.S. The same Christmas I got *The Keys of Marinus*, I also got *The Abominable Snowmen*. For some reason, probably a misunderstanding of something I'd read in *Doctor Who Weekly*, I was certain it was a purely historical story. That's despite the huge great monster on the front cover...

It's Never a Final Goodbye

Doctor Who and the Nightmare of Eden
by Tony Green

Favourite *Doctor Who* book: *The Cybermen* by Gerry Davis

The last Target novel I read, *Full Circle*, was in 1987 as I waited for the paper shop where I did my morning round to open. I was always early and killed the time on those bitter mornings by reading a book small enough to fit in my anorak pocket until Mr Pavis unlocked the door and invited me in with the welcoming grunt of a man who had spent twenty years in the RAF and barracked paperboys with the same vigour as a poorly turned-out recruit. Once I realised being insanely early was unnecessary, I set my alarm a few minutes later and arrived with the lights of the shop already on, Mr Pavis rounding on a customer for coming in before he was ready.

Just like in adulthood when you see a friend for what ultimately becomes the last time, you never say, 'Cheerio, send a card to my funeral if you happen to hear about it.' It's always, 'Let's not leave it so long next time.' I didn't know *Full Circle* would be my last Target book and it was always in my mind to read another. Soon the time I might have spent reading Target novels was absorbed by comics, mandatory reading for school and, ultimately, a telly in my room.

Many years later, I developed a yearning for the joys of things past. This was probably linked to the loss of my father but I've always been nostalgic by nature. I dug out my old Space Marines, grasping back for the time when the only thing I had to worry about in life was the application of a +4 armour save. I pulled out my old *2000 ADs* and framed a few of the most iconic covers. I picked up a Target *Doctor Who* novel...

I chose *The Nightmare of Eden* because it was a story I had not yet seen and so could read without any preconceptions – just like I did all those others in the mid-1980s. But, as with anything else one locks onto to regain the joys of a lost youth, something was missing. After a few chapters, I put the book down and went to help my friend assemble a wardrobe. The book stayed on my bedside table for a few weeks before being cleared away. I won't pick it up again. Today, my coat pocket is too small to fit the book into ... and it makes me sad.

Maybe it isn't a final parting. Perhaps one day I'll pick up another of these lovely little books again. I hope so.

'Let's not leave it so long next time.'

Horns of a Dilemma

Doctor Who and the Horns of Nimon
by Eddy Vortex
Favourite *Doctor Who* book: *The Daemons*
by Barry Letts

What can one say about *Doctor Who and the Horns of Nimon*? It was a pedestrian novelisation of a sub-par story. Now, don't get me wrong, I think Terrance Dicks is fantastic, but at the time he was almost the sole writer, writing nine of that year's ten novelisations, producing manuscripts that were practically a screen-to-page transference with only minor embellishments, and certainly in the lower end of page counts.

Anyway, enough of that, let me tell you a story about what life was like around the time of *The Horns of Nimon*. All sitting comfortably... good.

Back in the days of yore, long before disillusionment with the Moff or the fans moaning about anything, the Internet notwithstanding, *The Horns of Nimon* was by most reckonings the worst *Doctor Who* story ever made. If you thought being a *Doctor Who* fan in the late 1970s or early 1980s was embarrassing, these episodes did nothing to lessen that. Try doing a school book report on it, you'll see what I mean. Even in parts of fandom, it was the story that was never to be named and was referred to as (the dreaded) One-Oh-Eight.

As a twelve-year-old watching, to say it was a disappointing story is giving it far too much credit. It was impossible to suspend belief, because if they weren't going to take it seriously, why bother? When the news broke that Graham Williams was leaving and John Nathan-Turner would be the new producer *and with Barry Letts* exec-producing, there were high-fives and hallelujahs all round. It was seen as the first step in the right direction to regain a better, more acceptable *Doctor Who*, though hindsight makes us reconsider that too. It may have taken another ten years but declining quality ensured that the show was finally on permanent hiatus.

Before being successfully relaunched in 2005, this hiatus became known as The Wilderness Years and at some time during that period, the Williams revisionists started to appear, fans who had re-evaluated their own opinions or at least measured his tenure against other eras and said, 'You know what, *The Horns of Nimon* was meant to be satirical, and it was clever.' This ethereal 'They' published their thoughts through various forums, and lo, they looked down with contempt on all and any that proclaimed that the story was still, in fact, crap.

Meanwhile back in the 1980s, fandom, ironically, was still building strongly around the world. A large number of fan clubs and fanzines sprung up in a short time and everyman and his K-9 wanted to produce or be published in a fanzine, mainly to complain about the quality of the most recent *Doctor Who* stories and how story x or season y or Doctor Z wasn't a patch on the last story / season / Doctor. Of course, most of these clubs and fanzines died out fairly quickly (it turned out that this was hard work). There was no inter-web-super-info-spam-way and news about the series was still obtained from reading newsletters delivered six to twelve times a year, produced on a gestetner (look it up) because even affordable, reliable photocopying was not yet available, and don't even talk about offset printing. But still we joined as many clubs and subscribed to as many fanzines as we could afford, even some of the ones overseas, and they all needed names to show you how clever the editors were. Some names alluded to something you'd probably never dreamt of being able to watch back in 1980 (looking at you Space Museum / Steel Sky / Web Planet); others were cryptically incongruous (Zerinza / Vipod Mor); and later on some just used plain childish humour (Toilet of Rassilon). Outside of the eternal DWAS tomes of TARDIS and Celestial Toyroom, fanzines were often amateurish and folded rather quickly, though some of the better ones that lasted many years improved in quality in both visual presentation and content, with many of these fanzines attempting their own comic strips and/or novelisations of stories.

Reflecting on this today, the production of some of the fanzines by shall we say 'dedicated' fans was obviously a desire to leave some sort of legacy throughout the annals of fandom history. Like the Phil Morris wannabees of today who want to be forever remembered as being the finder of *The Tenth Planet* part four because they were the 128th caller to Sierra Leone to ask them if they are sure that the TV Station burnt down, or for making another YouTube video about the missing episode plight that will somehow strike sense into the hoarders and get them to return *The Space Pirates*.

Anyway, I digress and must get down from my soapbox. 1980 was also the era when the collecting of the affordable video cassette was a dream and even recording the show with a personal VCR was in its infancy. The fannish life consisted of going out each and every month to meet people and discuss *Doctor Who*, read and swap fanzines about *Doctor Who*, and of course moan about the latest episode.

Time moves on and we all mature and our tastes and likes change. The show, like the Doctor, also changes over time and you do see things in a new light, as did fandom when the VCR became affordable and access to copies of old episodes became possible. Meeting with fellow *Doctor Who* fans really became an excuse to see episodes you

197

hadn't seen before. There was less social interaction as everyone had to stay quiet whilst the episodes were on. Later on, when you could buy episodes on video and, later, DVD, the need to meet people just kind of evaporated.

Fan clubs still exist today, as do some fanzines. The original editors of those early 'zines started doing some of that professionally and worked for the likes of Starburst and the fan clubs once again focus on social events as quite frankly everyone has probably got every episode of *Doctor Who* they want that is available. It's quite nice that some 35 years later, fandom has come full circle.

So, we come to the end of my short little tragical history tour and its reflection time. New episodes were made and it wasn't long before a *Timelash* or a *Delta and the Bannermen* came along, and now I can look back and say, 'maybe *The Horns of Nimon* isn't all that bad.' I look at it today and readily acknowledge it by its name and not its story number.

Love and Monster

Doctor Who and the Monster of Peladon
by Andrew Curnow
Favourite *Doctor Who* book: *The Gallifrey Chronicles*
by Lance Parkin

I've got almost the full set of Target books on my bookshelf and almost every one of them carries with it a very clear recollection of where and when I got it. Granted, in the case of the mid-eighties that mostly means 'it came through the letter box' because at that time I was getting them on subscription from John Fitton Books & Magazines. That aside though, and just at random, there's *Logopolis*, which I picked up en route to a holiday in Scotland at Easter 1982; *Dragonfire*, purchased from the back streets of St Ives in 1988; *The Tenth Planet* and *The Tomb of the Cybermen*, bought together in a branch of Bulloughs one glorious 'Cyber-Saturday' in 1978; *The Monster of Peladon*, which came from the Carlisle branch of WH Smiths in July 1982.

Ah, the Carlisle branch of WH Smiths! I've not been there since...well, since July 1982 in fact, so it may not be the same now. (It may not even be there now!) From fading memory, though, it was a sprawling two-storey shop, one whose floors seemed to stretch on and on into an unseeable distance. Downstairs there was stationary and magazines and toys and in 1978 you could buy a Palitoy Stormtrooper there for 99p. Upstairs, reached by a glorious, sweeping, Norma Desmond-style staircase, were the books.

It's a shop that can be thanked for many a book, not just *The Monster of Peladon*. I saw *Destiny of the Daleks* there in 1979 only a few weeks after it had aired and, believing that I had grasped the workings of the release schedule, I put 'the French one' on my list to Santa that year. The very first time my brother and I were allowed to catch the bus into town without our parents was the shopping expedition during which I picked up *State of Decay* – so although I should be enraged at the cover's gaudy pink logo and Tom wearing the wrong jacket, I can't help but love it. I bought *The Green Death* there and read it in a single sitting and on the same day bought the glory that is and is Jean Marc Lofficier's *Programme Guide*, which somehow achieved the impossible and replaced *The Making of Doctor Who* as THE most important Doctor Who book ever written. *The Doomsday Weapon* (in its burgundy Delgado reprint incarnation) came from there too – a present from my Aunt who was holidaying with us at the time.

A present of a Target book was a great thing back then. I was given

The Day of the Daleks as an unbirthday present on my brother's 10th birthday. It took a chapter or four before I realised that I had mistaken time-travelling guerrillas for time-travelling gorillas (and in my defence the confusion was fuelled by the fact that, surely, that's one of the gorillas on the front cover) but for a time at least it was my favourite of the lot.

The Monster of Peladon was a present too, a spontaneous purchase by my Dad one Thursday evening. We had gone into WH Smiths to pick up a new football for my brother, and in the interests of fair play Dad asked if there was anything I'd like. Whenever I've told this story in the past I've always remarked on it being uncharacteristic of him, as a man not generally given to bursts of spontaneity – however, I can't help but recall that earlier the same year there had been similarly spontaneous and unexpected purchases of both the *Doctor Who* and *Blake's 7* Summer Special magazines, so maybe I do Dad an injustice. Maybe I was just spoiled (and to be fair, the phrase 'unbirthday present' which I've used so casually in an earlier paragraph probably clinches it).

It wasn't the latest book to have been released but *The Curse of Peladon* had only just been repeated in an unheralded and unexpected series of repeats on Monday nights. (Perhaps, like my Dad, the BBC had discovered some previously-unexpected reserves of spontaneity.) So, with my C90 audio recording of *The Curse of Peladon* still ringing in my ears, the sequel was an obvious and irresistible choice. (I'm sure the Pertwee fans would like it if I said here that it was a case of serendipity.)

Today, whether we're referring to the books or the TV shows, I know that *The Monster of Peladon* is not a patch on its predecessor. I could see that the sequel was a much slimmer volume than the original even in 1982, but I could also see that unlike the original it contained the actual words to the Doctor's Venusian lullaby, on page 51. At the time that sort of thing seemed to matter a great deal. Nowadays we probably look back and consider the very best of the Targets to be those that expand and enhance and even completely rewrite the original, but I certainly went through a phase where my test of quality was how close the book was to the TV version. I even went as far as putting bookmarks into each book at the point where the cliffhangers would have come on TV – an easy task in the case of a Terrance Dicks, not so easy with a John Lydecker. I suspect it was the many wasted hours spent trying to find the episode 6 cliffhanger inside *Doctor Who and the War Games* that finally made me give it up.

The Monster of Peladon turned out to be the very last book I ever got from the Carlisle branch of WH Smiths. It was also the last Target book I got before an unpleasant sort of snobbery kicked in. The onset of adolescent hormones and the growth of a more sneering side of fandom with an increasing sense of entitlement combined so that I began to look down my nose at the prospect of a new Terrance Dicks book. Ian Marter was giving his books a more brutal, edgy style; and in a very exciting move, original screenwriters from the 1960s were being brought in to novelise their own stories. Which meant that the slim, by the numbers, straightforward adaptations seemed second-rate by comparison.

I was of course quite wrong. Yes, his first few Target books are still extraordinary children's books today – but actually, in a different way, so are all the others. That they even exist, for one thing. I wouldn't be able to boast about having almost the complete set if it wasn't for Terrance's work (either that, or it wouldn't be much of a boast because 'the complete set' would only be about a dozen books). A victim of its own success, the more popular the range became, the greater the need was to get more of them out – and by adapting them in a simpler fashion, Dicks was able to give us something close to a book a month. But that's not the main brilliance of them, which is something I've only come to appreciate more recently.

By adopting a 'house style' of straightforward adaptation, it gives us an entirely new perspective on certain stories. Opinions formed on the basis of watching the TV version can be very much different when reading the book instead. Only in the crazy world of Target books could I make the following claim without being immediately sectioned: *The Monster of Peladon* is as good as *The Talons of Weng-Chiang*. It genuinely is. Get both books together (go on do it now, I can wait) and compare the opening pages. With great economy, and great precision, the opening page of each one sets up the world in which it is set – whether it's the old-time world of a class-ridden Victorian London, or the alien world of a planet previously visited by the Doctor. Before the action has properly begun, every reader, whether they are a dyed in the wool fanboy, or somebody who has never even seen an episode of *Doctor Who* is, as it were, on the same page.

That's the other brilliance of these books of Terrance's. It's as if he's treating each one like it might be the first *Doctor Who* book that the reader has ever picked up. Ian Marter's *The Invasion* (much as I love it) faithfully starts with the TARDIS and its crew reconstituted, exactly as it did on TV following on from the end of *The Mind Robber* the week before. That's fine for a fan who knows what's going on, but it's totally baffling and alienating for any first-timer. Compare that with a Terrance book – before the Doctor's even arrived, he's brought the new reader up to speed.

That's also why his famous shorthand descriptions work so well. We may chuckle at the 'impossibly large control room' variously piloted by a man with a 'pleasant, open face' or a 'shock of prematurely white hair' but it means that even if you've never heard of Peter Davison or Jon Pertwee, and even if they're not on the cover of the book, the new reader has an idea of who the hero is. Compare that to John Lucarotti's *The Aztecs* which, again much as I love it, fails on this score by totally failing to describe the regulars in any way at all.

The last reason why I now rate those Terrance Dicks books so highly is because, surely, they must have helped to get kids reading in the 1970s and 1980s. Nowadays we have the Quick Reads campaign; back then we had libraries and Terrance Dicks. I haven't done any research into that claim of course, but consider - there's nothing daunting or off-putting about his books. They're just challenging enough to make the novice reader pleased at learning a new word ('capacious' was a particular favourite of mine) but they're not so dense and wordy and impenetrable that they are abandoned before the end of the first chapter. His marvellous sense of economy, getting straight to the point, but accurately so, and his straightforward way of making each book a page turner, making each chapter not too long but not too short either, all these things combine to make them unscary books, friendly, welcoming, encouraging.

So I look back on the day I was bought *The Monster of Peladon* with a mix of affection and melancholy, as being in hindsight the end of an era. I can't in all honesty recall exactly how I responded as I read the book, whether I rattled through it, or whether I managed to make it last a week or so. What I do remember, though, is the thrill of getting it, and that's really what it's all about, isn't it?

Market Forces

Doctor Who and the Creature from the Pit
by Daniel Seymour
Favourite *Doctor Who* book: *Damaged Goods*
by Russell T Davies

Wimborne Market on the south coast of England in the late 1980s was my own personal nirvana for the seeking and acquisition of *Doctor Who* items. Although I couldn't afford much with my pocket money (a pound a week), I liked to browse these items and dream of owning them anyway. I was twelve years old and every Sunday morning I went there very early in the day with my family, whose primary purpose for visiting was to stock up on bargains for the house; boring items like foodstuffs, clothes and such like. My reason for going was to have a look at the goodies on offer at the stall run by the man I referred to as 'The *Doctor Who* Man', who sold from his stall in a dark corner of the market an abundance of used, rare (even at the time) *Doctor Who* items (and other sci fi mechanise of which I took no notice as I was a Whovian).

The treasure trove that interested me the most were the large dusty boxes he had laid out on a wobbly, dusty trestle table which contained (faded spine always showing first) lots of used, precious Target books. I think they were his own copies and used to wonder why he was selling them when, if I had them all in my possession, I would never ever part with them. It was fun running a finger along the uneven line of spines of these books and occasionally stopping to pull one out to read the blurb and examine the book for its 'usage factor' (i.e. worth parting money with). I believe they may have all been first editions and in hindsight I should have snapped them all up but being a kid I didn't have the money. At that time I was reading at the rate of one Target book per weekend, and on one particular Saturday I had just finished *Death to the Daleks* so now was a perfect time to buy a new Target book.

I couldn't take my time choosing that day because my family were pushed for time, so I hurriedly plumped for *Doctor Who and the Creature from the Pit*, not a satisfactory choice because I thought the volume was too slim and the spine didn't look as vibrant as the rest of the range, being typed in small lettering. In those days I was a little too fussy when parting with money and always pictured how the spine would look on my shelf. I think to this day my award for best spine goes to *Paradise Towers*, a combination of orange background and white lettering which worked well for some reason. The story itself is in my top five so, yes, I'm an odd fan with weird tastes.

203

I started reading *The Creature from the Pit* that same November evening; it was dark, rainy and cold outside, which to me was the perfect atmosphere to read a Target novel. This combination of novel and weather noise and lamplight proved to be a perfect mix, as very easily I was able to get into this story of dark dangerous pits full of despair and bleak, overgrown forests where all manner of horrible beasts and wolfweeds lurk. The fact that Enya's *Oronico Flow* was playing on the radio in the next room bolstered my fantastical experience of this novel.

When the Doctor made it to Lady Adrasta's citadel early in the novel, I could image that being a place similar in vein to the castle from *The Brain of Morbius* with crashing thunder outside, lit only by candlelight. It probably wasn't described as such in the novel but my imagination tends to embellish these stories with personal touches. The Doctor's journey through the tunnels under Chloris and subsequent encounter with Organon reminded me of scenes in *The Hobbit* when Bilbo became separated from the dwarves in the mountain before he meets Gollum: Organan was a friendlier character but the tunnels were just as dark and scary. In my mind the wolfweeds were able to thrash and generally lash out long twigs and branches and the creature itself, Erato, was gloopy and gelatinous and I could almost feel the slime envelop me when it 'attacked'. (My primary memory of Erato from TV was similar albeit slower, not seen as much and without appendages which, watching it now, I discover is painfully untrue.)

Although I was not really happy with the conclusion (the creature turned out to be a good guy!), I darn well enjoyed the journey to it and it left me wanting to read more of these types of fantasy/gothic *Doctor Who* stories. The following week I had another pound coin to spend which immediately went on a copy of *The Ribos Operation* plucked from that same dusty box.

Once I found a copy of *The Hitchhiker's Guide to the Galaxy* erroneously placed there next to a copy of *The Horns of Nimon*. Even at my young age I appreciated some of the humour David Fisher used in *The Creature from the Pit*; thinking about it now I wonder if the stallholder knew what he was doing.

The Enemy of My Family

Doctor Who and the Enemy of the World
by Robert Smith?

Favourite *Doctor Who* book: *Remembrance of the Daleks*
by Ben Aaronovitch

I nearly got killed reading *The Enemy of the World*.

I was nine years old and we'd won the holiday of a lifetime. Well, sort of. We were a poor, working-class family and my aunt had entered a competition and won a stay at a cottage. Which sounds lovely... only it was deep in the Australian bush, about six hours' drive in a car full of four kids including my baby sister. (My childless aunt sensibly made her own way there). The cottage was of the classic Australian variety: weather-beaten, remote and only one door. Which doesn't seem like much, but that's where I almost died.

My mother had forgotten to bring bedsheets, so we had to journey into the local town to buy some. While we were there, I asked to look in the local bookstore, as I often would whenever I was dragged along on shopping expeditions. At the bookstore, I always had one goal: to look for *Doctor Who* novelisations. I preferred the Tom Baker ones, but I was okay with Jon Pertwee at a pinch. We didn't have much money, so I was only allowed to buy them once in a while. However, today I was given some cash and told I could buy a book if I wanted.

Being way out in the boonies, the local bookstore had just one *Doctor Who* novelisation: a solitary copy of *The Enemy of the World*. I'd never heard of the story, but it had the logo on it, so I snapped it up. Recommended Retail Price: $3.50.

I started reading the book in the car while waiting for my parents. (It was the early 1980s; that sort of thing happened back then.) Despite the story being wholly unfamiliar to me, I loved it. I wasn't sure who was on the cover, although I was fairly sure the bald guy must have been the Doctor. Or rather, the Doctor in his guise as Salamander. (Who else would they put on the cover? Besides, the book does point out that Salamander's hair was slicked back.) I couldn't quite tell if the woman in the space helmet and huge collar was Victoria, Astrid or Fariah, though I later decided it had to be Victoria. This is how I visualised this TARDIS team for the next several years.

When we finally got back to the cottage, my parents and siblings were hanging around by the car, but all I wanted to do was go inside and read so I walked up to the only door, little realising that this was almost the last thing I ever did. There were four steps up to it and they had no backs. As I went to climb the steps, my head buried in this wonderful book, a sudden movement made me jump. That involuntary jump saved my life.

It turned out that, this being Australia and all, there was a snake living under the house. And not just any snake: one of the world's deadliest. (As I said, it was Australia.) The snake's major point of entry was the missing backs from the four steps leading up to the house. So if you went to walk up the steps, the snake would dart out and try to bite you.

Furthermore, this wasn't a problem that you could do anything about. The only way to get at the snake was to put your arm into the crevice, a la Peter Davison in All Creatures Great and Small. Which wasn't the wisest idea, all things considered. We were way out of the way from anywhere, so there wasn't anyone to call; you just had to suck it up and coexist with a venomous creature actively trying to kill you. Ah, Australia.

The solution was to leave the door open at all times and for everyone to take a running jump at the entrance. So you'd leap over the stairs into the doorway. The snake would invariably dart out anyway, but — fuelled by fear — we were quick enough. Even my mother, who was jumping my ring these at all than a not the way evolution isn't happening to humans. Australians aren't incredibly hardy by chance, you know.

My response was to stay inside most of the time. Fortunately, I had *The Enemy of the World* to keep me company. I read that book as quickly as I could. Then I read it again. The fact that it was set at least partly in Australia was great, even though every character in *Doctor Who* talked like Crocodile Dundee in my head. By the end of the vacation, I knew that book backwards. Ian Marter's style was vivid and engaging, bringing it to life beautifully.

When I finally got to see the episodes in 2013, I had the unusual experience of watching the film of a book I loved, where the film was almost exactly what was in my mind's eye. Which, weirdly, made *The Enemy of the World* a more successful visualisation than *The Lord of the Rings*. Giles Kent even had an actual Australian accent — although Rod's attempt at one is so terrible, it took me several minutes to figure out what he was even attempting.

And what, you may be wondering, became of the snake? My cousin sorted it out. He was a decade older than me and hitchhiking his way around the country. He sat by the hole in the steps for hours, patiently waiting for the snake to emerge. Eventually it did, and he grabbed it by the neck, extracted it from its lair, killed it and hung its body on the fence, presumably as a warning to all the other snakes in the area that this house was not to be messed with.

As I said, it was Australia. The place where you can go swimming in your long johns, get strafed by bullets fired from a hovercraft and meet the enemy of the world — and where the enemy of my family finally met its fate. I guess I'm just glad that the snake wasn't a doppelganger for any of my family members. Now that's scary.

First Things First (and Necessarily in That Order)

Doctor Who and an Unearthly Child
by Erika Ensign
Favourite *Doctor Who* book: *Companion Piece*
by L.M. Myles and Liz Barr

I love beginnings. Always have. *Star Wars* is my favourite of the original trilogy. *The Fellowship of the Ring* is my favourite of *The Lord of the Rings* – whether it be the film or the book (yes, even Tom Bombadil). Meeting new characters and watching them take their first steps into a larger world is the kind of thing that reels me in like no continuation or conclusion ever can.

Like most people, I didn't start watching *Doctor Who* from the beginning. My childhood was a mishmash of episodes from all different eras because I saw whatever my mom was watching. My first experience with Target novelisations was the same —I had access to the random assortment of books my mom had collected.

As many fans have done with the televised series, so I tried to do with Target books. I've heard it called 'The Pilgrimage'—where you start at the beginning and go through all the stories in order (all the stories you have access to, anyway). I'm a big fan of order, so this always appealed to me. When I decided to read Mom's Target novelisations, I started at the beginning with *Doctor Who and an Unearthly Child* by Terrance Dicks. I can't tell you how happy I was that she had the very first book.

I read along as Barbara and Ian laid in wait for Susan to arrive at the junkyard. As they discovered the mysterious police box that felt alive. As the Doctor whisked them away to prehistoric times. As Za and Kal vied for control of the clan of cave-dwellers. As the newly-formed team TARDIS developed their relationships and were captured, escaped, were re-captured and re-escaped. It was delightful. I continued with other books, but eventually life got in the way and I stopped reading at whatever book I'd gotten to.

Then one day, I decided it was time to return to the Target world. But, being a very left-brained nerd-girl, I felt it was my duty to start again at the beginning. To do otherwise wouldn't have been right. So I dove back into *Doctor Who and an Unearthly Child* and re-experienced the genesis of that first TARDIS crew before moving on to other volumes.

Enter life, once again, and I stopped reading before I got through all the available books.

Lather, rinse, repeat.

Confession: I stole – ahem – borrowed many of my mom's Target books when I went away to college. Surrounding myself with comfort from home was a natural thing to do. However, as nice as it was to have her books around, I wanted my own. The geek gods must have smiled on me because I discovered a local used book store with a huge selection of Target novelisations. As a poor college student, I couldn't afford much in the way of luxury purchases, so these books became my reward for completing a paper or midterm — occasionally they were just a treat on a day I was feeling down. It didn't happen a lot, but it was often enough to grow my little collection bit by bit.

When I picked up a new book, did I go home and dive into it like a normal person would? Why, no. No, I didn't. Because that obsessive love of order and organisation took over nearly every time. That's right. It was back to *Doctor Who and an Unearthly Child* again. And again. And again. Because when you're in college, life happens faster and more frequently than as a child at home. And each time I dropped the books for a while, I felt compelled to start back at the beginning again. By this point, I have no idea how many times I've read that slim volume.

When I moved from Wisconsin to Canada, I sold all my Target books. It was a necessary but painful act, especially since I'm pretty certain I never got around to reading many of the later novels. I just tell myself that I read *Doctor Who and an Unearthly Child* enough times to make up for it.

I look forward to reading all the other essays in this book once it's been published. I just hope I can get through them all before life gets in the way...

Chapter 3

Flashpoint

1982 – 1987

The Target range increasingly invites original script-writers to adapt
their own stories, but 17 books are still by Terrance Dicks. The first
73 books are allocated library numbers alphabetically; from *Time-
Flight* onwards they are numbered as they come out. Many books are
~~now given photographic covers until the final stretch. Nigel~~
Robinson spends three years as range editor; innovations include two
original novels.

Also in these years

Breakfast TV begins in Britain... the IRA blow up a hotel in Brighton
during the Conservative Party Conference... *Star Wars* moves from
the cinema to American defence policy... Rock Hudson dies... Andy
Murray born... Live Aid makes musical and charity history... *Top Gun*
makes a star out of Tom Cruise... *Doctor Who* goes on hiatus...

Batty

Doctor Who and the State of Decay
by Vince Stadon
Favourite *Doctor Who* book: *The Writer's Tale*
by Russell T Davies and Benjamin Cook

When I was a kid, I wanted to grow up to be an immortal alien vampire with a fruity Welsh accent who could summon at will all the bats in the world to attack people, just like my dad. He also wanted to be an immortal alien vampire with a fruity Welsh accent who could summon at will all the bats in the world to attack people, rather than to continue to be a rather melancholy foreman of a ragbag crew working for ICI, endlessly painting the Severn Bridge the same dreary shade of grey. He told me of his dream to switch jobs from boss painter to unearthly immortal bloodsucker over breakfast one morning, directly after he'd told me not to read *Doctor Who and the State of Decay* by Terrance Dicks at the table.

'Put your book down, son,' he'd said, 'You're not in a sodding library.'

I put the book down and spooned down a gloop of soggy Shredded Wheat.

'I remember that Docteroo,' added my Dad, after a gulp of strong tea. 'There was a bloke with a fruity Welsh accent who kept all them bats.' I nodded, even though I knew that Aukon – the vampire we were discussing – didn't actually keep bats in the way smelly Old Man Richardson up the road kept unhealthy-looking carrier pigeons on his roof; he had dominion over them, in much the way that my mum did over my dad.

'Easy life, that, lad,' sighed my dad, as he folded up his *Daily Mirror* to carry under his arm when he walked to the bus stop, ''avin' Welsh bats do all the graft for you. Fair play to the bloke, we'd all of us jump at the chance to 'ave all them bats do the graft for us if we could.'

I don't know why Aukon's bats had suddenly become Welsh – could bats squeak in a Welsh accent? Did they form male bat voice choirs? Did they squeak on and on about Rugby matches? – but I let the matter slide. My dad trudged wearily out the door, and I watched him head down the garden path, ungainly sidestepping around my younger brother's discarded Raleigh Tomahawk, following the manoeuvre with a depressed shake of the head. I fancied I saw him look up to the skies before he walked out of my view. Perhaps he was musing on what it would feel like to be in command of an army of bats. Though bats are of course nocturnal ('They come out at dusk, you know,' says the Doctor on page 19), so he would have a hell of a time getting an army

211

of bats to do anything at 7.15 on a sunny May morning. Unless the bats were on their way back to their bat-caves after a late night bender feeling considerably worse for wear, rather like my highly-strung Auntie Evelyn from down Devon would when she came to stay with us after she'd been dumped by her latest bit-of-rough boyfriend.

I gulped down the last of my Shredded Wheat sludge, then picked up my copy of *Doctor Who and the State of Decay* by Terrance Dicks. I stared again at the cover. The cover featured a quite baffling illustration by Andrew Skilleter. Doctor Who seemed to be wearing some kind of baggy black smock with massive, off-white triangular shirt collars, and Aukon, the immortal alien vampire with a fruity Welsh accent who could summon at will all the bats in the world to attack people, seemed to be balancing a giant vampire bat on his thumbs. I was 93 pages into the 125-page book, and there had been absolutely no mention whatsoever of Aukon balancing really big vampire bats on his thumbs. I shared Doctor Who's suspicions that there was something horrible hiding under the sinister Tower ('What monstrous creature stirs beneath the Tower, waking from its thousand-year sleep?' ponders the blurb on the back cover) and I wondered if it was a cave filled with massive vampire bats, and that maybe Doctor Who, Romana, K-9 and some irritating stowaway kid named Adric would confront Aukon (and the other two vampires, who were a bit dreary) and Aukon would amaze the time-travellers by balancing a big bat on the tips of his thumbs.

I was big on bats when I was twelve. Batty about them. I'd watched some *Dracula* films, with a variety of dapper Counts turning into a variety of flappy bats (the best one was the tall, thin black-and-white Dracula with the pencil moustache and the top hat, who morphed into a bat during a brilliant fight with Frankenstein and the Wolf-Man). I had *The Surprising World of Bats* by Christian Dietz on permanent loan from Horfield Library (along with *Doctor Who and the Space War* by Malcolm Hulke, which I could never finish reading for some reason, even though there were some really good bits in it). I had several toy rubber bats of various sizes and quality, including one that made a squeaking sound if you punched it really hard on the back of the head. I had munched through dozens of packets of bat-shaped crisps called Bats. I was always doodling bats on my school exercise books and had copied the big bat that was balanced on Aukon's thumbs onto the front of my English homework book, but I'd drawn the proportions slightly wrong so it looked like it had a head several times bigger than its body, like Mr Trenchard, who taught French. The same English homework book had on its rear cover a drawing of the poster of *Return of the Jedi*, if the *Return of the Jedi* poster had lots of bats on it, which it didn't, unlike my drawing of it, which did, and was therefore much better. All sorts of things could be improved by adding lots of bats, which was pretty much the extent of my world-view when I was twelve. Certainly the best bits of *Doctor Who and the State of Decay* were the bits with lots of bats, and *Doctor Who and the Space War* would be considerably enlivened by having a new bit with the Draconians being savagely attacked by giant vampire bats (on the moon). I hadn't seen *Return of the Jedi*, but I had no doubt that Darth Vader could kick some serious Jedi arse if he had an army of giant space-bats at his command, possibly giant robot space-bats that could shoot laser beams out of their eyes. Mr Trenchard's tedious French lessons would definitely be much more interesting if he was forced to teach masculine noun endings converted to the feminine form to a class of bored twelve-year olds whilst fending off an attack by an army of angry bats (le chauve-souris).

At dusk, my dad came home, wolfed down a plate of bangers and mash, flopped into his favourite armchair and fell asleep. He smelled of tobacco and paint. As always on a school night, I went to bed just before 10pm, after the BBC evening news. I shared a bedroom with my younger brother, who was invariably already sound asleep by the time I went to bed, and I didn't want to wake him, so I would read by torchlight, hidden under a makeshift tent of pillows and blankets. Under the bed covers, I finished reading *Doctor Who and the State of Decay*. We had been right to be suspicious of the Tower, Doctor Who and I: there was indeed a giant monster vampire bat slumbering underneath it. Disappointingly, Doctor Who killed it before it took wing and started to wreak bloody havoc throughout the universe, but Doctor Who was always killing monsters, so it hardly came as a surprise. I drifted off to sleep listening to the faint sounds of *International Golf* floating up from the television downstairs, and dreamed, I think, of K-9 speaking French to Aukon, the immortal alien vampire with a fruity Welsh accent who could summon at will all the bats in the world to attack people.

213

Zero Point: Between the Positive and the Negative

Doctor Who and Warriors' Gate
by Shaqui Le Vesconte
Favourite *Doctor Who* book: *Battlefield* by Marc Platt

It's a very weird dichotomy.

Doctor Who novelisations, for me, were not just a means of finding out what stories were like you hadn't seen. Up until the point where I started work in the late 1980s, I had every single one published. At a time before the internet or DVD or even VHS, they were archives. Resources.

By that, I expected each to be a reasonable reflection of the story it was based on. I was that pedantic as a fan, I wanted the dialogue and prose to be an exact recreation of what we saw on television. In hindsight it's obvious some of the earliest and best in the range didn't do that, going beyond budget and production restraints to give a much fuller literary experience. The more recent stories were usually handled by Terrance Dicks and were as faithful and straightforward as can be expected.

This attitude might have been born out of the disappointment I had after seeing the first television screening of the 1953 film *The War of the Worlds*, then being lent the original novel by an aunt. I was already devouring Target novelisations at quite a rate even then, so it came as something of a shock to my aunt, expecting me, possibly 9 or 10 years of age, to struggle through the chapters, only to be told I was more than halfway through the book in just a few days! However, the greater shock was mine, as the novel wasn't set in America in the 1950s, but England and – so the text on the back informed me – before man had even learnt to fly. Such was my culture shock at this radical shift in both time and space, when the unnamed protagonist encounters a Martian War Machine striding through the forest at night, I at first imagined him driving a car rather than, as the later description and graphic adaptation in Doctor Who Weekly made clear, a horse and cart. That's not to say I hated the book. I still have a massive appreciation of the period setting of the novel, though that might be due more to the chronologically accurate Jeff Wayne version released a few years later. But perhaps that's why I buried myself in the safe and secure universe of *Doctor Who* noveldom. The collars and cuffs usually matched.

I am also quite an avid Gerry Anderson fan and acquired the novelisations for *Space:1999* in parallel with *Doctor Who* when

214

published shortly after. These, to my annoyance, were not so faithful to their television counterparts. I still liked them, and still have them, but it just wasn't the same. *The War of the Worlds* may have been the start but these cemented my greater affection for *Doctor Who* novels.

Then came *Warriors' Gate*.

To say I was impressed by this story on TV is an understatement. It was a story I audio recorded, and the compact cassettes allowed me to relive the adventure over and over to the point where I had all but memorised the dialogue and Peter Howell's evocative music score. It took what seemed a long, long while for the novelisation to appear, originally – if I recall correctly – announced for the end of 1981 but not appearing until around the Easter of the following year. I can still remember the absolute glee of finally finding it in the local Dillons bookshop one Saturday morning, rushing home with a copy and even ringing another fan to say it was finally out, such was my veritably erupting enthusiasm! I then sat on the sofa and started to bury myself in it.

That's when the disappointment began to settle in.

Okay, so some earlier novelisations had begun in not quite the same way as on television, such as David Whitaker's *The Daleks*, for example, and even Terrance Dicks himself with *The Auton Invasion* and *Day of the Daleks*. Fair enough, with the Antonine Killer at this point. But glancing at the opening pages, there was no contents page. No chapters! What? I considered myself a speedy reader, often finishing a Target book in a day (or two, if interrupted) but this meant no convenient breaks! It was, and I believe still is, the only novelisation aside from the same author's *Terminus* to do this. Was he a sadist? Slim novel, should be a doddle, but further in, the departures from the version I knew and loved became more evident and more difficult for this televisually sensitive fan to, well, visualise. Why were Aldo and Royce sidelined, introduced so late as to almost be an afterthought? Who were Nestor and Jos? Actually, come to think of it, who was this John Lydecker anyway, as Steve Gallagher had been mentioned as author in the *Doctor Who Monthly* previews? These questions and more surfaced. Occasionally, familiar bits appeared as a vague reassurance this was the same story but it was like two different writers were vying for the same space, with the result a bit like watching a game of tennis. Or flipping a coin. Heads, one version (TV). Tails, the other.

I hated it.

It was almost like my precious world of cosy, easy-to-read, none-too-taxing-to-imagine novels had been hijacked the same way E.C. Tubb, John Rankine, Brian Ball and Michael Butterworth did with *Space:1999*. They turned them into distorted mirror images, a gateway to an inaccurate nightmare instead of relived dreams. The names might be the same but the whole emphasis, separated cruelly from the episodes as broadcast, was just wrong.

The *Warriors' Gate* novelisation stayed in my collection, largely unrevisited until last year, whereas I have frequently dipped into so many of the others.

Years later, Powys Media in the USA acquired the rights to publish new novels based on *Space:1999*. The massive tome that was the Year Two Omnibus collected together all six of Michael Butterworth's novelisations with some new material to segue them into one epic hardback. The book arrived from the States in due course, and I prepared to relive the episodes.

I hated it.

The biggest irony is that some twenty-five years earlier, it would have been exactly the kind of *Space:1999* novelisation I had wanted to read. It was obvious the brief was to make it as much like what had been televised as possible. That, to me, older and hopefully wiser with an appreciation of what of a novelisation should be, was its failing. It was an awful fannish wish fulfilment to drag the prose down to the limitations of production some thirty years earlier, rather than – as I had come to appreciate – make the novelisations proper science-fiction adventures in their own rights.

Of course, *Doctor Who* had already been there. Steve Gallagher was one of the earliest precedents of script writers wanting to write their own novelisations, after Terrance Dicks had helmed the range for so many years, wishing to fill in the gaps that budget couldn't even touch. Others followed, and towards the inevitable end, we were treated to two books which told the stories as seen on television, but embellished them to an outstanding degree, giving us insights into both major and minor characters alike, with future (or alternate) histories, supporting prose and flashbacks. These were *Remembrance of the Daleks* and *Battlefield*. The latter is still my candidate for best Doctor Who novelisation ever.

In hindsight, seeing the DVD extras about the production of *Warriors' Gate*, and reading the In-Vision analysis, I can re-read the novelisation and bemoan what we never got and now never will. The reassuringly familiar scenes now read as perfunctory contractual obligation to fall in line with the rest of the novelisations at the time. That isn't to put Gallagher down, as he apparently had to add these at short notice and jury rig them into his existing prose, which was probably what contributed to its delayed release.

Knowing this makes me mourn the other novels which could have been so much more if their original authors had been interested at the time. How would *The Stones of Blood* and *The Androids of Tara* have sparkled from the pen of David Fisher? What mystical layers could Christopher Bailey have revealed for *Kinda* and *Snakedance*? And had he not passed away, could The Mysterious Planet have benefitted from the wry authorship of Robert Holmes, alongside earlier classics such as *The Deadly Assassin*? Such tantalising possibilities...

That's not to put down Terrance Dicks either. He did after all keep the line going for many years, through thick and thin book spines, when others seemingly dismissed them. Until this juncture. This gateway between the universes of limited television production, innovative though Warriors' Gate was at the time, and literary imagination, sadly chained to it when deserving to be free.

From this point, gladly, there was no turning back.

The Vandals Were Quite Decent Chaps

Doctor Who and the Keeper of Traken
by Christopher Bryant

Favourite *Doctor Who* book: *The Writer's Tale: The Final Chapter*
by Russell T Davies and Benjamin Cook

My copy of *The Keeper of Traken* is damaged. Almost a quarter of the front cover has been torn away, leaving Sarah Sutton resembling the half-faced android from *Deep Breath*. I've no idea how this happened, but whenever I see an undamaged copy of this book, it looks... wrong, somehow.

Truth be told, I'm not much of a collector. My stash of Target books was never completed and never will be. I wanted the books so I could read them, at which point they became a collection, but I had no urge to buy different editions or pay through the nose on eBay. I wasn't even careful with the copies I bought.

(This is a trigger warning: if you are a little more obsessive about your books than me, you may want to look away now.)

The Keeper of Traken is far from the only Target book in a less-than-presentable condition. *The Mind of Evil* is another book with a torn cover, this time removing the TOR from the neon logo at the top. Thankfully, young me rectified this by redrawing the missing section (poorly) on the page beneath.

Writing in a book? Scandalous! Horrifying! Not something that worried me in my adolescent days. In dozens of my Target books, the careful prose of the author is interrupted by my own additions in blue biro. A favourite pastime was to allocate titles to sections of the text: so, for example, when Clara explains to Steven and Dodo how to play their game in *The Celestial Toymaker*, I headed that section 'THE RULES'. A quick flick through similarly-vandalised texts reveals the memorable sections entitled 'ETTIS TRAPS THE DOCTOR' and 'THE XERONS FIND THE TRAIL', as well as more generic headings such as 'WARNINGS' (the opening section of *Inferno*) or 'THE BETRAYAL' (which ends chapter 9 of *The War Games*). Spoilers clearly didn't worry me ('THE DEATH OF TALOR'), while page 114 of *The Androids of Tara* alarmingly announces one section with the word 'PENETRATION'.

Why was I doing all this? Did I think it improved my re-reading experience? No: mainly, I was bored. Often, these doodlings were carried out underneath the desk during lessons, where my *Doctor Who* books were the only things I had to doodle on.

Sometimes, my scrawl has a more obvious intent. Most of them have my name written inside, but for some reason *Four to Doomsday* also contains the ominous warning: 'LOSE IT AND DIE!' Really, young me, *Four to Doomsday* isn't worth it.

In many books, I have revealed an obsession with cast lists, writing a full dramatis personae for the novelisation in the inside cover (*The Cave Monsters* seems to have given me particular trouble). Within a year or so, I would discover Jean-Marc Lofficier and would never look back.

Some of the books have suffered from far less cerebral vandalism. On the front cover of *Earthshock*, Peter Davison has gained a beard, glasses and a pork pie hat. He is similarly defaced on *The Visitation*, with his torso additionally obscured by a sticker advising people to pay their TV licence. Worst of all, I have drawn a label onto the planet Ravalox on the front cover of *The Mysterious Planet* saying, 'If lost, please return to the Milky Way!' My sides.

The most abused book of all is *The Leisure Hive*, where I have actually drawn over the words on many of the pages, making David Fisher's prose partially illegible, with sketches inspired by a word on the page, such as 'law' or 'aliens'. My depiction of the word 'Klout' is at least entertaining, but not as much as the original novel.

Time for a few utterly inexplicable ones? How about the legend inside *The Time Warrior*: 'IOU one tooth'? Whose handwriting do I find inside *The Krotons* bizarrely commenting that 'This song is typical of Erasure'? What's with this list of books inside *The Sensorites*, beginning with a couple of Target novels before some books I read at school (*Carrie's War*, *Wind in the Willows*) and then three that I've never even heard of. I've just Googled *Thursday in Paris* and would swear it was completely new to me... but here it is, in blue biro, immortalised in the late 1980s in a Nigel Robinson book.

As it turns out, I am a collector. My collection isn't of pristine blue spines or first editions: it's far more personal than that. Hidden inside my Target books, or sometimes outside, are pieces of evidence, fragments of young me, pickled in time. Entropy came for Nyssa's face, but my drawing of Peter Davison's *Black Orchid* mask remains. A person is the sum of their memories; a Target fan even more so.

219

London Calling

Doctor Who and the Leisure Hive
by Christopher Payne
Favourite *Doctor Who* book: *Turn Left* by Andy X Cable

London is synonymous with *Doctor Who*.

The old, majestic city has been the backdrop for so many classic moments: Daleks on Westminster Bridge, Cybermen on the steps of St Paul's, incredibly realistic dinosaurs terrorising the third Doctor outside Moorgate tube station, spaceships crashing into Big Ben, Capaldi chatting up a dinosaur on the South Bank...the list is endless.

London is also where my earliest and maybe my fondest memories of *Doctor Who* were too. Both my parents came from London and during my early childhood I spent a lot of time visiting the city as we lived further out in the sticks. My Dad's family stayed in the East End for many years after my parents decided to fly the nest and head out to darkest Essex, but on Saturdays my parents would take me and my sister to Plaistow in the East End for our regular family gathering. The journey seemed like an eternity in the car and I often wondered if it would be much quicker in the TARDIS, but the wait was made easier and super-exciting by the thought of seeing my Nan, Grandad, and a large cast of outrageous, cockney characters. The fact that there would be a new *Doctor Who* episode at teatime and potentially a new *Doctor Who* Target book just added to my giddiness. As a young child who was already an avid fan, Saturday was THE important day of the week, the resolution to the cliff-hanger made all the more enjoyable by my family gathered round the old custard and jelly. Even Nan's incredible roast potatoes came in second to new *Doctor Who*.

Saturdays were almost military in their routine: leave early, a few cups of Rosie Lee on arrival, then Dad would wait for his brothers and Grandad would spruce himself up, the smell of pomade always fresh on his hair. Then the gentleman would head off to the Green Gate pub for a few 'liveners'. Nan and sometimes my Mum would take me, my sister and any of our cousins who wanted a walk up to Plaistow High Street where I would be chomping at the bit for a detour to WH Smiths or Woolworths, purveyors of the finest *Doctor Who* Target books. Nan or Mum would treat me (not every week) to a new book and I would marvel at the classic curved logo and the thrilling cover illustrations or, once I was more confident, read the plot summary on the back to influence my choice. Once back at Nan's house, I would lose myself in my new book and play with my Tom Baker, Cyberman and Giant Robot dolls (my sister had Leela) happily as the afternoon passed by. The men would return, Grandad would have a cheeky nap and then the

220

family would gather around the telly for the early evening. The football scores would be checked for the pools results (ask your own old person about this civilised form of sports gambling) and I would settle onto Grandad's lap with Tom Baker, ready for the most exciting 25 minutes of the week. There is a wonderful Polaroid of me sitting with Grandad; he is still in his waistcoat and shirt and my eyes are fixed onto the screen. After tea, the evenings would be a never-ending party; an open front door, helping Aunt Rose make endless pots of tea, listening to bizarre stories from people I had never met, eating pie, mash and liquor from George's Pie Shop, dancing to incredible music and then trying to sleep on the floor in the front room with 20 other people, unable to sleep with excitement and the constant car headlights that lit up the room (like that horrible white effect on the 80s end titles).

Then it changed.

It wasn't the change of Doctor that made me confused or sad - Tom was defining for me, but I was now nine years old and understood the programme more when Peter Davison took over. The abominable move to Monday and Tuesday nights didn't alter our little Saturday adventure, but meant that I didn't sit on Grandad's lap for as long as I just wasn't as into *The Dukes of Hazzard*. The unexpected Target re-branding did however take some getting used to and a trip to WH Smiths in early 1982 was where I first noticed the unfolding horror. On one particular Saturday, the shelves contained only the garish new neon logo and none of them featured any of the old Doctors on the cover. That classic curved logo which had always been an integral part of the books' identity was nowhere to be found - and why were all the old Doctors missing from those exciting cover illustrations?

Confounded and a little scared, I considered my options; maybe it was David Haig's young, encouraging face or the warm soothing orange tones but I plumped for *The Leisure Hive*, my first Target book from this intimidating new range and from the new eighties *Doctor Who*. Although comfortingly familiar as a read, it did seem somewhat more complex than others (it really isn't, by the way, despite Bidmead's attempts at 'hard science'). As the months passed, the Target range got less enchanting with rubbish photomontage covers or illustrated ones that never featured any of the old Doctors. As I began to get older and more distracted by other things, the family trips became more about the party and the interaction with these incredibly large, gregarious family characters and their stories (and their language) and less about *Doctor Who*.

Eventually, everybody left the East End. The family gatherings stopped, Doctor Who went away, the Target books ended and everything became a memory. Like many fans, I lost my way for a

221

while (Mum swears she didn't give all my *Doctor Who* stuff away, so it must be on a parallel earth with Professor Stahlmann). I have recently been lost in happy nostalgia reading the current crop of factual tomes dedicated to the Target range and still get the same warm feelings of joy and innocent thrills that I did from those original Target novelisations, especially the wonderful illustrations on the covers, which remind me of blissfully happy times with my family. I have managed to replace many of my Target Books, just on the odd whim popping into an old bookshop or at a car boot sale, but I have never come across *The Leisure Hive* and I still get a nervous twitch when I see a Target book with the wrong logo for that particular Doctor. I spent three years living in London with my wife and visited many of the old haunts, but they didn't stir the same feelings in me the way looking at those old Target books does.

My son is now two years old and he gets me to tell him *Doctor Who* stories at bedtime (Planet of the Teddy Bears is a particular favourite, Chibnall take note), plays with my model TARDIS and always wants to see my Target books. He hasn't even seen *Doctor Who* on TV yet (although he does keep trying to play with my DVD collection) or been to London and when he does he will not have that large family to surround him or that 25-minute tea time TV treat. He often sees my Mum, now his Nan, and I wonder if they will ever pop out to WH Smiths to buy a little Target book together, you know, one of these new-fangled reprints, with the imperious gold logo which looks impressive but lacks a certain old school charm. Whatever his (and my newborn son's) journey, I hope they will experience their own *Doctor Who* magic just as I did, maybe with their Nan, maybe through those wonderful old Target books.

To Lilian, my Nan, finally reunited with Grandad for the last great adventure in time and space.

The Re-Visitation

Doctor Who – The Visitation by Lee Rawlings

Favourite *Doctor Who* book: *The Dinosaur Invasion*
by Malcolm Hulke

D.J Brooking. That was the name above the shop window. Through the glass were displays of new books and art materials. I remember the shop sign having white clear plastic letters on a brown wooden background. In the yellowy warm lights I could see a couple talking to the store owner. The grim, wet Parkstone on a Saturday afternoon reflected lights off the pavements and it felt like it didn't need me in the picture, which was fine because I loathed wet Saturday afternoons. The decision to go in should have been easy. But it wasn't. It was a battle of nerves. My hand gripped the door handle and I pushed.

I was twelve and my Target experience was reading my older brother's collection of books. I would sneak into his room whilst ingesting the tart smell of Humbrol paint rising from his freshly-painted lead Napoleonic figures. I would turn to his shelves of *Doctor Who* books and get stuck into as many pages as I could. These were adventures I had never seen on television and they were all so exciting, exploding off the page and into my young brain. I longed for my own collection of books and I finally got my wish on that dull Saturday afternoon.

I needed to know if any more stories had been released. According my friend Rabbetts and my other *Doctor Who* friends at school, there had been a title released recently starring Peter Davison and also new exciting releases from the show's past, like the first ever story, *An Unearthly Child*. The promise of these releases really excited me and I was now getting a good enough amount of pocket money a week. But where to buy them from? I was surprised to find the answer when I wasn't looking for it. I was idly walking through Parkstone one Saturday and D.J. Brooking caught my eye.

It was a modern book store; well, for the 1980s. The carpet was made of beige and brown squares, the same colour as the shopkeeper's pullover. The wooden desk looked like a semi-circular raft, untethered and floating away from the wall with just a spinner of bookmarks, a rack of cards, a stapler and a till for company. The bell went 'ding' twice as I pushed the slightly jammed and stubborn door open. I was a very shy boy and the three faces in the shop now looking at me nearly made me walk straight back out in to the street again. Shyness is misunderstood; it can actually hurt and my ribs and chest were tight with anxiety, yet I carried on because I had to know if they had the books I was looking for. I proudly overcame enough of my invisible

223

pain and strode past the desk. If you have ever seen Adric in *State of Decay* striding awkwardly through the TARDIS... well, that was my style traversing that beige carpet; unnatural and forced.

I managed a wobbly smile directed at nobody in particular and headed to where I could see books lined up at the far end, just to the left: and my oh my, they had great books. There were hundreds of shiny new science fiction books: Harry Harrison, Douglas Adams, Isaac Asimov and a very special book with a blue cover. I wasn't a massive reader as a child, but I can safely say when I spotted this book on the shelf in front of me, it changed my reading life. This moment was a milestone as this book would be mine and no one else's. It was not hastily borrowed from my brother's book shelf, it wasn't a school library copy; this would be my very own copy to read carefully and slowly, revisiting those exciting adventures whenever I wanted!

So it is a shame then that I left empty handed.

The book in question was *The Visitation*. I picked up the book and gazed at the cover. I didn't even notice the garish design and not very exciting photo of Peter Davison because to me on that day, this book was the most exciting thing I had ever found in a shop, ever. I had watched this story not long ago, so this felt relevant, modern and fresh and it would be mine, all mine. Nothing in the world would stop me now! Except that when I looked for the money to pay for the new treasure, I was short. It is hard to imagine now but the book was just over a pound to buy - a pound! You can't even buy a ginger pop for that nowadays. I searched desperately but I couldn't find my one pound note anywhere. I was crestfallen and almost asked if I could put it by to collect another time, but that would mean talking to the tall thin curly haired shopkeeper in the beige top, busying about like an insect looking for pollen. My shyness flushed my cheeks and my palms became sweaty. No, I couldn't do it. It was alright, I told myself, I would go home tonight and look in my football boot money box, check if I had enough and come back next week.

After the longest week at school ever, I ran to the bookstore and made for the shelf like a rat up Pudding Lane. I didn't even take that much notice of the rain until I got home later and could feel my socks were damp and squishy. I had managed to find a new determination, a new and exciting fire was bubbling inside. This strength found me bolting for the corner of the shop where the books were. My hand went to the shelf... but it wasn't there. The book had gone. I looked and looked but someone else must have bought it. Bought my book.

My heart fell to my ankles and I felt I was going to burst into tears. You see, I hadn't grasped the concept that you could order another copy. I thought that once it had gone that was it, your chance was gone. So when Mr Brooking asked me what I was looking for, I believed it was a false hope. I blinked, was breathless from nerves and just said 'Doctor Who'. He smiled and simply said 'Which one would you like?' I left that shop with a head full of possibilities. I could order any book I wanted without paying upfront? Amazing!

I scooted up a week later to check if it had come in. I was no longer shy in D.J. Brookings. No sir! The moment I saw him disappear around the back of the shop and come back with *The Visitation* felt the happiest I had ever been. I paid the money, he wrapped it into a brown paper bag and I held it tight all the way home. I ran a mile without stopping. This all sounds like an episode of some 1970s children's TV show but it is true. As a child, the biggest things that affect you are the smallest and *Doctor Who* was more important to me than life itself. I crashed into my house and threw myself into my bed, opened the paper bag and brought the book out.

The smell was a good start. I love the smell of books. The older the book, the deeper the smell. History itself emanates from just a whiff of its decaying pages. Whose shelf had it lived on? Whose lives had it been involved with? Whose domestic historical soap operas had it witnessed? It is fascinating to ruminate about the story of ancient tomes, but what of new books? The smell of promise! Newly minted imagination in a block of brand new sliced and glued paper. No history at all because its history starts when you first read it. So new books are as exciting as old ones and *The Visitation* was now in my hands. The book still has the receipt inside the last time I looked.

As for the story, everything about it was excellent. I read that book cover to cover and relived the story in my head easily. It was exciting, scary and clever and I loved it. Of course, when I look back at the episodes now I realise they have faults but at the time it was new and different. A diamond-encrusted robot in Death's cowl, a fish thing with a terrifying face letting diseased rats into London, a hammy Richard Mace, creepy villagers, the TARDIS crew in peril: well, I just thought it was as good as any blockbuster at the pictures. I didn't know who Eric Saward was but I knew he could write a cracking fun story. It stood proudly on my shelf, soon to be part of a much larger collection, even to the point where my brother and I merged our collections for a while. My dad put a whole shelving unit upon the landing at the top of the stairs just for the *Doctor Who* collection. Every time I went to bed I would lie half on the landing, half with my legs on the stairs staring at the books and their curious titles. What was a Zarbi? There were still stories I hadn't read from earlier in the Doctor's timeline so I would simply pick one out and read it. Night-time dreams were full of Daleks and dinosaurs climbing over our play parks and fields. Halcyon days.

If D.J. Brooking's bookstore was the catalyst for my fan gene to kick

225

off, I feel as if I should seek out the shop again and go and say hello. I could walk in hoping it will look exactly the same as it was when I was a boy (it won't) and meet the same curly haired owner (I won't) and find *Doctor Who* books for the new generation in the same spot in the shop like all those years ago (they won't be, will they?). Well, the first step would be to have a quick tap of the futuristic electronic tablet and find Google Street View. The next few lines are a dialogue of my mind:

'Ah, here we are then, yes Parkstone, oh look, that shop's gone and that one, no paper shop either, that's a shame I used to buy my fizzy sweets there, ok here we go then, should be somewhere around here... jumping Jehoshaphat! It's still there! Same lettering too! Wait a moment, you can go inside the shop with this photo attachment link. What the...! No...it looks the same! Was this taken in the 1980s? No! There are modern books in the window... I wonder if the owner is in one of these...'

After a rather excitable evening of nostalgic gushing over a shop in a town in the southern parts of England, I decided to drive to the shop and meet the man and the place that started my insatiable appetite for collecting *Doctor Who* books. I will tell him about the influence it has had on me and that he himself is now in a book about the book I bought from him. This could turn into a paradox machine if I'm not careful. I will go down just before Christmas, walk in, buy a new *Doctor Who* book, take it to the counter and let the story rip. Who knows what may happen. Who knows?

So the day was not rainy but warm and sunny, the shop looked like the Google photo, the window still had books in them and the door opened fine, no jamming. As I stared at the same counter and crossed the same carpet I couldn't help thinking I had walked through a timeslip. It was the same owner from all those years ago. The curly-haired man was a bit greyer and older but essentially the same person. Even the jumper was even similar to that beige pullover. I told him my story and started to feel the old emotions of my childhood wash over me. I held fast, being a much more confident adult and finished the story by punctuating it with the fact they would be in this very essay in a *Doctor Who* book.

Much to my disappointment, he seemed not that bothered or even listening. I realised it was a strange story to take in while stock taking and dealing with phone orders. It wasn't the right time for that story. I mentioned my library work which interested them more and I had a very fascinating chat about Kindles killing books and art materials for twenty minutes. I found out they no longer stock *Doctor Who* books. He asked me if I remembered a boy called Rabbetts who was very keen on them and was in all the time back in the 1980s snapping them up from the shelves.

Maybe Rabbetts bought that copy before I could buy it all those years ago? Maybe I should look him up and find out? Time for another revisitation.

Home

Doctor Who – Full Circle by Jason Wilson

Favourite *Doctor Who* book: *Blood Heat* by Jim Mortimore

Full Circle is, in part, about Home. For Romana and Adric, Home is a sterile, lifeless boredom to which they don't want to return. For the outlers, Home is the cave of their self-imposed exile. The community dreams of returning Home to Terradon only to find it's not that simple. Adric finds a Home in the TARDIS only for it to break up in *Warriors' Gate*. Finally, of course, in *Earthshock*, he yearns for his roots, too late.

Adric irritates a lot of people, but I clicked with his sense of home and Home being moveable feasts, of being slightly rootless. Between the TV and book versions of *Full Circle*, I learned that Home was shifting again for me. Parental army service had made childhood a pleasant but peripatetic affair, with stints in various parts of England and Germany. Germany fuelled my lifelong love of Bratwurst, but other than that our army brat culture was mostly English: oddly, it was in a German playground that I first heard of *Blake's Seven*.

These bases were homes; Home was our then base in Millom, Cumbria. Though Home for me would not be marked by suffering or tragedy as Adric's were, we shared perhaps a sense that our self-definition would be defined by other things than place. Coming Home meant not living out of army packing crates for a bit and familiar comforts: the infant school at the end of the road; book swapping from our stockpile in the old deactivated chest freezer; monthly food trips to Barrow which meant the Book Corner. While I can remember where I got most of my Targets, *Full Circle* eludes me: Bertram A Watts in Sheringham is most likely, or maybe the newsagent in Spixworth where I got some Davison books.

Finally, we migrated to Norfolk. Season 19 would be our last in the North; 20 and 21 would be seen in Sheringham (my apologies to our faithful and long deceased Labrador who greeted me at the station as I returned home from school in Norwich only to be spurned so I could hurtle home for *Warriors of the Deep*); 22 in Spixworth and finally 23 in Norwich which has been Home since.

I wonder if he could have settled back in E-Space had that trip been possible? I've been to some parts of Cumbria since but never Millom. One day... not sure what I will find there now though.

Something Completely Different

Doctor Who – Logopolis by Cody Schell
Favourite *Doctor Who* book: *Verdigris* by Paul Magrs

I love collecting Blu-rays from the Criterion Collection. Criterion releases an amazing amount of films, all set in different times and places, with beautiful and bizarre cover art. I can visit a disturbing version of 1970's Japan in Nobuhiko Obayashi's *House* then travel to gorgeous 1950's Brazil in Macel Camus' *Black Orpheus*. From Brazil I can go to *Brazil*, the Terry Gilliam kind, and from there I can dance in *The Red Shoes* to dozens of other places.

I'm always torn between arranging the disc cases alphabetically, chronologically, by director or by genre! But my favourite way to arrange them on the shelf is by spine number. *Zazie dans le metro* – Spine number 570. *Harold and Maude* – Spine number 608. *Judex* – Spine number 710. These are fine films, and this is an adult and intellectual interest. I'm so glad I've grown up and changed...

...Hang on a second, Mr 'Adult'. I'm still that thirteen-year-old kid that bought *Doctor Who* books and obsessively arranged and rearranged them on the shelf! I arranged them by spine number, alphabetically, even by colour. But the most sensible way to arrange them was by the order that the stories were broadcast. (Arranging them by spine number was very useful in figuring out which ones I still needed to get, however.)

I made lists of what I had, of what I needed, and made notations about which ones weren't even released yet. (Hmmm, lots of Dalek ones, it seemed.) Multiple times a week I harassed Barb and Jerome, the employees at the local book store, asking them to special order books for me, and check on availability of others. They were so kind to look them up in their microfiche. 'That's *Keeper of Traken*, spelled T. r. a. k...'

Sometimes I could order them from the Intergalactic Trading Post – a mail order catalogue for nerds. But in the 1980s, this involved begging my mother to write a check, mail the check and then waiting 4-6 weeks for the books to arrive. That was a painful and anxiety-ridden process.

I looked for *Doctor Who* books in every second-hand shop and used bookstore that I visited, but there were never, ever *Doctor Who* books to be found. It didn't stop me from looking! Sometimes it was more about collecting than actually reading the books. I'm pretty sure I never actually read many of them.

I'll be honest. I could have really cared less about Mestor's reasons for kidnapping twin geniuses. I didn't stay awake at night wondering why there were Yeti in the Underground. Space Pirates didn't hold my attention. At the time, I bought Target novels for pretty much only one reason. I wanted to read everything and anything I could about the TARDIS.

Upon getting a new *Doctor Who* novelisation, I skimmed the text for *that* word in all caps. (Failing that, I was happy to find SIDRAT, DARDIS or TOMTIT.) Once I found *that* word, I quickly checked for any information about gleaming white hallways, or roundels inset into the walls. I hoped for paragraphs detailing exactly how many doors down from the console room particular rooms were located. I wanted to know more about the Food/Drink Synthesizer. Was there only one level in the TARDIS, or was there an upstairs and a downstairs? If so, were there elevators? Which panel on the console did what things? I had to know!

At the age of thirteen, *Logopolis* was one of my favourite novelisations, because it was brimming with TARDIS information. Not only was it about the TARDIS, but it was about the Master's TARDIS. It was even about the TARDIS landing inside this other TARDIS! Wait... the TARDIS ends up being inside of itself? (I think?) There's a back door!?

This was a jackpot of information.

Adric was my identification character. He was also very curious about the workings of the TARDIS and the theories behind it. I've heard the term 'Chameleon Circuit' originated in the Target novels. I still don't know if this is true, but I read and re-read all the relevant passages in Logopolis so many times that I imagined I'd have a good shot at getting the device to work if I were to ever chance upon a fully functional TT Capsule.

I enjoyed reading *Logopolis* all the way through. I thought it read somewhat like *Alice In Wonderland* or *The Phantom Tollbooth*. It's full of important-sounding concepts that are also quite silly at the same time: People getting shrunk, rabbit holes into other universes, mathematical recitations that change reality.

The stories surrounding *Logopolis* also have a touch of the fairy-tale and this grouping of novelisations was my favourite: the princess and the evil statue, the mountain town inside of itself, the cats who live behind the mirrors. These were the novelisations I read from cover to cover, over and over. Anything could happen in *Doctor Who*.

As a book-loving kid, *The Phantom Tollbooth* was one of my favourites. I always wanted to love *Alice in Wonderland*, but somehow, just never did. I knew it was supposed to be 'mad' but it just wasn't accessible somehow.

Logopolis is full of many of those Phantom Tollbooth moments. People dressed strangely, talking about nonsense math concepts. Yet I realise now there are people who don't find *Logopolis* to be their cup of tea. Some people wanted to read about action, robot fights and dashing historical figures. Not me, I wanted to explore the technological haunted-house that was, is and will be the TARDIS – the machine from so far in the future that its futuristic gleam had long faded and was full of forgotten memories and dusty mementos.

Falling into this same TARDIS content-rich category were the novelisations of *The Invasion of Time*, *The Edge of Destruction*, and *The Time Monster*. I also loved any book that described the operation or malfunction of the Chameleon Circuit: *An Unearthly Child*, *Attack of the Cybermen*. I read about the HADS in *The Krotons*, the State of Temporal Grace in *The Hand of Fear* and the Power Room in *The Mind Robber* (although it was called 'the Power Chamber' in that book).

Years later, when I had the chance to see most of these episodes, I was transported back to the age I was when I read the Target novels. Things weren't usually as I expected them to be, but at the back of my mind were the images I envisioned and imagined. In many ways, the books were the 'real' version to me and the TV show a pale imitation. They'll always have been my first introduction to most pre-2005 *Doctor Who* stories.

For me, the Fifth Doctor's first words will always be: 'Well, that's the end of that, but it's probably the beginning of something completely different.'

They Teach Them Nothing in the Preparation Centres

Doctor Who and the Sunmakers
by Bel Tolley
Favourite *Doctor Who* book: *Goth Opera* by Paul Cornell

'He's copied that out of *Brave New World*.'

'What's *Brave New World*?'

If I haven't heard of something I usually ask my mum, and she pretty much always tells me. I can't remember anything that she's ever declined to tell us. She tells us the meanings of rude words and the names of members of the Bloomsbury set. She was the one who explained to me what abortion was when I'd just been told that it was wrong by someone who didn't explain what it was. Mum never thought that there was anything to be gained by not knowing something. I think that's why I don't ever remember not being allowed to watch anything on the television. We know which programmes she didn't like because she told us, but she never stopped us watching them. She told us that she thought *Family Fortunes* was depressing because it rewarded the most predicable answer, but she still let us watch the show so we could decide whether she was right or not. Maybe we should have examined her biases a bit more, but at least we knew that they were biases, because she'd told us what bias was. She liked us to watch *Blue Peter, Newsround, Jackanory* and anything hosted by Tony Hart, but we were never made to watch them. I think we developed a far greater appreciation of ambitious children's television than we would have done if she had. She herself rarely got the chance to sit down and watch television; though programmes I can remember watching with her include *Antiques Roadshow, Monty Python, Last of the Summer Wine, Talking Heads*, a repeat of *Abigail's Party* and of course the most disturbing programme of all, the news. She didn't decide that anything was unsuitable for children, or assume that we would be bored.

She also loved to take us to libraries. I can see why: taking my own children to the library is one of my favourite activities now. Looking back, though, she'd probably taken us to the library in the hope of getting away from *Doctor Who* for a while, so it must have grated on her that we only seemed to want to get out Target novelisations. (She didn't get away from *Doctor Who* on the way to and from the library, as we probably made her listen to the BBC audio collection cassette of *The Evil of the Daleks* in the car. I can't say for certain that we did that, but we usually did.) *Doctor Who* wasn't on air at the time and if you

232

wanted a conversation in the playground about it you had to have it with one of the teachers.

'*Brave New World* is a book set in the future,' Mum told me, 'where people are graded alphabetically like they are here, and they wear colour-coded clothes like they do in this book.'

This is my main memory of *Doctor Who and the Sunmakers*: it brought *Brave New World* into my life and actually made me want to read it. I had to read it if there was a *Doctor Who* book like it. This is the way to introduce children to classic literature, finding some that's a bit like something they're already obsessed with. It'll mean telling them that something they love is probably full of plagiarism, but most things are and they've got to come to terms with that at some point.

I doubt if Mum had much sympathy with Robert Holmes moaning about his tax bill. She grew up in a working class family shortly after the war and brought us up to be grateful for the welfare state (and she does, still, consider the BBC to be a part of it).

She bought me a copy of *Brave New World*. At first I was disappointed by it. It just wasn't horrible enough. The inhabitants of Aldous Huxley's nightmare vision of Britain got to have casual sex and go to the cinema, whereas the inhabitants of Robert Holmes's Pluto were lucky if they got half an hour's unpaid leave to watch a gassing. When I complained to Mum about it, she pointed out that a lot of societies don't really seem that bad. Even a dictatorship would have to present itself as something that wouldn't seem that bad to most people. It was my first encounter with more subtle sci fi than *Doctor Who* offered. Still, it was pleasingly *Doctor Who*-like (it was exotically strange while being comfortingly middle class and British) and so I liked it.

To me, *The Sunmakers* is one of my favourite childhood books - it's not a TV programme I remember fondly because I never saw it until many years later, and it wasn't as good as the book. Terrance Dicks might not have been the genius that Bob was, but if you want to be pleasantly scared by something that's not likely to happen then this is the book for you. What actually happened under the rule of The Company is horrific enough that all you need is the words on the page to bring it home. Citizens of Pluto are referred to as 'work units', are destroyed on an allotted 'death day', accept this fate without question and have to pay for the privilege. Reading that is enough. You don't need to be distracted by cheap sets, or Tom Baker and Louise Jameson's total lack of pleasure in working together. No *Doctor Who* story benefits from being viewed for the first time as an adult.

Reading Huxley's book was like reading an unusually rich and textured *Doctor Who* book. *Doctor Who and the Sunmakers* was the first dystopian novel I ever read and it gave me a taste for them.

I hope I'll be able to take my mum's approach to raising and educating my children. It won't be easy: there are things that it's always going to be difficult to talk to children about, from where babies come from to where meat does, and like everyone I have plenty of my own personal untouchable subjects. You could say that there's no need, as if my kids want to know something they can always Google it, or use whatever will replace Google, and that's true, but... only if they already know what it is they want to know.

And you know what? *Family Fortunes* is brilliant. Without it there would be no *Pointless*, which is essentially the same show in reverse. And I'm grateful to Mum for letting me find that out.

Love at First Flight

Doctor Who – Time-Flight by Jamie Austin
Favourite *Doctor Who* book: *Script Doctor*
by Andrew Cartmel

Back in the early 1980s, there was a rather lovely girl at my school. She was in the year above me and was the oblivious recipient of my heart-rending crush. Conversations with my peers revealed that I was far from alone in my admiration. Completely unassuming, humorous and a pleasure to talk to, she was blessed with the flaxen hair and easy confidence that one now readily associates with TV advertisements for sanitary towels. She had an additional charm: she watched – and read about - *Doctor Who*. She was a kindred spirit who, one lunchtime, gave me a copy of *Time-Flight*; a casual act of kindness on her part which led us to being happily married some ten years later.

Well, no, sadly the last part is not true, but that moment of unexpected generosity has ensured that, for me, *Time-Flight* is forever associated with a beautiful innocence, evoking happy memories.

Nor is it alone. You see, unheeded, the Target books effortlessly wove themselves into the fabric of my early development and, bar a particularly dramatic spell of projectile vomiting a short time after receiving *The Talons of Weng-Chiang* (something which has coloured my appreciation of the story ever since), they provide very pleasant memories indeed, their titles spring-boarding into myriad recollections that would otherwise long since be forgotten. Consequently, I can recall that I first experienced the Doctor's struggles against the Weed Creature on a school trip to a nuclear power station, read of the Fang Rock horror amid an approaching thunderstorm and concentrated on the (thankfully truncated) antics of the Space Pirates while sitting at the back of a tedious Shakespeare lecture about... well, I forget what, but I do know that the Doctor's favourite marble is green and that he likes drawing pins - usually. You see, *every* Target book has a story of its own, way beyond its television and text counterpart – a personal story, forming a catalogue of associations. *The Dalek Invasion of Earth* = dentist; *The Loch Ness Monster* = school book club; *Dragonfire* = mock English exam; *Full Circle* = Woolworths; *Harry Sullivan's War* = an argument in W H Smiths. I could go on, not yet having touched upon the likes of 'rude newsagent', 'Oscar Wilde', 'porridge' or 'coach crashing into tractor' to name but four. Yet, despite these potential excitements, and likely due to the bias of unrequited love, *Time-Flight* itself stands tall.

This story was overshadowed on TV by the unfortunate necessity of trailing the budget-sapping *Earthshock* – a story with Cyber-smashing/Adric-bashing 'fan-pleaser' hard-wired into its DNA – but Peter Grimwade's novelisation had no such baggage. Unencumbered by scheduling, *Doctor Who - Time-Flight* stood as an adventure in its own right. Of course, this was where Target excelled: the writer's imagination let loose; Grimwade's vision unfettered by the cramped realities of TC8. In prose, the Doctor's crew *were* stranded in prehistoric times every bit as much as the Giant Robot was able to tackle an army not made by Palitoy and the Axonite blob blanket was a convincing threat.

There was far more to the novel than papering over questionable effects work (which, truth be told, never took me out of *Doctor Who* stories anyway). You see, it was hard not to be swept along by the exuberance and sheer breadth of imagination that Peter Grimwade brought to his *Doctor Who* adventures. Look at the structure of *Time-Flight* – a deceptively simple opening wherein Concorde vanishes. It's an interesting hook with a number of obvious plot directions opening up immediately. Fortunately, Grimwade eschews them all, weaving a tale of pre-history, crashed alien craft, illusions and one of the Master's most successful disguises ever. There is an astonishing wealth of material here, Grimwade's skill lying in his ability to intertwine the everyday and the fantastic.

And then there's the cover, which is simply beautiful. Like the story, it is deceptively simple at first. 'It's only a BBC publicity photograph,' you might think. But look again. The incongruity of Davison's old English style set against the far-from-being-retired Concorde, itself pointing towards the space-age neon *Doctor Who* logo. As separate elements, by rights they should be unconnected, their juxtaposition a nonsense – and yet it works. Beautifully too.

The subversion of the everyday is one of the great strengths of *Doctor Who* and Peter Grimwade understood this perfectly. The cover, like the text, epitomised the new, breathless approach that typified the wonderful John Nathan-Turner era. Imaginative and bold in execution, there was suddenly a sense that *anything* was possible. Nothing was off limits, especially where the new borderline insanity of the Master was concerned. *Doctor Who* suddenly had an edge, its stories thrilling and brimming with ideas. Peter Grimwade's excellent juxtapositions and boundless imagination were vital parts of this shift and he remains one of the unsung heroes of classic *Doctor Who*.

Time-Flight is glorious, the novel resurrecting pleasant memories. In fact, as I grow older the Target novels have increasingly taken on a new facet, immediately recalling happy times with cherished individuals whose loss is an aching void: getting *The Dalek Omnibus* as a Christmas present from my Gran and Grandad (both kindness personified), sharing *The Creature from the Pit* with my clearly

236

bemused Nan, and the copy of *The Two Doctors* bought for me by my father are just three examples among many.

The early 1980s went, but *Time-Flight* kept on giving. Back in the days of video tape, I won a signed copy of the Fifth Doctor's Concorde-based antics. The news of this genuinely exciting event took a little while to reach me. I had missed several telephone calls in fact, having been engrossed in some complicated alcohol-fuelled trampoline acrobatics; itself an unexpected opportunity very kindly offered to a group of fifty of us by a rather hospitable – if exiled - Eastern European monarch.

All absolutely true. My reality was finally catching up with Peter Grimwade's *Doctor Who* – a reality where anything could happen. A reality to be embraced!

The Library Cactus Terror

Doctor Who – Meglos by Chris Orton

Favourite *Doctor Who* book: *Remembrance of the Daleks*
by Ben Aaronovitch

'Never judge a book by its cover,' everybody always says. Wise words indeed, and something that most of us have probably learned not to do, but would you judge an entire building by the cover of one of the books that it contained? Well I did. In a way. Sort of.

The building in question was my local library and the star date was the mid-1980s. Thanks to my parents, I was always encouraged to read. I read storybooks, I read textbooks, I read comics, I read just about anything and back then the library was one of my main ports of call. Back then, books were more expensive than they are today and, with money tight at times, the little single-storey building in our town's market place was a great place to get your reading fix. They had all sorts of great stuff: I went through all of the *Asterix* books (umpteen times), all of the Tintin books (umpteen times), *Agaton Sax*, devoured Roald Dahl's back catalogue (umpteen times) and many, many other things too. So, as a fan of the television version, it was only natural that I would want to take out the hardback *Doctor Who* books I spotted one day on the shelves for older readers.

However, there only ever appeared to be three titles that I remember seeing in our library: *Doctor Who and the Cybermen*, *Doctor Who and the Zarbi* and one that went by the mysterious name of *Meglos*. Growing up with Peter Davison as my first proper Doctor, these titles were a bit of a mystery and I didn't really recognise them: were they adventures that the Fifth Doctor had experienced and that I had missed? Or were they all-new stories in book form? They surely can't have been from 'my' era, as they appeared to have other people on the covers in the role of our hero. Until I had seen the books in the library, my exposure to pre-Davison *Doctor Who* had been very limited. I was aware that there had been earlier Doctors of course, as I had caught the very end of Tom Baker's era, but these tales were all brand new to me. On some occasions the titles weren't there, so they must have been borrowed fairly regularly, but sure as eggs is eggs the books kept returning. Including *Meglos*.

It was this book that caused me to become a tad wary of one of my very favourite places. *Meglos* featured somebody on the cover who was of course the Doctor, but there was something very wrong about the image. This is what spooked me about the library. The picture looked *terrifying*. It was the Fourth Doctor, but his face was all spiky. What on Gallifrey had gone wrong with him? Had he had a terrible accident

238

whilst out collecting gooseberries? Was this some radical form of intergalactic acupuncture? Or was it perhaps a robot version of the Doctor? There are spikes sticking out of his face, for goodness sake! Why would the library have *this* horrific thing in their collection? Surely you can't let children see this sort of thing?

I didn't like it one bit and from then on the cover of the book slightly troubled me. I borrowed the two other books, but was reluctant to even go near *Meglos*. I just didn't like looking at it at all. The Doctor – my hero – shouldn't look like *that*. Purely because of this single book I became wary of venturing into the section where the titles for older children were housed, as I knew that *it* might be there. I could often see it in my mind's eye for a whole week, between each visit and I felt slightly wary of even going to the library. It all sounds rather illogical but at the age of seven or eight a mind fired up by a programme like *Doctor Who* can work in very strange ways.

Somehow my wariness subsided and I continued my weekly visits to the library, devouring more and more books with each visit. I became eager to explore the adventures that had occurred years before I was even aware of the show and began to seek out other titles. A cousin gave me brand new paperback copies of *The Dæmons* and *Destiny of the Daleks* in exchange for some *Star Wars* comics that I had and I'm fairly sure that lots of birthday money would have been spent in WH Smiths on Target novels. With my first pay cheque (a £10 voucher that I was given after having completed a spell of work experience at the age of 16) I bought *Ghost Light* and *Remembrance of the Daleks* (which I would come to consider the finest of all of the *Doctor Who* novelisations) in Durham's branch of Smiths. By this point, the titles were all being reprinted and I wanted to try to get through the lot. Amongst the dozens of titles I read, one name stood out above all others: that of Terrance Dicks...

Just how did this man manage to write quite so many books? Whilst his work may not have been anything particularly spectacular or refined, it was never anything less than eminently solid, exciting and readable and just the job for young bibliophiles like myself. This one writer must have been responsible for getting tens of thousands of children to read in the 1970s and beyond. Before your Charlie Higson and your Anthony Horowitz, we had Terrance. And his was the name emblazoned on the cover and spine of *Meglos*...

The fact that our library had those few *Doctor Who* titles was enough to keep me visiting week after week: slim in size, with straightforward language, the Target novelisations were the ideal way to progress from simpler material to more grown-up reading matter; they became a gateway to 'proper' reading for me. By continuing to visit the library, I gained an interest in a wider spectrum of reading matter than might have been the case had I not bothered going. A glance up at the shelf above or below the Target books could reveal a whole range of other fascinating things and open up even more worlds of the fantastic and informative. As you can see from the title of this piece, it even taught me Latin (this, of course, isn't true - I had to look it up on a translation website the other day, but the point remains). The library become one of my essential tools for research when I experienced the two-year spell of examinations between the ages of sixteen and eighteen because back then, believe it or not, there was no internet. This is where you went to do your research.

Perhaps inevitably though, other distractions got the better of me and my visits began to decline as I grew older. I continued reading *Doctor Who* books, but by this point the titles were stories that were probably too broad and deep for the children's section of any library or bookshop, and featured scenes scarier than any cactus-faced character. But without those first Target novelisations, I very probably wouldn't have gone anywhere near the Virgin New Adventures.

(But did I ever eventually get around to actually reading *Meglos*? Of course I did, albeit at a slightly older age. Up the time that I around the age of fourteen, I would probably have been just about brave enough to gaze upon that terrifying cover without having a funny turn. I read the book a good fifteen years before I ever managed to see the television episodes upon which it was based, and I think that I preferred the written word in this instance.)

Not so long ago, when he was only three, I introduced my son to the very same library and he is currently gaining a real love and appreciation of books. The same lady who stamped my *Doctor Who* books thirty years earlier stamped *Hugless Douglas and the Big Sleep*, *The Great Cheese Robbery* and *Those Magnificent Sheep in their Flying Machine* just the other day. The choice of titles overwhelmed my boy to begin with, but we began making a regular pilgrimage to this little haven of learning. Sadly, the hours at our branch were recently cut from around forty a week to just twenty, but it still manages to thrive. I only hope and dearly wish that our little library can survive any further forthcoming - and probably inevitable - public service cuts and will still be there in years to come when my son becomes a father. It would be fantastic to think that he could show his children the magic of the place in the same way that I did for him and my Dad did for me. (*Meglos* isn't there any more, by the way.)

So kids, do your best to support your local library. Yes, there are plenty of other things to do with your time and lots of other ways to consume reading matter, but these places really do matter. Libraries will entertain you, they will educate you, fire your imagination and will be one of the best friends you will ever have. They may even make you a little anxious as it did me, but being a bit scared is probably quite a healthy aspect of growing up. In this age when there are forces that would seek to throw public libraries onto the scrapheap and allow market forces to take control, they really do need us more than ever before.

If you are small and are reading this, don't let a strange image of the cover of a book put you off in any way. Even if you don't like the picture or design that you see, always be prepared to give it a go as it will reward you in many ways.

Doctor Who and The One I Never Finished

Doctor Who – Castrovalva
by Lucy Hyndman
Favourite *Doctor Who* book: *The Five Doctors*
by Terrance Dicks

We were poor. This was something that I never realised as a kid and in fact I was in my late twenties when I had this astounding realisation. It has to be said that this is entirely due to my mother. (The not realising, not the being poor bit. That was my alcoholic father's fault.) She did the most amazing job of keeping our family together, with a roof over our heads and food on the table and clean clothes on our backs. You see, to me the poor kids were the ones with dirty clothes, dirty faces. They were the kids who didn't get books for Christmas and birthdays, who didn't even have books in their houses. Imagine how poor you must be not to have books! Of course back then it didn't occur to me that the latest swish 22 inch TV set with remote control and CEEFAX, 8 bit computer game consoles and two cars parked on the verge probably meant that they weren't that poor. Their parents just weren't that bothered with them.

Like a lot of people back then, we rented our TV from Radio Rentals and I can remember being incredibly excited when we were due an upgrade and Mum said she could afford the extra 35p a week to have one with a remote control and CEEFAX. 35p. It seems almost laughable now, but back then and to us, it was a big deal.

I had homemade and/or hand-me-down clothes, my sister cut my hair, and outside of the things I received for Christmas and birthdays, if I wanted anything I had to save for it. Most of my book collection therefore is second hand, including most of my Target novelisations.

I was always excited to go to the library to see what books were on their sale table as whilst I couldn't, as a child, take out adult books, I could buy them. There, and in second-hand book stores, as I went from child to teen I got my hands on plenty of *Doctor Who* books along with the big four: at 12, I bought and read *1984*, *Brave New World*, *Fahrenheit 451* and *Flowers for Algernon*. Up until that point, I had mostly read children's science fiction, including a lot of Douglas Hill, as well as the *Star Wars* and *Doctor Who* novelisations, The few short story collections from Nebula prize winners that were sold off in the library were the only grown up science fiction I had read.

One of the reasons I loved the Target books was that they didn't seem like kids' books. They were more like adult books that I could easily understand. I was conscientious with my pocket money. At the age of thirteen, I was receiving £1 a week pocket money, always paid in 20p pieces as I would divide it up between my money boxes. One was my donation to the RSPCA, where our dog Susie had come from. One was my subscription to the *Star Wars* fan club (£11 a year I believe, sent by postal order). One was for buying birthday and Christmas presents for other people. The other 40p a week was mine to spend. Mostly it went on books. I had *Doctor Who* cups and posters, the magazine on order from the newsagents, a trip to the Longleat exhibition as my summer holiday treat one year, no toys - couldn't afford those – but books were available and affordable and *Castrovalva* was one of them. It cost me 15p from the library.

I always imagine the cover is black, but it isn't. There's much more blue, with stars on it. The spine is black, though, and I think that's where my memory fools me because I've seen the spine so much and very rarely looked at the cover.

Castrovalva is the book I've never finished.

It was *Doctor Who* and I desperately wanted to enjoy it. Just as I had all the others. I loved the episodes it came from. It started my interest in M.C Escher and his peculiar brand of warped perspective art and it was sciency and I liked sciency! The book was written by Christopher H Bidmead and wasn't he supposed to be all sciency too having had articles published in *New Scientist*?

As expected from the novelisation of a story by the man who wrote the TV story, it all seems in order. The characters are perfectly drawn and recognisable. I can hear their voices and see their movements and gestures in my head. It is written with a comfortable pace and the explanations for the Doctor's predicament and solution are sound.

So what was not to like?

I'd start off okay, reading along merrily, then there would come a point where it would tail off. I'd put it down and pick it up again days later, read a very few lines – sometimes even the same lines I'd already read, the way you do when you're tired and falling asleep reading. Then eventually it'd go back on the shelf unfinished and I would have started something else. It annoyed me and each time I came back to it I think I came back slightly annoyed. That isn't a good state of mind to read in. Hmmm...catch-22. Now I realise it was nothing to do with the story or the author or my ability to read and understand. It was just one of those books.

I run a children's book group at the library where I work, the same one I used to buy my books from as a kid. There are plenty of really good children's and teens' books around today but there isn't anything that feels like the Target books did to me. There are collections of books based around a theme (especially if you are a younger reader) that are eminently collectable but nothing of which I am aware that ties into one strong character; that covers a broad base of topics and wide range of writing styles; that keeps the interest alive. Maybe that's because children today aren't deprived like we were. (Cue *Monty Python* Four Yorkshiremen sketch.) If you have a favourite film or television series or cartoon, you can most likely watch it on DVD or online wherever you are. For us, as one of our few links outside of broadcast seasons, Target books had a huge importance. Times have changed and maybe they are just of their time. I am glad to have been around then, though, to enjoy them.

Over the years, I've realised that you don't *have* to like every book. One of our rules is that if you don't like it – don't read it. As long as you've given it a go and can say why you didn't carry on with it (boring is a perfectly acceptable answer and opinion) and read something else instead, I am happy. Our main goal for the group is to have *fun*. That won't happen if I force kids to read.

I've come to the conclusion that it's absolutely fine not to finish a book. In fact, with so many good books to read, it's imperative that sometimes you do sideline that book that just isn't doing it for you. Even if it is *Doctor Who*.

Judgemental

Doctor Who – Four To Doomsday
by Steven Alexander
Favourite Doctor Who book: *Cybermen* by David Banks

Trapped in the early nineties and bereft of ideas, I offered to take my younger self to the discount book store at the Harlequin Centre.

I was dismayed at Steven's choice of clothing, a garish patterned shirt from Mad House that I'd remembered being smart. I couldn't believe he was wearing it in public, yet he was the one who was embarrassed, making me walk five paces behind him. I asked Steven why he was ashamed to be seen with me given that we were literally the same person. He told me that people would think I was his dad and that the only people who took their dads shopping were sad cases.

I caught up with him at the *Doctor Who* novels. If I'd have been allowed to keep pace with him, I might have directed him to something more literary, but here we were. He was holding the re-issue of *Four to Doomsday* and he commented on how much better the artwork cover was than the original photograph. An older teenage boy chipped in and said that it was a shame that the spines were blue because they looked wrong on the bookshelf.

Steven put the book down and said he didn't want it. I said that back in the future I spent twice the cost of a Target novel on lunch every day and that I could buy him all of the *Doctor Who* books he didn't have. Steven grunted and then he managed to subtly creep out of the shop at high speed, a skill that I never knew I had.

I found him and asked what was wrong. He said that he didn't want to end up like him. That teenage boy was geeky, a weirdo, he was spotty and ugly. His face was so covered in acne that he looked like Monarch, the green space-toad who peered out from the cover of *Four to Doomsday*.

I was shocked by Steven's attitude. I started telling him that he would be nothing like that geeky boy, but then I realised that I was being as cruel as he was. That boy was who he was, a human being deserving respect and kindness. Steven shouldn't be so judgemental because eventually it would turn him into one of the bullies he was so afraid of.

That was when I realised – I couldn't save him from the years to come.

The Earth Shook

Doctor Who – Earthshock by Clay Dockery
Favourite *Doctor Who* book: The *About Time* books
by Lawrence Miles and Tat Wood

Earthshock is not a particularly great *Doctor Who* serial. The story is slow to get started, the Cybermen are doing the same thing they always do, the supporting characters are not well-developed, and the TARDIS team are locked into the same familiar set of discussions and distractions.

And then, abruptly, at the very end, it all changes.

Adric is dead.

The Cybermen are defeated, the show will go on, but for the first time a TARDIS team, and the Doctor, are fundamentally affected by the death of a companion. (No, the death of Katarina doesn't count, it should have been Vicki... but I digress.) This loss will haunt Davison's fifth Doctor until his last moments. It is an effective bit of television, ɯ ɒdɪɪɒ ɪ ɒllɪᵤᵧ ɒɪlɒᵤɪlɪ, ɒ ᵢ ɒᵢ Λdᵣɪɒ'ɒ ɒhɒɪɪɒᵣɒ d Ьɒᵢᵧɒᵢ Iↄ ɪɒ ɒ ɯɒɯᵢɒᵢ that can shape and reshape a viewer's experience of the show.

But the moment may be even more emotionally evocative in Ian Marter's Target novelisation. The build-up is much more intense, and there is a palpable sense of dread to every decision Adric makes in the final chapter, aptly titled 'Triumph and Tragedy'. The Doctor's simultaneous decisions back on the TARDIS are placed in stark relief: he thinks the resolution will be simple and that he will win the day as usual. By being able to follow each decision by each character, it is much easier to see the calculation behind the decisions and to follow the Doctor's shift from triumph to hubris to grief.

The use of Adric's gold, star-shaped badge - his award for his mathematical prowess that both saves the world and ultimately seals him in the place for his doom – to also defeat the Cyberleader in the TARDIS is clear in both stories, but the novelisation allows the symbolism to drip with intensity and underscores the fated tragedy even more than the visuals.

Then the novel ends, not with an extended sequence, or recap of the characters' thoughts, or even with the silent processing time the of the television episode. Instead, the Doctor stares at the ruined gold star badge and the novel ends with the line: 'With a sad smile he dropped it into his pocket and turned resignedly toward the console...'

There is nothing after the ellipsis.

Return to the Centre of the Known Universe

Doctor Who – Terminus by Richard Martin

Favourite *Doctor Who* book: *Interference*
by Lawrence Miles

Sometime in the late 1980s, I stowed my copy of *Terminus* in a box alongside sundry other Targets and shoved the lot on top of a wardrobe at my parents' home in a quiet North-Western suburb of Sydney, Australia.

I was packing away a whole geographical layer of my life – primary school years of awkwardness and social isolation, then happier memories from early high school, when fandom led to rewarding friendships with a few like-minded souls. At some point, we all jettisoned *Doctor Who* – to be honest it was pretty easy to let go during the post-Davison era of the show. Instead we discovered girls and rock music and our love of the series was left behind in all the excitement, a slightly embarrassing phase that we'd grown out of.

I packed it all away carefully, knowing that one day I'd open the box again and rummage around in the artefacts of childhood enthusiasm. As a *Doctor Who* fan, I guess I've never quite accepted the impossibility of time travel and I'm always fascinated by the way memory and nostalgia can influence our sense of the present and our sense of self.

Turns out I opened the box as a 41-year-old father of two, brushing away the dust and cobwebs while my partner Olivia kept Henry, Guy and my parents company in the living room. The same house in the same suburb where I grew up, a fixed point in time, or in my timeline at least.

Terminus was just as I remembered – a little thicker than the average Target and featuring a lurid orange cover that I had thoughtfully covered in 'sticky back plastic' (known in Australia by the brand name Contact) – a misguided attempt to protect it from the ravages of time. My nine-year-old self had written his name on the title page and then one year later I'd updated this with my newer signature – they are virtually indistinguishable, but both have a nifty 80s zappiness to them.

The Target photo covers get a lot of stick, but I remember loving them; in the pre-video era even a drab publicity still could be a bit exciting. *Terminus* has that wonderfully non-dynamic picture of Davison fiddling around with a vice-thing while the Black Guardian floats in the background like an evil woodwork teacher.

247

In 1983 the book's lack of chapter breaks felt pretty avant-garde for kids' lit, and I certainly felt a sense of achievement when I made it to the end (on the second or third attempt). Is it fanciful to ascribe a later-life taste for 'difficult' art to the satisfaction I gained from ploughing through *Terminus*? If we accept that Terrance Dicks was responsible for thousands of kids' love of reading, then perhaps it is not too much of a stretch to imagine that 'John Lydecker' got a handful onto James Joyce or Patrick White.

Strangely, in my one clear memory of reading *Terminus* I'm waiting for a bus at Wynyard Station in the centre of Sydney – which, at that time, was the terminus for many of the city's bus routes. Perhaps that's just my mind playing tricks.

The story itself plays impressively fast and loose with a number of SF concepts that may not hold up to adult scrutiny, but to a nine-year-old the Centre of the Known Universe was pretty heady stuff. I particularly enjoyed the TARDIS scenes at the beginning, the sense of threat encroaching on a 'safe space' and the uncertainty around Turlough's motivations and intentions. JNT got plenty of things wrong, but I think the notion of the untrustworthy companion was an interesting innovation, and I certainly identified with the character.

I met Mark Strickson once, in the early 2000s, during the time he was producing wildlife documentaries in Australia. We chatted at a post-production studio about the difficulties of getting cabs in Sydney. I didn't realize who it was until after he'd left and enjoyed the thought of a such a casual encounter with someone who had been a childhood hero (or anti-hero).

Doctor Who has featured in my work life quite a few times. I work as a promo producer, scripting and editing the trailers for television shows. Over the years I've been fortunate enough to cut *Doctor Who* spots for a number of different Australian channels, and have even done a few small jobs for the local arm of the BBC. The occasions I've been able to work on *Doctor Who* have always been happy times; it is always a pleasure and a privilege to be paid to sit down and watch an episode and my inner nine-year-old is delighted. It's a lovely feeling when one's enthusiasms and work converge and I think people who regularly obtain that sense of deep satisfaction from their work are extremely fortunate.

Having exhumed them, I'm not sure what I'll do with my old Targets now. I might keep a couple for the kids, but I think I'll probably give most of them to a charity store or second-hand bookshop. My sons are aware of the current incarnation of *Doctor Who*, and I think that's great. However I'm not particularly keen to actively instil in them the strain of fandom from my own childhood – that of reading for escapism, over-identification with an imaginary world, and the completionist's mentality.

Doctor Who was an important part of my childhood and continues to be a fondly-regarded presence in my life, but as I've grown older, I've also grown uncertain of the wisdom and worth of hoarding physical evidence of the past. Over the years I've ditched magazines, comics, NAs and EDAs. Now, having written this essay, I think it's time to jettison yet another part of that history. The dictionary defines a terminus as an end to something, but implicit in that is the beginning of another journey. Onwards...

A Cover Like Burnt Orange

Doctor Who – Arc of Infinity by Steven B

Favourite *Doctor Who* book: *Castrovalva*
by Christopher H Bidmead

The 1990s were a long time ago. A colourful, forward-looking moment in time; the young counted down the ticking clock to something monumental, perched as we then were on the verge of an imminent third millennium. This was to be the anointed moment when we would ascend to maturity – legal, physical and symbolic; when we were to inherit at last the Earth in a much-promised glory of the coming 21st century. Enthused by The New and each prospect and all aspects of it, the decades and eras that came before seemed, to those who cared to notice, to disperse, disappear, dematerialise before us. We began to forget. But some of us remembered.

Retreating once again out of the sun of that present into the past of yet another library, I remember finding in its silence, on a still and sunny seaside afternoon, a brach but battered, orange and yellow unfamiliar Terrance Dicks. The photo montage of a youthful blonde Doctor threatened (it would turn out) at impulse laser point by a distinguished old Time Lord in Prydonian robes, rather listlessly arranged under a bright neon logo, promised much, not merely in terms of its narrative, but more importantly with regard to its ethos, its promise, its very New-ness. Even its title suggested a kind of story that I had never before seen in my then still-burgeoning experience of *Doctor Who*. I clutched the new-found old treasure from 1983 in my anticipatory hands all the way home, eager to disappear into its past.

What only occurred to me much later was that this ancient relic – by its cover alone – summarised, in inverse, what was happening around me during that time: The Old no longer threatened The New. At some point between its own time and mine, the future had killed the past, turning around the threat of that impulse laser – nay, demat gun – but going one step further than the past was ever able to in its threats against its own future. The New had – at some point, entirely unnoticed – eradicated The Old from our memory of Time.

It was the 1990s. 1983, 1973, 1963 was a long, long time ago. In fact, that time was dead – and so was *Doctor Who*.

Nobody cared. No-one remembered.

Well, almost nobody.

Sliding Doctors

Doctor Who – The Five Doctors by Rob Irwin

Favourite *Doctor Who* book: *A Celebration* by Peter Haining

My local library in the 1980s was a dark, low-slung, claustrophobic piece of architecture that smelled funny. Compared with the much larger, brighter and friendlier libraries that have now sprung up in the area, it was basically a medieval dungeon with books. Make no mistake, if you told me that during its eventual decommissioning they found skeletons propped up in the darkest corners - forgotten readers from decades past - I wouldn't bat an eyelid.

Despite this, starting in February of 1987, nothing was going to stop me from becoming a regular visitor to that odd little place, now that I had started high school and was hanging around right outside its doors every afternoon as I waited for a bus to take me home. I would walk through those doors, smell that weird semi-antiseptic odour that seemed to permeate its walls and move silently through the stacks, through the gloom, to where a certain cache of books were located.

You see, the reason behind these visits into the underworld was simple. I was in my first flush of fully-fledged *Doctor Who* fandom. Although I'd first been shown the program in the late 1970s (initially fleeing the room in terror at the theme music), and had certainly watched it and discussed stories with my older brother during the 1980s, I'd recently taken that big step into what I'd call 'proper' fandom with *Doctor Who Magazine* #119 (Dec 1986). As this had happened in the absence of knowing anyone else who wanted to talk to me about the program (the aforementioned older brother had finished school and had a job), I found the best thing I could do for my new-found hunger was to borrow tons and tons of Target novels and live out the adventures in my own headspace. A path well-trod by many fans.

I even got into the habit of photocopying Target covers and pasting them into an exercise book. I don't really remember why I started doing this, but I think the general idea was to make an archive of things I never thought I could own. After all, these books were older than myself in some cases; they were like antiques to me. I could then gaze upon the covers when I was at home - without having to borrow them - and feel like I owned them. Well, the images at least. I realise this might sound incredibly weird, but I quite liked the artwork and there were few ways an 11-year-old could cheaply compile a collection like that in 1987. It would be years before we all got on the Internet and started scanning and sharing images with ridiculous ease.

Time passed and I started looking through lists of old TV stories to

251

give me a sense of what other books might be available. Some titles I remembered well, thanks to the repeat schedule of *Doctor Who* in Australia and the slow trickle of VHS releases. For other stories, I was uncertain if I'd ever seen them before. Such a story was *The Five Doctors*. Had I seen it when it aired a little over three years earlier? When you're 11 years of age, going on for 12, three years earlier seemed like an eternity ago. It's basically a quarter of your whole life. There was only one thing to do - to track down that Target novelisation!

I made my way to a row of computer terminals in the library where you could search for books. I duly tapped in the details and was initially elated to find *The Five Doctors*, but then instantly deflated when I realised it was located at another branch of the library. This meant it would have to be ordered in. How long would that take? A week, perhaps? A week! That's forever when you're 11 and you want something right now. I mean, anything could happen in that week. I might go off *Doctor Who*. I might forget I ordered it. The USSR might launch an attack and destroy life as we know it. These were all real fears to my prepubescent mind.

Next to these terminals was an information desk. Huge and wooden, multiple librarians sat on the other side of the desk and I always got the sense that they didn't like kids being in their workplace. Regardless, I asked if I could have *The Five Doctors* ordered from the other branch. The necessary bureaucracy was concluded and the deed was done.

At this moment, an older boy approached me.

Had he heard correctly, he politely asked me; had I just requested a copy of *The Five Doctors*? I said yes without thinking, but then suddenly wondered what was about to happen. Who went up to a stranger and asked them about *Doctor Who* of all things? Was I about to get beaten up by anti-Whovian forces? I braced myself but shouldn't have worried because, within seconds, he told me his name was Mark and he ran the local *Doctor Who* club, Timeflight. He explained how they would meet and watch old episodes (he had *The Five Doctors* and plenty more) and also made their own magazine. It all sounded very grand and, at last, people I could talk to about *Doctor Who*! Forgetting that I hadn't known him three minutes earlier, I provided my phone number, as well as my favourite Doctor and companion ('for his files'), and he said he'd be in touch.

I soon found myself attending Timeflight meetings; seeing all the old episodes as Mark had promised was amazing. This progressed into writing and drawing for the fanzine and attending events put on by the much-larger Australasian *Doctor Who* Fan Club. That progressed into attending conventions, meeting the stars of the show, tape trading with other fans, making fan films where I was cast as the Doctor (even though I'd never acted in my life), and finally, making my own fanzine.

All of this, you will note, because I was overheard requesting *The Five Doctors* at the library.

Even today, in 2016, I sometimes wonder what would have happened if I'd never requested that book at that precise moment, or if Mark had not gone to the library that day. There are any number of possibilities which aren't weird or outrageous in the slightest. Things that could have happened very easily instead. I guess they're the usual sorts of questions people ask themselves after a major event happens in their lives, either for good or bad. Because, while a non-Whovian might laugh, this was absolutely a major event in my life. I just breezed through some of the experiences that joining Timeflight afforded me, but I could write whole essays just on the making of our fanzine, or the fan films, or the conventions we attended. I could write about how the club was my first real brush with things like councils, committees and elections and the things people will do if they see such roles as desirable and important. I could tell you all about the time we ended up on a TV show, in cosplay (not that it was called cosplay in those days), for *Doctor Who*'s 25th anniversary.

There are so many connections I've made, skills I've learned and interests that have been fostered as a result of being in that fan group during my pre-teens and teens, rippling through time throughout the rest of my life, that it's clearly one of my most formative events. Does that sound a little much? I don't feel I'm overstating it in the slightest. For example, I later became a journalist and magazine editor - and can genuinely trace it back to making fanzines. I can pick up the phone, right now, and talk to the EP of one of Australia's top morning TV programs. Why? Because he was in Timeflight, later parlaying his interest in fan films and video editing into a long and successful career in television production. I think about the guy who was best man at both my weddings - clearly an important person to me – who was a school chum of some other Timeflight members. I think about a later hobby – tabletop wargaming - and how a couple of the guys I still play with are former Timeflight members. I scroll through my Facebook contacts and note many friends from that era are still in my life when friends from other eras have dropped away.

I also ponder whether my love of *Doctor Who* would have progressed in the way it did - especially after 1989 - or whether the lack of contact with other fans would have meant interest in the series quietly slipped away? What makes this especially stunning to me is that I genuinely believe there's a better than average chance I wouldn't have come across Timeflight without that chance meeting in the library. The club didn't go out of its way to market itself in the local area. I never would have noticed it.

In closing, I'm quite confident that anyone reading this book can point to *Doctor Who* as a significant force in their lives and probably the reason certain life events have occurred. Still, I'm intrigued as to how many people have had their whole life in fandom hinge on simply saying the name of a Target novel aloud and still be reaping the benefits of that moment decades later? I try not to believe in fate or things that were 'meant to be', which leaves me thinking that, for a moment in 1987, I was simply one of the luckiest people on the planet. The wind blew in the right direction and my life was forever changed.

All thanks to the Target novelisation of *The Five Doctors*.

Location, Location, Location

Doctor Who – Mawdryn Undead
by Ian Farrington
Favourite *Doctor Who* book: *Doctor Who On Location*
by Richard Bignell

It's a cold day in January 2016 and I'm heading north out of central London. Now that the Piccadilly Line is above ground, the city is flashing by the windows, while my train carriage is full of commuters and tourists and other travellers. But I'm not paying any attention. Instead I'm reading the novelisation of *Mawdryn Undead* for the first time in years.

The book was written by Peter Grimwade, adapting his own TV scripts, and published in January 1984. A large chunk of the action takes place at Brendan School, a grand institution set in what the book calls rolling parkland. So when the story had been made for television, the production team needed a suitable filming location.

After half an hour or so on the tube, I reach the end of the Piccadilly Line. I put my book back in my bag and walk through Cockfosters Station, turn right and walk up Cockfosters Road. (Note for overseas readers: yes, there really is a part of London called Cockfosters.) After a few minutes, I reach an attractive stone-and-brick gateway: the western entrance to Trent Country Park.

Covering 320 hectares, this public park was once part of Henry IV's hunting grounds. After politician Philip Sassoon purchased the estate in 1909, the fourteenth-century house – Trent Park – became famed in society for its lavish hospitality. Winston Churchill, Charlie Chaplin and George Bernard Shaw all stayed there. Then during the Second World War it was used to hold captured German pilots and officers whose private conversations were bugged by British intelligence. Later the site became a training college then, from 1974, a campus of Middlesex University. But Trent Park and its associated modern buildings have stood empty since the university sold them in 2012.

As I enter the park, the ground surrounding the paved areas is sodden thanks to recent heavy rain. I pass a war memorial then hit a very long, straight road. There are dog-walkers and I spot ducks on a small pond. At the end of the road is a quaint lodge and just beyond it is a column topped by a stone pineapple (no, honestly). Finally, here I am. Trent Park itself, the house so familiar from the TV production of *Mawdryn Undead* where it stood in for Brendan School. Here's the courtyard where Turlough and his friend Hippo steal the Brigadier's Humber Tourer. Annoyingly, though, I can't get too close. The house is enclosed by temporary metal railings and I can see workmen bringing out rubbish and throwing it into skips. There are no vintage cars today, just white vans.

Trent Park is still as pretty and impressive as it was in August 1982 when the cast and crew of *Mawdryn Undead* assembled for a three-day location shoot. Redbrick with lovely detailing, the building is shaped like a capital E. In his novelisation, Peter Grimwade wrote of Brendan School belonging to a 'bygone world of landed wealth and privilege' – and that's easy to feel with Trent Park. Sadly, though, some ground-floor windows are now boarded up. I stand next to the barrier, looking through at the courtyard. I take out my paperback and skim through the opening few pages. Grimwade's invented history dates Brendan School as a Queen Anne-era building, previously the seat of the Mulle-Heskiths but sold in 1922 after the death of Sir Barrie Mulle-Heskith. None of the 'rose-gardens, arbors and wisteria pergola' mentioned in the book are evident in real life.

Behind me is a grassy area and I spot another filming location. Just over there is where Tegan bumped into some students carrying Silver Jubilee flags. I walk across, slightly uphill, and am now close to the complete other buildings – unfortunately, these are also encircled by barriers. On my side of the barrier is a disused bus stop – a television scene between the Brigadier and Tegan was filmed here - but I'm disappointed that so much of the site is out-of-bounds.

Oh, wait – there's a gap between the barriers over there. It seems to be a public footpath, so I see where it goes. On one side is a pretty, well-kept, white house; on the other are numerous overgrown and neglected outbuildings. I think under all this foliage will be areas used for filming *Doctor Who*. (I already know that the Brigadier's clapperboard hut has long since been demolished, so I certainly won't be seeing that.) As I hit a secluded lane with a row of cottages, almost by accident I stumble across the field where Turlough crashed the Brig's car.

It's now 3pm and the park will be closing in an hour. It's time to seek out the Obelisk, a key location. I have a printed Google map, which gives me a vague idea of its general position. It's the other side of the house, though, so I double back on myself. I'm slightly shocked to realise that I need to pass a 'Keep out' sign I hadn't previously spotted! Part of me hopes I get challenged. Perhaps a workman will ask me why I'm trespassing. It would make a fun anecdote, if nothing else. However, the men seem less than interested and barely even look at me.

In the novelisation, the Obelisk is visible from where Turlough and Hippo steal the car, but the theft is said to take place at the back of the building, not the front where the scene was filmed in 1982. So I find a footpath to the west of Trent Park, which leads me through some thick woodland. I'm off the concrete pavements now. The ground is sodden and slippery, especially as I head down into a valley. I'm just passing a small lake and starting to admit that I'm lost when I see it. To the north, on top of a long rise, is the Obelisk. It juts up on the horizon, visible only because a stretch of forest was long ago cut away to create an open area – known as the Vista – from the summit to the house. In the book, Turlough thinks of the Obelisk as a 'sombre pinnacle that dominated the horizon, silhouetted against the sky like a sword of some Angel of Death.' It's certainly big.

The only way I can get closer is to leave the footpath and climb the grassy slope. We've had a lot of rain lately and I can see that the ground is wet through. I risk it and regret my decision straight away. This part of the park was once used for pheasant shooting. I doubt the birds had as much trouble as I'm having now. Soon my feet are sinking with each step. Mud is caking my trainers and I nearly fall on my arse, but I keep going. Close by, I can see a woman walking her dog. She's wearing Wellington boots. Clever. Bloody hell – I'm now sinking into what is becoming actual mud. I carry on, squelching with each step as I climb the long rise. About two-thirds of the way up, I have to cross a small steam with a flat wooden bridge, after which the ground starts to level out.

I'm short of breath as I reach the summit. I take consolation from the fact that in the book the Brigadier 'wheezes like a grampus' as he climbs the hill – even if he'd earlier chided Ibbotson about being unfit ('If you took more exercise…'). I'm also completely devoid of clean shoes, but the Obelisk is superbly impressive and well worth the sacrifice. Twenty metres tall, it originally stood in Bedfordshire. Philip Sassoon bought and moved it here as recently as 1933. As I get closer, I can see it has an inscription marking the 1702 birth of the son of the Duke and (as the Obelisk spells it) Dutchess of Kent. Peter Grimwade had other ideas: in his novelisation, we're told the structure was erected in memory to General Rufus Mulle-Heskith.

In front of it is a bench, sadly not the one seen on TV: this one's only been here since 2008. I sit down, necessarily after my dogged schlep. For the first time, I look back through the Vista. What a wonderful sight. Grimwade's description of it in the book, which I now dig out and reread, mentions the sun dappling the lake at the bottom of the valley. Well, I think I can see the lake in the distance but I'm here in January, not the cricket season of the story. To my left is the area where the transmat capsule landed although the small stone plinths that were added for the filming are, of course, nowhere to be seen. I have the entire area to myself. It's peaceful and serene and rather wonderful.

I find myself reading more and more of *Mawdryn Undead*, even going back over chapters I did earlier today. In the story, the Brigadier can't remember an event from a few years previously. It now occurs to me that I once had a similar experience. Having only watched *Doctor Who* occasionally as child, I became a serious fan in the early 1990s. One of the first VHS tapes I bought was *Mawdryn Undead*, a serial that to my knowledge I'd never seen before. However, as I watched Part One, I realised I was instinctively humming along to Paddy Kingsland's incidental music. It was clearly buried deep somewhere in my brain. I must have seen the episode on transmission when I was a toddler.

I soon sought out the novelisation. I think I found it in a charity shop. As with many of the Target books, it combines a faithful recreation of a TV serial with lovely flashes of extra detail and richer characterisation. Rediscovering it today and taking a tour of the 'real' Brendan School is a delightful experience.

After my rest, it's time to move on. Not wanting to brave the squelchy Vista in reverse, I instead turn west and pass where the TARDIS prop stood during the 1982 filming. A footpath leads me through dense woods and I slowly loop back round to the bottom of the valley. As I walk, I don't think about my foot cold and wet and caked in mud, but about Turlough and Hippo, the Brigadier's car, the Silver Jubilee, flashback sequences and the Blinovitch Limitation Effect. And I smile.

Getting Away with It

Doctor Who – Kinda by Rob Irwin

Favourite *Doctor Who* book: *A Celebration* by Peter Haining

My overriding memory of school in 1987 – my first year of high school – is that it was an endless summer, spent in rooms that smelt of new carpet and youthful imagination.

Okay, so maybe it rained once in a while and perhaps some of my chums weren't the sharpest tools in the shed, but that new carpet smell? That was always present. Our school, you see, was brand-new. Many buildings it would later feature had yet to be started, let alone built. Something that was in place from Day One, however, was a library. Although it started in a temporary location (which would later become a pair of classrooms), it was always a space I felt comfortable in, and where we'd sometimes be encouraged to lie on the floor and read.

At first I duly obliged with what I thought I should be reading. Being a touch precocious, I remember devouring Orwell's *1984* in a bid to impress my English teacher, at an age when most of the other kids around me were struggling to really understand *Animal Farm*. Then I realised something interesting. The library had a set of novels by Ian Fleming. Furthermore, it seemed that I could spend these reading periods with James Bond shooting people, shagging women and driving fast cars rather than reading 'proper' literature. This was outrageous! I felt I was onto something. Had any of my chums caught on to this?

With Bond exhausted, I then found a shelf full of *Doctor Who* novels I didn't own! Enter *Kinda*. To this day, I cannot look at its photo cover or even think of the Target novelisation in general without smelling that new carpet, or feeling the hard floor on my shoulder blades as I would lie on my back, chuckling to myself that I was somehow getting away with it and reading fun stuff, rather than what I thought the school would be wanting me to read.

In the end, of course, the joke was on me. The Target novels fired our imaginations, taught us useful (and maybe not so useful) turns of phrase, and encouraged us to read at an age when it didn't really matter whether it was *1984* or *Kinda*: it was just reading that mattered.

Did you feel like you were getting away with it, too? If you're reading this, I daresay you did!

The Legend Returns

Doctor Who – Snakedance
by Jack Dexter
Favourite *Doctor Who* book: *The Programme Guide*
by Jean-Marc Lofficier

Jack gazed distractedly out of the window as the City Dart pulled up to the bus stop at the bottom of Park Street and heaved an impatient sigh. At this rate, the shop was going to be closed before he got there. It was the second time he had had to race down Chester Park Road, hop on a number five City Dart bus and make his way into town that day. On his first visit, he had spotted the book in a shop window and had known right there and then, he had to own it. Unfortunately, however, he had been one pound and twenty-seven pence short of the cover price, so had dashed home again (which was no mean feat, as it entailed a six-mile bus ride, a twenty-minute walk and a considerable degree of patience with an erratic bus timetable), retrieved some money stashed in an old Quality Street tin on his bedroom shelf and headed back into town, hoping he could return before the shop shut. He checked his watch. It was 4:32pm. The shop didn't close until 5:00pm, but his sense of urgency did not desert him as he alighted from the bus.

Forbidden Planet was the name of the shop in question, located halfway up a steep hill of Georgian buildings crowned with a Victorian Gothic university. The shop was small and unobtrusive and specialised in merchandise associated with the science fiction, horror and fantasy genres. As Jack approached, he quickly checked the window display – it was still there, taking centre stage.

He had always been passionate about books, but why he should feel so entranced by this particular book was beyond Jack's comprehension. *Doctor Who – Snakedance* was another Terrance Dicks-penned story, the sequel to *Kinda*, and if its predecessor was anything to go by (not to mention the *Doctor Who Monthly* review), it wasn't going to light up the literary world, but that didn't overly concern the thirteen-year-old. While other authors had a tendency to flesh out the original story, to add description, background and context, with a Terrance Dicks novel the reader knew what he or she was getting from the get-go; a solid, straightforward retelling of the script, more or less as it had unfolded on screen.

When Jack read a story from a previous Doctor, a story that had been transmitted years earlier, he had a sense of it being before his time and engaged with it differently than he would a novelisation of a script that had first been transmitted that same year. No matter how much he enjoyed the older books, his scant knowledge of the regular characters, aliens and worlds somehow made the older novels feel less accessible than the contemporary adventures of the fifth Doctor. Perhaps it was all a question of context.

It was nearly a year since *Snakedance* had been shown on the telly. The first cliffhanger was still fresh in Jack's memory: Tegan laughing maniacally, the snake skull, the crystal ball exploding as it heralded the coming of the Mara. In the books you were able to read people's thoughts, not just their words and actions. Perhaps it was the thrill of digesting in prose what he had recently witnessed on screen that made *Snakedance* so appealing.

Pushing open the shop door, Jack scurried inside and navigated his way through a forest of ephemera to reach the till. He had become a familiar customer over the last few months. The stout, grey-haired man perched on a wooden stool with his back to the window display knew immediately what the young lad had returned for and with a wry smile retrieved the book without saying a word. Jack thanked him, paid the £5.95 cover price and then, with a considerable amount of satisfaction, departed.

Minutes later, the City Dart was trundling back to Chester Park Road with a very satisfied passenger on board. Jack withdrew the book from the shop bag and quickly read the back-cover blurb before opening the book and devouring the first page.

Jack gazed distractedly out of the window as he tried to think of something deep and meaningful to write. The problem was that no matter how hard he tried he couldn't think of anything, let alone something deep and meaningful, to say about the story at all. He scratched his head and with a blank expression sought inspiration from the ceiling of his bedroom-cum-study. He was probably thinking too hard. He could, he supposed, write about Buddhist mysticism and how it related to Christopher Bailey's script. Or describe his appreciation of Andrew Skilleter's stunning cover artwork. Wax lyrical about Terrance Dicks being the 'spiritual uncle' of the series, perhaps. As he contemplated, he thought to himself: 'This is all too obvious a start for an essay about my passion for the *Doctor Who* Target book range'.

He rubbed his eyes and closed his laptop. It was late and he was tired. Earlier that day, he had manoeuvred his most cumbersome item of furniture into the corner of the bedroom in his recently renovated flat. He wandered over to the Police Box-shaped cabinet, turned the Yale key inside its lock pushed open the double doors to reveal a bespoke bookcase packed spine-to-spine with WH Allen, Longbow and

261

Wingate titles and carefully took one particular title from a shelf. A coiled serpent with its jaws engulfing a planet sprung from the cover. Woven into the neon logo was an emblematic, mid waist portrait of Peter Davison. The cover artwork was as striking today as it had been when he had first seen it more than thirty years ago.

This copy of *Doctor Who – Snakedance,* however, was not the same one he had originally purchased in 1984. The extensive collection of Target books Jack had amassed throughout his teens had disappeared within months of him letting his home to a particularly unscrupulous tenant. He had bought it again on eBay several years later. A seller had listed a dozen or so mint *Doctor Who* hardbacks on the site and in a wave of nostalgic enthusiasm Jack had snapped up as many as he could afford to bid for. When it arrived in the post a few days later, he had instantly been transported back to his teens and had caught the collecting bug all over again.

Jack made himself a coffee and wandered back to his desk with caffeine-fuelled determination. He had had months to write this essay and it was already a late submission – a very late submission. In addition to this, it was not a well-written piece, and to top things off he still hadn't worked out what it was about this particular book which had made it his title of choice in the first place. The cover? The Doctor? The adversary? The companions? The plot? The prose? Maybe it was a combination of all of these and maybe it was something he had yet to consider.

It had been a while since Target novelisations were the principal (and often sole) medium for fans to re-experience the show. Now that all the stories that existed in the BBC archives had been released on DVD, the novelisation range could have seemed redundant in 2016, but Jack's TARDIS bookcase continued to dominate the room. Like the Mara, the legend of WH Allen and its paperback imprint, Target, could never belong only to the past.

A Little Bit of *Who* in an Age of Romance

Doctor Who – Enlightenment
by Christine Grit
Favourite *Doctor Who* book: *Engines of War* by George Mann

When I was studying in the wonderful Dutch city of Groningen, of which I assume most readers will not have heard, in the 1980s (approximately thirty years ago) my friends and I were in the habit of swapping romance novels during exam periods. Now, I expect most readers will think, 'What's such a silly habit got to do with our beloved Target books?' Don't worry, I'll explain later.

During this period, we had picked up the habit of making up a 'talking novel': I would be sitting with a friend in the pub, glass of red wine in hand, and together we would 'write' a romantic novel according to the rules of the Mills & Boon range. These books were quite boring and all written according to a certain, easily copied, formula: the men would obviously be good-looking with strong chins and be very masculine, while the female leads would not precisely fit into the stereotypical view of beauty (but would still be thin); the protagonist and antagonist would always meet in some tropical place; the male would be dominant, but the woman would not accept that, leading to lots of verbal fights; usually there would be an absolutely beautiful woman present who would be a real bitch. After some adventure (such as a threatening situation for the female lead involving a nasty, ugly islander, encouraged by the bitch woman, with the male lead saving her in the nick of time) both leads would suddenly realise that they loved each other all along. Wedding bells and stuff would generally follow.

Pretty predictable, all of them, so we would imagine all kinds of divergent paths for our stories, accompanied by a lot of laughs during the course of the evening, especially when we lost count of the numbers of glasses of wine swallowed. How did we get to know the formula of these books so well? We must have read loads of these silly books, no? We did. Now why would a bunch of studying girls read this kind of nonsense anyway? We should have known better, right? We did know - we just didn't want to acknowledge it.

Anyone who was ever a university student will remember the exam periods when one had to study night after night with hardly any social life at all. That's all part of the game. It was perfectly okay with me as most of my friends were undergoing the same lack of social mingling, except for that moment late in the evenings when one would put the

263

books down, finally calling it a day. I could never go to bed immediately but needed a diversion before being able to fall asleep. Dutch telly being what it was (and fundamentally still is), my choice would be to read a book. However, the books I generally liked to read required many hours of reading to be able to finish them and to my great regret, once I start reading I want to finish the book, even if that means it's suddenly five in the morning and I still haven't gone to bed yet. Not the best timing if you're having an exam at 8.30! My solution was to read a Mill & Boon novel, or a similar kind of book in Dutch. It would take less than an hour to read from beginning to end, and I would be totally diverted from the subject of my studies! Many of my fellow students had the same problem and so we started a swapping pool of these romantic novels. None of us wanted to keep them afterwards: we openly acknowledged they were bad (the grammar generally was abominable), but they were the perfect sleeping draught in times of woe (yes, we called the times of study that).

I suddenly got shocked out of my complacency when one of the pool books turned out to be *Enlightenment*. I didn't know of the existence of novelisations of *Doctor Who* stories, so it was a nice surprise! In fact, I've always remembered how pleased I was that this book turned out to be totally different from the ones with the strong chins, but could still be read within the hour. What a joy! Although I imagined the Doctor as being the one with the scarf and I didn't understand why he was travelling with Tegan and Turlough, two total strangers to me, the book stirred a bit of nostalgia as I remembered that favourite show of mine which I hadn't seen for many years. I never found out who actually dropped that book into our pool of swappable books, but I do know I was very, very grateful. After all, a story of pirates in space did offer a totally different kind of diversion than the strong chins, arguments and predictable adventures in the regular Mills & Boon fare.

Was *Enlightenment* a game changer? Alas, no, I can't say that it was. The next day, I was reading one of the boring Mills & Boon stories again and the Target book went back into the pool. Strangely enough, only one of my study mates mentioned the difference in tone and type of adventure in this particular book, but I expect the others didn't even read past page 5 when they realised this book wasn't a romance, but a swashbuckling adventure of a Time Lord.

However, reading this book did make me pick up and buy many more of the Target books after I had finished studying. I even bought this particular one to be able to re-read it. All of them had their positive points, not least by having more variety than strong chinned men and tropical locations! They become an ideal diversion whenever I arrived home rather late: always a quick read, just enough to forget the troubles encountered during the day.

And the 'talking novels'? One can hardly blame a girl for continuing to like the set up in the pub. These sessions, filled with squeals of laughter, remained a perfect antidote to dreary and complicated stuff until we started working and had real life personal woes to discuss when we met. I did manage to include a monster or two in the stories after reading *Enlightenment*, but that's just about as far as it went.

The Sequel Nobody Wanted

Doctor Who and the Dominators by Nick Walters
Favourite *Doctor Who* book: *The Writer's Tale*
by Russell T Davies and Benjamin Cook

As you may know, dear reader, there is a sequel to *The Dominators*, and I wrote it. *Mutually Assured Domination* is a novel in Candy Jar Books' range of adventures featuring Colonel Lethbridge-Stewart. It's set between the events of *The Web of Fear* and *The Invasion* and pitches Lethbridge-Stewart against the fearsome Dominators and their terrifying robotic servants, the Quarks. It was a real honour and a privilege, in fact the pinnacle of my writing career, to pen the follow-up to one of the greatest and most fondly-remembered stories of the classic series. Often voted the best *Doctor Who* story of all time, *The Dominators* is *Doctor Who* at its very best, with the mercurial Second Doctor as played by Patrick Troughton battling the series' best-realised and most terrifying foes in a gripping, pulse-pounding adventure set on the most convincingly depicted alien planet ever seen on television, supported by a stellar cast of the best actors ever to tread the boards clad in the most beautiful costumes – AAAAAAAAAAAAAARGH! I can't go on!

Of course, *The Dominators* is not one of the greatest and most fondly-remembered *Doctor Who* stories of all time. The Dominators and Quarks are minor league bad guys. Dulkis remains stolidly unconvincing. The actors, bless them, try, but – leads and Dominators aside – none of them really stand out. And the less said about the costumes, the better. In the polls, *The Dominators* typically languishes sullenly near, though not quite at, the bottom. Oh, it's far from the worst, but it's nowhere near even approaching the outer reaches of the best. Mediocrity is its legacy. No, the real honour for me in writing *Mutually Assured Domination* lay in crafting the early adventures of Lethbridge-Stewart. Writing a follow-up to *The Dominators* was a challenge at best, and a poisoned chalice at worst. Who really wanted to see a sequel to that story? Who was having sleepless nights pining for the return of the Dominators and the Quarks? Nobody, that's who – but I was commissioned to write it, with the brief of doing to the Dominators and Quarks what Lawrence Miles did to the Krotons in *Alien Bodies*. That is, making them a convincing and credible threat and taking them beyond what we saw on screen. What Lawrence Miles would have done will, for now, have to remain fan conjecture, and you'll have to make do with what I have done with them.

So what did I do with them? My aim was twofold: firstly, to take the Dominators deadly seriously, have them pose a real threat; and secondly, to have fun with them. The first aim was essential in creating a threat for Lethbridge-Stewart to combat. You can't have a silly and ineffectual foe. The second aim was because one of the joys of The Dominators – yes, joys, bear with me! – is the squabbling between Navigator Rago and Probationer Toba. The latter's unswerving instinct to destroy and the former's prissy worrying about conserving Quark energy - and the ensuing bickering - is (for me) the highlight of the story. So I took that relationship as the basis for my two Dominators, Navigator Deka and Probationer Azbo. (Anyone care to guess where I got that name from?) They squabble endlessly, as Rago and Toba did, about the conflict between the lust to DESTROY! and the need to conserve Quark energy. There is, however, another layer of authority in the story, in the form of Director Vaar, who is overseeing the Dominator operation on Earth. He is from the upper echelons of Dominator society and he takes the strategic view, sees the bigger picture and is more of a businessman than his underlings. He wears a big-shouldered business suit, mingles with politicians and appears on *Panorama* to be interviewed by Robin Day. His plan, Project M, is – well, spoilers, obviously. But it's not good news for the human race. So – comedy, but also credibility.

I realise I have not yet once mentioned the Target novelisation of *The Dominators*, by Ian Marter, which is what I am meant to be writing about. This book was equally as important for me in writing *Mutually Assured Domination* as the TV programme. Marter brought a darker, grittier, more graphic approach to the Target books, as anyone who read *The Ark in Space* will attest. His description of Noah's mutation remains one of the most gruesome pieces of *Doctor Who* writing. His use of the word 'bastard' in *The Enemy of The World* was our Sex Pistols and arguably where the New Adventures were truly born. And his description of the Dominators was where I took my cue. Marter makes the Dominators hulking, cadaverous Frankenstein's monsters with red-rimmed green eyes and padded gloves which creak when they move their fingers (a nice touch, that).

As for the Quarks, say what you like about them, but they actually are that most over-used of clichés, iconic. Their bizarre look makes them stand out in the *Doctor Who* monster gallery and that's against some strong competition. They have transcended the story in which they feature remain one of the more memorable one-off foes of the black and white era. Their unique shape, their shuffling gait and their chirruping voices combine to make an odd and rather disconcerting whole. *The Dominators* doesn't do them justice, however, and they are rather slow moving and easily defeated.

In the Target book, Marter describes them in some detail and has them 'cackling harshly' all over the place in order to make them seem threatening. It works, but in *Mutually Assured Domination* I decided to take it to the next level, and taking my inspiration from the Transformers, turned them into what one character calls 'Swiss army Jack-in-the-Boxes': able to extend their appendages and deploy a terrifying range of weapons from their casings. Again, fun was to be had, mainly in characters' initial reactions to them, but the idea was to realise the full potential of the Quarks and make them as deadly as the Daleks. Now there's an idea – Quarks versus Daleks! Before I wrote about them, my money would be on the latter, but now I'm not so sure.

Nobody may have particularly wanted a sequel to *The Dominators*, but just in case they did, I hope I have done the characters justice. What next for me, I wonder? *Terror of the Plasmatons*?

Darling It's Better Down Where It's Wetter

Doctor Who – Warriors of the Deep
by Dylan Rees
Favourite *Doctor Who* book: *Script Doctor*
by Andrew Cartmel

I became a *Doctor Who* fan in 1989, just in time to catch the Doctor disappearing into the sunset chasing the promise of a cold cup of tea. I doubt I knew it was the end, as for me it was just the beginning of a life-long relationship with the show. While there was no new series on the horizon, there was always new *Doctor Who* to discover thanks to the ever increasing video releases from the BBC and, later, UK Gold repeats from across the show's 26 seasons. *Doctor Who Magazine* and various factual volumes informed me of stories I'd yet to see, but with no way to speed up those releases, I would frustratedly dream of a day when I had seen every existing episode. It was a feat that would take me roughly ten years, with my final story being the official BBC VHS of *Paradise Towers*.

A few years into my fandom, my mother found a copy of *Junior Doctor Who and the Giant Robot* in our local library. She read me the book each night before bed and soon more titles followed - *The Androids of Tara*, *The Horns of Nimon* and *The Greatest Show in the Galaxy* were some of the first titles I remember her reading to me. As I became a stronger reader, I began to tackle the books solo, picking up used copies at car boot sales, conventions and second-hand shops. While I collected them all (what sort of fan would I be if it was incomplete) I would only ever read the titles I hadn't seen before. I saw no need to experience *Day of the Daleks* through a book when I had the 'real' thing on VHS.

So keen was I to read these books that I wouldn't read anything else, much to the frustration of my teachers. When we were asked to complete a book report over a school term, we were given various genres of books we had to cover. Needless to say, Science Fiction, Fantasy and Adventure were the first three ticked off (all with Target titles) but then I covered Historical with *The Gunfighters*, Romance with *The Novel of the Film* (well, the Doctor kisses a girl in it!), Factual with *The Making of Doctor Who* and Biography with *Who on Earth is Tom Baker*. This severally irked my teacher, who put a red line through romance and historical. As revenge, I bought a novelisation of *Baywatch* and wrote a lengthy book review about the romantic exploits in that. (My *Baywatch* fandom lasted no more than the length

269

of that book; it was just the most ridiculous thing I could find to read.)

One of the advantages of growing up in a pre-internet age (that distant time known as the 1990s) was not being exposed to fan opinion. I didn't know which serials were held in high esteem and which were considered clunkers, so I approached each new book or video with an innocent sense of optimism: of course it would be great, it's *Doctor Who*. In fact there are only two stories I remember not enjoying on first experiencing them: the first was the novelisation of *The Myth Makers*, which I just couldn't get my young mind round, and the second was the VHS of *The Daleks*, which I thought was as dull as Dodo in a disco.

Many stories intrigued me thanks to stills I'd seen in various publications. Oh, how I longed to see *Attack of the Cybermen* with its desolate alien landscapes or *Time and the Rani* with the terrifying Tetraps. When I found the books of said titles, they would be quickly assimilated so I could at least experience them that way. But the story I most wanted to see was one that could only be a classic - *Warriors of the Deep*. It featured a team-up between the Sea Devils and the Silurians and a huge dinosaur like creature called the Myrka. How could this be anything less than spectacular?

I managed to pick up a copy of the Virgin reprint of the novel from a local bookshop in the mid-1990s complete with a dark and brooding cover depicting an ocean base and the redesigned monsters in all their glory. The novel was basically a conspiracy thriller with a bleak interpretation of the future with the foreboding shadow of nuclear war hanging over the plot. The characters were realistic, the monsters had a motive and represented a genuine threat and the Myrka was a terrifying, biomechanical creature of extreme strength and power. (I should point out that I had seen pictures of the Myrka and knew full well what I was getting; I maintain to this day that it is a great design that moves badly and is shot unsympathetically.)

My next exposure to the story was the audio book read by Peter Davison. This suitably ramped up the tension of the script combining Davison's narrative with sparse eerie music to tell a chilling version of what was fast becoming one of my favourite *Doctor Who* stories. The world these interpretations presented was a palpable one that appealed to my young mind in the same way that things like *The Terminator* or Tim Burton's *Batman* did; it was a dark, gritty version of the future.

Shortly after the audio release of *Warriors of the Deep*, the VHS finally hit the shelves. I was so excited to finally see this classic in all its glory that I purchased it on the week of its release from my local fan club. Now most people would expect this moment to be a massive disappointment, as we all know this story is not well loved within fan circles. But no, for twelve-year-old me this was nothing short of the masterpiece I hoped it would be. Because I had yet to get to an age where things like special effects or directorial style mattered, it was all about the story. That is what captured my imagination and that's what all good *Doctor Who* had. Indeed, as a child my parents allowed me to watch films and television programmes way beyond my age range if they were engaging and obviously fictional. By age eight or nine I was one of the few kids in my school to have seen all the *Nightmare on Elm Street* films as well as things like *Terminator*, *Robocop* and *Predator* because they weren't real and my parents saw no danger in exposing me to them. Yes, they frightened me, but only in the same way that *Doctor Who* frightened me. I would never be allowed to watch something like *Goodfellas* or *Midnight Express* because these were real stories where real people carried out real atrocities on people. But a Cyberman shooting down a man was the same as Robocop shooting down a criminal and the gooey death of the Sea Devils was no different from the Terminator being crushed.

All these years later, I still have a great fondness for Warriors of the Deep. Yes, the Myrka looks rubbish but other televised stories are well loved despite the awful giant rat, the mutant clams and the Mummies with boobs. Yes, the Silurian and Sea Devils redesigns are a little ropey, but the Primords look like bad Halloween costumes, the Yeti look like oversized lumbering cuddly kids' toys and the less said about Scaroth the better. You want badly directed? Try *The Dalek Invasion of Earth*, *The Green Death* or *The Tenth Planet* on for size. My point here isn't to try and pick holes in classics, but to point out that the team behind those productions were dealing with the limitations of the day in order to pull off an impossible task, that of bringing to life a fantastical story on a BBC budget. And at the heart of each of those tales is a great story: so when I think of *Inferno*, I see the terrifying Primords that the script promised and the target book delivered and when I see the Myrka I see the hideous deadly nightmare that Terrance Dicks brought to life in his novelisation. Because this is where *Doctor Who* was the most successful - in impressing these petrifying images in the minds of its young fans and not providing cannon fodder for cynical old fan boys. While in many ways the Target book is the definitive version of *Warriors of The Deep*, the same could be said to be true of many classic stories.

No Sacrifice

Doctor Who and the Aztecs
by Claire and Katie Lambeth

Favourite *Doctor Who* book: *The Plotters* by Gareth Roberts
and *The Empire of Glass* by Andy Lane

Unlike the sacrifice depicted in the story, it was no sacrifice at all for us to read the Target book of *The Aztecs*. This particular book was one of the first of the range we had ever bought, as in honesty we'd never really heard of the books before, having just discovered our love for all things Hartnell era. We had no idea what to expect from *The Aztecs* book other than the fact it was linked to the TV serial. It was also nice to see it was written by John Lucarotti who had written the TV story as well as other good historical serials. History stories especially interest us.

We'd watched some classic *Doctor Who* together as kids. As twin sisters, sharing an interest meant we could enthuse about it together and come up with little stories, so it was pretty exciting when the programme returned in 2005 and took us right back to being little kids again. It was later, however, when we both were studying at university that we sampled the early 1960s episodes and found we wanted to consume everything relating to it. We purchased some Ian and Barbara-focused novels before realising there was a whole range of books, one for each classic story. We decided to start collecting the Hartnell era books and bought a whole bunch in a short space of time. Sadly there's a few we still need to get, though recently we did find an omnibus of *The Myth Makers* and *The Gunfighters* at a vintage emporium looking all lonely and dusty.

We made sure to buy just the one copy of *The Aztecs,* having made the mistake of obtaining three copies of *Doctor Who and the Daleks* on a previous occasion (talk about twin dilemmas). Of course, one copy between two of us meant we had to either read it one at a time or share the reading duties. We foolishly thought it'd be funny to read most of it aloud, taking it in turns almost to re-enact the story we already knew so well from the DVD. With us doing our best impressions, believing we were recording an audio play rather than plainly reading aloud, we felt we were re-living the story again but in an entirely different way. Reading aloud offers a lot in the way of amusement too. If you'd ever heard either of us trying to pronounce Aztec names like Huitzilipochtli, you'd never think Hartnell's fluffs were anything to laugh about.

We also like to take notes on what we're reading as we go. When we read the books, we have many little coloured post-it notes sticking out of the pages as we're keen to remember particular moments or talk about the characters and post snippets on our blogs. We also like to note down the good quotes. Sometimes our post-it notes are scattered throughout the book in a combination of colours and it becomes impossible to remember why we even stuck a note on that bit in the first place because the whole book is full of great little moments so where do we draw the line? It's a good job the book is relatively short otherwise it would take just as long to write down the good parts as it would to read it in the first place!

We came to the range late and really we're still catching up. In fact we're still only on the Hartnell era books but we enjoy savouring the ones we have read and slowly collecting the ones we haven't, watching them fill up the shelf along with all of our other Hartnell era-related books, DVDs and audios. We've also gone on to collect the audiobook versions of the Target novels. When we're feeling lazy it's nice to have a professional read it out, especially if it's William Russell or Peter Purves.

The truth is that we love sharing the stories with each other but we also love sharing the stories with everyone else who loves it in the greater fandom community. *The Aztecs* is one of our favourite Target books and one we hope to re-read many more times. The book remains very true to the episodes - and of course it doesn't have to; many of the range we've read divert quite a bit. Full of memorable moments and witty lines, it feels such a joy to re-visit.

Will there be another book that will eclipse this one?

273

The Cover of Fear

Doctor Who – Inferno by Chris Dale

Favourite *Doctor Who* book: *The Face of the Enemy*
by David A McIntee

I'm of the generation that grew up without the Doctor. Born in 1985 (a 'child of the hiatus', if you will), by the time I was of an age to appreciate the series it had already left our screens.

Oh, it was a dark time without him. Actually it wasn't, because you can't really miss what you never had, but looking back it would have been nice to have had the show around during my formative years. I was aware of it owing to the BBC2 repeats in the early 1990s (Friday evenings after *Thunderbirds*, which <u>was</u> a huge part of my formative years) but had no real interest in seeing it. Being something of a wimp at the time (and to be fair, nothing much has changed since) its reputation for scariness put me off, and the one episode I did sit through (round a neighbour's house while my parents were out) I did so with mild indifference. *The Sea Devils* episode 3, if you were wondering.

If *Doctor Who* was off limits on-screen, the primary school I went to was a different story. Despite the show having been off-air for at least five years by that time, several classrooms still had a fairly substantial collection of ageing Target novels on the carousels in the books corner, and for some reason I don't think I'll ever understand I found myself drawn to these more than anything else. I couldn't name a single non-*Doctor Who* title they had, yet I vividly remember flicking through books like *The Tenth Planet*, *The Dalek Invasion of Earth* and *The Time Warrior*. I seem to recall *The Auton Invasion* was renamed The Octopus in the Toilet, because kids think they're funny like that. However, one stayed where it was, never to be touched under any circumstances. The book with The Scariest Cover I Had Ever Seen Ever.

To say my first sight of the *Inferno* cover was a shock is putting it mildly. Looking at it now, I still find it a little unsettling and can't believe that what was ostensibly a children's book was published with such cover artwork. It's chilling. The original production still that it was based on, of actor Ian Fairbairn as the mutated Bromley lurking atop the refinery complex, isn't too scary - but cover artist Nick Spender took that photo and ramped up the horror with the addition of the glowing eyes and drool plus a hellish backdrop of the sky literally burning. It fit the tone and content of the bleakest story in *Doctor Who*'s history absolutely beautifully, but to the eight-year-old me, discovering that book ten years after it was published it was pure nightmare fuel. The back cover blurb generously described the effects of the green slime on humans as 'grotesquely debilitating' and judging by the cover art, that's a generous description if ever I saw one.

You see, on a lot of the Target covers not much is happening. It's largely just a few characters standing around amidst one or two other recognisable images from the story. *Inferno*'s cover presents you with the world going up in flames – but don't worry, kids! There's a rabid seemingly-demon-possessed man here who would gladly kill you in a mindless bloodthirsty rage long before that happens. Crumbs. It's certainly worlds away from photographs of Peter Davison standing around looking bored, that's for sure.

When I did finally get into Doctor Who in the early 2000s, its uniquely doom-laden atmosphere instantly made *Inferno* my all-time favourite story (ah, 6am three hour long *Doctor Who* omnibuses on UK Gold, how I miss you) and checking the novelisation out from the library revealed it to be a brisk, well-written retelling of the serial. I began to cobble together a small collection of Targets of my own and tried to acquire the books from my old school, only to discover they'd been thrown away just a few months earlier because nobody was reading them. Hardly a loss on the level of a missing episode, but still a frustrating near-miss nevertheless.

Flash forward to 2007. I'm now into my twenties and at my very first convention, the London Film and Comic Con. Highlights of the weekend included meeting Tom 'Tom Baker' Baker and Nana 'how can one lady be so sweet I don't know but she manages it' Visitor, but Ian Fairbairn was also going to be there, so I was looking forward to meeting him and telling him about my first encounter with that infamous cover.

It wasn't until I was on the train coming home from the event that I realised I totally forgot to stop by his table. He'd been there all day, I'd seen him from a distance...but just never got around to saying hi. So I wrote to him instead, telling the story of my first encounter with his front cover alter ego and he responded by sending me a signed copy of the photo the artwork was based on. A brief exchange of letters followed (it turned out he had no idea that he appeared on the cover until a fan pointed it out to him at a convention!) but sadly, despite him being a convention regular, our paths never crossed and I never had the chance to meet Ian in person before he passed away in 2014. From everything I've heard, and from that limited interaction I had with him, he seems to have been a very nice man as well as a reliable member of the Douglas Camfield stable of recurring actors. I do however very much regret that moment in 2007 when I missed the chance to find out for sure.

It's nice that that image of him as Bromley has lived on over the years, being used on the covers for *Inferno* DVD releases on both sides of the pond and lurking on store shelves ready to scare a whole new generation of kids – but somehow it never looks as frightening there as it did on the Target cover. It's as much a credit to Nick Spender as it was to Ian that something as simple as a picture of a guy looking a bit poorly and in serious need of a shave can have been so memorably transformed into a nightmare vision from hell, and if it ever gets a reprint I hope they don't change it even a little bit. I want this book out there on the nation's bookshelves with that beautifully horrible cover completely intact, waiting for some unsuspecting little kid to stumble across it and get the coolant scared out of them.

So once the new series came along, I ended up giving my meagre collection of Targets to the school – including my copy of *Inferno*. It seemed the right thing to do.

The Clan Destine

Doctor Who and the Highlanders by Simon Brett

Favourite *Doctor Who* book: *A Celebration* by Peter Haining

After a brief spell of frustrated cursing at a lack of ordered logic, I remove my copy of *The Highlanders* from its hiding place, slotted amongst roughly-organised piles of Target paperbacks, all secreted away on one of the top shelves of a bedroom wardrobe. Under ideal circumstances, these items would be sitting beautifully arranged in their natural, multi-coloured rainbow barcode of chronological pedantry. Not in this house. Not now. Now I have children. As much as I still live and breathe many of my childhood passions, there is only so much obstinate geekery that one family can take, and as yet there are no signs of interest amongst my daughters. Still, maybe one day they will breathe fresh air again on our bookshelves should Barbie no longer be the preferred icon.

Despite the very subtle possibility that maybe I'm being a bad fan by letting real life dictate how my love for *Doctor Who* physically manifests itself, the good condition in which I find the book disperses any negativity and I give my thirteen-year-old self a small pat on the back for looking after the book so well. I even momentarily question if this is actually my original copy as the spine does not show any sign of creasing. I turn to the inside cover and as irritating as it is reassuring, there in all its clumsy glory my name is written in blue ballpoint pen - curly and vastly more readable than the 'doctor' handwriting that now passes for my scrawl today. (Not *that* kind of Doctor, obviously.) But then I remember - I read this book extremely quickly, within a day of buying it. It scarcely had time to reshape itself as I held it open, such was the speed it was digested.

One thing is for certain: my copy of *The Highlanders* still retains more spine than that of the 13-year-old who originally purchased the book 32 years ago. If that boy had half of the backbone of the book into which he threw himself for a weekend in 1984, then maybe pushing for a date with a certain girl in the year below would have sent his life into a slightly different direction - and maybe this book wouldn't have been read quite as enthusiastically as I probably would have had other things on my mind. If my memory serves me well, she had actually agreed to meet one Saturday, but instead had to work for her father at the last minute. Despite the offer of meeting another time, I had assumed that this was a brush off and never asked again. Still, over the space of several hours of mindful solid reading, I had escaped to another, simpler time.

I'm sorry to say that my recall of the book's content itself is lacking

277

in detail, but it represents a maturing and a realisation that story and character could lead me astray as easily as any number of science fiction clichés and fantastical monsters. Up to this point, I had experienced a frustrating mental block that repeatedly steered me away from the 'pure' historicals – the *Doctor Who* stories based in the past with a distinct dearth of science fiction elements. In my self-imposed ignorance, I had seen very little point in delving into history if there were no creatures to be seen. Where was the fun in the Doctor stepping into dusty reality when imagination was such a rich source of adventure and escape? It seems that following *The Highlanders*, the makers of the television show felt much the same - Patrick Troughton included - and the serial was to be the last of its kind bar *Black Orchid* in 1982. I'm no longer sure that this should have been such a lengthy and blinkered existence for The Doctor and his companions – such was *The Highlanders'* effect on me. Its substantial story, character and humour trapped me in its pages and at no point did I look for the twinkling lights - they were all there in the Doctor's smile.

Gerry Davis's novel carried me along without the aid of a shiny metal surface that filled in the details of transforming my onscreen fix being a *Doctor Who* fan - in my head, anyway. To this day, as much as I love the incredible imagination and aspirational fireworks of *Doctor Who*'s world, it is the personalities, the humour and the heart that keeps me coming back and keeps me caring.

That particular period of Target publishing, accompanied by the regular reports in *Doctor Who Monthly* (as it was known at that time), held a feeling of tremendous excitement for me. Since around the early 1980s, the publishers had begun to cherry pick many of the so far unconverted scripts from the show's dim and distant past in a mostly classy and intelligent manner. Beautifully painted, realistic artwork for the covers coupled with many of the serial's original creators returning to their babies opened fresh windows into the past only previously hinted at on the printed page and, at its most effective and popular, focusing on episodes long lost to the short-sighted erasing machines.

Much as you may question a person's qualification to call themselves a true fan having only heard one album by a particular musician, I was unready in 1984 to call myself a Troughton devotee publicly. Yet in my heart, no other Doctor or indeed era held quite the same fascination for me. Indeed, the only Troughton serial that I had seen as a televisual whole was *The Krotons*, broadcast as part of *The Five Faces of Doctor Who* season on BBC2 in 1981. At this point, VHS releases were only in their infancy and were almost certainly out of the financial reach of a teenager yet to earn anything on his own paper round: we wouldn't own a family player for at least another year.

Here, albeit in prose form, was not only the earliest example of a Troughton story but also the introduction of Jamie McCrimmon, already one of my favourite companions.

To this day, many of the Troughton episodes remain a lost or undiscovered treasure trove making them all the more magical and mysterious as the era itself continues to be the least represented in video form. The Target novelisations of that era remain a precious insight into what once was. Whether the lack of visual material gives a somewhat skewed perception of that time in the show's history is certainly debatable, but even so, if that is another reason to find it so fascinating I feel that factor is as good as any other. Sometimes less really is more.

And then every now and then when we get lucky and we get more, then a little bit more – it's all the more wonderful.

In less wonderful circumstances, my interest in the girl in the year below me faded when I discovered that she smoked. I seem to remember being prudishly repelled by the offer of a cigarette at a Saturday afternoon showing of something like *Police Academy 2* at the local cinema. Not long after that, she moved away from the area. While my morality has somewhat cooled and these things have been as lost in time as episodes lost to BBC costing sheets, the Patrick Troughton era of *Doctor Who* is now publicly my favourite of what some call 'classic' *Doctor Who*. It seems that some things are just not meant to be – while some just are.

He Said the Earth Was...Hungry

Doctor Who – Frontios by Alun Harris

Favourite *Doctor Who* book: *The Programme Guide*
by Jean-Marc Lofficier

Episode One

We all have our favourites. We have our favourite Doctor, our favourite story, our favourite season. It never ends. I particularly like dialogue. There's nothing more satisfying than a quotable line which can work in any set of circumstances ('I don't work for anyone. I'm just having fun.') or a piece of dialogue from the series which never fails to inspire ('Just go forward in all your beliefs...'). There's dialogue which is exciting ('So you see, I'm not going to let you stop me now!') or sad ('There should have been another way.') or funny ('Really, Doctor; you'll be consulting the entrails of sheep next.').

One of my favourite lines from the series isn't even in the series – it's from Doctor Who and the Dinosaur Invasion ('Really, Sarah! I take you in the TARDIS to Outer Space, to another Time in the history of the Universe, and what really excites you? – *Woolworths*!'). It doesn't matter that it's never said on-screen, because it's part of the programme now. Everyone who's read the book knows it, just as they know that the Doctor takes the safety off Trenchard's revolver to give him a noble and heroic death (Malcolm Hulke again – the writer who also gave us poor Shughie McPherson. Mac Hulke's contribution to the mythology of *Doctor Who* is sadly understated.)

Doctor Who relied on dialogue. No, not just on dialogue – on *good* dialogue. For a series that often didn't have the budget to convey what it was trying to achieve, much of the effect is achieved by words. With just a couple of lines in *The Ribos Operation*, Robert Holmes does more to convey the credibility of Ribos as a real planet than any number of expensive model shots could have done. Holmes, on form, is particularly good at world-building. The entirety of society on Inter Minor is explained to the audience by dialogue between three characters. We don't need to see President Zarb at all, nor an immigration debate in Inter Minor's Parliament.

Atmosphere is vital to any form of narrative, whether that's a novel or an episode of a television series. *The Horror of Fang Rock* is spooky enough, but when Tom Baker says 'Gentlemen, I've got news for you: this lighthouse is under attack and by morning we might all be dead,' it hits the audience hard. It's a great line, perfectly stating the horror of the situation, and that Tom Baker delivers it so well makes it work even better – stern-faced, it would have been too grim, but by smiling (and then briefly laughing afterwards) Tom manages to make it simultaneously scarier, but also at the same time reassuring. Terrance Dicks is dreadfully under-rated for his dialogue. *The Five Doctors*, for instance, is chock-full of some of the most beautiful, quotable dialogue of the entire series. Forget the terrible line 'No, not the mind probe' (and stop blaming Paul Jerricho for his delivery – you try saying it out loud convincingly. It's impossible!) and revel in 'A man is the sum of his memories' or look at some of his atmospheric lines from *State of Decay*, which make the most of the gothic atmosphere.

Frontios contains my single favourite line from the whole of *Doctor Who*. I've never seen it praised in print before and I've never understood why. It sums up in one sentence just what *Doctor Who* feels like to me:

'When I was very small, I was sitting on his knee in the state room, and I asked him why we couldn't go underground any more. And he said - it was a child's answer, it seemed quite sensible at the time – he said the earth was...hungry.' This is *Doctor Who* in a nutshell. It's chilling, it's evocative, it's mysterious, it's alarming and it's quite, quite brilliant. It's also perfectly present in the novelisation, and Christopher H. Bidmead deserves every kind of praise imaginable for such a truly gorgeous line.

Episode Two

When you remember something, you're not actually remembering the event itself; you're remembering the last time you remembered it, at least according to contemporary psychological thinking. Memory, then, is fallible, coloured as much by the distance of time as our own recollections. When *Tomb of the Cybermen* was returned, a lot of people were disappointed because it didn't live up to their memories of the story. It's understandable, of course – they'd not seen it for twenty-five years. All they had to go on were their memories and the Gerry Davis novelisation. Prose is a particularly evocative medium; the writer can describe something up to a point, leaving the reader to fill in the rest. Quite what the viewers of *Tomb of the Cybermen* were expecting when it was found is another matter: there were enough episodes from the rest of the season to give them an idea of the production values of the time, and the editing. There are no camera angles in prose, of course, no rapid cuts. Just imagination. Still, that twenty-five year gap was a very long one. Every time the original viewers described the story to a fellow fan, their memories shifted, ever so slightly. They manufactured their own memories.

Faced with the lazy criticism of 'the show's not as good as it used to be,' JNT's standard reply was a weary, 'the memory cheats'. He was

281

right, though; the memory does cheat. It edits, it ignores the blur of the edges and fills in its own finer details. It's not done deliberately by any means but the memory does cheat. My own recollection of seeing *Frontios* is a prime example: I distinctly remember someone being dragged under the ground, screaming horribly all the time. I don't even know where this memory comes from. It's certainly not from the televised story, which features only three people being dragged under the earth, none of whom scream. It's not from the novelisation either – Bidmead wrings a great deal of horror from Plantagenet's silent scream as he's drawn into the ground (somewhat more successfully on paper than was managed on screen), but not a noise is made.

It's my imagination.

Frontios really struck me as a child – every aspect of the story appealed to me. The characters, the dialogue, the music (Kingsland's finest score), the very notion of creatures lurking beneath the ground sucking people down to their lair. I wouldn't go so far as to say I was haunted by the story, but it certainly left me with a strong impression (perhaps aided by the fact that I missed episode four) and over the years my own imagination cheated me, drawing on the themes Bidmead offered and exaggerating them.

JNT was right.

Episode Three

There's always been a debate (or at least there was while they were being published) as to what the Target range was for. Was it to provide an accurate recording of the story that had been shown? (By now you're probably quite aware that the books provided the only way to 'see' an old *Doctor Who* story. I'm sure this has been mentioned several times.) Was it a chance for the original author to tell the story they wanted to tell, without budgetary restraints, or for the adapter to open the story up according to their own tastes, resolve plot holes and expand the tale to fit the book? It's obviously none of those things; it was to tell a rattling good story that readers would enjoy. Whilst I'm sure all deserved praise has been heaped upon those authors who were able to do something fresh (Dennis Spooner's books being particularly notable examples), I do hope those authors who managed to straddle both bridges haven't been forgotten. Malcolm Hulke was particularly good at adding to his own stories without departing too far from the original. Terrance Dicks could throw in an exciting prologue (or, memorably in the case of *Pyramids of Mars*, an epilogue so good I still consider it a part of the TV version) and still tell you exactly what happened on screen. He even shows Susan being dragged into the Death Zone for good measure.

Christopher Bidmead's *Frontios* is another example of this latter group of authors: he adds to his story without deviating from the original – in this case simply by adding gore and depth. Ian Marter may be the one noted for featuring body horror in his novels, but Bidmead played at it too. On TV the excavating machine is just that – a machine. On paper, though, it's 'a repellent sight: a huge and hideous assembly of parts of human bodies, shaped something in the form of a giant Tractator.' On TV it's clunky and doesn't look entirely fit for purpose, made (except for the human operator) solidly of metal. In the novel 'white bones tipped with metal cutters scraped against the rock, while rotting hands polished the smooth surface.' On TV it's a not very convincing prop. In the book it's 'a machine built from the dead'. Obviously you couldn't show this nightmarish creation at 6.50 pm (you'd be hard-pressed to convincingly realise it at 9pm with ten times the money available), but in the novel it works a treat. It's *horrible*, the sort of thing that would keep Mary Whitehouse awake at night and exactly the sort of thing that young readers want to have crawling around their imaginations. The Tractators here aren't dancers trapped in (admittedly very impressive) unwieldy costumes, but huge silver woodlice which can curl up into balls and move with liquid grace, something which makes them genuinely unnerving.

Bidmead's approach is, I think, by far the most satisfying. He adds background the TV series didn't have time to do; he creates Frontios as a real colony on a real planet, something a studio-bound production can't show; and, without going too far himself, he adds the sort of gore the BBC wouldn't be able to transmit. He also tells a rattling good story. What more could one expect from a Target novel?

Episode Four

I didn't see episode four of *Frontios* on transmission. I saw episodes one to three, but for reasons I've now forgotten I was sent to bed early the night of the final instalment. At this point it's necessary to explain that my parents would never have considered such a disproportionate punishment – I was at boarding school. (My parents lived abroad and they decided to send me to a school back in England which happened to be near my grandparents. I could write a book the size of the one you're currently holding explaining why this was A Very Bad And Selfish Thing to do, but I'll save you the time and myself the introspection by just saying that I wasn't happy. I also identified quite strongly with Turlough as a result of my own exile.) If I had to guess, I imagine I was being punished for talking after I should have gone to sleep. Whatever I'd done wrong, this was my punishment. I wouldn't say I was scarred by the incident in any way, and even at the age of

283

eight I was aware that Mr Hartwell wasn't aware just how unfair his punishment was, although I didn't resent him any the less for this knowledge. What Dickens says about children and injustice is quite true and I recall desperately hoping that someone would invent a watch that could show television and let me have one so that I wouldn't miss the last part of a story that I was particularly enjoying. That wouldn't happen in reality for several more years, so I did indeed miss episode four, not watching it until years later when someone gave me a pirate video.

By then I'd read the novel, so I knew what happened, and the last episode didn't disappoint when I finally caught up with it. There is, though, still an episode four of *Frontios* that lives in my imagination. The other boys in the dorm (or at least those who weren't also sent to bed early, because presumably I wasn't talking to myself and someone else must have been punished with me) would have told me what happened in those missing twenty five minutes, and coupled with reading the Target book shortly after, I then had a perfectly good episode four of my own. Mine is quite clearly better than the televised one, because mine has an unlimited budget. Mine has Bidmead's horrid excavating machine and his mobile Tractators, but it also has the cast of the TV version, meaning I have the best of both worlds. This is probably where I have my faulty memory from – the Tractators are dragging people into the earth nastily all the time in my episode four. The spooky horror of 'he said the earth was...hungry' sets the tone throughout mine, and Bidmead's body horror is present throughout.

So there are now three *Frontios*es in existence – TV's, Bidmead's and mine. To this day I'm not sure which I prefer, but all three are magical in their own right.

Expiation

Doctor Who – Planet of Fire
by Zoë Mackay
Favourite *Doctor Who* book: *Companion Piece*
by L.M. Myles and Liz Barr

I have always had a problem with authority. In any situation where my impulses conflict with rules or instructions laid down from on high, I instinctively fold like a pack of cards and do whatever I'm told. It's one of the reasons that I've always been drawn to the Doctor: his rebellious, insubordinate, nature.

My copy of *Planet of Fire* is in hardback. It's the only hardback Target book I have.

My copy of *Planet of Fire* has a school library lending record stuck inside the front cover.

My copy of *Planet of Fire* is... well, it's ... Look, I stole it.

It's important to realise how out of character the *Planet of Fire* incident was. I didn't intend to steal it. It wasn't a prize that I admired from afar and there certainly wasn't a planning meeting with complicated diagrams and bad Cockney accents. I just wanted to read it and as I didn't have my library card that day, I thought I could just borrow it unofficially until lunch.

Only, at lunch, I played cricket.

The book came home with me. I didn't take it back the next day. I probably just forgot. I remember being overcome by a suffusion of guilt. I faced up to this overflowing of emotion in a cold, rational, way: I hid the book under a pile of others and endeavoured to forget entirely about its existence.

Days turned into weeks, weeks into years. I left school and the book remained unreturned, the crime undetected. It's been nearly three decades and it still sits on my shelf, radiating waves of guilt whenever I look at it. I try not to look too often.

At the end of *Planet of Fire*, Turlough decides to face his responsibilities, choosing to return to Trion on the rescue ship. He leaves behind the excitement and uncertainty of travelling with the Doctor for a more mundane, grown-up life.

Most of us grow up in tiny steps, and it's never a completed process. Thirty years after I stole the book, perhaps it's not too late for me to return it. Perhaps I could send it back with a note of apology, maybe a small donation.

Maybe next week. Or, even, next year. Yes, I think next year I'll send it back. I am not yet willing to give up *my* adventures with the Doctor.

The Caves of Memory

Doctor Who and the Caves of Androzani
by Don Klees
Favourite *Doctor Who* book: *Ghost Light – the Script Book*
by Marc Platt

On reflection, it feels a bit redundant to call these books a gateway to another world. After all, that could be said of almost any remotely decent book, and even at their most perfunctory, Target Books' *Doctor Who* novelisations were more than just remotely decent.

Obviously, not every story to be adapted was equally good, nor was every writer equally suited to translating a television drama into prose. Even within a given author's books, there were often major swings of quality. Malcolm Hulke's *Doctor Who and the Cave Monsters* was compulsively readable, but *Doctor Who and the Doomsday Weapon* was tough to get through, even if it did have the Master in it. Likewise, there was a big difference between Terrance Dicks' wonderful early books and his somewhat by-the-numbers efforts from the late 1970s and early 1980s. Regardless, each and every one was valuable, particularly those which adapted stories that weren't readily available in America at the time (a category that covered most stories before and after Tom Baker's first few seasons).

As one of the kids who first encountered *Doctor Who* on Saturday mornings on New York TV station WOR (but missed some of the explanatory voice-over added for Americans), it was a few years before I learned how many Doctors there had already been or that there were more to come. Fortunately, this revelation coincided with the wider availability of the Target novelisations in US bookstores offering a clearer path to learn more about the show's past and present.

This was especially welcome, because by 1983 both WOR and my local PBS station had stopped showing the programme at all. Aside from some Tom Baker episodes recorded on my mother's VCR and a few later ones seen on trips or at a convention my father took me to (where, fittingly, one of the guests was Terrance Dicks), the books truly were *Doctor Who* for me. Later on, I'd learn that my perceived wasteland was actually quite typical for UK fans, but teenagers aren't usually famed for their empathy.

One of my better lessons in empathy at the time came courtesy of Terrance Dicks and his novelisation of Peter Davison's final story, Robert Holmes's *The Caves of Androzani*. Thanks to the aforementioned convention showing Colin Baker's debut story, I'd seen as many episodes with the new Doctor as I'd seen with his predecessor. While Baker's mercurial performance ensured that my opinion of Davison as good but not especially exciting would remain unchallenged, it also underscored the need to learn how his incarnation of the Doctor met his end. It would be a while before I'd get to experience on-screen what even my teenage mind could tell was a story of great heroism and self-sacrifice, but as he had many times before, Terrance Dicks came to the rescue.

Before the show's 21st century revival, it was pretty much undisputed that Robert Holmes was *Doctor Who*'s very best writer. At the very least, he was the classic series writer who most consistently brought out the best in others, particularly in print. Whether it was the quality of the characters and writing or simply a desire to do right by his friend, Dicks' writing always seemed to display an added spark when adapting Holmes's stories.

Balancing exposition and action is key to the art of adaptation, especially when presenting the kind of textured worlds Holmes excelled at creating in his TV scripts. With just a single page, Dicks ably sets the scene – not just Androzani Minor with its 'desert rocky plains and seething mud volcanoes' but also the guerrilla war revolving around the valuable substance Spectrox. Very soon, the Doctor and Peri are deposited in the middle of this deadly environment as the TARDIS arrives with the 'wheezing groaning sound' so familiar to readers of the Target novelisations.

The description of Davison's incarnation of the Doctor as having a 'pleasant open face' is similarly familiar, and some might point to such recurring phrases as signs of a lack of ability or imagination on the writer's part. Alternatively, they reflect an understanding that for many readers (like myself) his books would be the collective memory of their *Doctor Who* experience. His consistency in describing the various Doctors as well as other recurring elements of the show – confirming that, however our mind's eye envisioned them, we were all 'looking' at fundamentally the same thing – was a key underpinning of this approach.

What remains most striking about *The Caves of Androzani* is how well it balances all of its plot lines without losing sight of the fact that, even if the supporting characters are more colourful, the Doctor is still the hero. The quiet resolve which I would later recognise in Peter Davison's onscreen performance is on display throughout the book, particularly in a scene where the Doctor waves off a threat from an armed adversary:

Abandoning the idea, he levelled his machine-pistol at the Doctor. 'All right, snoop. Hands in the air. Come over and open that door.'
    'Why?'

'Because I'll kill you if you don't!'

The Doctor laughed. 'Not a very persuasive argument, actually, Stotz, because I'm going to die anyway. Unless of course...'

It was a foregone conclusion that the alternative path the Doctor envisioned would work out for him and Peri, even if it was bound to be a little rocky, but learning how was still no less compelling. In the current culture of hyper-sensitivity about 'spoilers', it's amusing to think how many key plot twists American *Doctor Who* fans actually sought out via the books prior to seeing them on TV in the 1980s.

Something else the Target novels did exceptionally well was to camouflage moments where the production itself wasn't up to the task. Finding out that the comparisons of the 'Magma Beast' to a Tyrannosaurus Rex were a bit generous would turn out to be one of the few disappointing aspects of seeing *The Caves of Androzani* on TV. On the page, though, the creature was simply another compelling link in the chain of events. More than that, like virtually all of the novelisations, it was *Doctor Who* as we wanted – and imagined – it to be.

I Found Kuiju's Monkey

Doctor Who – Marco Polo
by Simon Kemp
Favourite *Doctor Who* book: The *About Time* books
by Lawrence Miles and Tat Wood

Marco Polo was one of those Target novels I bought at the time it came out but didn't actually read until many years later. Sporadically, I get the urge to watch/read/listen to all *Doctor Who*, in all formats, in order, using one of the lists available on the internet, and so in 2010 I listened to the *Marco Polo* audios for the first time, read the novelisation and watched the Loose Cannon reconstruction. I was captivated by the story in all formats.

The novelisation is perhaps not the most celebrated of the range. In the mid-1980s, many of the Hartnell historicals were given innovative treatments when novelised, such as the series of letters that comprised the adaptation of *The Myth Makers*. Such a treatment could have worked well for *Marco Polo*, given the inserts in the TV version as Marco reads from his journal while a map of the journey is displayed on the screen, but such devices are totally absent here, which does seem like a missed opportunity. The character of Marco dominates the story and the book could have been written in the first person from his perspective. It would also have been good to return to the old idea of having illustrations in the novel, at least in so far as including maps of the journey (the audio has the advantage here by including the map in the CD case).

The story in the novelisation is quite streamlined, as it deals with seven episodes in 136 pages of text, but there are few significant changes to the action or the plot. What changes I noted were more towards the end, with more details given about Ping-Cho running away, while it is made more explicit that she will end up with Ling-Tau. In fact, the novel does not really provide any more detail about Marco and the other characters´ thoughts and motivations than the TV script, though the dialogue, especially when Kublai Khan appears, is astounding. As an aside, it's interesting that Dennis Spooner is usually credited as introducing humour into *Doctor Who* in *The Reign of Terror* and *The Romans*, but I personally find (the Mighty) Kublai Khan hysterical. 'We discussed our lamented uncle, Jenghis, saying he was the warrior of the family...Nothing frightened him. We are but a poor planner, an administrator of sorts.'

While not adding much to the characterisation, the novelisation does contain some very nice descriptive passages. Ping-Cho's beautiful clothes, worn while reciting the long poem about the Hashashins, are

289

described in detail, while the layout and style of the buildings of the Summer Palace at Shang-Tu and the palace at Peking also receive detailed descriptions.

The audio and the novelisation combined to give me a substantial interest in China and its history. Previously I'd never thought of China as being at the top of my list of countries to visit, but I was now intrigued and when I saw that a big astronomy conference of the International Astronomical was taking place in Beijing in 2012, I jumped at the chance to go and spend two weeks in China. Of course I was eager to identify any traces of Marco there, and follow in his footsteps.

I made my first trip into the centre of Beijing on the Friday afternoon. Getting off the metro at Tiananmen Square and making my way through airport-style security past the mausoleum of Chairman Mao, I headed south along the Qianmen shopping street, turned off into one of the hutongs (old alleyways) and found a restaurant that looked ok. I selected from among the hundreds of photos on the menu, but when the food arrived it was somewhat disappointing, particularly as I found that most authentic Chinese cooking was incredibly delicious. But the most memorable moment was when a man walked by cradling a small monkey in his arms. He passed by too quickly to get a photograph, but I do remember the wide-open-mouthed expression of the white woman on the next table, so I know I didn't imagine it. The spirit of Kuiju and Tutte Lemkow was still alive in Beijing that Friday afternoon and I imagined that it was a fairly common thing to see monkeys being carried around, or on people's shoulders. However, I saw no other one on that or the subsequent trips I have made and my girlfriend assures me that she's never seen one in Beijing, and she's spent most of her life there.

Of course, after re-reading the Target novel, I found that John Lucarotti didn't even mention Kuiju's monkey in it. Maybe it wasn't in the camera script, or maybe he just thought the idea was too ridiculous, that someone would walk around Cathay carrying a monkey. Well, we all know better now don't we?

Much of Beijing has been continually rebuilt during its history. Even the famous buildings like the Forbidden City and the Summer Palace were being rebuilt in the nineteenth and early twentieth centuries, while much of the centre was bulldozed by Chairman Mao, and so little survives from Marco's time. I did find some old trees in the parkland in the beautiful Temple of Heaven which were said to be eight hundred years old; also the Summer Palace contains a gateway dedicated to the god Wenchang, which sounds a bit familiar from another story.

On later trips to Beijing, I went to the National Museum and saw portraits of Kublai Khan and Genghis Khan which I have seen used to illustrate other articles on the Marco Polo serial, in books and on the internet. I have also seen one part of the Great Wall of China (reached by cable-car, which was a huge challenge to my vertigo!), and the Beijing City Walls, though the construction of the walls that survive was begun in the fifteenth century. I even have a hope to one day follow in the footsteps of Marco's journey with the Doctor and his companions. (Well, the more practical bits anyway...I don't plan to be 15,000 feet up in Tibet or in the areas affected by Uyghur violence, so I'll probably skip the more western parts.) But I'm sure from Dunhuang onwards it could be fun. Maybe I'll persuade my girlfriend to go there for our honeymoon.

Hodcombe, All Ye Faithful

Doctor Who – The Awakening by Iain Martin
Favourite *Doctor Who* book: *Warlock* by Andrew Cartmel

Once you pop, they say, you can't stop, and that was certainly the case with the Doctor and me. It wasn't reciprocal, of course: I doubt the itinerant Gallifreyan's bookshelves are rammed with Target novelisations of *I, Iain Martin – Mindwarp* (in which our eleven-year-old hero raids Uncle Keith's drinks cabinet with disastrous albeit precocious results), *Iain Martin and the Crimson Horror* (which was about acne and was, at times, genuinely horrific) or even *Iain Martin and the Edge of Destruction* (about those first few years at Uni and the discovery of fast food).

My bedroom shelves went from housing a few tatty Roald Dahls, the original paperback of *The Hitchhiker's Guide to the Galaxy* and some rubbish reference books to holding a ginormous collection of Target books in a very short space of time, all stemming from my first ~~title, a paperback copy of Eric Pringle's The Awakening~~. As I recall, it was a gift from my Dad, and very possibly he had picked up that one purely by chance, because there's no way he could have known that *The Awakening* was and remains my favourite Classic Era story.

Whoah, I hear you say, back it up. Dial it down. W, I hear you snarl, TF? No, really. *The Awakening* was one of my very favourite *Doctor Who* adventures ever. Here's why.

The scary, goggle eyed loon who terrified me as a tiny had transformed into the heroic and quintessentially English fifth Doctor and I was a devoted fan of the show. Each episode, you'd sit cross-legged on the living room carpet watching your heroes charging about star-liners, alien citadels and lunar quarries, wistfully yearning to be part of the adventure. It was escapism from the mundanities of your own quiet, humdrum childhood; your own dull village, town or city, with its grassy nooks, sleepy lanes and dull churches.

Only when the Doctor came to Little Hodcombe, charging along said country lanes, being captured on said grassy nooks and discovering alien monsters hiding in the aforementioned dull church, did I begin to cotton on to the fact that peril, excitement and adventure could, potentially, lurk around every corner.

Every single corner.

I think this realisation is what kick-started my creative imagination and at the time, it just turned me into a very tedious little jerk who liked to pretend he was the Doctor during family outings to Sainsbury's, dangled down the stairs from his umbrella to imitate the end of *Dragonfire* Part One and spent all his inconsiderable disposable income on short novelisations of TV stories – that he'd *never* after all get to see for himself – in second-hand bookshops. Eventually, it would turn me into a writer.

It's December 2009. Shortly after Christmas. In a few days, I'm going to abandon the UK. I'm about to leave my job at the head office of the UK's last chain bookseller to move to the Middle East to try a slightly different role in a whole new bookselling environment. My childhood love of books has led me into a career working with...yes, you guessed it.

Emigrating requires a certain amount of upheaval. The West London flat has to go and almost everything needs to be charity-shopped, or else jettisoned. Charity shops have already, snootily, refused my VHS collection. They've been dismissive of a great many of my books. The old, yellowy-brown-paged Target books? They don't stand a chance.

Today, I am about to do something massive. To permanently sever the cord that connects me to my childhood. To make the leap to a new life, you need to be agile, streamlined and above all clutter-free. If you collect and hoard stuff, if it lines your shelves, it tricks your brain into thinking you're still basically in your childhood. You're trapped, frozen in time, your eyes absorbing a thousand subliminal reminders throughout the day convincing you that you're still a child because you just glimpsed the familiar and comforting 1981 paperback cover of *The Hitch-Hiker's Guide to the Galaxy*. It holds you back, because you think all this stuff is crucial to who you are, and defending your curated Library of You becomes the most essential thing in life.

However, I put my trust in Neil Hannon from The Divine Comedy who was comprehensively burgled at around the age of thirty, lost virtually everything he owned and announced he'd genuinely never felt so liberated as a result.

Don't be a slave to your possessions. Don't have anything in your life you can't walk away from in thirty seconds. I put all my Target books into black bin bags. I had about a hundred, I guess. But there was one I picked up, singled out and muttered a heartbroken goodbye to. A faded, tattered book, front and back covers held on with Sellotape. The monster on the front looked like a woodcut of a mediaeval devil. The name on the spine was Eric Pringle. I said goodbye to *The Awakening*. And thanked it for making me into me.

Then I put all my Target books into black bin bags.

I visited Greyfriars Bookshop, the second-hand bookshop on East Hill, most afternoons after school, on the off-chance that someone had been along during the day and sold on to them a huge and thrilling stash of Target books which I hadn't read yet. Obviously, some of my collection were bought new: copies of *The Giant Robot* and *The Sea Devils* for my 12th birthday – Thanks, Mrs Chittock! I purchased in Boots by my father who, by this point, no doubt wished I'd shut the hell up with regard to *Doctor Who*, copies of *Castrovalva* and *Logopolis* ordered in specially to the bookshop at the foot of East Hill which is now long, long gone. Otherwise my needs were fulfilled at Ace Comics in Colchester, where I'd make a weekly pilgrimage to see if the novelisation of *Remembrance of the Daleks* had arrived yet. I think all my *The Trial of a Time Lord* books came from there and all my Sylvesters too. To this day, I wish the book of *Mindwarp* had had a blue spine. It wasn't much to ask. I'm not an aggressively anal *Doctor Who* fan, after all. I gave that up in about 1993 when it was apparent that the show really and truly wasn't coming back and, if I wanted to do things with girls, I'd need to relaunch myself not as a massive nerd but as a sophisticated and erudite man about town. (I'll let you know how this reputation works out if it ever actually happens.)

The novelisations dried up. A few Hartnell Dalek jamborees from John Peel (no, not that one) and *The Paradise of Death* and...well, it was probably all over then. I had moved on to adult pastures by this point. Stories too broad and too deep for the small screen. Each month I'd pick up a New Adventure. I loved these books no doubt because they felt very much like a continuation of the Target line. They were a comforting presence, much like say a long woolly scarf, and acted like a cross between a safety net and a comfort blanket, connecting me to my childhood even as I made my first steps in the direction of notional adulthood. I was at school when *Timewyrm: Genesys* was published in June 1991. When we met Bernice in *Love and War*, I was entering 6th Form. In *First Frontier*, an old enemy returned just in time for me to move to Canterbury and begin my degree. By the time we got to *Twilight of the Gods* in 1999, I was, in common with a huge number of my fellow university graduates, working in a shop and wondering how one got a hold of one of these so-called 'graduate jobs' which paid a sensible wage that we'd all been told to expect.

I recall a lacuna between *Survival* and *Timewyrm: Genesys* where I would read and re-read the Target books, in order. Yet once the New Adventures began, I don't think I revisited a Target book. I'm not sure why I would, now. Maybe there'd be joy to be had in Saward's excellent novelisation of *The Twin Dilemma* or Ian Briggs's *The Curse of Fenric* novelisation, which remains a New Adventure in all but livery, but I'm not sure that, as a grown-up, I could cope with a Terrance. And there's no reason why I should.

But if I still had them all, one rainy afternoon in Autumn, I would like to sit with my back against the radiator and revisit *The Awakening*. One last time.

It's six years since I threw away all my Target books. I'm still in the Middle East, enjoying a cup of coffee in a Dubai restaurant. I only have a few weeks left; then another new job is bringing me back to live in the UK. When I left, David Tennant was still the Doctor (for a matter of hours). Lots has changed since then. I have, too: I'm still working with books but as a publisher now, rather than a bookseller. It's my job to travel the world and sing the praises of our new titles – and backlists – to booksellers who might choose to stock them. I also write a series of eBooks, ongoing adventures set in space, with a mysterious central character who regularly locks horns with monsters, aliens, despots and madmen. Did I end up here because of my lukewarm English Literature degree? Did I end up here because of a considered decision to spend my life working in the sphere of books?

No. I ended up here because when I was a little kid, my Dad bought me a copy of a *Doctor Who* novelisation which caused a deep and powerful awakening in me.

The Castle was Bigger in the Book

Doctor Who – The Mind of Evil
by L.M.Myles
Favourite *Doctor Who* book: *The Discontinuity Guide*
by Paul Cornell, Martin Day and Keith Topping

I always feel a little gutted when I think I've missed out on a bit of *Doctor Who* fandom I could have loved, and my memory often tricks me into thinking the Target novelisations are one of those things. A little sadness will descend over me when I hear someone expounding on how the unfussy prose of Terrance Dicks helped them learn to read, or how their imagination conjured up the most wonderful images, far superior to what they eventually saw when they watched the story on television, as they adventured along with the Doctor.

This is, obviously, a bit silly of me. I know that. What makes it extra silly is that I did grow up reading the Targets and I did have the delight of learning about some adventures first in prose and I did have that terribly non-enviable experience of seeing onscreen a pale imitation of what I'd imagined. (Oh, *The Happiness Patrol* go-kart!) As a child, I also went through a long phase where I was wholly uninterested in any other books when visiting the library: every time, it was straight to the *Doctor Who* Target novelisation shelf. I learned what an epistolary novel was thanks to *The Romans*, as well as what it felt like for an adaptation to horridly betray the source (*Genesis of the Daleks* – I was furious at the Time Lord telling the Doctor that the universe was 'younger' instead of 'less than half its present size' because it assumed you couldn't work out that meant younger from what he'd said...yes, I know, it's trivial; but at the time, this seemed terribly important.)

One of my most vivid reads was *The Mind of Evil*. I was eight years old, more or less, and it was the biannual trip to the mobile school library. This was a large van packed with books that went around rural schools so we could all choose a book to have on loan for the next six months: a well-conceived recipe for lost books, six months being approximately forever when you're eight years old. I remember being terribly excited to find *The Mind of Evil* (in amongst *The Babysitters' Club* and *Sweet Valley High*) for it was not just a *Doctor Who* Target novelisation but a story I'd never seen or read before. I knew a little about it, thanks to an entirely non-obsessive reading of *Doctor Who Magazine* and various non-fiction volumes that illuminated the history of the show. I knew it was the last story to exist wholly in black and white, thanks to the colour prints being lost. I knew more or less what happened and that fandom opinion at the time was generally favourable towards it.

My recollection of reading it is a fascination with how vast and exciting a story it was and how vividly it came to life, my mind's eye stubbornly deciding that the whole thing should be in black and white. I recall how complicated it seemed to me, how ambitious; simply being in writing instead of onscreen seemed to lend credence and authority to the story. There was also something deliciously indulgent about getting to enjoy a new *Doctor Who* story in book form: no distractions, no worries that something would seem absurd or cheap. My suspension of disbelief, hardy at the worst of times, was invulnerable, and fear at the Doctor's inevitable defeat and the destruction of the Earth was a heady thing.

Of course, the Doctor saved the day, but he didn't manage to save everyone with it. There's seldom been a death in *Doctor Who* that hit me harder than Barnham's sad, pointless end in the final pages of *The Mind of Evil*'s novelisation. A minor character, one of dozens to die in the show, yet I still remember the punch I felt right in the middle of my chest as Terrance Dicks despatched him with a ruthless efficiency of words.

It was with trepidation that I first watched the story, not wanting my experience of the novelisation to be tarnished by the limits of the budget and television in general. Marvellously, that never happened. If anything, my memory of the book and the story onscreen merged into a platonic ideal, each enhanced by the other. It remains one of my favourite *Doctor Who* stories, though I would never dare read it again, for fear of ruining a valued memory. Nor can I really believe it in colour. 'Unrealistic!' cries my brain, impossible to ignore.

So since I did enjoy the Target novelisations growing up, why does my memory insist on telling me otherwise if not harshly reminded of the truth? I think it's because they weren't that profound, life-altering experience I hear from so many other fans. They didn't teach me to read, or awaken a lifelong love of reading in me, or changed how I saw the world. They were one small part of my childhood books, and I enjoyed them. And that's something good in and off itself, and instead of lamenting their lack of a profound influence on me, I should appreciate them for the joy they did bring.

Cotton Tale

Doctor Who – The Myth Makers by Miles Northcott

Favourite *Doctor Who* book: *The Myth Makers* by Donald Cotton

There are some things in life that you can't do without. I'm not talking about the obvious things such as food, water & air, although quite clearly these are useful at times; I'm talking about things like music, love and humour. Unlike the aforementioned essentials, these three are things which can define a person (although I can name one or two people who could be defined by food). We all know someone who lives and breathes music and as such that becomes a fundamental part of who they are. Similarly, we all know someone who is so in love with someone or something that it is impossible to think of them without that concept in your head. Well, as far as I am concerned, the thing that defines me more than anything else is humour. Anyone who thinks it might yet be food can go and do one.

There are folks I know who might think that *Doctor Who* defines me and in some ways they would be right, as the show has dominated most of my life and has without doubt been one of the things that has shaped me into the man I am today. (Okay, stop it now! I know who you are and you can stop banging on about food!) When I was knee-high to a grasshopper (admittedly an eight-foot grasshopper), I started devouring (no, not my dinner! I won't warn you again!) the Target novels and some of the stories – such as *The Cave Monsters* and *The Loch Ness Monster* – made me think about environmental concerns, whilst the Doctor's policy of non-aggression struck a chord with me and made me a lover not a fighter. The moral code of the series is one that I follow and so yes, *Doctor Who* is a very big part of me...but humour is bigger.

I always liked comedy shows from Hancock to Monty Python (no, I do not want a 'waffer thin mint', thank you very much!) and many, many more, but in 1980 I discovered the Goons: Peter Sellers became my second hero (behind Tom Baker) and in 1981 became the first person outside of my family who reduced me to tears when he died. Their madcap, zany antics appealed to me at the deepest level, but what really resonated was how, despite being surreal and off the wall, they were *clever* too. Things like the classic Bluebottle & Eccles 'What time is it?' sketch, where Eccles always knows the time because he has it written on a piece of paper, made me laugh and admire in equal quantities and still, after 35 years of knowing it, makes me chortle. I absorbed that Goonery into my very being and became the school joker, never able to pass up an opportunity to try to raise a smile, or better yet a belly laugh, in others. Today I am the same and my inability to resist going down the comedy route has occasionally left me in deep water, so at times I have to fight my natural instincts out of respect or good taste.

There had always been humour in *Doctor Who*; it is an essential part of all good drama in order to balance the darker side of a piece or simply amuse for the sake of it. Some of the good Doctor's greatest tales are liberally laced with comedy (particularly in the Patrick Troughton era and whenever Tom Baker is let off the leash) and even the darker, harder hitting stories contain some (*Genesis of the Daleks*, for example, has moments such as the Doctor asking his interrogator for tea). It is well-recognised by anyone who knows me that *City of Death*, one of the funniest of all *Doctor Who* stories, is my all-time favourite.

Then, in 1985, well into the Target run and with an already heaving bookshelf (I said bookshelf, not fridge! You can leave now, thank you!), along came *The Myth Makers* by Donald Cotton. These were the days before DVDs and not long into the videotape era, so all I knew of the story was from the various programme guides and magazines. One thing I did know was that it was a pure historical, which by and large were predominantly toward the tail end of my preferred stories. The only hint I had about the treasure that was about to rain down on me was what I knew of the episode titles, both the official ones and the ones Donald Cotton had wanted to use, which had greatly amused me when I first heard of them, but I had no guarantee that the book would follow that format. I need not have worried however, as this novelisation was utterly brilliant and was devoured in one sitting (no! Not like my dinner!) It left me with a huge grin & a warm, tingly feeling of satisfaction. I was, in fact, sorely tempted to pick it back up & re-read it again straight away, such was the delight I got from it. (No, not Turkish Delight!)

Written mainly in the first person, from Homer's perspective, this was page after page of laugh out loud dialogue and description. Cotton brought the various historical figures to life with gusto and made it easy to have an emotional response to everyone, even the minor characters; the writing was both funny and clever and I adored every page. I would say, indeed, that Cotton's comedic style fitted this story like a glove – a cotton glove! Despite other stories being better and subsequent novelisations being brilliantly penned, this remains my favourite of the entire series and one I always look forward to reading – after all, who couldn't adore a story with chapters entitled 'Small Prophet, Quick Return', 'Zeus Ex Machina' and 'Doctor in the Horse'? I heartily recommend this one to anyone.

Okay, now that's done I need to grab a sandwich. I'm starving!

Harry Sullivan and the Invasion

Doctor Who – The Invasion by Steve Herbert
Favourite *Doctor Who* book: *Harry Sullivan's War*
by Ian Marter

I first discovered Target books in our local library in Keynsham where I'd take out three or four books at a time and read each one over the course of a day/evening/late at night under the covers. One of the first was *The Web of Fear* (but I didn't recognise the Doctor: the character on the front cover looked nothing like any Doctor I knew, and it would be years before I'd finally get to see Patrick Troughton as the Doctor for the first time). It would soon become common for me to go into a shop and come out with a pile of Target books.

So on to my favourite Target contributor, Ian Marter, actor, journalist and author. Without a doubt, the best male *Doctor Who* companion ever! Harry Sullivan wasn't just an imbecile, he was a hero and a short-lived companion who, to this day, I wish had been in the show until it limped that he was.

My interests are very broad. I love science fiction, but I love so much more: I love the thrill of motor sport – I watched endless Grand Prix and Indy 500's when I was young so when I saw a report on the 1955 tragedy at Le Mans written by a certain Ian Marter in a Sunday newspaper colour supplement magazine at my Gran's, I cut it out and stuck it in a scrap book that I had for years and still have somewhere to this day. It was the only example of his work in journalism I ever saw and another reason that made Ian a firm favourite of mine. I so wish I knew more about him.

Target books were a thing of my childhood. Soon after growing up, the majority of my collection would be gone. Lost, thrown out, left up in the attic. Anything that was left, along with copies of the New and Missing Adventures, were auctioned off on eBay, something I'd later regret.

Many years later, I walked into a market stall in Bath and saw a few piles of Target books and, looking through, I pulled out three by Ian and bought them. Then at a *Doctor Who* Convention in Slough a few weeks later, I found a copy of *The Invasion* which I bartered down to two pounds. So, slowly, I'm beginning to revisit the Target book range. I can't for sure remember if I ever owned *The Invasion* this book before, so last year I began reading it for possibly the first time ever.

The televised *Invasion* is a longer-than-normal eight episode story with two complete episodes missing from the archives, though these missing episodes would be the first to be animated on its DVD release. Before that we only had the audio version, various reconstructions and the novelisation itself to have any idea of how those two episodes might have looked. They remain missing. Of course, when Ian wrote the adaption he would have had to rely on the use of scripts for the two missing episodes. But by having the scripts available, Marter's adaptation is able to include deleted and alternative scenes. He writes in a more adult tone than others, say Terrance Dicks, would ever write. And in reviews online, there is the suggestion that Marter's books could have been the inspiration for the New Adventures. There are certainly more gory descriptions than any other Target author. Plus, after adapting an eight episode story, he had a larger page count than many previous books.

When I was younger and was only just beginning to read Target books, I struggled with Ian's *The Sontaran Experiment*. But I read *The Enemy of the World* a few years later and loved it, though the one surviving episode back then didn't expire me to want to see the full classic story again. When *The Web of Fear* and *The Enemy of the World* were discovered, I loved *Enemy* more. Target novels filled so many gaps of stories I'd never seen and to be honest without a miracle there was no chance of seeing those episodes ever. But to have a writer of Ian's calibre filling a few of those gaps was really a wonderful thing. It was such a shame that Ian never saw his final book, *Harry Sullivan's War*, in print.

If only Ian had lived on and written more wonderful books.

Fire and Chaos

Doctor Who – The Krotons by Zoë Mackay
Favourite *Doctor Who* book: *Companion Piece*
by L.M. Myles and Liz Barr

In early 1986, Rupert Murdoch moved the production of his newspapers from Fleet Street to Wapping, after the failure of negotiations with the print unions. Night after night, the news brought images of protests, of violence, of a building with the kind of security usually associated with prisons or defence facilities: high walls, barbed wire. The protests and disorder spread through the streets. Wapping became a place with dangerous associations.

It was also home to The Who Shop.

I'd seen the advert for it in *Doctor Who Magazine* and it instantly became a trip that I wanted to make. However, it required planning, as I would need to travel from the far North...London. To an unadventurous ten-year-old, East London might as well have been another world. It was remote and dangerous and none of the reassuring blue Tube lines went there. I mitigated the risk in the only way I could; I went with my Mum.

Wapping was poised on the brink of a transformation. For decades it had been in decay, the shipping and commerce that had built it long gone. Warehouses were derelict, abandoned. Like much of the rest of London, if you knew where to look, the scars of the war were still visible: houses missing from terraces like teeth knocked from a mouth; odd, unexpected, patches of scrubland full of brambles clawing through rubble. Places to play for those who had the chutzpah to climb the fence or risk the displeasure of unnamed (and possibly imagined) authority figures. Nowhere in London was this more obvious than Docklands. Without the money, desire or need to rebuild, row after row of Victorian warehouses stood silent and gaunt. Intimidating in both scale and the austere grandeur of the architecture, the area was forbidding and desolate.

It's unsurprising that some of the most iconic Doctor Who images come from nearby. *Resurrection of the Daleks* was filmed at Shad Thames, just the other side of the river. *The Dalek Invasion of Earth* has scenes shot at St. Katherine's Wharves, before they were pulled down to be replaced by a different sort of carbuncle – the Tower Hotel, built in 1973. There wasn't much set-dressing needed to evoke a post-invasion city.

Into this wasteland my Mum and I adventured, armed with only a London *A to Z* and an address. Our goal was little short of utopia: an entire shop devoted to *Doctor Who*. We weren't going for anything in particular, just to visit it, and with a budget that was unspecified and would be revealed to be ... disappointing.

As a relatively new fan – technically, I had been a devotee since 1981, but a childcare arrangement that saw me stuck in a neighbour's home three evenings a week (a home where, of all horrors, they watched ITV exclusively) had limited the number of episodes of seasons 19 and 20 I had been able to watch – I was aware of only two things. Firstly, that *Doctor Who* was the greatest television series ever and secondly, that Patrick Troughton's Second Doctor, with Jamie and Zoe as his companions, were my favourite TARDIS team.

There was only one problem: I had no idea why.

Most of my exposure to *Doctor Who* had come from the Target novelisations. A sympathetic primary school teacher had fed me her son's collection, loaning them one at a time, dispensing adventure like a drug. I had two of my own – *Doctor Who and the Cybermen* and *Doctor Who and The Auton Invasion* – which were both thrilling, though a source of some long-term confusion. The Second Doctor was the star of the former, but there's no Zoe. None of the novels I had borrowed from the library, or been lent by the teacher, had featured my favourite team – they were mostly Fourth Doctor stories. My devotion to the Second Doctor, Jamie, and Zoe was as inexplicable as it was unshakeable.

The only sign of The Who Shop was a little card by a doorbell. The walk from the station, through the wild streets of Wapping, had seemed to take forever. Above us, the warehouse loomed, the red brick bones covered in layers of soot. I was terrified. Had I been alone, I would have run away, but one of the advantages in travelling with a parent is that they're not going to tolerate that kind of nonsense. My Mum rang the bell and a friendly man admitted us. I recall a staircase and a corridor with a Cyberman lurking at the end. I was fascinated – who knew Cybermen existed outside of the BBC! In the shop itself, there was a wide variety of treasures, most of which have gone from my memory. It was at this point, as I looked around, that the budget was revealed. I could have a book. One. One book. That was it.

I browsed and fretted. There were thousands of books here. All five doctors were amply represented. How was I to choose? Why was I being made to? After a time, I stopped chafing at the unfairness of life and settled down. It had to be one from my favourite Doctor, one that I was unlikely to be lent, one with my favourite team. There it was. *The Krotons*. It called to me. It had the second Doctor. It had Jamie and Zoe. Best of all, it had a picture of some sort of robot on the front cover and that was a sure sign of quality.

Once I had it selected, like a government IT programme I pleaded for more budget. I was met with resistance and it wasn't until we reached the till that some flexibility emerged. I could have, in addition to my book ... a bookmark! There was one with a photo of the second Doctor (from, I now realise, *The Three Doctors*). My haul was complete, and our visit was over.

I was a third of the way through reading *The Krotons* before I felt the touch of creeping familiarity. Was it possible that I had read it before? Now, *The Krotons* is not exactly a cornucopia overflowing with originality. There are a group of people, the Gonds, oppressed by robotic overlords, the Krotons. The Doctor, Jamie, and Zoe arrive by chance. There is much running around and the Krotons are defeated and overthrown. It's a well-worn template for *Doctor Who*. The prose style – Terrance Dicks at his functional average – is not distinctive. Perhaps I was just recognising the structure and the tone?

As I continued to read, that feeling grew. I started to predict events. Pictures of the action appeared in my mind – not, in itself, unusual, but these were in black and white and slightly grainy. I was more endowed with a voracious reading appetite than a predilection for self-analysis, so I put the feeling aside and read on. It would be a decade before the rise of the internet, when I could look up the stories included in *The Five Faces of Doctor Who* repeat season and realise that this ... this was the story. This story, in all its derivative glory, was the story that had made me a *Doctor Who* fan. A story that had such an impact on me that I had wiped it completely from my mind, emerging from watching it clutching only an olive branch which read 'The Second Doctor, Jamie and Zoe are the best'. Not *The Three Doctors* or *Carnival Of Monsters* (both of which I remember clearly), but *The Krotons*.

The bookmark had less of an impact.

There are few notable things about *The Krotons*. The scenes with the Hall of Learning are a lot of fun, the Krotons themselves – a crystalline life form – are moderately thematically interesting, and their referring to the Doctor and Zoe as 'Doctorgond' and 'Zoegond' suggest amusingly poor database design. The Gonds' names appear to have been generated from Terry Nation's trademarked Scrabble Bag method of futuristic name generation, a game that poor Eelek lost. Perhaps the most interesting element, though, is what happens at the end. The Krotons are destroyed, as is pretty much all of the Gond infrastructure and way of life. Their city has a giant hole in it and still lies in the middle of a wasteland. For all Thara's assertions, Eelek is still likely to be causing trouble. What does the future hold for them? After centuries of oppression, what kind of world will they build for themselves? We never find out. The TARDIS leaves and, to our knowledge, never returns. Out of fire and chaos, a new order grows. Is it certain that it will be better than that which preceded it?

Rupert Murdoch won his battle with the unions. Within a few years, all of the former Fleet Street papers had moved out to Wapping. The Docklands Light Railway was built and the area regenerated. The warehouse occupied by The Who Shop has been cleaned and renovated and it now houses, amongst other businesses, a boutique coffee shop. The area is inhabited and alive, if pricey. The Who Shop itself moved to Barking, where it has a proper sign and doors and now features a museum and hosts regular events. London today bears few signs of the war: a station missing a dome, a ruined church which has been turned into a garden. You need to know where to look to see it at all. Wapping's shabby dreams of past glory have been replaced by an artisanal gloss.

I hope the Gonds found a way to build a utopia. Somehow, I doubt it.

When it's Easier to Find Symbiotic Nuclei than Dodge an Anniversary

Doctor Who – The Two Doctors by Matt Goddard

Favourite *Doctor Who* book: *Cybermen* by David Banks

The Two Doctors is special, although it's often done its best to keep that under an Andalucian thicket. Fortunately, some have found it out.

On screen, that first and always foremost home to *Doctor Who*, *The Two Doctors* is an anomaly. Through skill, imagination and circumstance during those oh so difficult mid-80s, it is a serial that delights in the unexpected and confounds itself at almost every turn: as contrary as the sixth Doctor. It is the only multi-Doctor story in the classic era not attached to an anniversary. It was substantial enough to form the show's final six-part adventure, but that was masked by the curious 45-minute format that the show assumed in the mid 1980s, turning it into three episodes. It featured one of the production's occasional sojourns abroad, although plans chopped and the changed to the point where Holmes was put through the wringer to rewrite the script's New Orleans setting to a rather arbitrary Seville. It featured an odd mix of two Doctors separated by four incarnations, which stuck out even in a mercurial season that revelled the show's history, sometimes more successfully than others. And it was during this story's original broadcast that the BBC announced the show's hiatus and an end to a continuous run of nearly 22 years.

Who better to first realise the potential of *The Two Doctors* than Target, not only seizing upon the story to become their one hundredth release, but also luring Robert Holmes to adapt his own script (no mean feat, considering that he'd previously struggled and failed to novelise *The Time Warrior*); it would become his only novelisation. Before I'd seen barely any of his stories on screen, one novel from the pen of Holmes was enough to double my vocabulary, or so it felt during that short reading.

There's still a buzz seeing classic Target books lined up (even if randomly) in a car boot sale or a memorabilia shop. At jumble sales, fetes, wherever there was a book stall I'd scan it twice, once for James Bond, second for *Doctor Who*. Pan then Target. I still recall countless Saturdays spent visiting the same bookshops during the very early 1990s, finding an unchanging selection stacked on the shelves, mostly the later books, with the stunning covers mostly by Alister Pearson. I'd never caught *Delta and the Bannermen* on broadcast, but I probably read the back copy of that book than anything else at the time.

Still, with a necessarily eclectic collection strategy, it's little surprise I can barely remember where I got most of my Target book collection, from the battered first edition of *Carnival of Monsters* long missing its spine, as if chewed off by a lazy Drashig, to the later editions I preciously slipped into clear book protectors, vainly hoping it would halt the effects of the time stream on their pristine covers. I remember being gifted *The Power of the Daleks* for Christmas, miraculously featuring a Pearson cover I'd not pawed at in book stores; it was a story I severely doubted I'd ever see onscreen. Not so with *The Two Doctors*.

The cover of Target's hundredth novel was a strange one, emblazoned with a star proclaiming it a first edition (just like the serial itself, the range was well aware of its heritage and audience). The star sat on a curious but effective cover by Andrew Skilleter, which nodded to the Seville setting and the serial's familiar antagonists, but boiled the pairing of the Doctors down to a giant angular heart formed by two TARDISes, pointing to the author's name. Most noteworthy of all, above the image, below the headline that proclaimed yes, this was the hundredth novel (an achievement rewarded with an introduction by producer John Nathan-Turner), was the show's mid-1980s logo: the familiar neon piping in shape, but shining in gold.

There that gold emblem sat on a shelf in the Longleat shop. After the control room and the looping mirrored corridors, I just had to buy something while I was there. I had no idea if *Pyramids of Mars* as book 50, *The Face of Evil* as 25 or *Meglos* as 75, had been emblazoned in anniversary colours when they were released (they weren't) but I definitely knew that logo was gold because it was the hundredth novel and that was a big thing. I'd no idea it was the final issue of 1985, nor the first adaptation of a story with the sixth Doctor, but it was already special and irresistible, even more so because I'd never really heard of it before, let alone thought about watching it.

When I did watch it, it came in the midst of the BBC's furious VHS release schedule of 1993. Seized for the good of the franchise again, *The Two Doctors* appeared not only with special thirtieth anniversary branding, but in the birthday month itself. That was soon a well-worn tape sitting in the same room as the well-thumbed novelisation.

Jumping forward ten years, through the digital revolution, 2003's fortieth anniversary worked the magic again. Once more *The Two Doctors* gained a birthday release, the Sixth Doctor's entry among a DVD selection featuring all the Doctors, beaten back to a September release by the combined might of *The Three Doctors*. By the time I picked up my copy in the *Bred for War* DVD box set, it was the forty-fifth anniversary year of 2008 and the show had returned to the small screen, bringing the Sontarans with it. The year before, *Time Crash* pulled the tenth and fifth Doctors together with no pretence of an anniversary.

There's no doubt that, if it somehow knew all of this, *The Two Doctors* would have tried to remove itself from all these key dates in the show's history. That's exactly what this contrary adventure would have done. But I can see through that like a Sontaran torture projection thanks to that showy cover full of self-celebration I saw in Longleat a quarter of a century ago. So, it's a good thing that Target figured it out first.

The First Chance, the Last Chance and the Wise Owl

Doctor Who – The Gunfighters
by Mark Trevor Owen
Favourite *Doctor Who* book: *About Time* series
by Tat Wood and Lawrence Miles

The novelisation of *The Gunfighters* is a funny book, in many senses of the word. It was published when I was fourteen. As some of you may recall, absolutely nothing is funny when you're fourteen. Everything is a very serious business indeed. Jokes and laughs are for silly children, not mature, misunderstood creatures such as me at that age.

Luckily from my point of view, *Doctor Who* on television was being very serious at the time. The episodes shown recently had been almost invariably swaggering, smile-free affairs, garnished with gore and set upon a lake of ponderously earnest continuity references. It was almost perfectly finessed to appeal exclusively to fourteen-year-old boys. Rather less fortuitously, senior management at the BBC had decided to force an eighteen month break into the transmission schedule of *Doctor Who*, while they considered ways to broaden the appeal of the show beyond pimply adolescents; and to amortise the setup of *Eastenders*.

It's hard to convey what a blow this was to those who weren't there or weren't that geeky. Nowadays, whenever *Doctor Who* has one of its games of Management Musical Chairs and the next series is delayed for a bit, a consoling rewatch of a previous episode or seven is only the touch of a button away. It's a strangely cherished myth that at this time, the novelisations were the only other source of *Doctor Who*. There was actually quite a range of media and what posterity has mercifully glossed over is just how odd so much of it was.

There was the annual, purchased each year by doting parents, clearly unaware of what hallucinogenic insanity they were sliding under the Christmas tree. There was the beginning of the range of VHS releases of the stories, a few titles inelegantly hacked into omnibus editions and flogged for the equivalent of an entire year of my pocket money. There was a new range of comic books launched around that time: in a curious marketing strategy they were printed to squint-inducingly Lilliputian dimensions, allowing them to be given away inside packets of crisps.

The novelisations, however, remained dependably consistent. Recent years might have seen an increasing number of them written by the original authors of the TV source material, keen to add their own flourishes, but few deviated wildly from the template honed by the master craftsman Terrance Dicks.

Then A Man Named Cotton moseyed into town...

The Wise Owl bookshop was the sort of place guaranteed to produce online gales of nostalgic sighs. Not just an independent bookshop, but one granted the luxury of specialisation, it was an independent bookshop that only sold children's books. Of course, my fourteen-year-old self regarded *Doctor Who* novelisations as works as serious and mature as his own temperament but with other local booksellers failing to keep up with the latest releases, Wise Owl offered a safe nest. The titles were released on a monthly basis, ensuring a regular supply of fresh material that the TV version of *Doctor Who* was currently unable to match. Occasionally, a book would, for reasons unknown, fail to make it onto the Wise Owl shelves. One of those was *The Myth Makers*, Donald Cotton's first contribution to the range, published the previous year. The review in *Doctor Who Magazine* had indicated that that book was rather different to the norm, but this gave me no immediate cause for concern. We were, as I mentioned before, in a phase of the novelisations trying different things. Those published under the pseudonym John Lydecker dispensed with chapter breaks; those written by Ian Marter slipped in the occasional swear word. As far as I knew though, the novelisations remained broadly formulaic in a way young nerds found reassuring. All that was about to change, thanks to a book with a stetson-wearing William Hartnell on its cover.

I knew very little about the TV version of *The Gunfighters*. Black and white tales from the First Doctor were not something I seriously thought we'd ever watch, bar the very occasional repeat. All I knew was that it was the almost inevitable 'TARDIS lands in the Wild West' one and had a reputation as the very worst *Doctor Who* story of all, due to the opinions of a small group of influential fans. I already knew that this was no yardstick – many a poorly-regarded TV story had inspired an enjoyable novelisation – so I handed over the princely sum of £1.60 for the latest addition to my library, still leaving 10p for the bus fare home. The book opened...and so did my definition of what made *Doctor Who*.

From the elusive opening dedication 'For TAMSIN, with coloured moon clouds' onwards, *The Gunfighters* made it abundantly clear that, like a sharp-shooter in the Last Chance Saloon, it had no respect for the established way of doing things. The conventional linear structure so beloved of both televised and novelised *Doctor Who* was thrown aside in a genre-bending free association of first-person narrative, obscure classical allusions (Johnny Ringo studies Caesar's *Gallic Wars*) and dialogue that read like PG Wodehouse after a few shots of redeye. Along the way, Donald Cotton even found time to break a particularly notorious taboo, as we have *Doctor Who*'s first ever sex scene. (In the TV version, the Doctor interrupts Doc Holliday and his lady friend Kate having a bit of a cuddle. In the book, they're rather more involved. I'm sure the staff at Wise Owl were blissfully unaware.)

My teenage incarnation found all this quite shocking, and not just the stuff with Holliday and Kate. Was this whirl of allusion, wordplay and random moments of violence actually *Doctor Who*? Yes, of course it was. Had I read Cotton's earlier book, *The Myth Makers*, I might have been better prepared for this wild, Wild West assault on my preconceived ideas; but this was my earliest opportunity to see the world of *Doctor Who* through the particular prism of Donald Cotton. A first chance at the Last Chance Saloon to make an attempt at his impish style.

Of course, something as flexible and brilliant as *Doctor Who* can never be restricted in the range of styles and formats it can use. The series of novelisations would continue to experiment and broaden their scope, as more writers brought their own ideas to add to the mix. (There would be one more rule-breaking novelisation from Mr Cotton, but I'll leave that for somebody else to champion.) A couple of years after *The Gunfighters* arrived in Wise Owl, like Wyatt Earp riding into Tombstone, *Doctor Who* on television would break away from the insecure macho continuity-fests and find fresh ways to tell its tales. A few more years after that would see me leave home to study the greats of literature. I might not have carried a ten-volume edition of Caesar in my saddlebag, like a certain gunslinger did, but thanks to a humble Target Books novelisation, I already knew there really was no way to keep a good idea restricted in a tidy little box. As all *Doctor Who* admirers should know, little boxes can contain more than their outward appearance suggests. As can little books.

Lost (in Time) in a Book!

Doctor Who and the Time Monster
by Stephen Candy
Favourite *Doctor Who* book: *Timewyrm: Exodus*
by Terrance Dicks

I'll start with a confession. I have never seen the television version of *The Time Monster*. I never got around to buying the VHS version and the DVD was part of a box-set of stories-that-make-you-go-meh. I have, however, read the novelisation by the mighty Terrance Dicks. It is worth saying, although I am sure many others in this very book will also say it, that the legacy of happiness and enjoyment created by that one man should stand alongside any other, perhaps better known, children's author (or any author for that matter.)

So many great stories written and script-edited for television by him and then so many more novelised and enjoyed in print, as well as his original fiction. (Go and find a copy of Dicks' Virgin New Adventure Timewyrm: Exodus and read it right away. It has everything you could want from a *Doctor Who* story: a well characterised Doctor and companion, clever plot twists, nods to TV series continuity, use of time travel, alternate histories... a veritable showcase of why *Doctor Who* fans almost universally love his writing.) Anyhow, back to *The Time Monster*. It's not my favourite book. As I've just said, it's not even my favourite book by this author. I've read a lot of books, but only once have I experienced what happened with this one.

While at primary school, I swiftly worked my way through their collection of *Doctor Who* novelisations. This process would continue into secondary school, where the library was thankfully much larger and where I played a five-year game of cat-and-mouse with the school librarian involving me replacing all the books on display stands with *Doctor Who* ones. One lunchtime, I was reading *The Time Monster*, enjoying the tale while blissfully unaware that Kronos the Chronovore was a punningly clever name for a creature that can eat time. I was sat in class in my usual seat and carried on reading. Eventually I came around to thinking 'it's been quite a long lunch break' and I looked up from the book. The whole class was halfway through the afternoon's lesson! I had been sufficiently engrossed in my reading that I had failed to notice everyone tidying up from playtime, the register being taken (no memory of answering my name) and the next lesson starting. I was truly lost in the story. My classmates had, helpfully, left me to carry on reading, or else hadn't even noticed I wasn't doing the lesson as I tended to be a quiet student in those days.

The memory of genuinely being unaware of what was going on

around me while I was reading has stayed with me to this day, although it has never happened again since. I've continued to be a voracious reader and put my enthusiasm for reading down to my early experiences with the Target range. (A Whovian cliché, yes, but certainly the truth.)

Now I think I will treat myself to a re-read of the book and might actually get the story on disc to see it on screen for the first time!

Postcards from an Alternate Future

Doctor Who and the Twin Dilemma by Graeme Burk
Favourite *Doctor Who* book: *Damaged Goods*
by Russell T Davies

It's a cliché to say that the Target Novels were the only access fans had with *Doctor Who*'s past, but for fans like myself living in North America in the mid-1980s, it was also the only access fans had to *Doctor Who*'s present and future.

I bought Eric Saward's novelisation of *The Twin Dilemma* from Pick of the Crop Toys and Books in Oakville, Ontario in early 1986. (I paid $3.95 for it, according to the price still written in pencil on the inside front cover.) Pick of the Crop was on Lakeshore Road, a short bus ride from High School. I always felt self-conscious buying *Doctor Who* books there. It was a toyshop with a side-line in books, clearly for younger kids, but they stocked Target novels. I made my first purchase of a novelisation there (*Doctor Who and the War Games*; I still have a Pavlovian response of excitement every time I see that cover with its stylised searchlights) and the thing that kept me self-consciously going to a kiddie store was that they were one of the first places in town to get newly-published novelisations.

And new novelisations meant new *Doctor Who*.

While *The Twin Dilemma* was broadcast on British TV in early 1984, it hadn't transmitted anywhere near Southern Ontario, where I lived. We were reliant on *Doctor Who* from two public broadcasters – one American, one Canadian – and neither had broadcast it. The most recent thing I had seen transmitted was a 'movie format' version of *The Caves of Androzani* which I saw in the spring of 1985 on the Buffalo PBS station. (I also got to see fourth generation copies of *The Two Doctors* and *Attack of the Cybermen* courtesy of a friend who was well connected in Canadian fandom, but that's another story.)

I have to digress here at this point to offer another cliché: things were different back then. And the attitudes of fans to what was going to happen next in *Doctor Who* was especially different. We're nowadays so precious about spoilers. There was none of that in the 1980s, particularly in North America when new episodes of *Doctor Who* might broadcast a year or two (or more) after their UK transmission. I knew every single major plot revelation of *The Five Doctors* – Borusa was behind it! The Yeti appear for a scene! The Raston Warrior robot slaughters the Cybermen! – even *before* I read the novelisation. It was all, I suppose, a *carpe diem* approach to

314

spoilers: who knows when we'll see it, let's find out about everything that happens.

Consequently, I was often reliant on Target to fill me in not just on *Doctor Who*'s past, but what was, for me, its future. The first time I did that was with *Mawdryn Undead* and I continued with a number of Season 20 and 21 stories. *The Twin Dilemma* was just the latest one. These books were postcards from the future: a tantalising glimpse of what would happen in the world of *Doctor Who* as soon as WNED Buffalo got around to showing it.

But, here's the thing: *The Twin Dilemma* novelisation was even better than that.

One of the first sentences of Eric Saward's novelisation is a description of Archie Sylvest's home which was 'as pleasing today as when it was first built in 1810, some five hundred years earlier' – a way of situating the story in the future without saying so that tickled my imagination when I read it thirty years ago. And then we get into the second chapter where the new Doctor has split his jacket open from the added girth of his regeneration (which turned out to be a nod to the fact that they did have to let out Peter Davison's clothes for Colin Baker to wear them!) We have a digression to explain what regeneration was (something created by a hormone Time Lords possess called lindos) and the story of a Time Lord, Councillor Verne, who, after regenerating from a really good-looking man into an ordinary one, tried to regenerate into something better looking and eventually became a puddle.

At that point, *The Twin Dilemma* had me.

It was bold, it was mad, it was discursive. In short, it was Eric Saward writing like Douglas Adams. I loved Douglas Adams – when I was sixteen, my favourite novel was *The Hitchhiker's Guide to the Galaxy* – and I loved Eric Saward writing like him. I adored the wonderful digressions throughout the book that ranged from the story of Azmael's acrimonious parting from the Time Lords to the Doctor musing about Adric (and actually contextualised Adric's awkwardness and death – '...the boy had died without the Doctor ever being able to fully praise, help or ultimately like' – in a way that was terribly moving). And I was enthralled by the deft way Saward would move from visceral death to a punchline.

However, what really caught my imagination was the way Saward captured how dangerous the Doctor's unstable regeneration was. Part of that trick is achieved easily (he says from the critical distance of a fan – as a writer I know it's bloody hard) by using Peri's point of view, which does two things: one, the Doctor becomes incredibly scary as Peri muses about what a deranged Time Lord might be capable of doing. Two, we now have an interlocutor to interpret and explain what

315

particular fugue state the Doctor is in: acting like a hermit, a coward, Sherlock Holmes (albeit an ineffective version of him). Furthermore, the Doctor is moving between personalities at any particular moment – which adds to how scary the unstable regeneration is.

Plus, we get Peri's reaction to the Doctor's new clothes: 'The whole ensemble was finished off with a waistcoat which looked as though someone had been sick on. (For all Peri knew, someone had.) [sic]'

It was vivid writing. It had a deft and weird sense of humour I hadn't seen on screen in *Doctor Who* in a while (and honestly didn't manifest itself on screen in that era except for *Revelation of the Daleks*). And the Gallifreyan mythos was cool too.

Of course the cliché I'm probably expected to utter next is, 'And I was so disappointed when I finally got to see *The Twin Dilemma* and it was nothing like how it was in the book.' But the truth is actually a lot muddier. I was not all that bothered when I finally saw *The Twin Dilemma* about six months later when it was broadcast on PBS. Everything Saward had in the novelisation about the Doctor's fugue states simply added a layer to my understanding of what was going on in the TV version. If I felt any dissonance between the TV version and the novelisation, it was in the interpretation of Nestor and the Gastropods, which had seemed more fearsome and visceral (more was made of how their slug trails destroyed the gorgeous architecture). The thing I really remember really bothering me was Hugo Lang becoming such a boring character.

It was only as I got older and rewatched *The Twin Dilemma* that I found the TV version wanting compared to the book. I began to suspect that the novelisation was Eric Saward atoning for his guilt that he didn't do more to rewrite Anthony Steven's TV script. (Saward even outright mocks one of the worst lines of the script, 'I'm the Doctor, whether you like it or not', adding in the narration, 'The statement was as bland and sterile as it sounded'). Because, honestly, if the version that was in the book was onscreen it would never be at the bottom of *Doctor Who Magazine*'s polls decades later: a version where the fear Peri is experiencing is made more explicit, and where the Doctor's fugue states are better explained and show that the Doctor is currently bereft of an actual personality.

If the novelisations were postcards from the future, *The Twin Dilemma* is a postcard from an alternate future. And I was happy to live in the future with Seedle Warriors, the hormone called lindos and the Doctor randomly believing he's Sherlock Holmes.

And yet, the novelisation taught me something more than that. It taught me the power of vivid, even lurid, prose. And I still remember that prose with the same excitement that I had when I first read it at a bus stop outside Pick of the Crop Books in Oakville, Ontario.

316

Rill Seeker

Doctor Who – Galaxy Four by Cliff Chapman
Favourite *Doctor Who* book: *Alien Bodies* by Lawrence Miles

Four Hundred Dawns

So many moments, elements, occasions threaten to be the dawn of my fandom. Seeing the Cushing movies; *Revelation of the Daleks*; bits of the trial; getting *Genesis of the Daleks* on audio; renting videos; owning *The Robots of Death*... but my first few Target books are a pretty special memory. A big batch, bought for me by my grandmother from St Paul's Bookshop in Parliament Square, Ramsey, Isle of Man. *The Invasion* thrilled me, *The King's Demons* seemed so much better than the television version, *The Mark of the Rani* was purple, in cover and prose, and *The Savages*... I don't remember much about, much like most people to this day.

The majority of this batch were published in 1985 or 1986 and I'd have been five or six when given them. One of them had a red cover, which was my favourite colour for a long time. These things matter when your age is in single figures. (My favourite colour is now purple, but red still has a place in my heart when it comes to wine on my lips and lipstick on sexy space ladies). Oh yes, and there were sexy space ladies on it. It was called *Galaxy Four*.

Trap of Steel

'...Vicki was cutting Stephen's hair.' Now, I don't know about you, but whilst I appreciate the idea of having a moment of calm before an adventure kicks in, I don't want to read about a haircut. When I was five, I hated having my hair cut. I believe it's common in children. It may be some Samson-related fear of losing one's innate superpowers when one loses one's locks. It may be because a strange person you don't know or trust is coming at your head with *sharp things*. For this reason, and probably because *The Invasion* was much better, I seem to recall I started *Galaxy Four* and then quickly gave up on it. I know I did eventually finish it, possibly around the age of nine or ten when I started rabidly consuming other novelisations at the town library, having exhausted the school library's stock. I remember loving *The Mutants* and *The Android Invasion* (oh, the disappointments when I saw those).

The thing about *Galaxy Four* though, was that you couldn't see it, not until years later when a long clip turned up on that video that came with *The Ice Warriors*. It exemplifies for me how novelisations are really the best way to experience missing stories. Whereas I can't sit through a recon because they constantly pull me out of a story by recycling the same photo for what feels like hours, and my attention wanders with soundtracks alone, I can keep my disbelief suspended by an animation or a book. *Galaxy Four* seems an exceptionally faithful book, even down to it being split into four chapters of around 25 to 30 pages each. Where it digresses are a few little zooms into the minds of characters – awkwardly, as without chapter breaks, the switches from omni-narration into POV character narration jars, especially when we're in the Doctor's mind one minute, Stephen's the next, and Maaga's after that. Maaga's characterisation reflects some of the steady strength Stephanie Bidmead gave it on TV that was only really apparent once *Air Lock* surfaced. The Doctor's thoughts betray this as a product of the 1980s mop-up operation the Target novelisations went through, with foreshadowing for the first regeneration and a truly bizarre section where the Doctor muses on how God treats him.

It's hard to know what to make of Emms, but from what I gather he was an Australian, like Antony Coburn before him; the Doctor's cantankerous nature mixed meshes with a clichéd no nonsense Aussie sensibility. And a race of Warrior Women seems less progressively feminist-orientated than some kind of revenge on a really hot woman whom he once fancied. On the one hand, William Emms, that's a feminism fail. On the other... dude, we've all been there. I can't ask Emms, he's dead. So I won't guess how he feels about commentators judging work from the Sixties, and novelised in the Eighties. At times, there's the bizarre juxtaposition of visualising the Hartnell Doctor giving it large like Connery's Bond. 'I'm a scientist, woman, I know these things!' he exclaims at one point, and you panic and hope there's a God so you can hope to Her/Him/It that that line never appeared in the broadcast version, or that they never find that episode in full so we're spared the indignity of discussions online for ever more. And yet, with a female guest cast of more than one, a rarity for classic Doctor Who, *Galaxy Four* passes the Bechdel test in that it has female characters having conversations that aren't about blokes. It also essentially portrays women as capable, yet flawed, and not dependent upon the male sex.

Air Lock

The *Galaxy Four* novelisation was one of the first Doctor Who things I owned. The significance of sitting in the BFI cinema, catching my breath as Mark Gatiss gave way to the Hartnell titles and then seeing the opening five minutes of *Air Lock* was rather special, back in 2011. It had been an awful year, but a truly lovely end to it. The direction was great (okay, well, great in comparison to, say, a Richard Martin episode) and the Chumbleys were a bit more visually interesting than they'd seemed. I'd love to see the rest of it. I don't assume we ever will, despite the rumours to the contrary, but I was and am grateful to have a flavour of it. And I'll still return to the book, not the recon, to contextualise it.

Seeing it and reading it over again, is *Galaxy Four* a reaction to, and a comment upon, the Daleks? The Drahvins as beautiful blonde Thals, but this time evil? The goodies being the ugly mutants with the weird domed travel machines on a dead planet? It's the old trope of the SF Amazonian story, but it does seem to have a spin on it, a critical evaluation of the notion of beauty equalling goodness. And it could be done again. Here we are today, and we are yet to see a chunkier, brass-plated, dirtied-down Chumbley voiced by Nick Briggs. Moffat has only sort-of brought the Drahvins back (they're name-checked as one of the ships in *The Pandorica Opens*.) It's not beyond imagination to suggest his successor will consider bringing them back on screen.

The Exploding Planet

I still own that novelisation. I'm very pleased about that. It's in pretty good nick too – minimal imprints from being leant on to draw things. *Galaxy Four* has lived in three houses, but I've been in many more. It hasn't travelled with me: it's still at my mum's, in a box in my old bedroom. I can't pretend it's the most amazing *Doctor Who* story, or the most amazing novelisation, but it's there, in my life, significant at the beginning, and the height of my fandom.

It's a simple story: basic, sort-of done before, a bit sexist, with some dodgy dialogue and in some respects, best forgotten. They didn't know better in the sixties and they were trying to be progressive within a low-budget family teatime sci-fi show destined to live no longer than the planet. They say if the DWAS had got a request in to screen it at their 1978 event a few weeks earlier, we might have had the whole story for ever. I think this was proven apocryphal later, but it's still nice to imagine. And for stories that have been done before, that are a bit sexist, with dodgy dialogue, and are in some respects best forgotten, we can be thankful they're a thing of the sixties and will never be a problem for *Doctor Who* again. Hopefully.

'Bad? *Bad*? BAD?'

Doctor Who – Timelash by Simon Paramore

Favourite *Doctor Who* book: *The Discontinuity Guide*
by Paul Cornell, Martin Day and Keith Topping

I can't remember a time when I wasn't a *Doctor Who* fan. I literally can't; my earliest memory is a *Doctor Who* memory. I am four years old, sitting on the floor, in front of the television. My favourite programme has just finished and Peter Howell's bouncy reworking of the *Doctor Who* theme bursts out, as Peter Davison's face fills the screen and dissolves into countless stars. And four-year-old me, already a precocious reader, struggles to decipher the word 'Turlough'.

Even at the age of four, I loved *Doctor Who* books. I was fortunate enough to live across the road from a library, and the library was fortunate enough to contain a vast array of *Doctor Who* books. I am sure there were many Target novelisations, but I was too young for novels. At that age I was attracted to *Doctor Who* picture books, and there were actually quite a few. On the whole they were actually reference books full of production codes and explanations of special effects and makeup. But my four-year-old eyes turned to the pictures – different, older, black-and-white Doctors; Sea Devils and Yetis and Cybermen. I remember that there was a large feature on Michael Wisher in one book, full of behind-the-scenes photos from *Genesis of the Daleks*. Four-year-old me lapped it up.

Naturally, as my reading improved, I moved onto the Target novels and would seek out as many as I could. My primary school only had one – *Meglos* – which I read at least fifty times. For a long time, it was my only experience of the fourth Doctor. The picture on the cover made such an impression on me that when I actually met Tom Baker, around that time, walking through a village in Kent, it was not the lack of scarf or curls or sonic screwdriver that surprised me – it was the lack of cactus spines!

Although I was an avid viewer, I was the only member of my family who was. Neither of my parents watched the show and did not really understand how important it was to me. This meant that when the programme was broadcast on Saturday evenings, we were often out rather than tuning in for the Doctor's latest adventures. As a result, I missed some episodes on transmission, having to fill in the gaps from my imagination, but the new format of two-part stories in season 22 meant that I occasionally missed entire stories. As I got older, this proved to be something of a double-edged sword as it meant that I occasionally found a Target novel of a 1980s story that I had never seen. This always filled me with anticipation and joy. On one such occasion, when I was about twelve, I managed to acquire a copy of *Timelash*.

I can vividly remember first seeing the cover of *Timelash*. The main thing that attracted me to it was obviously the neon logo, which I loved finding because it meant it was a story from my era. Beyond that, two things stood out for me. Firstly, this book was not written by Terrance Dicks, unlike most that I had so far read (to this day, I cannot consider any description of the TARDIS sound to be accurate if it does not use the words 'wheezing' and 'groaning'). The second thing that stood out was the hideously twisted face of the Borad. Interestingly, this face is deliberately hidden for much of the TV story, in anticipation of the big reveal. He spends most of the first half Davrosing around in the shadows, his features obscured by darkness – very rare for the JNT era! But here the Borad is revealed from the start, somewhat spoiling the later revelation that he is now half-Morlox.

But what of the actual book? As a twelve-year-old child, I found it a fascinating read. There were so many intriguing little gems in here for me. For a start, there was the mention of the Doctor having visited Karfel before, albeit with a different face and different companions. By this time, I knew much more about the earlier Doctors, but was still hazy on the details. I remember genuinely believing that this must be a reference to an old Jon Pertwee story, or why else would the author have put it there? In my mind, *Timelash* was obviously a sequel of sorts, with the Doctor returning to a planet he had previously visited long before; I was hugely disappointed when I discovered the truth.

Something else that grabbed the attention of twelve-year-old me was the character of Herbert. By the age of twelve, I was already very interested in science fiction and had recently read H.G. Wells' *The Time Machine*. (A quick interjection here – if you've never read it, go and do so. Seriously. It is an easy read for Victorian fiction and still stands up as an excellent piece of literature.) As a fan of that book, his inclusion as a character delighted me. I seem to remember knowing that Herbert was H.G. Wells from the start; either I had read a synopsis somewhere or I had flicked through the book and seen his name at the end. For me, knowing Herbert's identity did not spoil the story, it added an extra bit of interest. It was one of many things that I enjoyed about *Timelash*. I loved this book when I was twelve. In my imagination, Karfel was so alien and real, the Borad was such a menacing figure and the actual Timelash was a spectacular passageway through time and space.

Oh, to be twelve again.

I have returned to this story twice in recent months. The first time was when I recently re-watched most of the Colin Baker era, and while

321

many of the stories are better than their reputations would suggest, *Timelash* is most certainly not. The sets, costumes, characterisations and plot are all disappointing. As usual, Colin does his best to be heroic and wonderful, while every aspect of the production seems hell bent on preventing him from doing so. Paul Darrow is nowhere near as good as he should be and Herbert is just annoying. And as for the Timelash being filled with tinsel...

The production values in the imagination of twelve-year-old me were just so much higher. *Timelash* was a fantastic story when my mind was filling in the gaps. The TV version could never live up to the magic of the glorious Target novel. But, of course, when I recently found my battered old copy of the glorious Target book, I found that it was not glorious at all. It did not have any of the sparkle and wonder and excitement that I remembered. It was full of dull prose, hardly any dialogue and nothing to excite the senses at all. Where I had remembered an intriguing and fast-paced story, there was, in fact, nothing of the sort. But was that part of the magic of the Target range? Even bad Target books could fuel the imagination of young *Doctor Who* fans. And this one was bad. Reading *Timelash* now, with an adult's mind and far more experience of good literature, it is nothing special at all.

But it was special once. When I was twelve, the Doctor's adventure on Karfel was spectacular.

Vislor of the Wanderers

Turlough and the Earthlink Dilemma by Pete Murphy

Favourite *Doctor Who* book: *The Doctor Who Role-Playing Game* by
Cubicle 7

I really hated school, and I'm very thankful for *Doctor Who* novels and
Association Football.

After being 'asked to leave' my local comprehensive school, I found
myself in the unenviable position of going to an all-boys boarding
college, which ended up being the most bizarre time of my life and I
detested it. The whole ethos of the school was about achieving the
highest marks and passing exams, things in which I had no interest.
During my eighteen months at the school there were two things I was
interested in: *Doctor Who* and football. If I was not playing football or
listening out for the latest results, I would be sat reading a Target
book, normally in the library.

The school day would start with lessons at 08:30 and finish at
17:00. I would be sent out of a lesson at least once a day, which was
fine by me. If I hadn't mocked a teacher by the end of lessons, I would
consider it a bad day. The majority of teachers were full of their own
self-importance and took themselves very seriously. I didn't dislike all
the teachers: I got on well with the Sports/PE teacher, who was a
Doctor Who fan who had *The Five Doctors* on video, which he copied
for me.

I got on with most of my school mates and even though they thought
the school work was important, they found my antics amusing. As I
was able to make people laugh, I was treated well. Only one pupil (that
I was aware of) took a dislike to me: he was a couple of years older
than me and slightly bigger. I somehow managed to get in a scrape
with him and when he asked me for a fight I agreed, but only on the
condition I could choose the place. He would have beaten me and as
the exams were approaching, I decided to have our confrontation
during one of them. As soon as he realised I was serious and didn't
care about the consequences, he changed his mind and let it go. I'm
sure his Mummy and Daddy would have had something to say about
him getting expelled.

On Saturday we would have half a day off which would be our own
time. I would either go into the local town to pick up the latest *Doctor
Who* book or watch Bolton Wanderers at home. Then in 1986 it was
announced that Target would be publishing a line of original novels
based upon the companions of *Doctor Who*. I was extremely happy
about this, as two books in one month would help me escape the boring
tedium of school. The first of this series to be released was going to be

323

Turlough and the Earthlink Dilemma.

On Saturday 17th May 1986 after dinner, I got changed out of my pretentious school uniform and caught the bus into town. Following my usual routine, I went to WH Smith in the centre of town and then to the local record shop and the game and hobby shop, in which I often bought the latest FASA *Doctor Who Role Playing Game* supplements and Citadel *Doctor Who* figures. The next shop was John Menzies, the shop which stocked Target books. On this particular Saturday they had both *Timelash* and the Turlough novel. I picked them both up and bought them, caught the bus back to college and straight away started reading *Timelash*, intending to leave the Turlough novel until I'd finished the first book.

The following Tuesday, I was called to the headmaster's office, which was a regular occurrence so didn't bother me. It was good news: a couple of weeks, earlier Bolton had won the semi-final of the Football League Trophy and they were on the way to Wembley and I was going! I was going to be picked up on Friday evening and go with the Bolton fans from Burnden Stadium and travel down on Saturday morning.

Over the next couple of days, I finished *Timelash* and decided to leave Turlough for the journey to Wembley. The rest of the week really dragged. On Friday afternoon I had double Science with a teacher of whom a lot of pupils were scared, but I just thought he was a bit of a sad plonker. This was followed by double sports which meant football. We always had enough boys for two complete eleven-a-side matches. One match would be for the boys who were not interested in playing or were no good and I was always in the other match.

I don't know what happened to me in that game: maybe I was looking forward to being able to leave school but I was buzzing and had a great game. I also managed to score the best goal I ever scored. It was in the second half, with our team losing, when the opposition had a throw-in in our half. I anticipated who the player was going to throw it to and knew that I could get the better of him. I have played in my mind what happened next quite a few times since but if you'd told me when I tackled that player what I would do next, I wouldn't have believed you. I took the ball and ran into their half and kept running. I beat one player, then another, then another (who happened to be one of the best defenders in our school). The next moment, I was curling the ball round the goalkeeper with my left foot (I was predominantly right-footed) and watching it hit the back of the net.

I turned around to complete silence, I thought I had done something wrong. The defender who I just beat said 'Brilliant' and I was then mobbed by my own team mates. Our team went on to beat the opposition and after the match I went to have a shower, got changed into my own clothes and waited for my lift, pleased to be out of the school uniform.

Saturday came and we got on one of the Bolton Wanderers Supporters coaches and travelled down to Wembley. I remember reading *Turlough and the Earthlink Dilemma* on the journey. It has had a lot of bad reviews but I have a special fondness for it and always remember reading it on my first trip to Wembley and associate it with the goal I scored the day before.

Bolton lost to Bristol City 3-0.

'Words, Words, Words...'

Doctor Who – The Mark of the Rani
by Cliff Chapman
Favourite *Doctor Who* book: *Alien Bodies* by Lawrence Miles

'In general, prefer small ordinary words to unusual portentous ones,' says Alastair Fowler in *How to Write* (OUP, 2006). He's largely ignored here.

There is a beauty, a fascination and a sense of fun in archaic or unusual words. I still make a little burble of joy when I learn a new word. I am a fan of linguistics, an advocate of vocabulary. I rue the dumbing down of things. The dialogue in *The Mark of the Rani* is florid like few other *Doctor Who* stories... but the novelisation takes this even further. I celebrate the Bakers' efforts to educate and entertain. I'm sad we won't see *Doctor Who* assume that its audience is intellectually curious for a while. I'm even sadder that in trying to push for academically-minded adventure, the Bakers didn't really see the wood land mines for the tree land mines.

Violent miners in bath house! Master is scarecrow! Trolley Mine Shaft! Landmine trees! Dinosaur embryos! It's all good, they're great scenes, great images, but they don't really connect. *The Mark of the Rani*'s problem is that it's merely a few set pieces that don't tie together, peppered with fancy words to distract you. We are told characters are sweet and jovial right after they've kicked the soot out of someone... it's more of an emotional hop on one leg than a journey. The Rani is clearly a product of Thatcher's Britain... a woman who's allowed to be every bit as clever and devious and cool as the Doctor or the Master, as long as she basically behaves like a man. Peri, once again in *Doctor Who*, does absolutely nothing of use... which is a shame. Why not write the book entirely from her perspective? And as for the prose... so many ellipses!

Yet it's hard to hate *The Mark of the Rani*. It's a whizzably entertaining read, and at least some of that is intentional. It's got more intellectual curiosity and a more Doctorish Doctor than most of Season 22. And at least the Doctor isn't perpetrating a lot of the violence... for a change. It's not great, it makes little sense, but all it wants to do is teach children a little bit about history, and make them look up words in a dictionary... I mean, you suspect another motive?

'Obdurate... Equivocating... Chivvied and beguiled... chuntering indignantly, the Doctor followed obediently.'

326

Two Trips with One Book

Doctor Who – The King's Demons
by Johnny Spandrell
Favourite *Doctor Who* book: *The Zarbi* by Bill Strutton

Late afternoon, getting dark. I'm on a train, and not a good one either. A red rattler. It's noisy, there's no heating and my seat's lumpy. It's going to be a long trip home from Sydney. Three hours.

It's the end of a day's shopping. My mum, y'see, likes to escape from the country and head for the big smoke. Dad can't abide cities. So I'm my mother's travelling companion. It's 1986 and I'm twelve. I'm happy to trail around behind her on these occasions, as long as I get to go to the Galaxy Bookshop, a specialist sci-fi bolt hole and a haven for nerds of all varieties. Like the TARDIS, it periodically shifts locations, but I'm always able to find it. I'm a Target-seeking missile, and it has more *Doctor Who* books per square metre than any other store.

Galaxy was always worth the trip because they flew books in from the UK ahead of the Australian release schedule, *Doctor Who* books you couldn't get anywhere else! Beyond exciting. On this particular day, I secured book 108, *The King's Demons*. Oh yes, I know the numbers.

I'm a fan of this story. Saw it on the telly. It stars my favourite Doctor. It's set on my birthday! It has a shapeshifting android! It's a long trip home, but for me it evaporates. I'm engrossed.

Late afternoon, getting dark. I'm on a plane, travelling for work. Aged 43, I'm re-reading *The King's Demons* and thinking about the story it emerged from.

The TV version, loved by young me, now feels inconsequential – a whimper that ended the celebratory season 20. Even its big move, the introduction of a new robot companion, is undermined when the shiny mannequin has to be shuffled quietly off stage because all it can do is lean precariously and say its lines at the wrong times. No wonder it's not allowed out unaccompanied on VHS and DVD: like Kamelion, it seems *The King's Demons* can't stand up on its own.

But the Target books are great equalisers. *The King's Demons* might be an underwhelming TV story but in book form, it commands the same shelf space as any other story – In fact, at 153 pages, it's luxurious by Target standards. Inside those pages, Terence Dudley elaborates and embellishes. For him, this is no small deal. He relishes historical detail and obscure vocabulary, and wraps it all in elegant, if occasionally pompous, prose. Freed from the limitations of TV production, Kamelion's a fully functioning technological wonder, the Master's disguise is foolproof and the Doctor sounds just like Jon Pertwee. On top of it all, it finds time to mention the Doctor's bum.

I smile at its sheer audacity. This mouse of a TV story that roars as a book, finally legitimised. My journey home evaporates. I'm engrossed again.

Slip Back in Time

Doctor Who - Slipback by Mike Morgan
Favourite *Doctor Who* book: *Remembrance of the Daleks*
by Ben Aaaronovitch

It's not easy trying to be Douglas Adams. It was hard enough for Douglas Adams and he had the genius to mostly get away with it.

I bought the Target novelisation of *Slipback* a few months after its release, in 1987. The Cold War was winding down. With Gorbachev's glasnost and perestroika policies, the spectre of Mutually Assured Destruction was receding. Reagan had just challenged Gorbachev to tear down the Wall, I had survived school long enough to reach the relatively violence-free Lower Sixth, and I was finally going to find out what had happened in the episodes of the Radio 4 play I'd managed to miss on their original broadcast. Life was looking up, all things considered.

Quite how I missed half of the six ten-minute episodes of *Slipback's* radio run during 1985, I'm not sure. The run had started the day before my fifteenth birthday, the best birthday present a boy fuming about *Doctor Who*'s hiatus could imagine. Then I forgot the start time, then I couldn't find the station on my small transistor radio. Like all fifteen-year-olds, I was a disaster zone masquerading as something partially functional. Unfortunately, so was *Slipback*.

The novelisation was a shining hope for something better, but its 'Captain Slarn as a Vogon' cover, a sly jest from artist Paul Mark Tams, tells you everything. Eric Saward takes his thin script, designed to cover short ten-minute bursts, and madly fleshes it out for print form. To give him some credit, he manages to write like Douglas Adams for nearly two whole chapters before gradually abandoning the effort. From then on, the book is full of throwaway ideas, most of which were subsequently thrown away. At least those first two chapters are an easy read, but they're a blatant reworking of ideas from *The Hitchhiker's Guide to the Galaxy*, as everyone who's ever read *Slipback* has observed. In the end, it's a story that tries to be funny but isn't, not really.

On the plus side, we still haven't all died in a thermonuclear war, so that's good.

Not Reading Stories

Doctor Who and the Savages by Tom Henry

Favourite *Doctor Who* book: *Running Through Corridors*
by Robert Shearman and Toby Hadoke

In 2012, *You and Who*, edited by J.R.Southall, was released. The Daddy of this series of *Doctor Who* books, it is a lovely book, containing all sorts of reminiscences by a variety of fans of the show. When I think back on reading it, the second most likely thing to pop in my head is a feeling of great warmth; that such a large number of people, throughout the generations, have been touched by this daft little science-fiction show. It's a patchwork of love stories; not only to the show, but to parents, partners, siblings and offspring. It's a great testimony to those that organised the work, and those that took part.

Second most likely.

The most likely thing to pop in my head are the words 'What? You did what?' as my brain squirms in impotent rage and jealousy. For example, let's take a quote from Al No's excellent piece on *Terror of the Zygons* in which he discusses Terrance Dicks' novelisation, *Doctor Who and the Loch Ness Monster*:

> 'It took me the whole weekend – with breaks to go and climb and fall off things – but I'd read the whole book by Sunday.'

You did what, Al? Read an entire storybook in 48 hours? Not just found the pages with the dodgy line drawings and, perhaps, if feeling particularly committed, read the line of relevant text copied below? Not just flicked to the back page, seen that the finish is 108 pages of child-friendly print away and thought 'That's gonna take me forever'?

The whole book is full of anecdotes of eager eight-year-olds discovering *Doctor Who and the Stones of Blood* on the Tuesday and having devoured every book with a diamond logo by Friday afternoon, camping out in their local library, surviving only on cheese puffs and parental love.

This was not my experience.

You see, my history with Target novelisations is my history of having a constant reminder that I don't read much: at least, not as much as I would like. I have definitely read fewer stories than I would like to be able to boast I have. I spent an awful lot of my formative years in libraries, not reading. I remember being seven years old in Beccles library, with their glorious collection of *Doctor Who* hardbacks, bright-coloured spines with big blocky writing. I would spend a perfectly contented forty minutes or so, taking ten books from

330

the shelf and looking at the covers – beautiful, evocative covers of space octopi and expanding robots – deciding on the four that I would take home. Once selected, and stared at on the car journey back, I would ignore these books and watch *The Five Doctors* on VHS on a loop.

Soon afterwards, my brother Dan read *Doctor Who – The Savages* to me and my sister on a long car and ferry journey from Birmingham to the south of Ireland. Quite what I was doing having stuff read to me at eight years old I don't know, but he enjoyed reading and I enjoyed *Doctor Who* that I didn't have to read. I'm pretty sure that this was the first *Doctor Who fiction* book that I completed. At some point on this holiday, I attempted to get Dan to read Jean-Marc Lofficier's *The Terrestrial Index*. For those of you unfamiliar with the works of Jean-Marc, he wrote programme guides that were essentially long, reasonably-accurate lists of *Doctor Who*-based facts. *The Terrestrial Index* was an attempt to document every *Doctor Who* story ever told – TV, comic, novel – often in table form. The first section was a table of every televised story with companions, monster, number of episodes and so on and so forth. Dan didn't think much of these tables. He humorously suggested that this was a waste of time after the third entry and stopped after the fourth. We soon went back to fiction for the communal book reading.

A year or so later, Jean-Marc published *The Universal Databank,* which was an encyclopaedia of *Doctor Who* television adventures. My main memory of it, perhaps distorted, was that every entry for a character consisted of the same four things: where they worked/lived, what their profession was, which Doctor and companion they met and, if killed, how they were killed. And I loved it. What a wonderfully economical way of experiencing stories. This wasn't reading one story, this was reading a hundred and sixty stories all at once, without wasting time on things like dialogue, description or the things characters did before they were killed.

From about the age of nine or ten, I used to get the bus into Birmingham City Centre to the various spots where *Doctor Who*-related items were sold. Nothing made me happier than being in Nostalgia & Comics, reading through old Doctor Who Magazines and DWBs before the fat grumpy bloke told me to move on, which I did to Readers' World a street or two away, where I would stare through the glass counter at their large Target book collection. I would read the plot summary and then make the decision to buy the book, take it home and not read it.

My great loves were finding out how *Doctor Who* stories were made and seeing how popular they were. I still adore reading reviews, whatever the quality. I love it when Doctor Who Magazine publishes its occasional list of *Doctor Who* stories ranked from top to bottom from its readership. I remember being thirteen years old, creating a spreadsheet that listed my favourite *Doctor Who* from top to bottom, and then, using the =RAND() function to create fictional lists of reader's favourites. I can still remember every production code. I think I largely got into sport because you can admit to doing this kind of nonsense and no-one bats an eyelid.

I did read some fiction. I must have read *The Savages* at some point by myself as I can see the tell-tale sign that I had read it (the book has lost its back cover). I can't remember anything about the experience. When I began buying the *Missing Adventures* they cost a fiver, so I knew that I had to read them to justify not spending the money on videos. The worst ones took me forever: something unreadable like *A Device of Death* took me about three months, a miserable, unrewarding experience and I would spend much time being distracted by slapping a tennis ball against a wall.

Even so, my dream at that age was to be a fiction writer. All those reviews, programme guides, the excellent Matrix Data Bank and Andrew Pixley's excellent Doctor Who Magazine Archives were all inspired by fiction. I think, even though I was never able to read stories, and struggle to write anything - I have played about thirty games of online eight ball pool trying to piece this together – I'm still attracted by the romantic image of the prose writer. I wanted to be one of those people of whom it was said, 'I took his book off the shelf and devoured it in a weekend.'

I was never a reader or writer of stories. I got a job in electoral services and fill up spreadsheets full of long lists of staff, premises, electors and postal voters. It's a good job, and one that I feel I have been building towards all my life. And I'm quietly confident that no one will look at what I do and go 'You did what?' in a fit of impotent rage and jealousy...

Just Pick Up a Quill and Write Something

Doctor Who – Fury from the Deep
by Thomas H Marwede
Favourite Doctor Who book: *The Programme Guide*
by Jean-Marc Lofficier

My passion for collecting *Doctor Who* books and memorabilia has waxed and waned over the last forty years.

In the beginning, there was a television program known as *Doctor Who* which was also known in my mind as *The Show*, and from the first time I watched it, it was everything to me: I was hooked, enthralled and devoted to it. Not to mention ostracised, made fun of and laughed at for it, as watching *The Show* was not the 'cool' thing to admit to (unlike in this day and age). Discussions of the previous night's episode were usually done in hushed whispers in the school library after giving the secret Masonic handshake in conjunction with the applicable signs and countersigns.

I digress. Anyway, I was a late starter to the collecting game and did not start buying the Target books until around 1978. Soon after that, I done found me fandom (hallelujah!) and this eye-widening discovery made all of that angst at school seem insignificant. I didn't care about them anymore; I had found a place where others were just like me, where I could discuss *The Show* to my heart's content, where every nuance could be dissected, discussed and reviewed, and collections could be compared, including all those wonderful Target books. For the first time in my life, I felt included and wanted. I was 'one of us' and I went into full-on fan mode. As soon as VCRs became available, I started videotaping every episode; I had my mum knit me a fourteen-foot scarf and collected everything I could find including Doctor Who Weeklies and Monthlies, magazine clippings, badges, fanzines, and, importantly, those Target novelisations. This was my life for ten years.

However, time moves on and things change. Towards the end of the eighties I, what, grew up? No, that's not it; the reality is I grew apart from *The Show*. It was in a death spiral and I was not overly interested in the current episodes and had become less interested in the history of *The Show* and even my collection. I had broadened my horizons and discovered other shows and interests; moreover, I was working and found out about that relationship thing that can exist (with a Not We). I was making plans for a future beyond the next Target release. Soon I would be getting married, building a house and starting a family, all of which required funds and, since I was getting little enjoyment from my collection, I went and sold or gave away everything. So bye-bye complete set of Doctor Who Weeklies and Monthlies...sayonara scarf...auf weidersehen badges...farewell videos, fanzines and clippings...hasta la vista to the complete set of Targets. Except one. *Fury from the Deep*. That one I kept.

I ask myself now, nearly thirty years later: 'Why did I keep *Fury from the Deep*?' Was it because it was a better-written novelisation than, say, *The Auton Invasion*, *The Crusaders*, *The Tenth Planet* or *The Cave Monsters*? No, and it isn't. Was it because it was the rarest Target book? Don't think so. Was it because it was the consummate Troughton and just a fantastic story? Maybe. Okay, for the sake of transparency I will admit that the TV version of *Fury from the Deep* is one of my all-time favourites and my number one choice in the hopeful return category. But I don't think I kept it for any of those reasons. I think it may have been nostalgia.

Now this was a period of self-discovery outside *Doctor Who*. I had stumbled across *Red Dwarf* and that instantly became the all new *The Show*, with all of the desire for collecting. I had also expanded my interests and read and collected other books. So during my own personal wilderness years, I had built up a nice little library of literary science fiction books and other TV Tie In books: *Blake's 7*, *Callan*, *Red Dwarf*, *The Avengers* and *The Prisoner* sitting on the shelves alongside Philip K. Dick, Harry Harrison, Douglas Adams, John Wyndham and some new bloke called Terry Pratchett. Amongst these sat my one and only *Doctor Who* book. Then I found out that John Peel had novelised the last two Troughtons under the Virgin imprint and decided to re-read *Fury from the Deep*. This made me realise how much I missed *Doctor Who* and so off I went and bought *The Power of the Daleks* and *The Evil of the Daleks*. Soon afterwards, the third edition of *The Programme Guide* appeared and I bought that too.

Now that *Doctor Who* collecting itch decided that it was time to stop sleeping and began playing a long game for ultimate control of my soul. Occasional purchases started to happen – the Handbooks and other reference books – but I still had it under control, honest. But the itch was back in force and it was game over man. I felt the need, the need to read. The passion had moved away from *Red Dwarf* and *Doctor Who* re-took the mantle of *The Show* in my head. I started to buy Target books again wherever I could find them, scouring the second-hand bookshops on a regular basis, and then, with a heralding of trumpets, came eBay. Oh my giddy aunt, what a find. We've all been there, surely: type in 'Doctor Who' Books' and browse hundreds of books, thousands of listings, good, fine, very fine conditions, bargain prices, right there, buy it and it'll be delivered to your door from anywhere in the world. It was paradise, and I was revelling in it.

Then the series starts to come out on DVD so you just have to buy all of them, don't you? Then what happens? A new series, that's what, and so you start collecting Doctor Who Magazine again, and find old issues, and then new toys (they're not toys, they're action figures!) were being released, what joy! And you just have to have them all. All of it thanks the novelisation of *Fury from the Deep*.

Eventually, it came to pass that I just had too much stuff. Too. Much. Stuff. Wow, that's difficult to say. The passion fled the collecting game again (see, it waned) and I came to the realisation that I did not need to have everything to continue appreciating the show. Over a hundred Target books sat on my shelves, competing for space with books from Adams to Wyndham, I had a filing cabinet full of magazines and more toys (stop calling them toys, they're action figures!) than could be displayed and appreciated (still in original packaging). It was time to be pragmatic and selective: what did I really want to keep this time? Decisions, decisions...was I ever going to go back and read Doctor Who Weekly issue 32 again? Or any other issue for that matter? The toys (sorry, action figures), keep some and get rid of the rest. And as for the books, most will go but I will also keep more than I did last time. That itch for collecting *Doctor Who* stuff is still there just under the skin and I still have too much stuff, as the Not We keeps telling me, but one thing you can be sure of though is that I still have my copy of *Fury from the Deep*.

Sullivan. Harry Sullivan

Harry Sullivan's War by Warren Frey
Favourite Doctor Who book: *A Celebration* by Peter Haining

As an actor, Ian Marter charmed us in his onscreen persona of Harry Sullivan. Who better to continue the adventures of his most notable role than the only man who knew him from the inside?

I originally read this novel at age twelve. I read each and every Target book I could get my hands on once I'd exhausted the paltry supply at the local library. One of my fondest childhood memories is my mother coming home from a visit to Powell's Books in Portland, Oregon with over 30 Target novels I had not yet read. I devoured them in a week.

It wasn't enough. I needed more.

Two separate Edmonton bookstores dreaded my regular visits, because the first question out of my prepubescent mouth would be, 'Are there any new *Doctor Who* books this week?' As time went on, the supply of the new books dwindled and the range caught up with most of the stories available. So when I discovered that a new book was coming out, written about a companion by the actor who played the character onscreen, and it was an all-new adventure...I was enthused, if somewhat baffled.

How could they (the overlords of Target Books, whoever 'they' were) put out a story that wasn't based on a televised adventure? It beggared belief! Even though my young mind had no idea of the concept of canon, or of the endless wars fought by fans in its name, I had to know more about this mysterious artefact. Something about the whole enterprise seemed...off.

I dived into the adventure of one Surgeon Commander Harry Sullivan expecting...what? Certainly not for the book to take place just as our hero was turning forty. That was more than enough cognitive dissonance for my young mind. As the novel progressed, I could see it took a more adult tone than other Target books, yet confusingly hewed to most of the familiar plotting and encounter-chase-escape of many other *Doctor Who* adventures.

My initial impression of *Harry Sullivan's War* was wonder at the sheer 'newness' of it. While *Doctor Who* had arguably tackled the spy genre before during the Pertwee era, there was always an overlay of science fiction. *Harry Sullivan's War* had none of that. Besides guest appearances from Sarah Jane Smith and the Brigadier, this novel was pure Sullivan from start to finish. The only thing I could draw upon that was remotely similar was reading Vonda McIntyre's novelisation of *Star Trek III: The Search for Spock*, where scenes were expanded upon and made up out of whole cloth to flesh out the various threads of the story to novel length. Up until that point, I wasn't aware you could do such a thing with an established universe, and Marter's novel took the concept to a new level for my still-developing mind to digest. But although he had prior experience writing Target Books, Ian Marter stumbled with an original story.

You would think that as a teen I would be excited to see the occasional 'goddamn' and watered-down sexual tension mixed in with Sullivan's derring-do, but I wasn't titillated or even offended. It simply felt incongruous in a story ostensibly set in the *Doctor Who* universe. I've learned to enjoy the double entendres and other naughty shenanigans found in the 21^s century version of the TV series, but it still feels weird to this day when the Doctor says 'hell' onscreen and he isn't talking about a fiery furnace for the eternally damned.

When I was young, the story seemed perfectly serviceable, if a bit ridiculous. After finishing *Harry Sullivan's War* for the second time, it still seems ridiculous. I'm not sure it's a great story. It might not even be a good one. *Harry Sullivan's War* is cheap and pulpy spy nonsense, but that's not where it goes wrong. Pulp has its place, especially within the genre trappings of *Doctor Who*. I was excited to relive the thrilling spy adventures of UNIT's medical specialist as he took on thugs and did his best impression of James Bond on a BBC budget. But this book comes off much of the time as a fever dream of what a spy novel is like seen through the lens of a clueless, upper crust British male of a certain time. I suppose that might be the point.

At the start of my re-reading, I was struck by Marter's florid prose. His writing is not the spare, clipped style of Terrance Dicks: it's descriptive, sometimes overly so. Through it all, Harry comes off as a bit of a bumbler, a pompous, upper class military man blundering his way to victory. When I was a kid, that just seemed true to the character. Reading it now, with years of experience and cynicism under my belt, I detect a note of subtle satire. Marter took the 'Harry Sullivan is an imbecile!' line and ran with it, all while keeping him a likeable protagonist. Harry somehow falls upwards through increasingly dangerous episodes before a climactic battle on the sides of the Eiffel Tower ends in the possible, but unlikely death of our hero. There's even a touch of bedroom farce as Sullivan pursues a mysterious, dangerous woman while his friend's buxom sister makes increasingly ludicrous passes at him.

Maybe Marter disliked playing the character, or became sick of being identified with a mere job he'd done nearly a decade ago; maybe he saw this book as a way to poke fun at the whole enterprise, but I don't get that sense. Marter seemed to enjoy writing the Target novelisations, even if he did court fan controversy with the occasional curse word. Though he puts Harry through all manner of scrapes, he does so with an air of affection. He likes this upper-class oaf, maybe even identifies with him.

One more thing about *Harry Sullivan's War*: because it was taking place entirely in my head, all the exteriors were on 16mm film and all the interiors were shot on studio cameras on obvious sets. It just seemed right.

The Imagination Cheats

Doctor Who - The Celestial Toymaker
by Mark Coxwell
Favourite Doctor Who book: *Timewyrm: Exodus*
by Terrance Dicks

I don't like *The Celestial Toymaker*.

You might think that an unusual statement to make at the start of an article all about *The Celestial Toymaker*. You might even be wondering what made me choose this story to write about if I dislike it so much. Well, the truth is that this wasn't always the case. Once this story ranked amongst my all-time favourites. What happened to change that?

I've been a lifelong fan of *Doctor Who* and I mean that literally. One of my earliest memories (possibly even my very first memory) is of watching the opening scenes of *Full Circle* in 1980. But I had missed out on so much of the TV series up to that point. That was okay though, because I always had the novelisations. I think I've been a lover of books and reading almost as long as I've been a *Doctor Who* fan. Every three or four weeks I would take my regular trip down to my local library looking for something to read. And, more often than not, I would come away with at least one *Doctor Who* book. Sometimes I might choose a novelisation of a more recent story that I only dimly remembered, like *Earthshock*. Other times I'd find myself attracted to book with a particularly striking cover or an evocative name. I remember *Carnival of Monsters* appearing particularly intriguing on both those counts.

However, it was the books from the earliest days of the series that fascinated me the most. To my seven or eight-year-old brain, the William Hartnell era was ancient history. My only exposure to the First Doctor was his appearance in *The Five Doctors* and a few grainy black and white photographs I'd seen in reference books. Beyond that, I knew nothing of the First Doctor's era and reading those novelisations opened up a whole new world to me.

One thing I discovered quite quickly on reading the books was that the First Doctor's era told stories that you just didn't see at any other point in *Doctor Who*'s long history. One such story was *The Celestial Toymaker*.

They say don't judge a book by its cover but that's exactly what I did when I first saw it on the shelves of WH Smiths. The cover looked amazing and indeed still does today. Beautifully painted and striking with the eponymous Toymaker surrounded by clowns and playing cards, staring ominously out at the reader. It was hard to resist and, much like the Doctor and his companions, I found myself being lured into the Toymaker's world.

The story itself didn't disappoint either. It was everything that I'd hoped a story involving a magical Toymaker would be. Toys coming to life! The Doctor and his friends playing potentially lethal games! What more could I want? Admittedly I was a little disappointed that the toys weren't a little more modern than ballerina dolls or schoolboys from the early 1900s, but other than that the story was faultless.

What fascinated me most was the character of the Toymaker himself. Much of my reading as a child was of the fantasy variety, from Enid Blyton's *Faraway Tree* stories to *The Chronicles of Narnia* with a bit of Tolkien thrown in. So, to me, the Toymaker was another evil wizard: a powerful, menacing figure who could appear or disappear at will, bring inanimate objects to life with a wave of his hand or attempt to take control of your mind using magic mirrors. Perhaps most unsettling of all, they Toymaker is able to render the Doctor helpless for much of the story. To my mind there had never been a more powerful villain in *Doctor Who*.

My imagination was fired up by both the book and the character of the Toymaker. I read the book several times, often wondering why such an interesting and powerful villain had never been bought back. After all, the Doctor had never totally defeated him. A few years later I read *The Nightmare Fair* – the novelisation of the unmade re-match between the Toymaker and the Doctor – and decided that maybe it was just as well they hadn't brought him back after all.

For a long time, *The Celestial Toymaker* was my favourite *Doctor Who* novelisation and one of my favourite stories. I collected and read a huge number of novelisations during the late 1980s and into the 1990s and, although there were books that were better written or had a more compelling story to tell, none seemed to quite capture my imagination in the same way. But then, in 1991, something happened to change all that. I bought a video tape called *The Hartnell Years*. For those who missed out at the time, this was a rare opportunity to see classic episodes of *Doctor Who* that had not been seen since their original broadcast on television. One of the episodes on that video was the final episode of *The Celestial Toymaker*, entitled *The Final Test*. You can imagine my excitement as the opening titles started.

If you've seen the episode, then you might also be able to imagine my disappointment twenty-five minutes later as the closing credits rolled. It wasn't the first time I'd been disappointed when the original televised episodes failed to match the images in my head, but this particular disappointment hurt more than most.

In my mind, the Doctor's companions were on platforms raised high above a floor that crackled with electricity. In reality, the platforms were barely off the ground and the whole thing looked like a cheap game show. The Toymaker's office in the book was a wood-panelled affair with a ceiling that stretched into infinity rather than the *Play School* set that we saw on screen. Most disappointingly, the Toymaker's on-screen depiction was far from the all-powerful wizard figure that I had pictured when I read the book. There was little menace in his on-screen portrayal and he comes across as being a bit of a gullible idiot.

John Nathan-Turner used to say 'the memory cheats' when fans during the 1980s used to complain that the television series wasn't as good as it once was. Well, when I first watched *The Final Test*, I found myself thinking that the imagination also cheats. Just as some fans' memories of the early stories tainted their perception of the later episodes, I felt that the book had fooled me into imagining this story to be better than it was. It quickly plummeted down my list of favourite serials and the book has remained unread on my shelf ever since that unfortunate viewing in 1991. In fact, thanks to the rise of the video, my entire collection of novelisations remained untouched for many years. Perhaps I felt that now I had the 'real thing' on VHS, I no longer needed the alternative interpretation offered by the books. Perhaps I was afraid of being disappointed again.

I recently looked over the book again for the first time in over two decades. I was a little nervous. Would my feelings about the TV episodes now taint my opinion of the book? Happily, it was not to be the case. The book is still every bit as good as it was when I first read it and, for a time, I was able to forget what I'd seen on TV. *The Celestial Toymaker* is still far from my favourite television story but the book remains one of the best novelisations I have read.

The Shame of the Doctor

Doctor Who and the Seeds of Death by Steven Alexander
Favourite Doctor Who book: *Cybermen* by David Banks

'So Steven, you say you've been reading a lot. What books have you been reading?'

First year at secondary school. English. Miss Noble was asking the question. As time went on we found her to be a great teacher but at first she came across as terrifying and authoritarian.

The school was a boys-only school and had a competitive atmosphere that was similar to a barrel full of rats. Our school was rife with academic snobbery and the kids at the top of the intellectual pile could be way more brutal than the ones at the bottom.

In my mind, there was always an underlying sense of terror. Although physical violence was rare, there are many other methods for abuse. Laughing at people. Excluding them. General humiliation. I'd seen that any flaw that someone displayed could mark them out as a candidate for teasing. Indeed in some ways, I couldn't say whether I was justified in being afraid or whether it was something I'd constructed in my own head. There were others who suffered far worse than I ever did, but the last thing I wanted to happen was to join their ranks. So back on that particular day, as everyone in the class went up to the English teacher one at a time to tell what books they'd been reading, I started to worry.

I'd become a fan of *Doctor Who* at the tail end of primary school and for a few years I'd ploughed through a vast number of Target Novels. I'd read other things too, but the simple fact is that the *Doctor Who* novels are wonderful. The joy of tearing through them is sublime and that especially goes for the ones that have been compacted down to the point of anaemia, or dashed off by an author on the way to collect their pay cheque. Even novelisations like *The Horns of Nimon* and *Timelash* are evocative in their way. At the very least they display a rude economy of storytelling. If you want to understand the essentials of adventure story telling, the real nuts and bolts, then it's all there for you in those 144-page educational pamphlets.

The very first one I bought was *The Seeds of Death*, which I picked out from the rack at WH Smiths in Watford. It had a fabulous cover and starred the second Doctor (the one I knew for a fact to be the tall one with silver hair). My memories of reading it have long since gone, but just seeing it for that first time has stayed with me.

From that first seed (of Death), a collection started to grow. Target books took me on many adventures over the last few years of the 1980s, not only through all of time and space, but to book shops and

342

car boot sales across England. There was The Who Shop in West Ham where you could buy collection of five or six Target novels in a boxed set, or spend your money on some of the many factual *Doctor Who* books, all of which had been compiled by the celebrated historian Peter Haining. There was also Forbidden Planet near Tottenham Court Road with its carpets woven from rat's fur and a smelly basement full of ultra-rare Target novels, where for some reason I never bought the Bumper Edition *Fury from the Deep*. Since Forbidden Planet moved, they've had shiny linoleum floors. I really miss those carpets.

Neither of these official outlets could compare with the cornucopia of Who fiction though – Robin Hood's Bay in North Yorkshire.

If you've never been, Robin Hood's Bay is one of the most picturesque little villages in Britain. There are hotels and restaurants at the top of a hill and a narrow, cobbled street winding down to the bay. This street is flanked on either side by shops selling nick-nacks, shells and jewellery, but most of all selling second-hand books. Target books. There were a dozen tenth planets, all-but-one of the Key to Time series and a whole Citadel of Peladons, both monstrous and cursed. There were rare editions with covers I'd never seen before, covers very different from the ones in our local library. Most magical of all were the legends written in pencil on the inside covers. These messages would say things like '50p' and '20p', which brought delight to both the heart and the pocket. They also meant that I could walk out with a stack of *Doctor Who* books.

Back to the English lesson. This was the start of the 1990s, when *Doctor Who* was exactly as popular as acne. Telling the class that I'd been reading *Doctor Who* books would be like rolling my socks right up, putting on a tooth brace and gelling my hair with lard, or responding in a posh English accent to the German Guard saying 'Good luck'. I was sure that I'd become a marked man.

There was someone else in the class who shared my enjoyment of *Doctor Who* though, and that was my cousin. I think he was more successful than me in mixing with the cool kids. We'd been best friends since before primary school and we'd shared many childhood interests, from *Transformers* to *Turtles* and from *Warhammer* to *Who*. My cousin is smart and he would always kick my backside at *Warhammer 40K*. I'd be too concerned with getting the ultra-cool Terminator and Tyranid figurines down on the game board, while he would cheat outrageously by using strategy and tactics. Totally unfair!

We shared our collected *Doctor Who* books and videos. This seemed a great idea at the time, but anyone who's ever collected anything can see the obvious flaw in the plan. It's all good for the first few years and then you suddenly find that you have a bookshelf that's missing *Galaxy Four* and *The Mysterious Planet*, books that are long since out

343

of print and incredibly hard to find.

We also had different policies on how pristine the books should be kept. With some of my earlier paperbacks, I would bend back the spine to give it a 'used' look. I thought this gave any paperback novel a distinguished quality. I got over this insanity eventually, but I did notice my cousin becoming reluctant to lend me anything. I've always loved Target novels that have yellowing pages and curled up corners, they have a unique smell of decay about them. If you want to read a Target novel in your school lunch break, on the way to work, or sitting on the beach, then it's inevitable that it'll get introduced to chocolate, mud or even the salty sea-water of the English Channel. In my opinion, no book has character quite like an ex-library copy of *The Wheel in Space* that's been left in the garden for a month or two.

That was a hypothetical example, so you can breathe a big sigh of relief, though I did genuinely use spare copies of *Doctor Who and the Giant Robot* and *Doctor Who and the Loch Ness Monster* to prop up a wonky snooker table in the garage, which eventually resulted in their utter destruction. And if you think that's a sin, I once borrowed several books off a friend of the family and never returned them. He had an amazing collection of Target novels and I tore a chunk out of it. Outrageous! After three or four years of them sitting in the spare room, I finally put them on the shelf with my other books. One day, the bell of shame will surely ring loudly for that misdemeanour.

In the end, I didn't tell my school teacher what I'd been reading. I clammed up. 'Uh, uh... Well I have been reading things but not...'

Eventually she let me off the hook and I went back to sit down.

Which is one of the little monstrosities that make up school life. The Target novels are wonderful things that should be celebrated, yet I had felt ashamed to be reading them. I spent my school years afraid of those who found pleasure in cruelty. Not that they were themselves cruel, necessarily. At different times over the years I formed good relationships with almost everyone. Some didn't last, some came and went, but I found kindness and friendship at the most unexpected times from the least likely people. In the end though, I think we were all scarred by the competition. The winners became monsters and the losers became sad.

I think that we should imagine something better for our lives. We mustn't accept that 'Real Life' needs to be brutal. We should look for heroes who are never cruel or cowardly, heroes who are not swift to pass judgment, heroes who don't rely on violence or aggression to solve their problems. Our portrayal of them needs to be strong and clear, something that a child can take to their heart and believe in. Because, before we can bring heroism like that into our world, we have to imagine it.

344

Waiting for *Black Orchid*

Doctor Who – Black Orchid
by Paul Scoones
Favourite Doctor Who book: *The Television Companion*
by David J Howe and Stephen James Walker

I novelised *Black Orchid*.

In 1983, Peter Davison's first season screened in New Zealand, a year behind the UK. A year later, I had a set of that season's novelisations lined up on my bookshelves. The black, blue and red spines were carefully arranged in broadcast order. All, that is, except one. *Black Orchid* was missing.

New Target books appeared on sale with dependable regularity, but for a long time there was no sign of *Black Orchid*. Why did this one fall through the cracks? Perhaps the length was the issue. At only two parts, perhaps the usually unembellished approach to retelling the story by Target's author of choice, Terrance Dicks, would have produced an exceptionally slight adaptation. Was the historical setting, with no science fiction elements (other than the Doctor, his companions and the TARDIS of course), regarded as off-putting to Target's readers? Whatever the reason, I decided that if Target wasn't going to fill the gap, I would do it myself.

As a young teenage devoted fan of the series, I wanted to be a *Doctor Who* novelist. I taught myself to type motivated by an ambition to write Target books, so in early 1984 I novelised *Black Orchid*. I had an off-air audiotape recording of the story, so used this to transcribe the dialogue. To fill in the details of the story's action, I worked from a memory of my one and only viewing. Part One in particular was problematic due to that long sequence during the cricket match. There are lots of thuds, knocks and cheering but very little is spoken.

Armed with pages of hastily-scribbled transcript, I set about creating the novelisation on my typewriter, using pages cut to the same proportions as a Target book. With only two episodes to cover and no attempt at expanding or embellishing the story, I completed the task in about 50 pages. I drew a cover and glued the pages in to create a slim book that could fit between *The Visitation* and *Earthshock*. I was delighted with my achievement. The book stayed on my bookshelf for a couple of years but as I got older and became more discerning about such things, it began to look increasingly amateurish. Eventually, embarrassed by my efforts, I threw the book away.

Doctor Who books were released three months after the UK in New Zealand. Following the release of the novelisation of *Timelash*, the distribution of Target books in New Zealand was suspended. I spent ages looking in bookshops for any new titles: it was hugely frustrating. Then one day, nearly a year later, I spotted a new Target on the shelves. Normal service had been resumed. *Black Orchid* – the real one this time – was one of the first three titles (the others were *The Seeds of Death* and *Slipback*) to be made available.

That interruption in supply happened as my life was changing. In 1986, when I bought *Timelash*, I was in my last year of high school, in a suburb out on the western fringe of the city. I'd duck out at lunchtimes to visit a bookshop in the nearby suburban shopping centre to look for *Doctor Who* books. In 1987, when I bought *Black Orchid*, I was in my first year at university, in the heart of downtown Auckland. There were several good bookshops within easy walking distance of the campus in which to go looking for *Doctor Who* books.

At this time, I was re-evaluating my attitude to the novelisations. Target books had for a long time been hugely important to me as one of a precious few sources of information I had about the series. At university, I met other like-minded fans for the first time and through them started to see many new and old episodes on videotape, and to read a wide variety of fanzines. With access to this sudden deluge of fresh *Doctor Who* material, my interest in the Target books waned. I had once re-read the books many times over in order to soak in every detail, but with so much else to occupy my attention, each new book now only received a single reading.

For this reason, I've only read *Black Orchid* once. I admired it as an exemplary retelling of the story in an expanded form but felt no compelling desire to revisit it. I gave the book a favourable review in the first issue of Time Space Visualiser, the *Doctor Who* fanzine I started in 1987 which ran for 76 issues over twenty years. In the review I mentioned my own attempt at novelising the story and happily conceded that my own efforts were hardly worthy of consideration alongside Dudley's immeasurably superior version.

With the book read and reviewed, all that remained for me to do was to slot it into place on my shelves between *The Visitation* and *Earthshock*, a gap once occupied by a slim, typewritten adaptation of the same story.

Gary Russell Made Me Moan with Pleasure

Doctor Who and the Ark by **Michael Seely**
Favourite *Doctor Who* book: *The Sontaran Experiment*
by Ian Marter

The problem was the wait. Nine months waiting for a kid to be born is one thing, but a Target book could take up to a year! *The Ark* came out in paperback a year after a brief mention by *Doctor Who Magazine*. This was where every new book was conceived for me, usually accompanied by a few whimpers of anticipation when the author's name was Ian Marter.

The announcement was in March 1986 and followed a mouth-watering review by Gary Russell of (six months away, just six, practice your breathing exercises) *Fury from the Deep*. If you had money you could buy the hardback. That would reduce the wait by four months. Except shops that sold them were few and far between. The closest one I knew of was in Lowestoft, and that was practically in a different time zone. I was skint. Stuff libraries, I wanted to keep the books, not foster them.

'On Target' was my favourite section in DWM, which was, like the programme itself, recovering from the Cancellation Crisis of 1985. Sometimes the section featured an author's interview and occasionally Russell's review was better than the book. Whether he praised or damned them, every book had to be bought. Even *Brain Teasers and Mind Benders*. His thumb was firmly up when the review of *The Ark* came out in September, just as *Doctor Who* limped back onto the telly. He described how Paul Erickson's book was going to expand far beyond his original storyline, which *DWM* once printed in 1982 as what it was pleased to call an Archive – shoot-outs at waterfalls, tennis matches with invisible opponents and even a bit of philosophy thrown in.

1987 was my golden age for Target books, my seventh year of collecting. Each book outdid what came before. The problem was money. I started a part-time job and discovered the joys of blowing your earnings in one morning that same month: *The Ark* was part of that discovery. But you do anything for your babies.

Changing Faces

Doctor Who and the Mind Robber
by Kirk Kirkland
Favourite Doctor Who book: *The Brain of Morbius*
by Terrance Dicks

'Unlike anything else,' was the very first review I heard, from great friend and my 'Who-Guru' Steve, in late 1992. I couldn't track down the VHS video in those pre-Amazon days, but a few months later, I stumbled on the Target novelisation in a bookstore in the Little-Five-Points Arts district of Atlanta, Georgia.

Full disclosure: I'm a lifelong Sci Fi head. My earliest memory is of *The Invaders'* opening credits' saucer landing, circa 1968, and from there *Star Trek, Outer Limits, Lost in Space*, up to and including *Doctor Who* with the PBS omnibus reruns in the mid-1970s. Those were mostly Tom Baker; not a problem per se, but the mysterious black and white era always beckoned, and my guru had given me a special bug for the second Doctor. The one with the largest number of missing stories. I scoured episode synopses and tracked down what Target books I could find, which was very few, until I found *The Mind Robber*.

I recall that I read it on vacation, appropriately in the UK, with my new English wife to meet her family. A quick read, but it left me with a lot to ponder in the quiet moments afterwards, when I could lose myself in another reality and enjoy the infinite possibilities of creation. Reading it again now, I'm struck by more than the differences between the book and the serial, which in broad strokes are fairly few. The opening on Vesuvius as it's erupting is of course the most dramatic change, cutting the tale completely off from the dreary *The Dominators*. More is made of the Doctor's link to the mysterious 'Mind Robber' himself and the whole plot is more or less streamlined. Indeed, being a story of imagination unleashed, story-wise it works best as prose, unblemished by the restrictions imposed by budget, time and in this special case, chicken pox.

The book came at an important time. I had a new job at CNN that challenged my views of media and the nature of what was real and what was perceived. CNN was then the only 24-hour news network on cable and still run by Ted Turner who insisted the stories be vetted to be as accurate as possible. Days long gone in the modern day scramble for ratings uber alles and truth be damned. But *The Mind Robber* novelisation synchronistically fit right into the conundrum I was pondering at the time, of our emerging relationship with new media, then cable and 24-hour news, and our regressing relationship with classical literature, which seemed to be fading fast.

Within a few years, films such as *Scream* and TV series like *Dawson's Creek* would elevate pop culture to the fore and classical references were abandoned in the writer's rooms. Realistically, in American education, fewer and fewer of the classics were taught, if even tolerated, and to the young TV writers coming up, they held no interest. Being from an earlier era, with British writers raised on the classics, *The Mind Robber* is full of time-honoured characters: Gulliver and gorgons, knights and fairy tales. Drawn with much more than a passing interest, these characters shout a full-throated defence of their right to exist. Much of 1960s TV in the US is like this, from *Star Trek*'s love of Shakespeare to Dr Smith quoting Kipling, but by the 1990s that was lost, because it was lost to the writers growing up in the 1970s.

Re-reading the novel today, the conundrum is magnified. Today, social media has changed more than the landscape of our imaginations, it is even changing the very nature of how we relate to information, be it literature or any other art form, and with this, how we relate to each other. We are in the middle (or even at the beginning!) of an information revolution, one that is fuelling a scientific explosion and boiling a cultural kettle of disparate, often violently opposing attitudes and ideologies. The overwhelming flood of information made available to us through our suddenly ubiquitous smart phones is creating a generation, indeed generations to come, of *skimmers*, not *absorbers* of information. Why learn the date of the signing of the Magna Carta when you can look it up in an instant? The retention and recognition of classic characters and plot lines, and in the case of Gulliver himself, even dialogue that was in communal memory in the era that produced *The Mind Robber* is quickly passing into history. There is communal information today, though now it's stored in the Cloud, not our own memories. Is this a loss of immeasurable value, a weakening of human thought ability? Perhaps, but as is so often the case, change leads to unforeseen consequences, often unexpected and rarely wholly good or bad. Perhaps the ability of the current and next generations to skim and sort the information they need, as opposed to being walking 'Spock-like' computers themselves, will lead to greater, not lesser mental abilities.

On the dark side of this conundrum, I am left with a very recent experiment on the effect of this communal information overload on the current generation of children. Some sixty children were asked to unplug for eight hours. Only three managed actually to make it to the end, with several stating depression and even suicidal thoughts forced them back online. The experiment revealed the very real possibility of information addiction. A cutting-edge version of FOMO, perhaps. But unlike the Fear of Missing Out in the past, like forgoing a party or passing on a concert, these children have access to an entire planet of things offered to them, created for them, that are virtual, unconnected physically to another human being. And if this is a drug, like for the unfortunate Writer in *The Mind Robber*, it may be a trap, sucking them ever deeper into a cauldron of ultimately pointless 'content.' They may be neither able nor interested in retaining the information on display, ultimately losing the context of anything, rendering all meaning destitute. A bleak thought, but perhaps not inevitable.

Change seems to be only thing in our universe that is inevitable. Jamie changed his face in *The Mind Robber* as a result of a production crisis when Frazer Hines got chicken pox and the creative team utilized a creative solution to temporarily replace him. Men and women thinking on their feet, able to transcend the limited information available to them and 'make do'. I wonder, as we move forward, will the individuals of our species lose this ability, becoming just more cogs in the machine, like in so many *Doctor Who* and other Sci Fi stories? Or will we transcend this period, find balance with the technology we've created and thrive?

As our perceptions of ourselves, our species, our planet and its place in the universe is explored through this explosion of information and technology, ultimately we may find that the faces changing, for better or worse, are our own.

Going Nuclear

Doctor Who and the Faceless Ones
by Jamie Austin
Favourite *Doctor Who* book: *Script Doctor*
by Andrew Cartmel

By the 1980s, the nuclear industry had an image problem and so we school children spent an inordinate amount of time visiting nuclear power stations. On the monotonous coach journey, I would dive into a book: on this occasion, *The Faceless Ones*.

I had no preconceptions. I'd seen photographs of Patrick Troughton crouching next to an aeroplane wheel but, for all I knew, he was checking the tyre pressure (*Doctor Who Discovers Maintenance!*) – but what a glorious tale! Indeed, so engrossed in the adventure was I that when the accident occurred, I was desperately unprepared...

The rapid deceleration should have been a warning but, by then, I was busy hurtling forward at high velocity. In the days before seatbelts, we were blessed with eye-level metal ashtrays on the seat before us, making excellent receptacles upon which to bash the face. In deference to this, many of us duly did so. Luckily, injuries were minor. Bizarrely, a tractor had chugged out of a field straight on to the carriageway in front of our coach.

For me, *The Faceless Ones* will be forever imbued with a darker perspective. Context is everything: on that day, at that time, disaster seemed to teeter on a knife edge, ready to be tipped by an errant tractor or a runaway reactor. The power station itself, by the way, was the most *Doctor Who* place that I had been to: vast space-age concrete structures, all rigid lines and gleaming glass, probably the cover for some terrible secret, just like Gatwick Airport. Therein is the strength of stories like *The Faceless Ones* – the subversion. Nothing is what it seems to be: police boxes, aeroplanes, people.

Is it really coincidence that David McAllister's cover effortlessly taps into this notion of catastrophic accidents? Surely it can't be just down to a lack of decent reference photographs, can it? (Well, yes.) Nevertheless, from this deficit comes the most disturbing Target cover ever, with the TARDIS depicted materialising in the path of a landing passenger jet. On television, the low-flying stock footage makes it clear that the Doctor's careless parking has only casually endangered lives – the cover is far more ominous. The angle of the jet as it attempts to avoid the police box screams imminent catastrophe, effortlessly tapping into the 1960/70s preoccupation with air disasters. It's a heart-stopping piece of work and alarmingly grim for *Doctor Who* since, in reality, the pilots would have little chance of executing such a manoeuvre successfully. It is a chilling depiction of impending tragedy. It's also rather brilliant.

Invariably dismissed as superficial with a rushed ending, *The Faceless Ones* is far, far more – as the Doctor demonstrates throughout, it benefits us all to look a little harder. Here was a book where the hero questioned the obvious, spying burnt fibres and unused foreign stamps: he sought his own truth and, as a teenager, it was an attitude that I could relate to.

Journeys My Mother Sent Me On

Doctor Who and the Space Museum by Jason Elford
Favourite *Doctor Who* book: *Blood Heat* by Jim Mortimore

Circumstances can dictate that some books become more than the sum of their parts. They come to mean more than the stories told within the confines of the printed page. Other, more personal stories build round them making them uniquely valuable. Just seeing a title, taking a book off the shelf, flicking through the pages or reading the inscriptions inside create a physical connection to the past. Memories of all kinds, whether happy, sad or funny can come flooding back. My Target *Doctor Who* book range evokes many such memories, and certain titles are far more evocative than others.

The journey to *The Space Museum* began in 1984. I was five years old and despite being told I was an avid viewer, have few memories of watching *Doctor Who* during its original UK Broadcast. One of the earliest and most vivid is of the Doctor 'dying' in *The Caves of Androzani*. I cried! I was confused and upset. I didn't understand regeneration: the Doctor, my Doctor, was gone. Mum was sat next to me, gave me a cuddle and reassured me. Time passed and my memories of *Doctor Who* were pushed to the back of my subconscious, overtaken by the likes of *Transformers* and *He-Man*. But that scene made an impression and I would remember it soon enough.

By the time I was seven, thanks to mum's encouragement, I had become an avid reader. She began taking me to the local library and it was there I first saw two of them sitting on a shelf, front covers on display. *Doctor Who* books! The individual titles meant nothing to me and I didn't recognise the artwork on the covers but I remembered the words *Doctor Who*. The titles were checked out and taken home and at half past seven I went to bed and began reading. At eight, Mum came up and switched off the light. Ten minutes later, (giving her time to go downstairs, make a cuppa for my dad and resettle in the living room), the light went back on and I carried on reading. Later that evening, my parents came upstairs to bed and I was caught still awake and still reading. Pleased by my enthusiasm, but perturbed by the fact I was bound to be a grumpy little so-and-so in the morning, the light went out with a firm warning. Another ten minutes later, the light came back on and I continued my first all-night reading session.

I begrudgingly returned the books to the library and (probably due to the fact they had to be prised from my hands) was taken to buy a *Doctor Who* book of my very own. A wonderful pattern developed: when I finished a book, Mum would sit with me and talk about the adventure I had been on. From fighting Daleks on Skaro to exploring the Cybermen's tomb, I would recount and relive the stories with her. We would then go into town together and I would choose another book. So it went on and my book collection began to grow, stored in the bottom of my wardrobe. (Sharing a room with my brother meant there was no space for a bookcase. He would have to go!)

Then came Christmas Day 1990, the day I made my journey to *The Space Museum*. My parents had worked out that if a *Doctor Who* book was in my Christmas stocking, they would get a lie-in, so from 1986 it became a tradition for me to find one wrapped up at the end of my bed. In 1990, I unwrapped *The Space Museum* by Glyn Jones, looked over every inch of the cover artwork and began to read. Landing on the planet Xeros, my imagination, unlimited by budget and set constraints, created a fantastical, huge and sprawling space museum filled with every conceivable ship. The Moroks were mean, the Xerons were brave and I enjoyed the epic adventure set out before me. But *much* more than that, crossing all of time and space to join these adventures meant my parents got to stay asleep till nearly 10am on December 25th five years in a row. A Christmas Day miracle for anyone with children, as I have now learned.

The reason this book and this moment stands out is because *The Space Museum* would be the last Target book my mum would ever give me. By the end of the following year, I had started going to town on my own and had almost completed my *Doctor Who* book collection. Only three remained: *The Rescue, The Wheel in Space* and *Harry Sullivan's War*. Over the next couple of years, only a few new novelisations were released, up to *The Paradise of Death* in early 1994, which I bought on the day of release. Even though I was fifteen by now, Mum still insisted on sitting down and chatting about the books I was reading, though the discussions were more critical in approach. My brother still insisted on not moving out so I still couldn't put up bookcases!

I found *The Rescue* at a convention, the only one I have ever attended, and a friend gave me both *Harry Sullivan's War* and *The Wheel in Space*. I put them in the box with all my other Target books which, by late 1995, I had packed away. My Target collection was finally complete, eleven years after the half-remembered clips of *The Caves of Androzani*, nine years after seeing my first *Doctor Who* books at the library. Almost a year after Mum died.

Two decades later, I have finally been able to turn the box room of my house into a permanent library. I finally have my bookcases and my Target collection, unpacked, takes pride of place. My own children are nearly old enough to read them – maybe one day, one of them will tell me all about their journey to *The Space Museum*.

More Than Lunch

Doctor Who and the Sensorites by Jason Wilson

Favourite *Doctor Who* book: *Blood Heat* by Jim Mortimore

Was it London or Barrow in Furness? It was London; an unremembered bookshop somewhere, where I bought my first Target novel, *Revenge of the Cybermen*, in about 1978/79. We were starting to settle after a slightly nomadic few years owing to parental army service, allowing me to actually catch *Doctor Who* regularly and begin my lifelong love affair with it after a few years of catching it on the hoof in different bits of England and Germany. Settling meant I could collect books. Enter Target.

Amidst a few maternal murmurs along the lines that watching it was one thing, reading it was another, I bought it. It was, to my seven-year-old brain, creepy and evocative with scary plague infections and chilling villains – everything, not for the last time, that the TV version wouldn't be. And so the collection began (with a brief distraction, thanks to the Barrow in Furness book corner, by *Flash Gordon* novels in which I fortunately quickly lost interest). As the series entered the 1980s, it was fun to balance the Davison era with the older stories then available.

But valuable as they were, as I hit my teenage years the old Dicks-type quickies were starting to feel a bit thin. I noticed this with Davison stories, as great tales such as *Kinda* and *Snakedance* became wafer-thin books, their ideas left unexplored in a way that David Whitaker, Steve Gallagher or Malcolm Hulke would not have done. (I didn't yet have the chance to compare 1970s stories with the TV versions.) I read widely, dipping into some classics along with Helen Cresswell, and Susan Cooper's *The Dark is Rising* sequence (just the best children's fantasy ever written, sorry *Harry Potter* fans). *Dune* was there too, along with *Watership Down*, John Wyndham, Narnia, Alan Garner, the perennial *The Silver Sword*, T H White etc. Bernard Ashley and Robert Leeson offered a fantasy break with thought-provoking real-world stories. Returning to a quickie monthly Target such as, say, *The Robots of Death*, was enjoyable as a break from these weightier books – *Doctor Who* was something to be read alongside these – but the Target novels still felt like they needed to up their game a bit in terms of depth.

Somehow, they did. They got better again. They grew up with me. Well, to an extent. And just as this happened, after a period of waning owing to difficulty in finding them, the discovery that Jarrolds of Norwich had a whole flipping wall of the things got me going again.

I suppose the renewed upsurge, after the early great days of

Whitaker and Hulke and some early Dicks, had begun with Ian Marter even if, like early *Torchwood*, his brand of toughness sometimes seemed more adolescent than adult. There was no denying, though, the increased atmosphere of his books. Though he wasn't quite as good with characters, he was the best since Hulke at the time. Then 1984 was a watershed year: a drive to publish more of the early stories meant some of the original writers were coming on board to do them, and a lot of them were very good indeed.

As we got to the middle of the decade and the series began to come to the end of its rope, terrific sixties novelisations reminded us how iconic it had all once been and one day would be again. Nigel Robinson was a major part of this. He would be another strong editor as well as contributing some mean novelisations himself. He'd go on, of course, to write for the *New Adventures* range and it was with a thrill of pleasure that in 2013 I realised that he was going to write for the *Destiny of the Doctors* 50th anniversary audio series. Don't vanish again, Nigel, stick around and write for Big Finish, or give us a Capaldi novel. His finest hour was *The Edge of Destruction*, but *The Sensorites* was a decent and admonishing voyage into their obscure story.

Books have stories to tell about the place and circumstances in which you get them. I was on a school history trip to somewhere… can't remember where. Hot day. Thirsty. Lunch money jangling in pocket. It could buy me a sarnie and a coke. Or a Target book. Yeah. Dropped off on Surrey Street, off to Jarrolds. What would it be this time? What had I recently read? *The Aztecs* and *The Highlanders* together, then *The Dalek Invasion of Earth* and *The Invasion*. *The Sensorites* it was to be. I vaguely remembered the Doctor Who weekly early archive, but otherwise didn't know much about this one. Take a punt. You like this era and you have a crush on Susan.

That first season of *Doctor Who* did things that weren't always common afterwards: *The Keys of Marinus* gave us a planet of different climates and cultures; *The Sensorites* gave us a race where some were nice and some weren't, and the nasties could just be motivated by fear rather than evil. We'd just been studying the American West in history, and seen other instances where the clash of one culture with another had been less than benign. Robinson's epilogue, with Barbara's worrying about the safety of the Sense-Sphere's mineral deposits chimed well. This would, in part, be another book that out did its TV counterpart which, while far from dull, never quite lives up to a stunningly creepy first episode.

The book builds its mystery well: the sleeping astronauts, their mentally damaged colleague, Susan's telepathy attacking the Sensorites. Robinson evokes facing one's fears: on page 43, for instance, he tells us that the most basic fear is the fear of the unknown and takes time to tell us how wandering the ship evoked childhood fears for Ian and Barbara. In the way some of these Hartnell books make their characters live, we are almost back to *The Doomsday Weapon*, with John Ashe contemplating the Gospels as a story of sacrifice before giving his own life, a human warmth contrasted with the description of Captain Dent's soulless marriage (a computer stapling records together) – the details that make people live off the page. In *The Aztecs* we get Autloc referencing Christianity with its story of a possible better faith than the one he is starting to lose, again defined by a God-man who sacrifices himself, ironically brought by his people's future oppressors. I say this not to promote religion but because these telling details, marked by our defining cultural memes, form characters' turning points. In *The Sensorites* we get trips through people's primal fears and evocative descriptions about facing them for humans and Sensorites alike. Whatever planet we come from, we are as glorious, noble, teachable, petty, tribal, scared and messed up as each other.

Worth more than a Tesco sandwich for sure. Worth having no lunch. Mum tutted, Dad understood. I've sometimes wished we got novelisations of the new series. I might not make time for them all, but there are instances where they would be great additions, enhancing great episodes and developing lesser ones. After a morning spent wrestling with Civil Service IT systems, I hope I would be willing to sacrifice lunch again.

A La Recherche Du TARDIS Perdu

Doctor Who and the Reign of Terror
by Graham Peters
Favourite *Doctor Who* book: *The Doctor Who Annual 1981*

I was born in 1976. I discovered *Doctor Who* books in 1982. Somewhere in between those dates I watched *Doctor Who* on a ridiculous device called a television. I recall Davros in cobwebs, K9 getting his noggin knocked off and Basil Brush, who I think was in *State of Decay* (it's funny how the memory cheats, isn't it?). However, the telly box had limitations, particularly when you lived with your gran as I did: despite it being a colour set, the picture was invariably grey, white and pale green in hue. In order to rectify the situation, she would thump its plastic, mahogany-effect casing with genuine vehemence but alas to no avail. I therefore gave up on television forever which is just as well because as we all know *Doctor Who* is a rubbish TV show and quite frankly it'll never last, but the books, oh the books, they were something else.

We, my schoolmates and I, were blessed. Our school had what Roger Hargreaves might have called an extraordinarily long path, which was narrow and ran for about four hundred metres. It was fenced on either side and bisected the school fields of our school and the immediately adjacent Catholic primary. I'm not going to join the faith schools debate but however strange the religious divide seemed to me, we were all blessed, regardless of which of the schools we were from because at the end of the path was what I considered to be a utopia. Turn left to reach the play park, which featured in that era an improbably high slide and concrete slabs underfoot (boring health and safety hadn't arrived yet). Alternatively a right turn brought you to the small, modest, bijou public library. A glorified Portakabin it may have been, but to me it was an Aladdin's cave of delights holding treasures like *Meg and Mog*, *Green Eggs and Ham* and *Tintin and the Prisoners of the Sun*.

Yet the finest jewel was a book on the tall revolving rack that was clearly meant for readers older than my tender six years. Its plastic jacket gleamed in the incredible afternoon sun, that kind of incredible sunlight that only exists in autobiographical stories of childhood and 1970s Children's Film Foundation features. There on the rack was *Doctor Who and the Planet of the Daleks*. I reached up tentatively to lift its paperback perfection down into my adoring arms... 'No!' hollered my mother. 'You're not able to read that yet!' She was right, but I felt no less thwarted and sunk sulkily towards the picture book crate and *The Giant Jam Sandwich*.

In the weeks to come on other impossibly sunny days, for that's all there seemed to be, I gradually wore mum's resistance down and borrowed *Image of the Fendahl* and *The Zarbi* for the sole purpose of staring at their garish covers and imagining what horrors went on inside. This was the beginning of my love affair with *Doctor Who* books. I wasn't reading them to recreate the experience of watching TV episodes as some folks did, I was imagining my versions of the adventures based on the covers and what I understood from the limited reading I was able to do: and it was so, so much better than the TV. The version of *Image of the Fendahl* I read and imagined as a child was the most horrific story ever told, to seven-year-old me *The Power of Kroll* was actually funny, the Star books double pack of *The Dominators* and *The Krotons* became in my mind one continuous thrilling adventure. I co-created those versions; nowadays I can't find them anywhere on the page or in my head. No matter how closely I comb through any of the books, I can't recreate those readings. The Target books I borrowed gave me the chance to experience an atmosphere, let my imagination loose and enjoy being a little bit scared. It's that frisson of fear that means I will forever cherish the hardback edition of *The Invisible Enemy* and thus I spent more than I should've getting a copy on eBay. I'll always associate it with the night I first borrowed it from the library and clutched it tightly all the way home in the dark and fog. The combination of a *Doctor Who* story with a little atmosphere and imagination was my private heaven and grown-up me is foolishly desperate to get that feeling back.

One of the best examples of a Target book giving me the chance to escape into an atmospheric, mildly adventurous daydream is from 1990. I was thirteen and my parents and I, now in a home of our own with a functioning, possibly even teletext TV, were settling down to watch the final episode of *Waterfront Beat*. I had by this time relaxed my attitude towards televisual entertainment and had found this police drama serial mildly diverting. This season finale was much anticipated by us as it promised to reveal the identity of the bin-bag murderer who, as far as I can recollect, was murdering bin bags and throwing them off the Runcorn-Widnes bridge, though as I've said already, memory cheats. Unfortunately, there was a power cut and we were plunged into darkness.

I would love to tell you that in the subsequent hours we bonded as a family and learned much about ourselves but alas all we discovered was that Great Aunt Millicent (who lived in Yorkshire) enjoyed the last episode of *Waterfront Beat* but was unable to really explain it to my dad over the phone and most devastatingly, in the event of a blackout mum got first dibs on my Walkman. Whilst my dad toyed with the idea of phoning a few more relatives he hadn't caught up with for a while and mum listened to Roxy Music, I slunk off upstairs clutching a single candle to light my way and reached for my newly bought copy of *The Reign of Terror*. It was the forty-eighth *Doctor Who* book I owned, it says so in pencil on the inside cover (come on, I'm not the only one to do it, am I?)

Reading it by candlelight, I responded to the novel in an instinctive way, in a shallow, uneducated, kid-on-a-council-estate kind of way. You see, I figured that's what people had in those days – candles - and thus felt a bit more in tune with the novel and the era it was set in. The dark corners of my room helped me imagine the dank rooms and crumbling walls from the Doctor's favourite time in Earth history and I created a mise-en-scene in my head that helped me imagine a vibe to cling on to: that's what I needed as a reader in those days.

I enjoy re-reading my Target books. I never tire of *The Auton Invasion* or *Day of the Daleks*, *Remembrance of the Daleks* still impresses me and I have inexplicable soft spots for *Meglos* and *Paradise Towers*. However, for years I avoided revisiting *The Reign of Terror*. I knew whatever the reading conditions, it wouldn't generate the same atmosphere or trigger my imagination in the same magical way; I couldn't face the disappointment of being unable to recreate that feeling. Eventually I relented and lifted it from the shelf in 2010 (I know because the book is beside me now and I've found a restaurant receipt in it that I must've been using as a book mark). I read some of it again last night. Now I enjoy the book in a different way: the author sketches the supporting cast deftly and creates a real sense of continual peril for a feisty, intelligent TARDIS crew of adventurers.

The books, oh the books, they were something else, and do you know what? They still are. However, I, regrettably, have changed and I can't create them as I used to.

Quo Vadis, TARDIS?

Doctor Who and the Romans
by Roderick Murray
Favourite *Doctor Who* book: The *About Time* books
by Lawrence Miles and Tat Wood

Having lost interest in *Doctor Who* during the Colin Baker years, I only came back into the fold in November 1993 with the repeat of *Planet of the Daleks* on BBC1. Rescuing my old Target novels from the loft, I leafed through the pages and gazed at covers that I hadn't seen in years and slowly began to realise that by now there was now virtually a complete set of Hartnell and Troughton books available. I could finally cast aside the often dubious synopses which I'd relied on in the early days and find out what all those stories were actually about for myself.

I quickly amassed a huge pile of the Targets which had been published over the past decade. Eagerly working my way through them at a rate of one per night, I was desperately trying to get through the novelisations and catch up with the then relatively recent Virgin range. *The Romans* was one of those which I left towards the end, mainly because I always thought the original TV episodes were a load of old tosh.

The Romans on TV still bores me. Despite the perceived wisdom of fandom in general, I was never convinced that it was written as a comedy at all. *The Romans* is a vicious and horrific script, harsh and brutal, made all the worse by the fact that the miseries inflicted on the characters are instigated not by alien monsters but by other human beings. There are comedic elements in episode three, I'll concede that, but every time I watch it I come away with the impression that the humour comes from the performers themselves, largely Nero, with the rest of the cast following suit. I could never quite see it working as a novelisation, so every time I picked it up, I'd glance at the uncharacteristically dull cover artwork by Tony Masero – with its generic Nero who looks nothing like Derek Francis, and the rather bland portrayal of Hartnell from the worst publicity photograph I've ever seen of him - and end up putting it back down again. I read Donald Cotton's adaptation of *The Myth Makers* and *The Gunfighters* and loved them, despite knowing that the latter was the worst story ever in the history of the show because that's what *Doctor Who Weekly* had been telling me since my schooldays.

How was Cotton ever going to make *The Romans* work on the printed page? I genuinely couldn't see any way that he could ever do a straightforward prose adaptation. Then, one day, I finally started to read it and discovered that he hadn't. I found one of the few Target books that vastly outshines its TV equivalent and in doing so finally came to grips with the book that became my favourite in the entire range.

I love the way that Cotton largely scraps most of Dennis Spooner's actual scripts and just keeps the basic storyline, constructing his narrative from a series of letters which are supposed to be written by various characters and in doing so constructs what I think is the funniest, most witty and humorous version of any *Doctor Who* story in any medium.

Every time I read this book, there are all sorts of things which endear it to me. I love the way that Cotton's novelisation sweeps away all those dull scenes of playful dialogue with the crew in the Roman villa in episode one: they were never going to make scintillating prose, so they are simply trimmed or dropped entirely. Despite the economy of his narrative technique, I'm struck by how quietly and unobtrusively Cotton adds a mass of details into the storyline that were never there in the original scripts: in a few deft words we find out just why the crew can't get back into the Ship and simply go, and why Ian and Barbara are left behind when the Doctor takes Vicki off to Rome.

My favourite part of the book is the prologue and epilogue, framing the documents in sections supposedly written by the Roman historian Tacitus. I don't think I even knew who Tacitus was when I first read the book, but Cotton's skill is such that even if you don't know who Tacitus and Seutonius were, you can still pick up on the gag. The idea that these two noble Roman historians could sit playing practical jokes on one another by cobbling together fake documents and trying to trick the other into incorporating them into each other's histories of the Roman Empire is one of the funniest conceits in the most wonderfully sublime book of the entire series.

So if you've only ever sat through those rather turgid four episodes on TV, try digging it out and giving it a go.

362

Escape to Danger

Doctor Who and the Ambassadors of Death
by Christopher Stone
Favourite *Doctor Who* book: *Fury from the Deep*
by Victor Pemberton

It was the best of times, it was the worst of times – it was late 1986. Twelve Target novels were being released every year, but material was quickly running out. The bods at WH Allen HQ knew that the range could not go on forever and whispers could be heard in the doorways.

'We may not have much more time,' said one.

'The Target Books have a limited lifespan,' said another.

'They'll never survive,' said a third.

At this point, the prospect of a full run of novelisations of every television story looked highly unlikely. There were less than twenty stories remaining to be adapted. The two remaining Tom Baker stories were written by Douglas Adams and were contractually out of bounds. Peter Davison was just missing his Eric Saward Dalek story and Colin Baker's run looked unlikely to be complete for a similar reason (*Vengeance on Varos*, which had been cleared, was exceptionally delayed). Pertwee was missing just the one book, but given that *The Time Monster*, the penultimate Pertwee novel, had been released almost two years previously, hopes seemed slim.

Things weren't all bad. The Managing Director was attempting a licensing deal with a well-known chocolate firm attempting to exploit the fact that there was a complete run through from *Inferno* to *The Ribos Operation*. There were flaws with this strategy. The narrative in the books was not consistent: Jo Grant seemed to join UNIT twice and *The Space War* didn't segue into *Planet of the Daleks*. In the end, nothing would take off from Mars (confectionery).

However, there were still seven William Hartnell stories to be adapted, while Patrick Troughton was missing five. As the Hartnell stories formed the majority of the absentees, it was decided that a letter should be written to the original writers to offer substantial payment for novelising their scripts. Jane Shaw was head of this project: 'We have the contact details of the original writers and we need to put some pressure on them to allow our wonderful Target novelisations to continue. Quite frankly, we've got to get that rocket up their arses and get them motivated.'

The letter project went reasonably well and here are the results of the seven letters:

One – possibly a novelisation as long as it is less than 120 pages and has big print.

Two – further discussions necessary.

Three to Five – only if a prominent radio DJ writes the novel.

Six – original script missing and no chance of recovery.

Seven – it's on its way back after proof reading.

This positive news extended the Target range for another couple of years and all at HQ were happy and content so Jane received an unexpected bonus: as a reward, a promotional deal was done. She was flown to NASA and allowed to experience a routine flight in a space capsule, which would be used to advertise the extended Target range of world-class sci-fi novels. To reduce costs, this trip was double booked to allow the famous Dr Ruth to promote her book launch. Unfortunately, there was a problem. Along with these replies came two disturbing notes in plain brown envelopes and scrawled handwriting.

> The capsule will be smashed to fragments
> Your Doctor friend is as dead as a doornail

There was only one conclusion to be drawn from this: someone was threatening to kill Miss Shaw. Whether it was some random nutter mounting an attack on the Space Centre or a coherent plan by extreme DWAS members, the Target people didn't know, but they decided to go ahead with the event anyhow. With take-off imminent, Shaw joined Doctor Ruth and the other experienced astronauts – Michaels, Van Leyden and Lefee – in the cabin.

'All these pleasure trips,' said Van Leyden, the senior astronaut. 'It feels like we're being invaded by amateurs.'

A laugh permeated around the cabin of the capsule, lightening the pressure that the five people were feeling. It broke the ice as the tension mounted before lift-off. As the laughter dispersed, the safety checks were undertaken and the countdown descended towards zero. Shaw braced herself as the engines fired into life and the rocket took off from the launch pad. The g-forces almost made her pass out, but she had read enough first drafts to be able to stay awake through anything. She peered out the small window to her left and could see the Earth disappearing behind her as she journeyed for the first time into space.

Suddenly, there was some loud beeping from one of the consoles and Lefee sprung into life. His face looked worried and concerned. 'Someone's trying to break into our systems.'

'What do you mean?' questioned Van Leyden.

'The security protocols. They've started to crack the code.'

Shaw squirmed nervously in her seat, remembering the threats she had received. 'What's happening?'

'Someone's trying to access our systems, but we seem to have stopped them – for now,' said a worried looking Michaels.

The three astronauts were busy scanning the instruments, Dr Ruth still hadn't recovered from the g-force on take-off and Shaw was busy trying to distract herself from the panic. She pulled out the third draft of *The Ambassadors of Death* and began to read to calm her nerves.

'Large unidentified object approaching on collision course!' said an alarmed Lefee.

'Taking avoiding action – retro thrusters.' He was calm under pressure and steered the craft with precision. The passengers were grateful for their seat belts which held them in firmly while evasive action was taken. 'It's gonna be close'

With a matter of metres to spare, the huge rocket with the word 'Moffout' written in green spray paint on the side narrowly missed the capsule. Shaw dipped her head in shame and Michaels noted her disappointment.

'You know something of this?'

Shaw reluctantly nodded her head. 'It's the obsessive Whonatics. Some of them are from another planet.'

'Do you really think they're not human?' asked Lefee with a smile on his lips. It was the kind of question needed to allow everyone to relax a little, but it was clear everyone knew that this mission would have to be abandoned.

The emergency re-entry was as routine as could be expected in this situation. The careful preparation, the usual radio blackout and splashdown – an impact which woke Dr Ruth from her unconsciousness.

'Where are we?' she said. 'Have we left yet?'

'I'm afraid you've missed everything, the capsule has landed,' replied Shaw as she settled down to read Chapter 7...

'You must feed them radiation – or they'll die'

I'm sure this story was written by Terrance Dicks. It may or may not have been true, but it completed my range of Third Doctor novels and it was my moral duty to tell it.

Twinkling Eyes

K-9 And Company by Andrew Hampel
Favourite *Doctor Who* book: *Who on Earth is Tom Baker?*
by Tom Baker

In 1987 I was thirteen years old, a teenager. The only time of your life where you genuinely know better than anyone else, your ideas will change the world, and no one older has ever experienced the things that you are experiencing. This is the age where you form your loves, your passions, your identity, your social group and how to manage your feelings.

Like many thirteen-year-olds, I was in the metropolis of a bustling comprehensive school with a throng of chemically imbalanced fellow humans all evolving into adulthood at varying rates of hairiness, height and hormones. When the school term started in September, I'd just returned from a family holiday in Cornwall. It was on this holiday that a friend who had been a friend for a long time suddenly stopped being a friend, a companion and a playmate, and became something more. I'm not sure what the emotion was that I felt for my friend, but it made me tingle and it made me excited. It happened on the night of Monday 7th September at 7.35. I spent twenty-five minutes alone in a hotel room with my friend and what had been an innocent and exciting few years of fun and adventure turned into an awakening of passion, discovery and a desire to know more.

This was the evening I watched episode one of *Time and the Rani*.

After years of enjoying *Doctor Who* as a simple TV show, this was the evening where it became an obsession for dates, production notes and facts! I bought the *Doctor Who* Autumn Special to read on the journey home and it was the beginning of a deep and knowledgeable relationship. I hadn't purchased *Doctor Who Weekly* (as it was back in the seventies) since.... well, since the seventies. I decided there and then that I would be taking monthly delivery of *Doctor Who Magazine* from then on in. I used to love sitting by the radiator in my bedroom reading the latest Target novelisations being reviewed in 'Off the Shelf'. I knew all this information and knowledge I was lapping up would be great to discuss and philosophise over with fellow *Doctor Who* fans. Perhaps I could even convert the tall lads who played football to *Doctor Who*, they needed to know there was more to life than kicking a bag of wind around.

The thirteen-year-old me was very suave, sophisticated and a raconteur who would command an audience; I dressed with style, and I looked cool and iconic - not in a handsome way, but like Gary Numan or David Bowie in an alien-among-us way. In my own head. In reality,

I was spotty, had greasy, spiky and solid hair (hair gel was very new and overused at this time), was weedy and gangly in structure, and wore a long grey cardigan with pens and pencils in the pocket, black drainpipe trousers and a pair of deck shoes, finished off with a pair of black plastic rimmed spectacles with pint-glass-bottom lenses. In hindsight, I'm fairly sure a young David Tennant may have seen me and based the look of the tenth Doctor on my own unique image. It was an image that would set women's hearts all of a flutter in 2006 but, at the time, I was a standard geek decades before the chic set in.

When I got my Doctor Who Magazine out at break time, or started talking about *Doctor Who* as serious science fiction, I was ignored. My magazine would be snatched off me by the tall football lads who would then kick it around. At least I had shown them there was more to dribble with than a bag of wind!

What I needed was a killer topic of conversation. It was fine talking about how many Doctors there had been, or what TARDIS stood for, but these were lesson one for a *Doctor Who* fanatic. I needed a research project or a specialist topic. Then one day, opportunity came knocking at my door. I was reading the magazine by the radiator and I saw a preview for a new Target novelisation! I'd only just started to buy the Target books seriously and had a few that I'd picked up at jumble sales or that had been given to me, but I never really got into the books in a huge way until I started buying the season 24 adaptations.

The preview was for the novelisation of *K-9 and Company* by Terence Dudley. I remembered enjoying this on TV but there was no VHS of it at the time and it hadn't been repeated since Christmas Eve 1982. This was my opportunity for a specialist *Doctor Who* seminar to converse about at the *Two Ronnies*-style cocktail party in my head. I went to WH Smith to purchase the book and put it in my school bag for Monday break.

Monday morning was always a bit tough. Let's face it, tall lads kicking my stuff about might be cloakroom larks to them, but it made me feel rubbish and a target. I was bullied, simple as that. Monday was the day I had to return to it after the bliss of a weekend of comics, drawing and *Doctor Who*. First lesson on a Monday was Geography. I sat at the front with my mate Rich. I'm still mates with Rich – in fact, I'm godfather to his sons. Our teacher, Mr Wood, was tall and had a moustache. He looked like Basil Fawlty and therefore his nickname was Basil. I also still know Basil as he's the father of my mate Gid, and he still looks like Basil Fawlty.

We were studying Japan, and Basil had taught this so many times he spoke to us like a seasoned actor with a well-rehearsed script. It was the combination of Basil's height and his confidence in his material that meant he was sometimes oblivious to the desk-height front row. Behind me sat one of the football boys. He would wait until I was least aware, grab the back of my chair and rock it vigorously while shouting, 'Ride 'em Cowboy!' in his best Old Man Bonanza voice. This would happen several times in the lesson and, as you might expect, drove me crazy. I remember on that particular Monday getting exceptionally frustrated as I was given my sixth consecutive ride, pencils flying out of my cardigan and glasses falling off my face. I was launched off the chair and landed in a pile at Basil's feet

The whole class laughed and Basil asked for quiet as he directed me back to my chair. I sat down as my class mates pointed and sniggered. I looked around at various people shaking heads at me, grinning and emitting wild feral noises, or making faces insinuating I was stupid. Then I looked to the desk at my left and saw a face I'd never noticed before. This face also had a huge grin on it, but it wasn't mocking me. It was a smile, and a pleasant one at that, above it two twinkling eyes like beautiful jewels. It was a girl, a girl smiling at me. Why had I never noticed her?

'Are you Andrew?' she said in a chirpy enthusiastic voice.

'Err... Yes!' I replied

'My Mum's just started working with your mum. I'm Melanie,' she said excitedly.

I was a bit taken aback. Had she not just witnessed the humiliating attack on me? Or was this part of a more devious and evil ploy? I looked away and down to the map of Japan in the text book. I felt my face getting hot as I was aware the girl, Melanie, was still looking at me. I thought I'd better say something.

'Oh, at the Doctor's?' I said rather awkwardly - given my Mum worked at the Doctor's surgery and Melanie's mum was working with my Mum, this was probably a stupid response.

'Yes, that's right,' she replied, still smiling at me, eyes still twinkling like magical stars.

Who knows where the conversation would have gone next? The bell signalling break time sounded and throngs of books being flung into a heap, scraping chair legs and loud chatter meant that the discussion with Melanie was at an end. I had to re-focus anyway: I was about to reach greater levels of conversation with my new secret weapon.

I sat in the cloak room in full view of the varying species of teenagers. I got my copy of *K-9 and Company* out of my bag and started to read it, waiting for the interested parties to gather around and ask about the literary interpretation of witchcraft, soil analysis and robot dogs on dry stone walls. I didn't have to wait long.

'Excuse me,' said an excited sing-song voice.

I raised my head from my book and intellectually pushed my spectacles up my nose. My mouth then opened and my faux-intellect melted as my expression turned to one of gormless bewilderment. The voice was Melanie's.

'H-hello...' I offered.

'I wondered. If perhaps you'd like to go out with me?'

The gormless bewilderment looked at the twinkling eyes and the smile. I put my book in my bag and stood up as though Melanie's eyes had some kind of magnetic control over mine. In a breath I discovered what the feelings and bubbling chemicals inside me had meant, and what break-times were really for, and it wasn't about being over-affectionate in a romantic way for a TV show. We held hands and walked down the corridor.

'Is that a yes then?' asked Melanie.

'Affirmative,' I replied.

We Don't Need No Education

Doctor Who and the Massacre by Michael Seely
Favourite *Doctor Who* book: *The Sontaran Experiment*
by Ian Marter

The Target books are the reason I don't trust teachers.

We're in the mid-1980s. Reading a new Target book at break time would invite the usual passing comment from a teacher along the lines of, 'Reading that rubbish, are you?' But wait – hang on – don't you want me to read books? You're always banging on about the superiority of the printed word over the TV. I'm not reading comics, so that's got to be good, eh?

Why teachers were so dismissive of the programme isn't too difficult to work out. Wrong generation. What was I supposed to read? Not really interested in the social problems of another century, or Georgian women desperate for a husband with a nice thigh. You can get enough of that on an average boring Sunday night's telly. They could seldom give me an answer, apart from not to answer back.

An aunt once shoved a copy of *Swallows and Amazon* upon me. This was one of those tedious Edwardian books where children wore shorts and cardigans and had half a gallon of grease smeared upon their short back and sides. They were practically adults in miniature. They ate sandwiches on boats, came from a high income background and, well, not much else really. This wasn't the sort of time travel I was interested in. Teachers approved but when they saw me picking it up, questioned the look on my face, the same one which would one day greet a used nappy. It was set on the Norfolk Broads, which were only a few miles away, nice to visit, and where I plotted to dump the bodies of my enemies.

They were all so bloody grown up and were always surprised we didn't behave the same as they did, only shorter and spottier. Some teachers dictated their lessons like a Logopolitan monk and we had to write it all down until inwardly we were screaming for release by the Bell of Doom. Authority figures in cardigans and ties. A few of our teachers were nuns, no longer the psychopaths they had been when that aunt I mentioned attended the same Catholic High School some fifty years earlier. There were few really fit birds, as we used to say in those days, in our sing song broken voices.

The only thing I liked about teachers was their propensity to go on strike every now and then. If you were unlucky, the strike meant a few hours in the library, surrounded by all those earnest books. There were no *Doctor Who* books in the school library. Didn't matter, had them all at home anyway. Had they been there, it would have been nice to browse. An unreality check from the tedium of classes. If you were lucky, school was shut down, which also happened on Baker Days (named not after Tom, but Kenneth, one of the more destructive education secretaries). More time at home to spend with my true teacher.

Doctor Who was my teacher, or rather I would have liked it to have been. Most days at school found me with a Target book tucked inside my blazer's inner pocket. I chose topics that got as close to *Doctor Who* as possible, sometimes without realising it. (True, it wasn't always reliable. You shouldn't treat flu cases in the manner the Doctor did in *The Ark*.) I tried to sneak a few pages of *The Savages* during a start of term school mass, which we all had to endure for our moral instruction, but I was sitting next to a teacher. Ah well, just stroke the cover. Maybe it will soak in through my fingers.

Doctor Who books gave you an inherited knowledge. Nothing terribly deep but enough to get you an extra mark or two. Mr History mentions the Huguenots. I pipe up about the St Bartholomew's Day massacre, thanks to John Lucarotti. Oh yes, I could make the connection, get a quizzical look from Teacher before a smirk as he guessed the source of my knowledge. One track mind, eh? Being Catholics, we didn't have to feel too ashamed by the murder of the Huguenots by Catholics in 1572. After all, they were only French. 'Write about what you know!' barks one teacher. You try to write an essay which either featured or mentioned *Doctor Who*. The teacher would groan and mark you down. Why can't he write about the political situation in El Salvador?

Of course I had other interests, I used to think, but only one passion. It wasn't as if I had question marks stitched into my shirt collars or preached the gospel of Malcolm Hulke on the stairwells in a Roy Skelton Dalek voice. I didn't wave Doctor Who Magazine around and shout production code numbers under the noses of startled eleven-year-olds.

As a teenager, you were supposed to have grown out of it. I was reliably informed by family and teachers alike that as I progressed through high school, I would perhaps feel increasingly ashamed of liking *Doctor Who*. Really. Oddly enough, I was seldom troubled by the kids who wouldn't touch *Doctor Who* with a remote control on the end of a barge pole. In fact, there were a number of people like me, and yet we didn't necessarily gravitate towards each other to coalesce into a Super Fan, stomping down the corridors, looking for *Star Trek* fans to bully. I was often asked to identify and explain specific *Doctor Who* memories. Even a teacher asked me once on a field trip. Some of my friends borrowed the books. One found *The Dinosaur Invasion* hilariously funny with the author's asides explaining what 'nark' and 'stool pigeon' meant. He was a refugee from what was once called Rhodesia and was Hard as Nails. Yet there he was, flicking through a *Doctor Who* book.

The exams came in 1987, during the months of *The Faceless Ones* and *The Space Museum*. (You call them May and June.) 1987 is still the most golden of years for Target books, with *The Massacre* at the peak. A brand-new re-imagining of a lost story, one you could only read a short synopsis for in an ancient DWM if you could find it in a second-hand comic book shop. 1987 was dripping with excellent books and I had been lucky enough to see some of the classic stories now being adapted, thanks to pirated videos at the local *Doctor Who* group. (I was never one to compare the book with the television stories. Pointless. Two different worlds. I loved them equally, or not, as the case may be. Two versions of *Slipback*? Cor yeah.)

I crawled out of school with some unremarkable exam results but wasn't terribly worried. They were to be the last of the ordinary levels before something else took their place. A Levels next. That would kill it, though, of course and by then Target books would probably become a thing of the past, and the series too. The books followed me around the world. I went to Taiwan for about six months after my A levels. I was amazed to find the Targets were on sale in various specialised book shops dotted through the capital. They were quite expensive purchases as they were imports. I was in Heaven.

What was I doing in Taiwan? I was teaching English as a second language in the evenings. Those poor kids never stopped learning. I wasn't qualified, couldn't speak Chinese, not even Hokkien (thanks *The Mind of Evil*). Had they known I was only eighteen, I would have been out on my ear! Yet, I enjoyed it, especially the *power*. They called me Sir and stood up when I entered a room. Sometimes I let them sit down. I couldn't teach them Target books, but we used Ladybird books and one had a picture of a Dalek in it, would you believe. The *Start with English* books (American English) had nothing. A for Apple, B for bear, apparently. Bloody kids. What was the point in teaching them? They'll only read rubbish.

The New Number Who

Doctor Who and the Macra Terror
by David M Barsky
Favourite *Doctor Who* book: *Day of the Daleks*
by Terrance Dicks

I am not the first – nor will I be the last – to notice that *The Macra Terror* resembles Patrick McGoohan's weird and wonderful ITV television series, *The Prisoner*. I have been a fan of *The Prisoner* since the mid-1980s and so, for this essay, I decided to watch the Loose Cannon reconstruction and read the novelisation (for the first time) on the fiftieth anniversary of the UK broadcast premiere of the first *Prisoner* episode, *Arrival*. And boy, I'm glad I did.

Written by Ian Stuart Black, the author of the teleplay, the novel itself is a disappointment, presenting little more beyond the dialogue heard on screen. Other writers of the era who also toiled behind the typewriter some twenty years later really went for broke with the opportunity to enhance the stories, but Black clearly had no aspirations to emulate Donald Cotton or John Lucarotti, despite having once achieved some degree of success as a novelist.

Why was I expecting more? Perhaps Black's key role in developing *Danger Man*, McGoohan's earlier hit television series, led me to believe I was in for an intriguing read. Although after a bit of research, I failed to find any concrete evidence proving the two men talked about any concepts tackled by both programmes, *The Macra Terror* aired a mere six months prior to *The Prisoner's* ITV debut. Surely there had to be some sort of collaboration during the coinciding periods of development? Yet, the deep political and social issues *The Macra Terror* hinted at would not be further extrapolated within the pages of Target's 123rd *Doctor Who* release.

Of course, I'm not-so-patiently awaiting the day that *The Macra Terror* is found in the basement of some rural Senegalese television station. But my first reading of the novelisation while concurrently re-watching McGoohan's seventeen-episode opus offered something the as-broadcast serial will never be able to present: colour. The vivid pageantry of *The Prisoner's* costumes and set pieces were rainbowing through my mind's eye with each and every page turn of Black's feebly illustrative prose.

Reading the novelisation after watching the McGoohan series had them bounding about in my mind with the agility of *The Prisoner's* village watchdog, Rover. I was happily seeing many things that just weren't initially portrayed on television if the serial's sparse surviving footage is any indication; the production team realised the massive, shuffling Macra less convincingly than any Corman-esque beastie. I also pictured a more physical Second Doctor, a surrogate Number 6, as he crept about, a man alone, on the outskirts of the colony in search of Medok, the only person who knew the truth about the Macra's power over the colonists.

For me, the telesnaps and fan-recorded soundtrack combined with Ian Stuart Black's lean prose version will forever be woven into *The Prisoner* as a sort of missing eighteenth episode. As for the original televised version of this *Doctor Who* story: I still hope to one day 'be seeing you.'

Chapter 4

An End and a Beginning

1988 – 1991

Nigel Robinson hands over to Jo Thurm, who is succeeded by Peter Darvill-Evans: he will be the range's last editor. With all but a few televised stories now novelised, the imprint comes to an end. WH Allen are now Virgin Publishing, who have some new ideas.

Also in these years

The Berlin wall comes down... Margaret Thatcher is replaced by John Major... George Bush (the first one) becomes US President... Freddie Mercury dies... Rihanna is born... Nirvana release *Nevermind*... The Teenage Mutant Ninja Turtles arrive in cinemas... Sylvester McCoy and Sophie Aldred walk off into the distance as *Doctor Who* disappears from TV screens...

An Unfinished Journey

Doctor Who and the Rescue
by Mark Trevor Owen
Favourite *Doctor Who* book: The *About Time* books
by Lawrence Miles and Tat Wood

After more than half a century of *Doctor Who*, we've inevitably lost a number of the major players from the programme's history. The death of writer and actor Ian Marter on his 42nd birthday always feels like one of the cruellest.

At the time of his death, he left the novelisation of *The Rescue* at the first draft stage. The redrafts and revisions normally undertaken by an author were finished by Target Books editor Nigel Robinson. It's to his credit that the published book never feels less than Marter-esque.

The book left incomplete by Marter begins with an incomplete TARDIS crew, as the Doctor's granddaughter Susan has just left (to money I could Cumarino according to Doctor Who and the Crusaders but that is very much another book.) It seems appropriate then that for me, *The Rescue* holds another 'incomplete' association. It's the only one of the Target novelisations that I don't own in paperback, although I do possess a copy, one of the comparatively small number of novelisations that I have as a WH Allen-published hardback.

My years of collecting the paperbacks began on holiday to the UK when I was ten. Some were purchased pristine, with that wonderful 'new book' scent. Others arrived via charity shops, or as hand-me-downs from older cousins. Some, rather depressingly, were library discards as the absence of *Doctor Who* from television reduced demand for the books. Several years after the range ceased publication, I got my last-but-one Target book (*The Wheel in Space* if I recall correctly) and for a while acquiring a copy of *The Rescue* was on my to-do list.

Since then, the internet has arrived, and everything's for sale. I've just checked eBay and I could buy a copy of *The Rescue* in paperback right now. It would be an expensive collectors' item, but I could fill that final gap in my collection.

But I don't want to. I find something quite comforting about the idea that the collecting of Target books is technically still a part of my life. While there's always one more left to find, the paperback adventures go on.

'Stop it, Gargoyle!'

Doctor Who and the Terror of the Vervoids
by Michael S Collins
Favourite *Doctor Who* book: *The Eight Doctors*
by Terrance Dicks

In retrospect, I picked the wrong year to turn four. It was 1990. Having taught myself to read and write at some point in the recent past, I had also, at some point, fallen interested in the TV show *Doctor Who*. Or maybe I had taken a toddler's liking for my great hero Jon Pertwee, and his most famous TV show followed. As all of this happened before school, the memories are practically prehistoric in terms of the autobiographical. However the bug hit, by 1990, I was writing stories involving me, a Stegosaurus, an Iguanodon, Jon Pertwee, Sooty and the *Why Don't You* gang taking on an evil witch.

There was no new *Doctor Who* on the TV in 1990. Nor in 1991. Ditto 1992. In 1993...actually, there was *Dimensions in Time*, the first actual episodes on TV in my fan life, meaning I can't help but unconditionally love it, despite its reputation. Beyond these occasional crumbs, there was only one way to get into the series, in the days before I'd even heard of UK Gold: the Target novelisations.

Luckily, the libraries were full of these, mostly from the second and fourth Doctors' eras. I devoured as many as possible. The Mitchell Library book sale was a great thing to look forward to each October, as they sold off older library books cheaply, with children's books as expensive as 50p a pop. There came a time, either 1992 or 1993, when the Mitchell sale (which I am delighted to hear they have just started up again after a long absence) had a lot of *Doctor Who* novels. The entire Pertwee run! I looked at my pocket money, sighed, and picked out the four which had the most interesting titles. My dad, who likes to claim he wasn't a fan of the show, despite often possessing mysteriously contemporary knowledge about it at times, was trying to act unsuspiciously. The big box of books under his arm suggested he was up to something.

The mystery of the box wasn't lifted until we had driven home. Mum and dad had looked into their limited budget and bought every single Target novel at the sale, even *Inferno*, of which the cover scared younger me so much I hid it behind the bookcase, and didn't read it until much later (at which point, it became a favourite).

One of the stories which stood out, though, was *Terror of the Vervoids*. How could it not? A spaceship screeching off into the distance, the giant looming figure of a hideous monster, and the words *The Trial of a Time Lord* all yelled from the front cover. The Doctor on

377

trial? 'Answering a distress call, the Doctor and Mel arrive on the liner just as a series of grisly murders begin.' Who the hell was Mel? Someone who appears in fewer Doctor Who episodes than Kevin Stoney, my adult self later found out. But the description of the tale was too enticing to miss out on, as was my uncle's description (for he had actually seen this story on the TV, which seemed incredible and ancient to my young mind) of 'Agatha Christie in space with monsters'. By 1994, I had already read *The ABC Murders* and *And Then There Were None* – my mum had failed utterly in trying to covert me to Star Trek, but had succeeded in getting me into Christie and John Wyndham.

I read the first line. 'At the apex of the cosmic evolutionary scale is the ultimate refinement of creation – a society comprised of Time Lords.' I didn't understand many of those words, so my brain translated it into 'Time Lords were superheroes'. By the end of Chapter One, my vocabulary had been introduced to words such as 'ebullience', 'recess', and many others. This didn't matter; it added colour and intrigue to what swiftly develops into quite a ripping yarn...with a higher body count than *Where Eagles Dare*, admittedly. One of the great things about reading the book was that it left the reveal of the traitor as suspenseful as the writers no doubt hoped on the screen, whereas, when I finally saw the TV version, the casting of Malcolm Tierney would have sort of given the game away. That's a bit like watching a new Christie adaptation with a cast of Peter Davison, Billie Piper and Ian Richardson. I wonder who could possibly have dunnit.

I enjoyed the novel, though. And it was clearly a sequel to some other *Doctor Who* story I hadn't read. 'On the previous occasion the Doctor's path crossed mine, I found myself involved in a web of mayhem and intrigue!' I spent hours poring over my Lofficier to find reference to which story the Commodore had previously appeared in. The line 'Whoever's been dumped in there has been pulverised into fragments and sent floating into space! In my book that's murder!' made me laugh even then. However, unlike other sections of fandom, I assumed at the time (and still do) that it, and many other Pip-and-Jane-isms are intended to be humorous. You can't write the 'Killer insects! Look out, they kill!' line without tongue firmly in cheek.

This novelisation had a profound effect on me. I instantly tried to rip it off. I was by this point writing stories loosely based on *Doctor Who* adventures: in one, I had accidentally had Davros and the Cybermen kill off the Doctor on Page 6, which required the Time Lords to send Jamie and the Second Doctor forward in time to save the day. That made sense in the context of an eight-year-old's mind, I'm sure. *Terror of the Vervoids* was to bring The Gargoyle into existence. The Gargoyle was a man who basically acted exactly like a Vervoid. He hid out at an airport which was full of people, and would sneak up on them

378

and kill them. (There are times when I am grateful I wasn't born a decade later – at school that year, I wrote a story in which the Yeti attacked and half of us died. It was praised for its creativity, whereas nowadays, it would no doubt have the anti-terror police detaining everyone!) I read the finished masterpiece to my family, which ended with a climactic scene in which The Gargoyle held everyone left alive hostage in a big room.

> *'Stop this, Gargoyle,' said the Commodore, but The Gargoyle shot him.*

It seemed an innocuous line. My aunt started laughing, however, and it was one of those laughs where the person is desperate not to laugh for fear of causing offence and that just makes the whole laughing urge worse so that their entire body starts shaking and they collapse in large hysterical guffaws. So I read the line again, three times. The reaction was the same each time.

I understand that *Terror of the Vervoids* isn't massively popular in fan circles, but it's also held a nostalgic glow for me. The book introduced me to the world of Pip and Jane Baker's ideas, and far from scaring off this child reader, their use of the full spectre of the vocabulary range piqued my curiosity. You might articulate, coherently and lucidly, that they certified and qualified me to proliferate and augment my sophisticated erudite meditation in ascertaining and attaching contemporaneous and salubrious words to my own prose. Or something like that.

Or in short, it was fun. I thought it was fun, and I still think it was fun.

Irregular Chanting

Doctor Who and the Time Meddler by Ian Millsted

Favourite *Doctor Who* book: *The Target Book*
by David J Howe

I came to the Target *Doctor Who* books late. I don't know why, really, as I was aware of their existence from early on. Perhaps it was to do with money. If I had pocket money to spend, I tended to prioritise buying comics and if my parents were buying books for me, they probably went for something more traditional.

I watched my first episode of Doctor Who in 1971: episode two of *The Dæmons*. I think my elder brother, and probably big sister as well, had been watching for a while and Mum had been using the window of opportunity while they were amused to let me have a bath (a logistical matter in a family of four children that I probably didn't fully appreciate at age four). In any case, once I'd watched one episode, I wasn't missing the next one. But, before I knew it, the programme finished for a summer break. When it came back, it was the talk of the playground. We played Daleks and Ogrons and Sea Devils.

Sometime around 1974, our class teacher (it may have been the improbably named Mrs Perfect) put a poster up showing covers of the Target *Doctor Who* novelisations published to that date. She never made reference to it; it just appeared. Possibly there was a damp mark that needed covering up in the demountable hut where we were based. There were actual *Doctor Who* books as well. Not all of them, but a few – hardbacks available to borrow for when we read for pleasure. I studied the poster extensively and discussed the stories with friends in the class. We pointed to the stories we remembered watching and wondered about the ones from the olden days. *Doctor Who and the Crusaders*! That sounded like a team up of two of my favourite TV series: *Doctor Who* and *Desert Crusader* (a mostly forgotten French series dubbed into English which I recall, possibly incorrectly, as having lots of swordfights and chaps chasing each other on horses). We noted that the Daleks had fought the Doctor in his earliest version, of whom we were now aware since watching *The Three Doctors*. But I don't remember actually reading any of the books. I was probably working my way through the *Doctor Dolittle* series at the time.

I watched the TV series avidly as Pertwee became Baker. I collected the Weetabix cards. I read the *Doctor Who Summer Special* that Mum bought for my brother and me until the cover fell off. The Target books, though, went unread.

I think it was The Five Faces of *Doctor Who* that changed things. I'd gone from watching every episode to just watching most of the time.

If I was out with friends then, too bad. We didn't have a video recorder. Somehow, though, sitting down to watch the first episode of *An Unearthly Child* on a dark Autumn evening sparked a whole new interest in this thing I'd been taking for granted. The eerie patterns onscreen and that music! The sense of history and of watching *Doctor Who* that was still *Doctor Who* but unlike anything I'd been watching drew me in. And, of course, that first ever episode is a real corker. I wanted to know more. I wanted to know everything.

There were ways I could explore that history. I read Doctor Who Monthly when I could get a copy. I bought that big book by Peter Haining. And then there were the Target books. Some I borrowed from the library and some were given to me. I even bought a couple in a bookshop in Sweden while on a family holiday.

The early- to mid-1980s was a good time to be collecting Target books. Most of the 1970s titles could be found in second hand shops and the publishers were doing a great job on maintaining a release schedule which mixed recent adventures with older stories. I was buying the releases new each month and, being particularly keen to read all the Hartnell/Troughton stories, I devoured *The Time Meddler* as soon as it came out.

The Time Meddler is a great story in both prose and screen format. Having come to it in book form first, I still found the TV serial a great watch when I caught the BBC2 screening a few years later. It is a story that couldn't be done now. We know too much and the Doctor knows too much. But we can still travel in time to when we knew nothing of Time Lords or Gallifrey or, even, regenerations. We can imagine what it must have been like to see a guest character who has a TARDIS; who must come from the same planet as the Doctor and Susan...wherever that might be.

Nigel Robinson's novelisation does a great job of teasing out the slow reveal of who and what The Monk is. He also makes good decisions about which parts of the screen dialogue he should use verbatim and which to incorporate more generally into the narrative. Robinson takes the opportunity to flesh out the backgrounds of some of the supporting characters, making their actions logical consequences of who they are. He clearly enjoys writing the Monk himself, using prose to substitute for Peter Butterworth's skilled performance, showing us a crafty, witty and, I just have to say it, meddling monk.

Before you get to any of that, you are treated to a two-page prologue which is really part of the TV serial *The Chase*. In this instance, we see the climax of that story from the point of view of an outsider and it works really well. This entrance of Steven into the TARDIS echoes that of Ian in David Whitaker's novelisation of *The Daleks* – I don't know if

Robinson intended it that way, but I hope so!

Another reason why I should have been paying more attention to the Target books is that they were all printed in Tiptree, Essex, just a few miles from where I lived. Tiptree is probably best known for jam: indeed, it was an exported jar of Tiptree jam that once got picked up by an American woman in a store just at the time she was casting around for a pseudonym for her science fiction stories, a chance that led Alice Sheldon to go by the name of James Tiptree Jr. But I digress. Tiptree should also be known as the location of the Anchor book printers. Just think about all those thousands of *Doctor Who* books being printed almost under my nose.

The cover of the Target edition is by Jeff Cummins, who does an admirable job. We are presented with a portrait of the Monk against an atmospheric backdrop. Cummins made no attempt to do a likeness of Peter Butterworth, for whatever reasons, but I think that adds to the book being an entity in its own right, which is as it should be. The lack of likeness also lets us ponder who else might have played the role if the Monk had returned in later decades. I'll leave that one with you.

As I cannot turn to Target books, or to an old *The Time Meddler*, I like to think that if this book had been out in 1974, my friends and I would have been playing games in the playground where the Monk teamed up with the Master. My round face might have put me in the frame to be the Monk, even though I usually tried to be the Brig. Mark Gatiss recently said in an interview that *Doctor Who* will still be watched in a hundred years. I think he is right but I hope that *Doctor Who* is also still being read in a hundred years. It is possible that in that future readers will once again come to *The Time Meddler* not knowing that there are other Time Lords and TARDISes and turn the pages to find out more.

Starting All Over Again

Doctor Who – The Mysterious Planet
by Simon Hart
Favourite *Doctor Who* book: *Cybermen* by David Banks

The Mysterious Planet was the book that completed my collection and where it should have all finished. Obviously, I kept up with the intermittent Target Books that came after the summer of 1990, but that was it. As I headed off to university in 1993, the books were carefully packed up and put away, not to reappear on my shelves for many years.

There's something about the Target Books and the special place that they have in the childhoods of us fans of a certain age that means they never really go away. The talking book versions have become new favourites for a long car journey, with their readers breathing new life into old prose. It's lovely to hear the books in this new medium. For me, it reawakens memories of sitting on the sofa curled up next to my Mum as she read them to me when I was small. I'm sure I'm not the only fan who joins in with the old familiar phrases as they're read out: 'The Police Box that wasn't a Police Box at all...many sided console...' and, of course, the all-time favourite 'with a wheezing groaning sound, the TARDIS faded away...'

Inspired by my friends Richard and Si, who've started collecting the books for the first or second time, I've started collecting them again too. I'm going for it this time round, collecting the different covers, the different logos and all the blue spine 1990s editions I missed the first time. Just to make it difficult for myself, I'm aiming to buy them all in shops again this time around too. I could jump on eBay and buy them all straight away, but where's the fun in that? This way I'm back to spotting a Target logo on a spine from a hundred paces, getting the old tingle of excitement as I find one I've not yet got.

I'm doing surprisingly well so far, but I'm far from having a truly complete set. So, have any of you got a spare copy of the 1990s reprint of *Carnival of Monsters* going spare?

383

The Visitor in the Night-Time

Doctor Who – Time and the Rani
by Brendan Jones

Favourite *Doctor Who* book: *Timeline* by Jon Preddle

The boy sat in the darkened domicile, the soft undulation of the bedspread twitching with the nervous motion of his legs. A white alarm clock squatted beside the bed, illuminating the darkness mildly with its green liquid crystal display. However, it was not the light from this, nor the streetlamp outside in the claustrophobic expanse of night that kept him awake.

It was what the light illuminated that was bothering him.

The boy, Brendan, pushed the covers to the foot of the bed, and traversed the room's uneven surface strewn with clothing, and toys which his mother had frustratedly christened a 'floordrobe.' Following the shaft of light from outside, Brendan peered at the small bookcase next to the door. His pelmet of brown hair was cropped short, and he had reached just shy of five foot tall in his young life. His eyes strained in the brackish light (he was, in an act of great rebellion, not wearing his glasses), and read the spines of the books there, and frowned.

Oh, this is hopeless!

Did *Warriors of the Deep* come before or after *The Awakening*?

It was easy all the way up to *Logopolis*, Brendan thought to himself. They were all in order in *The Doctor Who Programme Guide*. Even after that, everything up to *The Five Doctors* was in *Doctor Who: A Celebration*. But after *that* he had to go by memory, and the episodes his Dad recorded off the TV.

His Dad had not recorded *The Awakening*.

Brendan was pretty confident that all of his Colin Baker and Sylvester McCoy Target novelisations were in the right order, although he was missing some. As he read the spines, he frowned at one of them, a novel he had not read all of – just the first chapter, again and again. He started to pull at the book off the shelf, but a sudden soporific state swept over him, and the book sat, its spine half an inch out of line with his others.

He shrugged, carefully picked his way across the cornucopia of child's paraphernalia in the room, and tried to sleep. Just as he succeeded, he thought to himself how nice it would be if the Doctor would come and help him put *The Awakening* in its correct place on the shelf...

'Hello, Brendan,' said the man, quietly, but brightly. 'I understand you

384

need some help with your books.'

The noise must have woken Brendan – a strange echoing, scraping sound, mixed in with a sound like his cousin's asthma attacks. In the far corner of the room, between the window and his desk, sat a tall, blue box.

The man crossed to the bookcase and Brendan almost cried out, not in fear, but knowing how only he knew how to navigate the mess of the floor safely. The stranger, however, came to no harm: even when he slipped on a stuffed bear, his foot skewed out to one side and quickly fell back into step.

This, Brendan reasoned, was because the man was a dream. Simple really. Unless...

The man, in his neat suit, knitted jumper and pale hat, bent to inspect the titles.

'Are you...' Brendan whispered, '...the Doctor?'

The man continued to smile, and rubbed his chin. 'Well, I know all of my adventures, so reason dictates...'

'...that you are the Doctor!' Brendan interjected excitedly, then clapped a hand to his mouth. He listened closely, and was certain he hadn't woken his parents in the next room.

The man turned back to the bookcase and deftly moved a blue-spined book one position to the right.

'*The Awakening* happened here,' he explained, 'after that sad business with Icthar and Sauvix.'

The Doctor and Brendan then stared at each other, one unsure of what to say and one sure of what the other would say next. Brendan finally pointed to the box.

'Is that...'

The Doctor simply nodded. 'I might even let you have a look inside.' The boy's eyes lit up, but the Doctor grabbed at the book that was out of alignment on the bottom shelf.

'...but first, why does this one bother you?'

Brendan's jaw gaped, before he returned weakly, 'It doesn't bother me.'

The Doctor tutted, then read from the book. '*Time and the Rrrrrrrani*,' he said, rolling the R around his mouth like it was a tumbler in his circus act. This convinced Brendan more than ever that this was the Doctor.

'I like that one. On TV,' he explained.

'But not the book?' asked the Doctor.

'No.'

'Why not?'

'Because... because you die in it.'

The Doctor shrugged. 'I die in lots of books.' To prove his point, he deftly, without looking at the covers, pulled out the novelisations of *The Tenth Planet, The War Games, Planet of the Spiders, Logopolis* and *The Caves of Androzani*, and brandished them at the boy. 'So what's so bad about this one?'

'It's not...it's not the same as what's on TV!'

The Doctor sat on the edge of the bed, his nose in the opening pages of the book.

'You mean, the bit with Mel exercising? And the energy bolts? And the tumultuous buffeting?'

Brendan looked up in surprise.

'Is that how you pronounce it? Buffeting? Buffeting. There's a really nice buffet over in Leumeah,' he muttered, putting a hard T sound into the end of buffet.

'No, no,' the Doctor chuckled. 'A buffet is a place you get food. To be buffeted is to be knocked around, quite violently.'

'Oh.' The boy was glad to know this, but seemed quite crestfallen to have looked so stupid in front of the Doctor.

'So, when you thought it said tumultuous buffeting...' The Doctor trailed off, dropping the T in the last word.

'I thought you'd been eating in the console room and the food went everywhere.'

The two of them chuckled as loudly as they dared.

'I really liked the Sixth Doctor,' said Brendan.

'Well, he was rather enjoyable to be.'

'I liked his coat.'

The Doctor raised his eyes in mock dismay, and Brendan decided not to mention that he and his mother had made a replica of the coat for his coming birthday.

'It wasn't fair.'

'And that's why you don't like this book?' The Doctor waved the Tetrap-covered tome in Brendan's face.

'I like the first chapter. I read it again and again, but then I can't read on any more. The bit where he gets to go properly. Where...' Brendan, like most boys at the age of ten, didn't like crying. Especially not in front of the Doctor.

'Where you got to say goodbye.'

It was like the Doctor could read his mind, but of course the Doctor could read his mind. Brendan just nodded, and took the book from the Doctor.

'It was just so silly of you,' Brendan remonstrated, still staring at the book, 'forgetting to set the HADS.'

'I know! Boy, was my face red! Well, actually it was all swirly and blue, I seem to recall.'

The Doctor had been trying to make a joke. No joy. He tried another tack.

'But you can still watch the Sixth Doctor. And the Seventh, eh?' he added wryly.

'But I know there's no more new ones coming. They stopped making new *Doctor Who* four years ago.' He looked up from the book. 'I only found out this week.'

The Doctor smiled sadly, but then gestured at the bookcase.

'But you've got all these to read! And I know that you've not read very many of them at all. So, why so sad?'

Brendan hadn't really thought about this. He took some time as he looked around the messy room, then finally back to the Doctor. 'Because it's all over now. And I didn't know. I thought there was more coming.'

The Doctor nodded. 'You wanted to say goodbye.'

Silence fell between them. The Doctor scooped up the book.

'What did you like about this one? *Time and the Rani*, on the TV?'

'Um...' Brendan was less erudite now, thinking on his feet. 'I really like Mel. She's funny, and brave. The Tetraps were scary, and the Rani is much better than the Master.'

'Good! What else?' The Doctor's blue grey eyes seemed to glow beneath his hat, which Brendan would later know to be a trilby.

'Oh! The Lakertyans. I like to run like them in the playground at school. Nobody knows what I'm doing, but that's OK.'

'Good! Because, firstly, and I don't expect you to fully understand this, but nobody knows what they're doing either.'

The Doctor was right. Brendan didn't understand at all. But that wasn't the important bit!

'But, secondly, and this is the clever bit: the Tetraps, Mel, the Rani, Ikona, Faroon, Beyus – they're all in here.' The Doctor's voice lowered to a whisper as he tapped the cover of the book with a crooked finger. 'You may have to wait for some new stories, maybe for a long time, but you still have all the old ones that you love. And sometimes there are all the extra bits you didn't see on TV, right here!'

Brendan looked at the book, back to the Doctor, then over to the bookcase. Finally, he replied, 'But that's really sad!'

'Yes,' said the Doctor.

'But... it's really good too, because I can watch them again, or read them.'

'Yes,' repeated the Doctor.

'How can it be sad and good at the same time?' Brendan put his hands on his hips, a strange gesture, given he was sitting up in bed in his Mickey Mouse pyjamas, under *Star Wars* bed linen.

'Because,' the Doctor's face was half lit by the street light, and half in total shadow, 'most of the good things in the world are a little bit

387

sad as well.'

The boy's young mind struggled with this, until he thought he saw the point. 'Because, one day... maybe it will stop?'

The Doctor nodded. 'However, there is always time to rrrrrevisit the good bits.' Brendan loved that rolling sound, but hadn't learned how to do it himself yet.

The boy smiled, and he laid back down in bed. The Doctor raised his eyebrows in surprise.

'Not coming into the TARDIS?'

'I've got school tomorrow, Doctor. Try to come back on a Saturday.'

'School?' The Doctor was indignant. 'And supposing I can't get here on Saturday?'

Brendan hadn't thought of this. He ran over the Doctor's words again in his head, and made his decision.

'Well, if you can't get back here on Saturday, you might not get me back in time for school. My Mum and Dad would be really worried.'

Brendan was very tired now, very suddenly. His voice became broken and muffled.

'Thanks for rescuing me my books.'

The Doctor stood and pointed at the book.

'Do you mind if I borrow this?'

'Why?'

'Oh, I just need it for a...thing I'm doing.'

The Doctor stepped lightly back to the ship and looked back at the boy as he stirred once more.

'I'd like to...go in the TARDIS...one day.'

Then, he was asleep.

Inside the oscillating lights of the console room, the man engaged the blue stabilisers, switched on the HADS as the boy had recommended, and smiled at the image on the scanner.

'Don't worry, Brendan. We get here one day. But that's another story.'

Brendan activated the controls for a short hop to 2017, and the room shuddered with anticipation of the next adventure!

Even More Me

Doctor Who – Vengeance on Varos
by Stephen Webb
Favourite *Doctor Who* book: *Lungbarrow* by Marc Platt

Stating that Ol' Sixie is your favourite Doctor isn't exactly common in this fandom, but perhaps more telling is that it isn't exactly easy either. Let's face it, choking your companion in your first story followed by an eight-month hiatus allowing everyone to sit and stew on just how awful you (and your costume) are is a pretty deep hole for anyone to crawl out of.

In 2013, Peter Davison wrote and directed *The Five(ish) Doctors Reboot*. There is a scene where Colin Baker is trying to persuade his family to watch *Vengeance on Varos* with him because even though his DVD 'mysteriously went missing', he has a new copy – a special edition – that he proudly proclaims features 'even more me!' That scene is what initially sparked my interest in Colin Baker's Doctor so I ordered my own copy of *Vengeance on Varos* to experience it for myself. While watching I discovered a foundation that made his Doctor not only more interesting than I expected, but also relatable in a way that I wasn't anticipating. In an exchange between the Doctor and Peri in which he realises the TARDIS has lost power and that they are stuck inside a void, the Doctor sits down dejectedly with all the emo force of an angsty teen and says:

> 'It's all right for you Peri. You've only got one life, you'll age here in the TARDIS and then die. Me, I shall go on regenerating until my all my lives are spent.'

Despite all the bravado and arrogance established in his two previous stories suggesting that he doesn't care what anyone thinks of him, this exchange illustrated to me a sense of insecurity and vulnerability in the Doctor. Yes, it was still problematic the way he carelessly and unemotionally mused about Peri's death, but it showed layers and an honesty about his feelings regarding his own place and mortality that we hadn't yet seen before. The idea that this Doctor might be so afraid of being alone that he chooses to mask that insecurity with a cocksure attitude and garish clothing was extremely intriguing. He was using arrogance and his contrarian attitude as a shield from either feeling or allowing himself to care. The notion has been explored many time in the modern series: 'Is not having a companion so you don't experience the pressure of losing them and the pain when they are gone worth pushing them away and not knowing them from the start?'

The one issue I had with this scene was that I felt like they missed the mark with the 'womp womp' style musical cue at the end and wanted to explore whether Philip Martin had expanded on this line in the novelisation and played it more seriously. I was surprised to see that the Target novel didn't feature this exchange at all. I have always found this to be one of the most interesting and defining moments of the Sixth Doctor's character, especially outside of the Big Finish catalogue, and it was just missing. The novelisations usually do a fantastic job of keeping the TV storyline in place almost verbatim and expanding on the ideas and concepts within, but this time I was let down, not so much because it wasn't there, but because I didn't know why it wasn't.

I've wondered over the years if this played into the now famous conflicts between upper management at the BBC not caring for Colin Baker and the desire for cancellation of the show. Were they were doubling down on trying to make him unlikeable? Maybe it was it just as simple as Philip Martin deciding he didn't like that line? Whatever the reason, I started looking beyond the issues with story, design, and costume (though I still maintain that his coat is beautiful), and started to explore the idea that things aren't always what they seem with this incarnation of the Doctor. Sure, he is abrasive, offensive, and flawed, but perhaps he is imploring you to peel back to the next layer because there just might be 'even more me.'

Stop Singing *The Locomotion* Please, I'm trying to Read About Professor Zaroff's Motivation

Doctor Who and the Underwater Menace
by David McDonnell-Pascoe
Favourite *Doctor Who* book: *The Sixties*
by David J Howe, Mark Stammers and Stephen James Walker

When it comes to holidays, what are the most important things to take care of before you set off?

1.   Your route.
2.   Your means of getting there.
3.   Your accommodation.
4.   Your holiday reading.

In 1988, all I had to think about was the last item on that list and I didn't need to think twice about what I was taking.

My childhood was not filled with holidays abroad (cue violins). My parents both worked hard, and when they had down time, they preferred to spend it with friends or visiting relatives up country. As we lived in Falmouth, these trips to see my mother's family in Hertfordshire counted as family holidays. I got a fabulous fortnight with my god-parents in Lincoln when I was 11 which took in Alton Towers and a trip to Portman Road, Ipswich to see us play Aston Villa on the opening day of the 1987-88 season: a 1-1 draw as I'm sure you already know.

I didn't have any great pining to go abroad, remembering a 1984 holiday in which we travelled with another family in a Dormobile across France, part of Germany and down into Spain. It had been a good holiday: we stayed in a villa with a pool, the weather was good and we went on some nice outings, but even at eight years old, I was betraying signs of the Brit abroad. I didn't like the food; although I wasn't under any pressure to cope with the language, I didn't feel comfortable about not knowing what people were saying or what signs meant; and the oldest child in the other family annoyed the hell out of me by constantly playing *Now That's What I Call Music 4*, which featured *Against All Odds (Take A Look at Me Now)* by Phil Collins, which I found simultaneously irritating and upsetting. Yes, it was nice to say that I had been to Spain, but I was happy to be home.

Things changed when I went to secondary school in 1987. Among all of the new changes which this brings, one of the most enjoyable was doing some lessons which I never experienced in primary school.

This included languages and I particularly enjoyed French. At some point in early 1988, my parents reflected that it had been nearly four years since we had taken a holiday away from the UK and given that it was close (we could do the Plymouth-Roscoff ferry) and that my mum and I had both developed an understanding of the language (she was going to a night school course), then France would be the ideal place.

I was told that I could bring a friend if I wanted, so I asked my best mate at the time, Kevin, if he wanted to come and he said yes. However, our other friend Norman, with all the subtlety you'd expect of a twelve-year-old boy, let it be known that he would be happy to join us on holiday, if we could possibly manage it...I mean no problem if we couldn't...but still, if there was any way...

Needless to say, through gritted teeth, my parents, paid for five tickets for ten days at a Haven Holiday camp in Les Sables D'Olonne on the western coast of France.

When I think back to 1988, there were two constants in my life that year: one was Kevin and Norman, and the other was *Doctor Who* novelisations. From the I beginning that night dropping in 1987 when my dad bought me a copy of Ian Marter's novelisation of *The Reign of Terror* through to Ben Aaronovitch's peerless take on his own *Remembrance of the Daleks* and John Peel's adaptation of *The Chase,* I was buying, on average, two novelisations a month. Little did I know that I would eventually be writing a blog about the life and works of a different John Peel...

Between charity shops and WH Smith, I sought out as many books as was possible. This was especially important through early 1988 as we didn't get a video in our house until late September of that year. It felt like we were the last family in the world to have one, but I don't think Norman or Kevin did either until about a year or so later, when Norman blew his paper round money on a Betamax. They may have seen him coming. Eventually, BBC videos won out over Target books for me, but only when they started to appear with the same frequency that the books had done.

If you had asked me by the end of 1988 who my favourite author was I would have answered, without hesitation, that it was Nigel Robinson, former editor of the Target range and author of three cracking novelisations that I read and re-read (which I didn't often with any book). In *The Time Meddler,* with its wonderful evocation of 1066 Northumbria, Robinson had been so good at making the Meddling Monk appear genuinely frightening and evil that I was actually rather disappointed in Peter Butterworth's more mischievous original performance when I finally saw the story on BBC2 in that unexpected 1992 repeat run. The book was given to me as a twelfth birthday present in 1988 and I have wonderful memories of starting to read it after a Sunday birthday swim and lunch with Kev and Norman. One of those days that pops up in childhood where you wish you could bottle the day and live it whenever things get more stressful, which they inevitably would do.

The Edge of Destruction offered Robinson a chance to expand on the nearest thing to a stage play that *Doctor Who* offered – all of the action set in the TARDIS and plenty of internal monologues for the Doctor, Ian, Barbara and Susan as they responded in their different ways to the seemingly malignant forces that had invaded the impregnable Ship.

But the book which led to me rating Robinson so highly was *The Underwater Menace,* the much derided 1967 story involving Fish People, Atlantean Gods and mad scientists. I bought it together with *The Stones of Blood* and *The War Games* and it sticks in my mind for a couple of reasons:

1) There was a competition being run on the back inside cover to win a trip to the *Doctor Who* studios and meet Sylvester McCoy during the recording of Season 26 (somehow Target had got ahead of the curve there).

2) It may have been the last of the novelisations to offer the chance to get those posters they used to advertise in the back covers. You could have the cover to the *Death to the Daleks* novel or a photo of the Doctor and Linx fighting at the end of *The Time Warrior.*

3) Polly thinking they had landed in Cornwall at the start of the story which naturally struck a chord with me.

4) '*Nothing in the world can stop me now!*'

5) The fact that the end of the novel led to a story, *The Moonbase,* which had been novelised over a decade earlier.

Had I not been on a cross channel ferry for several hours, it may not have happened, but barring a few broken off moments to go roaming around the ferry with Kevin and Norman, I read the book pretty much straight through, which I never managed with any other *Doctor Who* novel, and I did so because it was, in my opinion, the best page-turner I ever read in the whole range. That's not to do down the two other books I took to Les Sables D'Olonne, but they both had to be taken at a more leisurely pace, between trips to the onsite pool, outings and trying to chat up the other girls staying at the camp (and annoying their fathers in the process). I got *The War Games* autographed by a blues guitarist who played at the campsite bar and read *The Stones of Blood* in long car trips when the three of us decided to stop driving my parents to distraction by taking it in turns to sing Kylie Minogue's cover of *The Locomotion*, one word at a time. No iPhones in those days you see, so you had to make your own entertainment.

I may have taken three books out with me, but I came back with another two when we chanced upon some French language books about *Docteur Who* and his adventures with the Daleks and in the Crusades. They were published by Garanciere Books and saw Hartnell sharing cover space with the disembodied heads of a pair of identical twins, who I think were editors of the range. I bought both books because my parents thought that it might continue to help my French at school. However, when I was asked in a French lesson later that year to write down my favourite book, I thought back to the summer and put down *The Underwater Menace* (I didn't have the skill to translate it as *La Menace Sous-Marine*).

The holiday was a bit of an end of an era. In the months that followed it, Kevin and I started to drift apart – there was no falling out or big row, we just started hanging out with different people. Norman still came round quite frequently, but it was a different vibe as our teens started to dawn on us. By the end of that year, my parents had clubbed together with a group of their friends to buy a holiday home in the Dordogne and a year after the Les Sables D'Olonne trip, I was on my way down there with my parents and had the back of the car to myself, reading *Attack of the Cybermen*. That was a great book, but worryingly it didn't feature a competition offering a chance to meet Sylvester McCoy during the making of Season 27...

Targeting the Space Wheel

Doctor Who and the Wheel in Space
by Alex Townsend
Favourite *Doctor Who* book: *Cybermen* by David Banks

It was 1988, I was eight years old, and I was in love with *Doctor Who*. The show formed part of my earliest memories, and as such was as much a part of my life as learning to tie my shoelaces, going to school and brushing my teeth. However, for something so firmly intertwined with my growing up, there seemed to be a distinct problem with *Doctor Who*, specifically that I could not access it whenever I wanted. In this way it proved similar to birthdays and Christmas: you knew it was coming at some point, but you had no choice but to wait. And even when you reached that glorious half hour when the show was on television, and you could soak up all that amazing, inventive imagery, it would always come to an end and leave you with nothing for a whole week, something I found wholly unacceptable.

In hindsight, it was a great pity I did not know more fans at this age, as it may have proven reassuring to know that I was not alone in this situation. In fact, some older fans would argue I was actually far better off than they had been, as I was getting into the show at the point where it *did* start to become available to buy on video, so what was I complaining about? Bear in mind though, that I was 8 years old, so a BBC video retailing at £10 may as well have cost £10 million as far as I was concerned.

However, those handful of early BBC videos proved awe-inspiring to me, their striking photo-montage covers being windows into the past of the show I was growing to love so much. The cover of *Spearhead from Space*, with its blank Auton faces and worried-looking Jon Pertwee, genuinely filled me with the kind of terror that furnishes you with a desire for more. I would regularly march into WHSmith and Woolworths and stare at the empty VHS boxes, drinking in the details of these other-worldly objects which had the potential to send me on the journey I so craved. My father, however, made it crystal clear that he would not be parting with the necessary money to acquire one. The disappointment of knowing this was short-lived, offset by my introduction to that most significant of all *Doctor Who* merchandise: the Target book.

A small independent bookseller in Hitchin, Hertfordshire called Burgess Books Ltd always carried a selection of Target titles past and present, and like the VHS-gazing visits to Smiths and Woolies, would become another regular stop in town, where I would sit cross-legged in front of the lowest shelf and flip through the *Doctor Who* books, desperate to spot a cover I had not seen before. The 1980s covers were just as striking to me as the video releases, possibly more so since some depicted the distant past of the show, combining enigmatic portraits of William Hartnell's Doctor with my beloved neon logo. Although I was delighted to receive *Terror of the Vervoids* and *Time and the Rani* for my eighth birthday, these were stories I already knew, and I was eager to explore past Doctors and their foes, some of which I may have glimpsed in a battered copy of *The Doctor Who Monster Book* donated by my sister's then-boyfriend. So when I acquired my third Target book, *The Wheel in Space*, my excitement was two-fold: not only did I have my first Cyberman book, but it also set a precedent that my father was clearly much happier to part with £1.99 than £9.99.

I was first drawn, perhaps wrongly, to the cover rather than the content. A Cyberman! But having only seen the silver giants in *The Five Doctors* and *Attack of the Cybermen*, this Cyberman was something new to me. Why does he only have three fingers? Why is he crying? And if those are tears, what is the one on his mouth meant to represent? All pertinent questions in the mind of a child, matched in importance only by the discovery that the Cybermen have guns in their chests! (Imagine the shock when I watched *Revenge of the Cybermen* a year later.) The blurb also proved enticing, including the mystery of what exactly a 'hostile Servo-Robot' could be, equalled only by the seemingly vital question, 'Who or what are the Cybermats?' At the time, this seemed like such a mystery, despite them being mentioned two sentences after the revelation that the Cybermen are the book's villains.

At the time of reading *The Wheel in Space*, I remember being thrilled about the idea of a small group of isolated humans being menaced by an invading force. The atmosphere of menace conjured up aboard the *Silver Carrier* and later on the Wheel itself is very well-realised, especially the idea that things driven by a malevolent alien intelligence are happening somewhere out of view. Terrance Dicks, by his own admission, doesn't like the Cybermen, and I remember being a little disappointed at how flat they seemed. They don't seem to say or do that much, and are repetitively described as giant silver forms with fiercely glowing chest units. Most importantly of course, this book was my introduction to the term 'wheezing, groaning sound'.

The Wheel in Space novelisation is a significant and very personal chapter in my life as a *Doctor Who* fan. It was my first foray into the show's past, my first experience of a story that was not something I had seen on television, my first glimpse of a monster realised very differently from what I had seen before, and my first inkling that there was a much larger and more varied universe to be explored than anything I had imagined. Over the years we have been lucky enough to have many lost First and Second Doctor stories returned to the BBC archives. Everyone has their particular hopes but the one I hold the most hope for is *The Wheel in Space*. Given that the two most recent discoveries hail from the same season as this story, I pray that one day soon, we will be able to venture out into the solar system, and finally relive those adventures with the Doctor, Jamie, Zoe and the Cybermen, aboard *The Wheel in Space*.

You're Not Signing on as a Martyr Yet

Doctor Who and the Ulimate Foe
by Andy Hicks
Favourite *Doctor Who* book: *Timewyrm: Revelation*
by Paul Cornell

In 1986, *Doctor Who*'s future was uncertain. What had seemed like a promising return-to-form had disintegrated into a convoluted season long story arc full of unsatisfying loose ends.

In 2008, I sold my collection of Doctor Who *novels to pay the rent. What had seemed like a promising career in rock-and-roll radio had disintegrated into a couple of weekend air-shifts and a series of unsatisfying temp jobs.*

Putting the Doctor on trial, while the show itself was also on trial, might conceivably have worked. Script editor Eric Saward had hired Robert Holmes, who he greatly respected, to set the stage for an epic fourteen-part story.

Two years previously, I had dropped all of my other part-time jobs to focus on radio, a plan that might conceivably have worked. The Program Director really liked me, and he was well-respected in the industry. The stage was set. Things were going to be epic.

Suddenly, Holmes died. Saward wanted to keep Holmes's original ending, with the Doctor and his alter-ego locked in eternal combat like Sherlock and Moriarty.

John Nathan-Turner insisted on a happy ending instead.

Saward quit.

Nathan-Turner hired Pip and Jane Baker to write a new ending from scratch. Fearing litigation, no-one told them of the original plans.

Suddenly, my old boss left, and the station died a little. The internet locked in eternal combat with the industry anyway, and the new folks in charge reacted by allowing for less on-air creativity, which made absolutely no sense. This also meant part-time DJs like me gradually got less work, which was, by that point, my only steady source of income.

The economy crashed.

Then the station went off the air.

So, in 2008, I sold my Doctor Who *books to pay rent. One of the books I kept was* The Ultimate Foe. *I wasn't sure why.*

It's 2017, and I think I know why.

People come and go. We all make mistakes. We all stand guilty of putting all our eggs into one basket. We are sentenced to a lifetime of turning lemons into lemonade.

And – honestly – bless those beleaguered Bakers. They had to pick up the pieces of a broken show and do the best they could. And then they had to write a Target novel, which – since this was a two-parter – needed a lot of padding. It can't have been much fun for them, though at least they got to fill it with lots of juicy, loquacious, purple prose.

So I kept *The Ultimate Foe*. I sold *The Crusaders* and *The Left-Handed Hummingbird* and *Lungbarrow*, but I kept this one. Why? To remind myself that, sometimes, through no fault of your own, you're caught between a turbine and a megabyte modem, and you just have to roll with it, man.

Or in other words: when life gives you carrots, make carrot juice. Pip and Jane would be proud.

Chapters in the Life of a Target Book Collector

The Edge of Destruction by Paul Driscoll
Favourite Doctor Who book: *Nightshade* by Mark Gatiss

AFTERSHOCK. 1974

I cover my ears and cower as the music of nightmares echoes throughout the auditorium. I keep forgetting I've had a birthday – I'm five and a big boy now. Too old to be frightened of the imaginary. But I don't like this, I don't like it one bit. Basil Brush was fun when I met him in that other theatre, but the Doctor, the Daleks and those horrid crab creatures?

Something was wrong from the start, and I don't just mean the alien invaders. What happened to the Doctor, that reassuring face who told me it would all be OK in the end? He faded away on a giant screen and another man in in his place.

'Don't worry son, you'll get used to it,' says Dad, and Mum just smiles. They both know more than they are letting on. They always do.

The next morning, my parents decide to take me to the local library. They point out to me a rack of *Doctor Who* books. Some have the unmistakable face of the real Doctor on the cover, but who are those imposters?

'Is that white haired man the one I saw in Wimbledon?'

'No, but he's the Doctor too. He's had different faces before you see. And he will again. On television next Saturday.'

They take me to the children's corner and ask me to pick a book, but I say that I don't want baby books anymore. I'm five now. I want to read about these other Doctors.

THE SEEDS OF SUSPICION. 1975

Lately, I've been staying up late, reading about the Doctor under the pillow, using a tiny red torch. I'm not allowed to stay up after lights out and I have to pretend to be asleep whenever my Mum pops her head through the door to check on me. The torch is hopeless, I keep having to take the cover off, refit the batteries and bang it a few times. I don't know all the big words, and I keep forgetting which page I'm on, but I'm starting to get into the stories.

The school are getting worried about me. I've been falling asleep in class and I'm not concentrating very well. But I can't help it, I simply cannot sleep without my fix of *Doctor Who* stories. School is boring anyway – Peter and Jane never do anything worth reading about.

I think I've been rumbled. The torch has disappeared. But as if that'll stop me. Wrapped in my blanket I sit by the window, popping my head behind the curtain. There's just enough light from the lamppost.

INSIDE THE MACHINE. 1977

I've been reading *Doctor Who* books for two years now and already I can get through a whole one in a week. The current Doctor is my favourite and the local library has some of his stories now too. I like the one with the giant robot the best.

The adventures are really coming to life and it's like I'm the other side of the sofa, in the heart of the action. When the Doctor is in his TARDIS, I'm inside the machine too. I swear I can hear it humming as I read. I can't believe I'm saying this, but I honestly think that this is better than watching it on the telly.

TRAPPED. 1983

Six years later and I'm still in the same three-bed terraced house in Croydon. I've just celebrated my fourteenth birthday. We're overcrowded now and I'm the oldest of six. The library isn't such fun anymore. They've stopped stocking new *Doctor Who* books and I go there to do my homework away from all the babies. When I'm not going to the library armed with schoolwork, I'm taking my little brothers and sisters to the play area outside. All the time I'm thinking, I could travel to bigger and better libraries and catch up on the other *Doctor Who* books. I could even start to save up my five pence a week pocket money to buy my own. It's such a wrench having to return them to the library. But my parents keep saying I'm not old enough to go to London on my own. What they really mean is that they need me to carry on babysitting.

LIKE A PERSON POSSESSED. 1984-1988

Freedom! In 1984 I made my first trip to London unaccompanied. I travelled on the number 12 armed with the Doctor Who Magazine Merchandise Special, my ticket to the comic mart in Westminster Central Hall. I loved that magazine even before I'd got John Nathan-Turner to sign it at the event. My favourite section has always been the article on the Target books. For the last four years I've been using it as a checklist. I've added to it each new publication, underlined the ones I bought and ticked those I read. I've even scored them with a complicated logarithm borrowed from primary school: asterisks. One star to five star and a specially drawn gold medal for the exceptionally good ones, like *The Auton Invasion* and *The Dæmons*.

I've left home to work as a volunteer in Central London with a missionary organisation. Full board and lodgings, free transport and a £6 per week allowance, used almost exclusively to buy *Doctor Who* books. I'm having issues with the more evangelical volunteers here, they seem to think that everyone we meet is Bible-bashing fodder. I'm experiencing a crisis of faith. I keep going AWOL, using my free tube pass to go hunting for more *Doctor Who* books.

One of the other volunteers genuinely thinks I'm the devil because I keep questioning my faith and read *Doctor Who* more than I do the bible. Most of my belongings stayed at my parents' house, but my Target collection simply had to come with me. Some of the covers seem to especially spook him out.

I *am* possessed though. Possessed or obsessed. I have to find them all and complete the collection. The hobby is taking up a lot of time, not just reading the books, but continuously rearranging them too. Sometimes I wants my own reading of random stories or I'll put them in broadcast, publication or alphabetical order. Mostly it's an excuse to see all the covers in their full glory. I can cover the whole floor of the prayer room if I lay them out side by side.

THE END OF TIME. 1991

Doctor Who is over. Well, on TV at least. I've started to collect the New Adventures now that the target range has come to an end. Oh and I've left the mission now. Was it a success, I hear you ask? The other volunteers rated their time according to how many people they'd 'saved' and so left disappointed (praise the Lord), but I judged it by how many *Doctor Who* books I'd ticked off the list. I left with only five gaps remaining (praise the Lord again).

My collection is almost complete now, thanks to Burton Books and their little ad in Doctor Who Magazine. But there is one elusive book, *The Edge of Destruction*. I've never seen it in the shops and it's not in stock anywhere. I've even tried Virgin Books directly.

You'd have thought that with just one left to collect, I'd pull out all the stops to find it, but in truth I'm beginning to resign myself to being the nearly man, the Jimmy White of Target book collectors.

THE HAUNTING. 1995

I keep dreaming of Target books. Broken memories of dusty second hand bookshops, the old library in Ashburton Park and London's

Forbidden Planet have converged to create a surreal bookshop with me as its only customer. It stands alone on a beach, bathed in the sunlight of a permanent summer. Bigger on the inside with long, winding corridors, the shop is staffed by hyperactive monkeys who climb spiralling ladders to reach the ever-moving, ever-growing top shelves.

Pristine copies of all the Target publications and hundreds more of previously untold *Doctor Who* stories are waiting for me, but the only book I want is, by all appearances, the least impressive of the lot – a battered, dog-eared copy of *The Edge of Destruction*. It's only priced at 15p, the same as the very first *Doctor Who* book I bought. But it's ever so slightly out of my reach. When the monkey climbs to fetch it for me, a game of cat and mouse ensues with the book moving around the shelves of its own volition. Finally, triumphantly he gets hold of it. He bows as he passes to me my object of desire. That's when this nightmare's punchline hits me, waking me up every time: for as soon as I touch it, the book slips through my fingers, turning into dust.

ACCUSATIONS. 1998

I'm living in Oxford, studying for a Masters. This place is second-hand bookshop heaven. I've been in the city for three years and picked up plenty of variant covers, but *The Edge of Destruction* has remained elusive. There is hope however – one option left to pursue. Apparently the Bodleian library has a copy of every single book published in the UK. The only snag is that you can't withdraw them. Now that my thesis is complete, I'm tempted to break the pledge I signed by smuggling out a copy of *The Edge of Destruction*.

Finding the book proves fruitless. The only *Edge of Destruction* here is a Hardy Boys spin off adventure. Search under *Doctor Who* and you will find thousands of entries - hell, they even have a copy of Nigel Robinson's crossword book in the vaults. But *The Edge of Destruction* is too rare or precious even for here, unless another fan has already swiped it.

THE BRINK OF DISASTER. 2005

The Doctor is back! On television at least. It's as if the show had been waiting for me to have children to enjoy it with, guilt-free. To gear them up for the new series, I'd planned to watch a DVD or two with them and then bring out the Target books, which after several house moves sit unloved in a box somewhere. But can I find them? I'm in a state of sheer panic, annoyed at myself for not having taken better care of them. I've had the whole house upside down and the books are

403

definitely not here. The only hope is a trip back to Croydon to see my parents as, between homes, I'd stored some belongings in their loft.

So I travelled back to the house and neighbourhood I grew up in. I'm happy to report that my Target books were indeed up in the loft. I've lost many material things over the years but none of them affected me as deeply as this. They are more than just books to me. Each one tells a story of how and where I acquired it, triggering associated memories of people and places that otherwise would have remained dormant.

A RACE AGAINST TIME. 2005

I think I must have inherited some kind of collectors' gene from my Mum, who is a Freddie Mercury fanatic. Her house is like a museum of Queen memorabilia. It turns out she is far more with the times than me: most of the items she's purchased are from eBay and tonight she's anxiously bidding on another rare collector's piece.

'You should use eBay for your *Doctor Who* collection,' she suggests.

'I don't trust online shopping, I'd rather trawl the charity shops and car boot sales. But then again there is one item I've been trying to get for years... I doubt it'll be there though.'

'You can find everything on eBay. What is it?'

To my astonishment, within twenty seconds, a near-mint copy of *The Edge of Destruction* fills the screen. The auction ends in half an hour and there are only two bidders so far. Mum enters the race for me.

'Twenty pounds? You'll need to put more on than that,' I say pessimistically.

'No. For now we wait,' she replies. 'We'll put a final bid on in the last ten seconds.'

EPILOGUE

Incredibly, we won. We won the book that finally, after all those years, completed my collection. All for a meagre £26.50. Three weeks later and *The Edge of Destruction* by Nigel Robinson was in my hands. The pearl of greatest worth. My personal holy grail. It seemed somehow fitting that my quest should have ended as it had begun: after all, my parents had introduced me to the Target range in the seventies and now forty years later I had my Mother to thank again.

Gingerly, I turned over the first couple of pages and following a tradition I'd kept since childhood, the first thing I did was read the chapter headings. Quite by coincidence, they told another story.

The Eleven-Year Itch

The Smugglers by J.R. Southall

Favourite Doctor Who book: *Doctor Who in an Exciting Adventure with the Daleks* by David Whitaker

It was, I suppose, the *Doctor Who* equivalent of the seven-year itch.

I'd discovered the Target books quite late, I think; I was eight years old when I walked into the Torquay branch of John Menzies one May morning in 1977 and discovered a whole shelf of them (in my memory it was a whole bookcase, but I realise this can't be true). My brain automatically went into a kind of spasm and once I was right again I knew I was leaving that shop with something from that shelf. The copy of *Doctor Who and the Planet of the Daleks* I took home with me that day cost 45p and probably left me with only 5p, but it was one of the best investments I ever made. It wasn't until later that week, when I'd read it from front cover to back, that I realised this story – the one I'd picked up because I wanted Daleks and an alien planet and a Doctor I could remember but who wasn't the over-familiar one currently on the telly – was the same story that also formed my earliest clear memory of the TV series. I was back in John Menzies the following Saturday, and every Saturday afterwards that I could persuade my parents we needed to go into town, and the collection grew, cementing my love for the television version and confirming my latent fanhood as something much more real.

By a curious coincidence, 1977 was also the year I began to realise that the TV series wasn't quite the perfect production I had thought. Prior to Graham Williams becoming producer (not that I knew any of this back then), I was too young to tell when a costume was just a costume, a set just a set or a performance merely learned lines and a bit of brio. Season Fifteen, on the other hand, wasn't quite up to the standard of what I'd been accustomed to – partly because of the change in producership and partly because I was growing older and recognising these things, of course – and I embarked upon a stage of fandom where I was subconsciously making comparisons between the cheaply-produced TV series I was watching and the budget-busting stories created in my imagination through reading the books. The TV series was bound to suffer, while the reputation of stories like *Genesis of the Daleks* and *Planet of the Spiders* only grew.

I made it through, though, and never stopped watching (not until 1986, at least). Season Eighteen was a gigantic wobble, as the sets became cheaper and cheaper and the acting more and more arch (in my estimation, given that I was getting older and more capable of spotting the joins with every new season that was broadcast) and now

405

even the funny bits had disappeared. By this point, sadly, the Target books were under-performing too. 1980 had seen a run of Dicks-by-numbers adaptations of recent TV stories which were to a twelve-year-old's imagination the equivalent of beans on white toast, minus the tomato sauce and the toasting process: barely digestible, in other words. I read each of these once and returned forthwith to the classic early releases, devouring *Death to the Daleks* and *The Auton Invasion* countless times as my patience with both the newer books and the TV programme that was spawning them grew thinner.

I wobbled as Peter Davison took over and John Lydecker penned a novelisation which failed to include useful chapter breaks; and when Colin Baker got his TARDIS keys after two years' worth of photographic covers on adaptations of recently-broadcast stories I hadn't liked in the first place, I was all but ready to give up. Even the recent fashion for going back and novelising the black and white stories barely interested me: unfamiliar Doctor and companion combinations, coupled with a dearth of familiar monsters and villains –and a heavy leaning towards historical tales, which featured no monsters at all – couldn't spark my dying interest.

When *The Trial of a Time Lord* turned up on TV, I stopped watching – after over a dozen years of never missing an episode (I even cried once, stuck in traffic on the way home from Exmouth, at the prospect of not making it home in time for the first few minutes of Tom Baker's final story; I might have hated Season Eighteen but I was still addicted to it). Simply didn't bother tuning in. This lasted only a few weeks, needless to say, and curiosity got the better of me to the extent that I didn't miss any more than maybe a third of Season 23, but still. I'd never deliberately not watched *Doctor Who* before.

By the autumn of 1988, the tables had turned a little. *Remembrance of the Daleks* had rekindled something of my excitement at the TV series, and the books, even the early ones, had lost their lustre. I was, by this point, struggling through A levels in subjects that provided about as much in the way of a fascination factor as cold tea and soft biscuits, and my Saturday morning lie-ins (being a teenager I was never one to get out of bed much before midday, even if I have contrarily never been much of a one for spending hours sleeping; my Saturday morning lie-ins then would usually be spent reading between the covers) had now left the Target novels behind for slightly more grown-up fare. I had, after eleven years, fallen out of love with the Target books.

That was when my revelation occurred.

There had been the occasional novel that had piqued my interest. Donald Cotton's books had felt silly and frivolous, but at least had provoked a little amusement in the reading, while Ian Marter's had generally proved a better read even if the stories themselves had left me rather cold: *The Invasion* is a fantastic serial, silly and serious in equal measure, but the book felt rather po-faced. *The Mind of Evil* and *The Time Monster* – stories from the age of *Doctor Who* that had previously given rise to adaptations that I'd read over and over and over again – had simply bored me. I was not, therefore, expecting anything very much from a Terrance Dicks novel from a period of the series that had never generated any enthusiasm on my part (even *The Tenth Planet* had left me bewilderingly bored, although *The Cybermen* had been one of my absolute favourites), featuring companions I'd never seen on the screen, a complete absence of monsters and a lack of any science fiction content whatsoever. So, with a heavy heart, I picked up *Doctor Who – The Smugglers* one November Saturday morning with the plan of forcing myself through it. No matter what else I might be reading at the time, I was still in the habit of buying the latest Target releases and struggling through them, given that by the age of nearly twenty they'd only cost me a couple of hours on a weekend once a month. We all know about the collector gene, after all.

The Smugglers came as a complete surprise. Expecting a similar reaction to the ones *The Underwater Menace* and *The Edge of Destruction* had given me – mild curiosity gradually drifting into complete disinterest, compounded by Terrance's current 'he said, she said' writing technique – I found myself experiencing the opposite response. Curiosity turned to absorption as I discovered I was turning the pages more and more furiously, fascinated to discover what would happen next and how the story would resolve itself. In Ben and Polly I found a pair of characters whose lives I cared about, whose well-being became paramount to the experience of reading the story; I realised I was following the trajectories of those two characters far more than I was the Doctor.

Looking back, I can see that the story isn't really all that; a recon has punctured any illusions on that score. The prose, similarly, is hardly less bland than in anything Terrance Dicks had written since around *The Robots of Death* in 1979, when the rot really set in – and in terms of the historical stories of the 1960s, I would eventually see that there was far more of interest in *The Reign of Terror* and *The Aztecs*, or the adaptations of *The Myth Makers* and *The Romans*.

In fact, I'd reacted to the novel of *The Smugglers* in the same way I might react to a matinee screening of *Moonfleet* or *Treasure Island*, as if it weren't a *Doctor Who* story at all, but simply a story in a genre I'd never much appreciated but that, for a couple of hours on a lazy Saturday, had grabbed my attention enough that I'd engaged with it completely.

It was a huge turning point, though, and 1989 would prove to be the year that both the novels and the TV series itself would fully hold my attention once again. For that, if for nothing else, *The Smugglers* will always be the story I'd most like to see returned to the BBC's archives, and the novelisation will always be the late-period Target book with the biggest, warmest, most assured place in my heart.

The Once and Future Kang

Paradise Towers by Jon Arnold

Favourite Doctor Who book: *The Scarlet Empress*
by Paul Magrs

The past and future of *Doctor Who* collided for me in my Christmas stocking in 1988. My stockings tended to be an eclectic mix of small gifts such as chocolates, paperbacks and whatever other bits and pieces could be fitted in to keep me from disturbing my parents until something close to a civilised hour. In adult life, I've come to appreciate their point of view that one of the finest Christmas gifts a parent can receive is at least half a night's sleep, but back then I was still eager to get on with tearing off the paper, particularly as the opening of presents involved each member of the family opening a present in their turn. Patience was a virtue yet to be learned.

That morning, just before dawn (actually around 3am, so that'll be dawn in Russia) I flicked on the lights and grabbed the stocking, which contained such magical treats as a digital alarm cube (with a natty rotating dial on top to tell you the time in various significant locations around the world), a chocolate orange and, most importantly, a VHS cassette and a paperback book: *The Seeds of Death* and *Paradise Towers*.

Unlikely as it seems, the item that pointed the way to the future was the monochrome VHS compilation, a hacked-together continuous edit of Troughton seeing off the Ice Warriors by setting the controls for the heart of the sun. My parents tended to be late technological adapters so 1988 was the year we finally bought a video recorder after years of my incessant nagging. *The Seeds of Death* was the first official *Doctor Who* release I owned and for all that it had two slapped-together publicity photos on the cover and six episodes crunched into one long story, I adored it. I'd been waiting to see more Troughton stories since *The Krotons* repeat in 1981 convinced me that he was clearly the best Doctor. I could actually finally see all the fabulous stories that until then I'd only known via the works of Richard Marson, Jean-Marc Lofficier and the Target authors. I spent as much as possible of Christmas Day hogging the TV, spending two hours spellbound at Troughton's antics (he's a genius you know, he told us so in the story). The fanboy's dream future was opening up: you could keep your jetpacks and hovercars, there were old *Doctor Who* stories available to watch just for me (until our recorder got temperamental and had one of its occasional tape-chewing fits). There hasn't been a birthday or Christmas since that I haven't had a *Doctor Who* story given to me.

The ghost of Christmases past was represented by Stephen Wyatt's

409

novelisation of his own story. *Paradise Towers* and I had gotten off on the wrong foot to begin with. It was part of Season 24, a season which nearly killed off my love of *Doctor Who*. It actually managed to enforce a trial separation period for me and my lifelong TV love. I was thirteen when it had been broadcast, a dangerous age when the world's adult distractions begin to creep in. Sex and drugs and rock and roll (or as close as could be found in the provinces - the front cover of a Madonna album, a cup of tea and the realisation that Radio 1 didn't stop broadcasting at teatime). An age where you're trying to define your personality, desperately trying to get people to take you seriously, particularly if you are one of the class spods peering at the world from behind a pair of thick lenses. What you don't need at that point is a series rediscovering a lightness of touch, not taking itself so seriously. Sinfully, I drifted away from the show, stopped buying Doctor Who Magazine (it took me years to find out what finally happened to Frobisher), stopped looking in the newspapers for the vanishingly few mentions of the series and, worst of all, stopped buying the Targets.

I wouldn't say I had been obsessed with the Target books if only because obsession was far too small a word to describe my childhood fascination with them. It began with the Five Faces of Doctor Who repeat season as after the showing of *The Three Doctors* I spied a brand spanking new copy of the novelisation in Newport WH Smith and pestered my parents – this was something I needed, don't bother with feeding me if needs be but I have to have this because I might never see it again. 34 years on, dog-eared, broken-spined and falling to pieces through love, it remains the item I'd save first in the event of a fire. Mind you; it got away lightly, as other books lost back covers or fell victim to a raspberryade spillage or just the rigours of being carried in a schoolbag. Being stick thin, scrawny and not particularly fast, I spent so many school lunchtimes absorbed in the Doctor's old adventures that I was banned from bringing them in (a ban I got around by stuffing them into the lining of my anorak when a seam split). On one infamous occasion, recalled by my mum to this day, for a trip to Bristol (a mere half hour or so) I came out carrying ten Target books, indecision I excused by pointing out that I'd need them in the event of a traffic jam. But in 1988 I'd lost the Target-buying habit, a Christmas 1987 copy of *The Macra Terror* being the point I pressed the pause button.

So, after one of my mum's typically large Christmas dinners, I arrived in the quiet of Christmas Day, post-*Top of the Pops* and Christmas film (*Back to the Future*) with nothing to do. So I picked up the book from my stocking, opened it and read the first line: 'Later, as he sat on his balcony eating the dog, Dr Robert Laing reflected on the unusual events that had taken place within this huge apartment

410

building during the previous three months...' (What, you thought you were going to get away without a *High Rise* joke?)

It's a cliché to say that the Target range at its best reflected the stories as they should've been, presenting the stories at their purest, without the hindrances of technology, budget and uneven casting or direction. Fourteen months earlier I'd seen a story burdened with miscasting (Howard Cooke just physically wrong for his role), lacklustre direction and inappropriate lighting. Now here it was without Richard Briers hamming it up or the amusingly unthreatening Pool Cleaner, where the ingenious slang and use of language by the different factions could dazzle. I already knew at some level that the books were my platonic ideal of *Doctor Who*; I'd still snap up the tapes but most of the time a budgetless imagination beat what was on screen hands down. And so my Christmas money went not on more videos but on repairing some of the damage I'd done by taking a year out of book collecting.

I thought the story ended on a 1993 trip to London, a trip to The Who Shop plugging the last hole in my collection when what I thought of as an extortionate £12 bought me *The Wheel in Space*. But as so often with *Doctor Who,* such endings are rarely neat; gaps still remain where *The Pirate Planet* and two 1980s Dalek stories should be. Or maybe the end should be at the 50th anniversary event at the ExCeL centre, where I got that threadbare copy of *The Three Doctors* signed by Sir Terrance himself, his autograph sitting alongside my eight year old self's assertion of ownership of the book. I got to say a proper thank you and was rewarded with a smile and observation of how well-read the book was. Or maybe it still shouldn't end there. Maybe I should look for the opportunity to track down Stephen Wyatt and get him to sign the far less battered but equally loved copy of *Paradise Towers*, for rekindling that past love in the face of the future.

Debbie and the Bannermen

Delta and the Bannermen by Jolyon Drake

Favourite Doctor Who book: *Placebo Effect* by Gary Russell

When Bernie and Debbie split up, I was terrified that I would lose *Delta and the Bannermen* forever.

Nine-year-old me was no expert in relationships. To be honest, 36-year-old me isn't much of an expert, but back then I had seen enough break-ups to know the routine. To follow my train of thought, it will help you to know that there are ten years between me and my next brother up, as I was, and am, the youngest of three. This means that a lot of my life experience, particularly in my younger years, was obtained vicariously through the actions of two older brothers, rather than through any excitement of my own.

The best thing about being the youngest is that you never have to babysit anyone. I suspect this was a constant source of irritation to Bernie and Donol, the much older teenage years as, being the elder two, they would often be called upon to babysit.

I was, and remain, very easy to occupy. Sit me down in front of an episode of *Doctor Who* with a cheese and marmite sandwich and I am happy. Pop a paperback in my hand and send me to bed with a glass of water and I will cause no trouble. I will read until I am asleep. Easy to please, that's me.

So, as my brothers had dated and babysat and dated and babysat, and occasionally had dates that involved babysitting, so I had got to know a few of the young ladies as they passed through. Splendid ladies, all of them. Some would bring sweets to keep little brother quiet and there's nothing a little brother loves more than to be given sweets by the latest girl.

Bernie is my biggest brother, in years if not in stature, and back in the day, he was romantically linked to Debbie. She had an open honest face, a smile for every occasion and, most memorably, became the first person ever to give me a piece of *Doctor Who* merchandise. I know, right? She was obviously the one.

I can still pretend to remember the moment that she passed me that carefully wrapped parcel on my ninth birthday. Peeling back the paper to reveal the Target logo and a sunburnt Sylvester McCoy smirking out from beneath the heading: *Doctor Who – Delta and the Bannermen*. But there's no use pretending. After all, there was a bouncy castle and a cake.

Weeks later though, this was all to come back and bite me when Bernie and Debbie split up. After all, we all know what happens when there's a break up, don't we? You know, there's that awkward moment when somebody turns up on the doorstep and brings back any stuff of yours that might've been left with them. And then there's an immediate expectation that you'll have bothered to thoughtfully pack up their stuff in exactly the same way, ready to pass that stuff back. And really, it depended which brother was involved in the break up as to how prepared they would be for the exchange of stuff.

Debbie was the kind of girl who sent her sister to our doorstep with a carrier bag of Bernie's belongings. Bernie was the kind of chap who would have her wait as he threw a few things together and send her away with the message that if there was anything else she wanted, she should let him know. Deep within me was an overwhelming concern that I had to return *Delta and the Bannermen*. This is a moment I don't have to pretend to remember, as these thoughts have remained with me through the years. Because if he had to give back everything from their relationship... would I have to give back everything from their relationship too?

These thoughts weighed heavy on my nine-year-old mind. What if she were to let him know that she wanted *Delta and the Bannermen* back? I would lose the only *Doctor Who* book in my collection. I hid the book and I sobbed. I appreciate that this is a difficult image for you, who might expect the more discerning fan to weep at the point of being given *Delta and the Bannermen*, rather than at the thought of it being taken away. Not even a cheese and marmite sandwich from my mother could bring me comfort in those hours of fear.

'What's wrong?' she asked.

'Nothing,' I replied, sniffing through the combination of tears and runny nose and mild hyperventilation that only an inconsolable child can speak through. 'I'm just sad that Bernie and Debbie have broken up.'

This certainly baffled my mother, who had never seen me fazed by any break-up my brothers may have had in the past. Indeed, even Bernie himself had not seemed very distressed.

'It's just one of those things,' she said. 'Some relationships don't last, but they will both meet other people and they will both be happy.'

'I just don't understand why her sister had to come and take back the stuff he had to return.' I suspect that this was wailed, but I am either over-dramatising now or was overreacting then.

'Well,' my mother said with a pause, about to deliver a lesson I would carry with me for life, 'it's important that when a relationship ends, you cut all ties. People don't want the reminder of things that have happened to get in the way of moving on and building a new future. And that's why they give their stuff back.'

I must have been satisfied by this answer, as I went to my bookshelf and I found my hidden copy of *Delta and the Bannerman*. For just a

413

moment I hugged the slender volume to my chest. I placed it into the hands of my mother and wiped my tears and my nose on my sleeve.

'Here,' I said. 'Give it back to Debbie so that Bernie can move on.'

'Is this the book that Debbie gave you for your birthday?' she asked.

'Yes,' I said.

'She won't come back for this. It was a gift. Nobody would expect you to give it back.'

Oh. It seems obvious now. In fact, it seems pretty stupid now. What had I been thinking?

You may be left wondering why this moment of trauma remains so vivid among the many tales of life moments we associate with our Target books. Well, primarily it's because my mother has never let me forget it. Some people dread introducing potential partners to their parents because of the baby photos that may be trotted out for all to see. For me, every girlfriend I ever introduce to her gets the whole, 'Whatever you do, don't give him any *Doctor Who* books.' (I love how my mother rightly assumes I will have outed myself as a full Tennant introducing .... If you break up. He'll cry at the thought of having to give them back, just like he did when Bernie and Debbie broke up.' Thanks for that.

Bernie has also delighted in this story as the years have gone by. I'm not sure how long afterwards he finally told me that Debbie hadn't really given me the book anyway. Knowing me and my interests so well, he had bought the book and wrapped it for me. Then, when he found that she had come to the party without even a bag of sweets for me, he gave her the book to give to me. He was good like that.

So, dear Delta, Billy and Ray, your relationships aren't really what I think about whenever I see your story sat on my shelf. Sorry about that.

Doctor Who is Required

Doctor Who and the War Machines
by Mark McManus
Favourite *Doctor Who* book: *Human Nature* by Paul Cornell

I didn't see any *Doctor Who* until I was nine years old. I don't know what my parents were thinking. I mean, I liked the *Star Wars* and *Superman* movies; on TV I couldn't get enough of *Terrahawks* or Sunday morning repeats of *Time Tunnel* and *Lost in Space*. It wouldn't have been a huge leap for them to make, but I had to find out about it myself. Specifically, I watched Part One of *The Happiness Patrol*, because other kids at school had been raving about *Remembrance of the Daleks* for a couple of weeks before. By the end of the season, I was completely hooked. This would be my new favourite programme and I would watch it every year.

Between Seasons 25 and 26, my dad died suddenly, and *Doctor Who*, especially the more readily-available Target books, became a welcome escape from the new harshness of life.

We moved house and I had to join a new school. We were given a book catalogue one day, and with it the opportunity to buy the novelisations of *The War Machines* and *Dragonfire*. I don't ever remember being given a book catalogue at school before or after that, but this timely intervention opened my eyes to the wider world of *Doctor Who* beyond watching it on television. I knew nothing of the Doctor's pre-Terra Alpha exploits, so naturally I assumed that these two books would tell consecutive stories. When they finally arrived, I read them immediately, noticing to my excitement that they were numbered 136 and 137 respectively.

I'd always loved reading: when I was younger, I devoured all the works of Roald Dahl, End Blyton and Douglas Hill that I could get my hands on. I would read by torchlight when I was supposed to be asleep and at school I'd be in trouble for starting my weekly library book in whatever lesson I had next. Realising that there were at least 135 other *Doctor Who* books available, I immediately wanted to start collecting the Target range.

Everywhere I went after that, I'd scour second-hand bookshops, charity shops and car boot sales. You could always find plenty of Target books in places like that in those days; they were maybe 20p or 50p a throw, and you could easily finish one in a single sitting. I would read and re-read these old paperbacks all the time. There was a simple pleasure in finding one that I didn't have and making space to slot them into the correct numerical order on my bookcase. I had no idea what was available, so if I could afford it I would just buy the books I didn't have when I found them. Nowadays I feel like some of that excitement is lost by always knowing exactly what is being released and when.

Reading *The War Machines* again now, I wonder what I must have made of it then. I had only briefly seen the TARDIS interior (in Part One of *The Greatest Show in the Galaxy*). Ian Stuart Black has the scanner sweeping the streets of London for a suitable landing spot and I do vaguely remember that I used to think that's how it worked. He effectively makes Dodo a co-pilot, describing her plotting their flight on a graph using the TARDIS computer, so I might have been left with an exaggerated sense of her abilities. I also notice that Black 'corrects' WOTAN's famous line ('Doctor Who is required') to 'The Doctor... is required.' But either meaning makes sense for me, as he could just as easily be talking about the show as the character.

So *The War Machines* was the first *Doctor Who* book I ever read and, in a way, the Target books are my era of *Doctor Who*, because I only got to see a handful of stories broadcast before the series was cancelled. They were a comfort around for me at a very difficult time in my life and set me on the road to being a life-long fan and collector. I often think it's worth remembering that even if you are not enjoying an era of the series, there might still be plenty of people for whom it is an important source of comfort or escape.

Turning Points

Dragonfire by David Kitchen
Favourite *Doctor Who* book: *Timewyrm: Exodus*
by Terrance Dicks

When something as large as an oil tanker turns, the beginning of the manoeuvre is at first more or less imperceptible. Yet inevitably there is a moment when it becomes incredibly obvious that the ship is now facing a different direction.

In *Doctor Who*, *Dragonfire* is that moment. It's not the start of the turn – that happens in *Paradise Towers*, and would only be noticed with hindsight. But it is the moment the audience realises that under Andrew Cartmel's vision the show's direction is changing, even if it would take another season for that turn to be completed.

So it is with the *Dragonfire* Target novel. For a couple of years previously, Target novels had been changing direction, becoming longer and deeper. But *Dragonfire* is the moment when it becomes clear how much they have changed.

But let's bring me into the story.

In 1987, my dad started taking me to meetings of the *Doctor Who* Club of Victoria. In those days, most meetings were still held in members' homes, with a couple of dozen fans squeezing around a living room TV showing a multi-generation copy of *The Ark*. At one of these meetings later that year, I saw *Dragonfire* for the first time on a bootleg video sent from the UK, giving me my first taste of Sylvester McCoy. It was *Doctor Who* at its best, exploring far-away worlds in distant galaxies and firing my young imagination.

Two years later, I was nine and reading the Target novel. And suddenly, there was... more. Of course, plot and events not seen on screen had been in Target novels before (even something from the 'just get them out every month' period like *Pyramids of Mars* had a wonderful prologue and epilogue added). Yet *Dragonfire* was the moment I realised that the novelisations were now going to be something a little more special, going deeper into the plot, with better understanding of the characters. Malcolm Hulke's style was not only back, but was the new normal.

Decades later, I can recall scenes such as Kane walking out of Ace's fridge as vividly as if it had been on screen. At that age I half-comprehended that the book was trying to tell me something more about the relationship between Ace and Glitz, without really understanding it. I just knew that this book was being a little bit more grown-up, and felt proud that it was including me in its more grown-up world.

For me, *Dragonfire* was the beginning of the McCoy years on screen and the novelisation was the dawning of the new golden age of Target books for my generation. From here, there would be more story, more character, more amazing covers by Alistair Pearson, who should be as linked to this new golden age of Target as Chris Acheillos is with the first golden age.

Dragonfire was my turning point from childhood to young adulthood. And there was so much more to come...

The Gangster's Guide to the Galaxy

Attack of the Cybermen by Fiona Moore
Favourite *Doctor Who* book: *The Completely Useless Encyclopedia*
by Steve Lyons and Chris Howarth

When I was in university, to practice my textual criticism skills ahead of a literature exam, I decided to apply them to a Target novelisation. I chose *Attack of the Cybermen* simply because it happened to be there to hand (I had brought two Target books with me, and it was a toss-up between that one and *The Robots of Death*), but it turned out to be an inspired selection. Although the original experiment was, for obvious reasons, hastily written and not very polished, I will here develop it and use *Attack of the Cybermen* to show how Saward was able to compensate for some of the flaws of the TV serial by shifting the focus, perspective and tone of the story when he wrote the novelisation, and how I was able, through close reading, to figure out the literary devices and tropes Saward had used in doing so.

Attack of the Cybermen, the TV serial, is generally held to be less good than its own novelisation: the serial is an uneven piece which seems to be trying to follow a particular trope of the Davison era, best represented by *The Caves of Androzani* – specifically, the conceit of a story in which the Doctor is very much on the side-lines of someone else's narrative. In this case, rather than, for instance, the Jacobean politics of Androzani Minor, the Doctor finds himself drawn into the story of space mercenary Lytton's deal with the Cryons: to help him escape from Earth, in exchange for preventing the Cybermen from rewriting their own timeline.

The difference is that in *The Caves of Androzani*, the Doctor gradually, imperceptibly, becomes a crucial part of the action, until, by the climax, what has been Morgus and Jek's story has now shifted to become the Doctor's. In *Attack of the Cybermen*, the Doctor spends the whole story as a peripheral character, one who could easily have been written out of the action (for instance by having Lytton, or one of his henchmen, imprisoned with Flast and becoming the agent of her pyrotechnic revenge on the Cybermen). On television, the fact that the Doctor is the official protagonist, and the Cyber Controller the official antagonist, requires the story to continually slow down the narrative to remind us of their presence in it. And, as this is a story with little room for the Doctor, he feels less a part of the action than someone shoehorned in out of necessity, simply because it's his name on the front titles rather than Lytton's. How, I wondered, was the novelisation able to rescue the story and compensate for these flaws?

The answer, a close reading revealed, was through a simple literary device: reframing the perspective. The tale is now told through the eyes of Lytton's henchman Charlie Griffiths (and secondarily Peri, playing much the same role to the Doctor), with periodic shifts into third person omniscient narration to provide background information, usually of a rather sardonically humorous sort, as when the narrator dryly explains how Lytton was not only aware that Russell was an undercover policeman, but was deliberately exploiting him to obtain explosives on demand. By changing this perspective, the story now reveals itself as a gangster version of *The Hitchhiker's Guide to the Galaxy*, with Griffiths as a twisted Arthur Dent figure, a petty criminal for whom an ordinary day leads to the discovery that someone close to him is an alien, following which he is transported away on a bewildering intergalactic caper.

More subtly, through analysing the early sections of the book, it became clear to me that Griffiths is also an unreliable narrator, ~~presenting himself in a flattering light which undermines the~~ ~~truth of his own perspective.~~ The description of his criminal career before meeting Lytton makes this clear: Charles Windsor Griffiths, whose full name turns out to be appropriately pompous, speaks of 'supplementing his mother's income' with the proceeds of crime, clearly attempting to construct himself as the stereotypical East End family-man gangster, selflessly helping his poor old mum, when it is equally clear that the 'supplements' benefit only himself. He worries idly about criminals holding up his mother's favourite shop because of the distress it would cause her, oblivious to the distress his own activities cause others. Seeing things through Griffiths' skewed perspective thus gave me a further change in genre: the tale of a gangster determined to present his actions to the best effect, summed up by the narrator's obituary:

> Charlie Griffiths had not led a particularly good life. Until he had met Lytton, neither had he been very successful. But in all his wildest dreams he never believed he would die on an alien planet with two million pounds' worth of uncut diamonds in his pocket. He hadn't wanted to die, but, whatever else could be said, he had done so in some style.

Griffiths' subjective narrative therefore made it very obvious, to a student who had been applying the same close-reading skills to *Oedipus Rex* earlier that term, that we are in hubris-and-nemesis territory here, a story of criminals whose clever plans will ultimately be undermined by the selfishness of their actions.

420

The resulting tale became streamlined and focused, and was shot through with the kind of ironies common to both Douglas Adams and the British gangster genre. As I read, I noted that the deaths of the various criminals echo each other through the narrative, as they are all down to personal flaws: chain-smoking criminal Payne's demise early on, when he becomes separated from the group while pretending to investigate a suspicious noise, but actually intending to sneak a crafty cigarette, conceptually prefigures Lytton's capture by the Cybermen, which, in the novelisation, is due to Lytton's arrogance in failing to check for a security camera near the time-ship, rather than, as in the TV version, down to simple bad luck. The Doctor is introduced into the story (on page 32, by which time the action is well underway) less as its protagonist and more as a complication, blundering into the middle of Lytton's plans and being, despite himself, drawn into the plot to foil the Cybermen. The Cyber Controller, in the novelisation, is absent until page 125, appearing only as a kind of end-of-level boss who defeats Lytton and is, in turn, defeated by the Doctor, whose gun rampage in Cyber Control in the penultimate scene thus becomes less the tying-up-loose-ends coda of the serial, and more the sort of act of satisfying revenge that one might expect in a modern British gangster story, or, indeed, in a Jacobean play.

The exercise, though, did more than simply help me prepare for my exam. It demonstrated clearly to me that not only was it possible to analyse *Doctor Who* in this way, but it was, actually, helpful, showing how you could discern authorial intention, identify the various literary and rhetorical devices the writers of the series were using, and bring out aspects of the text that, perhaps, had gone unnoticed up until then. It was exactly those sorts of analytical tools that I would later bring to the story reviews that I wrote, and co-wrote, for the Oxford University *Doctor Who* Society's zine Tides of Time, for the Doctor Who Appreciation Society's magazine Celestial Toyroom, for four of Telos Publishing's Unofficial and Unauthorised Guides (to *Blake's 7, The Prisoner* and both versions of *Battlestar Galactica*), and many other publications. But we all have to start somewhere, and I started with the novelisation of *Attack of the Cybermen*.

All the Fun of the Fair

Doctor Who – The Nightmare Fair
by Cory John Eadson
Favourite Doctor Who book: From A to Z by Gary Gillatt

The Nightmare Fair is a novelisation of a television story that might have been and, indeed, should have been.

Being a particular fan of the Colin Baker years, the slim but pacy Target offering from Graham Williams was a delight for me to peruse. Part of a three-book series novelising stories that might have made it to television in 1985, were it not for an awful error of judgement on the part of Michael Grade (no bias there, honest), not only is *The Nightmare Fair* the strongest of the triumvirate, but is also the one that shows the most progression in terms of characterisation. As Colin Baker's first full series developed, we saw a slow mellowing of his character. Yes, by the time we reached Necros he was still tetchy and a little ▓▓▓▓▓▓▓▓▓▓▓▓ ▓▓▓ ▓▓▓ ▓▓▓▓ ▓▓▓ ▓▓▓ ▓ ▓▓▓ ▓ ▓▓▓ ▓ ▓▓▓ clearly just a part of his persona as the Doctor. Graham Williams not only brings this to life beautifully in his novel, but we also see new aspects of 'Old Sixie'.

This is a Doctor who is clearly having a whale of a time in Blackpool! Although the Sixth Doctor had a certain Pertwee-esque pomposity about him, it feels absolutely right to plonk him in the middle of a funfair surrounded by rides and candy-floss, enjoying himself immensely. No funerals to attend, no TARDIS to refuel. This is the Doctor and his friend simply having fun.

Naturally, we can't keep things that way for long, and *The Nightmare Fair* has a fantastic ace up its sleeve in the villainy department; the Celestial Toymaker. Having such a colourful and arch enemy go up against an equally colourful Doctor against the garish backdrop of Blackpool is simply irresistible, and it works an absolute treat. Williams balances everything in his novelisation, making for a fast-paced read that nonetheless recreates the characters successfully.

Who knows where Doctor Who might have gone had this story made it to the screen? A fun, bright adventure that has a few continuity references for the fans (but not enough to trip the story up), and plenty for the 'regular' viewer to enjoy. A Doctor and companion who genuinely like each other's company, and a familiar location that families all over the country would recognise. *The Nightmare Fair* could have been the story that granted Colin Baker a longer tenure as the Doctor on television. Alas, it was never to be, but former producer Graham Williams has given us a tasty little side-step. A faithful piece of what might have been, or rather, should have been.

The story ends with the Doctor coaxing Peri back to the funfair, once the Toymaker is defeated. Instead of giving Blackpool up as a bad job, the Doctor wants to make good on his promise of showing Peri a good time around the funfair. And, grinning, she happily obliges.

How I wish we could have joined them for more.

Trial of a Librarian

Doctor Who - Mindwarp
by Christopher Bryant

Favourite *Doctor Who* book: *The Writer's Tale: The Final Chapter*
by Russell T Davies and Benjamin Cook

'Bryant, I wonder if you could help me with something,' Mr Phillips began. 'One of the boys in the year below said he saw someone walking away from the library with a pile of books under his jumper. I was wondering if you would have any idea who that was?'

This was 1989, my final term at the school, and I had had a complicated relationship with the library during the preceding six and a half years. Now, this may have been an expensive and eccentric school of the kind that aimed to turn out the most successful, most powerful and most deranged members of British society, but don't imagine anything grand when I refer to the library. It was one room, smaller than most classrooms in the flat, with bookshelves around three of the four walls and a couple of settees.

My earliest memory of the library comes from my second year at the school. I would have been seven or eight years old and I was sitting on my bunk bed in my dormitory enjoying a *Beano* annual borrowed from the library. Then I realised, criminal genius that I was, that all I had to do in order to own this book was to tear out the library sticker, for then nobody would be able to tell whence it had come and I would have committed the perfect crime.

So I stood at the dorm window, happily ripping the label from the inside cover and tossing the scraps into the garden. Satisfied, I turned around to see...him. The deputy head. Standing in the doorway. Waiting for me to turn around.

Instantly, I crumbled. My misdemeanour discovered, I began to blub. This was perfectly understandable: everyone was scared of this man and with good reason. Most of the boarders had been beaten with his enormous slipper for less serious crimes than theft. I knew I was in for it.

Surprisingly, he did not choose violence on this occasion. Instead, he sent me to see Mr Phillips after breakfast. This genial old man (they're all old when you're eight, aren't they? He was probably in his fifties) gloried in the roles of Head of English, Head of Latin and Librarian. The library was his domain, so the punishment was his decision.

In this case, the punishment was to be a red line. From my earlier comments, you're probably imagining a cane across the hand, but the line was caused by a pen and inflicted upon my page in the library record book. It meant that I was banned from using the library for the rest of term.

I can't remember now, but that must have been something of an ordeal. I was less than fond of breaktime activities that involved balls, voluntary exercise or other people. My preferred method of passing that thirty-minute gap between lessons was to sit in the library reading quietly. To have lost this privilege would have been a terrible blow.

Would you like to guess what I liked to read?

It wasn't just *Doctor Who*. Often it was *Asterix*, or Enid Blyton, or Tolkien, or another *Beano* annual. I was timid with my reading choices, in a way I berate children for now that I am myself a teacher in a not dissimilar school. I always knew where to find Jack London's *White Fang*, because I used to store my current reading book behind it. I must have read *Doctor Who and the Cybermen*, for instance, dozens of times in that library. When I think now of all the opportunities I ignored in that room...well, I'm still glad I spent so much time reading Target books, but perhaps I should have broadened my oeuvre a little.

Time passed and the red line was long forgotten. During my final years in the school, I became part of the librarian team and worked hard to make the library my own domain. I gave out red lines myself for such hideous behaviour as talking loudly in the library. All the while, I continued to read Target books.

Given that my exalted position in the library allowed me access to the pupils' record books, I could see who was reading what books and which ones were most popular. Therefore, I knew for a fact that almost no-one else in the school was reading *Doctor Who* books. They were missing out, obviously, but this was the 1980s and I seemed to be a lone voice of sanity at my particular school.

Why, then, did Mr Phillips continue to buy them? Surely he can't have just been humouring me? He even splashed out on Peter Haining's *The Doctor Who File*, arguably that esteemed chronicler's least essential book. I have a photo of the school library with the Haining book displayed unnecessarily prominently.

Back in 1989, I flung my desk open.

'Yes, sir, it was me.'

Front covers by Jeff Cummins and Chris Achilleos and Andrew Skilleter and Alister Pearson stared out from my open desk, completely masking the usual exercise books and pencil sharpenings. Mr Phillips looked at the library books, then back to me.

'These are the books I want to buy, sir.'

To be completely fair to me, the library had been known to sell off old stock before now. Once or twice a year, there would be a library sale in the basement where slightly worse-for-wear books would go for 10p or 20p a pop. Right now, I hold in my hand a copy of *Doctor Who and the Doomsday Weapon* (the 1979 edition) with ancient Sellotape keeping its front cover attached, although the back cover has long since disappeared. Inside, I can see the vestiges of the removed library label... no, honestly, I bought it! I can also see where the book's original owner, one M.J. Kelly, wrote his name.

Gently, Mr Phillips had to explain to me that he wasn't going to flog 80% of his library's *Doctor Who* collection to me just because I was leaving. It dawned upon me that I was really going to have to leave the books behind when I moved to secondary school. Suddenly, my Target collection had a massive hole in it.

I returned the books to the library, crestfallen. I no longer remember exactly which books were in that little collection – maybe *Pyramids of Mars* or *The Talons of Weng-Chiang*, which would explain why those are still missing from my shelf – but I know one thing for certain.

Mindwarp would not have been among them.

I remember the day Mr Phillips produced *Mindwarp* amongst a small stack of new purchases. I remember reading it. I remember the daft cover art and the unappealing story inside, complete with utterly crazy new fate for Peri.

That morning, in my dying days at that school, when I gathered up my literary favourites and stuffed them under my jumper (so I didn't drop any, you see) and arranged them in my desk ready to discuss them with Mr Phillips later that day, I would have let my hand drift past Philip Martin's second Target novelisation.

My nostalgia for the Target era knows few bounds, but even amongst such treasures there are inevitably a few duds not even worth 10p in a library sale. *Mindwarp* remained on the shelf as I left the school. I wonder if it's still there.

Better Executed

The Chase by Paul Castle

Favourite *Doctor Who* book: *Doctor Who in An Exciting Adventure
with the Daleks*
by David Whitaker

When I was twelve, back in 1989, my emergent obsession with *Doctor
Who* was primarily book-based. I had watched the television
programme ever since Peter Davison filled Tom Baker's boots (not to
mention trousers, shirt, waistcoat, overcoat and scarf), but television
was pretty much a throwaway medium. We'd rented a home video
recorder since the summer of 1988, but aside from the taped
adventures of the seventh Doctor and Ace, my video collection
consisted of nothing more than *The Empire Strikes Back, Transformers:
The Movie* and what I now know as *Transformers* Season 4. The long
history of *Doctor Who* was represented only by sketchy memories from
1980s broadcasts, a gradually growing personal library of the Target
novelisations and a couple of months' worth of *Doctor Who Magazine*.

The updated release of *The Doctor Who Programme Guide* that
summer was a revelation. For the first time ever, the series was
quantifiable. My books suddenly became individual pieces of a jigsaw
puzzle, with Jean-Marc Lofficier providing the whole picture. I started
compiling lists, something which I do to this day. My first listed all
stories in order of broadcast together with a tick box: coloured in for
available and left blank for unpublished. By 1989, the majority of
stories had been novelised, but being twelve, I felt the blanks in the
list were going to remain out of reach forever.

Incredible news came in the next magazine: the missing Dalek
stories from the first Doctor's era were to be out in time for Christmas.
They went straight on the Christmas list. Although Mum provided me
with both *The Chase* and the enticingly-entitled *The Mutation of Time*,
she was unfortunately unable to find a copy of *Mission to the Unknown*
(to this day, I've never read it), but the substituted omnibus edition of
The Dominators and *The Krotons* made me a lifelong fan of Jamie
McCrimmon and the Quarks, so the absence was more than made up
for. Anyway, let's cut to *The Chase*.

Quarks notwithstanding, *The Chase* was my favourite book that
Christmas and reading it again 26 years later (the age of the entire
telly series back in 1989), the reasons why are clear. The intervening
years have overwritten my memories of the novelisations with the
television episodes they were based on, so I'm coming to these books
afresh. What strikes me most is not how much this book differs from
the television episodes that I have grown to love dearly, but how

427

similar it is. John Peel wrote an introduction stating that it drew upon the original scripts more than the production, but aside from tightening up the plot and providing backgrounds to the times, peoples, and places involved, the story runs pretty much as it did on television. This is the kind of balance that any good adaptation should strive to achieve.

It's almost a shame that these books were destined not to be the epitome of archival *Doctor Who* but merely a footnote between the broadcast era and the home media era. Even with the current vogue for audiobooks giving the Targets a breath of new life, the original television episodes will always be the top dog. A shame, because when these books are written well, they are better; a refinement of the original teleplays, in some areas expanding the story, and in others trimming the excess.

Where *The Chase* truly benefits from John Peel's adaptation is with his portrayal of the Daleks. They are badass in a way they never were during the Hartnell era. Oh, they were marvellous on screen, but robbed of the visual presence and the immutability of their grating voices can fall slightly flat on paper. To compensate, Peel strips away all the *'Allo 'Allo* bumbling and stammering Daleks seen on TV and replaces them with hard-line SS officers. This shows clearly from their first encounter with the Aridian Elders, where the Dalek in charge of the time squad exterminates the first resistance, states its demands, and surmises that the Aridians will be killed rather than conquered when the time came. This insight into Dalek thought processes is where the value of prose can enrich their characterisation, making them colder, calculating, and more menacing than ever.

The work of John Peel passed out of fashion following his work with BBC Books, which is unfortunate as Peel's Hartnell and Troughton novelisations were applauded most highly at the time. I'd like to think that in some alternate universe out there, where television remained a throwaway medium and we had no inkling that seeing episodes a second time was even a thing, John Peel's five Dalek novelisations are regarded by fans as the greatest run of Dalek stories ever.

Intrigued and Repulsed by Evil

Doctor Who – The Ultimate Evil
by Chris Kocher
Favourite *Doctor Who* book: *Timewyrm: Exodus*
by Terrance Dicks

Some 'classic' *Doctor Who* stories were completed for television and later discarded from the archives – a decision that I hope causes recurring nightmares among BBC executives in today's on-demand, content-streaming world. Others were proposed and never made it to our TV screens. Thanks to Big Finish, many of those have now been recorded: some are heralded as rediscovered classics, while others clearly had good reasons for not being made.

In a 26-year history that seems picked clean, one story that's avoided a wider 21st century audience is Wally K. Daly's *The Ultimate Evil*. A script abandoned because of the 1986 hiatus, it later surfaced as a Target 'Missing Episodes' novel in 1989. A recent re-read of the book reveals how well it would fit into the sixth Doctor's era. With the scales-and-eyeball-antennae cover illustration as a reference, it's easy to imagine duplicitous arms dealer Dwarf Mordant in all of his 1980s rubber-monster glory. I can only imagine Mary Whitehouse's stern letters of complaint to the BBC when Mordant's 'hate ray' turns characters into bloodthirsty savages, but those scenes are in-keeping with the violent tone of Season 22.

On the other hand, there are a few too many ludicrous ideas: everyone on Tranquela can teleport but generally don't until an escape is required; a war arsenal is locked up for fifty years under penalty of death, then casually opened; a planet-wide treaty depends on each side having zero contact with the other; a continent of people is controlled by a computer that decides what is moral and what isn't (a situation the Doctor, strangely, does nothing about). And the Doctor saves the day by essentially telling Mordant to go and play elsewhere. Perhaps these problems could have been smoothed out with a good script edit – but in the chaos of the Colin Baker years, that never was a sure thing.

I can't imagine that *The Ultimate Evil* is anyone's favourite Target novel. It's not even a good *Doctor Who* story, although it's arguably better than some 'Lost Stories'. But as a snapshot of a moment in the show's history, the book serves as an intriguing 'what if'.

Another Master Plan for the Daleks

Doctor Who - Mission to the Unknown / The Mutation of Time
by Alwyn Ash
Favourite *Doctor Who* book: *Destiny of the Daleks*
by Terrance Dicks

I was never a big collector of *Doctor Who* Target books. For one thing, as a child I struggled to read and write, so my excursions into the novel were few and far between. Thankfully, I did find sanctuary in the pages of some of these wonderful titles, however, and specifically loved any of the Dalek adventures. For me, Target books were less about revisiting the current televised series (my Doctor was Peter Davison) and more about discovering something new, those classic black and white episodes that had aired long before I was even born. The Daleks' adventures were initiating to the imagination; their world were exciting prints. How I'm glad that Target was able to negotiate the rights to these with the Terry Nation estate!

John Peel (author of personal BBC Books favourites *War of the Daleks* and *Legacy of the Daleks*) penned both titles, starting with *Mission to the Unknown* and following that up with *The Mutation of Time*. In 1989 I was fifteen years old and, though I didn't know it at the time, *Doctor Who* was close to being taken off air altogether. My only video tape (in Betamax form) was that of *The Five Doctors* and my copy of *Genesis of the Daleks* and *Slipback* on double audio cassette kept me company in bed. I did not own much in the way of merchandise otherwise, except for a few magazines and a single postcard of the Fifth Doctor bought at the Blackpool exhibition in the days when the outside was an actual TARDIS (well, it certainly felt bigger on the inside!)

The Daleks' scheming towards their Master Plan felt epic, greater in design than any story I had either watched or read about before. Being a fan of the James Bond movies, the inclusion of super-villain Mavic Chen, Guardian of the Solar System, was genius, adding extra weight to the threat against both the Doctor and his companions, Katarina and Steven Taylor. On screen the Doctor was portrayed by William Hartnell, but in my youth and in print I only thought of him as 'the Doctor'; it helped to maintain the mystery. Peel's writing didn't feel out of reach, so no literacy struggle – instead, I was encouraged to keep turning each page, each chapter, until the very last page of the second book. The fact that it was a two-parter, and that I was able to get through it, gave me such confidence in my new-found exploration of the written word: I certainly thank Peel (and Target Books) for that!

25 years later and I'm just as attached to these adaptations, now including the splendid AudioGO audiobook releases narrated by Peter Purves and Jean Marsh, again published in two volumes. Perhaps as an adult I am more aware of the differences between the two parts, especially how the second instalment leans towards jest. That does not take away the power of its conclusion, however, involving the death of the Doctor's new ally Sara Kingdom. The first book killed off Trojan servant girl Katarina, bringing to an end her far too brief appearance in the Doctor's life. And here was me thinking Adric's demise in *Earthshock* was, erm, shocking!

My biggest regret is ever growing up. In my late twenties I lost interest in *Doctor Who* for a number of years and gave away my collection, including those books I had loved so dearly. Thankfully I didn't stay an adult for too long and, in recent years, have been recollecting via eBay. I still don't own clean copies of *Mission to the Unknown* or *The Mutation of Time* but will keep looking...

It's frustrating how some recollections remain out of complete reach. As a child, I once visited a fishing village someplace in Wales, where I grabbed copies of *The Five Doctors, Day of the Daleks* and *Death to the Daleks*. To this day I cannot recall the village or store (it might have been Fishguard or Tenby). It is a clouded memory I would like to sharpen. This is a reason why Target books have such importance: they inherit beautiful memories and a longing to reconnect with them on a deep, personal level in the years to come.

WH Smith was my source for John Peel's novelisations, as it would be for future purchases (did I mention *War* and *Legacy of the Daleks* earlier? Forgive me, but I was just as giddy for these at 23 as I had been at fifteen). These days I am old and grumpy, less likely to be overwhelmed by any new publication, but holding a second-hand copy of *Destiny of the Daleks* and seeing that cover by artist Andrew Skilleter does give me goosebumps – as does Alister Pearson's work on the two volumes of *The Daleks' Masterplan*!

I am a child again...

Novelisation Nemesis

Doctor Who - Silver Nemesis by Don Klees

Favourite *Doctor Who* book: *Ghost Light – the Script Book*
by Marc Platt

It wasn't my first choice. Of all the *Doctor Who* novels in the house –
a selection recently expanded by a large cache obtained at a used
bookstore – there were several others I'd have picked to read sooner.
Nevertheless, my youngest son wanted to read *Silver Nemesis* with me.

We'd been reading *Doctor Who* novelisations together for a while.
It started with *Planet of the Daleks*, read aloud to comfort him after a
vacation mishap. He said that I read it better than Jon Pertwee had.
While his sincerity was undeniable, it still struck me as an overly
generous assessment.

Generosity was not a feeling that came to mind for *Silver Nemesis*.
The TV version had underwhelmed me when it premiered in America
early in 1989. Having heard that scenes had been cut from the
broadcast version, I considered buying the novelisation when it was
released to see if any restored elements made for a more satisfying
narrative. For whatever reason, I ended up not getting it. Being a
college student, it's possible I was short on money and planned to pick
it up later. It never occurred to me that timing would be an issue for
either the show or the books. *Silver Nemesis* aside, the programme
itself seemed to be back on solid footing, and the Target novels seemed
virtually eternal.

However, while they outlasted the programme, at least in its
original form, the novelisations ultimately came to an end, at least in
their original form. By the mid-1990s, Target had become part of
Virgin Publishing, and the New Adventures books were clearly the
focus. When the BBC reclaimed the publishing of *Doctor Who* books
several years later, the novelisations became hard to find even in used
bookstores, leaving me to regret those not bought or lost along the
way.

Silver Nemesis was never one of those regrets. Though I grabbed it
as part of that motherlode, part of me firmly expected it to sit on the
shelf, but my son had other ideas. He shared the same hope my
younger self once held about the book's potential to improve upon an
inconsistent narrative. In the end, the book wasn't necessarily better,
but admittedly testing the hypothesis was fun.

The Day the Circus Came to Town

Doctor Who - The Greatest Show in the Galaxy
by Grant Bull
Favourite *Doctor Who* book: *Time and Relative*
by Kim Newman

I remember my Mum and Dad taking my sister and me to the circus when we were younger. I'm sure they took us more than once but this trip in particular was different. The circus tent has always been a bit of a fascination for me, the way it transforms an empty field into a spectacle. Its size and shape seems to be part of the act, the way it stands like it might fall in on itself at any moment. Then, once inside, the size grows: like a certain time machine, the dimensions inside are different. You are transported into an arena of entertainment, a centre stage, rows upon rows of benches: it's huge but then you are brought back to reality by the green and brown carpet of grass and mud. Then there is the outside and the Tetris like pattern of caravans of varying sizes depending on the success of the performer, living their lives in a box on wheels. Is this the dream or is it a cold stark reality?

On this one night, we passed through the heavy-duty vinyl doorway to find our seats. There was a warmth in the air though it was a cold evening, the warmth of a number of bodies in an enclosed space. The centre stage in its circle form was lit up as music rebounded off the plastic walls. We found our seats and waited for the show to begin. It began and we enjoyed it, daring, funny, entertaining, more words like this and then there was the interval. It was then that my sister and I moved seats. Behind us were rows of empty stalls going right to the back of the venue so we decided we would move upwards to get a more aerial view.

Then it happened...

In a moment of supposed entertainment, a gorilla ran out amongst the audience. It wasn't a real gorilla but to us it was and it was as real as the fear we felt. I didn't like it at all and my sister didn't like it either and we were disconnected from our Mum and Dad. The gorilla was causing trouble, much to the amusement of others, but to us it was torture. Mum and Dad were looking back at us with reassuring grins, but we weren't smiling. We wanted to be with them, to feel safe like they always made us feel, but we were too frightened to move in case we drew the attention of the gorilla. It seemed to go on forever until the 'fun' was over. When we were sure it was safe, we scampered down the steps to our original seats, into the comfort of our parents' company. Both shaken, we watched the rest of the show, one eye watching over shoulders for the rest of the night, just in case.

Don't get me wrong, it was a good night out but for the gorilla. If only someone had warned me; if only we had known what was coming...

Coda:

The skinny little boy sat on the cold playground, his parka coat wrapped tight around his small frame, bright blond hair hidden under its hood. His hands were warming inside black gloves, the tops bearing the character Ultra Magnus from the cartoon series *Transformers*. The gloves gripped a small comic, the bottom of the cover sporting the bubble writing logo of the crisp producer Golden Wonder. The comic had come free in his crisps and it had been carefully shoved into his coat pocket for later reading, that later being now. It was all new to him, something completely different, it was real, not cartoon, it had space and it had time and it had 'The Doctor'. He was hooked.

The bell rang for the end of playtime. The sea of bodies scrambled down from the helicopter climbing frame and whizzed past the boy's eyes in a blur. It was time to go back inside for the final lessons of the day with the promise of sweets and a packet of stickers from his loving Mum when the home time bell rang. As he stood up, using the brick wall behind him to extend his legs, there was a distant whooshing sound that made his head turn towards the playing field of Hatfield Primary School. There in the far corner beyond the pond stood a box. The boy rummaged in his pockets for the comic frantically and once found, he pulled it towards his confused eyes and glanced at the box on the cover.

The TARDIS!

In amazement, he looked back out onto the field but it was gone. Nothing there. Another daydream? But as he stepped forward, he inadvertently kicked a parcel along the floor in front of his feet. He looked around at the rapidly emptying playground. It was as if he was the only one who could see the package. Calmly, though his heart was racing fast, he knelt on the hard floor and delicately tore the brown paper away. There was a book inside and a hand-written note laid upon it, addressed 'To the boy who dreams'.

'A book from the future written by someone in the future about the future from a future friend. Read and believe, I will return and return again. Don't give up on me. I will always be there in some shape or form. Oh and don't fear the gorilla, it's just someone in a suit. Suits aren't that bad, though some are, but they are mostly men in ties.

434

'In your adventures always,

'The Doctor x

'PS – Hurry on to class now, you don't want to get in trouble with the headmistress!'

As if the person who wrote the note knew, Miss Nadal appeared right on time.

'Into class now please Grant, you don't want to be late.'

The boy quickly glanced at the cover of the book: *Doctor Who – The Greatest Show in the Galaxy* by Stephen Wyatt. The cover showed a character, presumably the Doctor, and below him a circus tent. A smile of impossible size spread across the boy's face. He clutched the book tightly to his chest and hurried up the steps into school.

Miss Nadal turned her attention to the corner of the field, for some reason unknown to her. There was nothing there, just a distant noise.

The bell for the end of the day rang and the half-asleep children who were sat on the carpet listening to the story being read aloud by their teacher awoke with an excited start. Coats, gloves and lunchboxes were gathered and they spilled out onto the playground. Grant ran to his Mum and hugged her tight. As much as he enjoyed school, this was the best part: stickers, sweets and walking home to watch cartoons before tea holding his Mum's hand.

'Don't forget darling, we are going to the circus tonight too.'

Grant's loose hand rested on the book he had placed in his coat pocket. A knowing smile appeared on his little face.

'I can't wait Mum, it's going to be great'.

Together they walked down Bow Lane, past the monkey tree, the length of Hillcross Avenue to the warmth of their loving home.

No gorilla could ruin this.

'A Giant Cat is Looking Intently Down at Us!'

Doctor Who - Planet of Giants
by David Guest
Favourite *Doctor Who* book: *The Dark Path*
by David A McIntee

There was only one question as I opened number 145 in the Target *Doctor Who* Library: would the novelisation of *Planet of Giants* by Terrance Dicks come anywhere near the brilliant scripted version I had written for a group of wild and wacky fellow fans to record?

The Grappenhall Recording Company (GRC), based in Warrington, had been recording their own interpretations of *Doctor Who* stories for quite a while when I met the three members at a DWAS convention in Birmingham in 1982. One of the gang used to type out scripts based on listening closely to the lines while watching the videos – in some cases these were the pirated copies of stories that were often difficult to see, let alone make out the words. Of course, the Target books helped to decipher some of the more obscure lines, though the earnest scriptwriter preferred to use a good listening ear and his memory in preparing the classics for the GRC to record for posterity.

We were soon joined by three other 'regulars' and it would be fair to say that most of our recording sessions took place in an atmosphere of barely controlled hysteria. The main scriptwriter had committed most of the stories to paper in his teens and there were many examples of excessive narration and, more particularly, hilarious instances of misheard dialogue.

We were amused to learn, for example, that the Great One in *Planet of the Spiders* was 'the size of a semi-detached house.' We guffawed during *The Ark in Space* when Sarah remarked, 'The Moose said, "Stick around and get killed!"' rather than the actual, 'Vamoose or stick around and be killed.' And we were helpless when in *Mawdryn Undead* the Brigadier opined that, 'A swan goes on till it drops' rather than his more stoic, 'This one goes on till he drops!'

A typical weekend get-together for the GRC included the recording of at least two stories and the watching of either the newest episode or the most recently obtained video of an older story. These were viewed with a complete lack of respect and seriousness: we enjoyed them but in a group we somehow couldn't stop finding the funny side in just about everything. *Planet of Giants* was, for some reason, a particular favourite and it was the story I decided to try my hand at scripting for the GRC. We had already settled which of us would portray the original TARDIS four (I was always the heroic Ian Chesterton, not least because I had fine-tuned delivering the line, 'Yes it is!' to perfection) and had had enormous fun recording a number of First Doctor stories on audio, as well as the pilot episode on video.

I wanted to capture the fun of our recordings with some of the childish amusement enjoyed while watching those early seasons together. The Target book was not yet available to help me out, but I included more than a few instances of deliberately inaccurate lines, for which my friend had become noted, and moments of such barking insanity that I really should have become a writer for Harry Hill.

So it was that I started reading the Target novelisation with trembling hands and a deep-seated feeling that it could never be as good as what I wrote, how the GRC had performed it, or even how it came across on television. One of the shorter novels – I read it in an hour while studying at theological college, which might explain a lot about where and who I am today as a Vicar in south west London – was it was actually a hugely-anticipated book, as it was the final story of the Hartnell era to be novelised. These things definitely mattered to avid *Doctor Who* followers trying to build up collections. The Target books were something to be collected with pride in an age before videos, DVDs and action figures. The first in my collection, proudly purchased with a book token in 1974, was *Doctor Who and the Day of the Daleks*, complete with illustrations – 30p spent to launch me on the road to collecting all of the titles, now stored in a police box cabinet. If by some mischance I missed a first edition, I would later try to find one in old bookstores and charity shops. I was furious when the cover design changed because it would ruin my perfect library.

I never did have to write to 14 Gloucester Road, London, enclosing cheque or postal order for the book price, plus 7p to cover packing and postage. All my books were proudly purchased on visits to WH Smith (extra pocket money might allow me to be reckless and buy two), or I would deliver lists of which titles I required to relatives enquiring about birthday or Christmas presents. At a push I would visit the local library, which had a very good Doctor Who section, and borrow unread novels in hardback – though of course this didn't stop me wanting to possess the paperbacks, much to the annoyance of my mother, who regularly accused me of hoarding rubbish.

The novelisation of *Planet of Giants* even takes me back to that first Target book I purchased as it ends with the chilling teaser that, 'Outside in the ruins of London the Daleks were waiting...' And the Daleks bring back a whole load of other memories of GRC recordings, especially sore throats and plenty of coughing when one of us attempted a Dalek voice too many.

Planet of Giants was important to me as it was the one and only serial I scripted for the GRC. On TV the serial had originally suffered when the final two episodes of what was originally a four-part story were edited together – something Terrance Dicks tried to put right by reinstating the cruelly cut action into his novelisation. The novel was certainly one of those cases where Terrance attempted to instil a sense of dramatic terror into a story that actually contained little. We had made fun of this in our recording with several comments along the lines of spotting a giant photograph of a dead man or constant references to nobody touching anything with their hands, to show up Barbara's general wetness in trying to keep her illness a secret from the others. (And just how many times did she ask for water in this serial?)

A good example of the different ways a scene was dealt with occurred at the end of episode one. A clearly disinterested cat, shown in close-up on screen, was greeted by Susan shrieking, 'Grandfather!' as Barbara turned away in horror and the end credits rolled. Episode two began with the Doctor's useful advice not to look directly into the cat's eyes before the creature simply wandered off. I decided in our version that it would be far more dramatic for Susan to scream and exclaim, 'A giant cat is looking intently down at us!' The Target novelisation racked up the tension thus, 'Looming over them, green eyes glowing balefully, was an enormous cat...'

It was this sort of thing that made me enjoy the *Planet of Giants* book more than I should. We had made inane comments while watching the video, we had sent it up mercilessly while recording my script, and now the novel was funny because it seemed to be taking it all so seriously. Maybe a modern writer would be tempted to venture into gently-mocking 'Honey, I Shrunk the TARDIS' territory, but Terrance had to write what was described in chapter one as 'the Doctor's most grotesque and terrifying adventure'.

If the TV story itself had been underwhelming, littered with some poor acting, at least our GRC version had been a loving pastiche which had given us a good laugh. We had turned the Doctor's small screen explanation that they had been 'reduced roughly to the size of an inch' into, 'roughly to the size of inch, depending on the size of the available props, backdrop or set.' We giggled at Ian's full explanation of the actions of ants when attacked, though in the early days of *Doctor Who* this was no doubt considered a fine example of imparting scientific knowledge. In my version Ian happened to have a handy Mitchell Beazley pocket guide to ants about his person and delivered a long lecture to Susan on these members of the formicidae family. The humour is obviously lost in the book as Terrance seeks to explain these lines as 'the science teacher in Ian reasserting itself'.

How could the written word even begin to capture the unintended

438

comedy value that could be expressed in sight or sound? I'm pretty sure neither the TV cast nor Terrance Dicks had quite as much fun with the story as we did; yes, we were incredibly silly, but we were affectionately sending up a series about which we were all passionate, and bonding together as fans and friends with at least one common interest.

Reading *Planet of Giants*, indeed reading any of the Target novelisations, brings it all back: not just watching the televised stories, but remembering the daft afternoons with friends never quite taking Doctor Who as seriously as we probably should have done. Reading the correct versions of lines purposely ruined in amateur audios has the power, more even than watching the original series, to bring a very large smile to the face. And I'm always reminded of the joy of being a child at heart.

I'm Glad You're Happy and I'm Happy You're Glad

Doctor Who - The Happiness Patrol
by Stephen Webb
Favourite *Doctor Who* book: *Lungbarrow* by Marc Platt

'What is your favourite story from *Doctor Who*?'

It is an easy enough question, right? Of course, without a little insight into the person you're asking, the answer is largely meaningless. Let's start there.

I have diagnosed social anxiety disorder. One of the 'bonus gifts' that comes with anxiety is extreme highs and lows. I have learned to manage it fairly well and my condition is exceptionally mild. From the moment I learned how to handle it, the overall de-stigmatisation of mental illnesses within our culture and society became an extremely important thing to me. *Doctor Who* is a programme that hasn't particularly shied away from looking into behaviour-based reasoning for characters doing strange things. As with anything, there have been varying degrees of success with that, but it always leads to an interesting discussion within and about the fandom.

So with all that in mind, let's get back to the easy question:

'What is your favourite story from *Doctor Who*?'

The looks that I get when I respond with '*The Happiness Patrol*' are like the looks when you tell someone that your favourite candies are those generically wrapped butterscotches that your grandma could produce from her purse like magic when you got antsy at church. I've found the response most people are looking for is generally 'I like it because it has a cool monster'. Yeah, my brainframe doesn't have that setting, but I'll try to be brief.

When I first watched *The Happiness Patrol* on television, the tone had me immediately hooked. I love the TARDIS being painted pink because the weathered blue was too drab, the punk-inspired pink wig uniforms the Happiness Patrol officers wore, and the ridiculous, yet terrifying, Kandyman being your executioner should you not uphold the one unbreakable law of the land on Terra Alpha - simply, always be happy. The notion that happiness is required served as an interesting parallel to the real lie in society that if you aren't completely happy, or at least putting on a facade of happiness at all times, then there is something wrong with you.

The thing that stood out the most to me, though, was the incidental music by Dominic Glynn and the music of Earl Sigma, the med student turned musician who wandered the streets with his harmonica,

440

shifting from flowing blues riffs to upbeat campfire fodder as necessary for survival. As much as I loved this story, I wondered how it could hold up in written form because the music in *The Happiness Patrol* could almost be billed as its own supporting character. I decided to read the Target novel by Graeme Curry, which happened to be my first novelisation of a *Doctor Who* story, to see if there was any way that same eerie tone could maintain. Not only was the tone still there, but I found it confirmed how much this story resonated with me. Removing the music took away that Spielberg/Williams sort of 'Okay, feel this emotion now!' thing that has always bothered me.

In many ways, the lack of music as a primary character in the Target novelisation made me think about new angles from which I identify with this story. The themes were solidified by seeing it in text and processing it in that medium, and it put an emphasis on a real issue that I see in culture regarding how, sociologically, we put such weight on maintaining the perception of normality. Mental illnesses are an invisible enemy, and that makes the looming threat for the person who has the disability all the more stressful while making it easier for those who don't to rationalise it away. In *The Happiness Patrol*, unhappiness is a crime because it is the perspective of the planet's ruler, Helen A, that unhappiness spreads like a virus and makes Terra Alpha a less pleasant place to be. This parallels common societal views that someone who is sad or even melancholy may be less desirable to be around than someone who is constantly upbeat and never down.

There is an exchange where Ace is talking to Susan Q about the auditions to join the Happiness Patrol (where the failure to entertain leads to death):

> *'I'm not Happiness Patrol material anyway. They stand for everything I hate. Like you said, smiling all the time - smiling when it doesn't mean anything. I'm not one of them.'*

Many people with varying mental illnesses would love nothing more than to be 'Happiness Patrol material'. The idea of just shutting down and smiling all the time and living in bliss is certainly appealing in some ways, but it simply isn't a setting that some people have. It doesn't make the conclusions that they are wired to come to any less valid or important.

The Doctor, as he almost always does, in the blink of an eye explains things in a clear and meaningful way that rings as true as any self-help book or therapist could state it:

> *'And what were these opportunities that you gave them?' he asked. 'A bag of sweets? A few tawdry party decorations? Bland soulless music?' He stared at her. 'Do these things make you happy?'*

441

> *Helen A was shaken. It was clear to the Doctor that she hadn't even considered this.*
>
> *'Of course they don't,' he snapped, answering his own question. 'Because they're cosmetic. Because real happiness is nothing if it doesn't exist side by side with sadness.'*

That exchange connects with me on such a basic, yet personal level. Light and dark, summer and winter, hot and cold – these things only work because they are perfectly complementary opposites. Everyone prefers one or the other, but that preference is fuelled directly by the endurance and experience of the opposite. We may view 'normal' as being directly balanced in the middle of the sliding scale, but my experiences tend to show that almost no one is perfectly balanced. We strive for that and we try and aide it in various ways from medication to meditation and beyond, but we may never reach 'normal'.

Helen A learns this lesson too, although it isn't until her beloved pet Fifi has been killed doing her bidding. Only then does she allow herself to experience real sorrow. The novel does an exceptionally better job at showing the love and devotion in this relationship than the television story which, always limited by budget, simply couldn't manage given the distracting ridiculousness of the Fifi prop. I was now able to feel more for Helen A and what she was going through.

We leave Helen A in the same position on the sliding scale that not only those of us that deal with mental illness are in, but the position that everyone is in on in some degree or another. She is navigating through her highs and lows by taking the extreme sorrow of a horrible loss and using it to learn from it and allowing herself to feel it and shape her. Like any of us, the goal is to come through it on the other side and have great days due to the experiences we've had and hope to have in the future. It gives us the belief that, with a little luck and a lot of hard work, happiness will prevail, even when we do realise that we aren't Happiness Patrol material.

You're Never Too Old to Enjoy Your Childhood

Doctor Who - The Space Pirates
by Iain Key
Favourite *Doctor Who* book: *A Celebration*
by Peter Haining

Preface
Irlam Train Station, 13th November 2013 around 4.55pm

The wind is blowing so hard that the trees on the opposite side of the station, the line that heads towards Liverpool, are almost bent in two; the rain lashes downward and then horizontally. I am protected to a degree by my Jack Wolfskin coat, although I have to keep adjusting my laptop bag as it annoyingly slips down from my right shoulder as I try to read the Kindle held in my right hand ...

I'm approaching my 44th birthday and I'm reading *Doctor Who and The Space Pirates* by Terrance Dicks.

I was first attracted to Doctor Who in 1975 although not allowed to watch it until 1977. I fell in love with the show in 1979, discovering Target novelisations and Doctor Who Weekly. I became obsessed in 1981 when I got *The Programme Guide* and the whole history of the show began to reveal itself to me.

I vividly remember watching the first episode of *Castrovalva* in January 1982 on my Dad's black and white portable... actually, that pretty much sums up most of the Peter Davison era... more often than not it would have been in the dining room after tea, other than *The Five Doctors,* which I was allowed to watch on the colour TV in the living room.

By 1984 I had an almost complete set of the Target Books; I'd joined the DWAS and had even been to a local group meeting in Redditch. I can't remember the actual address but my Dad drove me there in his Robin Reliant. The person holding the meeting had a full-size *Earthshock* Cyberman costume and an Ice Warrior too; at some point in the meeting, to everyone's amusement, the Ice Warrior's head fell off as I watched an episode of *Inferno* intently and cracked me on the back of my own. It hurt

By 1987 I was planning my first holiday without my parents. This would have been just before Sylvester McCoy made his debut. I'd begun to be a little disillusioned by the show and I needed money, so

443

with a little reluctance, I sorted through my *Doctor Who* collection and with my friend Paul took my collection to Paramount Book Exchange on Withy Grove in Manchester. Paul was one of my first friends to learn to drive and get a car and was also going on the holiday so was willing to sacrifice his Saturday morning in order for me to raise spending money for our trip to Newquay.

I think I got £60 for my almost complete set of Target Books and more than a hundred issues of Doctor Who Magazine from the near-legendary one-armed shop owner.

Christmas 2011. My wife buys me a Kindle. The first thing I do search online and acquire copies of every *Doctor Who* Target novelisation. They're loaded onto my Kindle, so when I'm travelling for work I have something to read. My love for show the show had been rekindled (no pun intended) over the intervening years as I started to collect the episodes released by the BBC, but for some reason I didn't go back to collect physical copies of the Target Books.

Unfortunately, by April 2012 my wife and I have acquired iPads and my Kindle is tidied away into a drawer.

In September 2013 I started a new job. For the first few months I have to travel to Irlam or Birchwood (the latter being a stop further then the former) to get up to speed with what's what and who's who. Almost as if by magic, the day before I am due to start, I find my Kindle.

I haven't commuted for work for many years, and although my journey is only going to be short, I decided that I needed something to distract me from the packed train and people pushing and shoving. And that's when my love of *Doctor Who* novelisations came back. Over the following few months, I read all those that I'd not seen, from *The Myth Makers* to *The Macra Terror*. Reading those novels again on the journeys to and from work, some for the first time, took me back to the long winter evenings of my early teens where they offered an escape into a magical world of 'new' *Doctor Who* adventures.

So then, there I am, November 2013, a couple of weeks from my birthday and the 50th Anniversary of *Doctor Who* and I finish reading the last 'missing' adventure. I hadn't been looking forward to *The Space Pirates* – it's a story which is often derided, possibly due to the lack of photos and only one episode existing. For Heaven's sake it doesn't even get a re-appraisal in *Hating to Love*... is it really hated that much? But I enjoyed it, maybe because Terrance Dicks is a master craftsman, maybe because he focussed on the story and characters rather than having to explain in detail the long scenes involving space craft. I may not feel the same way about the televised story if the missing episodes appear, but the book reminded me of why I fell in love with the programme so many years ago.

Epilogue
Summer 2016

After a change in personal circumstances, I found myself reconnecting again with my past, hunting down things which I'd sold or let go over the many years to pay bills and make ends meet. Speaking to a few people whose relationships and marriages have broken down, I believe this is the period known as 'finding yourself'.

I struck lucky and managed to buy an entire 'classic era' DVD collection for a reasonable price to replace my collection which I'd sold a couple of years earlier. I soon found myself sorting my newly purchased DVDs into transmission order, revisiting the sleeves and then putting them on the shelf. It gave me a warm glow, but something was missing. There was a space on the shelves.

I casually flicked through eBay, Amazon and eventually Shada on Gallifrey Base, looking for something but not knowing what...and then I saw it: 'Complete Set of Target Novels for Sale'. Again, a reasonable price: messages were exchanged and less than three days later I found myself sorting my newly-purchased Target book collection into transmission order, revisiting the gorgeously evocative sleeves, some of which I've not seen in close detail for almost thirty years. It took me a few hours to work through them and organise them onto shelves. When the job was finally done, I sat back and marvelled at my collection.

Now it felt complete.

Reaching out, I pulled *The Space Pirates* from between *The Seeds of Death* and *The War Games*. Sitting back, I opened it and began to read: *'Beacon Alpha One hung silently in the blackness of space, its complex shape recalling the technology of distant Earth...'*

À la Recherche du Dalek Perdu

Doctor Who - Remembrance of the Daleks
by Andrew Orton
Favourite *Doctor Who* book: *AHistory by Lance Parkin*

Number 154 in the You On Target Library

The Changing Face of the Author of This Book
This adventure features the 154th Author, whose physical
appearance later changed when you reached the end of this article
and turned the page.

1. Escape to Danger

In the wonder of a city sat the wonder of a man.

Far out in that swirling vortex of colours and shapes that is County
Durham, in that mysterious dimension of Durham where time and
space are one, sits a man. Wearing a stylish leather jacket, with a wide,
floppy-brimmed hat and unfeasibly long *****, was that strange
writer of charity pieces known only as Andrew Orton, a handsome
young man with a pleasant, closed face and a shock of dark hair.

With a wheezing, groaning sound he stood up, puffing on an asthma
inhaler and gesticulating wildly as he demonstrated a particularly
intelligent point. 'You see,' he began, 'the Target novelisations have a
peculiar place in the history of *Doctor Who*.' His contemporaries
nodded at his clear accuracy. 'New versions of all of our favourite
Doctor Who stories – and *The Twin Dilemma*...' they laughed at his
brilliant joke before he continued, '...which re-tell the stories of the
series in new and interesting ways. Occasionally, in the books of
Malcolm Hulke or Ian Marter, they provide fresh scenes, exciting
glimpses into things we never saw on telly. But you all know this. And
the key thing about the history of the series as a whole is its
delineation along some very simple lines.' He sighed, remembering the
last time he had attempted to write a piece for a charity anthology,
and hoped the argument playing out amongst he and his colleagues
right now was constructed somewhat better than that one was.

'I read all the Target novelisations between about 1990 and 1995,'
said Orton, handsomely. 'I came upon one of them in my primary
school's library – it was Terrance Dicks's *Doctor Who and the Giant
Robot*, with the comic book Peter Brookes cover – and read it. I was
already something of a burgeoning fan,' he explained, 'but that K1
robot looked fab and I gave it a shot.' He paused to consume a
triangular sandwich, probably the last one on the plate. 'They had

Doctor Who and the Green Death in there too (with the Alun Hood cover) and that was a bit trickier to get into because it was written properly, but it was still fun. The thing about the novelisations was,' he continued, as he pocketed the plate in one of his voluminous pockets, 'that they were very much school library fodder by that point, propped up alongside TV tie-in editions of *The Machine Gunners* from 1983, a battered *Choose Your Own Adventure* about a dangerous undersea journey, or some nonsense featuring *The Moomins* or somesuch: and crucially, they were inextricably linked in the mind of an impressionable but sturdy young youth with those other titles; the only survivors of the discarded remnants and detritus of a barely-stocked school library of fifteen years earlier.

'That was the thing about becoming a fan of *Doctor Who* in 1990, in a small Durhamshire town miles away from anyone else who was interested in the series: there weren't really many videos out yet and it wasn't on telly and you had no mates who watched it. It was a bit tricky to actually see the series. We had to rely on *Doctor Who Monthly*, and the odd Lofficier book, and whatever relics from a more prosperous time we could find on forgotten shelves of distant WH Smiths.

'What a world those books painted: Morka the Silurian. That opening of *Doctor Who and the Dinosaur Invasion* with Shughie McPherson ('A massive claw hit him in the face'). 'Through the ruin of a city stalked the ruin of a man.' 'And Channing smiled a terrible smile.' 'Although they didn't realise it, the Earth had just been conquered.' Words like 'unfeasibly' or 'transcendental' or 'dais' which never appeared in any other book ever written. Everyone in every book was called by their surname, except Jo or Sarah or Liz.

'Soon,' Orton said, moving expertly on to the next phase of his argument, 'I was picking the books up everywhere. I spent ages collecting them, ordering five at a time from Burton Books, having seen adverts for it in the beloved pages of the Monthly. Getting some through the library. And that day... that day when I walked into a second-hand bookshop in Saddler's Yard, and someone had left *their entire collection of Target novelisations there*, including all four of the rare *Trial of a Time Lord* books, *The Wheel in Space*, *Fury from the Deep*, everything. They were a pound each, and I was about thirteen and only had a fiver in my pocket. Argh! That day... I undertook one of the greatest choices in my life that day. I missed out on a first edition of *The Five Doctors* because I already had a copy of the reprint. I was so happy with my prizes (I went for the *Trial* books and *The Wheel in Space*) and read them when I got home; but was still marginally disappointed that I'd missed out on some others. I went back a week later and the entire collection had gone. It was probably one of you lot

447

that bought them.

'I also won the reading list competition at school one year when my diligently-completed recording sheet had 95 Target books on it (that and *Danny the Champion of the World*). My nearest competitor had eleven books. It seems likely I still have those reading lists somewhere. We like lists.

'In short,' he said, reaching a temporary conclusion, 'I would just like to say Klokleda Partha Menin Klatch.'

'Klokleda what?' they all asked.

'It's an old Venusian proverb,' he said, 'and roughly translated it means, 'Terrance Dicks was a genius and the novelisations were our history, our initiation and, most of all, our culture.' They were fantastic.' He sat back down. Although they didn't realise it, Orton had been perfectly correct.

A mumble rumbled around the room.

A massive thought hit him in the face. Some of the story he had recounted from his dais had sounded a little far-fetched. His colleagues had noticed it. They had started to mutter amongst themselves. Then suddenly, one of them stood up, accusingly, and pointed a finger.

'I'm not convinced by these stories! I think you've made them up for this book. I think you're exaggerating elements to make a good story because you've got nothing really interesting to say! Orton, you vile, treacherous degenerate, you're a damned stinking liar and a grotesquely ugly freak! J'accuse!' The rabble cheered.

And Orton smiled a brilliant smile.

2. Durham, January 2016, Sunday, 12:30

> One of the more distinctive features of Target's collection of re-interpretations of the *Doctor Who* stories is that as the range went on, so their style changed significantly. With the availability of VHS and the circulation of pirate copies of television stories – themselves the creation of the new, organised fandom – merely retelling the series was no longer feasible. Something different was called for. So a new breed of authors explored new avenues of fiction...
> *The Children of Dicks, Vol XIX*
> *by Njeri Ngugi (4065)*

'Shut up,' said Orton commandingly, and his opponent sat down, utterly defeated.

His work at deflating the impotent quorum of miserable, insignificant peoples done, Orton continued. The audience were with him again. 'Of course, it all changed by the late 1980s.' He leaned forward. 'The later Target novelisations were the template for a new range of adventures,' he said, assuredly. 'Uncle Terrance was in his fallow period, after his successes with early, exciting novels like *Day of the Daleks* and *The Auton Invasion*, and was now churning out books which were little more than television scripts with the words 'he said' and 'she said' at the end of every line,' he said.

'As things progressed, the new young authors of the later television stories began to see the novelisations in two new lights.' He paused, and ate a biscuit that he briefly offered to a companion but pulled away before she could take it. 'They began to see the novelisations as both an additional money-spinner, and as an opportunity to expand upon their themes and ideas: to complete their stories.' He knew, in his heart, that this meant more than just announcing that the novelisation of *Dragonfire* would explain why the Doctor climbed down that cliff-face – and he knew the others knew this too. What all this said about the original television stories was a moot point: for the novelisations themselves, it was magnificent.

'The novelisations became proto-New Adventures,' he proffered, a smile on his young-old face. 'What the Daleks call *Ka Quaron Falik*. They told the extra bits that the television stories could not, and expanded upon subjects not fully explored on screen, such as the back-story of Fenric, or the history of the Time Lords; things that the television series could not feasibly shoot.' He paused. 'They were excellent.'

He sat back in his chair, content that his point was made. There were a great number of these new, novel-style developments: *Battlefield*, with its future, red-haired Doctor, *The Curse of Fenric*, with its scenes of the Doctor and Fenric pulling bones from the sand to carve into chess-pieces, and *Remembrance of the Daleks*, with its images from early Time Lord society. That all gave way to a new way of writing *Doctor Who* literature. Essentially, when *Remembrance of the Daleks* came out in 1990, it was the first proper novel in the New Adventures style, and for many of the people who lived through the Wilderness Years, the New Adventures were the series.

And didn't they have trouble with the prototype...

A colossal shape hovered above, in the circle of the heavens, silhouetted by the massive bulk of a burning star.

Two figures stood beneath the statue of Helios holding the sun in the doughnut-shaped laboratory courtyard. One, an engineer, large and bearded; the other, a planner, with a moustache and a grand title.

'So, we meet again,' said one.

'This is my control centre,' said his companion.

'Where your plans are wrought.' There was a touch of irony in his voice.

'Plans indeed.'

'What say you?' asked the engineer.

'I want to change the world,' said the second. 'Change how our universe works. Bring down the government. We must needs use our power and position to create something new.'

'Modernisation.'

'I know not if it can be accomplished.'

'We can not do it alone. Where is the other?'

'He attends to his own affairs, Ben.'

A third figure appeared: mysterious, quiet and dark. He nodded to his companions. 'Ben, Andrew. What are you doing at TV Centre? Anyway, I've got this great idea for a thing set in a gothic house,' he announced. 'On Gallifrey. And what if the Doctor was like a vast mountain range in the distance? Powerful and enigmatic. And maybe we can make the companion the focus for a bit.'

'That's a great idea, Marc. It will work well with either of the ideas for the new companion, won't it, Andrew? The Welsh one or the London one?'

'Yes, it will. It'll be Ace.'

'It probably happened a bit like that,' said Orton. 'Even the misprint 'peeing over a shelf' could not detract from what the new breed of writers tried to achieve, being as it was a phrase that must appear at some point in any book on the novelisations, so I'm crowbarring it in here; I'm sure many other authors will too.

'As a result of these developments in the later novelisations, by young left-wing writers looking to say new things about society, the New Adventures range of novels would be born.' As Orton said this, he thought further on to the New Adventures, and the style of early-1990s liberalism and the sexual politic they embodied. 'What this entire change is about is the same debate that raged in the pages of Doctor Who Monthly at the time: trad v rad. Should *Doctor Who* be about old monsters or new people? The fact that characters started to have relationships when their audience started having relationships seems important.' He moved a chess-piece on a board he had been studying as he spoke. He had faith in his argument.

'As it happened, Terrance Dicks never adapted a McCoy television story. Most of the television series authors decided to write their own novelisations. Ben Aaronovitch decided to write a novel.' Orton stopped and thought for a while, unsure whether to reveal more of his thought processes and plans, or keep his cards close to his chest to ensure his scheme played out. He opted to continue.

'Thus a new series was formed, a melting pot of everything the series had been, was or could be. Proper series veterans Terrance Dicks, Andrew Cartmel, Ben Aaronovitch and Marc Platt all wrote for those New Adventures, along with an extraordinary collection of fresh young writers with things to say. Several of those went on to write for the new series of *Doctor Who* when it returned on television. *Remembrance of the Daleks* was the first rad novel that set *Doctor Who* on that trajectory, a ground-breaking work that defined what the next twenty years would bring. How complex things could be. How important the people were. It was magnificent. I read it back in the day and had no idea what most of it was about.' Orton sat down, exhausted, his point made, his argument proven.

Suddenly, a beautiful cropped-haired woman with a big gun in her hands erupted out of puterspace and screamed at the top of her voice at the memory of an eye-stalked alien pepperpot that can't be named that killed her father.

'Cruk it!' she said. 'It's all frocks and guns these days!' Then all her clothes fell off.

Things had changed.

Mission Improbable

Doctor Who – Mission to Magnus
by Ian Wheeler
Favourite *Doctor Who* book: *The Key to Time*
by Peter Haining

You know how it is. You're a twelve-year-old kid, your favourite TV show is *Doctor Who* and then suddenly, without warning, the BBC decides to take it off the air. They say it's just a hiatus and that the show hasn't been axed but you can't help but wonder if it will actually come back. When it does return for a fourteen-part story called *The Trial of a Time Lord*, you can't help thinking that you've missed something. What would it have been like if the BBC had carried on and made the stories that should have been produced and shown during that gap? Is it something you'll just have to wonder about for the rest of your life?

Target comes to the rescue. Good old Target. Target was the Doctor Who fan's greatest friend for many years, giving us permanent records of stories we could never hope to see, and in their final years, they did some mopping up of leftovers, including some of those elusive missing stories from Season 23. The third of these – an intriguing-looking Sil and Ice Warrior tale called *Mission to Magnus* – was probably the one I most regretted not seeing on TV.

I treasured my copy of Mission to Magnus when I got it, even more so when the cover artist Alister Pearson signed it for me at a convention. I told him how much I liked the cover. He winced as he clearly didn't like it himself! That's Alister for you – often very self-effacing about his own work but still one of the all-time great Target book cover illustrators.

So, did I like the story after I'd waited for it all that time? Frankly, I didn't and I'm glad it was never actually made. On paper, it had a lot going for it: a follow-up outing for Sil the Mentor, written by the character's creator Philip Martin, and the return of everybody's favourite Martians, the Ice Warriors. (For me, the lack of appearances by the Ice Warriors following the Jon Pertwee era is one of the great mysteries of *Doctor Who*. John Nathan-Turner loved bringing back old monsters. He possibly did it a little bit too much. Strange that he never brought back the Ice Warriors, given that they had so much potential and iconic status.)

The major problem with *Mission to Magnus* comes when the Doctor meets Anzor, another Time Lord, who bullied him at school. And the Doctor is scared of him. And that simply will not do. The Doctor is there to protect us, to show us that we should stand up to those who mean us harm. I was bullied myself at school and I'm sure many people reading this book were bullied too. But once a week, on a Saturday night, we didn't have to worry about the bullies because the Doctor was there for us. So to show the Doctor himself cowering in front of a bully would have greatly undermined the character and would have been one of the great mistakes of *Doctor Who*.

Mission to Magnus is a fun book but I'm glad it remains 'what might have been' rather than what was!

Dreadful Beginnings

Doctor Who – Ghost Light by AJ Hayes
Favourite *Doctor Who* book: *Lucifer Rising*
by Andy Lane and Jim Mortimore

It was 18th October 1989 and nine-year-old AJ was staying with my Granny. She was busy in the kitchen as I settled down to watch my favourite programme. I had been out for the two weeks before but was excited to catch up on the new story – and the *Radio Times* write-up made it look like it was a good 'un. Just as a bizarre woman in filthy rags placed a beetle in her mouth and giggled, my Granny came in with the tea. 'Oh dear what's this? No, I think we'd better look for something else,' she fussed, and changed the channel. I had just missed *Ghost Light*.

It wasn't until around five years later that I would get my hands on the Target book of *Ghost Light*. In the meantime, I had spent many an hour scouring the second-hand bookshops of the North East seaside town where I lived, and of anywhere else we visited. The New Adventures had started by then so I was spoiled with literary *Doctor Who* riches. I hadn't been reading the NAs in order and wasn't aware of all the televised stories, except from brief descriptions in various reference books. One of my absolute favourites was *Blood Heat* by Jim Mortimore. In that book, there was a character from Ace's past called Manisha. She had died in a terrible fire, but on an alternate Silurian earth she was alive and their meeting was a moment of extreme emotions for Ace. A bit of research revealed this was all linked to Gabriel Chase. It was time to read *Ghost Light*.

The second-hand Targets I had found were an exciting chase over several years but I didn't much like old books: they just felt a bit dirty to me. I sent off to Virgin for a copy of *Ghost Light* and it arrived in the post a week or two later – a pristine copy! Since then, I have received hundreds of new books delivered through my letterbox and it never fails to be tremendously exciting.

I had not yet read Marc Platt's *Cat's Cradle: Time's Crucible*, another NA which was available at the time, and which I would later find difficult to read. *Ghost Light* had the same dense style, but it fit the 19th century setting wonderfully, and every line was worth a re-read (just as well as I had to re-read plenty in order to work out what was going on). The extra detail of the novelisation is really marvellous, especially in the introductory flashback to Ace's childhood where she comes across the house for the first time. It shows her at a time in her life where she is starting to learn about being an adult, and about the real world. At this point, she is at her most primal and just wants to destroy something, a side to her that will be explored again in the following story.

The prose descriptions are also sumptuous, especially the lush fertile wildlife in the flashback where nature seems to be taking over the house, and indeed the human world. All very fitting with the themes of the story. Later, the house is in decay and Reverend Matthews crushes a line of ants without a second thought. Ace does not like 'dead things': another reason she has come to the wrong place. The atmosphere builds and builds – the oddness is there from the beginning, with the housekeeper bringing dinner and an ironed copy of The Times to a dungeon, before worrying about getting her duties completed by 'first light'. I like nothing better than to be set on edge, the feeling that something bad is about to happen but no-one yet knows what. This story had tension coming out of its ears.

Most of the things I loved about the NAs were here in prototype, such as the puppetmaster Doctor playing a complex strategy game against dark, higher forces, using his friends as he saw fit. 'Anyone who travelled in the TARDIS had a price to pay…their lives were in the Time Lord's hands.' Here, he brings Ace to the scene of her worst childhood memory, the house she burned down after her friend Manisha had hers firebombed. The place where she felt an evil presence and never wanted to return. Why has he brought her here? The answer is not entirely clear. The Doctor is setting her a test of initiative, to work out where and when the TARDIS has landed, and what may be going on in this place. He is oblivious to the fact that it may be distressing for her, or believes she will learn a valuable lesson. He may even have altogether greater ambitions for her, but all remains mysterious.

I'm sure the fact that I read the Virgin NAs in my mid-teens had a lot to do with their becoming easily my favourite era of *Doctor Who* as a whole, but they were an integral part of my growing up. The betrayals! The introspection! The terrible sense of dread! And it was all here in *Ghost Light*.

And Then the Day Came When I Knew I Had to Have Them All

Doctor Who – Survival by Mike Morgan
Favourite *Doctor Who* book: *Remembrance of the Daleks*
by Ben Aaaronovitch

When Rona Munro's novelisation of *Survival* was released in October 1990, I was in my third and final year at Staffordshire University. Student days were filled with beer, working shifts in the campus bar and rare bouts of intensive late-night study.

I was twenty years old – less than half my current age – and my interest in Target paperbacks extended only so far as keeping up with the most interesting looking of the new releases, primarily the adaptations of the Sylvester McCoy stories I'd watched only one or two years previously. Even then, I appreciated how much better the stories were on the printed page, how much less embarrassing the monsters were and how much more intriguing the Seventh Doctor was once the character was divorced from McCoy's sometimes unconvincing portrayal. When I read these stories instead of watching them, I didn't cringe. Like many fans who had stuck with the series throughout the 80s, I had far too much experience of cringing.

Oh, I knew the books were really meant for kids. For every *Remembrance of the Daleks* and *Terminus* in the Target range, there were at least ten on the level of a *Famous Five* story (and they were just as cliché ridden), but I blithely ignored that minor detail. The range was trying to become more mature and the recent covers had been simply beautiful: tremendously detailed works of art by Alister Pearson. I sometimes bought the books for the cover art alone.

Survival, too, had a stunning cover. The contents were less stellar, falling at the more juvenile end of the range's recent output. *Remembrance of the Daleks* is a book I read again and again. Likewise, *Battlefield* and *Ghost Light* are volumes whose pages I have cracked open many a time. *Survival*? Not so much.

I wasn't disappointed enough to stop reading. I wanted a hit of *Doctor Who* and the novelisations were my only source. It hardly needs to be said that the programme itself was gone by this point: *Survival* had been its last hurrah, only the year before.

Still furious at the low-key cancellation of the programme just as it was starting to improve again, I was far from convinced by the continuing claims that it would return one day soon. It's hard to credit, but in the months following the end of what we now call the classic series, bigwigs at the Beeb insisted with straight faces that they were interested in bringing the programme back, albeit produced by an independent company. What they were actually interested in was trying to create a new smash hit show they could claim personal credit for devising, spending their meagre budgets on various new series that history would soon forget rather than in investing wisely in the triumph of imagination they already had. The grass is always greener...

But this is an essay about the book, not the programme that spawned it, and the book, abjectly average though it was, had an impact. The impact was a cumulative affair, another brick in the cobblestoned path towards a burgeoning obsession. The people reading this collection of essays probably all share that obsession: the need to own, to possess, to hold in their suddenly perspiring mitts the entire range... even the thought of the quest is enough to make me smile.

Is it nostalgia that fuels such an urge, that can bring such happiness at the mere thought of what are, in the final analysis, just flimsy paperbacks? In the beginning, the drive to have more and more of the books was simply a result of not being able to afford the video tapes, and I wanted to know what happened in those stories I had never seen, never thought I would be able to buy for myself, never dreamed I would view in their full, restored glory.

But after a while, once I amassed a certain number of these slender volumes, a thought began to coagulate in the fecund underworld of my subconscious: *would it be so hard, would it be so terrible just to carry on buying these books until, until, until... one day, you'll have them all... them all...*

Impossible, I thought, there are too many, and some of them are far too expensive. And, come on, be serious, they're kids' books. No, it's completely out of the question. The grown-up thing to do is to go down the pub and blow far more money on beer, and then nurse a monumental hangover for the majority of the following day, quite obviously. That's the mature course of action, without question.

You know there are foreign language editions too, whispered the voice in tempting tones.

I put the idea behind me and focused on adult pursuits: beer, women, avoiding studying.

And then I graduated in the midst of a recession, and I was unemployed. For a long time.

Being unemployed is horrible: it destroys your soul. It brings on depression, poverty, ennui, and a thousand other complaints that sap you of your will to live. I needed something, anything, to cling to in the face of a sucking emotional maw of hopelessness and pointlessness.

457

I discovered charity shops sold *Doctor Who* Target paperbacks really cheaply (or they did in those days).

You have nothing else to do, said the voice. I had stopped collecting the books. I started collecting them again. They made me feel safe. They helped me ignore my life.

'Well,' I thought one day. 'I obviously like *Doctor Who* a lot. I should join a club. Meet some likeminded people. Get out of the house where I have been hiding from the world. Try not to be so miserable.' So I did.

I joined the Stoke-on-Trent *Doctor Who* club and went to various gatherings at the YMCA where they showed videos of old Jon Pertwee and Tom Baker stories. I made friends. Friends who gathered me into their social circles and made me feel loved. Friends I still have to this day. Friends like Lea, Ian, and Kath.

And I kept on collecting the novelisations. When I (finally) got a job, Virgin started printing the New Adventures, so they joined the stacks of Targets on my bookshelves. Saturdays fell into a ritual pattern: go to bookstore, buy latest *Doctor Who* book, go to pub, read book over beer and greasy food, meet up with friends, get utterly wasted. Fun times. No, *great* times.

Saturdays were my favourite day of the week. The other days? Eh, they were not as terrific. Work was awful. Something had to give. I moved to the far side of the world. I'm not exaggerating.

My friends helped me box up my books. They carefully put them into their storage areas and attics. They didn't want me to leave. But I needed to do something with my life. I needed to do more.

So, I found myself in Japan. I worked hard, I dove into the local culture (eventually) and I used the internet to buy more Target paperbacks. Well, of course I did! With a salary like that? What else was I going to use it for? I even made a special trip to a store in Tokyo so I could buy the Japanese language editions. The day had come – I knew I had to have them all, regardless of language. And yes, I even had to possess *Turlough and the Earthlink Dilemma*.

I am in the thrall of pure obsession, and I know I am. You know what? I regret nothing.

More than two decades have passed since I truly got into collecting Target paperbacks. Do I have them all yet? No, I don't; the quest continues. These days, the gaps in my collection are so small, the 'quest' is really just an occasional search online to see if *The Wheel in Space* has got any cheaper (nope, it hasn't). There are (I think) two others I need, but they're at the astronomical end of the price spectrum too. I console myself with the thought that I have virtually every other *Doctor Who* fiction book ever published, barring a few over-priced Big Finish anthologies. I certainly have enough to drive my wife to distraction.

Contrary to what my younger self thought, too, I have a great many of those TV stories on DVD now, and I can watch them when kids and work permit. My twenty-year-old self would never have believed it possible. My twenty-year-old self would have scoffed at the idea that my/our life could take this path: Japan and then America, a wife and then two children. My twenty-year-old self was, unsurprisingly, an idiot.

My wife says, 'You have the DVDs, do you really need the books too?' She eyes the shelf space like a predator, considering the unpacked boxes of her own books.

I pretend not to hear her. Yes, I need the novelisations. I'm sure you understand.

These days, I don't have as much time to read them, but I'm glad they're *there*. On the shelves, waiting.

Perhaps, given the theme of this essay, I should read *Survival* again. Go on, I will; I'll make time. The memory cheats, after all. It's been 25 years; surely it can't be as stultifyingly mediocre as I remember.

I find it quickly on my carefully organised shelves. I crack open the beautiful cover and I start to read...

No, it's still crap.

Thankfully, that's not the point.

You've Gotta Have Faith

Doctor Who – The Curse of Fenric
by Adam Lighterness
Favourite *Doctor Who* book: *Timewyrm: Exodus*
by Terrance Dicks

Target books! Oh, what a sharp twang of joy is let loose in my heart upon hearing those two words together. A rush of nostalgia grips me and I am instantly transported back to my youth. These books were as much a part of my childhood and early adult life as the TV series itself, Wolverine and Nightcrawler, Green Lantern and Green Arrow, the Muppets, the Bash Street Kids!

Doctor Who had always been around for me. I was born in 1977 and the programme was a staple of our household. I had a couple of clear memories of the grinning goon Tom Baker as the Doctor, but for the most part Davison, Baker and McCoy charted the course through my childhood. At some point I had been bought *Doctor Who – The Making of a Television Programme* which detailed the making of *The Visitation* (a personal favourite of my dad; even now he mentions that 'the aliens started it' whenever the Great Fire of London comes up). At the beginning of the book were pictures of the previous doctors – Baker I knew, Pertwee I knew from *Worzel Gummidge* and *SuperTed*...but who were these other two in black and white? William Hartnell and Patrick Troughton? Semi-mythical figures as far as I was concerned. Troughton was in a fur coat with his hands chained above him and Hartnell apparently arranging some sort of pyramid. My journey into geekdom would later place all of these pictures with their correct stories but there is still a wonderful feeling of nostalgia that rushes over me when I see one of the early stories and remember that initial step into the unknown.

My journey with Target started with the paperback of *Doctor Who and the Dinosaur Invasion*. It was the reprint edition with the Tyrannosaurus Rex outside St. Paul's Cathedral on the cover. My dad bought it for me when young and obviously thought that it was a good bet – Doctor Who *and* dinosaurs? Boy was he right. By this time, I would have been around ten years old. The series was going great guns – the girl who presented *Corners* was the companion, the Daleks and Cybermen made reappearances and there were wonderful new villains. The break at the end of the 25th series in 1988 allowed me more time to get acquainted with older Doctors. I made a trip to my local library, certain that I had seen some *Doctor Who* books on my last visit there. I wasn't to be disappointed. Everywhere I looked there seemed to be more of them – rows upon rows, hardbacks aplenty and lots more paperbacks squirrelled away on the revolving stands. The older, hardback books were what mainly caught my eye, rich in illustration and written by a variety of names – Dicks, Letts, Hulke, Grimwade, Holmes, Luccarotti, Marter – some of which I recognised but most were exotic and different.

I came away with copies of *Doctor Who and the Loch Ness Monster* (the Doctor had met the Loch Ness Monster? Of course he had, but how? And who with? And when?), *The Three Doctors* (complete with illustrations on the cover that left me under no illusions which three they were), *The Seeds of Doom* (looking like a big budget movie with an enormous monster on the roof of a country house) and *The Auton Invasion* (Jon Pertwee looking serious on the cover along with a young-looking Brigadier and another big space monster). I think I devoured the Loch Ness Monster story in an afternoon and went back for more (we were limited to six items in those days as opposed to the thirty I can get on a library card now). So began the journey – I would return to the library each week and cycle back with more new titles. Even now I can remember which library I got which book from and what cover and edition they were.

When the series returned in 1989, I had learnt a wealth of information about it. I had also been using my pocket money to begin my own collection and my shelf of paperbacks slowly began to grow as I played catch-up and discovered hidden gems and nuggets. I thought then (and still do) that the new series was great – the return of Bessie and the Brigadier (battling a demon no less), the Doctor as Merlin, a bizarre haunted house story, the return of the Master and a whole planet of cheetah people! But top of the list for me and still one of my all-time favourite stories was *The Curse of Fenric.*

I have always been interested in mythology: stories and legends, Gods, monsters and the eternal fight between good and evil. I was raised a Catholic so suppose it came with the package. The idea of the Doctor having a hand in various mythologies or even being a God to others is an interesting idea and has been touched upon in the series (both old and new). The old Norse myths were well known to me and Fenrir, Odin, Fricka, Heimdall, Tyr, Thor and Loki, the tree of life and the rainbow bridge were all familiar concepts to me and to see them incorporated into my favourite series was a joy.

I was confused by the lack of a TV series in 1990 but the Target novelisations caught up with the McCoy era and provided something of a cushion. There were also reprints of old novels so I was able to fill some holes in my collection. The latest artist was Alister Pearson and I was very impressed with his work. How could one man provide such wonderful and accurate work? When the novelisation of *The Curse of Fenric* appeared in November 1990, it was a major bonus for me

461

(although I still couldn't work out why they didn't come out in broadcast order!) and I snapped it up as soon as I saw it. I even ended up recreating the cover for an art project in school.

The book was everything that I had hoped for and more. It expanded on the broadcast version to great effect and Ian Briggs used every opportunity to build on the story that he has created. As well as the main narrative, we get several cutaway chapters to deal with different documents. The first is a young Millington's school essay on the fall of the Gods which shows the obsession of the young man with Fenric. 'The Curse of the Flask' fills in a big part of the backstory and charts the course of the flask from Turkey to Norway, as well as the trail of bodies the curse leaves in its wake. We then get a letter from Bram Stoker who seems inspired and invigorated after a visit to Maiden's Bay and a grisly discovery. What better inspiration for the story of Dracula?

The most interesting addition for me is a story from Arabia that is recounted by the mysterious Alee Sheyr and tells the story of the original battle between El Dok Tar and the evil Jinee Ahoo Fenfun. It's a twist on an old tale of three princes vying for the hand of a princess and apparently reveals how the Doctor defeated Fenric and where the flask started its journey. It also seemingly introduces a new companion as El Dok Tar takes the slave girl Zeleekha away with him, with her returning a couple of years later recounting her tales of journeys between the stars.

Touches like this made me fall in love with the book. Ian Briggs has obviously relished the opportunity to expand his tale and cement it in *Doctor Who* mythology. I loved the legend shrouding El Dok Tar and used it as my Dungeons and Dragons name for ages afterwards! Each character is given more of a background and fleshed out as well. Reverend Wainwright in particular, still mourning the loss of his parents and fighting to hold onto his faith during the war, cuts a tragic figure. Presented in the book as a young man rather than the silver haired Nicholas Parsons, you get a better sense of his internal struggles and it makes his death even sadder. Where the book makes clear that the Doctor takes faith from his past companions, Wainwright finds his faith in God slipping and pays the ultimate price. One can only hope there was a God to meet him on the other side.

The epilogue of the book adds to another *Doctor Who* mystery as well – the fate of Ace. It's something that has never been officially resolved. The epilogue picks up on the deleted scene from *Silver Nemesis* where the Doctor and Ace discover a portrait in Windsor Castle apparently of Ace in regency period costume. In the epilogue to Fenric, the Doctor and Ace (going by the name Dorothée) meet in Paris in 1887. Ace has obviously been there for some time and has ingratiated herself into Parisian life. They discuss Fenric and the nature of good and evil and Ace reveals that she's fallen for a Russian count named Sorin. This throws up an intriguing concept – what if Ace did end up marrying Sorin's grandfather? The machinations of Fenric indeed!

Target books rightly deserve their place in *Doctor Who* legend and they have made a significant impact in fans' lives. I recently unearthed my copies from the loft and remember them fondly. The joy of finding and starting a new one, of learning new adventures, of immersing further into the Who universe and meeting old Doctors and companions: for all of these things I am grateful. *The Curse of Fenric* certainly had an impact on me as I could see the opportunities for the novels and the show in general. My dog-eared copy was always close to me and I think it still stands as one of the best of the range and a great example of a job done right. For me, the Target books got better with age and *The Curse of Fenric* was part of a great final swansong.

A King, A Queen, An Ace and A Wild Card

Doctor Who – Battlefield by Nick Campbell
Favourite *Doctor Who* book: *The Scarlet Empress*
by Paul Magrs

In the summer of 1991, Marc Platt's novelisation of *Battlefield* was a landmark for the saddest of reasons, bookending a project begun in the heady, mercury-fuelled days of David Whitaker. Though there would be Pescatons come the autumn, *Battlefield* was the last TV story Virgin Books had the rights to adapt. More significantly, there were no more televised stories to come. To all intents and purposes, *Doctor Who* was done. Somewhere there was danger; somewhere there was injustice; somewhere else (the sci-fi shelves of WH Smith), the second in a series of New Adventures novels was just out. The wider population, though (and in 1991 that included eight-year-old me) had let the TARDIS slip away.

Three years later and, for me if no-one else, things had changed. No visit to my Nan in the little seaside town of Worthing was now complete without a trip to Badger (Second-Hand and Antiquarian) Books, and particularly its musty back room, with the atmosphere of a temple and the glorious totem pole that was a book carousel as tall as me, full of Target books. Years after that carousel mysteriously dematerialised, the thought of it still thrills my heart. Those books represented almost thirty years of stories still to yield their secrets, and I loved them as both texts and talismans. Through the work of Terrance Dicks, Ian Marter or David Whitaker, I experienced those stories as I imagined their most earnest and adoring viewers might have seen them. Moreover, they were the evidence of a once thriving cult, often with a name on the inside cover to prove it had all been real. They were the bardic songs of a long-lost king and the treasures of his people, both at once.

Between these books and the odd VHS, I was weaving and looping through time, discovering *Doctor Who* backwards and by instinct, choosing stories on the basis of covers and blurbs. (I thought I was so special.) I could write in praise now of *The Abominable Snowmen* (my first), *The Daleks* (my favourite), *The Five Doctors* (mindboggling), *The Rescue* (so cleverly done), *The Auton Invasion* (my other favourite) and the list runs on. But I'd like to consider what makes Marc Platt's *Battlefield* so special, even though I didn't read it for years afterward.

I was bumping through the twisty roads of North Wales on a single decker bus, between the fields, mountains and farm houses of a rural landscape, on the map almost diagonally opposite Sussex, which for years had been my home. I won't go into the circumstances of my great move north-west, but let's just say that on this particular bus-ride, Marc Platt's novel was very, very welcome escapism. You can't fail to be transported by it, I think. It's so dense with world-building detail, it can almost kid you there was a rogue year in the late 1990s when Charles was on the throne and we were all flinging £5 ecucoins about the place (and what an ambitious tribute all of that is to the years of PM Jeremy and his female successor).

I had come around to reading *Battlefield* now because at the age of 24 I had suddenly discovered King Arthur. I hadn't cared for that macho nonsense as child: it was only now that I happened to open my Mum's old Puffin edition of the tales (retold by ex-Inkling, Roger Lancelyn Green) that I saw it wasn't macho, at least not in any modern sense. Even in Puffin's version, it was arcane and uncanny and tragic and mystical. It was the Holy Grail and the Isle of Avalon and the Dolorous Stroke, it was refraining from erotic longing and yielding to forbidden passions and capitulating to terrible unavoidable fates. Moreover, it wasn't called the Matter of Britain for nothing: it was written into local folklore throughout the British Isles. Merlin himself was said to have stolen the young Arthur away to 'the deep and mysterious valleys of North Wales, which was then called Gwynedd' – as in Gwynedd, the place I now found myself to be living. My romantic heart was stirred. It was possibly even better than the fact *The Abominable Snowmen* was filmed about twenty minutes' walk from our house.

So here I was reading the novelisation of *Battlefield* to see what Marc had made of what Ben Aaronovitch had made of Britain's most enduring folk cultural hero, in an encounter with King Arthur.

Back in September 1989, I used to dare myself to watch the *Doctor Who* title sequence up to the start of the show, and then pounce on the TV to switch it off before something came on and terrified me. Across the country, TV viewers followed my example, for their own reasons. At the back of my mind, I was vaguely thinking I would watch the show one day soon, when I was a big tough boy like those at school, but for various reasons this was never going to happen, and at least one of these reasons is that only three and half million people watched *Battlefield*.

Obviously, ratings aren't everything. But even re-watching the show today, the TV version remains – and I say this with love – a bit of a mess. Despite some great work, and some fantastic moments, nothing quite coheres. *Doctor Who* has had many virtues over the years, from unorthodox heroism to teatime terror for tots, from brilliant cliff-hangers to bonkers costumes, but if there is one

465

consistent feature of *Doctor Who* that makes me love it, from Hartnell to Magrs, it's audacious creativity when others would take the easy path. *Battlefield* might be a victim of this mentality. *Doctor Who* was unloved, unfashionable, unwatched. Andrew Cartmel and Ben Aaronovitch could have turned in a cheap adventure with sexy leads and evil aliens, but they went for an ambitious story about parallel worlds: one that contrasted our fears and fantasies of the modern military with those of the 1970s and, indeed, the 470s and then to ask, where is the Doctor in this? Heroic? Moral? A figure of the past or of the moment?

They could have played it safe; instead they played a wild card.

Likewise, in 1991 nothing was stopping Marc Platt from writing an entirely straightforward adaptation of the story seen in 1989. (*Ghost Light* and *Survival*, both enjoyable novels, are faithful to the shooting script, even if they take things up a notch here and there.) The show was over. This particular story had its fans and its detractors. He could have opened Chapter One: 'It was a beautiful day in the garden centre, "Oh, show some enthusiasm, Alistair." ' did Brigadier Lethbridge-Stewart, hotly... Slip in a few lost scenes here and there and we would have been content.

Instead, Platt's novel begins in the ancient past, with Arthur's last battle and the loss of Excalibur. It proceeds, via a snatch of 29th Century Bardic Ballad, to Brigadier Bambera being recalled from action in Zimbabwe to a briefing in Geneva, followed by a disconcerting communion between Arthur's sword and the Doctor's TARDIS that nearly scuppers the ship entirely, till it sluggishly remembers 'that it had a pilot who was capable of taking over manual control.' After this comes a scene from the broadcast version, but it's completely rewritten: enhanced, expanded, electrically charged. Most importantly, the focus of the scene is on the mysterious message's appeal to 'Merlin...'

Platt takes an obvious cue from Aaronovitch's own *Remembrance* novelisation of the previous year, with backstory, dreams and childhood memories for almost every character. It feels like every detail of the broadcast version is enlarged, not gratuitously, but to get its due significance. When we finally see the Lethbridge-Stewarts, it's a flashback to their first reunion, where we see her propose to him. This isn't mere fan service: it means we actually care about their separation during the story, and makes Alistair's return to UNIT – which he refuses point blank until the Doctor is invoked – all the more significant.

Vague references to a storm on TV become a country-wide hurricane against whose ferocity other aspects of the story make renewed sense: the village is isolated, Bambera is stranded and the

466

nuclear convoy is driven almost into the lake. The missile itself, somewhat under-emphasised on telly until Morgaine tries to use it, looms over the novel. It's the dry tinder the Doctor keeps trying to prevent igniting amidst the constant battles. It's the emblem of a world still recognisably wracked with political tensions: it isn't just Morgaine's use of the missile against Carbury that the Doctor fears, but the ensuing response from the rest of the world.

At one point, Morgaine deliberately draws the Doctor to protect the missile so that Ace is more vulnerable. It's there onscreen, but in the novel the Doctor takes a much clearer gamble, and almost loses everything. This became more important when I was recently re-reading all the novels of the era. Reading *Remembrance* reminded me what a dangerous quantity this Doctor is: cute, clever and morally indignant, but also underhand and manipulative, capable of genocide without a lip-wobble. In the alternate dimension of the Target books, perhaps *Battlefield* can follow *Ghost Light* and *The Curse of Fenric*. Perhaps the story can be told differently.

For the first time, we witness the Doctor's self-doubt. He sees himself reflected in the stories of Merlin, faced with the fact that he will die again, and live anew, perhaps even more irresponsible than he is now. At times, he dreads the thought of being so 'enmeshed' in his own fate. These are ideas so good that inevitably they've since been explored in all sorts of ways (River Song, Trenzalore) but the use of Arthurian myth lends his anxiety a deeper grandeur, as well as the chance perhaps to reflect on his recent behaviour. Morgaine thinks he's a chess-player, when in fact it's all about poker and, ultimately, his faith in Ace.

The Brigadier ('le grand fromage') gets all the best lines, but this is ultimately Ace's novel. Her jealousy of the Brigadier's friendship with the Doctor comes from scenes cut from the broadcast version, but Platt makes it part of this ongoing narrative of her unique relationship with the Doctor. At one point, Ace tells Shou Yuing, 'I don't trust him to guard the Doctor's back. That's my job.' But on more than one occasion, he's described as her mentor, and she as his protégé. If the Doctor really is Merlin, that makes her 'the sorcerer's apprentice!' as she says, excitedly. Or is it Sir Lancelot? Is she an eternal warrior like the Brigadier, or an oncoming storm like the Doctor?

I have to say I particularly love Platt's description of the spaceship's destruction, a joint effort from friends past and present. The Doctor watches from afar, and sees two figures: one, 'solid and stentorian ... unblanching at [the explosion's] fury', the other 'tiny and nimble', capering about in 'a sort of dance of triumph'. It's somehow incredibly touching. Perhaps this is how the Doctor's friends appear to him – little, incredibly concentrated figures, more alike than they can see.

467

The Doctor's reconciliation with his identity, and Ace's with her own, are hard won, and done through the kaleidoscope re-readings of King Arthur. Is it all the same story? How can we go on telling it and making it new? And what happens to those stories when, like the Doctor finding out about Merlin, we read them out of order and back to front, in spirals and surprises?

(Like I said, I used to think I was special. But the young *Doctor Who* fans of the last ten years are reading these stories completely anew, and will go on doing so.)

I must also mention Merlin himself. In the prologue, we get a brief glimpse of him, with his curly red hair and afghan coat. In the closing chapter, the Doctor is resigned to his strange destiny. 'With luck he might spend several lifetimes avoiding it.' Two years after *Doctor Who* is supposedly over, Marc Platt, like the truest of fans, is looking to 'several lifetimes' more, and beyond: something even stranger, yet still recognisable.

I think that's the best spirit of all in which to tell this ongoing story

One Less Gap

Doctor Who – The Pescatons
by Matthew Kresal
Favourite *Doctor Who* book: *Human Nature*
by Paul Cornell

The Pescatons, both in its original audio drama form and as a novelisation published fifteen years later, stands out among the works of *Doctor Who* fiction: one of the earliest works made specifically for the audio medium was to be among the last stories to be novelised. It could have been a golden opportunity as well for something of a last hurrah for the range.

As an audio drama, *The Pescatons* was a rather limited affair. Victor Pemberton, a veteran of the Troughton era, was working with a lot of constraints – limited to just three actors and a 45-minute running time to fit on the LP – but the result turned out to be a highly enjoyable piece of work. After his excellent work novelising his own *Fury from the Deep*, one could only imagine what he might be able to do with this story in prose.

Sadly, I was left with what felt like a mixed bag between my fingers. Pemberton did take the opportunity to expand out the basics of the story, filling in characters and sequences that Tom Baker's narration had covered in a couple of line; he also allowed a wider scope of events beyond the Doctor and Sarah Jane, though strangely UNIT was still nowhere to be seen. Yet none of it really added depth to the story; it felt less like an expansion of the story I had enjoyed so much and more like filler material. Not necessarily bad... just underwhelming.

Maybe it was the limited page count. Pemberton wrote a bumper-sized volume for *Fury from the Deep* and *The Pescatons* was to be the last regularly-sized Target book. What could he have made of the story given the page count of one of John Peel's subsequent Dalek novelisations? Would it have been better? Would the characters who felt wooden have been given more depth? Or would it have involved even more filler?

We'll never know, of course. Yet I'm still glad to have it sitting on my shelf. It may not add much but it does have nice moments. Plus it's one less gap in the collection and, let's be honest, as fans we can't have that. Can we?

Chapter 5

Too Broad and Too Deep

1992 – 2017

Virgin Publishing are busy with a range of original fiction books
called *The New Adventures*, but find time to release three more
novelisations in 1993-4. The subsequent 23 years see a few more
novelisations emerge before, in 2011, when gaps begin to be filled as
Gareth Roberts adapts *Shada*. In 2011-13, then again in 2016, BBC
Books begins reissuing selected Target novelisations.

Also in these years

American gets its first black President... Britain votes to leave the
European Union... mobile phone technology advances far enough to
leave most of *Doctor Who* looking old-fashioned... Diana, Princess of
Wales, dies... *Top of the Pops* is taken off the air... Jon Pertwee
becomes the third Doctor to leave us... *Doctor Who* returns for one
night only in 1996, then makes a permanent comeback in 2005...

A New Hope

Doctor Who – The Power of the Daleks
by David Kitchen
Favourite *Doctor Who* book: *Timewyrm: Exodus*
by Terrance Dicks

'Which Doctor was your Doctor?'

It's a question that fills me, as a *Doctor Who* fan, with a strange mix of melancholy and joy. The questioner always wants to know which golden era of the show was being broadcast in my youth. If the question is asked of my dad, he can talk about Hartnell & Troughton, and coming home on cold winter nights from rugby practice as an eleven-year-old to watch those first stories. Many of my friends in fandom can get nostalgic and talk about discovering Tom Baker on the TV in the 1970s, whilst there are kids today who have a whole new series to discover and enjoy.

But I was born in 1980.

Whilst in my earliest days I was able to see the JNT era go out, and enjoyed the seemingly never-ending repeats of Pertwee and Baker on the ABC, by the time I was seven it was clear the show was already struggling, and had become something of an embarrassment in Australia, lumped in with the children's after school viewing. By the time I was nine years old, *Doctor Who* had been cancelled, seemingly forever.

I was also born in Australia. Even now, it's almost as far as you can get from UK fandom geographically (apart from our Kiwi cousins, of course) and in the pre-internet era that feeling of isolation from mainstream fandom was palpable, and in some ways defining.

All this meant that as I entered my prime geekdom years, ready to truly embrace *Doctor Who*, there was no *Doctor Who*.

Even the Target novels were starting to come to an end.

As long as I'd been alive, they'd been on the bookshelf, steadily growing in number. I remember fondly my dad reading me a chapter a night at bedtime from the latest Terrance Dicks adaption, and the first novel I read to myself aged seven was *The Dalek Invasion of Earth* (which was a surreal experience, as the story was nothing like the *Daleks – Invasion Earth: 2150AD* movie we had on tape). But soon there would be no more stories to novelise, and these books too would apparently end. What merchandise there was at this time seemed to be a desperate yearning for a simple past; Dapol figures, script books and poorly-researched reference books were the order of the day.

It's in this context that the novelisation of *The Power of the Daleks* feels so important to me: it was the start of something new. A new

471

hope. The beginning of *my* era of *Doctor Who*. When *The Power of the Daleks* was released in July 1993 I read it cover to cover in record time, followed two months later by the equally wonderful *The Evil of the Daleks*.

In my memory, this was the point at which *Doctor Who* fandom – both the professional and the amateur – decided that the future was ours for the taking, and didn't have to be defined by what had gone in the past. It perhaps also acknowledged that with no show on TV to hook new fans into *Doctor Who*, the average age of fandom was only going to increase as existing fans grew older and no one younger joined us.

The novel most obviously shows this in its increased length, more than double that of a traditional Target novel. This allowed for a slightly more evolved writing style, and for more time spent getting to know the characters and their motivations. Feelings and relationships that would have barely been hinted at in the past could now be explored, and the role of minor characters expanded.

This is especially fitting given the historic nature of this story. We all know just how important Patrick Troughton's first story in the role was to the history of *Doctor Who*. We all know that the show would never have survived were this moment done badly – and future debut stories for later Doctors demonstrate just how easy it is to blow these moments. So, having the longer page count to really explore the moment is of intense value to the reader, and I know just how much I revelled in that.

The story is also missing from the archives, and unable to be watched today. In this, *The Power of the Daleks* is similar to other Target novelisations, as it allows fans to experience and feel a story that we otherwise would not be able to. Yet it is perhaps difficult to remember how much it seemed that we'd never get this story in print, either. At the time the Target run was wrapping up the McCoy era, I remember a pervading and regretful acceptance in fandom that seven stories would never be novelised, including the two classic Troughton/Dalek adventures, which uniquely would be missing both on video and in print. They would be the most missing of missing stories.

As such, when I heard the news that John Peel would be allowed to write it (for our assumption was that permission to write Dalek stories was in the gift of Terry Nation personally), it was almost as though the episodes themselves had been found. I still remember today the wait for the publication date to come, and then the even more excruciating wait for copies to arrive in Australia – excruciating because you just didn't know *when* it would suddenly appear in the local book shop.

John Peel's novel, with his wholehearted embracing of continuity, feels like the transition to a new era. Freed from the old and familiar house style of the bulk of the Target run, Peel adds in a prologue linking this story with *Doctor Who* continuity forward and backward. References are made to the Cyber-invasion from *The Tenth Planet* – not unnaturally, as that was the preceding story – but also to characters and adventures not even conceived of in 1966, such as Sarah Jane Smith, or Allison Williams from *Remembrance of the Daleks*. IMC from *Colony in Space* (or rather, *Doctor Who and the Doomsday Weapon*) also form part of the story's background.

More than twenty years later, older and grumpier fans will disparaging dismiss these references as over the top. Some will coin the term 'fan service', while others will use a ruder word to conjure up the same idea. And perhaps it was a little over the top, but that didn't stop me lapping it up at the time, smiling at every little reference, feeling that this story really was part of one continuing history. Whilst imperfect in its execution, it was the start of an era that embraced the concept of a consistent *Doctor Who* universe, with a continuity that permeated throughout it.

One of the principal elements of this new era was Virgin's New Adventures range of books. These in fact started a little under two years before John Peel's books were published, but the announcement of his novelisations occurred just as Virgin's original novels were proving that they had staying power. It was all part of that new direction of *Doctor Who*. The New Adventures arrived the month I turned eleven and finished two months short of my 18th birthday. They weren't on TV, but for me they were there at the right time; they were my era of *Doctor Who*. Imperfect? Yes. Of their time? Unquestionably. But they were mine. And *The Power of the Daleks* will forever be the keystone which links the Virgin era, the TV series and the Target range. The missing link allowing evolution to happen, transitioning one version of the series into another.

Importantly, this age of *Doctor Who* long-form books was a gateway drug for me to the novels of other series. I quickly started buying the *Star Trek* original novels; it was Timothy Zahn's *Star Wars* trilogy beginning with *Heir to the Empire* that turned me into a fan more so than the films; my *Red Dwarf* novels were the only genre novels that others at high school wanted to read, allowing me for a brief moment to share my love of sci-fi. I doubt I would have embraced any of these had I not embraced *Doctor Who* books first. I even found and read the *Blake's 7* novel *Afterlife*...but not everything in this time can be wonderful.

Books like *The Power of the Daleks* and the Virgin range kept fandom alive, so that when I was a teenager there *was* a fandom for me to join and enjoy, and the friends I met then I still know today. To me, it represents the start of an era where *Doctor Who* grew up a little and found a new voice for a new time. *Doctor Who* chose not to fade away with the TV series, but neither did it decide to be shackled by what had gone before. As a result, it became something even more wonderful. There I was, a young boy in Australia starting high school, perfectly placed to enjoy it and let it help shape my teen years. My prime fandom years.

I may not have had an onscreen Doctor of my own, but this was my era.

The Human Factor

Doctor Who – The Evil of the Daleks
by Robert Morrison

Favourite *Doctor Who* book: *Time and Relative*
by Kim Newman

Unorthodox. I am the unorthodox *Doctor Who* fan. Whenever I talk about becoming a *Doctor Who* fan, I'm always fond of saying that I came to the show 'out of order'. That extends to what medium I experienced the show in, as much as to the order I watched the television stories in. We all have our *own* era of the show, and my era involved paperback books, the local library and second-hand book shops. My era is the 'Wilderness Era', and that is as unorthodox as you can get. I come from the 'Era of Books', although not necessarily in the way that you might think. I'm unorthodox, you see.

Books are, perhaps, an unconventional way to become a fan of a television series but that's what happened to me, and to understand it, we need to journey back in time. Consider the availability of *Doctor Who* in the early 1990s and then look at the *Doctor Who* landscape today. There's a new series (or at least a Christmas Special) every year on BBC1, with repeats on channels like BBC Three, Horror and Watch. Then there are Big Finish audios every month, lots of stories from BBC Books, and of course the entire history of the show is available on BBC DVD (in some cases Blu-ray). There's a birthday party of cakes and treats, a cornucopia, when it comes to *Doctor Who* today. We are spoiled with so many options. Fantastic!

That landscape was really very different in 1993, the year that I became a fan. Repeats were available on satellite (although I didn't have access), and the New Adventures were being published (although I wasn't aware of them at the time). All I had were the trickle of VHS releases (the Dalek Tin!) and the trickle of repeats on BBC2 (*Planet of the Daleks!*) while the only new *Doctor Who* stories that I experienced up until 1996 were *Dimensions in Time* and the TV Movie, as well as two Jon Pertwee radio plays, although any *Doctor Who* was 'new' to me at the time.

The 1990s, those were the days. Trying to pick up a non-digital radio signal! Watching *Doctor Who* on a portable television using an indoor aerial, getting fuzzy reception! Or, and this is the best one of all, lying on your bed reading a battered Target paperback that's at least twenty years old. I wouldn't have it any other way, because I have such touching memories of each and every one of those moments. Can you still find them in libraries? I haven't a clue! You can certainly pick them up cheaply on eBay.

When I consider my love of books, it is inevitably linked to the strong bond that I have with my parents. My Mum and Dad are my best friends in so many ways. I can go to them with anything, and they continue to guide me in my life. They've also introduced me to a lot of fun along the way. I vividly recall bedtime stories with my Mum, usually a spine-chilling tale by Roald Dahl. And I remember trailing round art galleries, libraries and, best of all, second-hand book stores with Dad. Sometimes he would come home having been to just such a store, and I can picture a battered binding of paper, with the words *The Green Death* across it, landing in the middle of my bed in front of me. I loved that little book, torn parts and all.

I don't remember the exact year that I found Target, since memory is an extremely funny thing. I had a good friend from swimming lessons who introduced me to the books. We visited the library and he recommended *Mission to the Unknown* and *The Mutation of Time*. I didn't used to know that they were television novelisations, or perhaps it simply didn't register with me it's surprising what doesn't when you're young, but from that point on I was hooked. I worked my way through the Target books with glee, as many of them as I could. It didn't matter how good or bad a story was supposed to be, I didn't know or care, I would read anything that sounded like a great adventure and there was one that was more epic than all of the rest.

The only Target novelisation that means as much to me as *The Green Death*, if not more, I didn't realise was a Target, because the inside said it was published by *Doctor Who Books, an imprint of Virgin Publishing*. As it transpired, it was the first and only Target that I bought brand new (well, that my dad bought new actually, he was the one who paid for it). *The Evil of the Daleks* was just sitting there on the shelf in John Menzies and it must have been the latter part of the year, very likely autumn, because I remember cold, wet days and dark evenings, with chimney smoke heady on the air. Take a deep breath!

I'd sink into Dad's chair after school and read *The Evil of the Daleks*. It was my favourite place to sit, when he wasn't around. I looked forward to him walking in from work, apart from having to find somewhere else to sit. What a read that book was though. Patrick Troughton was right, *The Evil of the Daleks* really is a *Doctor Who* film. A movie with a backstory, set in the past, present and the future, and set on Earth as well as an alien world. Books are all big budget in your head.

The Evil of the Daleks is entwined in how I became a *Doctor Who* fan, and it is eternally entwined in my memories of growing up, surrounded by a loving Mum and Dad. Memories of being surrounded by a loving family, that is what *The Evil of the Daleks* means to me.

476

It's the End...But is it Target?

Doctor Who – The Paradise of Death
by Jason Elford
Favourite *Doctor Who* book: *Blood Heat* by Jim Mortimore

The Paradise of Death was one of only four Target *Doctor Who* novelisations I knew about pre-publication and the last time I would be waiting at the local bookshop as it opened at 9am (late for school) so I could pick up my copy of the latest Target book. It was the end of the range and the end of an era, but I didn't quite realise it at the time.

By the 1990s, my limited knowledge of *Doctor Who* had begun to grow: lists of book titles copied from advertisements in the back of Target books were expanded to include stories I hadn't known about thanks to Doctor Who Magazine, a friend from secondary school involved in various fan groups and a copy of *The Programme Guide*. I started getting an allowance and going to town without mum, list in hand, to search for the titles required. Luckily, there was a plentiful supply available and I was buying books faster than I could read them, so the gaps diminished.

By November 1991, having purchased *The Pescatons* (the very first Target title I knew about pre-publication) I had only three books left to collect (all of which would remain stubbornly elusive till 1995). I had moved on to buying the New Adventures range, which I enjoyed, but they were different in style, tone and content. They were not Target books and though they were placed in chronological release order after *Survival*, they were never mixed up.

As each issue of DWM came out, I would scan for news of new Target releases – the blue-spined reprints were keeping the candle burning, but seven titles had never been published so there were gaps (I hated gaps). I assumed Target would get to these soon, but over the next three years only three books would be published under the Target banner: John Peel's two Daleks books and *The Paradise of Death*. The first two reduced the list to five unpublished stories, but the latter was a welcome bonus, adapting the previous year's radio broadcast.

Happy as I was to have this book in my collection, according to some fan discussions and even comments from the publishers, *The Paradise of Death* wasn't quite a Target book. An odd statement considering that the Target range had never been uniform. They were all different lengths, they had different writing styles, some differed in height... I was fascinated by the debates about whether the cover design, length or style that made it feel like it didn't fit in. One thing seemed to be discussed above all: the Target logo, that wonderful little emblem synonymous with the *Doctor Who* novelisations, was missing.

477

Okay I admit this was absolutely a minor thing; but I noticed (I laugh, somewhat nervously, at my fifteen-year-old geekiness) and other fans noticed too. *The Paradise of Death* was a novel with an identity crisis, stuck somewhere between the old, new and forthcoming styles of *Doctor Who* books.

I took my copy home and began reading that evening. As I opened the book, there, on the front title page, was the Target logo. A reassuring acknowledgement, even if a somewhat begrudging one hidden from plain sight, that this book belonged to the Target range. It was an okay story, not the best or worst I had read. It felt like a pastiche of the Pertwee era but, for me, captured the spirit of the Target books.

A follow-up radio play, *The Ghosts of N-Space*, was broadcast and then novelised as part of the Virgin *Missing Adventures* label in 1995. That was also the year I completed my Target collection and realised the Target era had truly come to an end. For me it had been a fantastic journey, full of amazing adventures. The Target novels had been an important part of my formative years as both an avid reader and a *Doctor Who* fan. Without the Target books, in all probability I wouldn't have become a fan.

When finally being able to put all my books up on shelves, I wondered how best to display my collection, a quandary shared by many fans as I later discovered on forums – I kid you not, there are whole threads (with photos) discussing this very topic. I decided to keep all the different sets together in publisher order. Target books went up first followed by the two Virgin ranges and then BBC Books. Then after 2005, up went the books based on the current series and, most recently, *Shada* and *City of Death*. *The Pirate Planet* is soon to be published as well – obviously not by Target books, but I am happy nonetheless. It will mean only two titles will remain on a very old list of mine needing to be officially published and crossed off.

As for *The Paradise of Death*, it sits proudly with the rest of my Target collection in the correct chronological place between *The Time Warrior* and *The Dinosaur Invasion*. It is without doubt a Target book....the last Target book.

The Case of the Missing Radio Drama

Doctor Who – The Ghosts of N-Space
by Stephen Hatcher
Favourite *Doctor Who* book: *Short Trips: The Centenarian*
ed. Ian Farrington

In February 1995, the excitement of the thirtieth anniversary had been replaced with the realisation that there was still no hope that the series would return to TV any time in the near future.

One bright spot remained. For me, the highlight of the anniversary year had been the radio serial *The Paradise of Death*. A sequel had been commissioned and recorded but as yet no broadcast date had been announced. For many, the written version of this story was how they first encountered it, but it would be the end of the decade before I was to get into those - so where was the radio serial?

In fact, as Barry Letts revealed in Doctor Who Magazine, *The Ghosts of N-Space* had originally been conceived as his contribution to the Virgin Missing Adventures novel range, and he had ended up working on the novel and radio script in tandem. So although many take this book for the novelisation of the radio serial, it has much more in common with its fellow Missing Adventures; it is a stand-alone novel in its own right.

It was January 1996, almost a year after the novel was published, when the BBC finally broadcast the story. The reason for that delay has never been explained, although the rumour at the time was that the powers that be realised that it was pretty awful. It is hard to disagree with that damning verdict. All the faults of the audio version remain very much in evidence in the book, in particular a very shaky science behind the 'ghosts', a plot that relies horribly on coincidence, including the risible suggestion that the Brigadier is part-Italian, and Jeremy Fitzoliver, probably the worst companion visited upon the Doctor in any medium.

However, I rather enjoyed the book, more so than the radio serial. It serves as a reminder of one of the key staging points in the so-called Wilderness Years, pointing the way forward to Big Finish and the new TV series. If for that alone, both versions of *The Ghosts of N-Space* are to be treasured.

These Shoes! They Fit Perfectly!

Doctor Who – The Novel of the Film
by Barnaby Eaton-Jones
Favourite *Doctor Who* book: *The Five Doctors*
by Terrance Dicks

We all knew it was coming. The publicity had been constant and the sense of excitement amongst the fan community was akin to Elvis Presley fans finding the King alive and well and living as a short order chef in their local diner. But here was the dilemma. *Doctor Who: The Novel of the Film* was released a good couple of weeks before the actual transmission date on BBC1. This is what happened with the twentieth anniversary special too and I'd been drawn to the shiny silver cover of the novelisation of *The Five Doctors* before watching the actual special. I'd bought it but didn't actually read it until afterwards. This wasn't going to be the case this time. Oh no.

In 1996, when the novelisation and the movie debuted, I was a bit of a mess. I'd been diagnosed with a long-term illness and had spent a few years bed-bound, at a time when I'd expected to have left home, accepted a place at RADA (Royal Academy of Dramatic Arts) and started living the high life in London as a carefree young creative soul. Hospitals scared me, because I'd been in and out of them so much, so the sequence in the novel where the Doctor is operated on had me sweating a lot when I read it. My anxiety levels were through the roof and I expected to pass away every time I had a relapse, so reading about the all-too-human demise of my non-human hero was not an easy thing to come to terms with (and I know I would be even more uncomfortable when watching it play out on television). For me, *Doctor Who* was an escape into a reality where I didn't worry about being unwell. I was drawn in and forgot about reality. Sure, there's death in *Doctor Who*, but it's never glorified or overly realistic. This seemed perfectly real and the Doctor seemed to have been plonked into an episode of Michael Crichton's *ER*.

Nonetheless, I recall reading the novelisation in one sitting. That's partly to do with loving the Doctor and partly to do with Gary Russell's writing. If you're a fan, you'll know that he's a big cheese in the world of our beloved Time Lord. A Baked Camembert, shall we say? With a hardened surface but, once open, containing a warm gooey inside. On a tangent, I first met the man himself at a Northampton *Doctor Who* convention in 2003, where I chatted one-on-one for an exceedingly long time in the fading hours of the evening after I'd performed a full-length comedy spoof called *Deja Vu of the Doctors*. I recall praising him highly for this novelisation and then getting a little insight into the sections he had to edit out to bring it in line with the supposed target audience age. If you've ever heard Gary speak on stage or had the chance to wag chins with the man, you'll know he's not only a fantastic storyteller but also a good listener, something that's too often rare in celebrities.

In his dedication at the start, Gary Russell says the book is for Terrance Dicks, 'who made me want to write a *Doctor Who* novelisation'. Another big name in *Doctor Who* culture. Terrance Dicks had a way of making you want to turn the page and, regardless of the story, you've got to be able to translate what is strong about a story and keep the reader engaged. Terrance Dicks did that with such effortless ease that it made you think that you too could write a story for the Doctor. I suspect many writers who read his novelisations as a child were initially inspired by his prose (current showrunner, Steven Moffat, has admitted this to be true of him, for example). So, the fact that Gary Russell delivers exactly the sort of novelisation that echoes those of his illustrious predecessor is a fitting tribute – especially as this book was published by Virgin, who took over the licence after Target, just before the BBC retained the licence and started publishing their own range. It bridged the gaps between the Target, Virgin and BBC styles without feeling like a badly-stitched patchwork.

The novelisation was created from an earlier (and more fleshed-out) draft of the script and added in some lovely linking touches with the original series. As this movie was a continuation of the series, rather than a reboot, these linking parts are perfectly in keeping with the narrative. The characters have more backstory and motivation because they have time to breath. However, and here was my only criticism, the new Doctor felt a little bland. The story starts, as you'll know, with the seventh Doctor nearing the end of his incarnation. In the movie, this is a nice little section with a voiceover by Paul McGann's eighth Doctor, which sets up the story in a quick and concise way without confusing a new viewer. In the novel, this is such a well-written and expanded section that you feel this is going to be a rather brilliant seventh Doctor adventure. It makes you sad that he is brought down in a hail of bullets and his life is cut short on the operating table afterwards.

So although I loved the story, didn't mind the romance and couldn't see how this wouldn't be the sort of well-received pilot that led into a new series (how wrong I was!), I came away from the book without getting a hook on who the new Doctor was. He didn't seem to have a personality of his own and interesting things happened around him. Now, I don't know if you're one of those people who like reading novels before seeing their adaptation in another form (be it film, television or radio), but I'm of the opinion that the media are so different that you can get as much enjoyment out of all of them, especially as they'll never be exactly the same. This is exactly what happened with the novelisation and the broadcast movie. I was surprised when I viewed the movie itself to see so little time spent with the other characters and how much personality Paul McGann injected into the role. Those lines that had appeared a little generic, or just not eccentric or witty or urgent enough, became, with Paul's breathless, urgent and enthusiastic delivery, all of those things that you wanted from a new Doctor. I suppose, and I'm just guessing, that the script was written so generically because it was written before anyone was cast and therefore they had nobody to tailor it to. The performance enhanced the lines written; the shoes fit because Paul McGann made the character his own.

Did it spoil the broadcast version to have read the novelisation beforehand? No. In this case, the novelisation provided much-needed detail that the movie version omitted. I wasn't so aware of the fast editing and speedy pace of the plot because I know the backstory and motivations of characters without it having to be spelt out on screen. With an actual series, I'm sure the novelisation wouldn't have been so fulfilling as there would have been that added extra time to include all that was cut. But as this was a movie-length pilot for a series, it had to be quicker and flashier; not giving you time to think or breathe as it rattled along. It works as a movie, for me, regardless. Maybe the naysayers would have glossed over the inconsistencies if they'd have read the novelisation before watching it?

Scream from a Parallel World

Doctor Who – The Scream of the Shalka
by Michael M Gilroy-Sinclair
Favourite *Doctor Who* book: *The Discontinuity Guide*
by Paul Cornell, Martin Day and Keith Topping

A good book can take you on a journey. A *Doctor Who* book can transport you anywhere. Especially a place that never was...

When I look at those bulging and incomplete Formica shelves full of well-thumbed titles that date back further than my own childhood, there are few that trigger a purely emotional response more than *The Scream of the Shalka*. This book takes me to an alternative 'now', a world where *Doctor Who* is on the BBC but on CBBC rather than BBC1. The show has become more cult than it ever was and has attracted some of the best writers in the world.

In this 'now' *Doctor Who* is seen across the world and is regarded as the most ground-breaking story-telling machine ever seen. This world has an animated ninth Doctor played by the other guy from *Withnail and I*, who still refuses to attend a convention. In this universe-spanning narrative, the Doctor's companion is the Master and has been played by Derek Jacobi for over a decade. There has never been a Time War. The producer, James Goss, has become a household name amongst the 'We' and the 'Not-We' haven't even noticed the show is back on screens.

On the forums, they have long ago given up arguing if this new format of their beloved show is truly canon and now simply revel in its complexity.

This is where my own personal reality kicks in. I was at Cosgrove Hall in Manchester during the time when the cell animation of *The Scream of the Shalka* was in its most basic form. Somewhere in Manchester, on an industrial estate near a funeral director, in the offices upstairs, far away from the puppet animation of Gerry Anderson's *Lavender Castle*, *Rotten Ralph* and *Rocky and the Dodos*, there was a secret *Doctor Who* just beyond my grasp.

Of course, in this new alternate 'now' the show has gone from Flash to full computer animation in a seamless evolution. It's left the web to exist on digital TV then returned to the web to be streamed by millions. There was even a brief dalliance with 3D to celebrate the fiftieth anniversary. Meanwhile, Saturday night belongs to ITV. A series of short-lived BBC revivals of shows from *Quatermass* and *The Tripods* to *Bugs* and even *Crime Traveller* have failed to fill this live-action teatime void.

So maybe it's for the best that this experiment never got further than one story. That this cartoon, this webcast from the back end of dial-up, has become a footnote in *Doctor Who* lore. It is fitting that the novelisation is not even a Target book, it's a BBC novelisation of a world that never existed, a map to a road that no one travelled. Which is the most *Doctor Who* thing ever.

So the next time you look at this book by the magnificent Paul Cornell, remember that it's a story that contains a strong black female companion as well as more comedy, pathos and drama than you can shake a singing rock worm at...and remember what might have been.

The Lost Adventure

Doctor Who – Shada
by Anthony Burdge
Favourite *Doctor Who* book: *An Unearthly Child*
by Terrance Dicks

In order to understand my feelings for the Gareth Roberts novelisation of *Shada*, I must offer a bit of personal history concerning my *Doctor Who* fandom, my love of literature and my admiration for Douglas Adams, who is one of my literary heroes. My first introduction into the Whovian universe via PBS in NYC during the mid-1980s was *The Hand of Fear*. *Doctor Who*, back then, was not the worldwide brand it is today. By the time I saw the episodes, they were years old and Tom Baker had already moved on. I had no knowledge of *Shada*: not the fact that it never completed filming, nor that scenes in *The Five Doctors* were taken from the un-broadcast serial, nor the 'canonicity hitches' implied therein. It would be a number of years until all would be revealed.

As a child with a thirst for literature, having grown up with avid bibliophiles as parents who first exposed me to Tolkien while *in utero*, I was a voracious reader. My library grew and grew and the books of Douglas Adams became treasures that I consistently re-read. Within the pages of *Dirk Gently's Holistic Detective Agency*, I was introduced to Professor Chronotis and his time machine and immediately thought of Doctor Who and his TARDIS, still having no knowledge of *Shada*.

The 1990s saw me graduate from high school, join the U.S. Navy, receive discharge in 1993 and attend classes at the local college. I cannot pinpoint the exact moment in time when I was introduced to *Shada*, but through discussion with a friend, this 'lost' *Doctor Who* story was mentioned and the character of Professor Chronotis and his college rooms-cum-TARDIS were noted. The connection was made, but since it was the Dark Ages of Pre-Google, the whole story would remain a mystery to me for some time

I began my exploration as a writer pretty much as I explored other works of fiction. While writing a *Star Trek: The Next Generation* screenplay (never submitted alas, but I still have the long-hand version), numerous fantasy stories inspired by Tolkien and bits of sci-fi, I became more serious in honing my craft. I read biographies, histories and other works that inspired my literary heroes. In 2002, I met my beloved wife Jessica, a fellow bibliophile and writer, aptly enough in the Tolkien section of a Greenwich Village Barnes and Noble. A year later we had our first official joint publication and now have a chunky list of publications to our credit. Together, we've sifted through a number of local authors' papers, and love learning about other independent scholars and academics doing the same first-hand research of their own.

I finally saw the existing sections of *Shada* a mere decade after it had been released on VHS and also stumbled across the Eighth Doctor Big Finish version, to which I obsessively listened quite a number of times. It almost goes without saying that I adored *Shada* in both versions. Now I could see more clearly how Douglas Adams utilised elements from *Shada* for his first Dirk Gently book, my adoration for both works grew exponentially. To me, it did not matter that the Whovian references were removed; I love the interconnectedness of all things!

Being a writer and book nerd (my wife and I are also avid book collectors), I'm especially intrigued when a story centres around a certain tome. Fan of H.P. Lovecraft that I am, I get fully invested in stories that concern the Necronomicon or other ancient dark texts (Point of note – I like stories surrounding ancient texts of nice things too, like the Redbook of Westmarch or the book from *The Neverending Story*.) In the case of *Shada*, it is The Worshipful and Ancient Law of Gallifrey, which was in the possession of Professor Chronotis and becomes the focus of investigation for Chris Parsons, Skagra and the Doctor.

Moving forward to 2011, one year after my first book was published with my wife as co-author and editor, we were involved in the local *Doctor Who* community and their monthly meet-ups at a New York pub. On occasion, special guests would be invited, such as Gary Russell, David J Howe and, at one especially memorable event, Gareth Roberts and Clayton Hickman. To my surprise, I learned from the organiser of this pub meet that Gareth Roberts was working on the novelisation of *Shada* based on varied drafts of the scripts and Douglas Adams' own papers. For some reason or other, this news had completely whooshed by me, which sounds quite similar to the noise a deadline makes. I must confess, I completely geeked out, not just in Whovian delight but in terms of my hoopyfroodedness.

So, when Roberts and Hickman went outside for a quick adulation to the tobacco gods, I turned to my wife and told her I was going to join them in an offering. Now, could I have waited for them to come back in to mingle? Sure. But stalking them outside was an ideal moment to talk. After the pleasantries of a quick reintroduction, our chat turned to the forthcoming <u>Shada</u>. Granted, Mr Roberts couldn't go into exquisite detail, but I asked about his work with Douglas Adams' papers. Remarking that it was a humbling experience, he talked about it literally being an opportunity of a lifetime – not just to work with the papers, but to work on Douglas Adams' own project, thereby helping to fulfil the original vision Adams had for the story. He hoped readers would enjoy what was to come and believe that he honoured Douglas Adams in every way.

I pre-ordered the book as soon as it became available and when it finally arrived I did not let the inspiring, enthusiastic chat I had had with Gareth Roberts colour my reading. Within the pages was a more complete story of Professor Chronotis, the book, Skagra, Shada, the Time Lords, and, of course, the Doctor. The narrative was pure Douglas Adams, especially the computer aboard Skagra's ship, complete with witty remarks reminiscent of Eddie from the Heart of Gold. The author's afterword explaining his work, acknowledging Clayton Hickman and their joint research to work out the kinks of the varied original Adams scripts, is nothing short of brilliant for me, the reader and independent scholar seeking to learn more about the mechanics of writing and construction of narrative.

This novel is a monumental achievement and honours Douglas Adams in every way. Roberts perfectly captures Adams' style and, personally, I cannot tell any difference between what either man wrote. I greatly admire what went into this novel, and shall cherish it and honour the combined authors by re-reading it time and again.

A Gallifreyan in Paris

Doctor Who – City of Death by Tony Cross

Favourite *Doctor Who* book: *Love and War* by Paul Cornell

For a long time, the most important fact about the novelisation of *City of Death* is that it did not exist.

As the Target range drew to a close and as *Doctor Who*'s absence from television began to look permanent, only a handful of televised stories escaped novelisation. Two of those – *The Pirate Planet* and *City of Death* – were written by Douglas Adams. There was also the faint possibility that one day they would get around to novelising *Shada*, Season 17's untelevised story. That too was a Douglas Adams script.

The problem was that Douglas Adams became an incredibly successful author and always said that if his stories were to be novelised, he would do the novelising. Understandably, he seemed in no rush to do so, which was hideously frustrating to the student *Doctor Who* fan (me) who was cluing in in having a complete set of Target novelisations. This became even more frustrating when Adams cannibalised themes and elements from both *Shada* and *City of Death* for his own novel, *Dirk Gently's Holistic Detective Agency*. That, I thought, was that.

There are occasional deaths of cultural figures that have a real emotional impact on you even when you have never met them in real life. They connect to you through their work, perhaps at a time in your life when you really needed to find someone you felt was on your wavelength. Douglas Adams was one of those for me ever since I stumbled across a copy of *The Hitchhiker's Guide to the Galaxy* in a Cornish second hand book shop. I then ransacked Gerrards Cross library for every Douglas Adams book I could find. Then I discovered the television series and finally the original beast itself, the radio series. This, I thought, was my kind of man. His death therefore was genuinely upsetting. All that Adams potential. All those lost books. Gone. Gone far, far too soon.

Time passed. *Doctor Who* returned to the television. No one novelises the new series, which is disappointing. To me, raised on Target novelisations and Virgin New Adventures, *Doctor Who* is as much a literary phenomenon as a television one and always will be. How better to get kids to read than offering up novelisations of their favourite stories? But perhaps times have changed. Target books were, often, our only access to *Doctor Who* but now everything is available. Perhaps people do not need novelisations anymore, but I still think it is an opportunity missed.

I got older and greyer and my *Doctor Who* DVD collection grew out of control. The world moved on. Then, somewhere in 2011 or 2012, they announced that BBC Books would be novelising *Shada*. They had given the task to Gareth Roberts, whose Missing Adventures featuring Romana and the fourth Doctor had been so good. This was great news.

The novel came out. I bought it. It's wonderful. Go buy it. But this isn't about *Shada*. This is about *City of Death*.

You need to know that *City of Death* is burned into my brain. I remember watching it on first broadcast, which makes it amongst the first *Doctor Who* stories of which I have clear memories. I remember enjoying it immensely and almost certainly missing any of the wit. At that age, *Doctor Who* was mostly about being scared and having an adventure. Lalla Ward's outfit certainly did not have the effect on me then that it would grow to have on me as I got older. What do you mean you don't care? Is no one interested in history!?

So *Shada* had been published and surely *City of Death* would be next. And lo it was. I will admit I knew next to nothing about author James Goss, although I was pretty confident they would not hand such a project to a rank amateur. (Apologies to James: ignorance is often said to be bliss but, in truth, most of the time it is just ignorance.) Having bought *Shada* in hardback, I pre-ordered *City of Death* from a well-known online retailer. I wasn't going to miss out on this.

The day came. The book arrived.

There is something majestic about a hardback book. It feels like a luxury. Sod your Rolex watches, your yachts and your Bentleys. Luxury for me would be a library of hardback books. They have a satisfying heft. Thus it was with *City of Death*, which came with the added weight of all that history. All the time I had waited for it, the assumption that it would never arrive; the loss of Douglas Adams.

I looked at it and before I opened it said quietly to myself: please let it be good. Let it be the *City of Death* that I remember.

It sits beside me now. Glowing. Of course it can't possibly be the *City of Death* I remembered. It's a book, not a television programme. It's by James Goss, not Douglas Adams: but it is good. Very good. It manages to remain attached to the original whilst becoming something new. The dialogue still glistens but there is a depth to the characters that we missed in the television series, which after all doesn't have time to dwell on the inner life of almost any character let alone the supporting cast. We learn more about Duggan, whose propensity to hit first and ask questions later makes him rather endearing in the end. We find out about what motivated Professor Kerensky and where Count Scarlioni found Hermann, the wonderful violent butler. Then there are Harrison and Elena, reverse engineered from one of the finest cameo appearances in *Doctor Who* history. The Countess, a beautiful woman probably, gets to breathe a little and

Scaroth himself is given a little more bite. Goss makes an interesting decision when he lets the reveal of Scaroth's identity be as much a surprise to...ah, but spoilers.

It ends well.

Time still passes. I still get older. But now I have a copy of *City of Death* to read and re-read. That list of novelisations that escaped gets shorter. Surely *The Pirate Planet* can't be far off? Then someone needs to have a word with the Terry Nation estate and Eric Saward. That, though, is a story for a whole other book.

Waiting for Douglas

Doctor Who – The Pirate Planet
by Anthony Brown
Favourite *Doctor Who* book: *The Curse of Peladon*
by Brian Hayles

I know almost to the minute the moment that Douglas Adams entered my life, though I can't say which day it actually was. It was just before 8am, between *Thought for the Day* and the headlines as the *Today* programme crackled out of my transistor radio as I got ready for school. I had no idea what it was, and on longwave it was almost incomprehensible, but someone was consoling a depressed robot, and it sounded like nothing except the *Doctor Who* theme music had ever sounded before.

That must have been March 15th or April 30th 1978, as by the time *The Hitchhiker's Guide to the Galaxy* got its second repeat the following November, *The Pirate Planet* had been broadcast; I was one of the few *Doctor Who* fans at school who already knew the name Douglas Adams when it popped up in the Radio Times as well as what it meant – a combination of wild SF ideas and even wilder humour.

But then, almost uniquely, the book failed to follow. Adams wouldn't let it go to the usual suspects (okay, Terrance Dicks) and when I slipped out of the school's imitation of The Great Egg Race to pick up my pre-ordered copy of his now-legendary book, I found it was already a second printing – the first sign of how unlikely it was that Adams would ever have the time to produce his version of his *Doctor Who* scripts, particularly the expanded, six-part version of *The Pirate Planet* he occasionally promised in interviews to distract attention from the delays to his latest project.

And then, after I'd had the pleasure of meeting him a few times – from a passing meeting at Imperial to a full hour as he launched the BBC-backed H2G2 website – he went and died on us. That seemed to be that...

Until, that is, 2016. Now, you'll note that I haven't mentioned the actual novelisation of *The Pirate Planet* much so far. I gave it one fast reading when it appeared in the shops unexpectedly early before Christmas 2016 and haven't had the chance to open it again before delivering this essay. But that's quite appropriate really, because the only deadlines Douglas ever met were the impossibly short ones.

The book we finally got isn't the one Douglas would have written. It certainly isn't the one Uncle Terry would have delivered if he'd just been given the assignment back in 1979, despite the taste for Adams humour he displays in his prologue to *The Horns of Nimon*. Instead, the script is used as a frame for ideas that Adams considered and put aside, from a totally different episode three resolution through to a Dalek cameo and a role for the Black Guardian, while the notes hint at even wilder ideas, including a female incarnation of the Master.

And that's how it should be: like Adams' scripts, the ideas are so packed that they're squeezing uncontrollably out of the cracks. That's why he could never control them enough to hit his deadlines.

Chapter 6

Meet the New Classics

2018 – 2020

Four adaptations of 21st century *Doctor Who* stories are released under the Target imprint with the tagline "Meet the new *Doctor Who* classics". Eric Saward novelises his own 1980s Dalek stories, meaning that the entire classic series is available in novelised form for the first time. Further novelisations are announced for 2020.

Also in these years

Prince Harry marries American actress Meghan Markle... Boris Johnson wins the biggest majority of any Prime Minister since 2001... Russell T Davies receives critical plaudits for his series *Years and Years*... Stan Lee dies... BritBox is made available to British subscribers, who can now access almost every existing episode of *Doctor Who* on their mobile phones... Jodie Whittaker's tenure as the first female Doctor begins with Chris Chibnall as showrunner...

Londoners Flee

Rose
By **Michael Seely**

The first time I read a *Doctor Who* book on a train journey to London was in 1984. It was *The Web of Fear*, which is about an attack on London by a hairy museum exhibit. By sheer coincidence – and this is true – the Lebanon embassy siege which started following the murder of a police woman was in full swing. I remember passing a road near Parliament, blocked off with a big blue plastic sheet with crowds of reporters waiting for developments.

This time, I was reading a *Doctor Who* book about an attack on London by shop window dummies (more connections: *The Auton Invasion* was the first Target book I ever read, back in 1980). Back in the 1980s, Target novelisations took me a well over week to read – and a week to get over my delight at my namesake encountering the Autons, albeit with that irritating additional 'e' which everyone seems to think should be there – whereas this time, *Rose* was easily read in the space of my two-hour journey.

I rarely keep up with *Doctor Who* news these days, so it came as a great surprise when these adaptations of episodes from the new series were announced. I witnessed other commentators approving of the idea because younger readers would experience the same thrill they felt in 1973 when they saw *The Auton Invasion* or *Day of the Daleks* appear in the shops. To be honest, I dislike any attempt from one generation to encourage another to wallow in their own nostalgia, which I experienced as a kid in the 1980s, hip deep in Thomas Beecham-conducted Mozart symphony recordings on fragile 78 gramophone records. ("Much better than the Boomtown Rats." Which is true, actually.) Were these books more an exercise in nostalgia for us forty- or fifty-somethings?

So, as modern youths like to begin sentences, I was a little cynical, as the modern series is so accessible we do not need TV tie-in books, unless it is another way of experiencing the story. But I am so glad they did it. Our Russell T Davies did what all of the best Target writers did when they were given the chance of retelling their story. He added, explained, expanded and threw in a few in-jokes, such as the Enoch estate neighbouring the Powell.

Davies loves writing about ordinary people's lives, it is how he gets into his story and drives that thing called plot. Davies introduced us to new characters, people caught up in the events and then, in some cases, killed them off: but he did not tap into his inner Ian Marter and

494

make their deaths too gory, which use to get disapproving tuts from the *Doctor Who Monthly* reviewer. These character expansions reminded me of some of my favourite Target moments, when the plot halted for a few pages and we had a biography instead. Professor Laskey in *Terror of the Vervoids*, for example, a moment which lifts a book I struggled to engage with in 1988, or Stael's motivation in *Image of the Fendahl*, which takes one whole page out of a mere 109, and shows how well Terrance Dicks understood his material.

Adapting your script into prose some thirteen years later gives you the benefit of hindsight, hence the descriptions in *Rose* of later Doctors and those yet to come. These paragraphs rapidly made the rounds on social media and while semi-interested observers like me went 'Ooh, really' the spoiler-allergic types were maddened. Although I can sympathise with them to a degree, these spoilers made me buy the physical book. And all the rest.

I got off the train at Stratford, the station with a ridiculous piece of bent ironwork called sculpture close to where the 2012 Olympics were held. The day after Britain won the right to hold that event, back in 2005, terrorists attacked London once more. On the tube. I could hear a repeated announcement: 'Would Inspector Sands please report to the operations room immediately?' I checked on Google. Typical. It is a not-so-secret code that something potentially unpleasant is happening.

I did what we humans usually do if we are not in a movie. Pretend nothing is wrong and nonchalantly head towards my tube journey. However, having just read *Rose*, I hastened my step a little and hoped nothing clinical would happen to me.

The Christmas Invasion of April

The Christmas Invasion
by Sean Alexander

There is a moment: a terrible moment, when you wake up, and you
suddenly realise, to your panic, that you've missed something.
('Doctor Who The Christmas Invasion' Prologue, by Jenny T Colgan)

Friday 13th April 2018. On this most superstitious of dates, I'm on my
way to London, specifically Forbidden Planet, to meet the writers of
the four new *Doctor Who* novelisations (and get my pre-ordered books
signed). For an old-school fan this is, of course, almost as exciting as
the television series coming back in 2005. The Target books have
become treasured life collections on my groaning bookshelves, and the
chance finally to add to them is like Christmas arriving in July. Or in
this case, April.

I get my connection from Crewe to London. Shortly after, we are
informed by a suspiciously automated-sounding voice that the train
will now be terminating at Crewe, which causes groans of irritation
and sighs of despair but the next train to London leaves well within
the window I've allowed myself to meet my friend Paul, dump our gear
at the local hostel and get to Oxford Street in time to beat the rush.

Finally, I arrive in London by 4.30 and greet Paul, who's having his
customary cappuccino in the nearest Costa. The hostel we've booked
for our overnight stay is the proverbial stone's throw away, and we
set off with good intentions. But both of us have neglected to
remember just how *big* London is, and the next half hour is spent
circling around like a pair of triangulating UFO spotters, desperately
seeking an efficient mobile signal. Google Maps comes to the rescue
only after we've passed our accommodation at least three times, and
even then the drama doesn't end: the hostel swipe cards don't open
anything, and we waste precious minutes trudging back and forth to
reception.

Legging it back to Euston with less than an hour now until the
signing begins, we rush through tube barriers and make our way to
Tottenham Court Road...except our sense of direction once again fails
us. Oxford Street is now the urban equivalent of Metebelis III, famous
blue planet of the Acteon Galaxy. Eventually, we emerge from a side
street to find an already considerable line of (mostly male, mostly
middle-aged) *Doctor Who* fans queuing in the politely gruff way only
we can. Not for nothing did we endure sixteen years without a
television series, and this latest wit' is a drop in the ocean by
comparison.

The line of people shifts and shuffles its slow way around the building like proles queuing for food in George Orwell's *Nineteen Eighty-Four*. Before long, Paul is complaining about his knees and I'm moaning about my back. We are, quite clearly, getting somewhat too old for this shift. At various times someone of greater importance than us is extracted from the line, promoted to the front and presumably gets home before twilight. As Friday teatime becomes Friday evening and night, a slow build-up of young, pretty people pass us, often with bemused expressions. One stops to ask who is it we're queuing to see – "*Doctor Who*'s most recent show-runners and executive producers" – and the girl totters away nonplussed on six-inch stilettos.

The final hour is mercifully brief by contrast. (Paul settles on calling his GP come Monday morning while I make a note to search out chiropractors on my return home.) And then the seemingly impossible happens: we find ourselves at the front of the queue and are shortly ushered inside. As eyes dart to see the figures sat behind tables, I catch sight of Russell T Davies (huge, gregarious and booming) and Steven Moffat (smaller, Scottish, and sporting a recently-acquired deep suntan). Both men are charm personified, thank us profusely for our patience in waiting, and react with sympathy to my tales of endurance getting here. Then, with books signed and approved selfie quickly snapped, I'm ushered down the line of Paul Cornell, Jenny Colgan and James Goss (who signs my copy of *City of Death* with the words THIS IS A FAKE in appropriately felt pen).

And then it's all over. Paul and I are back on the streets of London, where a 10 o'clock chill has descended. We wordlessly make our way to the nearest pub, get a round in and immediately compare our signed treasures. Pint follows pint, and Target Books are back on the shelves. If sales are good (maybe even astonishing, based on this evening's turnout) there should be more to come, launching a whole new quest to collect every story of the modern era in small paperback form. Maybe even some further signings to go to.

But Paul is already out. "Never again," he tells me over our third pint, knees still killing him.

"Never again," I agree, smiling. We're fooling no one, least of all ourselves. After all, we are both getting *far* too old for this sort of thing.

The Game Is On

The Day of the Doctor
by Robert Smith?

As I have mentioned elsewhere, I grew up in Australia where, throughout my childhood, looking for *Doctor Who* novelisations was one of the greatest pastimes I knew. I'd search everywhere possible, just in case. I loved these books. However, I loved the hunt even more. Trawling new and second-hand bookstores, just on the off-chance of finding something, was magnificent fun. It was invariably successful, too. Well, finding the books was. Affording them was a different matter, as I grew up with very little money.

In the 1980s, I got a summer job in a factory that paid about $2.50 an hour. Except I didn't see it that way: to me, it paid one *Doctor Who* book per hour. That was a fantastic way of getting through a mind-meltingly dull job. I'd while away the days thinking about the Target book numbering (I had it memorised by the end of the summer) and planning my next trip to a bookstore. It was the only thing that kept me sane. Finally, in my last year of high school, I completed my collection (and possibly my life) with *An Unearthly Child*. That seemed weirdly appropriate to end on.

Of course, there were other books to collect later on (the New Adventures and so forth) – I adored reading them, but there wasn't the same sense of search. I bought each one as it came out and later had a standing order at a bookstore, who would call me whenever the latest book arrived. Which was great; it just wasn't thrilling the way that hunting for the novelisations had been. Even later, there was the internet, which took any last vestiges of fun out of the game. If you want something, you simply order it and it turns up at your house. Ho hum.

Then, in 2018, four extra Target novelisations turned up. I was travelling in Asia when they first came out, because I'm now a professor on sabbatical who (nominally) lives in Canada, not some working-class kid in Australia. So I knew of them but figured I'd get around to ordering them some months later when I was home.

My travels took me to Sydney for a visit home and I was on a date when she suggested visiting a bookstore. (Words can't describe how amazing that sentence would have been to me once.) Lo and behold, there were *The Christmas Invasion* and *Twice Upon a Time*. I'd totally forgotten about them and now here were two of them staring me in the face. But weren't there two more?

Suddenly, the game was on. It had been thirty years since the heyday of my novelisation foraging, but baby I was back! Literally so, as I just happened to be in my hometown again. I found *Rose* pretty quickly. (Not quickly enough that I hadn't already finished *Twice Upon a Time*.) That left one more. A book I'd heard good things about. A novelisation of one of my favourite TV stories, bumper length a la *Fury from the Deep*. By Steven Moffat, no less.

I searched high and low. The joy was delicious, but the luck was poor. I figured I could always order it online when I got home, but I desperately didn't want to do that. Eventually, in Dymocks, the same bookstore where I'd bought many a novelisation in the past, having checked the most likely place for novelisations and only seen the other three, I wandered off to a different section because...

I should tell you that completing my novelisation collection wasn't the last joy I ever found in a bookstore. No, there's another kind, one that's indescribable if you haven't had the good fortune to experience it: looking for your own book. I do this all the time. Having written a bunch of them now, my aim isn't to buy books, it's to find out if a particular bookstore is carrying one of mine. This is just as delicious a thrill as the previous one. My publishers told me to ask the bookstores to let me sign any copies they stock. Which isn't what the search is about for me, but it does add some focus. I even found a copy of *Who's 50* in a bookstore in Kuala Lumpur, Malaysia, which proves that you really never know.

So I'm doing the egotistical author thing and looking around for any of my books in Dymocks. And, hurrah, I find a copy of *The Doctors Are In*. It was in the "performing arts" section, where books about TV shows are often stocked.

Sitting there, right next to my book, was a copy of *The Day of the Doctor*, misfiled with the non-fiction books, in the very same Dymocks I used to frequent — and right next to my very own book that was written by me oh my god I'm not worthy. Angels may have descended from heaven while singing and playing harps, I'm not sure. My search was over. My life complete. Again.

It doesn't hurt that *The Day of the Doctor* was a fantastic read. It's not only the best of the four, it may well be the best novelisation of all. Moffat's prose is stupendous, with layers and tricks and extra scenes and little bits of cleverness throughout. In short, it's everything you could possibly want from a novelisation and then some. Which is lovely. But the fact that it was the culmination of the kind of hunt that I'd thought lost forever was just sublime.

They say you can never go home again. They never said you weren't allowed to search for it.

Skip To The Good Bit

Doctor Who – Twice Upon a Time
by Johnny Spandrell

I read all the Target books as a young fanboy, but some were more
exciting than others. Some were landmark stories where big events
happened, like the Daleks showing up or old Doctors returning or
companions leaving to get married, cure diseases or become managers
of professional wrestlers. The most exciting of all were the stories
where the Doctor changed. No wonder the powers-that-be chose *Twice
Upon a Time* as one of the quartet of stories to restart this mighty
range. Regeneration stories were always the ones to snatch off the
library shelf.

So when I finally got my grubby little digits on *Twice Upon a Time,*
nostalgia gripped me and I did what I used to do with Target
novelisations of regeneration stories. I started at the end. Well, of
course I did! What kind of mad person wouldn't start at the end? I
wanted to read about the new Doctor. That's the most exciting bit! If
you were watching it on TV, you'd have to wade through all the actual
episodes to get to that eerie golden glow. But in book form, you could
cut out the guff about Ambushes and Captures and Escapes to Danger
and go straight to the main event.

The back-cover blurbs only fuelled this impatience. They would
subtly hint at the endings with expressions like, "the last thrilling
adventure of the first DOCTOR WHO". In the case of *Planet of the
Spiders,* it didn't bother to even mention the actual story and jumped
straight to spruiking the regeneration: "Read the last exciting
adventure of DR WHO's 3rd Incarnation!" It was a time before
spoilers, I suppose.

Twice Upon a Time features no such sensational headlines. (More's
the pity. "The last thrilling adventure of the first DOCTOR WHO...
again! And also the twelfth DOCTOR WHO, depending on how you
count.") But, as I eventually found when I went back and read the
whole thing, Paul Cornell does a bang-on impression of that old Target
style. He's a prolific *Doctor Who* author – books, comics, audios and,
oh that's right, TV episodes – but he puts aside his own idiosyncrasies
and writes in the way he remembers so well from his childhood. He
senses the great responsibility of writing a Target book.

Anyway, let's get straight to the end. I'll admit, I was disappointed
it didn't end a la *The Tenth Planet*:

"Allow me to introduce myself then. I am the *new* Doctor!"

500

Or the more elegiac ending of *Logopolis*:

> "Well, that's the end of that," said a voice they had not heard before. "But it's probably the beginning of something completely different."

(Of course, what I really wanted was a note on the frontispiece which said, "THE CHANGING SEX OF DOCTOR WHO: The cover illustration of this book portrays the twelfth DOCTOR WHO [We think. It could be the thirteenth or fourteenth] whose genitalia were transformed after he was mortally hugged by a Cyberman." Can't have everything, I guess.)

Famous last words. Target books had many of them. Cornell's great mentor, Terrance Dicks, for instance, would often end his with variations on a theme of, "The Doctor and his companions were on their way to new adventures." It's as familiar a Dicksism as a young/old face, a multisided console or that wheezing, groaning sound. Occasionally, though, he'd leave with an effortlessly perfect closing sentence. What about *An Unearthly Child*, with its "Out there on Skaro, the Daleks were waiting for him." Or *The Keeper of Traken,* with its "She seemed to hear the distant echo of mocking laughter." Or *Horror of Fang Rock* cheering everyone up with "No one was left alive to hear them."

Last words are important. They linger in the mind as vivid after-images. Malcolm Hulke liked to end his on wistful remarks. (My favourite is *The Space War,* when the defeated Master simply packed up his paperwork. "Oh well," he said to himself, "there's always tomorrow.") Donald Cotton's *The Gunfighters* ended with Doc Holliday drinking himself to death, and the story's narrator observing, "And I can't say I'm the least bit surprised." David Fisher underplayed the end of *The Leisure Hive* with the droll observation that, "it had after all been one of those days." David Whitaker's *The Crusaders* was the most poetic: "And the *Tardis* flashed on its way... searching for a new resting-place on a fresh horizon." As usual, Robert Holmes was the most elegant of all, ending *The Two Doctors* with the tantalizing. "Meanwhile, the Doctor and Peri..."

Cornell knows the importance of the punchy final sentence. He made a trademark of ending his *Doctor Who* novels with "Long ago, in an English [insert season here]". He closes *Twice Upon a Time* with "Towards her future" as our heroine plummets to the ground. (Let's hope the future's a cosy mattress). Sure, it's no, "The trouble with the Cybermen is one can never be entirely sure" but it's thoughtful and rings true. I like to think those words will resonate with young readers who raced to the back of the book first for many years to come.

And just think - surely this is not the end, but the beginning of a new range of *Doctor Who* novelisations, ready to entrance a new generation. There are loads of new famous last words to come. For a young fanboy who's grown up, that's unspeakably thrilling.

The Doctor and her readers are on their way to new adventures.

You've Got Mail

Doctor Who – Resurrection of the Daleks
by Russell Cook

A novelisation of *Resurrection of the Daleks* has over the past thirty five years had a number of false starts. In July 2019, it finally hit the bookshelves. Since then, certain information on the various attempts over the decades at persuading the writer of the story, Eric Saward, to put fingers keyboard has come to light. Presented here for the first time are unedited extracts from those communications.

1984 letter to an unnamed Target Books Editor at WH Allen from Eric Saward.

'Thank you very much for the offer to novelise my recently-transmitted story Resurrection of the Daleks. However, I will not be taking this up at the current time due to communication from Terry Nation's agent Roger Hancock with regards to the royalty payments for the project. Basically, I won't be getting any bar a small concession for typewriter ribbon and Tippex. They are very happy for me to write the book but feel the intellectual rights lie with Terry. He has gone on record saying all story ideas that contain the letters D A L E K in whatever order are his. The man is clearly suffering from a misplaced Andre Previn Syndrome. Sadly I won't be able to enter into any more correspondence on this as I'm currently in the process of not writing *Attack of the Cybermen* for the next season of *Doctor Who*. All good wishes, Eric.'

1984 letter to Eric Saward from unnamed Target Books Editor at WH Allen.

'Could we perhaps offer you an extra bottle of Tippex and the opportunity to contribute a recipe to the forthcoming *Doctor Who Cookbook*?'
Eric Saward's reply is not on record.

Some time later, things seemed to have moved on contractually. With *Doctor Who* off air and the Daleks not as centre stage as they once were, *Power of the Daleks* and *Evil of the Daleks* were in the process of being novelised and rumours abounded of the writer John Peel actually being paid! A brave soul approached the elusive Mr. Saward and received the following reply.

1993 letter to an unnamed Virgin Books Editor from Eric Saward.

'Thank you very much for your offer to novelise my long ago transmitted story *Resurrection of the Daleks*. However, I will not be taking this offer up at the current time due to you wanting me to write a novel that is the length of, as you emphasise, a New Adventure. If you need to be reminded of how a story should be written within a strict word count and should clearly be a faithful adaptation of the transmitted product, please read the enclosed copy of my novelisation of *The Twin Dilemma*. I'm off now to buy some Voxnic, Romulus and Remus the twin cats need feeding. Happy reading, Eric.'

1993 letter to Eric Saward from an unnamed Virgin Books Editor.

'Thank you for the copy of *The Twin Dilemma*. In case you change your mind, enclosed is *The Pit* as a template for a possible Resurrection novel."

Eric Saward's reply is not on record.

By the new millennium, novelisations had been sidelined by VHS tapes followed by DVD, instant access to stories from the past and *Resurrection of the Daleks* is available in these formats. However, there is a gradual surge in interest in the Target books when some are issued as audio books in unabridged form. Could it be that Resurrection could be released in this format?

2013 email from Eric Saward to unnamed producer at AudioGO

'Thank you for your recent email. It has been a long while since I have thought about *Resurrection of the Daleks* and the idea of adapting it as an audio book (surely you mean radio play?) is something that does appeal. Did you know that I started out in radio? It was tremendously exciting back in the pre-*Doctor Who* days when I was young and Terileptil free. I do have some thoughts as to how I could approach this rather exciting reimagining of the blood fest and body count that the story was and is to its many fans around the world. I think this could be a good time to reintroduce my detective and later theatrical hero Richard Mace who appeared in several of my radio plays and of course *The Visitation*! The Doctor could be sidelined and placed in a state of Tranquil Repose whilst Mace himself could engage Davros and the Daleks in a duel of words and clever dialogue?! I smell a winner, a real antidote to the Movellan virus! Look forward to hearing from you. With all good wishes, Eric.'

AudioGo's reply is not on record. Shortly afterwards the company ceased trading, but the two events are not apparently connected.

In 2018, BBC Books published the first new Target novelisations in over a quarter of a century. Titles such as *Rose* and *The Day of the Doctor* sold really well. There was an appetite for more. An approach was made again to Eric Saward to perhaps look at his scripts and how they would fare again in a different format.

2018 email from unnamed BBC books commissioning editor to Eric Saward.

'Eric, we at BBC books are really pleased with the sales of the latest batch of Target books. With that in mind, we would like to offer you the opportunity to novelise the fondly remembered (by certain age groups anyway!) *Resurrection of the Daleks* for BBC books! As you are aware, we are now part of Random House so we have the money to promote them ceaselessly and relentlessly even before you have put fingers to keyboard. Sounds like a winner eh? Do get in touch; a contract is attached.'

2018 email from Eric Saward to unnamed BBC books commissioning editor.

'Thank you for your recent communication. Bringing *Resurrection of the Daleks* kicking and violently screaming into the 21st century is too good an offer to turn down. I need to make you aware that contractually there are a few stipulations. Any spaceship that is an integral part of the plot in a vaguely threatening way is to be called Vipod Mor. Also I would like to reference my fondly remembered creations the Terileptils at every available opportunity. Looking forward, I think it is very important to reflect aspects of our cultural life within the proposed novelisation and therefore want to emulate the feel of an episode of the TV series Grand Designs when describing all things TARDIS. With that in mind an existential few pages describing the time machine's inner character will be, I feel, a major selling point for the book and certainly will not distract from the plot. You will be pleased to know that I've got a few ideas for modernising the character briefs of the Daleks: I would like to make them more lyrical, and singing to the tune of a Florence Foster Jenkins inspired reimagining of Davros. This is all rather exciting. Yes, I will do it; this writing will set me up above, well above something anyway. Contract printed off and signed! It's in the post. Love to you and yours. Eric x'

The reply from the unnamed BBC Books editor is not on record.

A Long Wait

Doctor Who – Revelation of the Daleks
by Christine Grit

It is here. Finally, it is here. A long-awaited book. The one book necessary to complete my collection. Not just any collection: my collection of Dalek novelisations. I guess everyone would assume I meant my collection of Target books (and it also makes that collection complete) but no, I started collecting the Dalek Target books, and only got into the other Targets much later (except for *Enlightenment*, as explained earlier in this volume), having not been able to finish my Dalek set.

Ever since I got the Dalek bug, I have tried to get my hands on anything Dalek. This obviously includes books, not just the novelisations, but also the various annuals from the 1970s, the space books and the Dalek book from the 1960s, the handbook and various standalone books (as well as various audio books and plays). One of my favourites is the *Dalek Survival Guide* (published in 2002), containing guidance about how to survive enforced captivity with a Dalek. The so-called Bride of Sacrifice (one of the ways to be carried by a Dalek in a safe manner) with accompanying illustration always makes me laugh out loud, as does the picture of a Dalek Death Squad surrounding a butterfly which is considered to be an intruder. I am aware this book is not to everybody's taste, but I love it!

Two novelisations were missing however: neither *Resurrection* nor *Revelation of the Daleks* had made it to an official version on paper. I tried to get myself an unofficial version online, but printing such a text and having it bound amateurishly really doesn't make up for having the real thing: a book.

I recall asking Eric Saward at the First Capitol Convention in Crawley (in 2015 I think), whether he would consider writing the novelisations. I thought that the way he had left the show had been the sole reason for him not to pick up the pen. I sincerely hoped that he would be willing as quite a lot of time had passed after all since then, especially as he had been willing to talk about *Revelation of the Daleks* on one of the special features on the DVD. He showed himself to be quite willing to write, but alas, he had not been asked (yet). And that was that. He did mention that it was up to the fans to ask for it, and that he would be available as the author.

I saw Eric again at another convention, and then a friend of mine asked a similar question without my foreknowledge, which made me realise there were actually quite a few people eagerly awaiting this novelisation. Perhaps there was someone from the BBC listening in?

However, it took until the beginning of 2019 for me to find out that both stories were to be adapted into books by Eric Saward. This made me happy and I immediately pre-ordered both books. The collection had to be finalised and completed!

And now *Revelation of the Daleks* has arrived. Not really a Target as I feel they should be, as my copy has a hard cover (my other Target hard cover is – yeah – *Resurrection of the Daleks*, and perhaps one could count the *Dalek Omnibus* which includes three classic novelisations) and there is no real cover art – or not the kind of cover art I would expect. No picture of the Doctor, Peri, the DJ or Davros although a (small) Dalek is present. I am pleased that there are going to be paperback versions as well, although the covers are yet to be revealed. If these will be in the more traditional style, I will have to pick those up too. Even though I already have copies of the hard cover!

I am going to close with some joyful remarks about the resurrection (pun intended) of the Target novelisations to cover the new series. That this actually means I will never – at least until there are no more stories with Daleks which is inconceivable - complete my collection of Dalek Target novelisations, is not a problem. In fact, it makes me very happy indeed that this tradition has been picked up again. It is good to know that in times of digitalisation, original novels and novellas and table books, a novelisation of a story still has its fans.

May this continue for a long, long time!

Afterword

By Nigel Robinson
Target Editor, 1984-1987

Target Books. For people of a certain age, two of the most evocative words ever. Some of the best books I ever read. Some of the best novelisations I ever commissioned. And, as one-time editor of the range, quite possibly the best job I ever had.

I blame Blackpool. One rainy day in July 1965, in a tiny kiosk on the resort's windswept North Pier, I spotted a copy of the Armada edition of *Doctor Who in An Exciting Adventure with the Daleks*. It was 2/6, a sizeable chunk of my pocket money, but I bought it. I was already a precocious reader of the likes of Enid Blyton but David Whitaker's splendid prose was the beginning of a lifelong love of books, and incidentally improved my vocabulary no end.

In the next few months, I must have read that book countless times. Even today, 51 (51!) years later I can still quote huge chunks of it from memory. I still remember Ian tearing his sports jacket on a door screw in his landlady's lodgings. The glass Dalek scares me even now. For me the TARDIS will forever be the 'the breadth and width of a middle-sized restaurant with room for about fifty tables', as Ian describes the console room in the book. And Barnes Common will be perpetually fogbound and the scene of a terrible car crash. And though I now have *An Exciting Adventure* on my shiny Kindle, I still own that original copy, its pages grubby and yellowing and its spine broken with use.

Two Julys later, I was in another Blackpool bookshop. The TV show was on a short break, but its absence was made bearable by my discovery there of a copy of the Green Dragon edition of *Doctor Who and the Crusaders* (suggested reading age 12–15 according to the cover). Once again, Whitaker's writing captivated me and today I can still remember the chaise longue, the bust of Napoleon, the Ormolu clock and the Martian chess set – and indeed later used them in my own novels. And I still wonder about the Talking Stones of Tyron in the seventeenth galaxy.

Move forward to July 1973 and I was in Blackpool once again, this time browsing in the book department of the big Woolworth's store which used to be beneath Blackpool Tower. Truth to be told, like any other randy post-pubescent teenager, I was sneaking a furtive look at the saucy *Confessions of a Window Cleaner* series, when I spotted a copy of *Doctor Who and the Zarbi*, alongside *The Daleks* and *The Crusaders*. At that time the Zarbi were my favourite monsters, after having encountered them on TV and in the first William Hartnell annual. Needless to say, I forgot about the *Confessions* series and bought that book, along with its two companion volumes with their iconic Achilleos covers.

Just a few months later, Target Books really kicked into gear as *The Auton Invasion* and *The Cave Monsters* were published, stories I had seen on TV but which I thought I would never have the opportunity to relive. From then on, I eagerly awaited the appearance of a new Target book, giving me the chance to enjoy again and again and again the fondly if hazily remembered adventures of the first three Doctors, as well as that new chap with the curly hair and ridiculously long scarf.

Some of those books were great, some less so, but they were so much a part of my teenage years that even today I can remember where I bought every single one of them – *The Giant Robot* from Woolworths in my home town of Preston (I hated the cover and the new logo); *The Cybermen* and *The Abominable Snowmen* by mail order, for some reason (maybe I was at that age when I felt slightly embarrassed about buying *Doctor Who* books); *The Mutants* from the Bold Street WH Smith in Liverpool; and, of course, quite a few from the bookshops of Blackpool.

Leaving University and with time on my hands, I set about writing a *Doctor Who* quiz book, which was quickly commissioned by WH Allen, who were then the publishers of the Target *Doctor Who* novelisations. Producer John Nathan-Turner and Script Editor Eric Saward graciously gave me the use of the script editor's office at the BBC with access to copies of all the past scripts. While it was a fan's delight reading the original scripts of the as yet unnovelised *The Daleks' Master Plan* or *The Mind Robber* (and sneaking a look at *Castrovalva,* which hadn't yet been transmitted), most of my actual research was done reading and rereading those wonderful Target Books, at that time the definitive record of the television programme.

It was that quiz book which led to my dream job as Editor of the Target Books. I had been editing and proof-reading the books on a freelance basis for a while now, but this was my chance to steer the series in the direction I wanted, exploring more of the past stories, especially featuring Hartnell, and encouraging the original writers to tackle their own scripts.

I was like a little boy again, eagerly awaiting the arrival of a new manuscript (and secretly, and a little smugly, delighting in the fact that I would be reading *The Space Museum*, or *The Two Doctors*, months before the general public would be!).

I have so many fond memories of my Target years, both professionally and as a fan. Tears of joy and laughter when I first read *The Myth Makers*, and then sharing some boozy publisher's lunches with its author, Donald Cotton, one of the most delightful and erudite men I have ever known. Astonishment at Victor Pemberton's *Fury from*

509

the Deep, which I felt was so good that I couldn't cut it down to its required word count of 40,000 and so published it as a 'bumper volume'. (This was Victor's first work of published fiction, I believe, and since then he has become a very successful writer of family sagas. I like to think that this was, in some small part, down to Target Books.) Desperately trying to find a contact for Paul Erickson and ask him to write his novelisation of *The Ark*. When all else had failed, someone helpfully suggested that I look in the phone book – and there he was. Breaking one of my own rules about continuity and asking John Lucarotti to include the Time Lords in his novelisation of *The Massacre*. I'm sure there was a good reason at the time but I've no idea what it was now!

There were lovely times with Pip and Jane Baker, who, I know, come in for a lot of flak, but were delightful people, whose stories were always based on solid scientific fact, and if you couldn't understand some of those long words they used, then what do you think a dictionary is for? (It's what I used which I was reading David Whitaker's *An Exciting Adventure*, after all, and my writing and reading became the richer for it.) Also dear Ian Marter, wonderful company, who always delivered to deadlines (unlike a couple of others I'm not going to mention here!) and who was writing *The Rescue*, as well as thinking about a sequel to spin-off *Harry Sullivan's War*, before his untimely death. And, of course, working with Terrance Dicks, whose knowledge and enthusiasm for the show, especially and not surprisingly for the Pertwee era, was infectious. I always looked forward to receiving his manuscripts, and would set aside a couple of hours in a corner of the office to avidly read them.

As far as I'm concerned, Terrance – and indeed the other Target authors – are up there with J.K. Rowling for getting kids to read and to love books – just as David Whitaker did for me way back then in Blackpool. And of course, many of those readers became writers themselves, myself included, and contributed to the ongoing story of *Doctor Who*.

Getting kids – and grown-ups – to read and to write. That, I think, is the most important legacy of Target Books.

It's such a shame that the Doctor and Peri never did get to Blackpool at the end of *Revelation of the Daleks*. I wonder what they would have discovered there?

"I've always seen everything as a job. At times it took up evenings and weekends, but it had to be done. And on time. That has been my work ethic all my life."

Terrance Dicks

"Well, that's the end of that. But it's probably the beginning of something completely different."

The Doctor, *Doctor Who – Logopolis*

Printed by Amazon Italia Logistica S.r.l.
Torrazza Piemonte (TO), Italy

11504181R10295